Lecture Notes in Computer Science 15995

Founding Editors

Gerhard Goos
Juris Hartmanis

AF167582

The series Lecture Notes in Computer Science (LNCS), including its subseries Lecture Notes in Artificial Intelligence (LNAI) and Lecture Notes in Bioinformatics (LNBI), has established itself as a medium for the publication of new developments in computer science and information technology research, teaching, and education.

LNCS enjoys close cooperation with the computer science R & D community, the series counts many renowned academics among its volume editors and paper authors, and collaborates with prestigious societies. Its mission is to serve this international community by providing an invaluable service, mainly focused on the publication of conference and workshop proceedings and postproceedings. LNCS commenced publication in 1973.

Bart Coppens · Bruno Volckaert ·
Vincent Naessens · Bjorn De Sutter
Editors

Availability, Reliability and Security

ARES 2025 International Workshops
Ghent, Belgium, August 11–14, 2025
Proceedings, Part II

 Springer

Editors
Bart Coppens 🆔
Ghent University
Ghent, Belgium

Bruno Volckaert 🆔
Ghent University
Ghent, Belgium

Vincent Naessens 🆔
KU Leuven
Ghent, Belgium

Bjorn De Sutter 🆔
Ghent University
Ghent, Belgium

ISSN 0302-9743   ISSN 1611-3349 (electronic)
Lecture Notes in Computer Science
ISBN 978-3-032-00632-5   ISBN 978-3-032-00633-2 (eBook)
https://doi.org/10.1007/978-3-032-00633-2

ARES Workshops 2025 Foreword

Alongside the main track of the 20th International Conference on Availability, Reliability and Security (ARES), the organizers received 17 regular workshop proposals, of which eventually 15 were accepted as workshops. A total of 173 papers were submitted over these workshops, of which 79 were accepted for publication and presentation at ARES 2025. All papers that were not desk rejected received a minimum of 3 double-blind reviews by TPC members, and in the case of conflicts of interest with the workshop organizers, the workshop chairs assigned reviewers and decided on the paper review ranking. As organizers, we believe the resulting workshops will allow for insightful discussions and interesting exchanges of ideas on advances made within the security field.

As workshop chairs we would like to use this space to thank all organizers for their hard work on promoting and managing their workshops. We'd also like to give a special thank you to the TPC members who provided—under strict time constraints—constructive reviews for both accepted and rejected papers. We sincerely believe the workshop programs contribute a lot to maintaining a vibrant ARES community. Therefore, from us to you, a massive thank you.

August 2025

Bart Coppens
Bruno Volckaert
Vincent Naessens
Bjorn De Sutter

ARES Workshops 2025 Organization

General Chair

Bjorn De Sutter   Ghent University, Belgium

General Workshop Chairs

Bart Coppens   Ghent University, Belgium
Bruno Volckaert   Ghent University, Belgium

Proceedings Chairs

Vincent Naessens   KU Leuven, Belgium
Michiel Willocx   KU Leuven, Belgium

Workshop Chairs

Aleksandra Mileva	Goce Delcev University, North Macedonia
Alessandro Aldini	University of Urbino, Italy
Amir Sharif	Fondazione Bruno Kessler, Italy
Amna Shifa	University of Galway, Ireland
Anastasija Collen	University of Geneva, Switzerland
Andrea Saracino	Scuola Superiore Universitaria Sant'Anna di Pisa, Italy
Andrew Marrington	Zayed University, UAE
Angelo Consoli	Scuola Universitaria Professionale della Svizzera Italiana (SUPSI), Switzerland
Artur Janicki	Warsaw University of Technology, Poland
Christoph Schmittner	Austrian Institute of Technology, Austria
Costas Lambrinoudakis	University of Piraeus, Greece
Daniela Pöhn	Universität der Bundeswehr München, Germany
Daniele Canavese	IRIT-CNRS, France
Gregorio Martinez Pérez	University of Murcia, Spain
Günther Pernul	University of Regensburg, Germany
Habtamu Abie	Norwegian Computing Center, Norway

Halvor Holtskog	Norwegian University of Science and Technology, Norway
Hamida Seba	University Lyon 1, France
Helge Janicke	Edith Cowan University, Australia
Javier Lopez	University of Malaga, Spain
Joerg Keller	FernUniversität in Hagen, Germany
Jorge Maestre Vidal	Indra, Spain
Kacper Gradoń	Warsaw University of Technology, Poland
Katarzyna Kamińska	Warsaw University of Technology, Poland
Kim-Kwang Raymond Choo	University of Texas at San Antonio, USA
Leandros Maglaras	De Montfort University, UK
Leonardo Regano	University of Cagliari, Italy
Luca Caviglione	CNR – IMATI, Italy
Mamoona Asghar	University of Galway, Ireland
Mansoor Ahmed	Maynooth University, Ireland
Marco Antonio Sotelo Monge	Indra, Spain
Marco Rasori	National Research Council, Italy
Markus Helfert	Maynooth University, Ireland
Marta Irene García Cid	Indra, Spain
Martin Husák	Masaryk University, Czech Republic
Martin Steinebach	Fraunhofer Institute SIT|ATHENE, Germany
Mauro Conti	University of Padua, Italy
Meriem Benyahya	University of Geneva, Switzerland
Mohamed Ali Kandi	IRIT-University of Toulouse, France
Mohamed-Lamine Messai	University Lyon 2, France
Muhammad Irfan Khalid	University of Agder, Norway
Nadia Kanwal	Keele University, UK
Nils Gruschka	University of Oslo, Norway
Pedro R. M. Inácio	Universidade da Beira Interior, Portugal
Peter Kieseberg	FH St. Pölten, Austria
Philipp Amann	Europol EC3, The Netherlands
Richard Overill	King's College London, UK
Richard Smith	De Montfort University, UK
Salvador Llopis Sanchez	Universitat Politècnica de Valencia, Spain
Sandeep Pirbhulal	Norwegian Computing Center, Oslo, Norway
Simone Fischer-Hübner	Karlstad University, Chalmers University of Technology & Gothenburg University, Sweden
Sokratis Katsikas	Norwegian University of Science and Technology, Norway
Stephen Fisher Davies	Airbus, UK
Steven Furnell	University of Nottingham, UK
Thomas Brandstetter	Limes Security/FHSTP, Austria

Virginia N. L. Franqueira   University of Kent, UK
Wojciech Mazurczyk   Warsaw University of Technology, Poland

CSA 2025 Preface

In an era of accelerating digital transformation, research and innovation are essential drivers for shaping tomorrow's cybersecurity solutions. As these technologies evolve, so too do the challenges in securing the digital domain. Keeping pace with these developments requires continuous exploration of cutting-edge approaches. Advancements in cyber situational awareness (CSA) and data-centric approaches are at the forefront of this transformation – transforming how communications and information systems anticipate evolving threats, manage risks dynamically, and support informed decision-making.

The Workshop on Recent Advances in Cyber Situational Awareness and Data-Centric Approaches (CSA 2025) within the 20th International Conference on Availability, Reliability and Security (ARES) conference, offered a mature platform for knowledge exchange at the intersection of technological innovation and cyber security. In its 6th edition, the workshop received a total of 18 paper submissions which resulted in 9 accepted papers after a peer review process. The accepted papers explore advances in cyber threat intelligence (CTI), natural language processing, quantum technologies, cyber deception, human-centric visualisation and data interoperability. The aim is not only to showcase theoretical and practical advances, but also to foster dialogue on the latest trends with a dual-use potentiality. In this context, selected contributions propose novel architectures, conduct testing and evaluation of results, or analyse meaningful frameworks for data analysis and processing. Together, these efforts will shape the next generation of cyber situational awareness tools and procedures, opening new opportunities for further research activities in the future. The outcome is a collection of high scientific quality contributions of leading-edge researchers from academia and industry. This volume contains revised versions of the selected papers that were presented at the 6th CSA Workshop.

August 2025

Salvador Llopis Sanchez
Marco Antonio Sotelo Monge
Marta Irene García Cid
Gregorio Martinez Pérez
Jorge Maestre Vidal

CSA 2025 Organization

Workshop Chairs

Salvador Llopis Sanchez   Universitat Politècnica de Valencia, Spain
Marco Antonio Sotelo Monge   Indra, Spain
Marta Irene García Cid   Indra, Spain
Gregorio Martinez Pérez   University of Murcia, Spain
Jorge Maestre Vidal   Indra, Spain

Program Committee

Nikolai Stoianov   Bulgarian Defence Institute, Bulgaria
Victor Villagrá González   Universidad Politécnica de Madrid, Spain
Joaquin Garcia-Alfaro   Telecom SudParis, France
Alberto Huertas Celdran   University of Zurich, Switzerland
Cataldo Basile   Politecnico di Torino, Italy
Miguel Páramo Castrillo   Indra, Digital Labs, Spain
Lorenzo Fernández Maimó   Universidad de Murcia, Spain
Manuel Gil Pérez   Universidad de Murcia, Spain
Alessandro Brighente   University of Padua, Italy
Fabio De Gaspari   Sapienza University of Rome, Italy
Georgios Kambourakis   University of the Aegean, Greece
Daniel Orlando Diaz Lopez   Universidad del Rosario, Colombia
Roumen Daton Medenou   Indra, Spain

RDGPT 2025 Preface

The First International Workshop on Responsible Data Governance, Privacy, and Digital Transformation was held on August 11–14, 2025 at Ghent, Belgium, in conjunction with the 20th International Conference on Availability, Reliability and Security (ARES 2025). Conceived as a forum for advancing both scholarship and practice, the workshop explored the pressing need to reconcile rapid digital innovation with rigorous accountability. Discussion ranged across data governance and evolving regulatory frameworks such as the GDPR and the EU AI Act, the design of ethical data-handling procedures and privacy-by-design architectures, emerging privacy-enhancing technologies and scalable privacy-management strategies, and the application of FAIR—Findable, Accessible, Interoperable and Reusable—principles to strengthen transparency and reproducibility. Contributors also examined how enterprise-level digital-transformation programmes can embed responsibility from the outset and how trustworthy, human-centred approaches to artificial intelligence can be realized in practice.

We invited authors to submit full manuscripts of up to 18 pages. For this inaugural edition, we received eight submissions, each assessed in a double-blind review by three independent experts from our interdisciplinary Program Committee. After this rigorous evaluation, four papers were accepted, yielding an acceptance rate of 50%. Guided by the reviewers' detailed feedback, the organising chairs selected these top-rated papers for oral presentation at the workshop and inclusion in the proceedings.

We extend our sincere thanks to every author for sharing their work, to the reviewers for their generous and timely evaluations, for their insights. We are also grateful to the ARES 2025 organizers for their unwavering support in hosting this inaugural edition of our workshop. Together we have taken an important step toward a future in which data-driven innovation proceeds hand-in-hand with privacy, fairness, and public trust.

August 2025

Mansoor Ahmed
Muhammad Irfan Khalid
Markus Helfert

RDGPT 2025 Organization

Workshop Chairs

Mansoor Ahmed   Maynooth University, Ireland
Muhammad Irfan Khalid   University of Agder, Norway
Markus Helfert   Maynooth University, Ireland

Program Committee

Farhan Safdar   Warsaw University of Technology, Poland
Aamir Anwar   University of Portsmouth, UK
Imtiaz Hussain   University of Management and Technology,
                                     Pakistan
Naveed Khan   Maynooth University, Ireland
Saif Ur Rehman Malik   Trinity College Dublin, Ireland
Tehreem Ashfaq   City St George's, University of London, UK
Syed Muhammad Usman   Bahria University Islamabad, Pakistan
Umair Yousuf   University of Calabria, Italy
Nadeem Yaqub   Beijing University of Technology, China
Azra Aryania   Maynooth University, Ireland

TrustBus 2025 Preface

Various of today's technologies (including generative AI, cloud and edge computing, and the Internet of Things) open new horizons to citizens, businesses and our whole society worldwide. All these developments ultimately aim to improve our quality of life, make it easier to generate wealth, and ensure that businesses remain competitive in the global marketplace. These developments have been made possible in a remarkably short time span because information and communication technologies move fast. Sometimes, they move too fast for society and governments. This explains why such rapid technological evolutions cannot be problem-free. In the domain of a digital society, concerns are raised regarding the lack of trust in electronic procedures and the extent to which information security and user privacy can be ensured.

The TrustBus series of events has a long tradition, dating back to 2004. In answer to the concerns mentioned above, the 22nd edition of the International Conference on Trust, Privacy and Security in Digital Society (TrustBus 2025) was held as an ARES 2025 workshop. It had the objective to provide an international and interdisciplinary forum for researchers and practitioners to exchange information regarding advancements in the state of the art and practice of trust and privacy in the digital society. Topics covered by TrustBus events include privacy enhancing technologies, privacy and identity management, secure authentication, access control and zero-trust technologies, security and privacy for data management, security management, security and trust for digital services, trust and legal compliance.

TrustBus 2025 received 17 submissions in total. All papers were peer-reviewed with a double-blind review process with at least three reviews per paper. PC members were requested to discuss and resolve any contradictory reviews. Any remaining contradictions were finally discussed by the PC chairs, who finally suggested the selected papers that were accepted. In total eight papers were accepted for TrustBus 2025.

We want to thank the members of the international Program Committee who all delivered their assigned reviews and contributed to the PC discussions. Moreover, we also thank the ARES program chairs and organisers for their support and guidance.

August 2025

Simone Fischer-Hübner
Steven Furnell

TrustBus 2025 Organization

Workshop Chairs

Simone Fischer-Hübner   Karlstad University, Chalmers University of
                               Technology & Gothenburg University, Sweden
Steven Furnell   University of Nottingham, UK
Sokratis Katsikas   Norwegian University of Science and Technology,
                               Norway
Costas Lambrinoudakis   University of Piraeus, Greece
Javier Lopez   University of Malaga, Spain
Günther Pernul   University of Regensburg, Germany

Program Committee

Reinhardt Botha   Noroff University College, Norway
Marijke Coetzee   North-West University, South Africa
Dionysios Demetis   University of Hull, UK
Vasiliki Diamantopoulou   University of the Aegean, Greece
Lynette Drevin   North-West University, South Africa
Davide Ferraris   University of Malaga, Spain
Stephen Flowerday   University of Tulsa, USA
Vasileios Gkioulos   Norwegian University of Science and Technology,
                               Norway
Stefanos Gritzalis   University of Piraeus, Greece
Paul Haskell-Dowland   Edith Cowan University, Australia
Yuxiang Hong   Hangzhou Dianzi University, China
Christos Kalloniatis   University of the Aegean, Greece
Georgios Kambourakis   University of the Aegean, Greece
Maria Karyda   University of the Aegean, Greece
Vasilios Katos   Bournemouth University, UK
Sokratis Katsikas   Norwegian University of Science and Technology,
                               Norway
Georgios Kavallieratos   Norwegian University of Science and Technology,
                               Norway
Joakim Kävrestad   Jönköping University, Sweden
Spyros Kokolakis   University of the Aegean, Greece
Costas Lambrinoudakis   University of Piraeus, Greece

Andrew M'manga	Bournemouth University, UK
Umi Asma Mokhtar	Universiti Kebangsaan Malaysia, Malaysia
Haris Mouratidis	University of Essex, UK
Martin Olivier	University of Pretoria, South Africa

Additional Reviewers

Thomas Baumer
Ioannis Chouchoulis
Johannes Grill
Chelsea Idensohn
Vyron Kampourakis
Jake Mead
Samantha Phillips
Ioannis Stylianou

Contents – Part II

**Proceedings of the First International Workshop on Responsible Data
Governance, Privacy, and Digital Transformation (RDGPT 2025)**

**Proceedings of the Twenty-Second International Workshop on Trust,
Privacy and Security in the Digital Society (TrustBus 2025)**

Proceedings of the Sixth Workshop on Recent Advances in Cyber Situational Awareness and Data-Centric Approaches (CSA 2025)

CSA 2025 Preface

In an era of accelerating digital transformation, research and innovation are essential drivers for shaping tomorrow's cybersecurity solutions. As these technologies evolve, so too do the challenges in securing the digital domain. Keeping pace with these developments requires continuous exploration of cutting-edge approaches. Advancements in cyber situational awareness (CSA) and data-centric approaches are at the forefront of this transformation – transforming how communications and information systems anticipate evolving threats, manage risks dynamically, and support informed decision-making.

The Workshop on Recent Advances in Cyber Situational Awareness and Data-Centric Approaches (CSA 2025) within the 20th International Conference on Availability, Reliability and Security (ARES) conference, offered a mature platform for knowledge exchange at the intersection of technological innovation and cyber security. In its 6th edition, the workshop received a total of 18 paper submissions which resulted in 9 accepted papers after a peer review process. The accepted papers explore advances in cyber threat intelligence (CTI), natural language processing, quantum technologies, cyber deception, human-centric visualisation and data interoperability. The aim is not only to showcase theoretical and practical advances, but also to foster dialogue on the latest trends with a dual-use potentiality. In this context, selected contributions propose novel architectures, conduct testing and evaluation of results, or analyse meaningful frameworks for data analysis and processing. Together, these efforts will shape the next generation of cyber situational awareness tools and procedures, opening new opportunities for further research activities in the future. The outcome is a collection of high scientific quality contributions of leading-edge researchers from academia and industry. This volume contains revised versions of the selected papers that were presented at the 6th CSA Workshop.

August 2025

Salvador Llopis Sanchez
Marco Antonio Sotelo Monge
Marta Irene García Cid
Gregorio Martinez Pérez
Jorge Maestre Vidal

CSA 2025 Organization

Workshop Chairs

Salvador Llopis Sanchez	Universitat Politècnica de Valencia, Spain
Marco Antonio Sotelo Monge	Indra, Spain
Marta Irene García Cid	Indra, Spain
Gregorio Martinez Pérez	University of Murcia, Spain
Jorge Maestre Vidal	Indra, Spain

Program Committee

Nikolai Stoianov	Bulgarian Defence Institute, Bulgaria
Victor Villagrá González	Universidad Politécnica de Madrid, Spain
Joaquin Garcia-Alfaro	Telecom SudParis, France
Alberto Huertas Celdran	University of Zurich, Switzerland
Cataldo Basile	Politecnico di Torino, Italy
Miguel Páramo Castrillo	Indra, Digital Labs, Spain
Lorenzo Fernández Maimó	Universidad de Murcia, Spain
Manuel Gil Pérez	Universidad de Murcia, Spain
Alessandro Brighente	University of Padua, Italy
Fabio De Gaspari	Sapienza University of Rome, Italy
Georgios Kambourakis	University of the Aegean, Greece
Daniel Orlando Diaz Lopez	Universidad del Rosario, Colombia
Roumen Daton Medenou	Indra, Spain

SC4OSINT: A Story Clustering Approach to Optimize OSINT Analysis

Elisabeth Woisetschläger, Medina Andresel, Florian Skopik(✉),
Benjamin Akhras, Peter Leitmann, Max Landauer, Markus Wurzenberger,
and Alexander Schindler

AIT Austrian Institute of Technology GmbH, Vienna, Austria
{elisabeth.woisetschlaeger,medina.andresel,florian.skopik}@ait.ac.at

Abstract. Cyber Threat Intelligence (CTI) has become an indispensable element of cybersecurity operations and any mechanism or tool that alleviates the workload of security analysts is highly valuable. Natural Language Processing (NLP) supports efficient processing of news articles, and enables us to group articles that report about the same story. This allows Open Source Intelligence (OSINT) analysts to manage information overload and focus only on essential events. Therefore, the contributions of this paper are manyfold: (i) We identify the relevant requirements for designing an OSINT clustering tool, (ii) present a solution that can support such requirements, and (iii) evaluate the solution considering the needs of OSINT analysts. Our clustering approach, denoted as SC4OSINT, is inspired by an existing semi-supervised graph-based story clustering method and adapted to the OSINT requirements. Unlike the original method, SC4OSINT is a fully unsupervised two-layer approach, which handles multilingual streaming data and uses sentence transformers to create fine-grained clusters. We evaluate SC4OSINT's story clustering by letting security experts rate the clustering quality across various model configurations. The results show that the best hyper-parameter configuration achieves an average rating of 4.19/5, demonstrating the efficiency of our approach.

Keywords: OSINT · CTI · NLP · Story-based Clustering · Streaming Data · Analysis Time Optimization · NER · User-based Evaluation · Taranis AI

1 Introduction

Cyber Threat Intelligence (CTI) is vital to cybersecurity operations, supporting tasks from vulnerability management to intrusion detection and risk mitigation to respond to emerging threats [14]. Yet, the volume of data from diverse feeds overwhelms analysts, increasing the risk of missed threats and costly consequences. Tools that reduce this burden while preserving accuracy are therefore

© The Author(s) 2025
B. Coppens et al. (Eds.): ARES 2025 Workshops, LNCS 15995, pp. 5–24, 2025.
https://doi.org/10.1007/978-3-032-00633-2_1

critical. The goal of our work is to alleviate the burden on analysts, enabling more efficient and timely ingestion of vital information. Story clustering aims to group related documents – represented as news items in this paper – into coherent stories, thereby significantly reducing redundancy in the analyst's workflow. For instance, major events like new software vulnerabilities or critical cloud outages are reported by many sources in varying styles and languages. Analysts face the cumbersome task of sorting through these repetitive reports to extract unique insights while maintaining an extensive understanding of the event.

By leveraging Natural Language Processing (NLP) techniques [4], story clustering methods group together related news items that report about the same event. This ensures that analysts can initially review a single representative cluster item instead of multiple redundant news items. Clustering cybersecurity is challenging, as articles often vary widely in length, style, and language (e.g., a blog article, a mailinglist entry, and a story of a tech magazine). Additionally, cybersecurity news is highly dynamic, with changing terminologies, such as novel advanced persistent threat (APT) group names, vulnerabilities, or software, emerging almost daily. In general, mistakenly clustering unrelated articles can lead to overlooking critical information, whereas treating related items separately is less ideal but tolerable. Moreover, certain text types, such as daily digests, research papers, or highly technical articles, may be less suitable for clustering due to their highly specialized content or the inclusion of multiple stories within a single news item. Furthermore, the solution must operate efficiently on standard CPUs under resource constraints, rather than relying on costly GPU infrastructures. To the best of our knowledge, there is no existing unsupervised clustering solution that can cope with all such requirements.

Our work draws inspiration from EventX [7], an existing story-based clustering approach, to better address the challenges inherent to Open Source Intelligence (OSINT) data, such as news feeds, blog posts, and cybersecurity articles. The existing approach employs keyword community detection [13] and a supervised classification method to determine whether two text passages describe the same event. An extension of this approach is essential due to the following limitations: (i) It employs a semi-supervised clustering method, making it unsuitable for the OSINT domain due to the lack of annotated data; (ii) it is incapable of handling multilingual data, which is critical for obtaining a broad range of security-relevant information necessary to efficiently respond to emerging threats; (iii) to handle streaming data, it compares each new event with all existing ones, which is time- and resource-intensive. This approach is unsuitable for OSINT due to the massive volume of streaming data. Additionally, the reliance on costly GPU clusters would further limit its adoption by Computer Emergency Response Teams; (iv) it considers all keywords as equally important, while we prioritize those most relevant to the OSINT domain.

Our approach SC4OSINT[1] (i.e., story clustering for OSINT) fulfills all above mentioned requirements, as it is a fully unsupervised approach, prioritizes the keywords that are relevant to the OSINT domain, handles multilingual and

---

[1] https://github.com/taranis-ai/story-clustering.

streaming data and is tailored for CPUs. Additionally, we present an OSINT evaluation dataset to address the lack of a pre-existing benchmark. This dataset also includes extracted keywords (tags in our use case). We apply SC4OSINT to this dataset and have security experts evaluate the clustering quality.

The main contributions of this paper are:

- **Motivation and Requirements:** We highlight the necessity of Open-Source Intelligence (OSINT) clustering in cybersecurity and outline specific requirements and design considerations.
- **Clustering Approach:** We propose a novel clustering method tailored to cybersecurity news items, designed for practical application with real-world OSINT data.
- **Dataset and Evaluation:** We introduce an OSINT dataset and demonstrate the efficacy of our approach through its application, followed by a detailed presentation and discussion of the evaluation results.

The remainder of this paper is structured as follows: Sect. 2 reviews related work, and Sect. 3 defines the problem and requirements. Section 4 presents SC4OSINT's components, including tagging, keyword community detection, and story-based clustering. Section 5 details the dataset, experiments, and user study, followed by the conclusion in Sect. 6.

2   Related Work

NLP [4] enables computers to process diverse forms of human language, from formal documents to informal messages, supporting applications like cyber situational awareness (CSA). Recent advances in deep learning and transformer models (e.g., BERT, GPT-3 [17]) have led to effective NLP-based CSA techniques for organizing and classifying text data [16]:

Named Entity Recognition (NER). NER, a subfield of NLP, extracts structured data by identifying key entities such as locations, persons, or cyber-specific terms like Advanced Persistent Threat (APT) groups [15]. It enhances clustering by providing domain-relevant features and is used in tools like TTPXHunter and TRAM to categorize Tactics, Techniques, and Procedures (TTPs) [11]. Our approach combines a multilingual NER model with word-matching to extract entities such as APTs, Indicators of Compromise (IoCs) and Common Vulnerabilities and Exposures (CVE) IDs (see Sect. 4.1).

Text-Based Clustering. Unsupervised methods like k-means and DBSCAN help reduce information overload in Computer Emergency Response Teams (CERT) analysis tools [6], but the lack of cybersecurity-specific text benchmarks limits evaluation of such NLP techniques in this context. While we share the goal of easing analyst workload, our approach applies more fine-grained clustering criteria (see Sect. 3). Ma et al. [8] propose an unsupervised clustering approach using Twitter data to extract and summarize threat information for infrastructure security. Their pipeline applies NER and filters infrastructure-specific features before clustering with HDBSCAN. Liu et al. [7] propose EventX, a semi-supervised method using keyword communities and a trained classifier to link event-related text. Inspired by this, we adapt the approach, due to lack of annotated data, with pre-trained models for keyword extraction and similarity detection, enabling dynamic clustering on streaming data. We further evaluate its impact on reducing information overload in the cybersecurity domain. Regarding supervised clustering, Riebe et al. [12] use an event detection method based on similarity metrics applied to Twitter data to create an alert system for CSA. Another supervised approach relies upon a novel cyber threat unified taxonomy to classify OSINT feed text based on tags and remove information with low value [9]. None of these approaches fully meet our requirements, as Twitter data lack the depth of information found in OSINT data, and focusing only on classification provides limited threat information. Furthermore, our approach extracts keywords not only using NER but also through a word-matching algorithm, and the extraction of Indicators of Compromise (IoCs).

3   Problem Statement

Open-source threat information is continuously growing, challenging security analysts in identifying the most relevant events. The main objective of SC4OSINT is to minimize the analysis time, however, there are several requirements, inherent to OSINT domain, to be considered. These requirements, outlined below, were identified through three workshops with experts from national CERTs.

R1: Analysis time shall be optimized. To reduce analysts time, similar news items must be clustered so they can be evaluated collectively. These clusters support further analysis, like automated summaries for decision-making. However, if clustering ignores news heterogeneity, unrelated items may be grouped together, risking missed information or requiring manual splitting, which is inefficient.

R2: The method shall account for heterogeneity of news items. We collect news items with Taranis AI [1], an OSINT platform, as described in Sect. 5.1, which integrates a variety of German and English OSINT sources, thus requiring a multilingual clustering approach. The wide thematic range of content, including special items like daily summaries, duplicates, and arXiv entries[2], influences clustering, thus must be handled differently. Feedback from analysts has shown that clustering these special items reduces the system's usability and increases the analysis time. Therefore, arXiv sources, daily reports and summaries shall be treated differently from the majority of regular news items, as they would negatively impact the clustering performance.

---

[2] https://arxiv.org/.

R3: The approach shall be unsupervised and handle streaming data. Due to lack of OSINT annotated data, an unsupervised clustering approach is required. As threat information is continuously generated, new items must be matched to existing clusters or form new ones to help analysts quickly spot trends and respond to threats. Incorrectly merging unrelated items, however, can slow analysis and hinder decision-making.

R4: The model shall run on-premise and shall be deployed on CPUs. Since OSINT is often combined with closed-source information (such as internal reports, analysts' comments, and conclusions), information processing must be handled on-premise. Additionally, only a minority of CERTs operate their own GPU clusters or have access to one for processing (confidential) data.

R5: The approach shall be evaluated by security experts. As the proposed unsupervised clustering approach is novel to the OSINT domain, its performance must be evaluated by security experts. To this end, we introduce an OSINT dataset and apply SC4OSINT to it. The resulting clusters must then be presented to the experts in a meaningful and verifiable manner.

R6: The model shall consider the last seven days of data. Through our collaboration with CERT analysts, we learned that only the most recent seven days of data are relevant for their analysis. Consequently, the clustering approach must focus on the last week of data. Additionally, to handle streaming data, clusters are updated using the most recent seven days of data.

Meeting these requirements is challenging, as state-of-the-art methods fall short (see Sect. 2). SC4OSINT introduces a novel, CPU-efficient unsupervised clustering approach for heterogeneous OSINT data streams. Additionally we provide a benchmark dataset for evaluating clustering quality.

4   Story Clustering for OSINT (SC4OSINT) Method

Our approach, inspired by EventX [7], follows three phases: pre-processing, community detection, and fine-grained clustering. As shown in Fig. 1, SC4OSINT introduces key modifications (highlighted in blue) to fulfill the OSINT requirements. The next subsections and Alg. 1 detail each phase and our innovations.

4.1   Pre-processing Phase

To extract keywords from OSINT data, we rely upon Taranis AI, an open-source OSINT platform. A *keyword*, also known as a *tag*, in a text document is an important word or group of words which describes a main topic or theme in the text. Thus, in the initial phase, Taranis AI extracts keywords, from each provided document (news item) in the input corpus (the collection of input documents). Unlike EventX's supervised keyword extraction, SC4OSINT employs an unsupervised method due to the lack of annotated data, and tailors its keyword extraction process to the security domain. These keywords are the basis for constructing one input keywords graph for the entire corpus. A *keywords graph*,

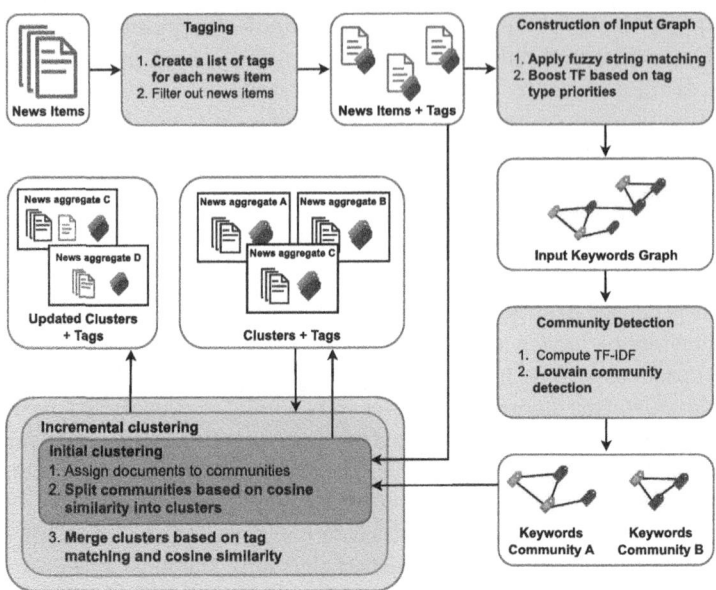

Fig. 1. Overview of the SC4OSINT approach.

is an undirected graph in which nodes represent keywords and edges represent co-occurrence of two keywords in the same document. EventX uses a supervised method to extract representative keywords [7], but this isn't applicable to our case due to the lack of a public model and annotated security data. Instead, we use fuzzy string matching to identify keyword co-occurrences. As in EventX, the resulting keyword graph represents key topics and supports keyword community detection.

Tagging. Taranis AI automatically assigns tags to each news item using a multilingual NER model, a word-matching algorithm, and/or the extraction of Indicators of Compromise (IoCs) and Common Vulnerabilities and Exposures (CVE) IDs. The tagging is tailored to the security domain, and the heterogeneity of news items (R2) is addressed.

In detail, Taranis AI performs NER tagging using the 'Flair' framework [2], with the standard 4-class multilingual NER model, covering English, German, Dutch, and Spanish. The four tag classes are person name (PER), location name (LOC), organization name (ORG), and miscellaneous name (MISC). Taranis AI only utilizes NER tags that are longer than two characters and have a confidence score[3] greater than 0.97. Both values were derived empirically by the developers of Taranis AI. Additionally, tags are extracted using a word-matching

---

[3] The confidence score in the 'Flair' framework is an optional value that specifies the label's confidence level, ranging from 0 to 1, with a default of 1.

Algorithm 1. SC4OSINT Algorithm

```
1   procedure InitialClustering(C = {⟨D₁, T₁⟩, . . . , ⟨Dₙ, Tₙ⟩})
2       for i ← 1 to n do
3           if size(Tᵢ) ≤ MT then
4               C ← C \ {⟨Dᵢ, Tᵢ⟩}                          ▷ Filter out documents based on MT
5           G ← CreateKeywordsGraph(C)                      ▷ Create co-occurrence graph
6       Compute TF-IDF for D₁, . . . , Dₙ
7       G₁, . . . Gₖ ← LouvainCommunityDetection(G, C)
8       for ⟨D, T⟩ ∈ C do                                  ▷ Doc to keywords community
9           ℓ ← argmax({sᵢ | sᵢ = KeywordsSim(Gᵢ, T), 1 ≤ i ≤ k})
10          Add D to the set of documents of community Gₗ
11      Let Sᵢ ← {D | D assigned to Gᵢ}, for 1 ≤ i ≤ k
12      A = ∅
13      for i ← 1 to k do
14          for unprocessed D ∈ Sᵢ do                      ▷ Initially all unprocessed
15              S_D ← ∅
16              for unprocessed D' ≠ D ∈ Sᵢ do
17                  Let D, D' denote the sentence embeddings of D, D'
18                  if CosineSimilarity(D, D') ≥ ST then
19                      Add D, D' to S_D and remove them from Sᵢ
20                  Mark D' as processed
21              Mark D as processed
22              Add Sᵢ and non-empty S_D to A
23      Return A = {S₁, . . . , Sₘ}                         ▷ Returning the story-based clusters

24  procedure IncremClustering(C = {⟨D₁, T₁⟩, . . . , ⟨Dₙ, Tₙ⟩}, A = {S₁, . . . , Sₘ})
25      A' ← InitialClustering(C)                           ▷ New clusters
26      for S' in A' do
27          Let maxScore = −1, superClsID = None
28          for S in A do                                   ▷ Iterate over existing clusters
29              Let U', resp. U, be the union of the tags of all documents in S', resp. S
30              if FuzzyStringMatching(U', U) ≥ 3 then
31                  Pick documents D, D' from S', and D'' from S, and let D, D', D'' denote their
                        sentence embeddings
32                  score₁ ← CosineSimilarity(D, D')
33                  score₂ ← CosineSimilarity(D, D'')
34                  if score₂ − score₁ ≥ DST then
35                      if score₂ ≥ ST and score₂ ≥ maxScore then
36                          maxScore ← score₂ and superClsID ← ID of S
37          if superClsID ≠ None then                       ▷ Merge clusters
38              Add each D' in S' to the cluster with superClsID in A
39          else Add S' to A
40      Return A                                            ▷ Returning the new and updated story-based clusters
```

algorithm by means of word lists provided by Taranis AI[4], which include vendors
and products, APT groups and operations, countries, and Austrian municipals[5]
Vendors and products are extracted based on CVE lists containing all current
CVE records[6] and the MITRE ATT&CK framework[7] is used to gather APT
group names. Countries and Austrian municipals are obtained with public lists
provided by country.io[8] and Umweltbundesamt[9], respectively. Tags are then cre-

---

[4] https://github.com/taranis-ai/wordlists (last accessed: 2024-11-19).

[5] Taranis AI uses a word list containing Austrian municipalities, as the validation of
the tool took place in Austria, involving experts from the Austrian national CERT.

[6] https://github.com/CVEProject/cvelistV5 (last accessed: 2024-11-19).

[7] https://attack.mitre.org/groups/ (last accessed: 2024-11-19).

[8] https://country.io/names.json.

[9] https://secure.umweltbundesamt.at/edm_portal/redaListOptimization.do?
seqCode=8yc33c74k8xcc2&6578706f7274=1&display=plain&d-49520-e=1.

ated by matching words (case-insensitive) from the word list with the content of the provided news item, using the regex word boundary '\b'. Further tagging is performed using the Python IOC finder library[10]. The following categories are extracted from news items: Bitcoin addresses (P2PKH, P2SH, and Bech32), CVEs, registry key paths, SSDeep hashes, file hashes (MD5, SHA1, SHA256, and SHA512), and IPv4 Classless Inter-Domain Routing (CIDR) addresses.

News items and their tags serve as input to the clustering algorithm. Items with fewer tags than the threshold MT are filtered out early, as they lack sufficient relevant information (lines 2–4 in Algorithm 1).

Construction of Input Keywords Graph. In the next step (line 5, Algorithm 1), we build the input keyword graph by using unique tags as nodes and connecting them via edges based on their co-occurrence in documents, edge weights are determined by the total number of co-occurrences in the corpus. To determine tag co-occurrence, we use fuzzy string matching (PolyFuzz[11]) with a 0.65 threshold to detect identical or slightly varied forms within a document. The input keyword graph also stores the term frequency (TF) and document frequency (DF) for each tag in the corpus, computed using again fuzzy string matching. These metrics are used in the community detection phase to compute the term frequency–inverse document frequency metric (TF-IDF) based on which the first clustering layer is created. Unlike EventX, the TF of certain security related keywords, such as CVEs and APTs, is boosted by applying a predefined priority order to the tag types (see Table 1). This is important as they do not appear as frequently as other tag types and might not be considered in the community detection phase as explain in the following section.

4.2   Keywords Community Detection Phase

This section describes SC4OSINT's community detection phase, the first clustering layer. In contrast to EventX, we use the Louvain method [3] instead of betweenness centrality due to its lower computational complexity (fulfilling R4) and ability to incorporate edge weights. SC4OSINT leverages this by weighting edges with keyword co-occurrence frequency, grouping frequently co-occurring terms into the same community.

Computing Document TF-IDF. We compute the TF-IDF [10] for each document (line 6 in Algorithm 1), which is a numerical representation of the relevant information in the document, used to compute cosine similarity between documents and keywords communities. Since TF-IDF metric favors tags with high TF and low DF, we boosted security relevant TF values, as previously described. Therefore, tags such as CVEs (which typically have low TF and low DF) obtain higher TF-IDF values. This metric is then used for the document-keyword community assignment, as described below.

---

[10] https://hightower.space/ioc-finder/ (last accessed: 2024-11-19).
[11] https://maartengr.github.io/PolyFuzz/.

Community Detection Method. The input keywords graph is used to construct keywords communities – densely connected sub-graphs, which are loosely connected to other sub-graphs. Given that keywords are nodes and edges represent co-occurrence, with frequency of co-occurrences as weights, a keywords community denotes a topic. To detect communities, we use the Louvain community detection method [3] (line 7 in Algorithm 1) since it is computationally more efficient than the approach used by EventX and it is based on modularity optimization. In this algorithm each node is initially considered its own community. Nodes are then moved to the neighboring community that yields the highest increase in modularity, computed by taking into account edge weights. This step is repeated until no further modularity improvement is possible.

Assign Documents to Keywords Communities. Once the keywords communities are constructed, documents can be assigned to them. This step is essential in grouping documents that share the same topic. The TF-IDF metric is computed for each community, and based on this, the TF-IDF cosine similarity between documents and communities. We then assign a community to each document in the corpus by selecting the community with the highest similarity score (lines 8–11 in Algorithm 1). This step results in news stories of documents that were assigned to the same community.

4.3   Fine-Grained Clustering Phase

SC4OSINT handles streaming data, essential for continuously generated threat information (R3). Unlike EventX, which uses a supervised classifier on document pairs, SC4OSINT leverages pre-trained embedding models for semantic-based clustering. Moreover, to update existing clusters with incoming news items, EventX's costly comparison of new and existing clusters limits its suitability for OSINT, while SC4OSINT offers a more efficient alternative (R4). SC4OSINT uses a two-layered approach: an *initial* clustering step that groups news items without modifying existing clusters, followed by *incremental* clustering, where new items are added to or form clusters, potentially merging with existing ones.

Initial Clustering. In this step, we split the created communities into clusters, representing more fine-grained news stories (lines 12–22 in Algorithm 1). For this, and to meet requirement R2, we use a pre-trained multilingual sentence transformer model[12] to create embeddings of the first five sentences of each news article's text. We then compute the cosine similarity between the embeddings of each document in a community. If the similarity is above a certain threshold – ST denoting *similarity threshold*, a new cluster is created containing the documents which have higher similarity compared to the others in the community. We use sentence transformers instead of bag-of-words approaches as it preserves the

---

[12] https://huggingface.co/sentence-transformers/paraphrase-multilingual-MiniLM-L12-v2.

semantical meaning of the text. Moreover, we only use the first five sentences of each document due to requirement R4 from Sect. 3, considering that news articles typically follow the same structure where the most critical information is presented at the beginning. The fine-grained clusters are then post-processed to create *news aggregates*, which represent news articles that report the same story. Finally, each cluster is assigned a set of tags by taking the union of the tag sets from all documents within the cluster.

Incremental Clustering. In the incremental clustering step, we first perform initial clustering on the new news items, followed by merging the newly created clusters with the existing ones (line 25 in Algorithm 1). In our novel approach we first verify whether the keywords community of each new cluster and the set of tags of the pre-existing cluster share at least three[13] keywords, using the fuzzy string matching approach (line 29–30 in Algorithm 1). If so, the title and the first 5 sentences of one randomly selected document in the old and new cluster are used to compute the cosine similarity using the above mentioned sentence-transformer model (lines 31–33 in Algorithm 1). If the difference in cosine similarity between the documents of each cluster (new and existing) exceeds a threshold – DST denoting *difference-similarity threshold*, the existing cluster is extended to include all news items from the new cluster (lines 34–36 in Algorithm 1). As shown in Fig. 1, the output of the incremental clustering can include both novel and updated news aggregates (lines 37-40 in Algorithm 1).

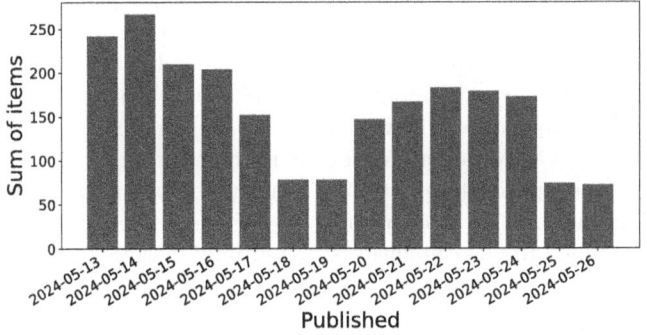

Fig. 2. Number of data items per day.

5   Evaluation

This section outlines the evaluation of our story clustering approach. Due to the lack of benchmarks, we created a dedicated evaluation dataset (R5) and tested

---

[13] A minimum of three keywords was chosen to ensure that similar clusters are not overlooked during comparison.

various hyper-parameter configurations. Feedback from security experts helped identify the optimal setup and assess its value for OSINT analysts.

5.1 Dataset

Creation of a Benchmark. Taranis AI collects news items from various publicly available sources. The admin user of the platform selects and configures these sources. Examples of relevant sources include Heise's security feed[14] and Help Net Security[15]. The platform automatically collects news items every eight hours and processes them for further use. This process involves extracting key information such as content, author, publication date, and title. The content is either directly sourced from the RSS feed or derived from the collected news item. When such extraction from the news item is needed, either the admin user provides an XPath expression specific to the source, or the extraction is performed using Trafilatura[16], a Python package for text processing. Additionally, tags are assigned to reflect the content of each news item (as described in Sect. 4).

In this work, we present a new OSINT dataset – AIT-OSINT-Summer2024, publicly available at Zenodo[17] consisting of news items stored in daily JSON files. To create the dataset, we utilized a Taranis AI instance to collect news items from 158 different open sources over a period of 12 weeks. Each day, the news items were gathered and exported by the platform over the previous two days into a JSON file. This overlapping content ensures that no information is lost due to time delays in the collection or export process. During post-processing, we merged all files, extracted unique news items, and organized them into files sorted by their creation dates. We filtered out items labeled with future dates or containing obvious errors from the retrieval phase, such as technical errors due to unreachable sources. Additionally, we removed attributes such as the user's relevance, ratings, and comments, as these pertain solely to the platform's usability and are not essential for the described algorithm. To fulfill requirement R6 we used only a subset of the entire dataset, applying incremental and initial clustering to one week of data at a time. Consequently, the first two weeks of data serve as the basis for all the experiments discussed in this paper.

Data Analysis. For the evaluation, we use 2,226 news items collected between May 13 and May 26, 2024, in German and English. Figure 2 shows the distribution of all news items; fewer items are published on weekends and a publication peak is recorded on May 14. Table 1 lists all tag types that occur within these two weeks, along with their priority and quantity. The priority of each tag type is used to weight the tags in the clustering algorithm (see Sect. 4). The total quantity of tags for each type is divided into quantities for the first and second week, respectively. The quantities per week is of importance, as we use the first

---

[14] https://www.heise.de/security/rss/news-atom.xml (last accessed: 2024-11-19).
[15] https://www.helpnetsecurity.com/feed (last accessed: 2024-11-19).
[16] https://trafilatura.readthedocs.io (last accessed: 2024-11-19).
[17] https://doi.org/10.5281/zenodo.14228995.

Table 1. Tag type frequencies

Tag Type	Priority	Quantity		
		Total	Week1	Week2
CVE	High	976	732	244
APT	High	133	68	65
SHA1	Mid-High	49	4	45
MD5	Mid-High	46	46	0
SHA256	Mid-High	60	51	9
Company	Mid-High	21	14	7
Registry key path	Mid-High	13	11	2
Bitcoin address	Mid-High	2	2	0
Country	Medium	2,461	1,844	617
ORG	Mid-Low	6,206	3,399	2,807
PER	Mid-Low	3,445	1,853	1,592
LOC	Mid-Low	1,586	902	684
MISC	Low	4,842	2,711	2,131
Cybersecurity	Low	760	442	318
IPv4 CIDR	Low	9	7	2
SSDeep hash	Low	4	4	0
SHA512	Low	1	1	0

week for initial clustering and the second for incremental clustering. Additionally, Table 1 indicates that tag types with medium priority or below are primarily assigned to the news items. Notably, tags of type 'ORG' are especially prevalent, representing organizations' names such as 'Apple'. Tag types of high and mid-high priority mostly occur in the first week, with CVEs being the most frequent. In general, more tags are assigned during the first week than during the second.

Figure 3 displays the ten most common tags in the dataset. 'Microsoft', 'Google' and 'Apple' are categorized as ORG tags. 'U.S.' represents a location (LOC), while 'ransomware' and 'phishing' fall under the tag type 'Cybersecurity', representing a word list. 'China', 'United States' represent Countries, and 'Windows' and 'Linux' are classified as MISC tags. Hereby, the tags 'U.S.', and 'United States' refer to the same country but are tagged with different techniques. Additionally, as stated above, the collected news items are in German or English, and thus tags can appear in multiple languages. Both effects (synonymity and multilingualism) must be considered in the clustering algorithm.

5.2 Experiments

The main goal of the experiments is to measure the quality of the clustering solution and to identify the optimal configuration based on the hyper-parameters

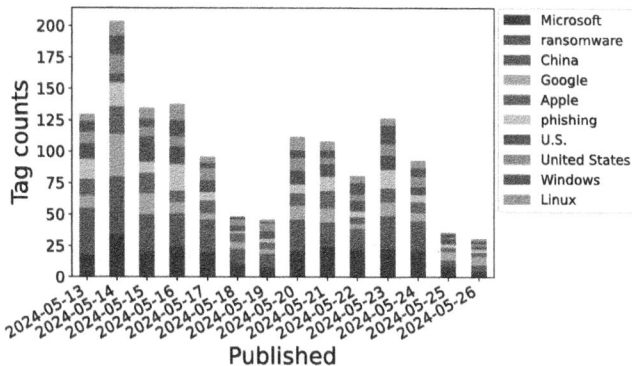

Fig. 3. Distribution of the 10 most common tags.

ST, MT, DST (see Sect. 4). For this, we use the first two weeks of the provided dataset as described in Sect. 5.1. Furthermore, the provided dataset does not include special sources such as arXiv or daily summaries (R2). Due to the lack of clustering benchmarks for OSINT, we perform a user-based evaluation, which allows for the assessment of the optimal hyper-parameter configuration as well as the overall quality of the clusters.

To identify the best configuration, we ran the initial clustering and incremental clustering for each $\text{Conf}_{\text{ST\_DST\_MT}}$, where $\text{ST} \in \{0.4, 0.45, 0.5, 0.55\}$, $\text{DST} \in \{0.2, 0.25, 0.3, 0.35\}$, $\text{MT} \in \{3, 5, 7, 9\}$. We initially observed that varying the hyper-parameter DST did not affect clustering results, indicating that ST (line 42 in Algorithm 1) plays a more critical role on this dataset. Thus, DST can be fixed, a random value 0.25 is used across all configurations, reducing the configuration space to 16 combinations of ST and MT. The next sections detail the configuration selection, clustering results, and user study design.

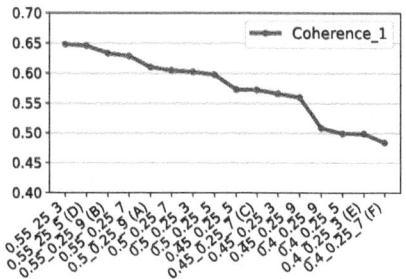

Fig. 4. Intra-cluster based coherence per configuration of the form ST_DST_MT.

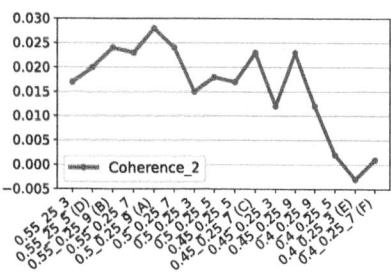

Fig. 5. Intra and inter-cluster coherence per configuration of the form ST_DST_MT.

Design of the User Study. In this section we present the analysis of the configurations and clusters obtained and the selection process for the user-based evaluation.

Selection of Configurations. Expert evaluation of all 16 remaining configurations is impractical due to the high number of resulting clusters. Therefore, we selected configurations for the user study based on coherence metrics. These metrics are calculated using cosine similarity between document title embeddings, applying the same sentence transformer model described in Sect. 4. We describe below the selection process:

(1) *Intra-cluster based coherence metric.* For each $Conf_{ST\_DST\_MT}$ we compute:

$$Coherence_1^{ST\_DST\_MT} = \frac{\sum_{i=1}^{n} intra\_sim_i}{n},$$

where n is the number of clusters obtained in the configuration[18], and $intra\_sim_i$ denotes the average pairwise cosine similarity of the titles of the documents in the cluster i.

The issue with this metric is that it does not account for inter-cluster relationships; therefore, a more comprehensive coherence metric is also used.

(2) *Intra and inter-cluster based coherence metric.* For each $Conf_{ST\_DST\_MT}$ we compute:

$$Coherence_2^{ST\_DST\_MT} = \frac{\sum_{i=1}^{n} intra\_sim_i - inter\_sim_i^k}{n},$$

where n is the number of clusters in the configuration[19], $intra\_sim_i$ is defined as above, and $inter\_sim_i^k$ is defined as the average cosine similarity between each item in cluster i and the nearest k news items from other clusters, averaged by the number of items in cluster i. In our experiments, we used $k = 5$[20].

Figure 4 and Fig. 5 display the results of these two metrics. Based on these results, we ranked all configurations using both metrics and selected configurations that performed well, moderately, and poorly across all configurations. Additionally, we considered the importance of selecting different values for hyperparameters ST and MT to ensure diverse samples and enable meaningful comparisons during evaluation. The resulting list of configurations selected in the evaluation is presented in Table 2.

Selection of News Aggregates. For the selected configurations, we take into account the $Coherence_1$ metric value for each cluster in the configuration. Therefore, for each configuration, based on this metric we split the clusters into those

---

[18] We discarded here the clusters with only one item.
[19] We allow here also clusters with only one item.
[20] Commonly used neighboring size value in clustering approaches.

Table 2. Configurations selected for evaluation based on performance across both coherence metrics.

Performance	Configuration	Value of ST	Value of MT
Good	Conf A	0.5	9
	Conf B	0.55	9
Mixed	Conf C	0.45	7
	Conf D	0.55	5
Poor	Conf E	0.4	3
	Conf F	0.4	7

with high coherence (≥ 0.6), middle coherence (≥ 0.4 and < 0.6) and low coherence (< 0.4). The goal was to select two non-trivial representatives per category in each configuration. Given the large number of resulting clusters in each category, the next selection criteria involved identifying clusters that were updated during incremental clustering, multilingual clusters (R2) and clusters with more than two items. Furthermore, to identify semantically overlapping clusters, we plotted all clusters for each configuration using Uniform Manifold Approximation and Projection (UMAP) [5] to reduce the dimensionality of the title embeddings. These embeddings were obtained using the same sentence embedding model as applied to the titles in the clustering process (see Sect. 5.2). Based on the visualization, we could identify overlapping (semantically close) clusters which were prioritized in the selection to assess the quality of non-trivial clusters. After this specialized selection, we choose two representative clusters per category, (i.e., 6 per configuration containing a balanced sample w.r.t. coherence). Due to updates during incremental clustering, some clusters appear in both initial and updated forms. As a result, users can evaluate 8 news aggregates for Conf A and Conf F, 7 for Conf B, and 6 each for Conf C, Conf D, and Conf E.

Evaluation User Interface. For the analyst, the distinction between initial and incremental clusters is irrelevant, as the focus is on optimizing analysis time regardless of the cluster type. Therefore, we present a list of all the selected configurations. These configurations along with their containing news aggregates are presented in a user interface (UI). The UI is implemented using Streamlit[21] and visualizes the news articles (title and link) and the tags for each cluster. Additionally, each user can rate the news aggregates based on their semantic similarity. A news aggregate is rated as good (5) if all its items are closely related (e.g., describing the same vulnerability). Conversely, a news aggregate is rated as poor (1) if its items are totally unrelated. Furthermore, the users can rate, on a scale from 1 (poor) to 5 (good), how accurately the tags provided for each news aggregate represent the news items within it.

---

[21] https://streamlit.io/.

Evaluation Setup. Our goal is to evaluate the impact of our clustering solution on improving the efficiency of OSINT analyst in processing recently gathered news articles (R1). For that, we asked in total 15 OSINT specialists to evaluate the selected news aggregates in terms of semantic relatedness and tags coverage. To minimize the workload for each user, we split them into two groups: one group evaluating Conf A-Conf C, and the other evaluating Conf D-Conf F. The groups are balanced in terms of their level of expertise. Furthermore, the users were not informed about the coherence metric results to avoid bias. In addition to the rating options described above, we allow users to rate the entire configuration and provide comments that can help interpret the results and suggest improvements.

5.3   Results

Table 3 summarizes the evaluation results obtained from security experts. In the following, we analyze these results to evaluate the quality of the tagging and the clustering approach, and to examine the impact of hyper-parameter values on the clustering outcome. Furthermore, we compare the user-based results with those based on coherence metrics.

Tagging Quality. The results in Table 3 indicate that, according to security experts, the tags were considered, on average, to be moderately effective in representing the articles within nearly all news aggregates across all configurations. As a result, the tags were rated as not particularly informative in fully describing the story conveyed by the items in the cluster. However, users noted in comments that aggregate tags generally cover most articles, suggesting usefulness for search but limited topic representation. Since Taranis AI assigns tags immediately after collecting them and SC4OSINT merges them when aggregates are created, maintaining a robust tag set is essential for keyword community detection—removing tags would harm incremental clustering accuracy. The roughly 1-point standard deviation in ratings aligns with evaluators comments. Given that most tags denote broad categories (e.g., countries, organizations, persons or "MISC"), SC4OSINT's strategy of prioritizing tag types and applying cosine similarity to form sub-clusters is crucial for sharper story-based clustering.

Semantics Quality. In terms of semantical relatedness, which refers to how well our solution SC4OSINT clusters semantically related articles, the overall semantics rating across all configurations is above ≥ 3.2 and thus *fair* to *good* (see Table 3). When examining the standard deviations of the average cluster semantics, it is evident that the range of ratings varies in each configuration. This indicates that the experts' understanding of a good cluster differs. Based on the size of the news aggregates, some users commented that they had more difficulties in evaluating larger news aggregates, stating that the items are only loosely related. As a result, these larger clusters were generally rated lower. This indicates that security experts are more focused on specific topics represented by smaller clusters rather than more general stories, which aligns with the comments

Table 3. Overall evaluation results. For each configuration, the number of evaluators, number of news aggregates (NAs), the average overall rating for the configuration, the average rating for news aggregates semantics and the average rating for news aggregates tags are presented. In parenthesis, the sample standard deviation average is presented for each metric.

Config.	#Evaluators	#NAs	Avg. overall rating	Avg. NAs semantics	Avg. NAs tags
Conf A	6	8	3.16 ($\pm$ 0.75)	3.29 ($\pm$ 1.13)	3.00 ($\pm$ 1.08)
Conf B	6	7	4.00 ($\pm$ 0.00)	4.19 ($\pm$ 0.61)	3.80 ($\pm$ 1.16)
Conf C	6	6	3.33 ($\pm$ 0.44)	3.44 ($\pm$ 0.77)	3.02 ($\pm$ 0.88)
Conf D	6	6	3.83 ($\pm$ 0.75)	3.88 ($\pm$ 0.87)	2.97 ($\pm$ 0.97)
Conf E	6	6	3.00 ($\pm$ 0.63)	3.30 ($\pm$ 1.11)	2.80 ($\pm$ 0.75)
Conf F	6	8	2.83 ($\pm$ 1.22)	3.14 ($\pm$ 0.91)	2.43 ($\pm$ 0.95)

provided by the users. Furthermore, this is supported by the fact that Conf B and Conf D, with the highest ST ratings, outperform Conf E and Conf F, which have the lowest ST ratings (i.e., higher ST leads to more fine-grained clusters).

Parameters Analysis. Examining each configuration represented in Table 3 individually, Conf B is evaluated as *good*, compared to the other configurations, in terms of overall rating and the average ratings for news aggregates semantics. In depth, all clusters with Conf B had an average semantic relatedness rating of over 3, with 5 out of 7 clusters scoring above 4.3. When examining the standard deviations of the average overall rating, it is evident that all experts rated Conf B identically. This is noteworthy, as Conf B is evaluated as the best overall configuration. In contrast, the range of ratings for the other configurations varies.

As outlined in Sect. 5.2, the configurations include different values for the ST and MT hyper-parameters. When observing the influence of the ST hyper-parameter, higher values (i.e., 0.55) result in better outcomes compared to lower values (i.e., 0.4), as evidenced by the better ratings of Conf B and Conf D over Conf E and Conf F. The overall rating of Conf A is lowered by two poorly rated news aggregates containing daily summaries. As noted by users and in line with R2, such articles should not be clustered, as they increase analysis time. This underscores the importance of expert evaluation and careful configuration selection to meet the requirements in Sect. 3. Notably, excluding summary clusters raises Conf A's average semantic rating to 3.66, making it the third-best configuration and further supporting the relevance of the ST hyper-parameter. The MT hyper-parameter primarily filters out documents with few tags, reducing the number of clustered items, but seems to have less influence on clustering quality than ST; its optimal value range remains inconclusive.

Coherence Metrics. Table 3 shows that security experts rated configurations Conf B and Conf D with the highest scores, while configurations Conf E and Conf

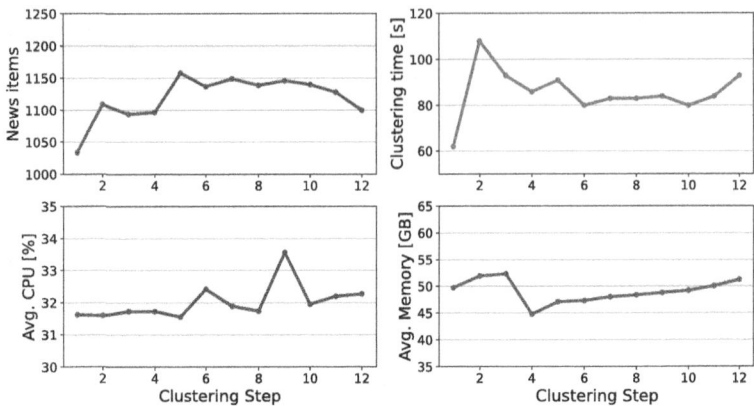

Fig. 6. Clustering performance analysis.

F received the lowest. When examining both coherence metrics shown in Fig. 4 and Fig. 5, it is evident that Conf B and Conf D also achieve higher scores than Conf E and Conf F. Based on this observation, it seems that *Coherence*$_2$ metric better distinguishes between *good* and *fair* configurations by considering inter-cluster similarity, revealing whether items in a cluster may belong elsewhere—a key factor in evaluating OSINT clusters. In future work, such metric can support expert evaluations due to the scarcity of available security experts.

Performance Analysis. Taranis AI was deployed using Docker (version 27.5.1) on a virtual machine (VM) with 64GB of RAM, an Intel© Xeon© Gold 6342 CPU (4 cores), and Ubuntu 24.04 LTS as the operating system. SC4OSINT was executed every 8 h on the deployed Taranis AI instance. SC4OSINT took into account the last 7 days of data (R6) in each clustering step regardless of whether initial or incremental clustering is applied. Figure 6 displays various performance metrics of 12 clustering steps. The first step represents initial clustering, followed by eleven incremental clustering steps. Incremental clustering requires more time than initial clustering, which is, however, not reflected in average CPU and memory usage. Further, no significant correlation is observed between the number of news items clustered and the other metrics.

6   Conclusions

Supporting security analysts in handling the volume of OSINT data is a major challenge. Automatically clustering news by story can boost efficiency, but existing NLP-based methods often rely on domain-specific labeled data, which are unavailable in the OSINT field. This paper presents SC4OSINT, an unsupervised story clustering approach tailored for OSINT streaming data. Inspired by existing methods but adapted to meet specific OSINT requirements, SC4OSINT also introduces a novel evaluation dataset for future research. A user study with security experts shows promising results, with most news clusters rated fair to good, and the best configuration scoring 4/5 in semantic similarity.

Acknowledgment. Funded by the European Union (EU) under the European Defence Fund (GA no. 101121403 - NEWSROOM and GA no. 101121418 - EUCINF). Views and opinions expressed are however those of the author(s) only and do not necessarily reflect those of the EU or the European Commission. Neither the EU nor the granting authority can be held responsible for them. This work is co-funded by the Austrian FFG Kiras project ASOC (GA no. FO999905301).

References

1. Taranis AI (2024). https://taranis.ai/
2. Akbik, A., Bergmann, T., Blythe, D., Rasul, K., Schweter, S., Vollgraf, R.: FLAIR: an easy-to-use framework for state-of-the-art NLP. In: NAACL 2019, pp. 54–59 (2019)
3. Blondel, V.D., Guillaume, J.L., Lambiotte, R., Lefebvre, E.: Fast unfolding of communities in large networks. J. Stat. Mech. Theory Exp. **2008**(10), P10008 (2008)
4. Chowdhary, K.R.: Natural Language Processing, pp. 603–649. Springer, New Delhi (2020)
5. Härdle, W.K., Simar, L., Fengler, M.R.: Uniform manifold approximation and projection, pp. 581–595. Springer, Cham (2024)
6. Kuehn, P., Kerk, M., Wendelborn, M., Reuter, C.: Clustering of threat information to mitigate information overload for computer emergency response teams. CoRR arxiv:2210.14067 (2022)
7. Liu, B., Han, F.X., Niu, D., Kong, L., Lai, K., Xu, Y.: Story forest: extracting events and telling stories from breaking news. ACM Trans. Knowl. Discov. Data **14**(3), 31:1–31:28 (2020)
8. Ma, C., et al.: FineCTI: a framework for mining fine-grained cyber threat information from twitter using NER model. In: 2023 IEEE 22nd International Conference on Trust, Security and Privacy in Computing and Communications (TrustCom), pp. 531–538 (2023)
9. Martins, C., Medeiros, I.: Generating quality threat intelligence leveraging OSINT and a cyber threat unified taxonomy. ACM Trans. Priv. Secur. **25**(3), 1–39 (2022)
10. Rajaraman, A., Ullman, J.D.: Data Mining, pp. 1–17. Cambridge University Press, Cambridge (2011)
11. Rani, N., Saha, B., Maurya, V., Shukla, S.: Ttpxhunter: actionable threat intelligence extraction as TTPS from finished cyber threat reports. Digit. Threats: Res. Pract. (2024)
12. Riebe, T., et al.: CySecAlert: an alert generation system for cyber security events using open source intelligence data. In: Gao, D., Li, Q., Guan, X., Liao, X. (eds.) ICICS 2021. LNCS, vol. 12918, pp. 429–446. Springer, Cham (2021). https://doi.org/10.1007/978-3-030-86890-1_24
13. Sayyadi, H., Raschid, L.: A graph analytical approach for topic detection. ACM Trans. Internet Technol. **13**(2) (2013)

14. Skopik, F.: Collaborative Cyber Threat Intelligence: Detecting and Responding to Advanced Cyber Attacks at the National Level. CRC Press, Boca Raton (2017)
15. Skopik, F., Akhras, B., Woisetschläger, E., Andresel, M., Wurzenberger, M., Landauer, M.: On the application of natural language processing for advanced OSINT analysis in cyber defence. In: Proceedings of the 19th International Conference on Availability, Reliability and Security. ARES 2024. Association for Computing Machinery, New York (2024)
16. Sun, N., et al.: Cyber threat intelligence mining for proactive cybersecurity defense: a survey and new perspectives. IEEE Commun. Surv. Tutorials **25**(3), 1748–1774 (2023)
17. Trummer, I.: From BERT to GPT-3 codex: harnessing the potential of very large language models for data management. Proc. VLDB Endow. **15**(12), 3770–3773 (2022)

Benign User Activities that Trigger False Positives in Intrusion Detection Systems: An Expert Survey

Max Landauer[1]([✉]), Florian Skopik[1], Markus Wurzenberger[1],
Teodor Sommestad[2], and Henrik Karlzén[2]

[1] Austrian Institute of Technology, Vienna, Austria
{max.landauer,florian.skopik,markus.wurzenberger}@ait.ac.at
[2] Swedish Defence Research Agency, Linkoping, Sweden
{teodor.sommestad,henrik.karlzen}@foi.se

Abstract. Simulations of normal user behavior are integral parts of cyber exercises where training and testing takes place in simulated environments. Specifically, benign user activities are essential to generate background traffic during cyber exercises and to estimate false positive rates when evaluating intrusion detection systems. Even though many user automation tools are available, developers typically only consider valid and compliant interactions with systems and applications when defining the scope of normal user behavior models. However, real legitimate users sometimes behave in ways that are non-compliant, erratic, or otherwise deviate from expected norms, and thereby generate suspicious yet benign traffic that triggers alerts from intrusion detection systems. To identify common activities in the vast space of possible user interactions and to support the design of realistic user behavior models, we assemble a list of 17 user activities that are commonly associated with false positives. We assess the relevance and frequencies of these event types with respect to their perceived priority, intent behind them, responsible actor, and circumstances in which they become noteworthy, through likert scale analysis of an expert study with 62 domain experts. Our findings reveal diverse perspectives among respondents and suggest that the behaviors leading to false positives can vary significantly between organizations.

Keywords: intrusion detection systems · false positives · user simulation

1 Introduction

Cyber attacks are a permanent threat to organizations and individuals alike. As the sophistication and severity of these attacks increase, so too does the need for realistic environments that facilitate security training and testing. Such environments are often referred to as *cyber ranges* and widely used for cyber exercises that enable cyber capacity building and awareness training as well as security tests that enable evaluation of intrusion detection systems [3,14,23].

© The Author(s) 2025
B. Coppens et al. (Eds.): ARES 2025 Workshops, LNCS 15995, pp. 25–43, 2025.
https://doi.org/10.1007/978-3-032-00633-2_2

When designing cyber ranges, developers usually focus on building relevant technical infrastructures that are representative for real-world scenarios and launching attacks against these systems. An often underappreciated aspect of cyber ranges is the simulation of realistic legitimate users that interact with services available in the cyber range infrastructure [10]. However, normal user simulation can be useful to enable attacks (e.g., phishing) or represent security-critical business processes (e.g., information sharing). Even more important, its primary purpose in cyber ranges is to generate background events and noise; without them, detection of attacker behavior would be trivial since almost any activity occurring on such an idle infrastructure would obviously originate from attack executions and defeat the purpose of exercises. Some cyber ranges therefore rely on humans to generate legitimate traffic [23]. Unfortunately, this strategy is expensive, difficult to reproduce, and causes issues with data sensitivity [22]. For this reason, most cyber ranges rely on simulations of attacker and benign user behavior [3,23]. Past research has shown that simulation of realistic normal behavior is generally more challenging than attack execution, which can often be pre-recorded or scripted since attacks are generally only executed once during an exercise and little variation is needed. In contrast, benign user behavior needs to be complex and extensive to appear realistic. Moreover, the range of activities that normal users carry out differs greatly from one application to another, which complicates the generation of simulation models [7].

Many tools for user simulation have been proposed in the past, but almost all of them focus on web navigation such as sending and receiving mails [6,7,10] or enable interaction with clients and graphical user interfaces of office applications such as document editing software [5,8,12,16,20]. An important aspect of normal user simulation that is generally neglected in existing simulations is that benign users sometimes behave erratic or non-compliant to policies of organizations even though they do not have any malicious intentions [4,10]. For example, normal users could use tools that produce suspicious network traffic even when they are using them for entirely benign activities [9].

Such suspicious but nonetheless benign behavior patterns have the potential to trigger intrusion detection systems and generate alerts; more precisely, false positive alerts since they are not related to any actual attack. Previous studies have shown that the vast majority of alerts generated by intrusion detection systems compose of these false positives [1,9]. Moreover, it is well known that false positives cause unnecessary analysis efforts and influence the decision process of cyber analysts [1,13]. It is thus important to model normal behavior in such a way that it triggers realistic volumes and types of false positives. In case that normal behavior is overly simplified, evaluation results of intrusion detection systems tested within cyber ranges may yield too low false positive rates [10]. Additionally, the scope of normal user behavior may have a direct effect on true positives when learning-based detectors are evaluated. For example, detection models trained on scenarios where benign users sometimes use incorrect login credentials – as they would in real life – may be less likely to detect brute-force login attempts than in scenarios with simplified user behavior where only valid logins occur and invalid ones are outliers.

Many public and widely used evaluation data sets have been criticized for lacking realistic behavior patterns that trigger false positives [2,15,17,19]. Despite these observations, little research has been conducted on the modeling of suspicious yet benign user activities in the past. With this paper we attempt to resolve this gap by analyzing benign user activities and their relation to false positives triggered by intrusion detection systems. To this end, we first identify groups of relevant user activities and group them into event types. We then develop a questionnaire and conduct a user study with security experts to analyze priorities, origin, intent, and circumstances of each event type. We summarize the contributions of this paper as follows.

- An identification of 17 normal behavior event types that cause false positives.
- A user survey to assess their relevance for tests and exercises.

The remainder of this paper is structured as follows. Section 2 reviews the background of normal user behavior simulation. Section 3 describes our strategies to identify and enumerate relevant benign event types. We present the results of our survey to assess our event types in Sect. 4 and discuss the implications of our findings in Sect. 5. Finally, Sect. 6 concludes the paper.

2   Related Work

Past research has analyzed false positives and their influence on alert triage, i.e., the process where human experts assess whether alerts indicate active threats that require immediate action. Alahmadi et al. [1] interviewed personnel of security operations centers and found that almost all alerts (up to 99%) are caused by so-called benign triggers, i.e., non-malicious user behavior. Their study shows that the sheer volume of these false positives leads to fatigue and incorrect decision making of analysts. Layman et al. [13] conduct a controlled experiment and find that higher levels of false alerts decrease the precision of decisions made by analysts and increase their time on task. Ho et al. [9] analyze alerts collected from a university network. They find that more than 90% of alerts are false positives and more than 90% of these false positives are caused by organizational policies. For example, such policies could be set in place to prevent peer-to-peer communication, which will trigger alerts even when used for benign activities.

Given the prevalence of alerts generated by suspicious yet benign behavior in real and productive networks, we review publications involving normal user simulations to check whether such behavior patterns are also reflected in the scopes of these models. Wright et al. [22] use state machines to simulate web browsing and document editing. Guttman et al. [8] propose a user simulation tool that interacts with web browsers, mail clients, office applications, FTP clients, chats, and telnet. Grimmer et al. [7] simulate users through scripts that automate web navigation, file uploads, and entering of text into forms. Creech et al.

[5] simulate web browsing and document preparation in order to create a normal behavior baseline for anomaly detection. Lashkari et al. [12] use three user profiles that interact with Gmail, Facebook, Skype, and Whatsapp. To evaluate deep packet inspection approaches, Megyesi et al. [16] automate user interaction with scripts or macros for Microsoft Windows programs, QuickTime, Flash, Bittorent, HTTP, SSL, DNS, Skype, Google, and ICMP. Van Sloun et al. [20] simulate direct interaction with GUI elements of web browsers, office applications, and mail clients to generate data sets for host-based intrusion detection evaluation. Dutta et al. [6] create bots that log into their accounts, send emails, browse websites, and create and modify documents based on observations from volunteers who interacted with their system. None of the aforementioned publications consider unusual user activities when defining the scope of their normal behavior models. Landauer et al. [10] use state machines to automate SSH interaction as well as web navigation in mail platforms and file shares. Even though their benign user models include entering of incorrect login credentials, they explicitly state that they did not purposefully design the models to trigger false positives, but mention that they could be generated as side-effects. Evaluation of intrusion detection systems on their data sets indeed shows that several benign user activities trigger alerts, such as correct and incorrect logins [11]; however, it remains unclear if they are representative for alerts from real users.

The realization that most evaluation data sets generated through simulations do not involve sufficiently complex and diverse user behavior is not a new one. Already in the year 2000, McHugh et al. [15] found that the background traffic contained in the DARPA data set, which was current at that time, is not representative for real Internet traffic. They state that real data involves legitimate but odd-looking traffic that could or should trigger intrusion detection systems, which is not the case in the analyzed data set. Further research has confirmed that the traffic in the DARPA data set is unusually uniform [2]. Sangster et al. [17] mention the small volume and low diversity of traffic generated during network warfare games that is not representative for production networks. A more recent review of existing data sets is provided by Sharafaldin et al. [19], who also criticize the lack of traffic diversity and volumes across most data sets and deem them unsuitable for estimating false positive rates that are accurate for real-world cases. To overcome this problem, the same authors propose an approach that analyzes features of real network statistics, such as packet sizes and the number of packets per flow, and recreates synthetic data following these distributions [18]. Unfortunately, this approach only generates synthetic network traffic but does not actually interact with applications within cyber ranges. Thus, it does not produce any system log data required to evaluate host-based intrusion detection systems.

In summary, most publications focusing on benign user simulation only model typical system interactions and assume that some false positives will be generated as by-products. Some authors are aware of issues with non-representative benign behavior, but have only resolved this by replicating distributions of real network traffic. None of the reviewed publications explicitly mention benign cases that should or even could appear suspicious for intrusion detection. We therefore assemble a set of relevant benign behavior patterns in the following section.

3   Analysis of Benign User Behavior Patterns

This section analyzes activities that are part of benign user behavior and have the potential to trigger intrusion detection systems. We first explain how we identify relevant types of events and which of their properties are used by analysts during triage. We then enumerate and describe each event type and provide examples.

3.1   Identification of Relevant Types of Benign Events

The literature contains numerous detailed models of attacker behavior, which is typically goal-oriented, follows well-known kill chains, and relies on techniques that can be systematically categorized using MITRE ATT&CK.[1] We argue that a comprehensive overview of user behavior relevant to cyber security is significantly more challenging to produce. The range of possible user activities is vast, the ways in which users can interact with systems are virtually limitless, and the specifics depend heavily on the operational context as well as the applications and services available to users [7]. Rather than focusing on specific protocols or applications as it has been done in previous literature [9], we therefore aim to identify abstract classes of activities that typically trigger false positives in intrusion detection systems in IT networks across many organizations.

We carried out our search for relevant types of benign events in three phases. Thereby, we internally discussed, refined, and iteratively grouped gathered events throughout all stages. First, we collected an initial list of events based on surveys that analyze the consequences of false positives on system operators [21]. For example, the questionnaire of Alahmadi et al. [1] involves several sources of alerts that can also be triggered as part of normal user and administrator activity, such as unusual outbound network traffic, log-in red flags, large number of requests for the same file, and several more. Second, we reviewed the open-source Sigma[2] database of intrusion detection signatures and selected those entries that contain the "falsepositives" field, which can be used by security analysts to state why the respective signature could be triggered by benign users. For example, a signature that detects suspicious file modifications mentions "Admin changing file permissions" as a potential source of false positives.[3] Third, we relied on interviews with practitioners such as security analysts that we reached through personal contacts. The discussions with these domain experts validated our identified set of relevant events and helped us to improve event descriptions and come up with real-world examples.

---

[1] https://attack.mitre.org/.

[2] https://github.com/SigmaHQ/sigma.

[3] Title: Chmod Suspicious Directory (id: 6419afd1-3742-47a5-a7e6-b50386cd15f8).

3.2 Event Types

After completing our search for user activities that trigger false positives in intrusion detection systems as outlined in the previous section, we ended up with 17 distinct types of events. We enumerate all events in the following without any particular order and provide some examples.

(1) **File Permissions.** Users changing permissions for files, e.g., setting files as executable, making folders accessible for everyone on the machine, or creating shared folders.

(2) **User Privileges.** Users changing the privileges of users or groups, e.g., adding new users to machines or servers, creating new user groups, increasing or decreasing privileges of other users, or adding privileges to user groups.

(3) **OS Configurations.** Users changing the configuration of operating systems, e.g., manipulating scheduled tasks, changing service settings, changing system recovery and backup configurations, or changing preferred applications of file extensions.

(4) **Many Copy-Operations.** Users copying a considerable amount of files within short time periods, e.g., copying many files to a folder and compressing them, sorting of many files, synchronizing folders to file servers of organizations, or creating backup copies of entire disks or databases.

(5) **Custom Scripts.** Users executing scripts for task automation, e.g., scraping of internal sites to gather information, sorting of files using PowerShell or bash, or using record-features for task automation in office applications.

(6) **Network commands.** Users executing complex network commands, e.g., executing software to capture network traffic, adjusting settings related to network interfaces, iptables, or the local firewall, or executing commands such as ifconfig, ping, tracert, or netstat.

(7) **System Commands.** Users executing complex system commands on machines, e.g., executing tools in Windows Sysinternals, using Event Viewer (Windows) or journalctl (Linux), executing applications as admin (Windows) or root (Linux), or changing settings such as whitelists or antivirus.

(8) **Software Installation.** Users installing new software or updates of existing software, e.g., running apt-get (Linux) or Windows Update, pressing the update button of any software, running msi-files or exe-files to install software.

(9) **Credential Updates.** Users changing password or credentials, e.g., changing of user account passwords or resetting passwords of web accounts.

(10) **Server Login.** Users logging onto servers, e.g., using remote desktop connections, PsExec, or ssh to check network interfaces or logging onto domain controllers, web servers, or mail servers.

(11) **Server Checks/Cleaning.** Users checking or cleaning servers, e.g., monitoring server performance metrics such as CPU usage, cleaning temporary files with Windows Disk Cleanup, or sifting through system logs.

(12) Server Reboot. Users rebooting servers, e.g., rebooting after system updates or crashes.

(13) Inbound Connections. Users initiating connections to services or machines in organization networks from external sources, e.g., creating VPN connections into organization networks or connecting to terminal servers.

(14) Software Execution. Users executing software on systems, e.g., executing unknown software, executing software that repeatedly crashes, or executing debugging tools.

(15) New Network Device. Users adding new machines or devices to the network, e.g., adding devices with new MAC addresses to the organization network or adding new machines to Windows domains.

(16) Failed Login. Users failing to logon to servers, e.g., entering wrong passwords sufficiently many times to cause that their accounts are blocked or attempting to login with alternative user names.

(17) Outbound Connections. Users initiating connections to external services or machines from within organization networks, e.g., uploading data to external repositories, using peer-to-peer protocols, or using legacy software to connect to remote servers.

3.3   Survey

We developed a questionnaire to assess the relevance of all event types enumerated in the previous section. Given that we are interested in the selection of events for simulations and cyber exercises, we consider event types as relevant if they are frequent in comparison to other events, likely triggered by normal user behavior, and have high impact on analysts, e.g., by occupying a significant amount of time for triage. To cover all aspects, we split our questionnaire into four categories: **(Q1) Priority**, which asks whether events are (Q1.1) important to monitor, (Q1.2) cause security alerts, (Q1.3) occupy analysts' time, and (Q1.4) lead to investigations. **(Q2) Origin**, which asks whether events are caused by users with (Q2.1) typical or normal privileges, (Q2.2) special or admin privileges, or (Q2.3) unauthorized actors. **(Q3) Intent**, which asks whether events are eventually determined to be caused with (Q3.1) malicious intent, (Q3.2) good intent, or (Q3.3) pose a real threat. **(Q4) Circumstances**, which asks about the unusual circumstances that are required so that analysts occupy their time with analyzing that event. Specifically, for each event we ask about its subject (e.g., the user triggering the event), object (e.g., the affected machine), timing (e.g., whether the event occurs outside of usual working hours such as weekends), and frequency (e.g., the number of times the event occurs in short time periods). Responses to questions of all categories are entered on a five point likert scale with the following levels: *Never, Rarely, Sometimes, Often,* and *Always*. Participants also had the option to select *Not Applicable* as a response to any question. To avoid any bias that originates from the order in which event types are presented to the participants, we configure the survey to randomize their order each time the survey is started by a new participant.

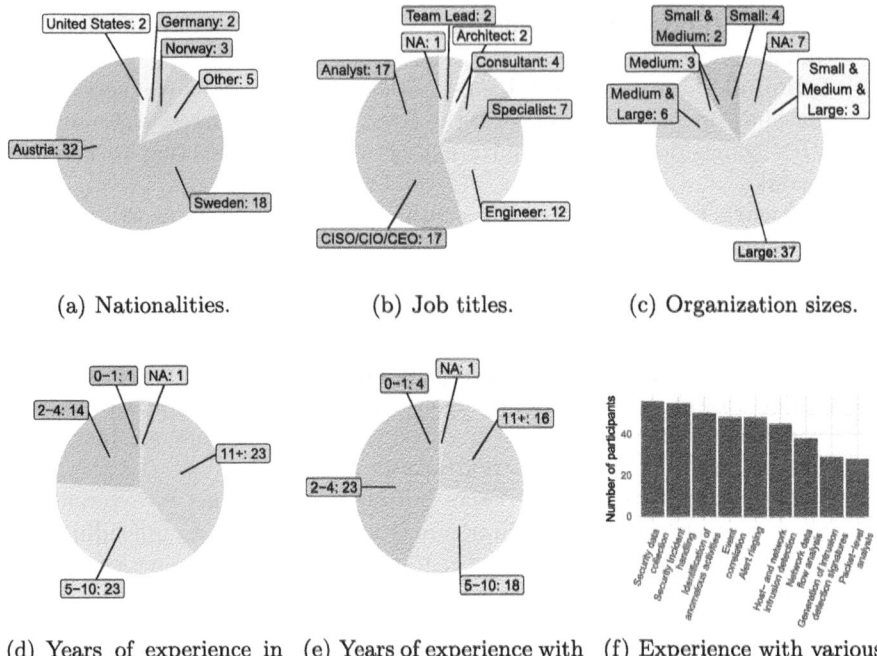

(a) Nationalities.   (b) Job titles.   (c) Organization sizes.

(d) Years of experience in   (e) Years of experience with   (f) Experience with various
cyber security.   security log/event analysis.   cyber security tasks.

Fig. 1. Demographics and background information of all 62 participants of our study.

We extended the survey with several questions about the background of participants, for example, their nationalities and experiences in the security domain, which we will describe in more detail in the following section. Moreover, on the first page of the survey, participants were informed about the purpose of this study and that their data and responses will be used and published in course of scientific research projects. The survey was conducted anonymously; however, participants had the option to provide their email address to enter a prize draw or to receive information about the study results. On the final page, we collected feedback about the survey itself.

The survey was hosted from September to December 2024 on a publicly accessible website. We gathered participants by sharing a link to the survey with professional contacts, on cyber security mailing lists, and within research projects. Moreover, we advertised the survey during a large cyber security events that took place in Austria in September 2024 and in Sweden in December 2024. In the end we obtained responses from 62 unique participants who rated at least one event type. We provide detailed results gathered from the survey in the following section.

4   Results

This sections presents the results of our survey. We first analyze the demographics of participants and then present their responses in detail.

4.1   Participants

This section presents some background information about the participants. Figure 1a shows their nationalities, which reveals that around 80% of all participants are either Austrian or Swedish. This is not surprising given that the authors of this paper are located in these two countries and leveraged personal contacts as well as national events to spread the survey. Figure 1b summarizes job titles, which shows that even though the majority of participants have technical roles (e.g., security engineers or analysts), there are also several managers among the participants. Figure 1c plots the sizes of organizations monitored by the participants. As visible in the plot, the vast majority of them are monitoring large organizations with more than 250 employees or more than 50 million Euro turnover. Figure 1d and Fig. 1e show the experience of participants in cyber security and security log/event analysis respectively, which ranges from newly employed to more than 10 years. Figure 1f shows the exact cyber security tasks where participants are experienced in; as visible, there is a significant number of people with experience in each of the mentioned tasks. In summary, even though there is a strong tendency that participants are monitoring large organizations either in Austria or Sweden, the demographics indicate that our respondents comprise a diverse mix of highly skilled cyber security experts.

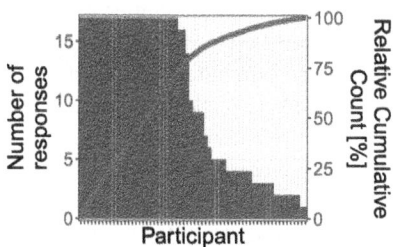

(a) Responses per participant.

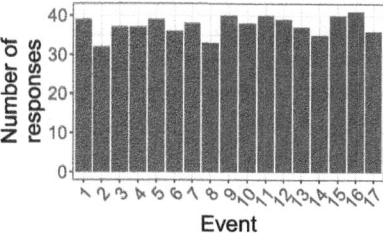

(b) Responses per question.

Fig. 2. Overview of the number of responses.

4.2   Responses

We first provide an overview of the responses received from participants. Figure 2a depicts the number of responses per participant, where each response corresponds to one event type assessed by the respective participant. As visible in the plot, 27 out of 62 participants have completed the entire survey; others have only assessed some of the event types. We use the responses from all participants independent from the number of event types they assessed for our survey. Even though some participants dropped out during the survey, we expect roughly the same number of responses for each event type as they are presented to participants in random order. Figure 2b depicts the number of responses per event type; on average, we have around 37 responses per event type at our disposal.

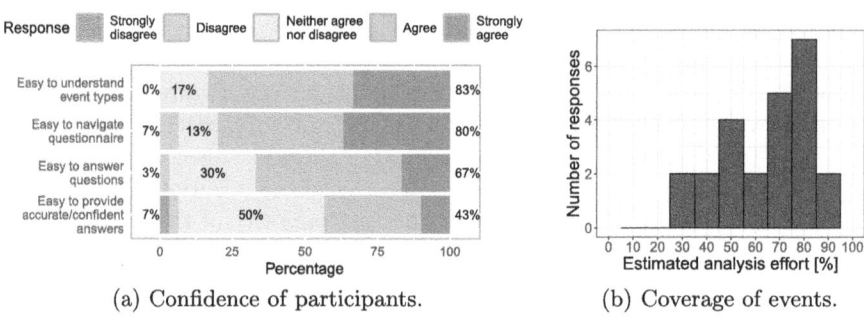

(a) Confidence of participants.   (b) Coverage of events.

Fig. 3. Feedback received from participants.

On the final page of the survey we ask participants about their opinion on the survey itself and how confident they are about their answers. Figure 3a shows that most users have positive feelings about the survey itself and found it easy to navigate the questionnaire and answer the questions. However, even though the vast majority seem to have no issues understanding the event types, they are less confident about the accuracy of their answers with only 43% agreeing or strongly agreeing on the last question. To estimate how many of the relevant log events we covered in our enumeration, we also ask participants to rate how much log analysis effort they believe is spent on the presented events altogether, where 0% means that the events covered in the survey cause no effort at all and 100% means that all events that cause effort are present in the survey. Figure 3b plots the results on a histogram, which reveals that the distribution is relatively spread out but peaks around 70%–80%. The average of 67% and median of 74% indicate that some participants believe that some normal behavior events are missing from our enumeration, even though no suggestions for events were stated in the free-form text field.

4.3   Event Type Priorities

This section provides visualizations for the responses of each question in our survey, which we count separately for each event type. Figure 4 displays plots of likert scales for questions related to (Q1) event priorities. As visible in plot Q1.1, most participants agree that it is important to monitor most of the event types;

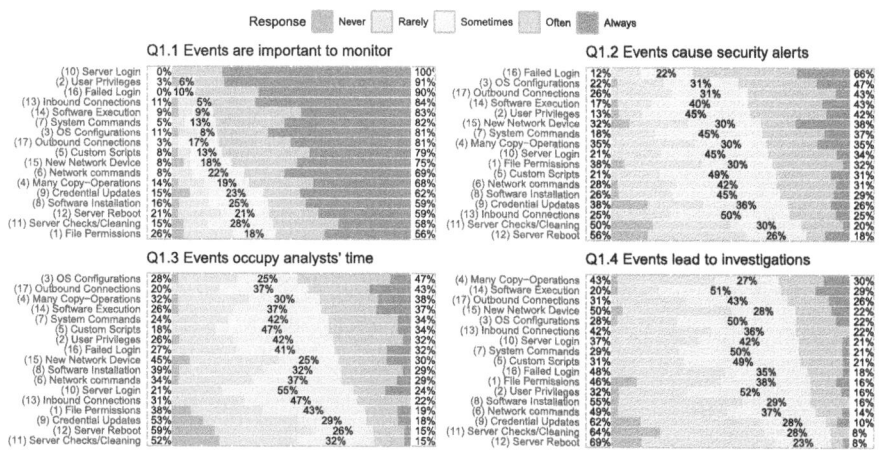

Fig. 4. Responses regarding priorities of analyzed events.

specifically, events related to *(10) Server Login* and *(2) User Privileges* yield high scores. There is less agreement among the participants for questions Q1.2-Q1.4, in particular, there are similar numbers of votes for the categories *Rarely*, *Sometimes*, and *Often*, while categories *Never* and *Always* are hardly used. Note that in each plot we sort the events by the aggregated number of votes for *Often* and *Always*; however, the order of events would be different when sorting by other categories, e.g., by aggregating votes of *Never* and *Rarely*. This caveat is also valid for the following likert plots in this paper and indicates that the displayed order of events should only be considered as a rough indicator rather than an exact assessment that allows to compare any two event types.

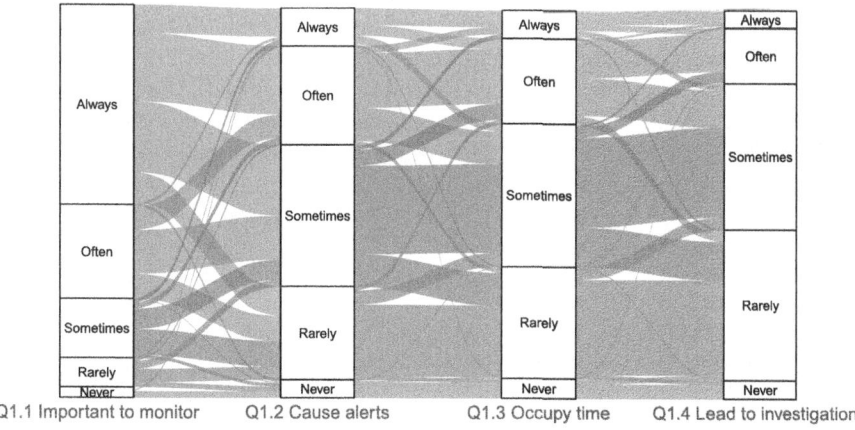

Fig. 5. Flow diagram of event priorities.

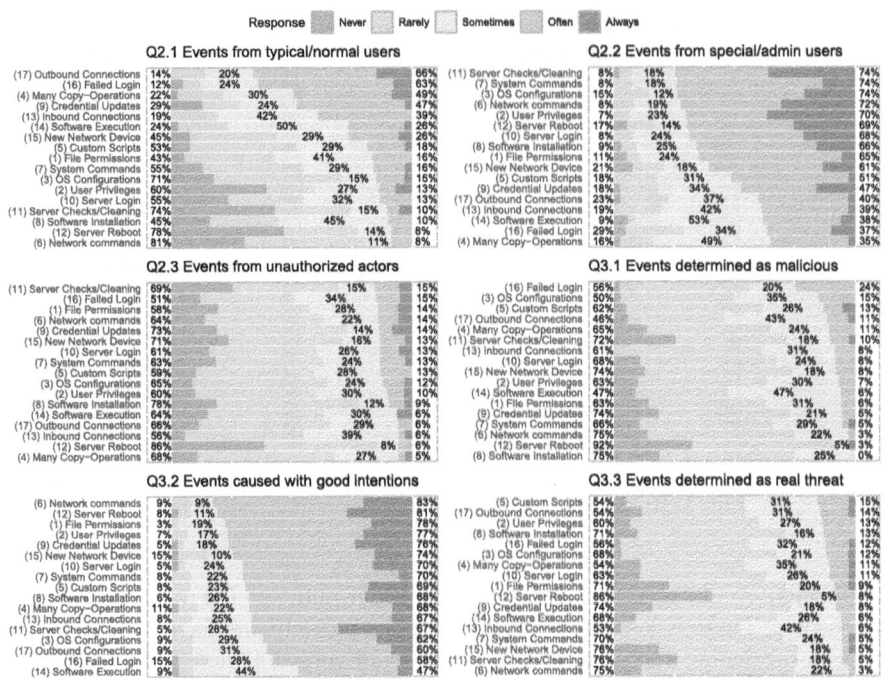

Fig. 6. Responses regarding origin and intent of analyzed events.

There are some logical dependencies between the four questions Q1.1-Q1.4. For example, those event types that are more likely to cause alerts (Q1.2) should also be the ones that are more likely to occupy analysts' time (Q1.3). To investigate these dependencies, we plot the responses as a flow diagram in Fig. 5. The plot confirms this assumption as most participants consistently selected the same categories for most event types when estimating their likelihood of causing security alerts (Q1.2), occupying analysts' time (Q1.3), and leading to investigations (Q1.4). However, the plot also shows that many of the events that are regarded as important to monitor (Q1.1) are not necessarily the ones that frequently cause alerts (Q1.2), since about half of the event types that should always be monitored only sometimes or rarely produce any alerts. On the other hand, those event types that are considered to be only sometimes or rarely important to monitor also hardly produce any alerts.

4.4 Influence of User Role

Figure 6 visualizes the responses to questions that deal with the origin of event types (Q2). Plot Q2.1 indicates that users with typical or normal privileges are most likely responsible for triggering false positives related to *(17) Outbound Connections*. This aligns with the findings from Ho et al. [9], who make certain application clients that generate outbound connections responsible for generating suspicious network traffic. Another highly ranked event type is *(16) Failed Login*. In comparison to normal users, plot Q2.2 shows that users with special or admin privileges are significantly more likely to frequently trigger false alerts corresponding to diverse event types. This is reasonable, since only privileged users have or should have the abilities and responsibilities to carry out activities that could trigger some of the highly ranked event types, such as the ones related to *(11) Server Checks/Cleaning* or *(3) OS Configurations*. Finally, plot Q2.3 shows that all event types are roughly equally likely to be generated by unauthorized actors, with low frequency overall in comparison to the two previous cases.

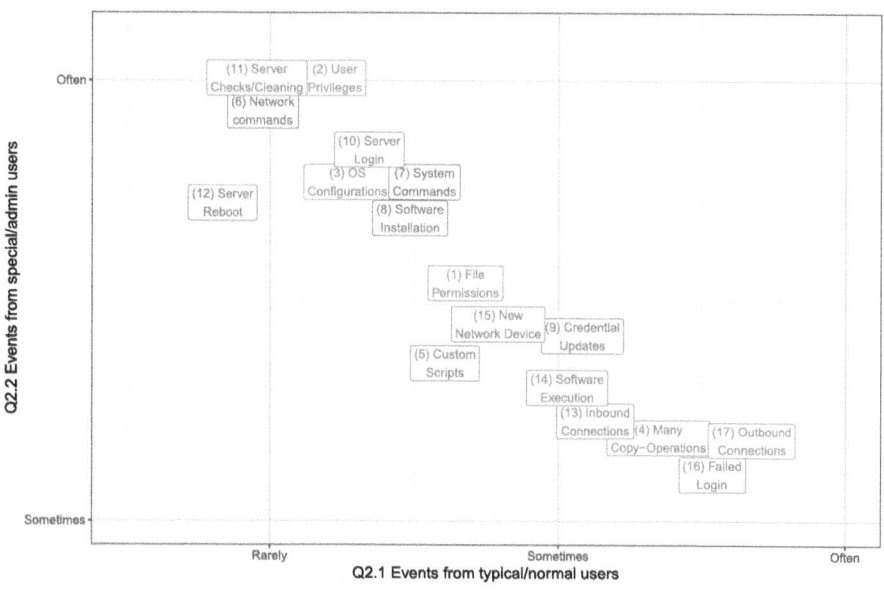

Fig. 7. Likelihood of events originating from privileged or unprivileged users.

Figure 7 allows to better understand the relation between event types generated by unprivileged (Q2.1) and privileged (Q2.2) users. The scatter plot places labels of each event type at the mean position of all responses, where we encode the five categories *Never* to *Always* with the numeric values 1 to 5 in order to compute the means. Despite some disagreement among the participants (cf. Figure 6), the means are roughly located along a diagonal line that stretches from the top left part of the plot, where event types that are often generated by privileged users but rarely by unprivileged users, to the bottom right, containing event types that are often generated by unprivileged users.

4.5   Intent Behind Events

Figure 6 also provides the plots corresponding to the intentions behind events that cause analysis efforts (Q3). The 17 event types included in the questionnaire were selected based on their perceived tendency to trigger false positives and unnecessary analysis efforts. Consistent with this, events requiring analysis were generally found to stem from good intentions (Q3.1) and were ultimately deemed non-malicious (Q3.2). Only a minority of events were eventually determined to be caused by actual threats (Q3.3). These results align with the findings from Alahmadi et al. [1], who conclude that the vast majority of events handled in Security Operation Centers are false positives that are not actually related to cyber attacks. They also support the notion that the 17 event types are relevant to consider in cyber security exercises and tests where analysis effort and false alerts are important.

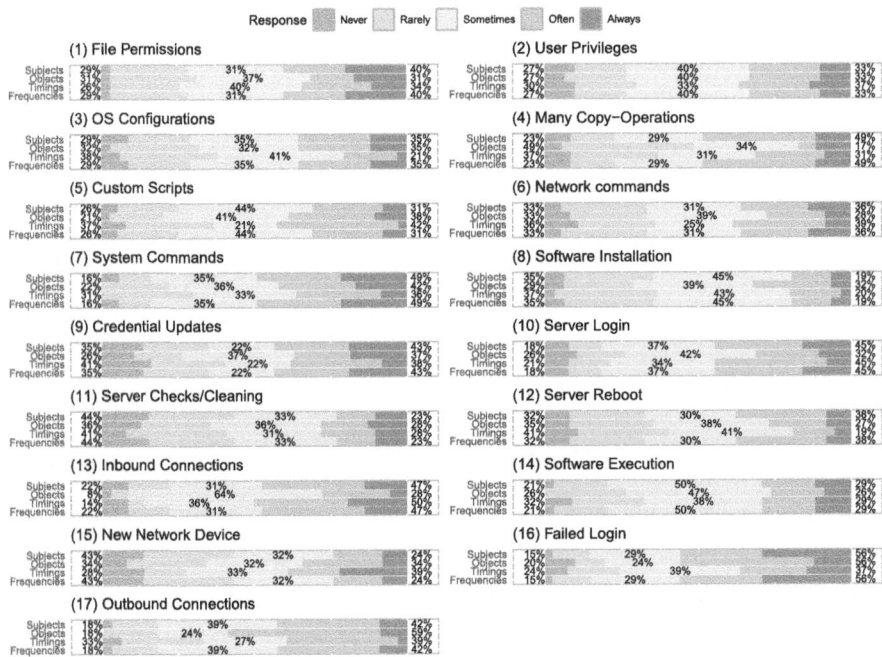

Fig. 8. Responses regarding the circumstances of analyzed events.

4.6   Circumstances of Event Occurrences

The final group of questions (Q4) concerns the circumstances of event occurrence and its relevance for analysis and triage. Figure 8 visualizes the responses for each of the four context attributes (subject, object, timing, frequency) separately for each event type. Once more, disagreement among participants is substantial and circumstances of most event types receive a fair share of responses across all categories. Thus, event simulations should consider the subject causing the event (e.g., user account), the object involved (e.g., server), the time (e.g., at night), and frequency (e.g., a burst). All of these can make events more or less interesting to an analyst.

5   Discussion

Realism of normal behavior simulations is critical when designing cyber exercises and test environments that aim to reflect real-world settings. In the sections below we discuss what event types to consider, which details to consider when events are simulated, and recommendations for future research.

5.1   Relevant Event Types

The study presented in this paper identified 17 abstract event types that can be associated with false alerts and are common across many organizational IT networks. We conducted a survey among practitioners to validate the relevance of this list and estimate how often these event types cause analysis efforts in operational networks. The results of our study suggest that all of the 17 event types can trigger intrusion detection systems even when responsible users have good intentions (cf. Sect. 4.5), and that the resulting false positives require manual review from security analysts (cf. Sect. 4.3). Thus, all event types stated in Sect. 3.2 deserve consideration when designing cyber security exercises or tests that involve challenging background events. Furthermore, as seen in Sect. 4.2, the event types covered in this survey appear to cover about two thirds of all events to consider.

We acknowledge that the presented rankings of event types (cf. Sects. 4.3–4.6) serve only as rough indicators and that no definitive trends can be drawn from our results. The reason for that is the substantial dispersion of responses observed for most questions of our survey. Interestingly, even though most participants claimed to understand the questionnaire and many exhibit confidence in their responses, their experiences with false positives seem to be highly individual. In fact, several participants use the free-form text field at the end of the survey to point out that they have made various experiences with false positives and that their occurrences depend on several factors. Foremost, they mention that the types and frequencies of false positives strongly depend on the tolerance of deployed detection systems. In addition, they state that alert assessment and triage often relies on domain knowledge about the networks, e.g., alerts from systems where no users should be active are automatically regarded as critical. One participant recognizes that even though they provided answers from their own perspective, they are aware that other analysts handle false positives differently. Based on the received responses and feedback, we thus conclude that security analysts experience different types of false positives at varying frequencies, which possibly depends on their area of expertise. Moreover, entire security teams may deal with different false positives depending on specific detection policies that vary across monitored organizations.

5.2 Simulating Events in Cyber Ranges

Our study provides guidance for developers in designing user behavior models that produce false positives during cyber exercises. Specifically, our results allow to decide which of the suspicious yet benign event types selected for implementation should be executed by network administrators or normal users (cf. Sect. 4.4). Moreover, the results of our study suggest that all four types of circumstances (subject, object, timing, and frequency) covered in the survey appear to be important across all event types (cf. Sect. 4.6). In alignment with the simulated security scenario, simulations should therefore include some variation to these attributes, e.g., by triggering false positives at unusual times or in bursts.

5.3 Recommendations for Future Research

Overall, the feedback on our questionnaire is positive. Most participants reported to understand the questions asked and many expressed confidence in their responses (cf. Sect. 4.2). Thus, the questionnaire may be suitable for reuse in future studies. To support future research on this topic, we point out some improvements that we derive from the free-text feedback. Two participants mention that they find the five point likert scale insufficient and propose to extend it to a seven point scale that additionally includes *Very Rarely* and *Almost Always* as choices. As an alternative, we suggest to use pairwise comparisons of event types to avoid having to deal with options such as *Sometimes* altogether, which can have different meaning to each participant. One participant states that the presented event types are too generic for accurate assessment; specifically, they mention that the impact of alerts related to *(6) Network commands* heavily depends on the exact command that is executed. It thus also stands to reason to further subdivide the list of events proposed in this paper or add technical aspects as contextual attributes (cf. Sect. 4.6), such as geographic location or connection details [13].

The sample in this survey is biased toward Europe, in particular, Austria and Sweden (cf. Sect. 4.1). However, similar studies could be applied to other populations to yield more generalizable results. With larger sample sizes, it may also be possible to identify differences between populations based on factors such as industrial sector, organizational size, and other characteristics.

Realistic simulation of normal user behavior remains challenging since the number and diversity of benign activities as well as the ways in which they can potentially be executed seem virtually endless. To handle this complexity, we recommend to develop and benchmark normal behavior models based on real user data collected from productive systems and avoid any simplifications, i.e., also recognize rare and suspicious activities as essential parts of the model. In particular, such comparisons could base on the number of diversity of alerts generated by a diverse set of intrusion detection systems, including both network-based and host-based as well as signature-based and anomaly-based approaches. Finally, we believe that future work could investigate to what degree large language models are useful to reduce manual effort when designing large and complex behavior models.

6 Conclusion

Simulations in cyber exercises and tests often neglect suspicious yet benign user activities, even though they are relevant sources of false positives in real-world networks. In this paper we therefore review existing literature, analyze detection signatures, and interview practitioners to enumerate 17 abstract event types that correspond to benign activities that often trigger intrusion detection systems. We then carry out a user study with 62 participants to assess the prevalence of these event types, their likeliness to influence the analysis and triage procedure, and whether they originate from benign users with or without special system privileges. The results of our study indicate that some event types are more frequently associated with false positives than others, such as changes to user privileges that are often carried out by privileged system administrators. At the same time, we observe significant disagreement among the participants of the study, which suggests that experiences with false positives are highly individual and depend on the operational context.

Acknowledgment. This work has received funding from the European Union - European Defence Fund under GA no. 101103385 (AInception). Views and opinions expressed are however those of the author(s) only and do not necessarily reflect those of the European Union. The European Union cannot be held responsible for them.

References

1. Alahmadi, B.A., Axon, L., Martinovic, I.: 99% false positives: a qualitative study of soc analysts' perspectives on security alarms. In: Proceedings of the 31st USENIX Security Symposium, pp. 2783–2800 (2022)
2. Brown, C., Cowperthwaite, A., Hijazi, A., Somayaji, A.: Analysis of the 1999 darpa/lincoln laboratory ids evaluation data with netadhict. In: Proceedings of the Symposium on Computational Intelligence for Security and Defense Applications, pp. 1–7. IEEE (2009)
3. Chouliaras, N., Kittes, G., Kantzavelou, I., Maglaras, L., Pantziou, G., Ferrag, M.A.: Cyber ranges and testbeds for education, training, and research. Appl. Sci. **11**(4), 1809 (2021)
4. Cram, W.A., Proudfoot, J., D'Arcy, J.: Seeing the forest and the trees: A meta-analysis of information security policy compliance literature (2017)
5. Creech, G., Hu, J.: Generation of a new ids test dataset: time to retire the kdd collection. In: Proceedings of the Wireless Communications and Networking Conference, pp. 4487–4492. IEEE (2013)

6. Dutta, P., Ryan, G., Zieba, A., Stolfo, S.: Simulated user bots: real time testing of insider threat detection systems. In: Proceedings of the Security and Privacy Workshops, pp. 228–236. IEEE (2018)

7. Grimmer, M., Röhling, M.M., Kreusel, D., Ganz, S.: A modern and sophisticated host based intrusion detection data set. IT-Sicherheit als Voraussetzung für eine erfolgreiche Digitalisierung **11**, 135–145 (2019)

8. Guttman, R.D., Hammerstein, J.A., Mattson, J.A., Schlackman, A.L.: Automated failure detection and attribution in virtual environments. In: Proceedings of the Symposium on Technologies for Homeland Security. pp. 1–5. IEEE (2015)

9. Ho, C.Y., Lai, Y.C., Chen, I.W., Wang, F.Y., Tai, W.H.: Statistical analysis of false positives and false negatives from real traffic with intrusion detection/prevention systems. IEEE Commun. Mag. **50**(3), 146–154 (2012)

10. Landauer, M., Skopik, F., Frank, M., Hotwagner, W., Wurzenberger, M., Rauber, A.: Maintainable log datasets for evaluation of intrusion detection systems. IEEE Trans. Dependable Secure Comput. **20**(4), 3466–3482 (2022)

11. Landauer, M., Skopik, F., Wurzenberger, M.: Introducing a new alert data set for multi-step attack analysis. In: Proceedings of the 17th Cyber Security Experimentation and Test Workshop, pp. 41–53 (2024)

12. Lashkari, A.H., Kadir, A.F.A., Taheri, L., Ghorbani, A.A.: Toward developing a systematic approach to generate benchmark android malware datasets and classification. In: Proceedings of the International Carnahan Conference on Security Technology, pp. 1–7. IEEE (2018)

13. Layman, L., Roden, W.: A controlled experiment on the impact of intrusion detection false alarm rate on analyst performance. In: Proceedings of the Human Factors and Ergonomics Society Annual Meeting. vol. 67, pp. 220–225. SAGE (2023)

14. Leitner, M., et al.: Enabling exercises, education and research with a comprehensive cyber range. J. Wirel. Mob. Networks, Ubiquitous Comput. Dependable Appl. **12**(4), 37–61 (2021)

15. McHugh, J.: Testing intrusion detection systems: a critique of the 1998 and 1999 darpa intrusion detection system evaluations as performed by lincoln laboratory. ACM Trans. Inf. Syst. Secur. **3**(4), 262–294 (2000)

16. Megyesi, P., Szabó, G., Molnár, S.: User behavior based traffic emulator: a framework for generating test data for dpi tools. Comput. Netw. **92**, 41–54 (2015)

17. Sangster, B., O'connor, T., Cook, T., Fanelli, R., Dean, E., Morrell, C., Conti, G.J.: Toward instrumenting network warfare competitions to generate labeled datasets. In: Proceedings of the 2nd Cyber Security Experimentation and Test Workshop (2009)

18. Sharafaldin, I., Gharib, A., Lashkari, A.H., Ghorbani, A.A., et al.: Towards a reliable intrusion detection benchmark dataset. Softw. Networking **2018**(1), 177–200 (2018)

19. Sharafaldin, I., Lashkari, A.H., Ghorbani, A.A.: Toward generating a new intrusion detection dataset and intrusion traffic characterization. In: Proceedings of the 4th International Conference on Information Systems Security and Privacy, pp. 108–116. SciTePress (2018)

20. van Sloun, C., Wehrle, K.: Poster: Vulcan–repurposing accessibility features for behavior-based intrusion detection dataset generation. In: Proceedings of the Conference on Computer and Communications Security, pp. 3543–3545 (2023)

21. Tjhai, G.C., Papadaki, M., Furnell, S., Clarke, N.L.: Investigating the problem of ids false alarms: an experimental study using snort. In: Proceedings of the 23rd International Information Security Conference, pp. 253–267. Springer (2008)

22. Wright, C.V., Connelly, C., Braje, T., Rabek, J.C., Rossey, L.M., Cunningham, R.K.: Generating client workloads and high-fidelity network traffic for controllable, repeatable experiments in computer security. In: Proceedings of the International workshop on Recent Advances in Intrusion Detection, pp. 218–237. Springer (2010)
23. Yamin, M.M., Katt, B., Gkioulos, V.: Cyber ranges and security testbeds: scenarios, functions, tools and architecture. Comput. Secur. **88**, 101636 (2020)

Enhancing Cyber Situational Awareness with AI: A Novel Pipeline Approach for Threat Intelligence Analysis and Enrichment

Dzenan Hamzic[1]([✉])(iD), Florian Skopik[1](iD), Max Landauer[1](iD),
Markus Wurzenberger[1](iD), and Andreas Rauber[2](iD)

[1] AIT Austrian Institute of Technology, Vienna, Austria
{dzenan.hamzic,florian.skopik,max.landauer,markus.wurzenberger}@ait.ac.at
[2] Vienna University of Technology, Vienna, Austria
rauber@ifs.tuwien.ac.at

Abstract. Cyber Situational Awareness (CSA) is crucial for understanding and anticipating developments across diverse domains. This paper introduces a novel approach employing advanced Artificial Intelligence (AI) and Natural Language Processing (NLP) techniques to effectively analyze and enrich Cyber Threat Intelligence (CTI) and Open Source Intelligence (OSINT) data. The paper designs an unified CTI and OSINT processing pipeline that integrates named entity recognition (NER), relationship extraction, classification, and summarization, addressing current limitations in CTI analysis. Notably, our evaluation of existing language models revealed significant shortcomings, with general-purpose tokenizers recognizing only 1.62% of specialized MITRE ATT&CK terms. In contrast, our pipeline achieves superior performance, notably surpassing state-of-the-art models in some important aspects. Practical military and civilian scenarios further demonstrate the pipeline's value in generating actionable intelligence, enabling complex reasoning by combining symbolic knowledge graphs and semantic vector search methods. Future developments focus on refining model scalability and enhancing analytical capabilities to increase the effectiveness, efficiency, and applicability of our approach.

Keywords: cyber situational awareness · cyber threat intelligence · nlp · defence industry · cti processing pipeline

1 Introduction

Cyber Situational awareness (CSA) refers to understanding what is happening in a given context and is essential across domains such as aviation, military operations, emergency response, healthcare, and power grid management [7]. More precisely, SA involves perceiving elements in the environment, understanding

© The Author(s) 2025
B. Coppens et al. (Eds.): ARES 2025 Workshops, LNCS 15995, pp. 44–62, 2025.
https://doi.org/10.1007/978-3-032-00633-2_3

their meaning, and anticipating future developments [13]. It relies on integrating diverse and distributed data sources [6].

Modern systems generate vast amounts of data reflecting internal states and external conditions. With advances in Internet and datalink technologies, data can be gathered from virtually anywhere. The challenge today lies not in data availability but in accessing, filtering, and retrieving relevant information efficiently [6].

Cyber Situational Awareness (CSA) focuses on the digital domain, utilizing data from various cyber sensors, including intrusion detection system (IDS) alerts and Cyber Threat Intelligence (CTI). This information often originates from Open Source Intelligence (OSINT) and is subsequently processed by analytical tools or directly assessed by decision-makers [23].

OSINT tools have emerged to address the task of collecting publicly available information for intelligence purposes. Although many such tools exist, they are often limited in scope-either focusing on a single source or integrating data from multiple platforms in a way that hinders streamlined processing and analysis. This limitation underscores the need for advanced intelligence systems capable of rapidly providing relevant insights and supporting the generation of actionable intelligence [15].

To maintain accurate CSA, it is crucial to correlate, filter, prioritize, and interpret large volumes of complex data. Artificial intelligence (AI) and natural language processing (NLP) offer promising solutions to automate these tasks, thereby supporting analysts and decision-makers in both strategic and operational contexts [3,16,21,23].

To address the challenges of processing unstructured, noisy, and high-volume CTI and OSINT data that posseses inconsistent formats, lack structure, and limit the use of automation, this paper presents a comprehensive AI- and NLP-driven analysis pipeline that enables end users (militaries, security operations centers, national and cross-border cyber hubs, etc.) to perform advanced document analysis through prompt-based interaction. The proposed solution enables efficient aggregation, extraction, and structuring of intelligence to enhance cyber threat detection and response in both military and civilian contexts.

The key contributions of this work are:

- Present a unified AI/NLP pipeline for processing, preparing, and enriching CTI and OSINT data.
- Address current limitations in OSINT/CTI analysis.
- Discuss and describe how the pipeline components can be implemented.
- Propose structured approaches for interpreting unstructured intelligence reports to support analytical workflows.
- Identify areas related to OSINT analysis that require further research.
- Illustrate the proposed approach through fictional but realistic military and civilian cybersecurity scenarios.

The remainder of this paper structures as follows: Sect. 2 reviews related work in CTI processing. Section 3 presents our OSINT analysis and enrichment pipeline. Section 4 demonstrates a practical example of pipeline usage. Section 5 illustrates fictional military and civil scenarios. Section 6 presents the conclusion and outlines future work.

2 Related Work

Recent advancements in CTI have increasingly focused on automating data extraction and analysis from heterogeneous sources to address challenges posed by large volumes of unstructured data. Chang [4] proposed an automated pipeline specifically designed to predict tactics and techniques according to the MITRE ATT&CK framework. This approach emphasized scalable data collection and preprocessing techniques, significantly reducing manual effort. However, it mainly focused on general CTI extraction without explicitly considering comprehensive structured information extraction and advanced relationship identification necessary for complex scenarios faced by various organizations, including military, governmental, and commercial entities.

To enhance CTI analysis further, recent studies have begun integrating AI comprehensively throughout the entire CTI processing lifecycle. Alevizos and Dekker [2] introduced a structured AI-enhanced CTI pipeline, leveraging neural networks for intelligence ingestion, collaborative human-AI analysis, and automated generation of predictive mitigation strategies. While this pipeline provides substantial improvements in automation, speed, and accuracy, it does not explicitly integrate structured knowledge graphs and semantic retrieval mechanisms. Consequently, it lacks the capability for complex multi-hop reasoning, crucial for comprehensive situational awareness and strategic decision-making across diverse organizational contexts.

Addressing domain-specific requirements, Zhou et al. [25] developed the CTI View framework, explicitly targeting Advanced Persistent Threat (APT) intelligence extraction. By employing customized NLP models, particularly a hybrid BERT-BiLSTM-CRF architecture enhanced with GRU layers, CTI View demonstrated superior performance in identifying critical threat entities and Indicators of Compromise (IOCs) from heterogeneous textual reports. Despite these advancements, the approach predominantly addresses entity extraction and did not incorporate advanced relationship extraction or reasoning capabilities, which are pivotal for constructing comprehensive cyber situational awareness frameworks applicable to multiple sectors.

In a similar vein, Alam et al. [1] introduced LADDER, an innovative knowledge extraction framework designed to extract and categorize attack patterns from CTI reports systematically. LADDER effectively addresses the extraction of complex attack patterns, mapping them comprehensively to the MITRE ATT&CK framework. Although LADDER significantly advances pattern extraction, it does not extensively address semantic retrieval or the integration of structured symbolic reasoning via knowledge graphs for enhanced query capabilities.

Li et al. [11] proposed AttacKG, a method for automatically extracting structured attack behavior graphs from CTI reports and constructing Technique

Knowledge Graphs (TKGs). AttacKG aggregates detailed technique-level knowledge across multiple CTI reports, providing valuable insights into the dependencies and interactions among attack entities. However, AttacKG primarily focuses on constructing knowledge graphs at the technique level without deeply integrating semantic retrieval methodologies or leveraging transformer-based NLP models for advanced textual analysis.

Further advancing the extraction and classification of tactics, techniques, and procedures (TTPs), Rani et al. [17] introduced TTPXHunter. This tool significantly enhances cybersecurity threat intelligence by automatically extracting actionable TTPs from cyber threat reports. It employs advanced natural language models fine-tuned on domain-specific data, achieving superior accuracy compared to previous approaches. Nonetheless, while effective in TTP extraction, TTPXHunter does not inherently support complex relationship extraction or multi-hop query capabilities through integrated symbolic knowledge graphs.

Rani et al. [19] also proposed CAPTAIN, a novel APT attribution method leveraging TTP sequences to identify threat actors accurately. CAPTAIN introduces a sophisticated similarity measure for comparing sequences of TTPs to attribute cyber-attacks to specific APT groups. While highly effective for attribution tasks, CAPTAIN primarily focuses on TTP-based attribution without explicitly integrating semantic search or advanced relationship reasoning across broader CTI applications.

Despite significant progress, the reviewed approaches share common limitations: They often lack comprehensive integration of entity extraction, relationship modeling, and semantic reasoning in a unified pipeline. Specifically, most solutions either focus narrowly on entity recognition, TTP extraction, or attack attribution, without supporting the full transformation of unstructured CTI into structured, queryable knowledge. Moreover, they frequently omit multi-hop reasoning capabilities by not combining symbolic knowledge graphs with semantic retrieval mechanisms. In response to these shared gaps, our paper proposes a holistic pipeline that integrates advanced NLP, transformer-based models, and dual-retrieval techniques-combining knowledge graphs for structured reasoning with vector search for semantic enrichment. This enables detailed, explainable, and context-aware cyber situational awareness applicable across organizational contexts, from military to civilian domains.

3   Method for CTI Analysis and Enrichment

The proposed OSINT analysis and enrichment pipeline (see Fig. 1) consists of eight sequential steps designed to enhance CTI texts for efficient storage, retrieval, and advanced analysis. The order of the steps is carefully chosen, and each step produces additional information which supports the model in the next step to perform a certain task. For example, the first step extracts the named entities from a textual report. The second step takes the named entities creates linked triplets, which are structured representations in the form (Subject, Relation, Object) that capture relationships between entities. The content is enriched with additional context and supports the model applied in step 3 to better understand and classify the given text. Also step 4 uses the information produced in steps 1 and 2 to categorize the report. Another example would be the ordered sequence of step 5, which performs the text-to-TTP task using the TTPFShot [9] framework to tag the OSINT texts with TTPs from the Mitre ATT&CK framework. Next step 6 identifies APT groups within the text. By enriching the text with TTP IDs, the model applied in step 6 may perform better at the task of labeling APT groups given the TTP IDs from step 5. Step 7 summarizes OSINT texts and connects them with the triplets generated from step 2, which eventually serve as additional information for the clustering in step 8. All steps serve the purpose of enriching the content, which is ultimately stored in two databases: a Vector DB for semantic similarity-based text retrieval, and a Graph DB for structured relationship reasoning.

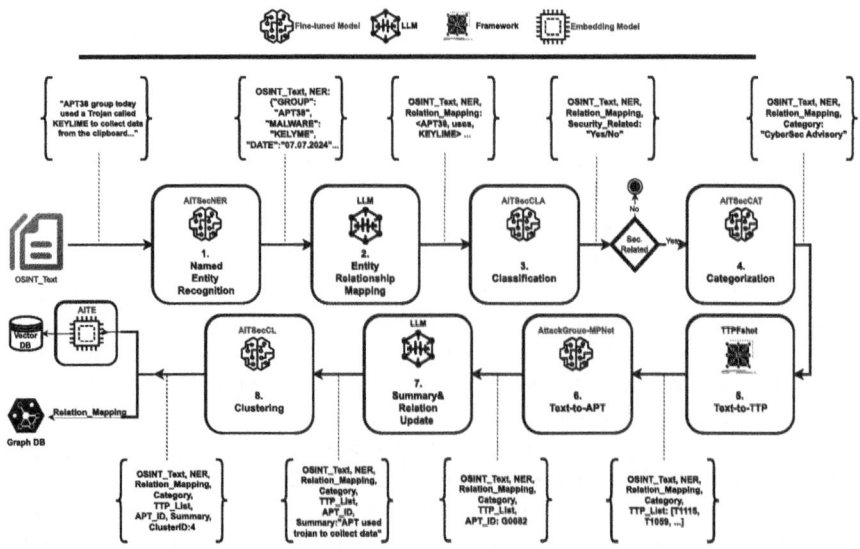

Fig. 1. OSINT analysis and enrichment pipeline.

The textual reports that serve as input to the pipeline are initially gathered and provided by external systems, such as Taranis AI[1], which is an OSINT tool that utilizes AI for information gathering and situational analysis. These reports are in a raw, unstructured text format and typically include a report title, timestamp, and body text.

The remaining sections describe each step in detail. Furthermore, each of the sections provides examples to support comprehension. Additionally, candidate solutions for each step are listed.

---

[1] https://taranis.ai/.

3.1   Step 1: Named Entity Recognition

The first step performs Named Entity Recognition (NER) on the input text, extracting critical entities such as attackers, victims, sectors, dates, malware names, IP addresses, and other cybersecurity-relevant terms. This step is necessary because the extracted entities are used in subsequent stages for triplet construction, classification and categorization, context enrichment, summarization, clustering, and as chunk metadata in the vector database to enable more precise retrieval.

While several specialized NER solutions for the CTI domain exist, most rely heavily on BERT-based models. These models face two key challenges: (1) limited context window length [5] and (2) poor tokenization of specialized CTI terminology [14]. For example, the term CVE-2021-44228 may be split into tokens like ["CVE", "-", "2021", "-", "442", "28"] by a general-purpose tokenizer, losing its semantic meaning. Such poor tokenization of CTI-specific terms can harm tasks like classification, relation extraction, and embedding generation. Consequently, further research is needed to evaluate existing tools comprehensively and potentially develop tailored NER models with custom tokenizers.

One promising candidate is the AITSecNER[2] model, a GLiNER-based [24] model fine-tuned on the AnnoCTR [10] dataset. However, AITSecNER is limited to a maximum input window of 384 tokens, restricting its usability on large CTI reports. Additionally, the motivation for developing custom NER models and tokenizers arises from our observation (see Table 1) that most commonly used security-focused transformer models do not adequately cover the MITRE ATT&CK dictionary of Groups and Software.

Table 1. Tokenizer Coverage of Mitre ATT&CK Software Dictionary

Tokenizer	Recognized	Unrecognized	Coverage (%)	Missing (%)
SecurityBERT	11	667	1.62%	98.38%
SecurityBERT+	11	667	1.62%	98.38%
SecBERT	225	453	33.19%	66.81%
ATTACKBERT	50	628	7.37%	92.63%

Table 1 presents the tokenization coverage of several prominent security-focused language models when applied to the Mitre ATT&CK dictionary of 687 Software-name entries. The results indicate that most tokenizers fail to represent the majority of these specialized terms as single tokens. Specifically, Security-BERT [8] and SecurityBERT+[3] cover only 1.62% of the terms, meaning 98.38% of the entries would be split into subwords or unknown tokens. ATTACKBERT[4]

---

[2] https://huggingface.co/selfconstruct3d/AITSecNER.
[3] https://huggingface.co/ehsanaghaei/SecureBERT_Plus.
[4] https://huggingface.co/basel/ATTACK-BERT.

performs slightly better at 7.37% coverage, while SecBERT [12] achieves the highest coverage of 33.19%. These findings motivate the need for developing domain-adapted tokenizers that can better preserve the semantic integrity of CTI-specific terminology.

One additional motivation for building a custom NER model stems from our evaluation of OpenAI's GPT-4o in a zero-shot setting on cybersecurity-specific entity extraction (Table 2). The evaluation is performed on the AnnoCTR dataset's [10] test split.

Table 2. LLM Performance per Entity Type

Entity Type	GT Entities	Predicted	Precision	Recall	F1-Score
TACTIC	21	2	0.000	0.000	0.000
CON	33	0	0.000	0.000	0.000
MALWARE	50	55	0.395	0.382	0.386
SECTOR	20	23	0.0567	0.0647	0.0589
TECHNIQUE	10	13	0.000	0.000	0.000
ORG	20	26	0.1333	0.1400	0.1350
DATE	45	48	0.380	0.380	0.380
LOC	20	20	0.0400	0.0233	0.0283

As Table 2 demonstrates, the zero-shot GPT-4o model struggles with extracting specialized CTI entities. Critical entity types such as TACTIC, TECHNIQUE, and CON (Cybersecurity Concepts) were either not identified or achieved zero F1-scores. Even common entity types like SECTOR, ORG, and LOC exhibit very low precision and recall, indicating frequent false positives or missed extractions.

Notably, the model performs slightly better for MALWARE and DATE entities, reaching F1-scores of 0.386 and 0.380 respectively. However, these results remain insufficient for operational CTI tasks where precise extraction of entities like TTPs, Groups, and Tools is crucial.

This evaluation confirms that general-purpose LLMs, even at the GPT-4o level, fail to capture the domain-specific semantics of cybersecurity texts. They lack the granularity needed to identify Mitre ATT&CK concepts, malware families, or organization names in threat reports. These findings reinforce the need for developing a dedicated CTI NER model with domain-adapted tokenizers and training on cybersecurity corpora to ensure reliable and accurate entity extraction for downstream analysis tasks.

3.2   Step 2: Entity Relationship Mapping

The second step proceeds with the output of step 1 and employs a LLM to construct relationship triplets in the format Subject-Relation-Object. For example, from the sentence *"APT29 used the SUNBURST malware to compromise Solar-Winds."*, the LLM extracts the triplets: (APT29, used, SUNBURST malware) and (SUNBURST malware, targeted, SolarWinds). These triplets capture key relationships between entities and form the basis for knowledge graph construction in the Graph DB. These triplets utilize NER-extracted entities and capture the relationships articulated within the OSINT text. This stage is crucial for clearly representing attacker actions and allows comparison with the Mitre ATT&CK-derived triplets to identify novel information. We validated our approach using a preliminary proof-of-concept. Figure 2 illustrates the prompt which we used in our premilary proof-of-concept for constructing triplets from entities and their relations provided in the original OSINT text.

```
Here are NER entities and annotations from a report.
Unique Entities and Labels (Entity => (Label)): {entities}

I am giving you the OSINT_report below.
OSINT_report: {text}

Construct the triplets
(connect the Entities using relations found in CTI_report)
from Entities in the form: Subject(Entity)-(uses, is-used-by, etc.)-Object(Entity).

Example: {
  "Summary (Triplets Only)": [
    {"Subject": "UNC2652", "Relation": "uses", "Object": "LNK"},
    {"Subject": "HTA", "Relation": "executes", "Object": "PowerShell"},
    {"Subject": "PowerShell", "Relation": "deploys", "Object": "BEACON"},
    {"Subject": "BEACON", "Relation": "communicates-via", "Object": "HTTPS"},
    {"Subject": "BEACON", "Relation": "uses-domain", "Object": "vesiderm.com"},
    {"Subject": "BEACON", "Relation": "uses-domain", "Object": "marketingkeepers.com"},
    {"Subject": "UNC2652", "Relation": "targets", "Object": "European-governments"},
    ...
  ]
}

Respond strictly in JSON format!
```

Fig. 2. Prompt template for relation extraction.

The extraction of relationship triplets represents a crucial step in transforming unstructured text into structured data. By leveraging a LLM to infer and generate Subject-Relation-Object triplets, this process effectively captures adversary tactics and operational linkages that might otherwise remain obscured in textual reports. The ability to align these extracted relationships with MITRE ATT&CK triplets allows for the detection of novel tactics and deviations from known attack patterns.

Our preliminary proof-of-concept demonstrates that this approach enhances situational awareness by structuring cybersecurity information in a machine-readable format. As Fig. 2 shows, our prompting strategy facilitates consistent and accurate extraction of triplets from CTI reports. However, further evaluation and revision is required to refine the prompt design, improve relation inference accuracy, and minimize hallucinated or spurious connections. Future work will focus on optimizing the triplet extraction process by incorporating domain-specific constraints and fine-tuning LLMs for improved precision in CTI tasks.

3.3   Step 3: Classification

The augmented report texts, enriched with extracted entities and their corresponding relationship triplets, proceed to the classification (Step 3). This stage serves as a critical filter to determine whether the processed report is relevant to cybersecurity and thus warrants further analysis within the pipeline. Given the heterogeneity of threat intelligence sources - ranging from generic news articles to detailed technical advisories - this filtering step is essential to avoid polluting downstream processes with irrelevant or off-topic content.

Currently, no comprehensive out-of-the-box solution exists that can reliably distinguish cybersecurity-relevant texts from non-relevant content in diverse OSINT datasets. To address this, our preliminary implementation leverages a zero-shot classification approach using the *bart-large-mnli* model[5]. The model is prompted with candidate categories (e.g., "cybersecurity report", "non-cybersecurity report") and infers the most probable class without requiring task-specific fine-tuning.

While this zero-shot approach enables rapid prototyping and preliminary filtering, our evaluation reveals (see Table 3) that general-purpose models such as *bart-large-mnli* struggle with the domain-specific nuances of CTI text. Reports containing ambiguous language, mixed cyber and non-cyber content, or implicit threat descriptions often result in misclassifications. This limitation highlights the need for a specialized classification model tailored to the CTI domain.

Table 3. Classificator Tokenizer Coverage of Mitre ATT&CK Software Dictionary

Tokenizer	Recognized	Unrecognized	Coverage (%)	Missing (%)
bart-large-mnli	10	668	1.47%	98.53%

To address this gap, we plan to develop AITSecCLA, a dedicated cybersecurity text classifier. AITSecCLA will be fine-tuned on a curated dataset of labeled CTI reports, ensuring better understanding of technical language, attack frameworks, malware families, and other domain-specific concepts. The goal is to significantly improve classification accuracy over general-purpose models, particularly in distinguishing subtle indicators of cyber threats embedded within complex narratives.

3.4   Step 4: Categorization

Step 4 extends the classification of step 3 and categorizes cybersecurity-relevant CTI texts to distinguish between different report types, with a particular focus

---

[5] https://huggingface.co/facebook/bart-large-mnli.

on identifying "Alert"-type reports. This step is crucial, as alerts represent high-priority, time-sensitive intelligence that often demands immediate attention from cybersecurity analysts and incident response teams.

To the best of our knowledge, there exist currently no out-of-the-box models available for this type of CTI-text categorization. Therefore, in our proof-of-concept (AITSecCAT), we consider using few-shot or zero-shot classification with the same model applied in the classification step, namely *bart-large-mnli*. Additionally, a large language model or a sentence transformer could be fine-tuned to perform this categorization task.

Accurately distinguishing alerts at this stage enables the pipeline to prioritize urgent intelligence for immediate action, while directing more detailed reports into deeper analysis paths-ultimately enhancing the pipeline's responsiveness and operational relevance.

3.5   Step 5: Text-to-TTP

Extracting TTPs is a crucial capability in cyber threat intelligence processing, as it enables direct mapping of observed adversary behaviors to the widely adopted MITRE ATT&CK framework, facilitating structured reasoning and comparative analysis.

Several existing solutions aim to extract TTPs from text, including TRAM[6], TTPHunter [18], and the current state-of-the-art, TTPXHunter [20]. However, both TRAM and TTPHunter are limited to mapping text to only the 50 most common TTPs. TTPXHunter improves on this by supporting up to 193 TTPs. Despite this advancement, none of these models supports the extraction of TTP subtechniques, and all require either resource-intensive model fine-tuning or time-consuming dataset augmentation during the initial setup.

An approach in this pipeline step is TTPFShot [9], which is a retrieval-augmented few-shot learning model specifically designed to extract Mitre ATT&CK TTPs, including subtechniques, from CTI text segments. This retrieval-based few-shot approach significantly reduces the need for large annotated datasets while maintaining high extraction accuracy, making it suitable for dynamic and evolving CTI datasets.

Preliminary evaluations (see Fig. 3) show that TTPFShot outperforms baseline models, including TTPXHunter, in terms of precision, recall, and F1-score when evaluated on the TTPHunter dataset[7]. Its ability to generalize from limited examples while maintaining strong alignment with the MITRE ATT&CK framework positions it as a state-of-the-art solution for TTP extraction.

---

[6] https://github.com/center-for-threat-informed-defense/tram.

[7] https://github.com/nanda-rani/TTPHunter-Automated-Extraction-of-Actionable-Intelligence-as-TTPs-from-Narrative-Threat-Reports/blob/main/Dataset/TTPHunter_dataset.csv.

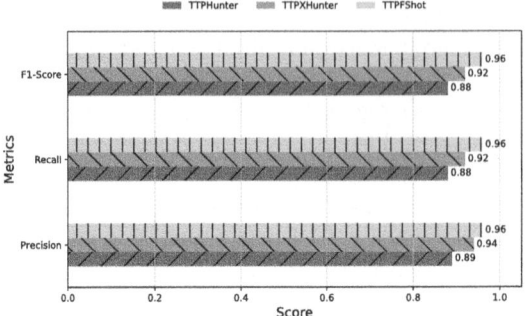

Fig. 3. TTPFShot performance comparison.

Table 4. Summary Evaluation Metrics

Metric	Our approach	BART CNN
ROUGE-1	0.0518	0.0283
ROUGE-2	0.0295	0.0278
ROUGE-L	0.0363	0.0283
METEOR Score	0.0166	0.0099

3.6   Step 6: Text-to-APT

Step 6 involves assigning Mitre ATT&CK APT Group IDs to text chunks. This step is essential for enriching chunk metadata, enabling retrieval based on APT Group IDs once the text chunks are stored in a database. Due to the lack of existing solutions for this specific task, we are actively developing a dedicated method. Our initial approach, the AttackGroup-MPNET model[8], is a variant of MPNet [22] fine-tuned on Mitre ATT&CK procedure descriptions, with an extended tokenizer tailored to the CTI domain. Alternatively, CAPTAIN [19] can be used at this stage as well, assuming TTP extraction has already been completed in Step 5.

3.7   Step 7: Summary and Relation Update

Using newly identified TTPs and APT IDs, Step 7 employs an LLM to update and expand the relation mapping with insights from earlier steps. Additionally, this step generates concise executive summaries derived directly from updated relations and identified entities. Based on initial experiments, this graph-enriched summarization offers superior quality compared to general-purpose summarization models.

To evaluate the quality of the generated summaries, we computed standard metrics such as ROUGE and METEOR. As shown in Table 4, our approach - which uses entity and relationship triplets within an LLM prompt guided by

---

[8] https://huggingface.co/selfconstruct3d/AttackGroup-MPNET.

the instruction "Generate summary using only the triplets"—outperforms the general-purpose summarization model BART CNN[9] across all evaluation metrics. These results demonstrate that leveraging structured knowledge in the form of entities and relationships may lead to more informative and contextually accurate summaries, especially for CTI reports.

3.8   Step 8: Clustering

Finally, Step 8 clusters the processed texts using a custom-trained embedding model, AITSecCL, which is currently being fine-tuned on cybersecurity-specific dictionaries and threat intelligence corpora[10]. This model builds on MPNet [22], adapted to the CTI domain. Once finalized, it will be used for clustering, assigning each text segment a cluster ID that identifies reports covering similar topics or related threat activities.

Clustering serves two primary purposes: (1) grouping intelligence related to the same incident or campaign, and (2) detecting emerging events or anomalies that deviate from existing patterns. This mechanism enhances situational awareness by enabling rapid correlation of new reports with known threat campaigns and by surfacing novel or previously unseen threats. The assigned cluster ID is carried forward and stored alongside each text chunk in the database, supporting efficient retrieval and downstream analysis.

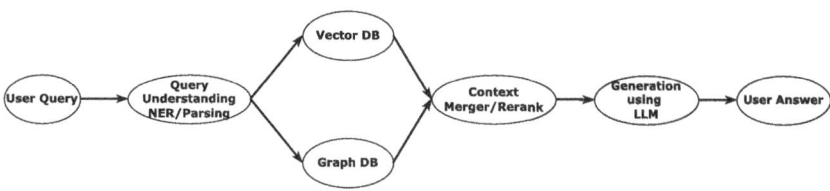

Fig. 4. Pipeline application example.

After the 8 steps of the pipeline, the data persistence occurs across two specialized databases. Text segments are chunked and embedded using our custom embedding model from the clustering step (see Sect. 3.8), optimized for cybersecurity-specific terminology, enriched by metadata from previous steps, and stored in a vector database. Concurrently, updated relation mappings are stored in a graph database. Both databases also retain metadata such as timestamps and source details, ensuring comprehensive data contextualization and traceability.

---

[9] https://huggingface.co/facebook/bart-large-cnn.
[10] https://huggingface.co/selfconstruct3d/mpnet-classification-finetuned-cyber-groups.

4 Pipline Application Example

The designed pipeline enables advanced information retrieval and reasoning by combining symbolic knowledge graphs and semantic vector searches. This dual retrieval mechanism significantly enhances the system's capability to answer complex, multi-hop,i.e., queries that require reasoning across multiple pieces of information-often spanning different documents or entities-and context rich queries that typical retrieval pipelines struggle to address due to their reliance on single-pass, shallow (semantic similarity only) retrieval and limited reasoning over disconnected facts.

As illustrated in Fig. 4, the process begins with query understanding, where entities, time frames, tactics, and targeted infrastructure are extracted using our custom NER model. The system then simultaneously queries:

- **Graph Database:** For structured relationship reasoning between actors, techniques, and assets based on pre-processed triplets.
- **Vector Database:** For semantically similar text segments enriched with metadata such as TTPs, infrastructure, clusters, and campaign context.

Both streams of information are merged and optionally reranked, balancing symbolic accuracy with semantic relevance. The merged context is passed to the LLM, which generates a detailed, context-aware answer.

4.1 Example Prompt and Detailed Pipeline Execution

To demonstrate the pipeline's practical utility, we present an example query (prompt) and generated answers, highlighting the system's ability to merge graph-based reasoning with semantically retrieved context for complex CTI tasks.

Example Prompt 1: "Which APT groups have used clipboard scraping techniques in the past year?"

Pipeline Execution:

- **NER and Parsing:** The system detects entities like "APT groups" and techniques such as "clipboard scraping".
- **Graph Query:** Traverses known relationships to find APT nodes linked to TTP nodes related to clipboard scraping (e.g., MITRE ATT&CK T1115).
- **Vector Search:** Retrieves semantically relevant report chunks mentioning clipboard scraping, APT operations, and similar cases.
- **Merging and Reranking:** Prioritizes graph hits with strong TTP-APT links and combines them with top vector matches.
- **LLM Answer Generation:** *"Based on available intelligence, APT38 and APT29 have both deployed clipboard scraping techniques over the past year. APT38 leveraged the KEYLIME trojan, while APT29 used CHOPSTICK malware, targeting clipboard memory to collect sensitive data."*

This example demonstrates how the hybrid pipeline:

- Handles multi-hop queries involving both cyber and physical components.
- Leverages symbolic knowledge graphs for explainable reasoning paths.
- Enriches factual retrieval with semantic context from vector-based similarity search.
- Produces LLM-generated answers grounded in structured and unstructured data sources.

Such capabilities are critical for advanced cyber threat intelligence scenarios, supporting analyst workflows in attribution, impact assessment, and proactive defense planning.

5 Military and Civil Use Cases

To demonstrate the practical potential of our proposed pipeline, we present two fictional but realistic use cases-one from the military domain and one from the civil sector where our hybrid retrieval pipeline (Fig. 4) supports situational awareness and decision-making. Both scenarios are illustrative mockups based on representative technologies and imaginable threat situations, showcasing how the system supports cybersecurity operations across different contexts.

5.1 Red and Blue Background

In this fictional scenario, the conflict involves two opposing sides: Red and Blue. Red is a hybrid threat actor combining a paramilitary group, the Heroic Brigades (HB), and an APT group, Teasing Mosquito (TM). Their goal is to destabilize Blue politically, economically, and socially, using influence operations, disinformation, and cyber-physical attacks—especially against critical energy infrastructure. Blue is a state-led coalition defending against Red's multi-domain hybrid threats. Blue aims to ensure societal stability, protect infrastructure, and counter disinformation and election interference. The confrontation spans several months, with Red's actions aligned to MITRE ATT&CK tactics and techniques. Red also collaborates with neutral hacker groups to purchase system access.

5.2 Scenario 1: Surveillance System Compromise

The framed content outlines how the pipeline components could work together to support situational awareness and threat analysis. A framed layout is used to clearly separate this illustrative example from the rest of the text. All data and actors are hypothetical.

Description: Red actors exploit leaked WiFi credentials for surveillance cameras to monitor Blue's mission activities.

Stage 1 – User Query:

```
Which APT groups have compromised our surveillance systems using WiFi credential leaks?
     Provide past examples and mitigation advice.
```

Stage 2 – Query Understanding (NER/Parsing):

– **Extracted Entities:** Surveillance Systems, APT Groups, WiFi Credential Leaks
– **Focused TTP:** Initial Access (MITRE ATT&CK TA0001)

Stage 3 – Graph Query:

```
MATCH (camera)-[r:COMPROMISED_BY]->(attacker:Actor)
RETURN camera, attacker
```

Example Result:

```
(Surveillance_Camera_A)-[COMPROMISED_BY]->(Teasing Mosquito APT)
```

Stage 4 – Vector DB Retrieval (Chunks + Metadata):
Similarity search: "Surveillance WiFi compromise initial access"
Retrieved Chunk:

```
"In 2023, attackers exploited leaked WiFi credentials to access surveillance feeds from
    cameras placed in forward operating bases."
```

Stage 5 – Context Merger and Reranking:

– **Graph Result:** Surveillance_Camera_A compromised by Teasing Mosquito APT
– **Vector Context:** Similar APT tactics observed in 2023
– Reranked for confirmed APT involvement

Stage 6 – LLM Generation (Merged Prompt):

```
Given that Surveillance_Camera_A was compromised by Teasing Mosquito APT, and historic
    reports show attackers using leaked WiFi credentials to access surveillance feeds
    in 2023, summarize the threat, intent, and suggest mitigation.
```

Stage 7 – LLM Answer (Final Assessment):

– **Threat Summary:** Teasing Mosquito APT compromised Surveillance_Camera_A via WiFi
leaks.
– **Intent:** Gather intelligence on troop movements and operational patterns.
– **Mitigation Recommendations:**
  - Rotate WiFi credentials
  - Disable compromised devices
  - Deploy traffic monitoring
  - Review remote access controls

5.3 Civil Scenario: Vulnerability Prioritization for Patch Management

In this mockup scenario, we walk through how a Security Operations Center (SOC) analyst might use our system to prioritize patching efforts after a newly reported CVE. The framed content shows step-by-step how the pipeline supports decision-making, from entity recognition to final recommendation generation.

Description: A SOC analyst needs to prioritize patching efforts after a new vulnerability (CVE) affecting their web infrastructure is reported.

Stage 1 – User Query:

```
Which active threat actors are currently exploiting CVE-2024-12345, and what is the
    impact? Should we prioritize patching our web servers?
```

Stage 2 – Query Understanding (NER/Parsing):

– **Extracted Entities:** CVE-2024-12345, Web Servers, Threat Actors
– **Focused TTP:** Exploitation for Initial Access (MITRE ATT&CK T1203)

Stage 3 – Graph Query:

```
MATCH (cve:CVE {id:'CVE-2024-12345'})<-[:EXPLOITS]-(group:APT)
RETURN group
```

Example Result:

```
(Scarlet Leopard APT exploits CVE-2024-12345)
```

Stage 4 – Vector DB Retrieval (Chunks + Metadata):
Similarity search: "Exploitation of CVE-2024-12345 by threat actors"
Retrieved Chunk:

```
"In March 2025, Scarlet Leopard APT exploited CVE-2024-12345 targeting Apache servers,
    leading to remote code execution in several financial organizations."
```

Stage 5 – Context Merging and Reranking:

– **Graph Result:** APT group confirmed exploiting CVE-2024-12345
– **Vector Context:** Active exploitation reported in the financial sector

Stage 6 – LLM Answer Generation (Merged Prompt):

```
Summarize the risk associated with CVE-2024-12345 based on APT activity and
    exploitation reports. Provide patching recommendations.
```

Stage 7 – LLM Answer (Final Assessment):

– **Threat Summary:** Scarlet Leopard APT is actively exploiting CVE-2024-12345 to achieve remote code execution on Apache web servers.
– **Impact:** Successful exploitation may lead to full system compromise and data exfiltration. Financial organizations have been targeted.
– **Mitigation Recommendations:**
  - Apply the latest security patch for CVE-2024-12345 immediately.
  - Audit Apache server configurations.
  - Monitor for signs of post-exploitation activities linked to Scarlet Leopard APT.

6   Conclusion

In this paper, we presented a comprehensive CSA framework specifically tailored for military and civilian cybersecurity applications, leveraging advanced AI and NLP techniques. Our unified pipeline significantly enhanced the analysis of CTI by improving named entity extraction, relationship mapping, identification of TTPs, attribution of APT groups, summarization quality, and clustering of threat reports.

The proposed framework integrates symbolic knowledge graphs with semantic retrieval methods to provide detailed, explainable, and contextually rich responses to complex cybersecurity queries. Through illustrative military and civilian scenarios, we demonstrated the practical utility and operational value of the pipeline, highlighting its ability to support real-time and strategic decision-making processes.

Pipeline improvements include the continuous refinement of entity extraction techniques, development of specialized cybersecurity classifiers for enhanced content relevance, and advancements in summarization methodologies through structured relationship extraction. Additionally, we emphasized the potential for improved clustering methods, enabling the identification of emerging threats and anomalies more effectively.

Future work will concentrate on enhancing the pipeline's scalability and robustness, refining AI model performance through extensive training on specialized datasets, and integrating additional cybersecurity data sources to further strengthen the situational awareness capabilities of our framework.

Acknowledgments. Funded by the European Union under the European Defence Fund (GA no. 101121403 - NEWSROOM and GA no. 101121418 - EUCINF). Views and opinions expressed are however those of the author(s) only and do not necessarily reflect those of the European Union or the European Commission. Neither the European Union nor the granting authority can be held responsible for them. This work is co-funded by the Austrian FFG Kiras project ASOC (GA no. FO999905301).

References

1. Alam, M.T., Bhusal, D., Park, Y., Rastogi, N.: Looking beyond IoCs: automatically extracting attack patterns from external CTI. In: Proceedings of the 26th International Symposium on Research in Attacks, Intrusions and Defenses (RAID '23). ACM (2023). https://doi.org/10.1145/3607199.3607208
2. Alevizos, L., Dekker, M.: Towards an AI-enhanced cyber threat intelligence processing pipeline. Electronics **13**(11), 2021 (2024). https://doi.org/10.3390/electronics13112021
3. Arazzi, M., et al.: NLP-Based Techniques for Cyber Threat Intelligence. arXiv preprint arXiv:2311.08807 (2023). https://arxiv.org/abs/2311.08807
4. Chang, C.H.: Cyber Threat Intelligence: A Pipeline to Classify Cyber Threats from Disparate Data Sources. Honours thesis, AiLECS Lab, Monash University (March 2022)
5. Ding, M., Zhou, C., Yang, H., Tang, J.: Cogltx: applying bert to long texts. Adv. Neural. Inf. Process. Syst. **33**, 12792–12804 (2020)
6. Endsley, M.R.: Theoretical underpinnings of situation awareness: a critical review. In: Endsley, M.R., Garland, D.J. (eds.) Situation Awareness Analysis and Measurement. Lawrence Erlbaum Associates, Mahwah, NJ (2000). https://www.researchgate.net/publication/292771806_Situation_awareness_analysis_and_measurement_chapter_theoretical_underpinnings_of_situation_awareness, accessed: 2025-04-07
7. Endsley, M.R.: Situation awareness. In: Salvendy, G., Karwowski, W. (eds.) Handbook of Human Factors and Ergonomics, chap. 17. Wiley (2021). https://doi.org/10.1002/9781119636113.ch17, https://doi.org/10.1002/9781119636113.ch17
8. Ferrag, M.A., Ndhlovu, M., Tihanyi, N., Cordeiro, L.C., Debbah, M., Lestable, T., Thandi, N.S.: Revolutionizing cyber threat detection with large language models: a privacy-preserving bert-based lightweight model for iot/iiot devices. IEEe Access **12**, 23733–23750 (2024)

9. Hamzic, D., Skopik, F., Landauer, M., Wurzenberger, M., Rauber, A.: Ttp classification with minimal labeled data: A retrieval-based few-shot learning approach (2025), to appear at the 20th International Conference on Availability, Reliability and Security (ARES 2025), August 11-14, 2025, Ghent, Belgium. Springer (2025)
10. Lange, L., Müller, M., Torbati, G.H., Milchevski, D., Grau, P., Pujari, S., Friedrich, A.: Annoctr: a dataset for detecting and linking entities, tactics, and techniques in cyber threat reports (2024). https://arxiv.org/abs/2404.07765
11. Li, Z., Zeng, J., Chen, Y., Liang, Z.: AttacKG: constructing technique knowledge graph from cyber threat intelligence reports. arXiv preprint arXiv:2111.07093 (2022). https://arxiv.org/abs/2111.07093
12. Liberato, M.: Secbert : analyzing reports using bert-like models, December 2022. http://essay.utwente.nl/93906/
13. Munir, A., Aved, A., Blasch, E.: Situational awareness: Techniques, challenges, and prospects. AI **3**(1), 55–77 (2022). https://doi.org/10.3390/ai3010005
14. Nayak, A., Timmapathini, H., Ponnalagu, K., Venkoparao, V.G.: Domain adaptation challenges of bert in tokenization and sub-word representations of out-of-vocabulary words. In: Proceedings of the first workshop on insights from negative results in NLP, pp. 1–5 (2020)
15. Pieterse, H., Van't Wout, C., Khan, Z., Serfontein, C.: Specialised media monitoring tool to observe situational awareness. In: Proceedings of the 17th International Conference on Information Warfare and Security, p. 244 (2022)
16. Rahman, M.R., Mahdavi-Hezaveh, R., Williams, L.: What are the attackers doing now? Automating cyber threat intelligence extraction from text on pace with the changing threat landscape: A survey. arXiv preprint arXiv:2109.06808 (2021), https://arxiv.org/abs/2109.06808
17. Rani, N., Saha, B., Maurya, V., Shukla, S.K.: Ttpxhunter: Actionable threat intelligence extraction as ttps from finished cyber threat reports. arXiv (2024). https://arxiv.org/abs/2403.03267
18. Rani, N., Saha, B., Maurya, V., Shukla, S.K.: Ttphunter: Automated extraction of actionable intelligence as ttps from narrative threat reports. In: Proceedings of the 2023 Australasian Computer Science Week, pp. 126–134 (2023)
19. Rani, N., Saha, B., Maurya, V., Shukla, S.K.: Chasing the Shadows: TTPs in Action to Attribute Advanced Persistent Threats. arXiv preprint arXiv:2409.16400 (2024). https://arxiv.org/abs/2409.16400
20. Rani, N., Saha, B., Maurya, V., Shukla, S.K.: Ttpxhunter: Actionable threat intelligence extraction as ttps from finished cyber threat reports. Digital Threats: Resand Practice **5**(4), 1–19 (2024)
21. Samtani, S., Li, W., Benjamin, V., Chen, H.: Informing cyber threat intelligence through dark web situational awareness: The azsecure hacker assets portal. Digital Threats **2**(4) (Oct 2021). https://doi.org/10.1145/3450972. https://doi.org/10.1145/3450972
22. Song, K., Tan, X., Qin, T., Lu, J., Liu, T.Y.: Mpnet: Masked and permuted pre-training for language understanding. Adv. Neural. Inf. Process. Syst. **33**, 16857–16867 (2020)
23. Wurzenberger, M., et al.: NEWSROOM: Towards automating cyber situational awareness processes and tools for cyber defence. In: Proceedings of the 19th International Conference on Availability, Reliability and Security (ARES 2024). Association for Computing Machinery, New York, NY, USA (2024). https://doi.org/10.1145/3664476.3670914, https://dl.acm.org/doi/10.1145/3664476.3670914

24. Zaratiana, U., Tomeh, N., Holat, P., Charnois, T.: Gliner: Generalist model for named entity recognition using bidirectional transformer (2023). https://arxiv.org/abs/2311.08526

25. Zhou, Y., Tang, Y., Yi, M., Xi, C., Lu, H.: CTI view: APT threat intelligence analysis system. Secur. Commun. Networks **2022**, 1–15 (2022). https://doi.org/10.1155/2022/9875199

Ontology-Based Model for Federated Systems Using JC3IEDM Taxonomies

Carlota M. Muñoz de Luna Eusebio[1,2]([✉]) [iD], Xavier Larriva-Novo[1]([✉]) [iD],
Carmen Sánchez-Zas[1]([✉]) [iD], Víctor A. Villagrá[1]([✉]) [iD], and Mateo Burgos[2]([✉]) [iD]

[1] Dpto. Ingeniería de Sistemas Telemáticos, ETSI Telecomunicación, Universidad Politécnica de Madrid, Madrid, Spain
`carlota.munozdeluna@alumnos.upm.es`,
`{xavier.larriva.novo,carmen.szas,victor.villagra}@upm.es`
[2] Cátedra ISDEFE Defensa y Seguridad, Universidad Politécnica de Madrid, Madrid, Spain
`mateo.burgos@upm.es`

Abstract. The combat cloud is an integrated information and communication system essential for modern military operations. It connects all battlefield components, including drones, soldiers, vehicles, satellites, and Command and Control centers, into a cohesive real-time network. This architecture significantly enhances situational awareness, threat analysis, and decision-making processes. However, the increasing complexity of multinational operations necessitates solutions that ensure both tactical interoperability and data sovereignty.

This paper introduces an ontological framework for the collaborative training of AI models through Federated Learning (FL), addressing integration challenges presented by traditional military standards like the JC3IEDM. While JC3IEDM offers a standardized vocabulary for defense systems, its complex structure often obstructs interoperability with domain-specific, lightweight ontologies typically used in AI applications.

To bridge this gap, we propose an ontology translator that acts as a semantic bridge between a domain-specific FL ontology and a JC3IEDM-based ontology derived from its logical schema. This translator effectively resolves conceptual mismatches, facilitating accurate transformations of entities and attributes. By implementing our framework, we enhance semantic interoperability among diverse systems while reinforcing data sovereignty and boosting real-time decision-making capabilities. These elements are critical for the success of future multinational military operations in an increasingly complex global landscape.

Keywords: Combat Cloud · Federated Learning · JC3IEDM · UAV · Ontology

1 Introduction

The increasing complexity of modern military operations, especially within multinational coalitions, necessitates information systems that are both tacti-

B. Coppens et al. (Eds.): ARES 2025 Workshops, LNCS 15995, pp. 63–79, 2025.
https://doi.org/10.1007/978-3-032-00633-2_4

cally interoperable and respectful of data sovereignty. In this context, the Combat Cloud has emerged as a transformative paradigm, a distributed, intelligent network that interconnects all elements on the battlefield, including UAVs, soldiers, vehicles, satellites, and command centers. This system enables real-time data sharing, threat analysis, and rapid decision-making, providing a strategic advantage.

The dynamic ecosystem of the Combat Cloud heavily relies on artificial intelligence (AI) and machine learning (ML) models to process large volumes of sensor data. However, traditional centralized training architectures prove inadequate for Combat Cloud environments due to constraints in bandwidth, latency, and privacy. To address these challenges, Federated Learning (FL) has been introduced as a decentralized learning technique. In FL, each node trains models locally and only shares parameters, thereby maintaining confidentiality and adhering to national policies.

Despite this advancement, a significant challenge persists: semantic interoperability. Each participating entity, such as a nation or organization, may describe its assets and data using distinct ontologies tailored to local systems, languages, or operational contexts. While this ensures autonomy and control, it hinders direct integration and coordination. Without a common semantic layer, collaborative AI becomes unfeasible.

In a federated, multinational defense environment, semantic heterogeneity between ontologies obstructs the integration of data and knowledge. This fragmentation occurs at two levels:

- **Conceptual**: Each organization employs its own modeling vocabulary and logic to represent key entities, such as drones, personnel, or servers.
- **Structural**: Even when two systems refer to the same concept, their underlying representations can differ.

In this context, **JC3IEDM** is a NATO-endorsed data model designed to provide interoperability across multinational military systems. However, its structure presents several challenges [6] that hinder direct integration with simpler, domain-specific ontologies:

1. Entity Overuse: Attributes in JC3IEDM are modeled as full entities (e.g., location, status, type) rather than properties, requiring intermediate relationships for what could otherwise be simple property mappings.
2. High Complexity: With 195 entities, 785 attributes, and 277 relations, JC3IEDM is overly generic and abstract, making its adoption difficult without expert knowledge. The accompanying documentation exceeds 1,000 pages.
3. Normalization Trade-offs: JC3IEDM strictly adheres to relational normalization principles, leading to fragmented representations (e.g., 22 entities just to define LOCATION), complicating semantic mapping and increasing transformation overhead.
4. Rigid Structure: The model struggles with unstructured data, such as images or documents, and mixes metadata into the logical model, complicating implementation.

5. Ambiguity in Type-Instance Distinction: The separation between OBJECT-TYPE and OBJECT-ITEM often results in redundant or static structures that offer limited utility for real-time decision-making in FL.

Consequently, although JC3IEDM is powerful and widely accepted, it lacks the flexibility and expressiveness required by dynamic, distributed, and AI-driven frameworks like Combat Cloud and FL.

This research work proposes a semantic integration framework that connects a domain-specific ontology, tailored for Federated Learning in Combat Cloud operations, with a JC3IEDM-based ontology via a bidirectional ontology translator.

This translator serves as a semantic mediator, enabling the transformation of individuals, properties, and relationships from one ontology to another.

- **A Federated Learning Ontology**: This models key actors (e.g., drones, pilots, servers), their attributes (e.g., operational status, autonomy), and their roles within the Edge–Fog–Cloud hierarchy.
- **A JC3IEDM Ontology**: Constructed from JC3IEDM's logical model, it incorporates standardized military entities and represents many attributes as linked classes.
- **A Manual Mapping Layer**: Defined via JSON files, this layer specifies how each class and property in the FL ontology maps to the JC3IEDM structure.
- **An Automated Translation Engine**: Implemented in Python using owlready2, this engine applies the mappings and generates corresponding instances.

2   Background

To support real-time decision-making in complex and dynamic military environments, modern defense systems increasingly rely on structured, interoperable data models and intelligent processing mechanisms. This article integrates several core concepts such as ontologies, Combat Cloud architectures, Federated Learning (FL), and the JC3IEDM interoperability model to enable semantic data exchange and collaborative model training across heterogeneous systems. Below, we describe each component and their interrelations in the proposed solution.

2.1   Ontologies

Ontologies [7] are one of the most popular tools for handling heterogeneous amounts of data when related entities stand out in the environments to be analyzed. In the context of military and cyberdefense applications, ontologies enable structured, machine-interpretable representations of knowledge, allowing disparate systems to reason over shared concepts consistently. In this research work, we develop two interconnected ontologies: a **domain-specific ontology** representing the entities involved in a federated learning military scenario (drones, servers, pilots, etc.), and an ontology derived from **JC3IEDM**, a standardized military data model.

These ontologies serve as the foundation for a semantic translator that bridges domain-specific semantics with NATO-standard military representations.

2.2   Combat Cloud

The emergence of a new paradigm called **Combat Cloud** is transforming the way military operations are conceived. The Combat Cloud arises in response to the need to operate as a network in order to achieve superiority in multi-domain environments (land, sea, air, space, and cyberspace) through comprehensive situational awareness [4].

This is achieved by capturing, sharing, fusing, and instantly processing large amounts of data from all connected assets, supporting precise and agile decision-making and ultimately achieving information superiority [5]. As shown in Fig. 1, the Combat Cloud infrastructure is divided into three domains:

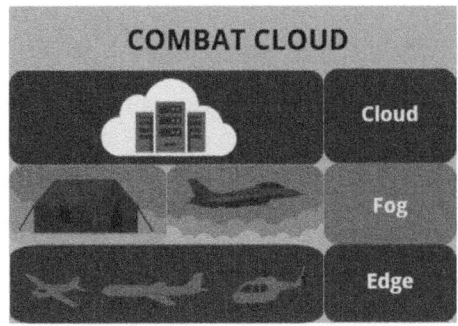

Fig. 1. Combat Cloud Domains

- **Cloud domain**: Handles large amounts of data using high-computing capacity systems, where the physical location is not critical for operations.
- **Fog domain**: Acts as an intermediary between Cloud and Edge, processing fewer data with limited computing power and positioned closer to the operational environment.
- **Edge domain**: Includes systems with effectors and/or sensors that generate low-level data consumed by the higher domains to produce more advanced information.

This architecture introduces distribution and heterogeneity challenges, particularly for AI applications, as data are distributed across multiple nodes with varying levels of connectivity and trust. Therefore, a key requirement is a learning methodology that respects locality and data sovereignty. This is where FL comes in.

2.3   Federated Learning

Federated Learning (FL) is a distributed machine learning paradigm in which multiple clients collaboratively train a global model without sharing raw data. Instead, only model parameters or gradients are exchanged. This approach is particularly suited to combat cloud environments where data are sensitive (e.g. surveillance footage, mission logs), communication is limited (e.g. intermittent satellite links) and nodes are autonomous and may belong to different nations or organisations.

In this project, FL is used to coordinate the training of object detection models between drones deployed by different organisations. Each drone trains locally on its collected data and contributes to a global model orchestrated by a central server. However, semantic interoperability remains a major hurdle, especially when clients belong to different military coalitions or use different data schemas. To address this, we incorporate a common semantic layer based on JC3IEDM.

2.4   The Joint Consultation, Command and Control Information Exchange Data Model (JC3IEDM)

JC3IEDM is a relational data model developed to standardise the exchange of information between military systems of different nations and organisations. It supports interoperability by defining a common vocabulary and structure for operational concepts [2].

JC3IEDM can be understood from three perspectives:

- **Conceptual Model**: Provides an abstract representation of military-relevant entities such as actions, objects, organisations and their relationships.
- **Logical Model**: Provides a detailed, normalised schema that defines the semantics of entity interactions, hierarchies and constraints. It is the basis for our ontology transformation.
- **Physical Model**: Specifies implementation-level structures for use in relational databases, such as keys and optimisation indexes.

Rather than modelling attributes as direct properties of entities, JC3IEDM often uses intermediate entities to represent status, location, classification or capabilities. For example, the location of a drone is not a property of the drone entity, but a relationship to an object-item-location entity. This architectural choice increases flexibility and reusability, but complicates direct mappings from simpler domain ontologies.

In this project, the JC3IEDM logical model is transformed into an OWL ontology. We map each relevant FL concept (e.g. *Dron, Servidor, Piloto*) to one or more JC3IEDM entities (e.g. Object-Item, Facility, Person), using intermediate entities and auxiliary classes where necessary. This mapping enables semantic translation of instances and reasoning across federated nodes, aligning decentralised AI workflows with standardised C2 structures.

2.5   Related Works

Situational Awareness (SA) is critical for interpreting not only the individual characteristics of objects but also the complex relationships established between them, especially in dynamic environments like military operations. This challenge has led to numerous research efforts aimed at enhancing the ability to identify and monitor these relationships through semantic technologies.

One significant contribution in this field is by Christopher J. Matheus and Mieczyslaw M. Kokar [1], who developed the Situation Awareness Assistant (SAWA) system. SAWA utilizes OWL ontologies to define domain-specific classes and properties and employs SWRL rules to detect complex relationships between objects. However, despite its innovation, SAWA faces notable limitations, such as implementation complexity, a lack of support for user-defined procedures, and inherent issues with SWRL's built-in functions.

Interoperability in military operations is further explored by [10], who proposed a formal ontology to capture the concepts and relationships of the C2IEDM model and its mapping with the OTH-T GOLD format using OWL. This approach structures classes and relationships to represent military entities and their evolution over time, enabling automated reasoning. However, challenges like semantic loss during the mapping of geopolitical codes and the heavy reliance on domain experts for ontology construction introduce subjectivity in complex scenarios.

Additionally, Matheus and Ulicny in [8] focused on automating the translation of the JC3IEDM model into an OWL ontology. Using XSLT scripts, they transformed entities, attributes, relationships, and codes into OWL elements. Although this approach effectively captured JC3IEDM's structural relationships, the ontology's massive size posed significant challenges for semantic reasoners. Moreover, the textual definitions of entities were not fully represented, limiting the capture of the true meaning of elements.

In a broader context, [9] integrated SAW-CORE and JC3IEDM into OWL ontologies to enhance contextual, spatial and temporal representation in C4ISR systems (Command, Control, Communications, Computers, Intelligence, Surveillance and Reconnaissance). While this integration marked significant progress in interoperability and decision-making, it still struggled to represent spatiotemporal and dynamic relationships due to JC3IEDM's general structure.

Expanding on situational awareness advancements, Chmielewski in [12] introduced an innovative approach by integrating ontological reasoning mechanisms with distributed services based on Geographic Information Systems (GIS). His proposal, embodied in the mCOP and tCOP platforms, aimed to improve data acquisition, object identification, and operational environment assessment. Leveraging the JC3IEDM model, these tools facilitated the semantic integration of heterogeneous data and automated reasoning, essential for decision-making in hybrid conflicts. Despite these advancements, challenges remain to ensure interoperability between C4I systems and efficiently managing large data volumes, highlighting the need for more adaptable and scalable solutions in military ontology development.

Finally, Wartik's work [11] emphasizes the formalization of JC3IEDM in OWL-DL, addressing business rules and hierarchical structures through an automated tool. Nevertheless, some complex rules could not be directly represented in OWL-DL, and the ontology's size remained a challenge for standard reasoners. Although smart partitioning strategies were proposed to mitigate this issue, their practical viability still requires further research.

Recent research underscores the crucial importance of semantic technologies in improving situational awareness (SA) during military operations, particularly in modeling entities and their intricate relationships. Notable systems such as SAWA utilized OWL and SWRL to derive contextual knowledge, though they encountered challenges related to expressiveness and usability. Other initiatives have sought to translate military frameworks like C2IEDM and JC3IEDM into OWL to facilitate automated reasoning and interoperability, but issues like semantic loss, ontology size, and insufficient spatiotemporal expressiveness continue to pose difficulties. Integration efforts, including SAW-CORE and GIS-based platforms (such as mCOP and tCOP), have made strides in the semantic representation of dynamic environments, yet problems with scalability and consistency across different systems remain unresolved. In summary, while the reviewed strategies lay important groundwork, they also reveal significant gaps, highlighting the need for more flexible, expressive, and computationally efficient semantic frameworks in defense applications.

3   Proposal

The exponential growth of Deep Learning (DL) and Machine Learning (ML) techniques has led to the centralization of model training in environments with access to large-scale, aggregated data. However, in the context of defense operations, this centralized approach poses serious limitations, including concerns regarding data privacy, sovereignty, and security. Data generated by millions of independent and geographically distributed devices, such as drones, edge sensors, and military units, cannot always be transmitted to a central server due to operational constraints, bandwidth limitations, or national policy restrictions. Federated Learning (FL) emerges as a fitting alternative for such environments. This approach enables each participating node to train a local model using its collected data while contributing to the development of a global object detection model without sharing sensitive information. The decentralized nature of FL ensures data privacy, compliance with national regulations, and effective use of distributed computational resources.

In this scenario, the system comprises the following key components:

– **Client Nodes**: Three Unmanned Aerial Vehicles (UAVs), which may belong to the same or different organizations and vary in storage and processing capabilities. Each UAV trains its local model and shares only the model parameters with the central server.
– **Command and Control (C2) Center**: This center coordinates all operational information received from the deployed UAVs. It processes real-time

video feeds from UAVs, applies the trained object detection model, and extracts actionable intelligence.

– **Cloud-based Central Server**: This server acts as the orchestrator of the FL process by aggregating model parameters from the UAVs, defining training rounds, determining the number of epochs, managing client participation, and establishing aggregation strategies (Fig. 2).

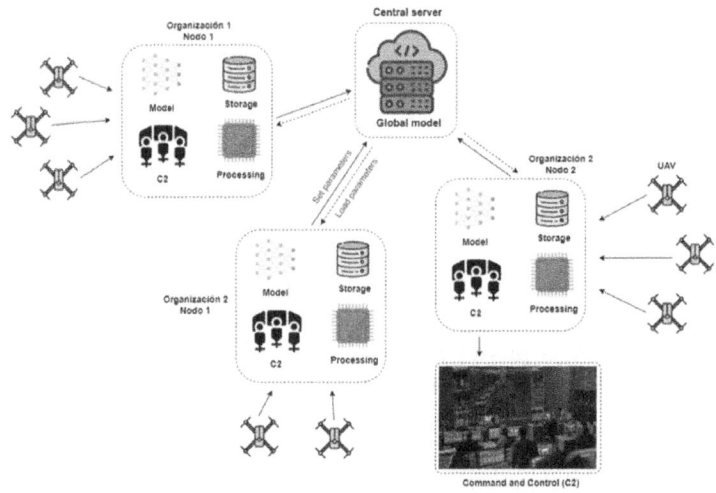

Fig. 2. Structure of FL scenario

Although FL supports decentralized and privacy-preserving learning, its full potential in defense contexts can only be realized if there is a shared understanding of data semantics among heterogeneous systems.

This is where JC3IEDM (Joint Consultation, Command and Control Information Exchange Data Model) becomes important. JC3IEDM is a NATO-endorsed relational data model designed to standardize the representation of military information across different systems and nations. It provides a common vocabulary and structured schema for entities such as personnel, equipment, actions, and events, ensuring interoperability in multinational operations. However, its rigid and deeply normalized schema can hinder seamless integration with lightweight, domain-specific ontologies that are more suited for distributed AI workflows.

To address this challenge, we propose a bidirectional ontology translator that bridges a domain-specific FL ontology, tailored for modeling entities and attributes within Combat Cloud layers, with a JC3IEDM-based ontology that standardizes military concepts. Acting as a semantic mediator, the translator resolves conceptual mismatches and enables meaningful interoperability between heterogeneous systems. This unified framework connects Federated Learning and

Combat Cloud environments through semantic alignment, enhancing real-time decision-making, preserving data sovereignty, and supporting AI collaboration in multinational defense scenarios.

This research outlines the context of the Combat Cloud and the need for semantic mediation in FL scenarios in Sect. 1. Section 2 presents the core concepts and related works, including ontologies, Combat Cloud architecture, FL, and JC3IEDM. Additionally, Sect. 3 describes the proposed solution: a semantic translation system between FL and JC3IEDM ontologies. Furthermore, Sect. 4 details the design and mapping strategies of the ontology translator, along with implementation techniques. Finally, Sect. 5 summarizes the main contributions of this work, presents the results obtained through a proposed use case, and outlines potential directions for future research and system optimization.

4 Design

In this section, the design of an ontology translator is detailed. This translator connects a domain-specific Federated Learning (FL) scenario ontology with a JC3IEDM model-based ontology. The design encompasses the manual creation of two ontologies and the mapping strategy to translate between them. The following section will describe the development of the FL scenario ontology and the JC3IEDM ontology. The subsequent presentation of the translator's design and mapping approach employs a Dron (drone) entity as a case study to illustrate how classes and properties are bridged.

4.1 Federated Learning Ontology

The FL scenario ontology was **manually crafted** to model the key entities and relationships in a federated learning-enabled Combat Cloud scenario. In light of the previously delineated scenarios, subsequent classes were identified and designated as OWL classes. For each class, relevant attributes were defined as OWL data properties (for literal values), and associations between entities were captured as object properties. The use of manual modeling ensured that the ontology faithfully reflected the domain semantics and requirements, resulting in the structure depicted in the Fig. 3.

Each **domain entity** was modelled as an OWL class with a rich set of properties. To illustrate this point, the Dron class, representing an unmanned aerial vehicle in the scenario, includes data properties for its operational status, flight autonomy, payload, and location. Specifically, a *estado_ operativo* property is employed to record the drone's operational status (e.g., active, grounded), an *autonomía_ vuelo* property is used to capture the drone's flight endurance or autonomy (e.g., maximum flight time), and an *ubicación* property denotes the drone's current location or coordinates. A *tipo* property is used to classify the type or role of the drone (such as a surveillance drone or combat drone), and a *carga_ útil* property represents any payload the drone carries. These attributes were selected to facilitate federated learning tasks. For instance, autonomy may dictate the duration for which a drone can participate in model training, and location may influence communication in the Combat Cloud.

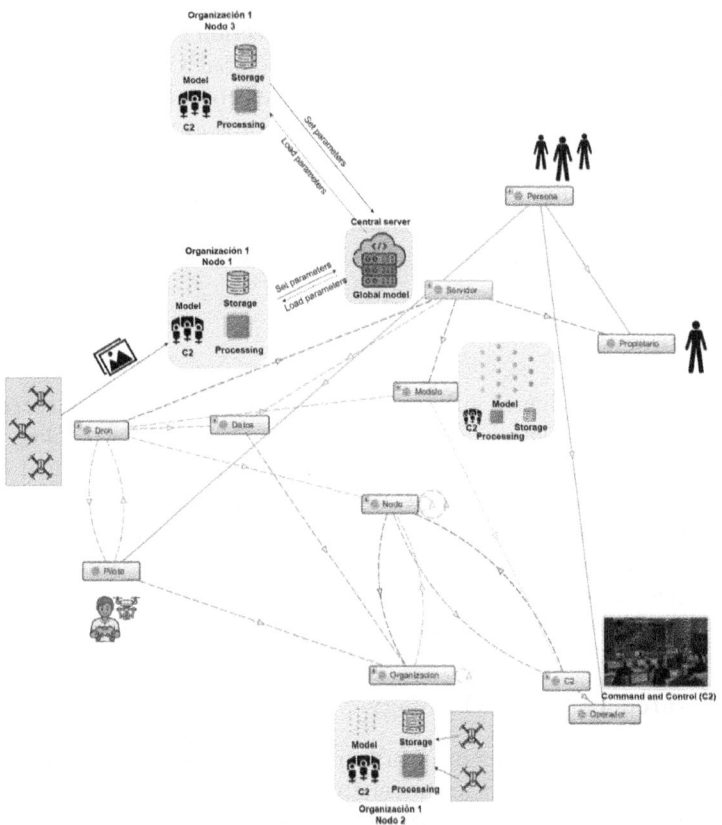

Fig. 3. Entities identification

Similarly, other actors in the scenario were modelled: The **Piloto** (Pilot) and **Operador** (Operator) classes represent human personnel with properties like license identifiers, training status, and system compatibility; **Servidor** (Server) and **Nodo** (Node) classes represent computational nodes (with properties such as IP address, storage capacity, and roles in command and control); and organizational entities like **Organización** (Organization) capture unit or team information (with properties for mission description, organizational type, members, etc.).

As shown in Fig. 4, the ontology encapsulates the semantic structure of the federated learning environment. Object properties interlink these classes to reflect relationships in the scenario. For example, the *pertenece_ a* property in the **Nodo** class (illustrated with a green arrow) links a node to an **Organización**,

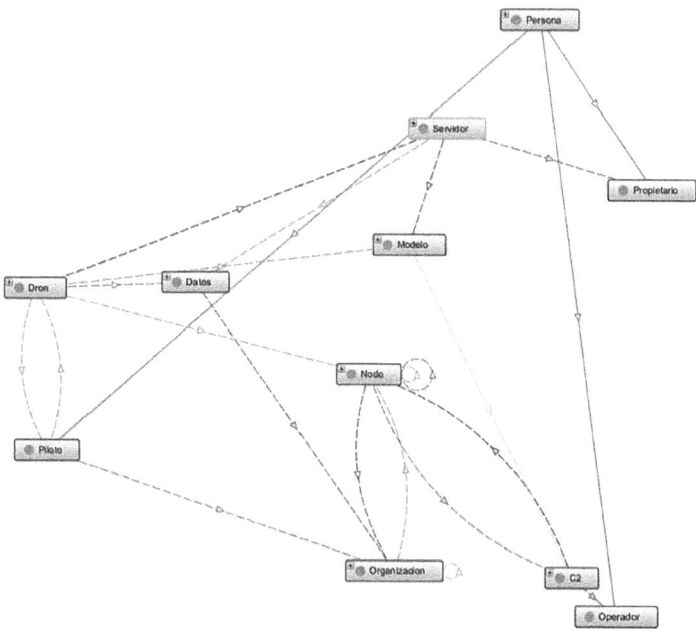

Fig. 4. FL ontology

indicating ownership or assignment. Similarly, the *interacción_con* property (illustrated with grey arrow) serves to define cooperation between nodes, particularly when they belong to the same organization. In this case, the relationship models collaborative behaviors such as sharing model parameters or coordinating training tasks in a federated learning setup. These semantic links are essential for enabling reasoning over distributed entities and maintaining interpretability across the Combat Cloud infrastructure. All classes and properties were defined in OWL using meaningful identifiers to maintain clarity. The resulting FL ontology provides a tailored conceptual model of the Combat Cloud federated learning environment, against which data instances (drones, pilots, servers, etc.) can be recorded.

4.2   JC3IEDM-Based Ontology

To enable interoperability with military systems, we built a second ontology derived from the (JC3IEDM) Joint Consultation, Command and Control Information Exchange Data Model logical schema. This JC3IEDM-based ontology was also created manually by converting the logical layer of the JC3IEDM (its core entities and relationships) into OWL classes and properties. Each principal entity in the JC3IEDM (such as Object-Item, Person, Organisation, Facility, Action, etc.) was mapped to an OWL class. The relationships represented by JC3IEDM as separate tables or associations were modeled either as properties of OWL objects or, when appropriate, as reified classes (OWL classes that stand for the relationship itself) to preserve the information content of the logical model [3].

We adhered closely to JC3IEDM's schema definitions when constructing the ontology. The JC3IEDM concept of a physical object is represented by the Object-Item class, while categorisations of objects are handled by an Object-Type class. In the ontology, an Object-item-type class was introduced as a reification of the "object is classified as a type" relationship: an instance of Object-item-type links an Object-Item individual to an Object-Type individual, mirroring the JC3IEDM approach to classifying objects. Similarly, status information that JC3IEDM manages (such as whether an object or person is operational) was captured with status classes (e.g., Object-item-status, Person-status), and capabilities or features are captured via classes like Object-item-capability. Many-to-many relationships from JC3IEDM, such as associations between organizations and resources, were also turned into intermediary classes like Object-item-association to allow additional details to be recorded if needed. Where the JC3IEDM model defines hierarchical or subtype structures, we reflected those as OWL subclass relationships. For instance, if JC3IEDM defines specific subcategories of capabilities or facility types, those were encoded as subclasses of a more general Capability or Facility class in the ontology [2].

During this ontology construction, we faced **practical modeling challenges**. One issue was **naming conflicts and conventions**: JC3IEDM uses many compound names and abbreviations that are not immediately OWL-friendly. We resolved naming conflicts by adopting composite identifiers and human-readable class names. In practice, this meant concatenating or slightly altering names to ensure uniqueness and clarity. For example, if two distinct JC3IEDM entities shared a generic name like "status" in different contexts, we disambiguated them as Object-item-status vs. Person-status in the ontology. We preserved JC3IEDM's meaning while adjusting syntax for OWL compliance (replacing spaces or special characters with hyphens or camelCase as needed).

Another challenge was handling **composite identifiers** and keys from the logical model. JC3IEDM tables often have composite primary keys (e.g., an association table key might combine IDs from related tables). In the OWL ontology, individuals are identified by URI rather than by numeric keys, so we did not carry over composite keys directly. Instead, we ensured each class and relationship instance could be uniquely identified by context (for example, an Object-item-type individual could be identified by a combination of the object's and type's identifiers in a single URI string). Additionally, we excluded implementation-level attributes from the ontology. The resulting ontology is a faithful OWL representation of JC3IEDM's logical layer, structured for ease of mapping and alignment with the FL ontology.

4.3 Design of the Ontology Translator

With both ontologies in place, we designed an **ontology translator** to map instances and knowledge between the FL scenario ontology and the JC3IEDM ontology. The mapping process was driven by semantic equivalence, i.e. the presence of a direct counterpart in JC3IEDM resulted in the establishment of a one-to-one mapping. For instance, the FL *Organización* class corresponds closely to the JC3IEDM Organisation class, and a domain *Persona* (person) corresponds to JC3IEDM's Person class. These direct mappings require the translator simply to convert an instance's type (class assertion) from the source ontology to the target ontology's class, preserving attribute values in the process. In a multitude of instances, numerous FL classes (particularly those designated for specific roles) are mapped to a solitary JC3IEDM class. For instance, the domain ontology distinguishes *Piloto* (pilot) and *Operador* (operator) as separate person subclasses, each with some unique attributes; however, the JC3IEDM ontology represents both as Person.

Although straightforward equivalences cover many mappings, some **structural mismatches** require the introduction of **auxiliary entities and intermediate relationships** in the translator. These arise not because an FL ontology property lacks an analog in JC3IEDM, but rather because JC3IEDM does not model attributes as simple properties of entities. Instead, it represents many attributes as separate entities, leading to situations where direct relationships between entities cannot be established. In such cases, the translator must introduce intermediate relations and auxiliary entities to bridge the semantic gap and accurately map the information.

The Fig. 5 illustrates the mapping of a *Dron* instance to its JC3IEDM counterparts, thereby demonstrating the creation of intermediate entities such as Object-item-type for type classification, Object-item-capability for autonomy, and Object-item-location for spatial position. Each arrow in the figure corresponds to a mapping relation that is handled by the translator (for example, an arrow from the *Dron*'s "*tipo*" attribute to the Object-Type class via an Object-item-type node).

Fig. 5. Drone translation

In essence, the ontology translator processes each class and property in the FL ontology according to a comprehensive mapping specification. This specification was recorded in mapping tables and JSON configuration files, which enumerate every source class and property alongside its target ontology equivalent. The translator implementation leverages these mappings to automate the conversion process. A custom ontology loader script iterates over instances in one ontology, and for each instance, it looks up the mapping rules to generate the corresponding individuals and relationships in the other ontology. These steps are encoded in the translator's code, which reads the JSON mapping definitions and programmatically generates the target ontology content.

In summary, the design of the translator enables seamless integration: it systematically maps classes (one-to-one or one-to-many with intermediates) and properties (attributes or links) between the two ontologies, maintaining semantic fidelity so that information about entities like drones, personnel, and resources remains consistent across the federated learning environment and the JC3IEDM-based interoperability framework.

5   Result

As mentioned in the introduction, the objective of this study is to address the issues of semantic interoperability and data sovereignty in multinational military operations. This section presents the results of implementing and evaluating the proposed bidirectional ontology translator, assessing its effectiveness in terms of mapping accuracy, semantic coverage and computational performance.

Integrating the DRON ontology into the JC3IEDM semantic framework has achieved functional and evaluative milestones. The results affirm the technical feasibility and practical relevance of the integration process, providing a robust connection between domain-specific knowledge and standardised defence ontologies.

Out of eleven defined entity types in the source model, ten were successfully mapped to the target ontology, achieving a 90% class-level mapping rate. This high percentage confirms the conceptual alignment between the operational domain and the military schema. Furthermore, 26 out of 40 properties were accurately mapped to their semantic equivalents, representing a 60% success rate at the attribute level. Among these 26 properties, 22 were successfully instantiated as relationships, resulting in a relation-building success rate of 81%. The only entity that could not be mapped was the class *Modelo*, which encapsulates artificial intelligence constructs such as training algorithms, performance metrics, and hyperparameters. These computational properties could not be aligned with any existing concepts in the JC3IEDM ontology, which currently lacks explicit support for AI-related operational elements. This layered analysis reveals a strong structural and semantic correspondence across ontological layers, while also identifying opportunities for extending the military schema to better accommodate modern, data-driven mission capabilities.

To validate the utility of the semantic model, a simulated mission scenario was implemented. The proposed operational scenario simulates a multinational alliance composed of ten partner nations, each contributing resources to a joint air defense mission. The architecture is structured around three primary coordination nodes and a central command and control center that maintains situational awareness and makes high-level strategic decisions. To ensure system resilience and prevent a single point of failure, two additional redundant nodes are deployed, acting as backups in case of disruption or overload in the main infrastructure.

Each nation operates a fleet of five unmanned aerial vehicles (UAVs), piloted by certified personnel trained in surveillance and reconnaissance operations. These UAVs are tasked with collecting high-resolution imagery data from their assigned sectors. Upon acquisition, the data is transmitted in real-time to the corresponding node.

Every node is equipped with a local AI model trained to perform object detection and threat assessment based on the incoming data stream. Once the local training cycle is completed, the updated model weights are transmitted to a centralized global server, which performs federated retraining by aggregating and optimizing the contributions from all nodes. This mechanism enables collaborative learning across the alliance while preserving local autonomy and reducing the need for raw data transfer, which is particularly critical in bandwidth-constrained or contested environments. From a technical performance perspective, the entire transformation process from data ingestion to ontology serialization was completed in just 4 s. This demonstrates that semantic translation can be achieved not only accurately, but efficiently—making the methodology suitable for real-time or near-real-time deployment environments.

6   Conclusion and Future Lines

The work presented here represents a comprehensive and methodical effort to semantically integrate operational UAV data into a structured military knowledge framework. Starting with the design and population of a domain-specific ontology, and continuing through the mapping of its entities and properties into the JC3IEDM military standard, this project has successfully demonstrated the feasibility and value of ontology-driven systems for defense operations.

The solution proposed effectively addresses the interoperability and data sovereignty challenges introduced at the beginning of this work. Through a rigorous mapping process, 10 out of 11 conceptual entities from the original ontology were accurately translated into the JC3IEDM model, achieving a 90% class-level mapping rate. Furthermore, 26 out of 40 properties were semantically aligned, with 22 of these correctly instantiated as inter-entity relationships, resulting in an impressive 81% relationship integration rate. These outcomes confirm the strong compatibility between the operational UAV domain and the JC3IEDM schema, especially for well-defined concepts such as drones, personnel, and infrastructure.

However, the process also exposed limitations in the military ontology standard when confronted with emerging technological elements. Notably, the entity *Modelo*, which includes AI constructs such as algorithms, performance metrics, and hyperparameters, could not be mapped due to the absence of corresponding classes in JC3IEDM. This gap highlights the need for semantic models to evolve alongside advancements in machine learning and autonomous systems.

To validate the applied ontology in a practical context, a defense scenario was modeled involving ten allied nations coordinating an air surveillance operation. The architecture included operational nodes and a centralized command structure, with federated learning capabilities implemented across local and global models. The ontology effectively supported the representation of UAV fleets, command hierarchies, operational data flow, and distributed intelligence processing, demonstrating both semantic integrity and operational realism.

In summary, this work achieved its primary objectives: building a coherent ontology, transforming it into an operationally valid format under JC3IEDM, and validating it through simulation. The system operated with high semantic accuracy, low computational costs, and real-world applicability, providing a strong foundation for future developments.

Looking ahead, integrating AI-specific semantics, automating error-handling in mappings, and deploying the ontology within live decision-support platforms represent promising directions. By pursuing these avenues, this project lays the groundwork for robust, intelligent, and interoperable systems that can support modern defense missions in a dynamic and data-driven world.

Acknowledgments. This work has been partially funded by the Catedra ISDEFE Seguridad y Defensa at the Universidad Politécnica de Madrid. The authors would like to thank the institutional support provided, which has contributed to the development of the results presented.

Disclosure of Interests. The authors have no competing interests to declare that are relevant to the content of this article.

References

1. Matheus, C.J., Kokar, M.M., Baclawski, K., Letkowski, J.J.: An application of semantic web technologies to situation awareness. In: International Semantic Web Conference, pp. 944–958. Springer (2005)
2. UK DMWG: JC3IEDM Overview – The Joint C3 Information Exchange Data Model Overview. Edition 3.1a. (2007)
3. Matheus, C.J., Ulicny, B.: On the Automatic Generation of an OWL Ontology based on the Joint C3 Information Exchange Data Model. Conference Paper (2007)
4. Joint Air Power Competence Centre: Multi-Domain Combat Cloud. https://www.japcc.org/essays/multi-domain-combat-cloud/. Accessed 20 Feb 2024
5. Demertzis, K., Kikiras, P., Skianis, C., Rantos, K., Iliadis, L., Stamoulis, G.: Federated Auto Meta-Ensemble Learning Framework for AI-Enabled Military Operations. Electronics **12**(2), Article 2 (2023). https://doi.org/10.3390/electronics12020430
6. Lasschuyt, E., van Hekken, M., Treurniet, W., Visser, M.: How to Make an Effective Information Exchange Data Model or The Good and Bad Aspects of the NATO JC3IEDM. TNO Physics and Electronics Laboratory, The Hague, The Netherlands (2004)

7. Mercier, C., Roux, L., Romero, M., Alexandre, F., Vieville, T.: Formalizing Problem Solving in Computational Thinking: an Ontology Approach. In: 2021 IEEE International Conference on Development and Learning (ICDL), pp. 1–8. IEEE (2021)
8. Matheus, C.J., Ulicny, B.: On the automatic generation of an OWL ontology based on the Joint C3 information exchange data model. In: 9th International Command and Control Research and Technology Symposium (ICCRTS). DoD Command and Control Research Program (2004)
9. Valiente, M.-C., Machín, R., García-Barriocanal, E., Sicilia, M.Á.: An ontology-based integrated approach to situation awareness for high-level information fusion in C4ISR. In: Salinesi, C., Pastor, O. (eds.) Advanced Information Systems Engineering Workshops, pp. 513–527. Springer, Heidelberg (2011)
10. Dorion, E., Matheus, C.J., Kokar, M.M.: Towards a formal ontology for military coalitions operations. In: 10th International Command and Control Research and Technology Symposium (ICCRTS): The Future of C2: Coalition Interoperability, McLean, VA, USA. DoD Command and Control Research Program (2005)
11. Wartik, S.: A JC3IEDM OWL-DL Ontology. Institute for Defense Analyses, Alexandria, VA (n.d.). Available upon request or internal distribution
12. Chmielewski, M.: Ontology-based methods and systems supporting situation awareness in hybrid conflicts utilising ontology reasoning mechanisms and GIS-based distributed services. In: Conference on Military Applications of Artificial Intelligence, Warsaw, Poland. Military University of Technology, Cybernetics Department (n.d.)

Large Language Models for Cyber Threat Intelligence: Extracting MITRE With LLMs

Andraž Krašovec$^{(\boxtimes)}$ (ID), Gary Steri (ID), Georgios Karopoulos (ID),
and Mirko Trapani (ID)

Joint Research Centre, European Commission, Ispra, Italy
andraz.krasovec@ec.europa.eu

Abstract. Cyber Threat Intelligence (CTI) reports provide information about emerging and current cyber threats, and their analysis is key for adopting appropriate countermeasures. Reports are typically in the form of long texts from which cybersecurity analysts extract essential elements and translate them into actionable steps. To summarise and share the findings of this analysis, sentences in the reports are often labelled with MITRE ATT&CK techniques that yield a better description of the identified attack patterns. However, this task can be very time-consuming and prone to both errors and biases of analysts.

In the literature, there have been some attempts to automate this process. Most commonly, researchers apply different pre-processing steps on the initial reports and then apply classification techniques, including approaches based on large language models (LLMs). Considering that reports are written in natural language, in this paper, we present an approach that relies entirely on LLMs and seeks to minimise preprocessing of reports and other human intervention, if not to replace, at least to ease the task of the analysts. We evaluate our approach on a real-world CTI report and an extensive dataset of MITRE-labelled sentences and reduce the number of potentially suitable techniques by up to 33× while retaining ground truth labels in up to 94.29% of the sentences.

Keywords: Cyber Threat Intelligence · Large Language Models · MITRE ATT&CK · Automated Labelling · Cyber Risk Identification

1 Introduction

The advancements in generative Artificial Intelligence (AI) and the growth in popularity of LLMs have seen the use of the latter in several fields. Cybersecurity is no exception, with applications spanning from spam detection, code security, or threat detection and response. When talking about cyber threats detection and response, CTI plays a fundamental role. Awareness of threats that could materialise can lead to better preparedness for early detection and quick and effective response.

© The Author(s) 2025
B. Coppens et al. (Eds.): ARES 2025 Workshops, LNCS 15995, pp. 80–89, 2025.
https://doi.org/10.1007/978-3-032-00633-2_5

CTI activities often rely on the collection of different sources of data about threats, including metadata coming from sensors or devices, or reports that describe general threats or specific events in a natural language. While metadata can be processed more easily in an automated way, CTI reports require the work of cybersecurity analysts to make sense of them, share the findings with other stakeholders, and finally provide actionable feedback. This analysis can be very time-consuming, can be subject to bias of each analyst, and ultimately can slow down the whole process, thus compromising the early preparation for defending against various threats.

The nature of CTI reports and the type of task expected by the analyst immediately trigger the idea of employing LLMs. The report is in the form of long text and has to be marked with labels corresponding to specific threats or attack techniques, so that these labels can easily be shared or further analysed to put countermeasures in place. A common reference for the labels is the ATT&CK Matrix from MITRE, consisting in the latest enterprise version (17.1) of an extensive set of fourteen adversary tactics describing 211 techniques and 468 sub-techniques. These numbers already give an idea of the complexity of the task and the likelihood of making mistakes. Even discarding the sub-techniques, an analyst has to choose from over two hundred techniques to label each part of the report that best matches the description. And this can be for dozens of sentences in the report, considering also that the same sentence could refer to several techniques. The help of an automatic tool is, therefore, extremely valuable.

The use of LLMs for this kind of task has already been proposed in the literature, even though with some preprocessing and intermediate steps relying on different types of techniques, such as machine learning processing and classifiers. In this paper, instead, we propose an approach that entirely relies on LLMs, attempting to minimise the preprocessing of the reports and to simplify the use of artificial intelligence to accomplish the task. The LLM becomes a first-level analyst; it does not substitute the human, however, it makes the task easier by reducing the amount of possible techniques to choose from for each sentence in the report. Ultimately, the final classification decision still lies with a human expert, however, the classification process is significantly reduced by the LLM's augmentation.

After analysing the related work in Sect. 2, Sect. 3 describes in detail the methodology we propose in this paper. Section 4 shows the results of our technique applied to different data sets, while Sect. 5 discusses common issues and challenges when implementing these techniques. Finally, Sect. 6 concludes the paper.

2   Related Work

With the proliferation of LLMs in recent years, their potential for various CTI tasks has become apparent. Perrina *et al.* [9], for example, propose a tool called AGIR for the automatic generation of intelligence reports from Structured Threat Information Expression (STIX) data. According to their estimations, the time required to draft a report using AGIR is reduced by more than 40%, compared to manual generation. Similarly, Liu *et al.* [7] focus on automated processing of CTI reports using ChatGPT to construct a CTI knowledge graph. This method consists of a pipeline where ChatGPT is used twice: first for extracting metadata from the unstructured textual CTI reports and later on for the selection of the SPO (subject-predicate-object) triplets to be used for the knowledge graph construction. CRUSH [10] is another multi-step approach to enhance CTI by developing an Enterprise Knowledge Graph (EKG) using LLMs such as GPT-3.5 and GPT-4. The authors demonstrate how LLMs can be utilized to automatically extract, infer, validate, and summarise information from various data sources to populate the EKG with entities, relationships, and properties. Other works also focus on transforming natural language CTI reports to structured forms [5,11] or summaries [3], quality assessment of human-performed CTI [12], and CTI reports deduplication [16]. With these generative tools being readily available to threat actors [4,13,15] and even lowering the knowledge threshold to perform more sophisticated attacks, it is imperative to investigate what effect LLMs can have on detection, prevention, and, in the case of this paper, collection, analysis, and dissemination of cyber threats.

Our approach classifies natural language reports according to the MITRE ATT&CK Matrix[1]. ATT&CK is a comprehensive knowledge base of adversarial tactics and techniques, already widely adopted by the community. It currently consists of over 200 adversary techniques, further split into over 400 sub-techniques, each with a detailed description, examples, possible mitigation, and detection procedures. Despite the adoption and robustness of the matrix, ATT&CK still faces some challenges, one major being the time required to classify natural language reports by cybersecurity experts. With natural language processing being one of the most prominent research directions in machine learning, automating report classification with ATT&CK is a topic of contemporary research. Most approaches rely on some sort of LLMs, either as encoder-only BERT [2] models that are fine-tuned for this specific task [6,8], or as encoder-decoder models that rely on carefully curated prompts to obtain ATT&CK techniques [11]. Convolutional neural networks (CNN) have also been utilised to perform the same task [14]. Compared to the state-of-the-art, we develop a method that relies solely on LLM prompting to perform all data processing and inference tasks.

3   Methodology

LLMs display great potential in processing long texts, focusing on important information, and providing competent summaries. Therefore, they are well-suited for the task we want to solve in this work. In this section, we present the details of our methodology.

---

[1] https://attack.mitre.org/.

3.1   CTI Datasets

Our ambition with this research is to alleviate the burden of analysts labelling natural language-written CTI reports with MITRE ATT&CK. Thus, we initially scrutinise our system on such reports, specifically from the repository of Orbinato *et al.* [8]. Their reports come with labels that are introduced on a report and not on a sentence-by-sentence basis. Initially, our intuition was that feeding complete reports to the LLM should yield the best results, as the LLM is then able to investigate multi-sentence dependencies and has more context to work with. However, a preliminary investigation on processing complete reports returned poor results. Thus, we opt to split and label the reports sentence-by-sentence.

We select a single report from the same dataset that describes activities of the FIN6 threat group[2] and split it into sentences by relying on the natural language processing Python library nltk[3]. Additional testing demonstrates that the same sentence splitting results can be achieved with an LLM. Next, each author (*i.e.*, four analysts in total) classifies the same report with ATT&CK. The resulting labels differ between the authors, however, we converge towards a common labelling result that we use as the ground truth in further analysis. Finally, we retain sentences with at least one MITRE technique accredited and discard the rest. In cases with multiple labels in a single sentence, we repeat the sentence with each assigned label.

Mapping MITRE to reports is a time-consuming process; therefore, to evaluate how well our approach generalises to a larger dataset, we employ the TRAM dataset[4]. TRAM consists of 12,945 sentences and phrases from CTI texts, labelled with MITRE ATT&CK. Similarly to our dataset, there are samples without corresponding labels, which we again discard. We repeat sentences with multiple labels as well. Altogether, we are left with 9,915 sentences to evaluate our approach.

We assume all data come from a trusted source; therefore, we do not investigate how robust our system would be in the case of adversarial inputs.

3.2   Prompting

Our prompting strategy consists of two separate steps to classify each sentence: 1) filtering through all MITRE techniques to recognise the ones that are potentially related to the sentence, and 2) ranking the recognised techniques from the most to the least probable. We rely on the mitreattack Python library[5] to obtain and manage the techniques' descriptions.

---

[2] https://attack.mitre.org/groups/G0037/.
[3] https://www.nltk.org/.
[4] https://github.com/center-for-threat-informed-defense/tram.
[5] https://github.com/mitre-attack/mitreattack-python.

Filtering MITRE Techniques. In the first step, we combine each technique description with a given sentence from a report and a request to build the following prompt:

```
You are a cybersecurity expert classifying a natural language cyber
threat intelligence text with MITRE attack techniques. You have a
description of a particular MITRE attack technique and a sentence
of text from a CTI report.
Based only on these two pieces of text, tell if the described MITRE
attack technique is present in the sentence. Do not rely on your
own knowledge of MITRE attack techniques.
Reply only with yes or no.
DESCRIPTION: {description}
CTI REPORT sentence: {sentence}
```

We tailored the request through iterations based on the replies we received from the model. In the current state of the prompt, we first provide context and the role to the model. Next, we tell the model to only reason from the presented content and disregard its own knowledge of MITRE. This part is crucial to obtain good results as the model's familiarity with the MITRE matrix is oftentimes obsolete and detrimental to the outcome. We conclude with the instruction to only reply with yes or no, which simplifies the answer extraction process from the reply. The final result of the filtering part is a set of MITRE techniques that the model deems connected to a given sentence.

Ranking MITRE Techniques. The second step refines the results obtained previously. The low number of positively predicted techniques from the previous step allows us to feed descriptions of all predicted techniques into a single prompt and ask the model to rank them:

```
You are a cybersecurity expert classifying a natural language cyber
threat intelligence text with MITRE attack techniques. We already
narrowed the selection of potential techniques to the most probable
ones.
Based only on the descriptions of these techniques, provided as a
python list, rank the techniques in order of the most related to
the least related to the report. Do not rely on your own knowledge
of MITRE attack techniques.
Only return a python list of indices for the ranking from the most
likely to the least likely related to the report. Include indices
of all descriptions.
Do not provide any explanation.
DESCRIPTIONS: {descriptions}
CTI REPORT sentence: {sentence}
```

Similarly to the first prompt, we provide context, instructions on the task and handling of its own knowledge of MITRE, and the formatting instructions. The model outputs a Python list. On occasion, the returned list is malformed, *e.g.*, missing brackets around the list. We handle such cases by relying on regular expressions.

3.3 LLM Infrastructure

The presented approach is computationally expensive. To reduce the environmental impact of our evaluation, we first perform a preliminary analysis on a subset of the TRAM dataset. We randomly select 100 samples from the dataset and utilise different LLMs with our approach to evaluate the performance of the models. We test Mixtral 8x7B, Llama 3.3 70B, and GPT-4o. In our testing, Llama performs best both in terms of coverage and accuracy, therefore, we opt to rely on it for the complete evaluation process. We rely on our internal LLM infrastructure [1] to build the system and generate experimental results.

4 Results

We separately evaluate the filtering and classification tasks to analyse the impact of each step. We first introduce the utilised evaluation metrics and evaluate our approach on the two datasets presented in Sect. 3.1.

4.1 Evaluation Metrics

We utilise different metrics for the filtering and classification tasks. For filtering, we are interested in the number of predicted labels and how many ground truth labels are retained in the predicted filtered set. In this regard, we report on two metrics. First is the average number of labels in the filtered set – #**filter**. It tells how many techniques, on average, the analyst must consider during labelling a given sentence. It also enables us to calculate the factor by which this space is reduced, compared to all available techniques. To measure the number of ground truth labels that are retained after our filtering operation, we introduce **coverage**. Coverage calculates the ratio between ground truths retained in the prediction set (y_{pred}) and all ground truths (y_{true}): $coverage = \frac{y_{pred}}{y_{true}}$. The main goal of our approach is to assist rather than replace a human analyst. Therefore, the #**filter and coverage metrics are the main focus of our evaluation process.**

In terms of classification, we scrutinise our approach with classification accuracy. Our datasets exclusively include a single ground truth label for each sample. Therefore, we can evaluate our approach by calculating the ratio of correctly predicted cases, *i.e.* cases where our prediction matches the ground truth, (hit) over all dataset samples (all). We coin two flavours of this metric – first one, **accuracy** (ACC), encompasses the calculation precisely as described above: $ACC = \frac{hit}{all}$, while **top-3 accuracy** ($TOP3$) takes into consideration the top three most probable predictions ($hit3$) and follows the same formula: $TOP3 : \frac{hit3}{all}$.

4.2 Filtering Results

The first step of our pipeline greatly reduces the number of potentially valid MITRE labels while retaining the majority of the ones deemed correct. We use version 15.1 of the MITRE ATT&CK matrix[6] that includes 203 techniques from which we choose. With the report data, our system selects 8.34 techniques on average, reducing the number of techniques taken into consideration by a factor of 24.34. At the same time, it retains the ground truth within the predicted techniques in 94.29% of cases. The more comprehensive TRAM dataset yields a 33.28× reduction in considered labels while covering the ground truth label in 84.84% of the cases as displayed in Table 1. These results display that our system can significantly reduce the number of techniques that should be considered when mapping to MITRE while retaining a high level of confidence. Consequently, the time required by the analyst to perform the classification task is greatly reduced due to the filtered set, while high accuracy can still be achieved due to the high coverage values.

4.3   Classification Results

To investigate the feasibility of automating the complete labelling pipeline, we task our LLM with ranking the filtered results to classify sentences with particular labels. This is a considerably more difficult task as it requires a more complex inference operation, compared to the binary nature of the filtering step. On the report dataset, our system predicts the correct label in 11.43% of the cases and includes it in the top three in 48.57%. Additionally, we calculate the metrics only on samples where the ground truth label was not excluded as a potential candidate by the filtering step. The results improve to 13.33% accuracy and 56.67% top-3 accuracy values. The results of the TRAM dataset continue to exhibit better results with 29.08% and 63.87% accuracy and top-3 accuracy respectively. These values increase to 34.87% and 76.57% when considering only samples with included ground truth label after the filtering for accuracy and top-3 accuracy, respectively.

Table 1. Results of the filtering (#filter and coverage), and classification (accuracy and top-3 accuracy) processes on the MITRE labelled report and TRAM sentences dataset.

Dataset	Samples	#filter	Coverage	Accuracy	Top-3 Acc
report	35	8.34	94.29%	11.43%	48.57%
TRAM	9915	6.10	84.84%	29.08%	63.87%

5   Discussion

A common obstacle with machine learning-based solutions is the lack of publicly available high-quality data, and MITRE classification is no different. This

---

[6] https://github.com/mitre-attack/attack-stix-data/blob/master/enterprise-attack/enterprise-attack-15.1.json.

is exacerbated by the volatility of the ground truth, which depends on the cybersecurity expert mapping ATT&CK techniques to CTI reports. In this work, we converge towards a single ground truth between four experts, however, that leads to more than quadruple the effort of an already time-consuming process. Sharing knowledge between experts and organisations can have an additional negative effect on the ground truth, as experts' bias and approach to mapping influence their decisions, contributing to further discrepancies in the selected techniques.

The classification results we achieve fall short of some state-of-the-art, more traditional deep learning approaches. Instead, our approach displays merit in the first step of our system – technique filtering, where we reduce the number of techniques that should be considered for classification by ∼97% while simultaneously retaining most of the relevant ones in the filtered set. Relying on LLMs for such a task yields additional benefits. For example, they can provide insight on *why* a certain technique should or should not be associated with a given report, assisting a cybersecurity expert to make an informed decision, instead of only producing a set of belonging techniques. Contingent on a deterministic output of LLMs, such an approach should also increase the uniformity of mapped techniques provided by different human experts.

While performant, our approach demands a substantial amount of computational resources. Further efforts should be put towards alleviating this concern by optimising the prompting strategy we employ in our current approach. For example, querying for multiple techniques in a single query or filtering by the MITRE tactic first could lead to significant savings in required computing power.

6   Conclusion

In this paper, we present an LLM-based approach to classify CTI reports with MITRE ATT&CK techniques. We split each report into sentences, then employ a two-stage classification strategy. In the first step, we filter out about 97% of all techniques, followed by a probability ranking of the remaining techniques that yields the end classification. We evaluate the approach on a sample CTI report that we label ourselves and validate it on a larger dataset of labelled sentences, where we achieve a coverage of correct techniques of 84.84% with 6.10 techniques remaining on average after the filtering process. We achieve an accuracy of 29.08% and top-3 accuracy of 63.87% with a baseline accuracy of 0.04%. The accuracy values are lower compared to results of a more targeted machine learning approach. Therefore, in our future work, we plan to improve on the classification results by employing specifically fine-tuned LLMs with newer, better-performing underlying models such as Llama 4. On the other hand, we also foresee testing distilled and quantised models that could be deployed in edge computing scenarios. Additionally, we intend to optimise our prompting strategy by querying about MITRE ATT&CK tactics first to lessen the computational burden of our current approach.

References

1. De Longueville, B., et al.: The proof is in the eating: dessons learnt from one year of generative AI adoption in a science-for-policy organisation. SSRN 5141665
2. Devlin, J., Chang, M.W., Lee, K., Toutanova, K.: Bert: pre-training of deep bidirectional transformers for language understanding. In: Proceedings of the 2019 Conference of the North American Chapter of the Association for Computational Linguistics: Human Language Technologies, Volume 1 (Long and Short Papers), pp. 4171–4186 (2019)
3. Fayyazi, R., Taghdimi, R., Yang, S.J.: Advancing TTP analysis: harnessing the power of encoder-only and decoder-only language models with retrieval augmented generation. arXiv preprint arXiv:2401.00280 (2024)
4. Gupta, M., Akiri, C., Aryal, K., Parker, E., Praharaj, L.: From ChatGPT to threatGPT: impact of generative AI in cybersecurity and privacy. IEEE Access **11**, 80218–80245 (2023)
5. Hu, Y., Zou, F., Han, J., Sun, X., Wang, Y.: LLM-TIKG: threat intelligence knowledge graph construction utilizing large language model. Comput. Secur. **145**, 103999 (2024)
6. Huang, Y.T., et al.: Mitretrieval: retrieving Mitre techniques from unstructured threat reports by fusion of deep learning and ontology. IEEE Trans. Network Serv. Manag. (2024)
7. Liu, J., Zhan, J.: Constructing knowledge graph from cyber threat intelligence using large language model. In: 2023 IEEE International Conference on Big Data (BigData), pp. 516–521. IEEE (2023)
8. Orbinato, V., Barbaraci, M., Natella, R., Cotroneo, D.: Automatic mapping of unstructured cyber threat intelligence: an experimental study:(practical experience report). In: 2022 IEEE 33rd International Symposium on Software Reliability Engineering (ISSRE), pp. 181–192. IEEE (2022)
9. Perrina, F., Marchiori, F., Conti, M., Verde, N.V.: AGIR: automating cyber threat intelligence reporting with natural language generation. In: 2023 IEEE International Conference on Big Data (BigData), pp. 3053–3062. IEEE (2023)
10. Sewak, M., Emani, V., Naresh, A.: Crush: Cybersecurity research using universal LLMs and semantic hypernetworks. In: EKG-LLM@ CIKM (2023)
11. Siracusano, G., et al.: Time for action: automated analysis of cyber threat intelligence in the wild. arXiv preprint arXiv:2307.10214 (2023)
12. Wu, Z., Tang, F., Zhao, M., Li, Y.: KGV: integrating large language models with knowledge graphs for cyber threat intelligence credibility assessment. arXiv preprint arXiv:2408.08088 (2024)
13. Yao, Y., Duan, J., Xu, K., Cai, Y., Sun, Z., Zhang, Y.: A survey on large language model (LLM) security and privacy: the good, the bad, and the ugly. High-Confidence Computing 100211 (2024)
14. Yu, Z., Wang, J., Tang, B., Lu, L.: Tactics and techniques classification in cyber threat intelligence. Comput. J. **66**(8), 1870–1881 (2023)
15. Zhang, J., et al.: When LLMs meet cybersecurity: a systematic literature review. Cybersecurity **8**(1), 1–41 (2025)
16. Zhang, T., Irsan, I.C., Thung, F., Lo, D.: Cupid: leveraging ChatGPT for more accurate duplicate bug report detection. arXiv preprint arXiv:2308.10022 (2023)

Enhancing Cyber Situation Awareness: Visualizing Advanced Persistent Threats as Complex Systems

Georgi Nikolov[1]([✉]) [iD], Margaret Varga[2]([✉]) [iD], April Rose Panganiban[3], Kaur Kullman[4] [iD], and Valérie Lavigne[5]

[1] Cyber Defence Lab, Royal Military Academy, Brussels, Belgium
g.nikolov@cylab.be
[2] University of Oxford, Oxford, UK
Margaret.Varga@seetru.com
[3] Air Force Research Laboratory, Dayton, OH, USA
april_rose.panganiban@us.af.mil
[4] Center for Space Sciences and Technology, University of Maryland, Baltimore County, MD, USA
digilience@coda.ee
[5] Defence R&D Canada, Québec, Canada
valerie.lavigne@ecn.forces.gc.ca
https://cylab.be

Abstract. In recent years the field of Information Technologies has become ubiquitous, it is used to implement and manage private, public, government and military installations. This has led to massive growth in the threat landscape, attackers have ample time, resources, technologies and tools to design highly sophisticated attacks implementing Zero-Day Vulnerabilities and complex algorithms using polymorphic behaviour, putting a major strain on defenders. Rapid advancement of Advanced Persistent Threats (APT) poses a major security risk for online services, but even more so for critical government, financial, healthcare and military infrastructures. The difficulty in counteracting APTs is amplified by the increasing challenge of identifying and preparing countermeasures in time. There is ample research and documentation available, describing the life-cycle of various APTs and their Tactics Techniques and Practices (TTPs), but a lack of deeper understanding hinders timely detection to halt the attack. To better understand APTs and how they function, we propose addressing emergent cyber attacks from the perspective of Complex Systems and the application of Visual Analytics and visualization to enhance the level of understanding and Situation Awareness. In this paper, we discuss how we can analyse APTs from a Complex System perspective, the visualization techniques and visual analytics approaches used and how they can be applied for better detection, understanding and management.

Keywords: Advanced Persistent Threat · Complex Systems · Visual Analytics · Visualization · Visual Hierarchy

© The Author(s), under exclusive license to Springer Nature Switzerland AG 2025
B. Coppens et al. (Eds.): ARES 2025 Workshops, LNCS 15995, pp. 90–107, 2025.
https://doi.org/10.1007/978-3-032-00633-2_6

1   Introduction

Over the years, our daily lives have become increasingly interconnected, with internet-facing devices enabling a wide range of activities, from streaming content to managing finances and controlling smart homes. Similarly, various infrastructures in healthcare, finance, industry, government, and military sectors have formed a complex cyber environment, enhancing oversight and management. This advancement is driven by new technologies and applications that facilitate connectivity and information exchange.

Despite efforts to manage the new distributed technologies, the growing complexity of integrated systems often leaves vulnerabilities that malicious actors exploit. High-profile attacks on public, private, and government organizations have become common, resulting in infrastructure disruptions and data theft. While many attacks are thwarted by experienced defenders and advanced detection capabilities [1, 32], the proliferation of free tools and information has led to more sophisticated and organized attacks, known as Advanced Persistent Threats (APTs). These threats have become more prominent due to geopolitical instability and technological advancements.

There has been much research on APTs [1, 4, 23], describing how APTs function and possible solutions. APTs are characterized by their stealthy, slow, and meticulous nature, aiming to steal information, conduct espionage, sabotage, or take control of target infrastructures. These threats are carried out by well-organized, often state-sponsored groups with deep knowledge of off-the-shelf applications and ample resources to exploit vulnerabilities. This creates a constant struggle between attackers and defenders, where attackers need only one successful attempt, while defenders must counter every possible attack.

The sophisticated nature of APTs has led to the application of various information technology theories to understand their Tactics, Techniques, and Procedures (TTPs) better. One approach is to model APTs using Complex Systems methodology. This paper explores APTs through the lens of Complex Systems, providing insights into their intricate and dynamic nature. Furthermore, we propose using Visual Analytics and visualization principles to enhance Cyber Situation Awareness [19, 28] for the better understanding and detection of such attacks.

In Sect. 2, we present our work on applying Complex Systems concepts to APTs. Section 3 discusses how APTs function, their impact, and how to model them as Complex Systems. Our main contribution, detailed in Sect. 4, is to illustrate ways to understand the cybersecurity domain, particularly APTs, using Visual Analytics and visualization. Multiple practical examples are discussed in Sect. 4.2, discussing the hierarchy of visualization and how to adapt the information to the intended audience, enhancing awareness at all levels of the hierarchy.

2   Complexity of Cyber Systems

In the Cyber Security Domain, a typical environment often consists of a variety of devices, each with different configurations and purposes, creating a complicated system. Companies use interconnected networks with users working on premises or remotely via a Virtual Private Network (VPN) connection. This creates a complicated infrastructure of a large number of machines that need to be monitored, maintained and managed. By carefully studying the components in the network(s), examining the deployed applications and restricting what can be installed inside the environment, the system administrators can have a good overview and in-depth understanding and knowledge of the network. Problems arise when we add the Human Factor to the equation [13]. By nature, human behaviour is difficult to predict and this is problematic when a high degree of predictability and controllability is required. By including humans as an integral part of a system, it changes from a complicated system to a complex one. This leads to an important shift in operational logic and different tactics need to be applied to manage such an environment [25]. Instead of reducing the system to its smaller simple components, the system needs to be regarded as a whole to detect patterns of emergent behaviour and how it propagates through the system and the non-linear changes it brings. This leads to another important aspect of complex systems: instead of viewing the system as a collection of individual simple components in isolation, it is considered as a "System of Systems". Indeed, a complex system can be composed of various interconnecting sub-systems, varying from simple to complicated or to other complex ones.

2.1   Management of Complex Cyber Systems

Sensitive infrastructures, such as healthcare, financial, industrial, government and military systems, are often the target of malicious actors. The non- deterministic nature of complex systems needs to be taken into account as it can have a severe impact on the stability, resilience, performance and possible vulnerabilities of the environment. These aspects are reinforced by the need for reliable, relevant and precise information to be transferred between segments of the environment in a timely and orderly fashion. Correct interpretation and overview of the environment are imperative for the secure exchange of information. For example, in the military command and control (C2) chain [16], as shown in Fig. 1, an in-depth understanding of the system leads to a high degree of Situation Awareness (SA) for effective decision making [7].

2.2   Situation Awareness in Complex Systems

In its established interpretation, SA was framed as an individual cognitive state that changes based on the dynamics between the human and their environment. Thus SA changes through this interaction and requires maintenance. Endsley's model [7] explains SA maintenance as a cycle, starting from perception of clues from the environment to interpretation of their meaning and resulting in

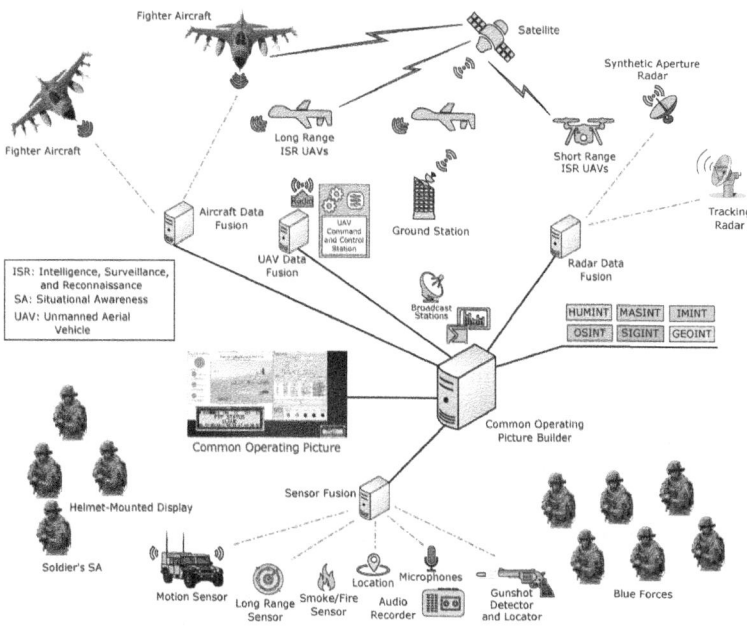

Fig. 1. Overview of military situation awareness as depicted in [16]

projection of a future outcome. Actions resulting from this process have the ability to change the environment, hopefully creating the desired result for the operator.

However, when SA is incorrect, these actions may create outcomes that result in inaccurate or erroneous projections of the operation, delaying or preventing ideal outcomes. Actions taken under poor SA can add noise to the system, thus adversely affecting future perceptual and interpretation stages of SA maintenance and carrying operators down the wrong decision-making path. Further inaccuracies in SA arise from the complexity of most operational environments where teams work together (adapting the environment) and exchange information. It is acknowledged that team SA is more than the aggregate and overlap of individual SA but arises from the communication between individual members with teammates shaping each other's SA [5]. As operational environments become more complex, a different view of SA is needed to account for the impact of technological advancements in AI. Technology has the ability to aid early stages of SA maintenance and foster team SA through communication aids. Additionally non-human agents form their own situation awareness by monitoring sensors, interpreting data and projecting courses of action to human operators, similarly to human teammates. These Sociotechnical interactions are accounted for in the Distributed Situation Awareness (DSA) model which treats SA as emerging from the interactions between all "agents" in the system (e.g. tools, documents, displays [21]). This approach shows good SA results from using different informational sources (teammates or agents) at the right time and occasionally reverting back to one's individual lens of SA. The DSA view captures how SA occurs in cyber defense and accounts for the complicated process of maintaining it in the presence of new sophisticated threats. Thus, viewing APT attacks and the defense against them as a complex system can directly improve SA for individuals working together in this system.

System intrusions in the form of an APT can lead to skewed, erroneous or often deliberately malicious data being injected into the information flow, perturbing SA. Compromised elements in the system can also be used for data exfiltration of, for example, personal information, threatening the safety of individuals. Malicious actors therefore gain entry to the system at different levels of the system, potentially confusing operators or manipulating their actions by injecting information. The complex nature of a cyber network makes it difficult to maintain awareness across the many connections and levels when threats arise. A better understanding of APTs is needed for proper cyber defense by extending the scope of SA to focus not only on what is happening in the field, but also on how information flows through the system, its origin and its validity.

Countermeasures (i.e., Intrusion Detection Systems (IDS), Intrusion Prevention Systems (IPS), Honeypots and the integration of Behaviour-based analysis) are integrated into a Security Information and Event Management (SIEM) architecture for further analysis and correlation. Though intended to assist, the abundance of alerts across various systems combined with time pressure to identify and stop a threat can lead to "alert fatigue" [24] and impairments to SA maintenance in the form of stress and burden on cognitive resources. Vulnerabilities in the operator provide fertile grounds for APTs to continue functioning in the background undetected. Therefore focusing on methods to enhance operator SA maintenance via visualizations and its evaluation [19] may aid in faster resolution of APTs.

3   Advanced Persistent Threats

3.1   Advanced Persistent Threat Definition

First, it is important to clarify the term APT in Information Technologies and literature as most Cyber Threat Intelligence (CTI) sources use APT to refer to organized groups responsible for cyber attacks on high-value targets. However, in scientific literature, APT can also refer to the specific attacks or campaigns by these groups.

In this paper, "APT" denotes a highly sophisticated and targeted cyber attack where an adversary gains unauthorized access and remains undetected for an extended period. APTs involve strategic planning, long-term objectives, and complex execution, often supported by nation-states or well-funded organizations. They are challenging to detect and counter due to dedicated spear phishing attacks, custom malware, and zero-day vulnerabilities. For a more in-depth look, Alshamrani et al. [1] provide an overview of APT techniques and tactics, along with case studies.

Table 1. Examples of APT groups targeting civilian infrastructures [15]

APT Group	Target Sector	Victims	Strategy	Impact
APT1 (China)	Commercial/ Industrial	Coca-Cola, Westinghouse	IP Theft, economic espionage	Loss of trade secrets and competitive advantage
APT28 (Russia)	Sports/ Health	WADA, IOC	Data leaks, phishing	Reputation damage, trust erosion
APT10 (China)	IT/ Managed Service	MSPs and client companies	Cloud access, lateral movement	Widespread data theft across sectors
Charming Kitten (Iran)	Academical/ Journalism	Academics, journalists	Credential theft, phishing	Surveillance, compromised communications
Lazarus Group (North Korea)	Media/ Entertainment	Sony Pictures	Destructive malware, data leaks	Operational disruption, public embarrassment
OceanLotus (Vietnam)	Civil Society/ Private Sector	NGOs, companies, media	Watering hole, document malware	Espionage, surveillance
APT33 (Iran)	Aviation/ Energy	Aerospace, energy firms	IP Reconnaissance, malware	Preparation for sabotage, IP theft

To illustrate the impact of APTs on different infrastructures, examples of attacks on the civilian sector are presented in Table 1. It is important to note that the information on these groups is source-dependent and often comes with a degree of vagueness.

3.2   APTs from a Complex System Perspective

As discussed previously, Advanced Persistent Threats are highly sophisticated attacks, often perpetrated by well-organized groups. More often than not, these groups are state sponsored, which leads to their targets often being financial, government or military.

Major effort has been done in the field of CTI to identify and collect information about APTs. Initially, a definition of their life cycle was proposed in the form of the Cyber Kill Chain [33], later expanded by MITRE [15, 22]. Platforms such as MITRE ATT&CK and MISP [31] offer a large collection of data, pertaining to the TTPs of APTs. All this information is often in text form, which requires long period of time to process and identify the key characteristics of advanced threats. Through the use of Knowledge Graphs [10], we can shorten this time and represent in a visual way the different APTs, offering a high degree of data exploration and analysis. This is shown in Fig. 2, a high level view of techniques used and their mitigation procedures.

The Knowledge Graph representation gives us a good high level overview, but to better understand how APTs work, we also need a way to follow the life cycle of a specific attack, as shown in Fig. 3, visualizing the initial stages and

Fig. 2. Knowledge Graph representation of APT29 and SolarWinds Compromise

how they interconnect. For this example, we chose to represent the SolarWinds APT [32].

Each phase of the attack, from Reconnaissance to Resource Development, relies on previously gathered information and decisions. Social engineering is crucial in the initial phases, as humans are the weakest link in any complex system. While regulations secure hardware and software, the Human Factor remains unpredictable. The vast amount of daily information produced in hybrid networks can put a lot of strain Security Operations Center (SOC) members. Sophisticated attacks often mimic benign activity, generating many false positives and true detections. This constant vigilance can lead to "Vigilance Decrement" reducing Situation Awareness (SA) and weakening detection [8].

To help mitigate this strain, a better understanding of APTs is needed, leading to quicker identification and detection of malicious activity. Modeling an APT as a complex system, there are four distinct levels we need to focus our attention on- the micro, meso, macro and meta levels. The four levels are part of the

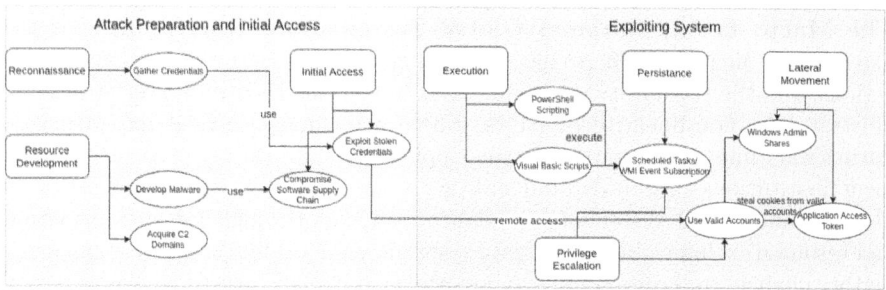

Fig. 3. Graph representation of the initial stages of the SolarWinds APT attack, based on data from MITRE ATT&CK

"system-based" approach for enhanced monitoring and management of the interactions and emergent behavior [25,26]. Each of these levels not only describes the scope of observation, but also has distinct characteristics and interactions within, and with other levels.

The Micro Level, Individual Actors and Attack Vectors. At the micro level, APTs focus on individual actions, starting with reconnaissance and using gathered information to create entry vectors. Social engineering is crucial in the initial stages, as demonstrated by SolarWinds [32], which combined social engineering and software supply chain attacks for initial access. Collecting user credentials through spear phishing, password spraying, and API abuse sets the attack in motion, leading to significant consequences due to system interdependence. This illustrates the non-linearity of complex systems- attackers adapt based on feedback from phishing victims or system defenses, leading to emergent behavior. Feedback loops are evident as attackers learn from public information and modify strategies to bypass security measures.

The Meso Level, Organizational Systems and Infrastructure. The meso level focuses on organizational systems, IT infrastructure, human elements, and internal security. Current infrastructures are tightly coupled and interconnected to facilitate data sharing and management, which can be beneficial but also exploitable by attackers. The SolarWinds attack exemplifies this, where attackers inserted a backdoor via a management product's software supply chain, making any network machines using the compromised software easy targets.

Large networks have numerous interconnected machines and applications, ranging from generic to highly specialized. Defending this vast array of potential targets is challenging, as minor vulnerabilities can initiate a cascade of system-wide issues. Incident response must be well planned and documented, as new attack vectors may emerge during the response. Defensive measures prompt attackers to evolve new methods to stay hidden and continue compromising the system.

The Macro Level, National/Global Systems and Ecosystems. At the macro level, the focus shifts to national and global networks, industry-wide interactions, and the regulatory environment. The Ukraine Electric Power attacks [3] illustrate the non-linearity of APTs, where attacking electrical infrastructure during war-time causes national-scale ripple effects, impacting civilians, government institutions, hospitals, and military operations. The interdependency of national and global systems can enhance resilience through faster information and resource exchange but also create systemic vulnerabilities. International regulatory changes and responses to cyber attacks influence future attack strategies, exemplifying the complex feedback loops in the global system.

The Meta Level: Sociopolitical, Economic and Technological Context. Advanced cyber attacks significantly impact societal, political, and economic landscapes. Economic growth can make a country a target for financial gain, while political interests can drive disinformation campaigns using APTs to steal information or damage opposition. Military institutions are prime targets for financial or strategic gains. The evolving sociopolitical, economic, and technological landscape leads to new forms of cyber warfare, shifting global power dynamics and initiating retaliatory measures and technological arms races.

APT System Levels Interaction. Each of the levels exhibits Feedback Loops, representing behavioral change within each specific scale. Furthermore, significant interactions between the different levels serve as feedback in between layers. This is represented in Fig. 4, showing the interaction between the different layers.

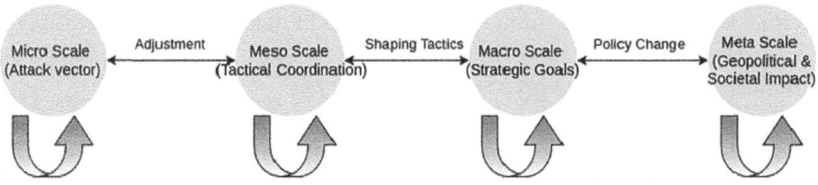

Fig. 4. Visual representation of the interactions between the different levels and the Feedback Loops inherent to the various levels

Micro-level breaches (e.g. phishing) impact the meso-level organizational structure. In response, the attackers will adapt their approach at the micro-level based on the aforementioned changes. Any vulnerabilities within one organization can propagate to industry-wide impacts and new defensive measures will lead to the implementation of new TTPs by adversaries. Further, national cyber strategies influence global cyber conflicts, shifting the power balance one way or another, which leads to the creation of new international agreements, or the break up of old ones, shaping the development of cyber capabilities for specific industries and environments.

4   Visualizing APTs as Complex Systems

The primary challenge in dealing with APTs is their detection, as they aim to remain hidden for extended periods for espionage, exfiltration, and sabotage. Analysts often use various tools to review the vast amount of network data for anomalies, but data heterogeneity complicates this task. Effective data visualization and the application of Visual Analytics can enhance Situation Awareness (SA) by representing different types of information uniformly, aiding in the identification and understanding of malicious activity [27]. Visual Analytics offers several advantages for APT awareness, including enhanced detection, discovery of hidden patterns, and transformation of raw data into intuitive visual representations, facilitating faster and more efficient decision-making [18]. Historical data and predictive models also support proactive defense strategies, while interactive visualizations improve communication and collaboration among stakeholders.

It is crucial to consider the intended audience for these visualizations, determining the appropriate level of detail and the message to be conveyed. The four levels described in Sect. 3.2 should be translated into visual forms that match the audience's experience and SA level.

4.1   Hierarchy of the APT Visualization

Selecting the appropriate visualization for cyber information depends on the users' knowledge, experience, objectives, tasks, and work environment. Users at different levels (micro, macro and above) require different views, and no single interface can address all needs. This is especially true in the military domain, where rapid and precise information comprehension is crucial for the advancement of mission objectives. Incorporating new forms of cyber symbology, as discussed in [29], can bridge data representation across levels and facilitate information exchange.

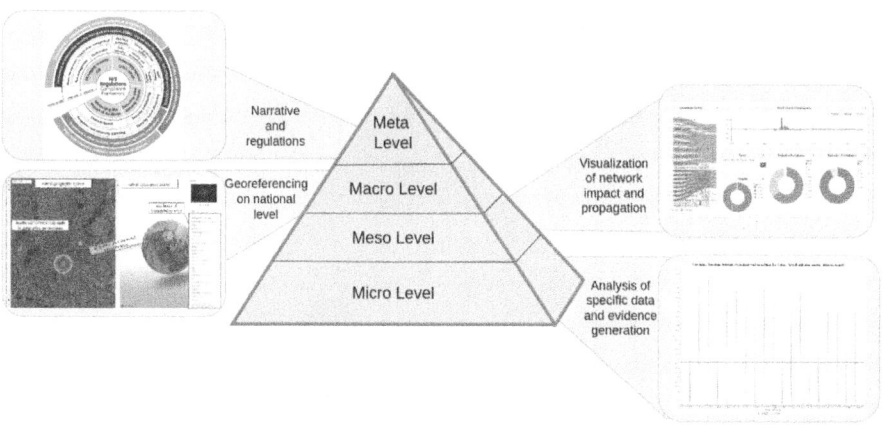

Fig. 5. Representing APT information at different levels of visualization [11,17]

The four levels of Complex Systems described in Sect. 3.2 can be visualized as a pyramid, with the micro level at the base and the meta level at the top. Figure 5 illustrates this, highlighting that most work in identifying and understanding APTs occurs at the micro level. At the micro level, analysts sift through data to detect abnormalities and indicators of suspicious activity, using proxy logs, network packets, endpoint logs, and other data types. Visualizations must offer functionalities to compare, filter, correlate, and dive deeper into the data [12]. As we move up the pyramid, data abstraction must match the intended audience's level of Situation Awareness (SA). The meso level will correlate data from individual end-points and create a high level overview of the network and the impact on the infrastructure. At the macro level, the gathered information needs to be abstracted so it can be applied to various infrastructures on national level. Finally, at the meta level, the impact on the sociopolitical and economical level needs to be evaluated. For each of the levels, the information needs to be adapted to suit the user's needs and goals. Even though the information is abstracted, moving through the levels provides greater awareness of the system structure and the connections between levels.

4.2   Practical Examples of APT Hierarchy Visualization

To better understand how Visual Analytics can be applied for APT detection, a collection of examples will be presented for each hierarchical level. The focus at each scale is very different and highly dependant on the user's area of expertise and the SA level.

Micro Level. The micro level focuses on specific points in the network, be that a specific connection, machine or application. The goal is to determine the cause

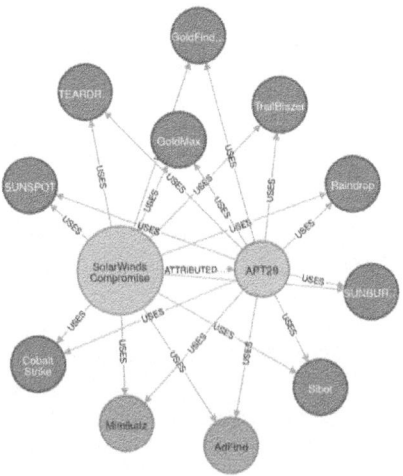

Fig. 6. Knowledge Graph representation of the SolarWinds malwares and tools used

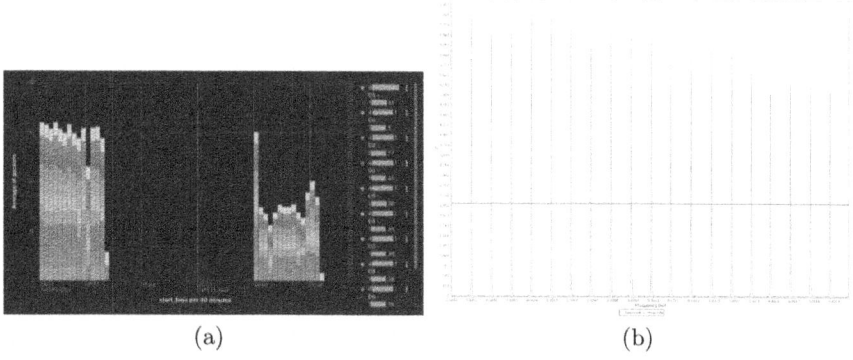

(a)   (b)

Fig. 7. (a) Bar graph visualization of netflow connections (b) Frequency spectrum visualization

of the abnormal behavior, following the chain of effect back from the malicious instance, discovered in the network. To do that, often analysts will focus on program execution, netflow and proxy logs.

A Knowledge Graph, as shown in Fig. 6, visually represents the APT, malware, and associated tools, aiding analysis of process execution on host machines. With AI detection tools, Knowledge Graphs are useful for both data exploration and model training.

When analyzing the flow of information in a network, the analyst must focus on specific connections established by internal hosts or internal machines and external servers. This is not always evident as in a day, thousands of connections are established. It is not easy to single out the suspicious ones for analysis, so to identify malicious connections, analysts often look for patterns that are abnormal in nature. These patterns are defined by characteristics such as periodicity, ports used, quantity of data exchanged, geo-location, etc. In Fig. 7, two examples of pattern visualizations are shown. In Fig. 7 (a) is a representation of the packet traffic between internal machines and a suspicious external server. The bar chart displays multiple characteristics of the connections such as the protocols used, duration of the connection and bytes exchanged. The information is shown for the duration of two days- this can be used to see if there is repetition and if there are common characteristics between the different connections. As shown in the figure, there seems to be a high degree of similarity between the various connections in regards to the number of packets exchanged and the frequency of connections. Regarding the frequency, Fig. 7 (b) showcases a more specialized visualization, focused on representing the frequency of a specific connection between a client and an external server. The frequency spectrum is a transformation of time-based data into the frequency domain aiming to detect certain periodicity spikes. APTs often use predetermined periodic time intervals of connection between an infected host and the C2 server to fetch new commands

(a)   (b)

Fig. 8. (a) Scanning/probing activities on multiple clients in the network [30] (b) System level overview of machines in the network [30]

or exfiltrate information. By detecting these periodic connections, we can better pin-point clients that need to be further investigated.

Meso Level. The meso level aims to describe the emergent behavior and feedback loops present on the organizational and infrastructure layer. Instead of focusing on a specific slice of data or one host in the network, the view is zoomed out to observe the network as a whole and the emergent behavior therein. Figure 8 shows how we can represent the network in two ways- Fig. 8 (a) a dashboard representation visualizes the scanning and probing activities that have been observed in the network. Such visualizations are useful to better discern anomalous behavior by comparing activities between clients and observing the evolution in time. To better asses how different machines in the network act, a visualization such as in Fig. 8 (b) can be useful- here a representation of the system helps to better visualize how the machines interact and their function

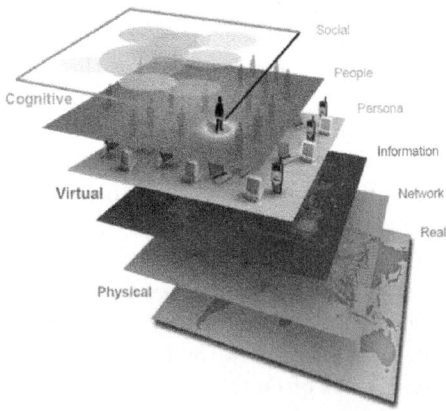

Fig. 9. Layered view of cyberspace. [20]

in the system. Figure 8 (a) is a user-centric based visualization where the user's experience and knowledge is leveraged to better understand the situation in the network. In Fig. 8 (b) a system-based approach helps to better understand how the system functions as a whole and the impact the emergent behavior may have on it.

Macro Level. At the macro level, there is value in leveraging concepts from the Activity Based Intelligence methodology [2]. More specifically, we want to leverage the concept of georeferencing to discover, i.e. to focus on spatially and temporally correlating data to discover key events, trends and patterns.

It is helpful to consider the multiple layers of the cyberspace shown in Fig. 9. Jiang et al. [11] proposed to visualize the multiple layers of cyber information, including meta level command and control relationship through a geo-cyber metaphor that can be represented with knowledge graphs and linked to the geographic environment (see Fig. 10 (a)).

Another example of geospatial visualization related to the cyber space is BubbleNet [14], as shown in Fig. 10 (b). It was designed as a cyber security dashboard to enable patterns identification and summarizations for users beyond network analysts, such as network managers.

Meta Level. As the meta level involves a wide range of information covering the sociopolitical, economic and technological contexts, multiple visualizations are required. At this level, we may be interested in visualizing the legal context surrounding the cyber environment. In some cases, meta level information regarding politics, legal aspects, cultural environment, and human involvement could be represented as knowledge graphs linked to geographical spaces (often at country-level precision) and also visualized using the geo-cyber metaphor [11].

Regarding the technological perspective, infographics representing the regulatory space and the cybersecurity technological landscape can give a quick

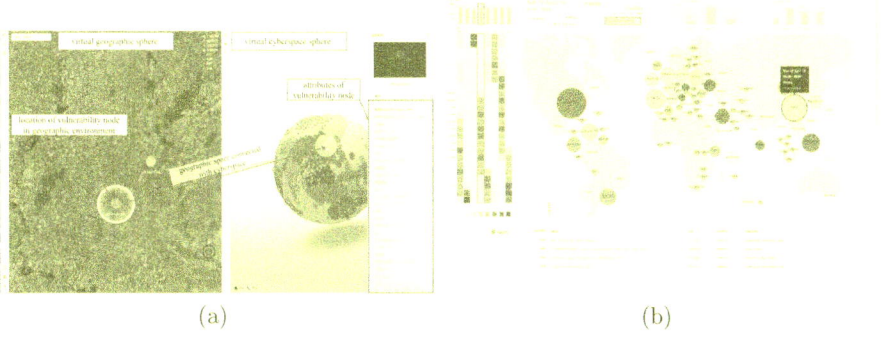

(a)   (b)

Fig. 10. (a) Visualizing the geo-cyber space with a geo-cyber metaphor represented with multi-layer knowledge graphs. [11] (b) BubbleNet dashboard example. [14].

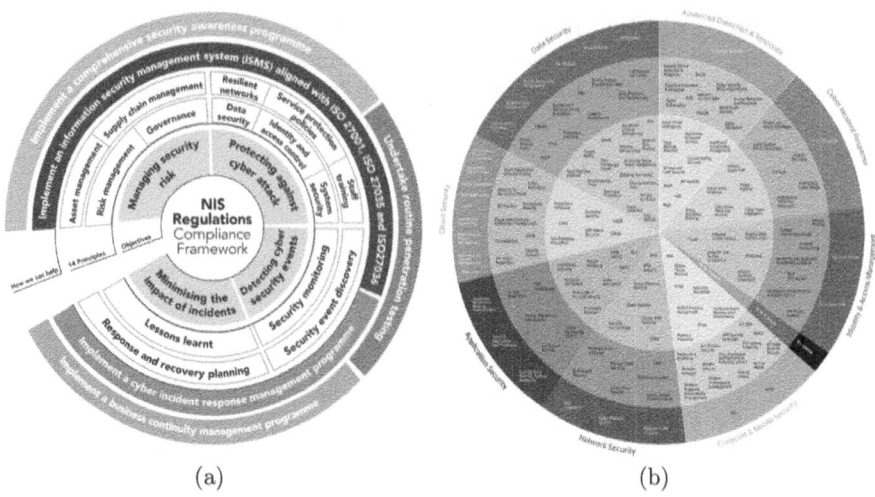

(a)   (b)

Fig. 11. (a) NIS Regulations: Cyber Assessment Framework. [17] (b) Cybersecurity tech radar. [6].

visual summary of this information. The NIS regulatory framework is depicted in Fig. 11 (a) from [17] through the use of concentric circle arcs that convey the hierarchical categorisation of the regulation framework. An example of technological cybersecurity context visualization is provided in Fig. 11 (b) from [6], where it is represented as a pie chart combining circle arcs divided by functions and a radial axis for expected temporal information.

The sociopolitical landscape involves narratives that surround cyber events, which are often discussed online within social media and discussion forums. For example, the HAITTON application (see Fig. 12) helps track and visualize online narratives [9].

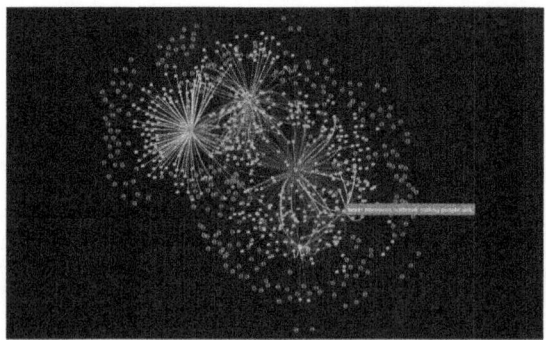

Fig. 12. HAITTON Knowledge graph view, linking posts and online actors to key narratives of interest. Note: These results are based on [9].

5 Conclusion

The success of an APT arises from the interaction of actions across micro, meso, macro, and meta scales, exploiting the interconnectedness of modern systems to create cascading effects and emergent outcomes. This emergent behavior is far more impactful than the sum of individual actions.

A complex systems perspective on APTs enhances understanding of their behaviors, enabling better detection, prevention, and resilience. This approach shifts focus from reactive measures to proactive, systemic solutions, addressing the interdependent and adaptive nature of cyber threats. Supporting proactive behavior requires enhanced SA of the APT's entry into and activity within the larger system. Examining feedback loops from both the attacker's and defender's viewpoints provides a dynamic insight of how APTs unfold, evolve and adapt. These perspectives reveal how actions and reactions at different scales direct escalation or containment, often in an unpredictable manner. Feedback loops within and between scales are critical to understanding the dynamic nature of these attacks. These loops enable adaptation, amplify effects, and create emergent behaviours. Through the understanding of APTs as complex, multi-scale phenomena, organizations can design defences that are adaptive and resilient to the long-term, sophisticated nature of these threats. Visualizations aimed at categorizing the different levels of the network assist in identifying cues, interpreting the extent of their impact across the entire system and allow for appropriate solutions. Additionally, they support a larger DSA view, where deeper understanding can be gained of the meso and meta scale components affected by a particular APT. This larger scale awareness of the impact of new APTs on a system can benefit detection from human operators and allow them to better train AI detection.

6 Future Work

In this paper, we have presented our work in the field of Complex Systems, its importance for the appropriate understanding and management of large-scale hybrid infrastructures. Further, through the application of complex system principles to the field of Advanced Persistent Threats, new ways are proposed for the application of Visual Analytics for their detection, developing new visualization techniques to enhance the Cyber Situation Awareness and bridge the gap between the levels of visualization hierarchy. Finally, specific evaluation techniques are needed for the assessment of the usefulness and usability of the visual tools, alongside methods for the correct evaluation of SA and its validity.

Acknowledgments. This is the work of the NATO Visual Analytics for Complex Systems Research Task Group.

References

1. Alshamrani, A., Myneni, S., Chowdhary, A., Huang, D.: A survey on advanced persistent threats: techniques, solutions, challenges, and research opportunities. IEEE Commun. Surv. Tutor. **21**(2), 1851–1877 (2019)
2. Atwood, C.P.: Activity-based intelligence: revolutionizing military intelligence analysis. J. Force Quart. **77**(2nd Quarter) (2015)
3. Case, D.U.: Analysis of the cyber attack on the Ukrainian power grid. Electr. Inf. Sharing Anal. center (E-ISAC) **388**(1-29), 3 (2016)
4. Chen, P., Desmet, L., Huygens, C.: A study on advanced persistent threats. In: Communications and Multimedia Security: 15th IFIP TC 6/TC 11 International Conference, CMS 2014, Aveiro, Portugal, September 25-26, 2014. Proceedings 15, pp. 63–72. Springer (2014)
5. Cooke, N.J., Gorman, J.C., Winner, J.L., Durso, F.: Team cognition. In: Handbook of Applied Cognition, vol. 2, pp. 239–268 (2007)
6. Eviden (2025). https://eviden.com/publications/tech-radar/cybersecurity/
7. Endsley, M.R., Connors, E.S.: Situation awareness: state of the art. In: 2008 IEEE Power and Energy Society General Meeting-Conversion and Delivery of Electrical Energy in the 21st Century, pp. 1–4. IEEE (2008)
8. Grier, R.A., et al.: The vigilance decrement reflects limitations in effortful attention, not mindlessness. Hum. Factors **45**(3), 349–359 (2003)
9. Riskaware (2025). https://www.riskaware.co.uk/insight/harnessing-the-power-of-ai-for-tracking-harmful-online-narratives/
10. Hogan, A., et al.: Knowledge graphs. ACM Comput. Surv. (CSUR) **54**(4), 1–37 (2021)
11. Jiang, B., You, X., Li, K., Li, T., Wang, X., Si, D.: Virtual geo-cyber environments: metaphorical visualization of virtual cyberspace with geographical knowledge. Int. J. Digit. Earth **17**(1), 2324959 (2024)
12. Liggett, K., Kullman, K.: Chapter 2 – human factors considerations for visual analytics, exploratory visual analytics. Technical report (2023). https://doi.org/10.14339/STO-TR-IST-141. NATO
13. Marble, J.L., Lawless, W.F., Mittu, R., Coyne, J., Abramson, M., Sibley, C.: The human factor in cybersecurity: robust & intelligent defense. In: Cyber Warfare: Building the Scientific Foundation, pp. 173–206 (2015)
14. McKenna, S., Staheli, D., Fulcher, C., Meyer, M.: Bubblenet: a cyber security dashboard for visualizing patterns. In: Computer Graphics Forum, vol. 35, pp. 281–290. Wiley Online Library (2016)
15. Mitre att&ck (2024). https://attack.mitre.org/
16. Munir, A., Aved, A., Blasch, E.: Situational awareness: techniques, challenges, and prospects. AI **3**(1), 55–77 (2022)
17. Nis (2025). https://www.ncsc.gov.uk/collection/cyber-assessment-framework/caf-supplementary-information
18. Nikolov, G., Debatty, T., Mees, W.: Detection through visualization for the multi-agent system for apt detection. In: Digital Transformation, Cybersecurity, and Resilience DIGILIENCE 2022 (2022). https://cylab.be/publications/43/2022-detection-through-visualization-for-the-multi-agent-system-for-apt-detection
19. Nikolov, G., Perez, A., Mees, W.: Evaluation of cyber situation awareness-theory, techniques and applications. In: Proceedings of the 19th International Conference on Availability, Reliability and Security, pp. 1–10 (2024)

20. Parish, M., Madahar, B.: Understanding cyberspace through cyber situational awareness. The Defence Science and Technology Laboratory: Wiltshire, UK (2016)
21. Stanton, N.A., Salmon, P.M., Walker, G.H., Salas, E., Hancock, P.A.: State-of-science: situation awareness in individuals, teams and systems. Ergonomics **60**(4), 449–466 (2017)
22. Strom, B.E., Applebaum, A., Miller, D.P., Nickels, K.C., Pennington, A.G., Thomas, C.B.: Mitre att&ck: Design and philosophy. In: Technical report. The MITRE Corporation (2018)
23. Tankard, C.: Advanced persistent threats and how to monitor and deter them. Netw. Secur. **2011**(8), 16–19 (2011)
24. Tariq, S., Baruwal Chhetri, M., Nepal, S., Paris, C.: Alert fatigue in security operations centres: research challenges and opportunities. ACM Comput. Surv. **57**(9), 1–38 (2025)
25. Traeber-Burdin, S., Varga, M.: How does systems thinking support the understanding of complex situations? In: 2022 IEEE International Symposium on Systems Engineering (ISSE), pp. 1–7. IEEE (2022)
26. Träber-Burdin, S., Varga, M.: Dealing with complex situations: towards a framework of understanding problems. In: 2022 IEEE International Conference on Systems, Man, and Cybernetics (SMC), pp. 1431–1436. IEEE (2022)
27. Varga, M., Winkelholz, C., Träber-Burdin, S., Bivall, P., Kullman, K.: Chapter 7 cyber situation awareness, exploratory visual analytics. Technical report. 10.14339/STO-TR-IST-141, NATO (2023)
28. Varga, M., Winkelholz, C., Traber-Burdin, S.: Cyber situation awareness. NATO/OTAN (STO-MP-IST-148) (2016)
29. Varga, M., Winkelholz, C., Träber-Burdin, S.: An exploration of cyber symbology. In: 2019 IEEE Symposium on Visualization for Cyber Security (VizSec), pp. 1–5. IEEE (2019)
30. Varga, M., Winkelholz, C., Traeber-Burdin, S.: Exploration of user centered and system based approaches to cyber situation awareness. Environment **1**, 2 (2018)
31. Wagner, C., Dulaunoy, A., Wagener, G., Iklody, A.: MISP: the design and implementation of a collaborative threat intelligence sharing platform. In: Proceedings of the 2016 ACM on Workshop on Information Sharing and Collaborative Security, pp. 49–56 (2016)
32. Wolff, E.D., GroWlEy, K.M., Lerner, M.O., Welling, M.B., Gruden, M.G., Canter, J.: Navigating the solarwinds supply chain attack. Procurement Law. **56**, 3 (2021)
33. Yadav, T., Rao, A.M.: Technical aspects of cyber kill chain. In: Security in Computing and Communications: Third International Symposium, SSCC 2015, Kochi, India, August 10–13, 2015. Proceedings 3, pp. 438–452. Springer (2015)

Quantum Security Mechanisms
for Defense Applications

Joan Bas[1]([✉]), Marta I. García-Cid[2], Francisco Sánchez[2], Konrad Wrona[3,4] [iD],
Joanna Sliwa[3,4], Federico Grasselli[5], Kadir Durak[6], Michal Krelina[7],
Armando Pinto[8], Nuno Silva[8], and Marco Piani[9]

[1] Centre Tecnologic de Telecomunicacions de Catalunya, Barcelona, Spain
joan.bas@cttc.es
[2] Indra Sistemas S.A, Madrid, Spain
{migarcia,fsjimenez}@indra.es
[3] NATO Communications and Information Agency, The Hague, The Netherlands
{joanna.sliwa,konrad.wrona}@ncia.nato.int
[4] Military University of Technology, Warsaw, Poland
[5] Leonardo Innovation Labs, Rome, Italy
federico.grasselli@leonardo.com
[6] Ozyegin University, Istanbul, Turkey
kadir.durak@ozyegin.edu.tr
[7] Czech Technical University in Prague, Prague, Czechia
michal.krelina@cvut.cz
[8] University of Aveiro, Aveiro, Portugal
{anp,nasilva}@ua.pt
[9] EvolutionQ Inc, Waterloo, Canada
marco.piani@evolutionq.com

Abstract. Many international organizations, such as the EU and
NATO, and national governments have launched strategic initiatives
supporting the migration to quantum-safe cryptography. Examples of
such initiatives are Spanish CCN (Cybersecurity Defence of Spanish Cyberspace) endorsing post-quantum cryptographic algorithms like
FrodoKEM and CRYSTALS-Kyber, and the European Union promoting
secure quantum infrastructure through programs like Quantum Flagship,
OpenQKD, and EuroQCI. Moreover, the efforts supported by the European Defence Fund reinforce the strategic importance of early quantum-
resilient adoption across civil and defense sectors, through projects such
as the Disruptive SDN secure communications for European Defence
(DISCRETION) or the Quantum Agile and Resilient Military Communications (Q-ARM). This paper focuses particularly on defense-related
quantum communication technologies, assessing not only quantum key
distribution but also advanced primitives like quantum oblivious transfer,
quantum digital signatures, and quantum secure direct communication,
among others. It highlights their respective vulnerabilities, criticality,
and potential countermeasures. Hybrid solutions that combine classical
and quantum-resistant encryption methods and cryptoagility are recommended to enhance resilience.

B. Coppens et al. (Eds.): ARES 2025 Workshops, LNCS 15995, pp. 108–121, 2025.
https://doi.org/10.1007/978-3-032-00633-2_7

Keywords: Post-quantum cryptography · quantum key distribution · quantum oblivious transfer · quantum digital signatures · quantum secure direct communication

1 Introduction

Quantum computing marks a transformative technological advancement, offering groundbreaking capabilities in many scientific areas such as molecular simulation and biology. However, it poses a serious threat to current cryptographic systems. A cryptographically relevant quantum computer, capable of running Shor's and Grover's algorithms, could break widely used encryption schemes like RSA (Rivest–Shamir–Adleman), elliptic curve cryptography, and Diffie-Hellman, potentially compromising global digital security. Though such machines are not yet realized, the risk is immediate due to the "Store Now, Decrypt Later" tactic, where adversaries collect encrypted data now to decrypt it later with future quantum capabilities. Mosca's theorem [33] underscores the urgency of transitioning to quantum-safe cryptography before this threat materializes. To address this, both post-quantum cryptography (PQC) and quantum cryptography are under active development. PQC provides cryptographic solutions based on mathematical problems different from those used in conventional cryptography, these solutions being resistant to Shor's algorithm. Quantum cryptography, on the other hand, provides mechanisms independent of mathematical formulations whose security depends on the basic principles of quantum mechanics.

Although many nations and international organizations, such as the National Security Agency in the USA and NATO, have advocated for the transition to post-quantum cryptography, it is crucial to acknowledge the limitations of the current PQC solutions. The new PQC algorithms, similarly to classical public-key cryptography algorithms, are not information-theoretically secure and rely on computational complexity assumptions for their security. Due to their recent development, the PQC algorithms are less well tested. The discovery of effective attacks against schemes such as Rainbow, GeMSS, and SIKE highlights the risks of relying on new methods that did not undergo sufficient scrutiny. These concerns are further heightened by the heavy reliance on a small set of hard computational problems, such as the Learning With Errors (LWE) problem and its variants (e.g., RLWE, PLWE), which form the foundation of major standards like ML-DSA (FIPS 204), SLH-DSA (FIPS 205) and ML-KEM (FIPS 203). A successful attack on these underlying computational complexity assumptions could undermine most of the current post-quantum migration efforts. For this reason, this paper also reviews additional quantum-based security primitives that could be of interest for securing military communications. However, also quantum-based security technologies, such as quantum key distribution (QKD), are not exempt from vulnerabilities in their implementation.

In this context, NATO, through its Science and Technology Organization (STO), is actively advancing research to integrate quantum communications into the military sphere. It has established three focused working groups: IST-217, dedicated to the development of a military-grade quantum Internet; IST-218, which examines multi-domain QKD for defense applications; and IST-219, which addresses the vulnerabilities inherent to quantum technologies. Specifically, this paper provides the initial outcomes of IST-219 regarding quantum primitives, such as QKD, Quantum Oblivious Transfer (QOT), Quantum Digital Signatures (QDS), Quantum Secret Sharing (QSS), Quantum Zero-Knowledge Proofs (QZKP), Multimodal Approaches (MA), and Quantum Secure Direct Communication (QSDC), highlighting their vulnerabilities and criticality.

The remainder of the paper is structured as follows. Section 2 provides an overview of the main QKD systems, covering their primary quantum state generation methods, corresponding protocols, and associated vulnerabilities - highlighting the most critical risks. Section 3 examines key quantum cryptographic primitives beyond QKD, focusing on the distinctions between purely quantum protocols and quantum-assisted (composite or hybrid) systems, along with their respective vulnerabilities and criticality. Particular attention is given to QKD implementations involving hardware components and the challenges they pose for formal security proofs. Finally, Sect. 4 presents the paper's main conclusions.

2   Quantum Key Distribution Overview

The aim of QKD is the generation of a completely random and secret cryptographic key shared between two legitimate parties. This key is intended for use in symmetric encryption algorithms. QKD protocols are said to be Information-Theoretic Secure (ITS) against both classical and quantum computational attacks due to their foundation on the laws of quantum mechanics [41]. In this section, we review the main encoding and protocols of QKD as well as their main vulnerabilities.

2.1   Protocols

Understanding QKD protocols begins with recognizing the different ways they can be categorized: (i) by physical implementation, (ii) by security assumptions, and (iii) by communication directionality. Physical implementation-based QKD protocols can be categorized as follows: (i) Discrete-Variable (DV) protocols use single photons with well-defined quantum states (e.g., polarization) (e.g. BB84 [6], B92 [5]); (ii) Continuous-Variable (CV) protocols utilize continuous attributes of light, such as phase and amplitude, allowing compatibility with standard telecom components (e.g. GG02 [21], No-switching protocol [26]); (iii) Entanglement-Based protocols rely on entangled photon pairs and Bell tests (e.g. E91 [11], BBM92 [7]); and (iv) Hybrid protocols combine elements of DV, CV, or entanglement with other techniques (e.g. based on Twin-Field QKD [53]).

Quantum protocols can also be categorized based on their security assumptions, often described using two parties: Alice (the sender) and Bob (the receiver). In the Prepare-and-Measure model, Alice prepares quantum states in specific bases and sends them to Bob, who measures the incoming states using appropriate detectors (e.g. BB84, B92). In the Entanglement-Based model, a central source distributes entangled particles to both Alice and Bob, who then perform independent measurements on their respective particles to obtain correlated outcomes (e.g. E91). The Measurement-Device-Independent model addresses vulnerabilities in measurement devices by having both Alice and Bob send their quantum states to a potentially untrusted third party, who performs a joint measurement. The protocol remains secure even if this third party or their equipment is compromised (e.g. MDI [53]). Regarding communication direction-ality, quantum protocols are categorized as follows: (i) Unidirectional, supporting only one-way quantum communication; and (ii) Bidirectional (Two-Way), allow-ing back-and-forth communication for tasks such as encoding or verification (e.g. Ping-Pong or LM05 Protocol [35]).

2.2   Vulnerabilites

While QKD offers theoretically unbreakable security grounded in the laws of quantum mechanics, practical implementations expose the system to various vulnerabilities stemming from adversarial strategies and device imperfections. A typical QKD protocol consists of a sequence of operations between two honest parties, Alice and Bob. It assumes prior authentication between those parties, for which different alternatives have been proposed, such as the use of Wegman-Carter-based authentication [1]. The aim of the communication is to achieve: i) *Correctness* of the keys generated by Alice and Bob (the keys must be iden-tical), and ii) *Secrecy* of the keys since only Alice and Bob should have any knowledge of the generated key. However, QKD has to face vulnerabilities in its implementation as reported in [8].

In classical systems, eavesdropping is undetectable by design. However, in quantum communication, any interaction with the quantum channel by an eaves-dropper (Eve) introduces detectable disturbances. These disturbances typically appear as increased error rates at the receiver, signaling potential eavesdropping attempts. Nonetheless, advanced attacks may be harder to detect, especially if Eve has access to quantum memory and sophisticated measurement strategies.

Attacks on QKD systems are typically categorized into three classes. In *indi-vidual attacks*, Eve interacts with each quantum signal separately, attaching an ancilla and measuring each one independently. Examples include intercept-resend and beam-splitting attacks. *Collective attacks* follow a similar interaction model, but Eve postpones her measurements to perform a joint measurement over all collected ancillae, allowing for greater information extraction.

The most general and powerful class is *coherent attacks*. In this case, Eve entangles all transmitted signals with a global ancilla and performs a global joint measurement. These attacks exploit the full power of quantum mechanics and are limited only by fundamental physical principles. Although theoretically detectable, they present a significant threat if the protocol or devices are not properly designed, since their detectability could be reduced.

Beyond theoretical attacks, real-world vulnerabilities arise from device imper-fections and side channels. Practical issues include detector blinding attacks, multi-photon emissions from imperfect sources (leading to photon number splitting), and miscalibrations [8]. These flaws can be exploited unless specifically addressed in the protocol.

To mitigate such vulnerabilities, newer protocols like Measurement-Device-Independent QKD (MDI-QKD) have been proposed. MDI-QKD neutralizes detection side attacks typically focused on the detectors by having both Alice and Bob send quantum states to a third-party measurement device, whose trustworthiness is not required. This significantly enhances practical security without sacrificing the benefits of QKD.

3   Quantum Cryptographic Primitives Beyond QKD

While QKD remains a cornerstone for securely sharing symmetric keys through quantum mechanics, e.g., [6,11,53], there are other quantum cryptographic primitives beyond QKD that hold significant promise for defense applications. Moreover, quantum cryptography still faces numerous challenges, including resistance to physical attacks, enabling autonomous authentication, managing hybrid keys, and certifying devices. As a result, exploring and developing quantum cryptographic primitives beyond QKD is critical to addressing these emerging needs.

3.1   Quantum Oblivious Transfer (QOT)

Oblivious Transfer (OT) primitive, especially the 1-out-of-2 variant [52], plays a foundational role in secure multiparty computation, enabling a sender to share one of two messages without knowing which was received [37]. Classical OT relies on public-key cryptography, which becomes insecure in the quantum era due to its dependence on problems like factorization and discrete logarithms.

QOT addresses these limitations. In the standard protocol, Alice encodes bits in photon polarization using random bases; Bob, unaware of the basis, can only partially retrieve information unless he waits to measure after Alice reveals the bases—an action that breaks the protocol if he has a quantum memory. This vulnerability is mitigated under the noisy-storage model, which assumes adversaries cannot store quantum data reliably for long.

Recent advances introduced oblivious keys, enabling a two-phase QOT, consisting of oblivious key distribution phase and oblivious transfer phase [38]. This framework uses hash-based commitments, secure even against quantum adversaries, based on the difficulty of finding collisions across thousands of hash functions in milliseconds. Furthermore, new protocols have been proposed that achieve simulation security in the plain model against malicious quantum polynomial-time adversaries, using one-way functions and quantum-enhanced commitment schemes.

3.2   Quantum Digital Signature (QDS)

Digital signatures ensure message integrity, authenticity, and non-repudiation. Widely used in modern communication, they are typically based on asymmetric cryptographic algorithms like RSA, Diffie-Hellman, or elliptic curves. However, these schemes are vulnerable to quantum attacks using Shor's algorithm. To counter this, PQC algorithms have emerged, notably through the NIST competition [42], which has already resulted in two signature standards: FIPS 204 [43] and FIPS 205 [44]. Simultaneously, quantum cryptography is exploring signature protocols whose security stems from quantum mechanics, akin to QKD.

Several QDS protocols have been proposed over the years. In 2001, the first QDS scheme [19], based on Lamport's one-way function, was proven to be information-theoretically secure, but it requires long-term quantum memories, making it impractical for current use. In 2014, a QDS protocol [10] was introduced that eliminated the need for quantum memories but relied on secure quantum channels and was vulnerable to coherent forging attacks. A 2016 scheme [3] improved upon this by utilizing secure classical channels through a symmetrization step, removing the need for secure quantum channels, though it limited message length and scalability. In 2021, an enhancement was made by eliminating the symmetrization step, improving efficiency, but the protocol remained restricted to signing short messages [32].

Additionally, Quantum-Assisted Digital Signatures (Q-DS) combine QKD-generated keys with classical cryptographic primitives. In 2023, a Q-DS protocol [17] was proposed that uses QKD-generated symmetric keys along with NIST-recommended hash functions and XOFs, enabling arbitrary-length messages and offering efficiency comparable to post-quantum cryptography (PQC). However, this scheme is limited to a single signer and two verifiers. In 2024, a refinement of this protocol [46] replaced hash functions with WC-MACs, while maintaining the same verifier limitations.

3.3   Quantum Secret Sharing (QSS)

Secret sharing is a cryptographic technique that splits a secret into multiple shares, requiring a threshold number t of them (in a (t, n)-scheme) to reconstruct the secret. Classical schemes like Shamir's and Blakley's [40] guarantee information-theoretic security using polynomial interpolation, assuming private channels—often established via QKD—exist between dealer and shareholders.

QSS aims to generate and share secrets using quantum properties such as multipartite entanglement. Most QSS schemes are (n, n)-threshold schemes where all participants must cooperate. The pioneering protocol by Hillery et al. [23] used GHZ states but was inefficient and insecure against internal adversaries [36].

Subsequent advances introduced measurement-device-independent setups [15] and graph states [4], improving protocols' robustness against photon loss and adversarial attacks. These protocols enable applications such as *Quantum Conference Key Agreement* (QCKA), though QSS generally leaks more error-correction information than QCKA. For a quantum bit error rate (QBER) q, QCKA requires $h(q)$ bits of correction, while QSS requires $h(Q)$, with $Q > q$ under most conditions due to noise in GHZ-based XOR operations.

Until recently, many QSS protocols lacked full security proofs, especially against dishonest insiders. This gap was addressed by Adesso et al. [25] and Walk et al. [49], who respectively provided composable security for continuous- and discrete-variable QSS, including finite-key effects. Their results show that entanglement-based QSS can outperform classical QKD-based sharing in constrained quantum networks.

To enhance practicality, newer QSS schemes avoid multipartite entanglement. A notable example is a $(2,2)$-threshold scheme based on Bell pairs [51], proven secure against both eavesdroppers and malicious users. However, it is limited in scalability and range. Another innovation by Chen et al. [22] uses a twin-field QKD approach to enable QSS over distances beyond 200 km, though with less general insider security.

Alternative protocols eliminate entanglement entirely by employing *sequential operations* on a single quantum system [31, 47]. These trade off entanglement distribution with challenges in routing and implementing random unitaries. One such protocol, by Qi et al. [20], achieves (n, n)-QSS via coherent-state injection and homodyne detection, requiring a shared phase reference and specific channel configurations.

Finally, Liu et al. [28] propose a practical QSS scheme that removes the need for phase-locking between participants. The dealer sends multiplexed coherent signals across parallel shareholder chains, who independently encode information. After traversing all paths, the dealer demultiplexes and detects the signals to extract shared keys. The setup enables scalable networks and supports classical secret sharing on top of parallel QKD channels.

3.4   Quantum Zero-Knowledge Proof (QZKP)

Zero-Knowledge Proofs (ZKPs) are cryptographic protocols enabling a prover to convince a verifier of knowledge without revealing the actual information. Introduced by Goldwasser, Micali, and Rackoff in 1985 [18], valid ZKPs must satisfy completeness, soundness, and zero-knowledge properties. ZKPs are divided into interactive, e.g., Fiat-Shamir [14], and non-interactive types like zk-SNARKs [39] and zk-STARKs [27], the latter being more scalable and avoiding trusted setups.

ZKPs have wide applications: authentication (with or without pre-shared secrets), privacy-preserving blockchain transactions (e.g., Zcash), anonymous payments, secure signatures, access control, and secure multi-party computation. However, many classical ZKPs depend on cryptographic assumptions (e.g., RSA, ECC) that are vulnerable to quantum algorithms like Shor's.

Post-quantum alternatives, such as lattice-based schemes (e.g., NTRU), zk-STARKs, or isogeny-based cryptography, offer quantum-resistant zero-knowledge protocols. Moreover, Quantum Zero-Knowledge Proofs (QZKPs) leverage quantum mechanics to ensure security beyond computational assumptions. For example, a QZKP authentication scheme using pre-shared secrets and key-derivation functions has been proposed in [16]. The protocol includes: (1) synchronization and key derivation; (2) transmission of quantum states encoded by that key; and (3) verification through QBER estimation. If QBER is within the threshold, authentication succeeds.

These quantum and post-quantum ZKP systems represent vital developments in building secure, future-proof authentication and privacy-preserving systems.

3.5   Multimodal Approaches (MA)

Multimodal solutions combine QKD with other cryptographic methods, such as post-quantum and traditional asymmetric cryptography, to provide layered security. This hybrid approach enhances resilience by leveraging the complementary strengths of different techniques.

A notable implementation is the Multimodal Key Establishment System (KES) by evolutionQ, which derives encryption keys from multiple cryptographic primitives. This approach offers several benefits, including strong computational security, as multiple layers provide backup protection in case one method fails. It also ensures forward secrecy, meaning past communications remain secure even if keys are compromised in the future. Additionally, the system provides post-compromise security, protecting future data after a compromise occurs. Furthermore, it offers identity theft protection, defending against impersonation even if the underlying infrastructure is breached.

Multimodal KES works with existing infrastructure and supports gradual integration of QKD. Keys are derived from two input shares: one from a quantum-safe authenticated key exchange (AKE) combining classical and post-quantum AKE, and another from an out-of-band secure channel.

The system includes Key Distribution Hubs (KDHs) and Multimodal Agents (MAs) installed at endpoints (e.g., Alice, Bob). MAs register with a KDH to retrieve and store pre-key data, enabling key derivation even without an active network connection. These pre-keys allow MAs to establish long-term, quantum-resistant keys.

A Multimodal KES includes two core components: a lightweight MA, deployed at endpoints or within applications, and a Key Distribution Network with at least one KDH. Registered MAs can establish secure keys with peers, made available through standard interfaces like ETSI GS QKD 014 [12], QKD 004 [13], KMIP [34], or SKIP [24].

3.6   Quantum Secure Direct Communication (QSDC)

QSDC is an innovative communication protocol that enables direct transmission of confidential information by exploiting fundamental quantum principles. Unlike traditional cryptographic approaches or QKD, QSDC transmits information without requiring prior key distribution, streamlining communication and enhancing security. It also provides unconditional security, leveraging quantum mechanics to detect any eavesdropping attempts. Additionally, the use of quantum entanglement and superposition enhances the system's robustness against interception by utilizing strongly correlated quantum states.

Compared to QKD, which separates key distribution from message transmission, QSDC directly encodes the message into quantum states. This reduces the complexity and potential points of failure in communication. QSDC and QKD both use quantum channels (e.g., fiber optics, free-space, satellite), but QSDC is particularly suitable for real-time, secure messaging. Although QSDC is still under development, it holds high potential for future secure communication systems, offering unmatched efficiency and resistance to quantum threats.

Various QSDC protocols exist, including: i) Ping-Pong Protocol [2], ii) Decoy State Protocol [29], iii) Quantum Relay Protocol [45], iv) Four-Party Protocol [48], v) Quantum Cryptographic Authentication Protocol [50], vi) MDI-QSDC [9] and vii) Quantum Repeater-Based QSDC [30]. These protocols differ in assumptions, functioning, security parameters, and vulnerabilities. The Ping-Pong Protocol is one of the earliest QSDC schemes, based on the use of entangled qubits sent back and forth between sender and receiver. While simple and intuitive, it is vulnerable to intercept-resend and denial-of-service attacks without additional safeguards. The Decoy State Protocol enhances QSDC security by introducing randomly inserted decoy photons to detect eavesdropping attempts, improving resistance against photon-number-splitting attacks. The Quantum Relay Protocol uses intermediate trusted nodes to extend communication range and detect interference, though it depends on node trustworthiness. The Four-Party Protocol adds a control center and an authenticator to manage and verify communications, enabling more secure and authenticated message exchange in multi-user environments. The Quantum Cryptographic Authentication Protocol integrates classical authentication with quantum transmission to ensure message origin and integrity, addressing identity verification along with confidentiality. The Measurement-Device-Independent QSDC (MDI-QSDC) removes vulnerabilities from measurement devices—often the weakest link in quantum systems—by letting an untrusted third party perform measurements without compromising security. Finally, the Quantum Repeater-Based QSDC introduces quantum repeaters to overcome distance limitations, allowing entanglement distribution and secure communication across long distances while maintaining high fidelity.

3.7   Vulnerabilities

Quantum systems face a range of vulnerabilities that can compromise their security. Imperfections in quantum devices, such as photon sources and detectors, can lead to weak entanglement, photon loss, or inaccuracies in measurements, which can weaken the system's reliability. Noise and decoherence in the quantum channel can distort signals and reduce the effectiveness of security protocols. In addition, eavesdropping attacks are a significant threat, with adversaries potentially intercepting photons without disturbing the system enough to trigger detection mechanisms. Sophisticated attacks, like photon-number-splitting or intercept-and-resend strategies, may allow an attacker to bypass security without detection. Other vulnerabilities include the risk of compromised relay stations or untrusted devices within the quantum network, which could manipulate data or introduce errors, undermining the integrity of the communication. These challenges highlight the ongoing need to enhance the robustness and resilience of quantum communication systems.

To mitigate vulnerabilities in quantum communication, techniques like entanglement purification, error correction, and regular calibration of photon sources and detectors can improve entanglement quality and reduce photon loss. To address photon-number-splitting attacks, using stronger decoy states and enhancing detection systems can help. Preventing relay manipulation involves implementing trust verification protocols and regular checks for errors in entanglement swapping. Reducing channel loss through better infrastructure and error correction, along with secure encryption of relay channels, also strengthens security. Overall, improving the robustness of entanglement swapping and ensuring the reliability of quantum communication channels are essential for secure communication.

Photon loss and detector imperfections are significant challenges in quantum communication, but the disturbance caused by eavesdropping remains a key advantage, as it enables detection of interception attempts. By using high-quality photon sources and robust detection methods, these vulnerabilities can be minimized, ensuring secure communication. Photon-number-splitting attacks pose a threat in the Decoy State Protocol, but improvements in detection techniques and protocol designs can mitigate this issue. The protocol is generally secure when properly implemented. Channel loss and relay manipulation are moderate concerns, which can be addressed through effective relay station management and error correction strategies. Overall, the severity of vulnerabilities is moderate, and risks can be controlled through careful monitoring and prevention of malicious behavior.

4   Conclusions and Future Directions

Quantum technologies are expected to significantly enhance secure military communications, offering strong protection against both classical and quantum-era threats. However, the integration of these technologies, especially those involving cryptographic primitives beyond standard QKD, requires rigorous security evaluation. This includes, in particular, emerging quantum-assisted and hybrid schemes, which often present new vulnerabilities related to hardware, protocol design, and unproven security assumptions. As NATO and allied forces move toward high quantum technology readiness, it is critical to anticipate adversarial exploitation and ensure that only thoroughly vetted systems are deployed. In this context, maintaining a well-defined and regularly updated list of secure, quantum-safe cryptographic schemes is essential to guide development, standardization, and operational use. Comprehensive vulnerability assessments and countermeasure strategies must be in place before these systems are introduced into mission-critical environments. In this regard, there are multiple ongoing activities at the defense level that aim to design, identify, develop, and implement quantum-safe solutions for military use cases. These activities take place within the collaboration frameworks provided by NATO STO activities, European Defence Program, and military national programs, such as the COINCIDENTE program from the Spanish government.

Quantum security mechanisms represent a transformative opportunity for enhancing the protection of sensitive information and communication in defense environments. Protocols such as quantum key distribution, quantum digital signatures, quantum secure direct communication, and other quantum cryptographic primitives offer the potential for information-theoretic security, making them highly attractive for high-assurance military applications. These tools can augment or even replace classical cryptographic systems in scenarios where resilience against advanced adversaries, including those with quantum capabilities, is essential.

Nevertheless, practical challenges persist. Issues such as photon loss, channel noise, hardware imperfections, and the limited maturity of device-independent quantum protocols must be addressed before widespread operational deployment. Additionally, the future impact of quantum computing on post-quantum cryptography highlights the need for layered and adaptable security architectures that integrate both quantum and classical techniques.

Importantly, the increasing complexity of modern military multi-domain operations (MDO)—spanning land, air, sea, space, and cyberspace—demands multi-domain quantum security solutions. Secure and interoperable communications across these domains require cryptographic mechanisms that can function robustly in diverse and contested environments. Quantum-secured networks, supported by technologies like Multi-Domain QKD and trusted relay architectures, can be essential for achieving mission assurance and strategic advantage in this context.

To prepare for this paradigm shift, continued investment in research, standardization, and experimentation under real-world conditions is crucial. NATO's ongoing initiatives, along with national defense programs, reflect a growing recognition that quantum technologies will play a pivotal role in securing MDO in the decades to come.

References

1. Abidin, A., Larsson, J.Å.: Direct proof of security of wegman-carter authentication with partially known key. Quantum Inf. Process. **13**, 2155–2170 (2014)
2. et al., D.P.: The evolution of quantum secure direct communication: on the road to the qinternet. IEEE Commun. Surv. Tutor. **26**(3), 1898–1949 (2024). third quarter
3. Amiri, R., Wallden, P., Kent, A., Andersson, E.: Secure quantum signatures using insecure quantum channels. Phys. Rev. A **93**(3), 032325 (2016)
4. Bell, B.A., et al.: Experimental demonstration of graph-state quantum secret sharing. Nat. Commun. **5**(1), 5480 (2014). https://doi.org/10.1038/ncomms6480
5. Bennett, C.H.: Quantum cryptography using any two nonorthogonal states. Phys. Rev. Lett. **68**(21), 3121 (1992)
6. Bennett, C.H., Brassard, G.: Quantum cryptography: public key distribution and coin tossing. Theoret. Comput. Sci. **560**, 7–11 (2014). https://doi.org/10.1016/j.

tcs.2014.05.025, theoretical Aspects of Quantum Cryptography – celebrating 30 years of BB84

7. Bennett, C.H., Brassard, G., Mermin, N.D.: Quantum cryptography without bell's theorem. Phys. Rev. Lett. **68**(5), 557 (1992)
8. BSI: Implementation attacks against QKD systems (2023). https://www.bsi.bund.de/EN/Service-Navi/Publikationen/Studien/QKD-Systems/Implementation_Attacks_QKD_Systems_node.html
9. Das, N., Paul, G.: Measurement device-independent quantum secure direct communication with user authentication. Quantum Inf. Process. **21**, 260 (2022). https://doi.org/10.1007/s11128-022-03572-z
10. Dunjko, V., Wallden, P., Andersson, E.: Quantum digital signatures without quantum memory. Phys. Rev. Lett. **112**(4), 040502 (2014)
11. Ekert, A.K.: Quantum cryptography based on bell's theorem. Phys. Rev. Lett. **67**(6), 661 (1991)
12. ETSI: Etsi gs 014: Quantum key distribution (QKD); protocol and data format of restbased key delivery API (2019)
13. ETSI: Etsi gs 004: Quantum key distribution (QKD); application interface (2020)
14. Fiat, A., Shamir, A.: How to prove yourself: practical solutions to identification and signature problems. In: Conference on the Theory and Application of Cryptographic Techniques, pp. 186–194. Springer (1986)
15. Fu, Y., Yin, H.L., Chen, T.Y., Chen, Z.B.: Long-distance measurement-device-independent multiparty quantum communication. Phys. Rev. Lett. **114**, 090501 (2015). https://doi.org/10.1103/PhysRevLett.114.090501
16. García-Cid, M.I., Bodanapu, D., Gatto, A., Martelli, P., Martín, V., Ortiz, L.: Experimental implementation of a quantum zero-knowledge proof for user authentication. Opt. Express **32**(9), 15955–15966 (2024)
17. García-Cid, M.I., Martín, R., Domingo, D., Martín, V., Ortiz, L.: Design and implementation of a quantum-assisted digital signature. Cryptography **9**(1), 11 (2025)
18. Goldwasser, S., Micali, S., Rackoff, C.: The knowledge complexity of interactive proof-systems. In: Providing Sound Foundations for Cryptography: On the Work of Shafi Goldwasser and Silvio Micali, pp. 203–225 (2019)
19. Gottesman, D., Chuang, I.: Quantum digital signatures. arXiv preprint quant-ph/0105032 (2001)
20. Grice, W.P., Qi, B.: Quantum secret sharing using weak coherent states. Phys. Rev. A **100**, 022339 (2019). https://doi.org/10.1103/PhysRevA.100.022339
21. Grosshans, F., Grangier, P.: Continuous variable quantum cryptography using coherent states. Phys. Rev. Lett. **88**, 057902 (2002). https://doi.org/10.1103/PhysRevLett.88.057902
22. Gu, J., Xie, Y.M., Liu, W.B., Fu, Y., Yin, H.L., Chen, Z.B.: Secure quantum secret sharing without signal disturbance monitoring. Opt. Express **29**(20), 32244–32255 (2021). https://doi.org/10.1364/OE.440365
23. Hillery, M., Bužek, V., Berthiaume, A.: Quantum secret sharing. Phys. Rev. A **59**, 1829–1834 (1999). https://doi.org/10.1103/PhysRevA.59.1829
24. IETF: Secure key integration protocol (2024). https://www.ietf.org/archive/id/draft-cisco-skip-00.html
25. Kogias, I., Xiang, Y., He, Q., Adesso, G.: Unconditional security of entanglement-based continuous-variable quantum secret sharing. Phys. Rev. A **95**, 012315 (2017). https://doi.org/10.1103/PhysRevA.95.012315
26. Lance, A.M., Symul, T., Sharma, V., Weedbrook, C., Ralph, T.C., Lam, P.K.: No-switching quantum key distribution using broadband modulated coherent light. Phys. Rev. Lett. **95**(18), 180503 (2005)

27. Lanet, J.L., Toma, C.: Innovative Security Solutions for Information Technology and Communications: 11th International Conference, SecITC 2018, Bucharest, Romania, November 8–9, 2018, Revised Selected Papers, vol. 11359. Springer (2019)
28. Liu, S., Lu, Z., Wang, P., Tian, Y., Wang, X., Li, Y.: Experimental demonstration of multiparty quantum secret sharing and conference key agreement. NPJ Quant. Inf. **9**(1), 92 (2023). https://doi.org/10.1038/s41534-023-00763-z
29. Lo, H.K., Ma, X., Chen, K.: Decoy state quantum key distribution. Phys. Rev. Lett. **94**, 230504 (2005). https://doi.org/10.1103/PhysRevLett.94.230504
30. Long, G.L., Pan, D., Sheng, Y.B., Xue, Q., Lu, J., Hanzo, L.: An evolutionary pathway for the quantum internet relying on secure classical repeaters. IEEE Network **36**(3), 82–88 (2022)
31. Lu, C., Miao, F., Hou, J., Meng, K.: Verifiable threshold quantum secret sharing with sequential communication. Quantum Inf. Process. **17**(11), 310 (2018)
32. Lu, Y.S., et al.: Efficient quantum digital signatures without symmetrization step. Opt. Express **29**(7), 10162–10171 (2021)
33. Mosca, M.: Cybersecurity in a quantum world: will we be ready? (2015). https://csrc.nist.gov/csrc/media/events/workshop-on-cybersecurity-in-a-post-quantum-world/documents/presentations/session8-mosca-michele.pdf
34. OASIS: Key management interoperability protocol specification (2019). https://docs.oasis-open.org/kmip/spec/v1.4/errata01/os/kmip-spec-v1.4-errata01-os-redlined.pdf
35. Pavičić, M.: How secure are two-way ping-pong and lm05 QKD protocols under a man-in-the-middle attack? Entropy **23**(2), 163 (2021)
36. Qin, S.J., Gao, F., Wen, Q.Y., Zhu, F.C.: Cryptanalysis of the hillery-bužek-berthiaume quantum secret-sharing protocol. Phys. Rev. A **76**, 062324 (2007). https://doi.org/10.1103/PhysRevA.76.062324
37. Rabin, M.O.: How to exchange secrets with oblivious transfer. Cryptology ePrint Archive (2005)
38. Santos, M.B., Mateus, P., Pinto, A.N.: Quantum oblivious transfer: a short review. Entropy **24**(7), 945 (2022)
39. Sasson, E.B., et al.: Zerocash: decentralized anonymous payments from bitcoin. In: 2014 IEEE Symposium on Security and Privacy, pp. 459–474. IEEE (2014)
40. Shamir, A.: How to share a secret. Commun. ACM **22**(11), 612–613 (1979). https://doi.org/10.1145/359168.359176
41. Shor, P.W., Preskill, J.: Simple proof of security of the bb84 quantum key distribution protocol. Phys. Rev. Lett. **85**(2), 441 (2000)
42. of Standards, N.I., Technologies: post-quantum cryptography (2016). https://csrc.nist.gov/projects/post-quantumcryptography
43. of Standards, N.I., Technologies: Module-lattice-based digital signature standard (2025). https://csrc.nist.gov/pubs/fips/204/final
44. of Standards, N.I., Technologies: Statelesshhash-based digital signature standard (2025). https://csrc.nist.gov/pubs/fips/205/final
45. Sánchez-Soto, L.L., Aguilar, G.H., Garcia-Escartín, J.C.: Quantum relays and entanglement swapping in quantum communications. J. Mod. Opt. (2007). https://doi.org/10.1080/09500340701324681
46. Tarable, A., Paganelli, R.P., Storelli, E., Gatto, A., Ferrari, M.: Generalized quantum-assisted digital signature. arXiv preprint arXiv:2406.19978 (2024)
47. Tavakoli, A., Herbauts, I., Żukowski, M., Bourennane, M.: Secret sharing with a single d-level quantum system. Phys. Rev. A **92**, 030302 (2015). https://doi.org/10.1103/PhysRevA.92.030302

48. Venegas-Andraca, S.E., Retamal, J.C., Eberly, R.B.: Four-party quantum communication with entanglement swapping. J. Mod. Opt. (2007). https://doi.org/10.1080/09500340701340527

49. Walk, N., Eisert, J.: Sharing classical secrets with continuous-variable entanglement: composable security and network coding advantage. PRX Quantum **2**, 040339 (2021). https://doi.org/10.1103/PRXQuantum.2.040339

50. Wang, S.: A quantum good authentication protocol (QGP) integrating quantum photonic channels and dilithium signatures. J. CS IAC **9**(1), 11–21 (2025)

51. Williams, B.P., Lukens, J.M., Peters, N.A., Qi, B., Grice, W.P.: Quantum secret sharing with polarization-entangled photon pairs. Phys. Rev. A **99**, 062311 (2019). https://doi.org/10.1103/PhysRevA.99.062311

52. Yadav, V.K., Andola, N., Verma, S., Venkatesan, S.: A survey of oblivious transfer protocol. ACM Comput. Surv. (CSUR) **54**(10s), 1–37 (2022)

53. Yin, H.L., Fu, Y.: Measurement-device-independent twin-field quantum key distribution. Sci. Rep. **9**(1), 3045 (2019)

Risk-Aware Adaptive Cyber Deception Guided by Large Language Models

David Lopes Antunes[1] , Pavlos Cheimonidis[2] , Eleftherios Batzolis[2] ,
Kyriakos Ovaliadis[2] , Salvador Llopis Sanchez[1] ,
and Konstantinos Rantos[2]([✉])

[1] Universidad Politecnica de Valencia, Valencia, Spain
{daan3,salllosa}@upv.edu.es
[2] Department of Informatics, Democritus University of Thrace, Komotini, Greece
{pcheimon,egbatzo,ovaliad,krantos}@cs.duth.gr

Abstract. Modern cyber threats demand defense strategies that are
adaptive, risk-aware, and capable of misdirecting adversaries in real
time. Traditional static deception systems lack the flexibility to respond
to evolving attack patterns and changing mission priorities. To address
this, we introduce a framework for risk-aware adaptive cyber deception
assisted by Large Language Models. The architecture integrates dynamic
risk assessment, AI-assisted deception strategy generation, and modular
deployment mechanisms. At its core, the Decision and Policy Engine
uses an LLM-driven agent to interpret MITRE CAPEC-aligned threat
intelligence and generate semantically rich deception recommendations.
These are then translated into executable deception playbooks by the
Dynamic Cyber Deception module, which manages tactic selection and
deployment. The framework includes a feedback loop where telemetry
and mission impact assessments inform ongoing refinement of deception
strategies, enabling mission-aware adaptation over time. This work lays
a foundation for the next generation of intelligent cyber defense systems
that combine structured risk models with language-model reasoning to
support resilient, adaptive, and context-driven deception capabilities.

Keywords: AI-driven Cyber Deception · Dynamic Risk Assessment ·
Common Attack Pattern Enumeration and Classification · Deception
Scheme · Adaptive Deception Playbooks

1 Introduction

Modern cyber-attacks are increasingly sophisticated, making it harder for organizations to defend against them using traditional security mechanisms. Static
defences, like firewalls and antivirus software, are no longer enough to keep pace
with the rapidly changing threat landscape. Attackers constantly adapt their
techniques, leaving defenders struggling to identify and mitigate new threats
quickly. To counter this, security systems must become more dynamic, intelligent, and proactive.

© The Author(s), under exclusive license to Springer Nature Switzerland AG 2025
B. Coppens et al. (Eds.): ARES 2025 Workshops, LNCS 15995, pp. 122–138, 2025.
https://doi.org/10.1007/978-3-032-00633-2_8

Dynamic Risk Assessment (DRA) provides a flexible and responsive approach to assessing cybersecurity risks by continuously updating threat probabilities and asset vulnerabilities based on real-time data [5]. Rather than depending solely on pre-defined rules or historical attack patterns, DRA techniques leverage probabilistic models like Bayesian Networks to assess the current threat landscape for the target environment. These models integrate internal data, such as network topologies and deployed assets, with external threat intelligence, like vulnerability databases and exploit prediction scores. In particular, public resources such as the Common Vulnerabilities and Exposures (CVE) catalog, the National Vulnerability Database (NVD), the Common Weakness Enumeration (CWE), and the Common Attack Pattern Enumeration and Classification (CAPEC) offer structured information about known vulnerabilities, software weaknesses, and attacker behaviours. By combining these sources, dynamic risk models deliver up-to-date assessments of which systems are most at risk at any given time, enabling more informed and adaptive decision-making.

Cyber deception, on the other hand, offers another proactive defence strategy by deliberately creating and managing deceptive elements such as honeypots, honeytokens, decoy applications, and fake data [12]. The goal of deception is to mislead and confuse attackers, delay their progress, and gather intelligence about their methods. Effective cyber deception increases the attacker's workload and uncertainty, making successful exploitation more difficult and costly. However, in many current systems, deception assets are deployed statically, without adapting to the evolving risk environment, and thus reducing their potential impact.

Cyber deception has the potential to contribute to the full spectrum of cyberspace operations (from purely Defence to Offense), especially in proactive and reactive defence against sophisticated cyber threats. In this paper, we utilise aspects of the taxonomy developed by Lopez *et al.* [4], and more specifically the defined tactics and techniques, and provide an enhanced set of categories for the deception mechanisms.

Their used AI-driven framework spans all defence phases: prevention, detection, reaction, and forensics, unlike previous limited-scope approaches. AI, especially Machine Learning and Deep Learning, is underutilized in Cyber Deception despite its potential to enhance deception adaptability and precision from Cybersecurity to Cyber Defence contexts. There are still key challenges to take into account, such as the absence of standardized evaluation metrics, limited use of multi-technique deception, insufficient attention to stealth and offensive tactics and the configuration of the underlying network infrastructure [11]. In this paper we adopt a more granular categorisation of cyber deception mechanisms than the one proposed in [4], comprising the following categories:

- Detect: this type of deception is designed to spot attacker early in the reconnaissance phase. It is used as early warning systems.
- Mislead (or misdirect): the goal is to trick attackers into going the wrong way. It is a manoeuvre in cyberspace for diverting the attacker.
- Engage (or interact): the goal is to prolong the interaction with the adversary to collect valuable intelligence.

- Respond: This type of deception aims to project power in cyberspace (offensive operations).

While dynamic risk assessment and cyber deception have each been studied extensively, existing approaches typically treat them as separate efforts. Risk models are often used to prioritize patches or firewall rules, while deception strategies are deployed independently, based on general assumptions about attacker behavior. There is a critical need for a unified methodology that uses dynamic, real-time risk insights to formulate and drive an organization's cyber deception strategy.

In this paper, we propose a novel methodology that connects dynamic risk assessment with the strategic planning and implementation of cyber deception. Our framework analyzes the results of continuous risk assessment to identify high-risk scenarios—situations where specific vulnerabilities, threat actors, or attack paths present the greatest danger. Based on these high-risk scenarios, we guide the selection and deployment of appropriate deception mechanisms, tailoring the deceptive environment to the current threat landscape. This creates a more responsive, intelligent defence posture that evolves as risks change over time.

The main contributions of this paper are:

- A novel adaptive cyber defence framework that unifies Dynamic Risk Assessment (DRA) with context-aware cyber deception to enable dynamic, mission-aligned defensive actions.
- A methodology for the formulation of cyber deception strategies by leveraging real-time high-risk scenario analysis combined with Large Language Models (LLMs) and specialised prompt engineering.
- A modular architecture for the selection, orchestration, and adaptive deployment of deception mechanisms, integrating semantic deception playbooks and dynamic feedback loops.
- An operational pipeline that links asset-level risk probabilities, CAPEC-based threat patterns, and deception scheme generation into a closed-loop, mission-driven cyber defense system.

The rest of this paper is structured as follows. Section 2 reviews related work. Section 3 presents our proposed methodology. Sections 4 and 5 conclude with a discussion of future work.

2   Related Work

Recent research has increasingly focused on proactive cyber defence approaches, particularly dynamic risk assessment and deception and the combination of these two has started attracting the research community.

Sengupta *et al.* [22] survey Moving Target Defence (MTD) techniques for network security, categorizing them based on what, when, and how movement occurs. They highlight the role of artificial intelligence and SDN/NFV technologies in enabling dynamic defences but do not directly integrate dynamic risk models with deception planning.

Li *et al.* [16] propose an optimal defensive deception framework for container-based cloud environments using Deep Reinforcement Learning (DRL). Their work focuses on adaptively deploying decoys based on system dynamics, but emphasizes placement optimization rather than a systematic methodology linking dynamic risk insights to broader deception strategy formulation.

De Faveri *et al.* [8] develop a multi-paradigm modeling approach to incorporate deception tactics into software design processes. Although this supports early-stage security engineering, it lacks a connection to dynamic operational risk updates or runtime deception adaptation.

Al-Shaer *et al.* [11] introduce the notion of autonomous cyber deception using dynamic decision-making frameworks, deep learning, and HoneyThings. Their work envisions automated deception, but focuses primarily on generating deceptive artifacts rather than structuring deception strategies based on evolving risk profiles.

Wang *et al.* [23] design a proactive deception decision-making model using Bayesian attack graphs and Stackelberg games to optimize honeypoint placement. While they integrate dynamic attack path analysis with deception deployment, their approach concentrates mainly on optimizing decoy allocation rather than developing deception strategies at the scenario level.

Huang and Zhu [10] present a multi-stage dynamic Bayesian game model to counter Advanced Persistent Threats (APTs) in cyber-physical systems. Their framework captures stealthy attacker-defender interactions, incorporating proactive defence and deception, but does not propose an explicit methodology for translating dynamic risk evaluation into deception planning.

In contrast to these prior efforts, our work introduces a novel methodology that systematically links dynamic risk assessment outputs to the formulation and implementation of an organization's cyber deception strategy. By identifying high-risk scenarios in real time, our framework leverages a Large Language Model (LLM) to assist in generating tailored deception strategies that dynamically align deception mechanisms with the current threat landscape. This integration of dynamic risk-driven reasoning, LLM-assisted strategy generation, and scenario-specific deception deployment represents a significant advancement over prior approaches that treat risk modeling and deception independently or statically.

3   Proposed Framework

Figure 1 depicts the proposed framework following a modular architecture where the various modules must interact in a sequential order. The framework operates as a closed-loop system linking real-time risk assessment to deception planning and deployment. The Information Collection and DRA modules identify high-risk assets and associated CAPEC attack patterns. The Decision and Policy Engine (DPE) interprets these CAPECs using an LLM-based specialist agent, producing tailored deception strategies structured as Deception Strategy Reports.

These strategies are then operationalized by the Dynamic Cyber Deception (DCD) module through structured deception playbooks, where each recommended technique is mapped to a corresponding deception tactic based on its category (Detection, Misdirection, Engagement, or Response) using a predefined association (as shown in Fig. 2). This ensures that high-level strategic objectives are consistently translated into actionable technical deployments within the playbooks.

Continuous telemetry feedback informs both the Mission Impact Assessment (MIA) and future refinement of deception schemes, ensuring that the defense posture remains contextually relevant, adaptive, and aligned with mission objectives. The modular architecture enables flexibility, human-in-the-loop operation during early stages, and supports incremental evolution toward full AI-orchestrated cyber deception.

3.1   Information Collection

Building on the principles of dynamic risk assessment, the *Information Collection* module systematically aggregates environment-specific data, including Common Platform Enumeration (CPE) identifiers, Common Vulnerabilities and Exposures (CVE) vulnerabilities, and Exploit Prediction Scoring System (EPSS) exploit likelihood scores, to inform targeted cyber deception strategies. The model's operation begins with the identification of all relevant assets within the target environment. For each identified asset, the model determines the corresponding CPEs, which are then matched against the National Vulnerability Database (NVD) [2] to extract associated vulnerability data in the form of CVE identifiers. These CVE-IDs are subsequently used to retrieve EPSS [1] scores. The collected EPSS scores serve as input to a Bayesian network, which enables the model to dynamically and proactively estimate the likelihood of exploitation, producing quantitative threat assessments tailored to the specific environment [6].

In the subsequent phase, the model employs a sequential approach to identify related Common Weakness Enumerations (CWEs). These CWEs are then used to detect associated Common Attack Pattern Enumerations and Classifications (CAPECs). It is important to note that a single CVE may map to multiple CWEs; in such cases, the model extracts and analyzes each identified CWE. Similarly, each CWE may be associated with multiple CAPECs, all of which are collected by our model for further analysis. These identified CAPECs, along with their associated descriptions, are then provided as input to the Decision and Policy Engine (DPE) through the DRA module.

3.2   Dynamic Risk Assessment Module

The *Dynamic Risk Assessment* module is responsible for integrating risk-related information (e.g., threat scores and impact levels) with target-specific contextual

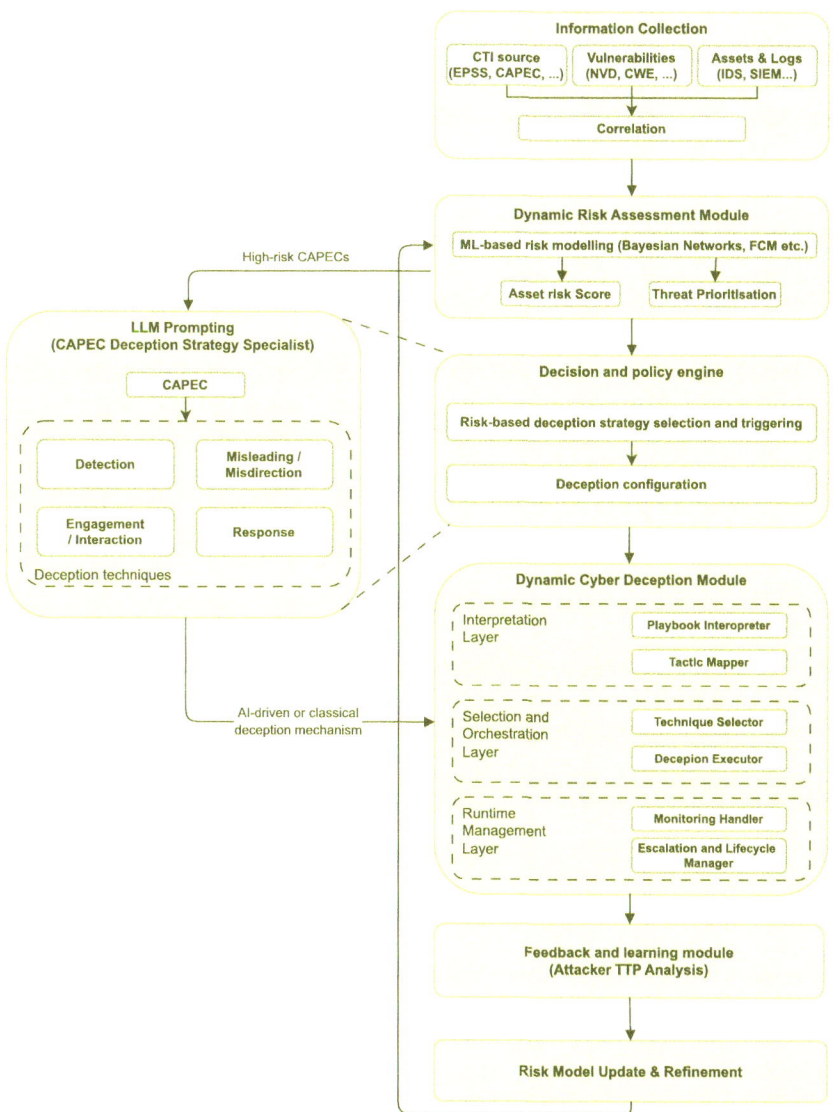

Fig. 1. Proposed framework for risk-driven cyber deception

data, such as network topology. This integration is performed using a Bayesian Network (BN) to generate quantitative risk estimates tailored to the operational environment. It is important to note that this approach is one of several possible methods for Dynamic Risk Assessment, chosen here based on the authors' previous work and expertise in Bayesian Network modelling.

Bayesian Networks (BNs) have been extensively applied in cybersecurity for dynamic risk assessment due to their ability to capture probabilistic relationships and update threat estimations as new data becomes available [6,7]. A BN is defined as $N = \{G, P\}$, where $G = \{V, E\}$ is a Directed Acyclic Graph (DAG) comprising nodes V and edges E, and P represents conditional probability distributions [13,14,19].

In our framework, we define two node types: (T) *threat nodes*, representing CVEs that may exploit system vulnerabilities, and (A) *asset nodes*, representing systems potentially impacted. Rather than relying on subjective expert input [18], we derive conditional probabilities from EPSS scores and CAPEC data, which are widely accepted in the cybersecurity domain.

Network structure reflects possible attack paths informed by asset connectivity and threat propagation. To define node logic, we adopt the AND/OR gate approach from [20]. OR gates are used when any threat can compromise an asset or an asset can be reached by many connected assets, while AND gates require multiple conditions, such as threat presence and previous asset compromise. The conditional probabilities are computed as:

$$P_d = 1 - \prod_{i=1}^{n} \left(1 - P_{(i)}\right) \tag{1}$$

$$P_c = \prod_{i=1}^{n} P(i) \tag{2}$$

This setup enables dynamic threat updates and risk calculation using the standard formulation [15]:

$$Risk = \sum_{i} P(A_i) \times S(A_i) \tag{3}$$

Here, $P(A_i)$ denotes the posterior threat probability for asset A_i, and $S(A_i)$ is its impact score. Impact levels reflect service degradation (Table 1), though the model can accommodate alternative schemes (e.g., confidentiality-integrity and availability (CIA) or financial metrics).

The primary output of the DRA Module is a set of quantitative risk scores assigned to each asset in the network. These scores capture both the estimated likelihood of exploitation and the potential impact of a successful attack, supporting informed and prioritized decision-making for cyber defence planning. In addition, this module also supplies the DPE with the relevant CAPECs identified by the information collection component.

Table 1. Impact Scale

Description	Impact Score
All services operational	0
Most services operational	1
Some services operational	2
No services operational	3

3.3 Decision and Policy Engine

The *Decision and Policy Engine* serves as the semantic interpretation layer of the framework, responsible for transforming structured threat intelligence, particularly MITRE CAPEC entries identified by the DRA module, into actionable deception strategies. At the heart of the DPE is an LLM specifically configured and prompted to act as a "CAPEC Deception Strategy Specialist" [3]. This specialized agent is designed to analyze a given CAPEC, understand its attack mechanics, and generate detailed, creative, and technically precise deception-based countermeasures.

Workflow and Output Generation. Upon receiving a high-risk CAPEC identifier and its associated context from the DRA module, the DPE invokes its specialized LLM agent. The agent processes this input based on its predefined system prompt, which guides it to first identify the specific CAPEC attack pattern, then provide an ultra-concise technical snapshot of the attack and its key enabling factors to ground the deception strategy, and ultimately generate a comprehensive Deception Strategy Report. This report is the primary output of the DPE and directly addresses the need for specific, actionable guidance.

The Deception Strategy Report is structured to include several key components, directly aligning with the capabilities of the "CAPEC Deception Strategy Specialist" agent. It details a set of recommended deception techniques which are specific deception tools and methods, such as credential honeytokens, fake vulnerable service honeypots, and deceptive API endpoints, directly relevant to countering the mechanics of the input CAPEC. This "set" of techniques is generated by the LLM agent based on its specialized knowledge of deception and the CAPEC landscape.

Furthermore, for every recommended deception technique, the report provides clearly defined strategic objectives, such as early detection of reconnaissance, misdirection of the attacker towards benign decoys, containment of malicious activity, or collection of attacker TTPs. These objectives are defined by the LLM agent itself, tailored to the specific CAPEC and the chosen deception tactic.

The agent also provides implementation guidance, offering practical advice on the optimal placement of these deception elements within the target environment (e.g., specific network segments, application layers, configuration files) and detailing crucial monitoring requirements (e.g., "alert on any access attempt to the honeytoken", "log all traffic interacting with the honeypot IP").

This guidance forms the strategic basis for the more detailed operational playbooks. Crucially, the report also establishes the basis for trigger logic; while the LLM agent does not generate executable Security Information and Event Management (SIEM) rules or complex alert conditions directly, its specification of "key monitoring points" and expected attacker interactions provides the necessary information for the subsequent DCD module to establish explicit trigger logic for high-confidence alerts or automated escalations. For instance, if the agent suggests monitoring a specific fake credential, the DCD module can then implement a trigger to alert when that credential is used.

Example Output of the "CAPEC Deception Strategy Specialist" Agent. To illustrate the output, consider an input of **CAPEC-126: Path Traversal**. The DPE's LLM agent might produce a Deception Strategy Report similar to the following (abbreviated):

```
### CAPEC Deception Strategy Report

**Attack Pattern:** CAPEC-126: Path Traversal (aka
    ↪ Directory Traversal)

**Threat Snapshot:** An attacker manipulates input
    ↪ parameters (e.g., in a URL or form field) with
    ↪ sequences like '../' to navigate outside the intended
    ↪ directory and access restricted files or directories
    ↪ on the server.

**Key Enabling Factor(s):**
*   Insufficient input validation and sanitization of user-
    ↪ supplied file paths.
*   Web server misconfiguration allowing access beyond the
    ↪ web root.


---


**Deception Strategy:**

**1. Technique:** Decoy Directory/File System
    *    **Details:** Create a set of directories and files
         ↪ within the web server's accessible paths that
         ↪ mimic sensitive system locations (e.g., '/etc/
         ↪ passwd-decoy', '/var/log/secret_system.log.decoy
         ↪ ', '../backup_config.ini.decoy'). These are not
         ↪ real sensitive files but are designed to attract
         ↪ path traversal attempts.
    *    **Strategic Goal:** Detect and identify attackers
         ↪ attempting path traversal by luring them to
```

⮡ access these specific decoy files/directories.
⮡ Successful access to a decoy is a high-fidelity
⮡ indicator of malicious intent.
* **Implementation & Monitoring:**
  * Placement: Strategically place links or
    ⮡ references to these decoys in less obvious
    ⮡ parts of the web application, or make them
    ⮡ discoverable if an attacker successfully
    ⮡ traverses one level up.
  * Monitoring: Monitor all access attempts to
    ⮡ these specific decoy files and directories.
    ⮡ Log the source IP, timestamp, and the exact
    ⮡ path requested.

2. Technique: Path Traversal Honeypot Listener
* **Details:** Configure a specific web application
  ⮡ endpoint or a dedicated lightweight honeypot
  ⮡ service that intentionally appears vulnerable to
  ⮡ path traversal. When an attacker attempts to use
  ⮡ '../' sequences against this endpoint, instead of
  ⮡ returning a real file or an error, it logs the
  ⮡ attempt and can optionally return a fake
  ⮡ directory listing or a "file" containing a
  ⮡ honeytoken.
* **Strategic Goal:** Actively solicit and capture
  ⮡ path traversal attempts, gather intelligence on
  ⮡ attacker TTPs (what files they are looking for),
  ⮡ and provide early warning of such reconnaissance.
* **Implementation & Monitoring:**
  * Placement: Can be a hidden endpoint on an
    ⮡ existing web server or a separate low-
    ⮡ interaction honeypot.
  * Monitoring: Log all incoming requests to this
    ⮡ listener, especially those containing path
    ⮡ traversal sequences. If a honeytoken is
    ⮡ returned, monitor for its activation.

- - -

Brief Contextual Notes:
* **Attacker Objective Hint:** Often used for information
  ⮡ gathering (e.g., finding configuration files,
  ⮡ credentials) or as a precursor to further
  ⮡ exploitation.
* **Deception Complexity:** (Technique 1: Simple to
  ⮡ Moderate), (Technique 2: Moderate)

This structured "Deception Strategy Report" serves as input to the DCD Module. It is the blueprint for constructing and operationalizing executable deception playbooks. The guidance provided by the DPE ensures that the deception mechanisms deployed are semantically rich, aligned with specific threats (CAPECs), and contribute directly to the strategic objectives of detection, misdirection, engagement, or response.

The DPE, powered by a specialized LLM agent acting as a "CAPEC Deception Strategy Specialist", transforms structured threat intelligence into dynamic and semantically rich deception strategies. By interpreting CAPEC data, the engine generates detailed Deception Strategy Reports (Deception Scheme) that recommend specific deception techniques, associate them with strategic objectives, and provide implementation and monitoring guidance. This output serves as the direct input for the DCD module, enabling the creation of context-aware, risk-aligned deception playbooks tailored to evolving threats and operational constraints.

3.4   Dynamic Cyber Deception Module

The purpose of the *Dynamic Cyber Deception* module is to execute deception playbooks based on recommendations provided by the DPE. Acting as a bridge between AI-driven decision modules and real-time deceptive actions, playbooks define when and how deception should be activated in response to specific attacker behaviors or risk levels, as well as the intended outcomes, i.e. whether to detect, mislead, engage, or respond to cyber attackers according to the deception categories identified in the framework (Fig. 1). In authors' views, the DCD module follows a human-based implementation where operators are responsible for interpreting high-level deception schemes/deception strategy reports, mapping tactics to executable techniques, deploying deception components, configuring monitoring, and managing the full lifecycle of each playbook. This manual workflow emphasizes the need for a structured transition plan toward automated execution in the future. A deception playbook is not merely an execution recipe, but a structured operational plan that translates the high-level deception scheme (from the DPE) into: tactical intent (why it is being used), technical deployment (how it is executed) and expected effects (what it is supposed to achieve).

The intended outcome is not inferred post-deployment but is embedded in the playbook structure to ensure consistent, goal-driven deception planning and evaluation. It instantiates both a "classical approach" - comprising, for instance, honey-X and MTD techniques - and an "AI-based approach" of adaptive and cognitive deception. Both technologies can coexist in a hybrid deception architecture. Human operators are responsible for interpreting and executing this specification, which highlights the need for a structured transition to automated orchestration as system maturity evolves. The DCD module may run immediate deception via a rapid response path and generates outputs shared with a feedback loop for continuous improvement. It is the "executor and tuner" of deception based on the input received from previous modules. Here is how the module can be functionally decomposed into three logical layers containing each one two submodules and services (as shown in Fig. 2) - in a structured way:

– **The Interpretation Layer** serves as the central coordination of two submodules: playbook interpreter and tactic mapper. The playbook interpreter parses DPE inputs, validates deception schema, and instantiates a runtime deception playbook while the tactic mapper maps the deception category (e.g., misleading) to a corresponding tactic (e.g., decoying or camouflage) using a predefined lookup table. The category-to-tactic mapping is a semantic grounding mechanism that refines high-level deception objectives into specific tactical intents. The original set of deception tactics proposed in the CYDEC framework [4] was designed to capture high-level cognitive strategies applicable to both offensive and defensive deception contexts. While valuable as a unifying taxonomy of intent, these tactics were not explicitly structured for implementation within adaptive, mission-aware cyber defence systems. In this work, the authors reinterpret and expand these tactics to align with four operationally distinct categories of deception (Fig. 2), targeting *detection, misdirection, engagement,* or *response* and thus, creating a practical bridge between strategic intent and automated execution. This expansion not only enhances the applicability of existing taxonomies but also provides the foundation for integrating deception planning into AI-driven decision systems and dynamic orchestration modules.

- **The Selection and Orchestration Layer** comprises two submodules: a Technique selector and a Deception executor. The first submodule, analyses the list of techniques provided by the DPE and selects the one that best implements the mapped tactic (based on priority, resource availability, or historical effectiveness). The latter submodule deploys the selected deception technique using orchestration tools (e.g., honeypot deployment, DNS manipulation, AI-generated content).

- **The Runtime Management Layer** manages telemetry setup, tracks attacker behaviour, and governs the playbook lifecycle including escalation or shutdown. These functions are operationalised by a Monitoring Handler and an Escalation and Lifecycle Manager.

In essence, playbooks incorporate trigger logic, placement and duration parameters, telemetry hooks, and escalation rules as defined by the LLM-generated scheme. This alignment ensures that each deception instance is semantically consistent, mission-relevant, and operationally effective within the adaptive deception loop. Unlike SODA [21], which synthesizes deception playbooks through offline malware analysis, the proposed model constructs deception playbooks based on semantic interpretations of elements provided by an LLM-driven DPE. SODA's playbooks are primarily malware-specific and centered around ploy-level API manipulation aligned with static deception strategies (e.g., Fake-Success, FakeFailure), whereas our approach defines playbooks as modular execution plans guided by high-level strategic objectives (e.g., detection, misdirection, engagement, response), linked to mapped tactics and techniques.

Together, the above-mentioned submodules form the active operational layer of the dynamic deception architecture, seamlessly integrating deception deployment with situational understanding. In the authors' opinion, implementation of the DCD module will include human oversight in key subcomponents. Specifically, the Technique Selector and Deception Executor submodules are envisaged

Deception Categories

	Detection	Misleading	Engagement	Response
Masking		●	●	●
Repackaging	●		●	
Dazzling	●	●		●
Mimicking		●	●	
Inventing	●			●
Decoying		●	●	
Concealment			●	●
Camouflage		●		●
False information	●			●
Lies	●			
Displays		●		●
Baits			●	

Fig. 2. Mapping of CYDEC tactics [4] with deception categories

to be operated manually or semi-automatically by human analysts during the proof-of-concept phase. This design choice ensures flexibility and interpretability in the early stages of system deployment, allowing expert judgment to guide the selection of deception techniques and validate operational execution in complex environments [17]. Furthermore, this human-in-the-loop approach enables iterative refinement of category-tactic-technique mappings and supports the safe evaluation of deception strategies prior to some type of possible automation. In production settings, these submodules are expected to evolve into policy-driven, AI-assisted orchestration services, but their manual control at this stage reflects a balance between experimental rigor, operational safety, and the incremental maturity of deception technology (Table 2).

3.5   Feedback and Improvement of the Model

The *Feedback Processor* serves as a critical analytical component within the deception architecture, transforming raw telemetry and attacker interaction data into actionable insights for system adaptation and learning. It continuously ingests data streams from the Monitoring Handler, including command sequences, engagement durations, and deception avoidance attempts. Utilizing advanced analytics, the processor assesses the effectiveness of deception activities, measuring indicators such as attacker persistence, confusion, and eventual disengagement. This analysis produces deception performance metrics that are structured and prioritized according to their relevance to ongoing operations and overall mission objectives. These metrics are then fed both to the MIA module, where they contribute to dynamic impact evaluation, and to the DPE module, facilitating continuous refinement of deception playbooks and orchestration policies based on empirical outcomes. Additionally, it has the potential of executing an adaptive tuning based on dynamic risk and MIA [9] - the latter being an external source of information. In a cyber situational awareness capability,

Table 2. Functional overview of Deception module subcomponents

Submodule	Purpose
Playbook Interpreter	Parses DPE inputs, validates schema, and instantiates a runtime deception playbook
Tactic Mapper	Maps the deception category to a corresponding tactic using a lookup table
Technique Selector	From the list of techniques provided by the DPE, selects the one that best implements the mapped tactic (based on priority, resource availability, or historical effectiveness)
Deception Executor	Deploys the selected deception technique using orchestration tools (e.g., honeypot deployment, DNS manipulation, AI-generated content)
Monitoring Handler	Installs required telemetry hooks as defined in the playbook and routes data to the Feedback Processor and MIA modules
Escalation and Lifecycle Manager	Monitors playbook triggers and conditions for escalation, timeout, or deactivation, and coordinates any runtime transitions

MIA evaluates how ongoing cyber events affect mission-critical capabilities. In doing so, the Feedback Processor closes the deception loop, ensuring that future engagements benefit from accumulated knowledge and tactical optimization.

4 Discussion

In the implementation of the framework provided in Fig. 1, some shortfalls may appear which are worth analysing. As mentioned in Sect. 3, LLM outputs map directly to deception categories (detect, mislead, engage, respond). Deception tactics associated with above-mentioned categories could be predictable or rigidly tied to CAPEC mappings to cope with a rapid adaption of cyber attackers's techniques. Therefore, Deception playbooks need to evolve dynamically, not just trigger based on category. Another possible limitation is that the DCD module produces attacker reactions which are captured to feed a MIA. MIA consumes information from deception activities and attacker reactions to provide its measurements. The proposed future work for the proposed architecture shall show how MIA influences upstream deception or LLM recommendations. DPE module is not directly fed with real-time attacker response data and it would affect the ability for the LLM-driven mechanism to refine recommendations based on deception effectiveness. Additionally, the modular approach and involvement of LLMs and agents may introduce processing latency. High-speed attacks (e.g. ransomware, data exfiltration) require faster LLM-based decision and deception deployment or at least, the possibility to find a compromise between effectiveness and speed. Moreover, explicit adversarial resistance is envisaged as a future work. Attackers may attempt to detect and evade LLM-driven deception systems. LLM and deception mechanisms may be vulnerable to: adversarial prompting, deception environment fingerprinting, or abuse of response deception to gain information. Successfully fingerprinting deception environments allows adversaries to bypass traps, reducing the effectiveness of cyber deception strategies.

The implementation of the DCD module requires careful orchestration of modular subcomponents capable of deploying and adapting deception strategies with human intervention in alignment with evolving threat conditions and mission priorities. Central to this is the integration of deception playbooks, which standardize the execution of deception schemes, ranging from detection and misdirection to environment manipulation and response deception, based on structured outputs from the DPE. Key aspects include the use of containerized microservices for flexible deployment, real-time telemetry collection for attacker interaction analysis, and a feedback mechanism to inform future deception strategies. At the framework level, seamless interoperability between the DRA process, and the DPE and DCD modules is critical to ensure context-aware and risk-aligned defensive actions. To ensure a coherent and logically structured operationalization of the framework, overlaps or inconsistencies between the inputs and outputs of the DPE and the DCD modules must be minimized. Clear interface definitions and modular boundaries are essential to maintain consistency, traceability, and semantic alignment across the system components. The definition of deception intensity within the DCD module must consider both the availability of operational resources and the assessed threat level. This intensity should be proportionally aligned with the threat actor's motivation and skills, enabling a calibrated response that avoids unnecessary system overhead. Furthermore, maintaining low-latency communication, ensuring scalability across distributed environments, and safeguarding against deception environment fingerprinting are essential to achieving a resilient, adaptive, and mission-aware cyber defence capability.

5   Conclusions

This work introduces a novel cyber defence framework that integrates DRA with AI-assisted cyber deception, aiming to enhance mission resilience through adaptive, risk-aligned defensive actions. Leveraging Large Language Models to interpret CAPEC-aligned threat intelligence, the system generates semantically rich deception strategies that guide deployment of structured deception playbooks.

The proposed framework establishes a modular, closed-loop architecture linking risk analysis, strategic reasoning, deception orchestration, and feedback-driven adaptation. While the current work focuses on the architectural foundation, future research will focus on the detailed development and operational refinement of the framework components, including the integration of feedback mechanisms, advanced deception environment and playbooks management, and optimisation of AI-driven strategy generation. Before DCD deployment of playbooks, alternative tactics and techniques analysis can be effectively supported through controlled testing environments or cyber ranges, allowing empirical evaluation of deception strategies and identification of the most effective solution for a given threat scenario. By bridging dynamic risk evaluation with proactive, context-aware cyber deception, this framework lays the groundwork for the next generation of intelligent and mission-driven cyber defence systems where cyber deception is an integral part of it.

Disclosure of Interests. The authors have no competing interests to declare that are relevant to the content of this article.

References

1. Exploit Prediction Scoring System (EPSS). www.first.org/epss/. Accessed 13 Aug 2024
2. National Vulnerability Database (NVD). www.nvd.nist.gov/. Accessed 10 Aug 2024
3. Batzolis, E.: Github - lefteris-b/system_prompts_for_deception_agents: System prompts for AI cyber deception agents. https://github.com/Lefteris-B/System_prompts_for_Deception_Agents (2025). Accessed 12 May 2025
4. Beltrán López, P., Gil Pérez, M., Nespoli, P.: Cyber Deception: State of the art, Trends and Open challenges (2024). https://doi.org/10.48550/arXiv.2409.07194, arXiv:2409.07194 [cs]
5. Cheimonidis, P., Rantos, K.: Dynamic risk assessment in cybersecurity: a systematic literature review. Future Internet **15**(10), 324 (2023)
6. Cheimonidis, P., Rantos, K.: A dynamic risk assessment and mitigation model. Appl. Sci. **15**(4), 2171 (2025)
7. Cheimonidis, P., Rantos, K.: A novel proactive and dynamic cyber risk assessment methodology. Comput. Secur. **154**, 104439 (2025)
8. De Faveri, C., Moreira, A., Amaral, V.: Multi-paradigm deception modeling for cyber defense. J. Syst. Softw. **141**, 32–51 (2018). https://doi.org/10.1016/j.jss.2018.03.031
9. Grimaila, M.R., Mills, R.F., Fortson, L.W.: Improving the cyber incident mission impact assessment (CIMIA) process. In: Proceedings of the 4th Annual Workshop on Cyber Security and Information Intelligence Research: Developing Strategies to Meet the Cyber Security and Information Intelligence Challenges Ahead. CSIIRW '08, Association for Computing Machinery, New York, NY, USA (2008). https://doi.org/10.1145/1413140.1413177
10. Huang, L., Zhu, Q.: A dynamic games approach to proactive defense strategies against advanced persistent threats in cyber-physical systems. Comput. Secur. **89** (2020). https://doi.org/10.1016/j.cose.2019.101660
11. Islam, M.M., Al-Shaer, E.: Active deception framework: an extensible development environment for adaptive cyber deception. In: 2020 IEEE Secure Development (SecDev), pp. 41–48. IEEE (2020)
12. Javadpour, A., Ja'fari, F., Taleb, T., Shojafar, M., Benzaïd, C.: A comprehensive survey on cyber deception techniques to improve honeypot performance. Comput. Secur. 103792 (2024)
13. Jensen, F., Nielsen, T.: Bayesian Networks and Decision Graphs. Springer, 2nd edn. (2007)
14. Johnson, P., Lagerström, R., Ekstedt, M., Franke, U.: Can the common vulnerability scoring system be trusted? A bayesian analysis. IEEE Trans. Dependable Secure Comput. **15**(6), 1002–1015 (2018)

15. Kaplan, S., Garrick, B.J.: On the quantitative definition of risk. Risk Anal. **1**(1), 11–27 (1981)
16. Li, H., Guo, Y., Sun, P., Wang, Y., Huo, S.: An optimal defensive deception framework for the container-based cloud with deep reinforcement learning. IET Inf. Secur. **16**(3), 178–192 (2022). https://doi.org/10.1049/ise2.12050
17. Llopis Sanchez, S., Lopes Antunes, D.: Operation assessment in cyberspace: Understanding the effects of cyber deception. In: Proceedings of the 19th International Conference on Availability, Reliability and Security. ARES '24, Association for Computing Machinery, New York, NY, USA (2024). https://doi.org/10.1145/3664476.3672355
18. Mkrtchyan, L., Podofillini, L., Dang, V.: Methods for building conditional probability tables of Bayesian belief networks from limited judgment: an evaluation for human reliability application. Reliab. Eng. Syst. Saf. **151**, 93–112 (2016). https://doi.org/10.1016/j.ress.2016.01.004
19. Peng, Y., Huang, K., Tu, W., Zhou, C.: A model-data integrated cyber security risk assessment method for industrial control systems. In: 2018 IEEE 7th Data Driven Control and Learning Systems Conference (DDCLS), pp. 344–349. IEEE (2018)
20. Poolsappasit, N., Dewri, R., Ray, I.: Dynamic security risk management using Bayesian attack graphs. IEEE Trans. Dependable Secure Comput. **9**(1), 61–74 (2012)
21. Sajid, M.S.I., et al.: SODA: a system for cyber deception orchestration and automation. In: Proceedings of the 37th Annual Computer Security Applications Conference, pp. 675–689. ACSAC '21, Association for Computing Machinery, New York, NY, USA (2021). https://doi.org/10.1145/3485832.3485918
22. Sengupta, S., Chowdhary, A., Sabur, A., Alshamrani, A., Huang, D., Kambhampati, S.: A survey of moving target defenses for network security. Tutorials IEEE Commun. Surv. Tutorials **22**(3), 1909–1941 (2020). https://doi.org/10.1109/COMST.2020.2982955 IEEE Commun. Surv. Tutorials **22**(3), 1909–1941 (2020). https://doi.org/10.1109/COMST.2020.2982955
23. Wang, R., Yang, C., Deng, X., Zhou, Y., Liu, Y., Tian, Z.: Turn the tables: proactive deception defense decision-making based on Bayesian attack graphs and Stackelberg games. Neurocomputing **638** (2025). https://doi.org/10.1016/j.neucom.2025.130139

Reducing Information Overload: Because Even Security Experts Need to Blink

Philipp Kuehn[(⊠)][ID], Markus Bayer[ID], Tobias Frey, Moritz Kerk,
and Christian Reuter[ID]

Science and Technology for Peace and Security (PEASEC),
Technical University of Darmstadt, Darmstadt, Germany
research@audacis.net

Abstract. Computer Security Incident Response Teams (CSIRTs) face
increasing challenges processing the growing volume of security-related
information. Daily manual analysis of threat reports, security advisories,
and vulnerability announcements leads to information overload, contributing to burnout and attrition among security professionals. Clustering such information to cope with the initial information volume
and enables security professionals to grasp the current overview of the
situation more easily and decide on actions. This work evaluates 196
combinations of clustering algorithms and embedding models across five
security-related datasets to identify optimal approaches for automated
information consolidation. We demonstrate that clustering can reduce
information overload by over 90 % while maintaining semantic coherence.
Our evaluation indicates a minimal need of configuration to successfully
cluster information within a reasonable timespan on consumer hardware.
The findings suggest that clustering approaches can significantly enhance
CSIRT operational efficiency while maintaining analytical integrity. However, complex threat reports require careful parameter tuning to achieve
acceptable performance, indicating areas for future optimization (The
code is made publicly available at the following URL: https://github.
com/PEASEC/reducing-information-overload)

Keywords: Security · Clustering · Natural Language Processing ·
Large Language Model

1 Introduction

The cybersecurity threat landscape continuously evolves, with attackers deploying increasingly sophisticated tactics while security findings proliferate across
multiple channels. Security personnel struggle to process high volumes of textual reports [12], impeding their primary mission of threat identification and
infrastructure protection. Despite existing frameworks like the Cyber Threat
Intelligence (CTI) cycle [41] and automation methods [17], information processing challenges persist. While CTI – the process of collecting and analyzing security data to derive actionable recommendations – can be aggregated in Threat

© The Author(s), under exclusive license to Springer Nature Switzerland AG 2025
B. Coppens et al. (Eds.): ARES 2025 Workshops, LNCS 15995, pp. 139–155, 2025.
https://doi.org/10.1007/978-3-032-00633-2_9

Intelligence Platforms (TIPs) [34], the diversity of sources and evolving threats creates significant information overload.

Computer Security Incident Response Teams (CSIRTs), as organizational security incident coordinators [43], require current threat intelligence for effective response. Studies reveal that 45% of CSIRT teams process only critical reports due to understaffing [9], while 13% lack capacity for new information and 11% cannot manage existing volumes. Recent research [12,16] reinforces these challenges, with 47.6 % of analysts reporting burnout and 46.6% identifying threat monitoring as their most time-consuming task. For 19.2 % of analysts, automating threat alert enrichment through incident correlation represents a critical priority [12]. Kaufhold et al. [16] highlight persistent manual processes in technical information exchange, redundancy checks, and general automation needs, underscoring the urgency for enhanced information processing solutions.

Goal. This research evaluates clustering algorithms' efficacy as part of a novel semi-automated threat analysis pipeline for CSIRTpersonnel. Such a system would ingest raw threat information from multiple sources, automatically clusters related threats using optimized embedding-clustering combinations, and presents the results to experts. This workflow transformation enables analysts to process substantially more threat data in less time, reducing information overload while maintaining comprehensive coverage. Rather than manually reviewing hundreds of individual alerts daily, analysts can first examine cluster summaries, prioritize clusters, and then investigate specific threats in detail. We assess various embedding-clustering algorithm combinations against derived requirements, with particular emphasis on threat messages and security advisories from both commercial vendors and security researchers. This investigation addresses our primary research question: *Which cluster algorithm and embedding combination is suitable to reduce CSIRT personnel's information overload (RQ)?*

Contributions. This work advances current research through two primary contributions: (i) introduction of THREATREPORT, a novel labeled threat report corpus (*C1*) and (ii) a comprehensive performance comparisons of 14 clustering algorithms on the created embeddings across the five diverse datasets (*C2*).

Outline. The remainder of this paper is structured as follows: Sect. 2 examines related work and identifies research gaps. Section 3 details our methodology, followed by our comprehensive evaluation results in Sect. 4. Section 5 discusses findings and limitations, while Sect. 6 summarizes our contributions.

2   Related Work

We present related work in embeddings, clustering, and evaluation, culminating in the identification of our research gap.

Embeddings. Embedding methods transform data points into vector representations where similarity is preserved through spatial proximity. These range from simple word frequency approaches to sophisticated language models encoding semantic relationships [35,47]. Document-level encoding presents unique challenges for threat intelligence processing. Traditional approaches include Bag of Words (BoW), which records absolute term frequencies using a global vocabulary, and Term Frequency-Inverse Document Frequency (TF-IDF), which weights terms by their document frequency [47]. Recent approaches use BERT [7], with Sentence- BERT (SBERT) specifically optimized for embedding longer text units [35]. The *MTEB* benchmark provides comprehensive performance comparisons of differently-sized language models (LLMs), including clustering efficacy [32].

Clustering. Clustering algorithms group data points based on similarity metrics such as cosine distance or silhouette scores [13,40,47]. Traditional methods range from centroid-based K-Means [24] requiring predefined cluster counts to density-based Density-Based Spatial Clustering of Applications with Noise (DBSCAN) [8] supporting arbitrary cluster shapes. Recent deep learning approaches leverage intermediate representations [19,20,26,27,29,36,44]. In security contexts, clustering facilitates log summarization [10], Android permission analysis [28], and cybersecurity event detection in social media [38] using various techniques from local sensitivity hashing to neural networks. Vulnerability management benefits from clustering through alternative vulnerability classification [2].

Evaluation. Text clustering evaluation employs both internal metrics (assessing compactness and separability without ground truth) [37] and external metrics (requiring labeled data) [47]. Rosenberg and Hirschberg [39] highlight limitations of traditional metrics like purity and entropy, particularly for edge cases. The V-measure framework [39] combines homogeneity (cluster label consistency) and completeness (label distribution) metrics, providing comprehensive clustering quality assessment. Recent frameworks [21] integrate multiple algorithms, datasets, and metrics for systematic evaluation.

Research Gap. While existing research addresses clustering of security information in natural language, it primarily focuses on short-form content (*e.g.*, social media posts) [38] or traditional embedding methods [18,38]. No comprehensive evaluation exists, which compares modern embedding-clustering combinations for longer security texts, such as security advisories or threat reports. This gap is particularly significant given the increasing volume and complexity of security documentation requiring efficient processing by CSIRT personnel.

3   Methodology

We present the data used in this work and the requirements for document embeddings, clustering algorithms, and evaluation metrics.

3.1   Text Corpora

This study employs multiple datasets to evaluate the selected clustering algorithms across three distinct use-cases: effectiveness in processing threat-related

Table 1. This table outlines the structural information of the datasets $c \in$ [$CySecAlert, MSE, ThreatReport, SBR, SMS$]. L_c is the sequence $len(dp_i)$ in character for all $dp_i \in c$. It shows the size $|L_c|$, the average length $\overline{L_c}$, the median $\widetilde{L_c}$, the minimum $\lfloor L_c \rfloor$ and maximum $\lceil L_c \rceil$ data point length, and the number of ground truth clusters ($\#L_c$) of c.

c	$|L_c|$	$\overline{L_c}$	$\widetilde{L_c}$	$\lfloor L_c \rfloor$	$\lceil L_c \rceil$	$\#L_c$
CySecAlert	13 306	136	119	6	486	2
MSE	3 001	284	277	57	686	2
ThreatReport	461	4 370	3 366	7	26 853	39
SBR	5 000	887	458	29	32 785	5
SMS	5 574	80	61	2	910	2

short messages and threat reports (use-case I), performance in handling security bug report (SBR) across diverse products (use-case II), and comparative analysis on non-security short messages (use-case III). Exemplar texts from each corpus are presented in Listing 1.1, while Table 1 provides a comprehensive overview of the datasets' structural characteristics.

For the security-centric analysis, we utilize three different datasets: CySe-cAlert [38], Microsoft Exchange (MSE) [5], and ThreatReport (self-labeled). The CySecAlert and MSE datasets comprise security-related short messages extracted from X (formerly Twitter). The ThreatReport dataset encompasses security-related content aggregated from news outlets and security feeds. While the former two datasets are representative for CSIRT data aggregations in crisis, the third represents data of the daily work of CSIRTs. In both areas the volume of information increased tremendously in recent years, while understaffing remained on a high level [14]. For product-specific analysis, the SBR dataset contains security-related messages from issue trackers spanning five distinct products [42]. Both former use-cases (I+II) address security related tasks. To establish a baseline for general text classification, we incorporate the UCI *SMS Spam Collection* [1], which features characteristics common to security domain texts, including abbreviations, non-standard nomenclature, and spam content.

The labeling of ThreatReport was done by two researchers in the field of information security. After the first independent labeling of 10 data points, both researchers discussed their labeling process and aligned differences. Afterward, both researchers continued independent on a half dataset each.

3.2 Operational Requirements for Automated CSIRT Information Processing

The automation of routine analytical tasks presents a critical opportunity for operational improvement, particularly in the identification of duplicate and related information within incoming data streams. Research indicates that security personnel estimate "half of their tasks to all of their tasks could be auto-

"*CyberRange : The Open-Source AWS Cyber Range [. . .]*"

(a) Example text for the CySecAlert dataset (use-case I).

"*SMBs need to take immediate action on #microsoft #exchange #vulnerabilities [URL] [. . .]*"

(b) Example text for the Microsoft Exchange dataset dataset (use-case I).

"*New CacheWarp AMD CPU attack lets hackers gain root in Linux VMs-November 14, 2023- 03:34 PM-2 A new software-based fault injection attack, CacheWarp, can let threat actors hack into AMD SEV-protected [. . .]*"

(c) Example text for the ThreatReport dataset (use-case I).

"*SYSCS_UTIL.SYSCS_COMPRESS_TABLE should create statistics if they do not exist There must be an entry in the SYSSTATISTICS table in order for the cardinality statistics in SYSSTATISTICS to be created with SYSCS_UTIL.SYSCS_COMPRESS_TABLE SYSCS_UTIL.SYSCS_COMPRESS_TABLE should create statistics if they don't exist. [. . .]*"

(d) Example text for the security bug report dataset dataset (use-case II).

"*Auction round 4. The highest bid is now £54. Next maximum bid is £71. To bid, send BIDS e. g. 10 (to bid £10) to 83383. Good luck*"

(e) Example text for the SMS dataset (use-case III).

Listing 1.1. Example texts from the different evaluation datasets (CySecAlert, MSE, ThreatReport, SBR, and SMS).

mated today" [12]. Drawing from multiple empirical studies [4,12,16], we establish the following core requirements for an effective CSIRT clustering system.

R1 **Reducing information overload for CSIRTs.:** The clustering system must demonstrably reduce the volume of information requiring manual review through effective cluster consolidation. Cluster homogeneity must be maximized through rigorous outlier management. The presence of misclassified data points would significantly compromise cluster integrity and negate the intended benefits of information reduction. Therefore, the system must prioritize classification accuracy over cluster completeness.

R2 **Unburden CSIRTs.:** The proposed algorithms must operate with minimal configuration requirements, eliminating the need for continuous model adjustment with emerging vulnerabilities or technologies. Model fine-tuning represents a significant operational overhead. While potentially more engaging than routine document review, such tasks divert resources from core responsibilities: threat identification, analysis, and stakeholder communication.

Table 2. Overview of the LLMs used in combination with SBERT (sorted alphabetically).

Huggingface Model ID ↓	Params
Alibaba-NLP/gte-base-en-v1.5	137M
jxm/cde-small-v1	281M
markusbayer/cysecbert	110M
meta-llama/Llama-3.2-1B	1.24B
meta-llama/Llama-3.2-3B	3.21B
mistralai/Mistral-7B-v0.1	7.24B
mistralai/Mistral-7B-v0.3	7.25B
NovaSearch/stella_en_1.5b_v5	1.54B
NovaSearch/stella_en_400M_v5	435M
nvidia/NV-Embed-v2	7.85B
sentence-transformers/all-MiniLM-L12-v1	33.4M
sentence-transformers/all-mpnet-base-v2	109M
thenlper/gte-large	335M
sentence-transformers/gtr-t5-xxl	4.86B

R3 **Retention of data.**: All alerts must remain accessible, regardless of their cluster assignability. The system should preserve outliers during analysis rather than forcing them into inappropriate clusters. Otherwise, important information might be either missed, due to being assigned to an outlier cluster or simply confuses personnel if found in wrong clusters. Either case would diminish the benefits of clustering the data due to lost trust in the system. This requirement aligns with information overload reduction by enabling a discrete outlier cluster for manual review, rather than discarding or misclassifying these data points.

R4 **Runtime performance.**: While not the primary optimization target, the system must complete clustering operations on new data and present results within an operationally acceptable timeframe, defined here as several minutes. The system might be run on-demand by CSIRT personnel in preparation of the daily inbound information review.

3.3 Embeddings, Clustering, and Evaluation

For the embedding process, we evaluate a diverse range of locally deployable LLMs. The selected models span from lightweight architectures with 33.4M parameters (all-MiniLM-L12-v1) to large-scale models with 7.85B parameters (NV-Embed-v2) [6, 15, 22, 23, 30, 31, 35, 45, 46]. We perform all embeddings using *sentence-transformers* [35] with the models enumerated in Table 2, utilizing computing infrastructure equipped with either NVidia A100 or NVidia H100

Table 3. Overview of used cluster algorithms, a short explanation, and the used parameters. If no parameter setting is displayed, we use the defaults selected by ClustPy [21], otherwise n_c is $n\_cluster$, m_s is $min\_samples$, and mp is $metric = precomputed$.

Algorithm	Description	Params
Partition-based Clustering		
K-Means [47]	Derive k clusters form centroid-based approach by minimizing within-cluster variance	n_c = 12
BF-K-Means	Bruteforce K-Means to find $k \in \left[2, \left\lceil \sqrt{|c|} \right\rceil \right]$ such that the silhouette score reaches a maximum (c is the dataset)	
SpecialK [11]	Determining optimal num. of clusters with probabilistic method to assess if clusters originate from a single distribution	
SkinnyDip [25]	Noise-robust clustering algorithm designed for datasets with up to 80 % noise, using Hartigan's dip test of unimodality and recursive univariate projection analysis	
Hierarchical Clustering		
Agg.-Clust. [33]	Hierarchical bottom-up clustering merging closest data points, creating cluster hierarchy via dendrogram	n_c = 12
Density-based Clustering		
DBSCAN [8]	Clusters dense regions separated by low-density areas. Robust to outliers, discovers arbitrarily shaped clusters	eps = 0.5 m_s = 2 mp
OPTICS [3]	Advanced density-based clustering handling varying cluster densities. Creates reachability plot for comprehensive structure analysis	m_s = 5 mp
Deep Clustering		
DKM [29]	Jointly learn data representations and cluster assignments through reparametrization for k-Means relying on gradient descent	n_c = 12
DDC [36]	Two-stage density-based image cluster framework using convolutional autoencoder and t-SNE for low dim. and density-based clustering	
DipEncoder [19]	Coupling the Hartigan's unsupervised Dip-test with an autoencoder to obtain cluster embeddings	n_c = 12
N2D [27]	Learns autoencoded embedding, uses UMAP for manifold learning, and applies shallow clustering algorithms	n_c = 12
DeepECT [26]	Builds cluster tree in embedding space, which allows selecting the number of clusters afterwards	
DEC [44]	Neural network clustering with iterative representation and cluster refinement	n_c = 12
DipDECK [20]	Advanced deep clustering with disentangled representation approach	

GPUs. Initial attempts to generate the embeddings on an Apple M4 system with 24 GB memory proved insufficient due to memory constraints.

Our clustering methodology incorporates algorithms from four major categories: *partition-based clustering, density-based clustering, hierarchical clustering,* and *deep clustering* [47], selected based on their prevalence, operational characteristics (*e.g.,* arbitrary cluster shape detection, parameter complexity), and MTEB ranking[1]. We prioritize algorithmic simplicity to assess performance

---

[1] https://huggingface.co/spaces/mteb/leaderboard.

under minimal parameter optimization. This approach aligns with *R2*, enabling CSIRTs to focus on core responsibilities without extensive hyperparameter tuning. Table 3 provides a comprehensive overview of the selected clustering algorithms. To evaluate the requirements *R2* and *R4* regarding operational burden and runtime performance, we conduct the clustering experiments on an Apple M4 system with 24 GB memory. This represents a worst-case scenario using consumer hardware, below typical CSIRT infrastructure capabilities.

The evaluation framework employs exclusively external metrics for two fundamental reasons. First, internal metrics introduce inherent bias when comparing diverse clustering algorithms, as certain algorithms optimize specific internal criteria (*e.g.*, K-Means for silhouette coefficient). Second, intrinsic evaluation metrics assess cluster morphology rather than semantic accuracy relative to ground truth. For CSIRT applications, semantic cohesion within clusters is paramount to prevent analytical confusion and redundant verification. We adopt the external metrics proposed by Rosenberg and Hirschberg [39]: *homogeneity*, *completeness*, and *V-measure*, with primary emphasis on *homogeneity*. Homogeneity $h \in [0,1] \subseteq \mathbb{R}$ quantifies intra-cluster uniformity, achieving its maximum of 1 when clusters perfectly align with ground truth [39]. While completeness $c \in [0,1] \subseteq \mathbb{R}$ measures object distribution across clusters, our focus on precision renders this metric secondary. V-measure $V_\beta = \frac{(1+\beta)hc}{(\beta*h)+c} \subseteq \mathbb{R}$ combines these metrics through their harmonic mean, reaching 1 for optimal clustering. We set $\beta = 0$, effectively reducing V-measure to homogeneity, prioritizing semantic consistency for CSIRT operations.

Our comprehensive evaluation encompasses 14 embedding models, 14 clustering algorithms across 5 datasets, measuring 8 distinct metrics while prioritizing *homogeneity*. Additional captured metrics include: *completeness*, *V-measure*, *silhouette coefficient*, *Adjusted Rand Index*, *Calinski-Harabasz index*, *Davies-Bouldin index*, and *runtime performance*. All metrics represent averages across 5 consecutive iterations, totaling 4 900 distinct experimental configurations.

4   Evaluation

Our evaluation methodology comprises three primary components. First, we analyze clustering performance across three distinct dataset categories: (i) CTI datasets, (ii) SBRs, and (iii) general short message data (UCI's SMS dataset). Second, we assess computational efficiency through runtime analysis of both embedding generation and clustering operations. Finally, we correlate these findings with our research questions and established requirements in the subsequent section.

4.1   Clustering Performance

Our analysis encompasses 196 distinct cluster-embedding combinations for each dataset, with results averaged across 5 consecutive executions. Clustering performance exhibits significant variation correlated with ground truth cluster car-

Table 4. Evaluation of the datasets sorted by homogeneity (H) with ranking (#). It shows the used evaluation combination: clustering algorithm (Algorithm), embedding model (Model), and metrics. The columns denote homogeneity (H), completeness (C), V-measure (V-M), Silhouette coefficient (Sil), Adjusted Rand Index (ARI), Calinski-Harabasz index (CH), Davies-Bouldin index (DB), runtime in seconds (t [s]), and number of predicted clusters (#C), respectively. Results are sorted in descending order by homogeneity ($\downarrow$). After the evaluation we evaluated the THREATREPORT dataset with the parameters $n\_clusters = 60$, denoted as THREATREPORT-60.

	Algorithm	Model	H $\downarrow$	C	V-M	Sil	ARI	CH	DB	t [s]	#C
	CYSECALERT (GT: $|c| = 13\,306$, #C = 2)					Use-case I (Threat Messages)					
1	K-Means	NV-Embed-v2	0.61	0.10	0.17	0.01	0.04	177.35	5.27	2.75	12.0
2	BF-KM	NV-Embed-v2	0.59	0.11	0.19	0.01	0.04	240.24	5.42	1.65	8.0
3	K-Means	stella_en_400M_v5	0.55	0.09	0.15	0.02	0.04	205.96	4.82	0.84	12.0
4	K-Means	stella_en_1.5b_v5	0.54	0.09	0.15	-0.01	0.03	212.45	4.85	0.88	12.0
5	BF-KM	stella_en_400M_v5	0.54	0.10	0.17	0.02	0.05	280.10	4.99	0.61	8.0
	MSE (GT: $|c| = 3\,001$, #C = 2)					Use-case I (Threat Messages)					
1	OPTICS	llama-3.2-1b	0.49	0.10	0.17	0.26	0.03	16.87	1.43	3.99	156.0
2	OPTICS	all-minilm-l12-v2	0.48	0.10	0.17	0.24	0.03	17.20	1.41	4.04	150.0
3	OPTICS	all-mpnet-base-v2	0.45	0.10	0.16	0.21	0.03	16.81	1.40	3.99	145.0
4	OPTICS	NV-Embed-v2	0.45	0.10	0.16	0.17	0.02	13.74	1.53	4.01	161.0
5	OPTICS	gte-base-en-v15	0.45	0.11	0.17	0.20	0.03	16.53	1.39	3.96	135.0
	THREATREPORT (GT: $|c| = 461$, #C = 39)					Use-case I (Threat Messages)					
1	DDC	gte-base-en-v15	0.34	0.30	0.32	0.02	0.03	6.90	2.26	2.90	30.4
2	DDC	all-minilm-l12-v2	0.33	0.29	0.31	-0.01	0.02	6.88	2.08	2.54	34.0
3	OPTICS	gte-large	0.32	0.34	0.33	0.08	0.05	9.28	2.16	0.10	23.0
4	OPTICS	stella_en_1.5b_v5	0.31	0.36	0.34	0.01	0.06	7.67	2.01	0.14	25.0
5	OPTICS	gte-base-en-v15	0.31	0.35	0.33	0.08	0.06	7.50	2.07	0.12	25.0
	THREATREPORT-*60* (GT: $|c| = 461$, #C = 39)					Use-case I (Threat Messages)					
1	Agg.-Clust.	gte-base-en-v15	0.51	0.33	0.40	0.27	0.02	9.26	1.65	0.03	60
2	Agg.-Clust.	all-mpnet-base-v2	0.50	0.33	0.40	0.27	0.02	10.59	1.55	0.03	60
3	Agg.-Clust.	stella_en_400M_v5	0.50	0.33	0.40	0.28	0.02	10.91	1.46	0.04	60
4	N2D	gte-base-en-v15	0.50	0.32	0.39	0.20	0.01	7.38	1.99	2.92	60
5	Agg.-Clust.	gtr-t5-xxl	0.50	0.32	0.39	0.26	0.02	9.25	1.63	0.02	60
	Security bug report (GT: $|c| = 5\,000$, #C = 5)					Use-case II (Product Security)					
1	DEC	stella_en_1.5b_v5	0.88	0.63	0.74	0.02	0.64	91.20	4.94	39.66	12.0
2	DKM	stella_en_1.5b_v5	0.87	0.62	0.72	-0.07	0.61	87.08	5.59	33.41	12.0
3	DeepECT	stella_en_1.5b_v5	0.86	0.47	0.61	-0.00	0.35	62.77	5.06	68.39	20.0
4	DEC	stella_en_400M_v5	0.86	0.60	0.71	0.02	0.60	96.50	6.44	39.52	12.0
5	DEC	gte-base-en-v15	0.84	0.58	0.68	0.04	0.57	93.44	4.97	34.88	12.0
	SMS (GT: $|c| = 5\,574$, #C = 2)					Use-case III (Generalization)					
1	K-Means	NV-Embed-v2	0.89	0.15	0.25	0.02	0.06	78.78	4.73	2.42	12.0
2	DKM	NV-Embed-v2	0.88	0.46	0.60	0.01	0.76	38.83	5.90	64.98	12.0
3	BF-KM	NV-Embed-v2	0.88	0.18	0.29	0.03	0.09	103.05	4.95	1.22	8.0
4	DDC	NV-Embed-v2	0.88	0.24	0.37	0.01	0.27	77.20	4.76	53.21	8.8
5	D.-Enc.	NV-Embed-v2	0.88	0.14	0.24	0.02	0.05	71.92	5.44	159.85	12.0

Table 5. Runtime results using the mean value of a total of 5 iterations for all datasets.

	K-Means	Agg.-Clust.	OPTICS	BF-K-Means	SkinnyDip	DDC	DEC	DeepECT	DipDECK	DipEncoder	DKM	N2D	DBSCAN	SpecialK
					CYSECALERT (GT: $|c| = 13\,306$, #C = 2)—Use-case I (Threat Messages)									
Min	0.54	8.08	302.67	0.40	0.06	76.83	92.82	180.59	56.18	219.19	78.87	73.20	–	–
Max	4.30	80.28	313.88	2.94	0.40	131.88	184.92	377.33	186.90	344.12	174.94	133.67	–	–
Mean	1.51	37.04	307.16	1.09	0.18	95.09	123.81	236.20	113.20	265.79	109.43	92.34	–	–
					MSE (GT: $|c| = 3\,001$, #C = 2)—Use-case I (Threat Messages)									
Min	0.11	0.45	3.96	0.07	1.05	14.40	17.65	38.47	27.49	55.66	15.43	15.07	0.07	–
Max	1.26	4.02	4.25	1.05	13.16	28.29	41.53	111.69	58.35	85.04	37.79	28.87	0.10	–
Mean	0.45	1.80	4.03	0.32	5.42	19.39	26.34	55.90	35.69	67.15	23.04	19.63	0.08	–
					THREATREPORT (GT: $|c| = 461$, #C = 39)—Use-case I (Threat Messages)									
Min	0.04	0.01	0.10	0.04	0.09	2.54	3.42	3.68	6.90	6.02	2.53	2.73	0.00	–
Max	0.32	0.15	0.20	0.21	1.31	4.78	8.15	15.24	14.11	12.07	6.50	5.94	0.00	–
Mean	0.11	0.06	0.13	0.08	0.48	3.37	4.88	8.57	9.25	8.38	4.02	3.59	0.00	–
					Security bug report (GT: $|c| = 5\,000$, #C = 5)—Use-case II (Product Security)									
Min	0.15	1.13	16.38	0.12	–	25.29	31.93	61.09	21.89	91.79	27.46	25.26	–	–
Max	0.74	2.99	17.33	1.17	–	30.70	39.66	88.85	48.51	105.60	33.83	29.55	–	–
Mean	0.37	2.36	16.99	0.34	–	28.24	36.80	70.54	36.37	95.85	31.33	28.09	–	–
					SMS (GT: $|c| = 5\,574$, #C = 2)—Use-case III (Generalization)									
Min	0.25	1.38	140.46	0.16	0.03	29.14	35.31	76.86	42.70	107.83	29.81	27.18	1.28	4.20
Max	2.49	13.43	176.86	1.59	1.01	55.41	78.64	176.91	94.06	171.19	73.11	58.07	1.44	21.56
Mean	0.92	6.70	149.56	0.69	0.34	39.96	54.16	112.33	64.32	128.59	46.51	40.02	1.39	13.83

dinality and dataset dimensionality. Table 4 presents the five highest-performing cluster-embedding combinations per dataset.

Partition-based clustering methodologies demonstrate superior performance on the CYSECALERT dataset. Model capacity shows limited correlation with performance, as evidenced by comparable results between *NV-Embed-v2* (7.85B parameters) and *stella_en_400M_v5* (435M parameters). While homogeneity metrics achieve a maximum of 0.61, additional metrics indicate significant cluster overlap. Completeness remains below 0.11, yielding a maximum V-measure of 0.19. Silhouette coefficient, Adjusted Rand Index, and Calinski-Harabasz index collectively indicate suboptimal cluster separation. The optimal configuration generates 12 clusters, achieving a 99.91 % reduction in dataset cardinality.

For the MSE dataset, density-based clustering, specifically OPTICS, achieves optimal performance. Homogeneity reaches 0.49, with superior performance from models below 1.24B parameters (Llama-3.2-1B) to 33M parameters. Auxiliary metrics suggest cluster overlap challenges, while achieving 94.80 % input reduction.

The THREATREPORT dataset exhibits optimal performance with deep and density-based clustering, achieving maximum homogeneity of 0.34. These results indicate insufficient performance for production deployment, necessitating enhanced fine-tuning procedures. Supplementary metrics corroborate suboptimal clustering performance. Despite achieving 93.41 % dimensional reduction, the clustering quality remains inadequate for operational deployment.

Deep clustering demonstrates superior performance on the SBR dataset, with *stella* models cf. Table 2 achieving homogeneity exceeding 0.86. This performance suggests that large-scale models like *NV-Embed-v2* are not prerequisite for optimal embedding generation. The configuration achieves 99.76 % dimensional reduction while maintaining high homogeneity. However, auxiliary metrics

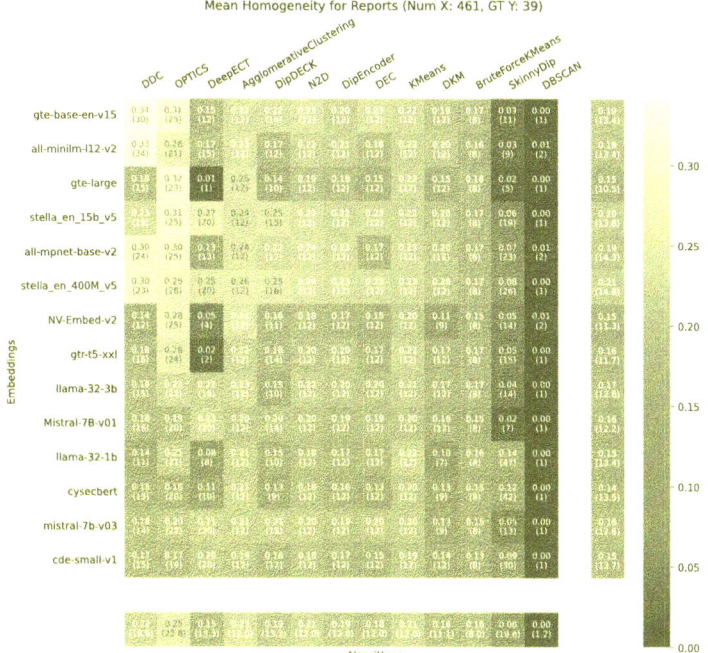

(a) Mean homogeneity of the THREATREPORT dataset.

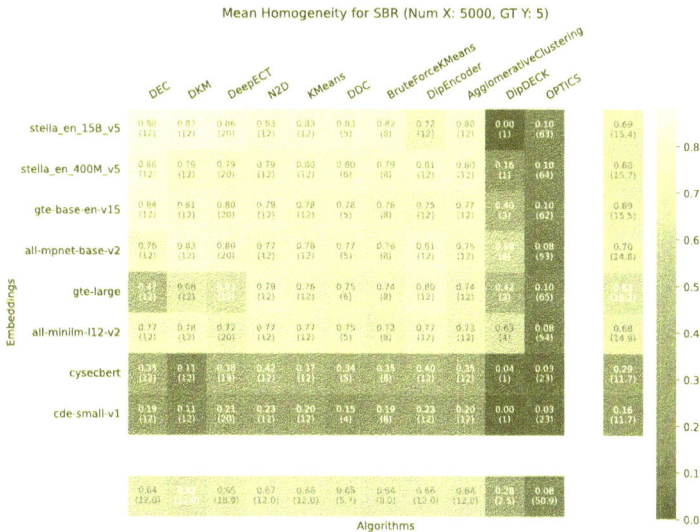

(b) Mean homogeneity of the SBR dataset.

Fig. 1. Result of the best and worst performing security related datasets with regard to the mean homogeneity over 5 consecutive runs. Columns show the clustering algorithms and rows the used embeddings. The separated column and row depict the mean over each column and row, respectively. The models and algorithms are sorted by the rows/columns sum (descending), such that the top left shows the highest result, while the bottom right shows the worst. Embeddings or clustering methods omitted did not run on the selected hardware.

indicate persistent cluster overlap challenges, with silhouette coefficients approximating 0.

For the general-purpose SMS dataset, partition-based and deep clustering algorithms paired with *NV-Embed-v2* achieve optimal performance. K-Means clustering achieves 99.78 % input reduction with exceptional homogeneity exceeding 0.88 across top-five configurations. However, secondary metrics continue to indicate cluster overlap challenges. Figure 1 depicts the best and worst performing security related datasets.

4.2   Runtime Performance

Runtime analysis encompasses both embedding generation and clustering operations, measured in seconds. Both phases demonstrate acceptable computational efficiency *cf.* Tables 4 and 6. Embedding generation peaks at 287 s for the CYSE-CALERT dataset, while requiring only 80 s for the SMS dataset. The CYSE-CALERT dataset exhibits minimum embedding time of 14.31 s with mean execution time of 84.15 s. When combined with clustering operations, DipEncoder requires maximum 344.12 s, while K-Means achieves optimal performance in 4.3 s, yielding total pipeline execution under 300 s. Comparable performance characteristics are observed across optimal cluster-embedding combinations: MSE achieves maximal runtime of 235 s (embed + OPTICS), THREATREPORT requires 220 s (embed + DDC), SBR completes in 300 s (embed + DeepECT), and SMS processing concludes in 155 s (embed + DKM).

Table 6. Tabular display of runtime statistics of embedding the different datasets.

Dataset	Min	Max	Mean	Median	Std
CYSECALERT	14.31	287.40	84.15	48.58	93.60
MSE	5.01	230.32	51.72	17.86	68.36
THREATREPORT	4.05	215.21	55.26	24.90	75.88
SBR	11.18	210.71	68.47	40.83	63.69
SMS	7.28	80.53	32.89	23.86	27.44

5   Discussion

This research evaluates the efficacy of clustering methods in mitigating information overload for CSIRT personnel. Our research question "Which cluster algorithm and embedding combination is suitable to reduce CERT personnel's information overload?" can be answered with qualified success.

Evaluation Results. No single combination universally excels across all CTI datasets, though several configurations show promising results. For immediate operational deployment, deep clustering combined with *stella* models achieves optimal performance on SBR data (homogeneity 0.88), while partition-based clustering with *NV-Embed-v2* performs well on general security data (CYSECALERT, homogeneity 0.61). The THREATREPORT dataset achieves only 0.34 homogeneity with default parameters, but subsequent analysis with adjusted parameters (n_clusters = 60 versus default 12) yields substantially improved results exceeding 0.5 homogeneity. The SBR dataset demonstrates exceptional potential with homogeneity exceeding 0.88, though cluster structure remains complex (silhouette scores approximating 0). Deep clustering methodologies effectively address these structural challenges. Our methodology generalizes well, evidenced by SMS dataset homogeneity nearing 0.9.

Requirements Fulfillment. All evaluated algorithms achieve data reduction exceeding 90 %, directly addressing requirement *R1* for information overload mitigation. Even with adjusted parameters, the THREATREPORT dataset maintains reduction rates above 86.98 %. The simplified configuration aligns with requirement *R2*, reducing operational burden while preserving original data points *R3*. Runtime performance satisfies requirement *R4*, with complete processing requiring approximately 5 min, potentially saving a single CSIRT over 3 750 h annually ($\sim$ 250 business days $\times$ 1.5 h) based on respondents' reported daily workload [16].

Implications. These findings suggest clustering offers domain-specific utility (*e.g.*, security bug report), while CSIRT applications may require algorithmic fine-tuning or careful dataset curation. This efficiency allows CSIRT personnel to preserve operational capacity for core infrastructure security responsibilities.

5.1 Limitations and Future Work

Our methodology exhibits several key limitations. Parameter optimization was intentionally omitted to align with requirement *R2*, though results suggest its necessity for heterogeneous CTI report processing. Our evaluation methodology is constrained by the limited number of consecutive runs (5), hardware restrictions (Apple M4, 24 GB memory), and consistently poor cluster separation indicated by silhouette scores approximating 0.

Dataset limitations include potential bias in the labeled THREATREPORT dataset and significant performance sensitivity to cluster count parameters (12 versus 60 clusters). While achieving high dimensional reduction (beyond 90 %), the long-term impact of false negatives on CSIRT operations remains unevaluated. Additionally, we excluded domain-specific features (*e.g.*, CVE ids, OWASP classifications) and foundational models (*e.g.*, Claude, DeepSeek, GPT) from our analysis.

Future work should address these limitations through expanded stability analysis, alternative distance metrics, systematic parameter sensitivity evaluation, and integration of domain-specific features while maintaining operational simplicity. The exploration of multilingual capabilities and assessment of false negative impact on operational efficiency present additional research opportunities.

6   Conclusion

This work investigated the application of clustering algorithms for reducing information overload in CSIRT operations. Through comprehensive evaluation of 196 cluster-embedding combinations across five datasets, we demonstrate that clustering can effectively reduce information processing requirements by over 90 % while maintaining semantic coherence. However, optimal performance requires careful selection of clustering approaches based on specific data characteristics.

Deep clustering combined with *stella* models demonstrates superior performance for structured security data (SBR, hom. 0.84), while partition-based clustering with *NV-Embed-v2* excels for general advisory content (CySecAlert, hom. 0.61). The more complex ThreatReport dataset requires parameter adjustment to achieve acceptable performance (hom. highlighting the need for domain-specific tuning. Runtime performance remains consistently efficient, with complete processing requiring around five minutes. Such a tool would save security staff precious time to perform more pressing tasks, which would ultimately improve the overall security stance of organizations.

While our evaluation demonstrates the potential for information overload reduction with clustering, several challenges remain. Future work should address cluster separation optimization, systematic parameter tuning, and integration of domain-specific features while maintaining operational simplicity. Despite these limitations, our findings suggest that clustering approaches, when properly configured, can significantly enhance CSIRT operational efficiency without compromising analytical integrity.

Acknowledgement. This work was supported by the German Federal Ministry for Education and Research (BMBF) in the project CYWARN (13N15407) and German Federal Ministry of Education and Research and the Hessian Ministry of Higher Education, Research, Science and the Arts within their joint support of the National Research Center for Applied Cybersecurity ATHENE.

The authors gratefully acknowledge the computing time provided to them on the high-performance computer Lichtenberg at the NHR Centers NHR4CES at TU Darmstadt. This is funded by the Federal Ministry of Education and Research, and the state governments participating on the basis of the resolutions of the GWK for national high performance computing at universities.

References

1. Almeida, T., Hidalgo, J.: SMS Spam Collection (2012). https://doi.org/10.24432/C5CC84

2. Anastasiadis, M., Aivatoglou, G., Spanos, G., Voulgaridis, A., Votis, K.: Combining text analysis techniques with unsupervised machine learning methodologies for improved software vulnerability management. In: CSR, pp. 273–278 (2022). https://doi.org/10.1109/CSR54599.2022.9850314

3. Ankerst, M., Breunig, M.M., Kriegel, H.P., Sander, J.: OPTICS: ordering points to identify the clustering structure. ACM SIGMOD Rec. **28**, 49–60 (1999). https://doi.org/10.1145/304181.304187

4. Basyurt, A.S., Fromm, J., Kuehn, P., Kaufhold, M.A., Mirabaie, M.: Help Wanted - Challenges in Data Collection, Analysis and Communication of Cyber Threats in Security Operation Centers. In: WI (2022)

5. Bayer, M., Frey, T., Reuter, C.: Multi-level fine-tuning, data augmentation, and few-shot learning for specialized cyber threat intelligence. Comput. Secur. **134**, 103430 (2023). https://doi.org/10.1016/j.cose.2023.103430

6. Bayer, M., Kuehn, P., Shanehsaz, R., Reuter, C.: CySecBERT: a domain-adapted language model for the cybersecurity domain. ACM Trans. Privacy Secur. (2024). https://doi.org/10.1145/3652594

7. Devlin, J., Chang, M.W., Lee, K., Toutanova, K.: BERT: pre-training of deep bidirectional transformers for language understanding. NORD'19 **1**, 4171–4186 (2018). https://doi.org/10.18653/v1/N19-1423

8. Ester, M., Kriegel, H.P., Sander, J., Xu, X.: A density-based algorithm for discovering clusters in large spatial databases with noise. In: Proceedings of the Second International Conference on Knowledge Discovery and Data Mining, pp. 226–231. AAAI Press (1996)

9. Gorzelak, K., Grudziecki, T., Jacewicz, P., Jaroszewski, P., Juszczyk, L, Kijews, P.: Proactive Detection of Network Security Incidents. Tech. rep, European Union Agency for Cybersecurity (2011)

10. Gove, R.: Automatic narrative summarization for visualizing cyber security logs and incident reports. IEEE Trans. Visual Comput. Graphics **28**, 1182–1190 (2022). https://doi.org/10.1109/TVCG.2021.3114843

11. Hess, S., Duivesteijn, W.: k is the magic number—inferring the number of clusters through nonparametric concentration inequalities. In: Brefeld, U., Fromont, E., Hotho, A., Knobbe, A., Maathuis, M., Robardet, C. (eds.) ECML PKDD 2019. LNCS (LNAI), vol. 11906, pp. 257–273. Springer, Cham (2020). https://doi.org/10.1007/978-3-030-46150-8_16

12. Hinchy, E.: Voice of the SOC Analyst. Tech. rep, Tines (2022)

13. Ignaczak, L., Goldschmidt, G., Costa, C.A.D., Righi, R.D.R.: Text mining in cybersecurity: a systematic literature review. ACM Comput. Surv. **54**, 140:1–140:36 (2021).https://doi.org/10.1145/3462477

14. ISACA: Companies' cybersecurity staffing worldwide in 2023 versus 2024. https://www.statista.com/statistics/1322073/cybersecurity-staffing-worldwide/ (2024)

15. Jiang, A.Q., et al.: Mistral 7B (2023). https://doi.org/10.48550/arXiv.2310.06825

16. Kaufhold, M.A., Riebe, T., Bayer, M., Reuter, C.: 'We do not have the capacity to monitor all media': a design case study on cyber situational awareness in computer emergency response teams. In: CHI'24, pp. 1–16. Association for Computing Machinery (2024). https://doi.org/10.1145/3613904.3642368

17. Kuehn, P., Bayer, M., Wendelborn, M., Reuter, C.: OVANA: an approach to analyze and improve the information quality of vulnerability databases. In: ARES'21, p. 11. ACM (2021). https://doi.org/10.1145/3465481.3465744
18. Le Sceller, Q., Karbab, E.B., Debbabi, M., Iqbal, F.: SONAR: automatic detection of cyber security events over the Twitter stream. In: ARES'17, pp. 1–11. ACM (2017). https://doi.org/10.1145/3098954.3098992
19. Leiber, C., Bauer, L.G.M., Neumayr, M., Plant, C., Böhm, C.: The DipEncoder: enforcing multimodality in autoencoders. In: Proceedings of the 28th ACM SIGKDD Conference on Knowledge Discovery and Data Mining, pp. 846–856. Association for Computing Machinery (2022). https://doi.org/10.1145/3534678.3539407
20. Leiber, C., Bauer, L.G.M., Schelling, B., Böhm, C., Plant, C.: Dip-based deep embedded clustering with k-estimation. In: Proceedings of the 27th ACM SIGKDD Conference on Knowledge Discovery & Data Mining, pp. 903–913. Association for Computing Machinery (2021). https://doi.org/10.1145/3447548.3467316
21. Leiber, C., Miklautz, L., Plant, C., Böhm, C.: Benchmarking deep clustering algorithms with ClustPy. In: ICDMW, pp. 625–632 (2023). https://doi.org/10.1109/ICDMW60847.2023.00087
22. Li, Z., Zhang, X., Zhang, Y., Long, D., Xie, P., Zhang, M.: Towards General Text Embeddings with Multi-stage Contrastive Learning (2023). https://doi.org/10.48550/arXiv.2308.03281
23. Liu, Z., et al.: SpinQuant: LLM quantization with learned rotations (2024). https://doi.org/10.48550/arXiv.2405.16406
24. Lloyd, S.: Least squares quantization in PCM. IEEE Trans. Inf. Theory **28**, 129–137 (1982). https://doi.org/10.1109/TIT.1982.1056489
25. Maurus, S., Plant, C.: Skinny-dip: clustering in a sea of noise. In: Proceedings of the 22nd ACM SIGKDD International Conference on Knowledge Discovery and Data Mining, pp. 1055–1064. Association for Computing Machinery (2016). https://doi.org/10.1145/2939672.2939740
26. Mautz, D., Plant, C., Böhm, C.: Deep embedded cluster tree. In: ICDM, pp. 1258–1263 (2019). https://doi.org/10.1109/ICDM.2019.00157
27. McConville, R., Santos-Rodríguez, R., Piechocki, R.J., Craddock, I.: N2D: (Not Too) deep clustering via clustering the local manifold of an autoencoded embedding. In: ICPR, pp. 5145–5152 (2021). https://doi.org/10.1109/ICPR48806.2021.9413131
28. Milosevic, N., Dehghantanha, A., Choo, K.: Machine learning aided Android malware classification. Comput. Electr. Eng. **61**, 266–274 (2017). https://doi.org/10.1016/j.compeleceng.2017.02.013
29. Moradi Fard, M., Thonet, T., Gaussier, E.: Deep k-means: jointly clustering with k-means and learning representations. Pattern Recogn. Lett. **138**, 185–192 (2020). https://doi.org/10.1016/j.patrec.2020.07.028
30. Moreira, G.d.S.P., Osmulski, R., Xu, M., Ak, R., Schifferer, B., Oldridge, E.: NV-Retriever: Improving text embedding models with effective hard-negative mining (2024). https://doi.org/10.48550/arXiv.2407.15831
31. Morris, J.X., Rush, A.M.: Contextual Document Embeddings (2024). https://doi.org/10.48550/arXiv.2410.02525
32. Muennighoff, N., Tazi, N., Magne, L., Reimers, N.: MTEB: Massive Text Embedding Benchmark (2023). https://doi.org/10.48550/arXiv.2210.07316
33. Nielsen, F.: Hierarchical clustering. In: Nielsen, F. (ed.) Introduction to HPC with MPI for Data Science, pp. 195–211. Springer International Publishing (2016). https://doi.org/10.1007/978-3-319-21903-5_8

34. Preuveneers, D., Joosen, W.: Privacy-preserving polyglot sharing and analysis of confidential cyber threat intelligence. In: ARES'22, pp. 1–11. Association for Computing Machinery (2022). https://doi.org/10.1145/3538969.3538982

35. Reimers, N., Gurevych, I.: Sentence-BERT: sentence embeddings using siamese BERT-networks. In: Inui, K., Jiang, J., Ng, V., Wan, X. (eds.) EMNLP-IJCNLP, pp. 3982–3992. Association for Computational Linguistics (2019). https://doi.org/10.18653/v1/D19-1410

36. Ren, Y., Wang, N., Li, M., Xu, Z.: Deep density-based image clustering. Knowl.-Based Syst. **197**, 105841 (2020). https://doi.org/10.1016/j.knosys.2020.105841

37. Rendón, E., Abundez, I., Arizmendi, A., Quiroz, E.M.: Internal versus external cluster validation indexes. Int. J. Comput. Commun. **5**, 27–34 (2011)

38. Riebe, T., et al.: CySecAlert: an alert generation system for cyber security events using open source intelligence data. In: Gao, D., Li, Q., Guan, X., Liao, X. (eds.) ICICS 2021. LNCS, vol. 12918, pp. 429–446. Springer, Cham (2021). https://doi.org/10.1007/978-3-030-86890-1_24

39. Rosenberg, A., Hirschberg, J.: V-measure: a conditional entropy-based external cluster evaluation measure. In: EMNLP-CoNLL, pp. 410–420. Association for Computational Linguistics (2007)

40. Rousseeuw, P.J.: Silhouettes: a graphical aid to the interpretation and validation of cluster analysis. J. Comput. Appl. Math. **20**, 53–65 (1987). https://doi.org/10.1016/0377-0427(87)90125-7

41. Sauerwein, C., Fischer, D., Rubsamen, M., Rosenberger, G., Stelzer, D., Breu, R.: From threat data to actionable intelligence: an exploratory analysis of the intelligence cycle implementation in cyber threat intelligence sharing platforms. In: ARES'21, pp. 1–9. Association for Computing Machinery (2021). https://doi.org/10.1145/3465481.3470048

42. Shu, R., Xia, T., Williams, L., Menzies, T.: Better Security Bug Report Classification via Hyperparameter Optimization (2019). https://doi.org/10.48550/arXiv.1905.06872

43. Skopik, F., Settanni, G., Fiedler, R.: A problem shared is a problem halved: a survey on the dimensions of collective cyber defense through security information sharing. C&S **60**, 154–176 (2016). https://doi.org/10.1016/j.cose.2016.04.003

44. Xie, J., Girshick, R., Farhadi, A.: Unsupervised deep embedding for clustering analysis. In: Proceedings of the 33rd International Conference on International Conference on Machine Learning - Volume 48, pp. 478–487. JMLR.org (2016)

45. Zhang, D., Li, J., Zeng, Z., Wang, F.: Jasper and Stella: distillation of SOTA embedding models (2025). https://doi.org/10.48550/arXiv.2412.19048

46. Zhang, X., et al.: mGTE: Generalized Long-Context Text Representation and Reranking Models for Multilingual Text Retrieval (2024). https://doi.org/10.48550/arXiv.2407.19669

47. Zong, C., Xia, R., Zhang, J.: Text Data Mining. Springer (2021). https://doi.org/10.1007/978-981-16-0100-2

Proceedings of the First International Workshop on Responsible Data Governance, Privacy, and Digital Transformation (RDGPT 2025)

RDGPT 2025 Preface

The First International Workshop on Responsible Data Governance, Privacy, and Digital Transformation was held on August 11–14, 2025 at Ghent, Belgium, in conjunction with the 20th International Conference on Availability, Reliability and Security (ARES 2025). Conceived as a forum for advancing both scholarship and practice, the workshop explored the pressing need to reconcile rapid digital innovation with rigorous accountability. Discussion ranged across data governance and evolving regulatory frameworks such as the GDPR and the EU AI Act, the design of ethical data-handling procedures and privacy-by-design architectures, emerging privacy-enhancing technologies and scalable privacy-management strategies, and the application of FAIR—Findable, Accessible, Interoperable and Reusable—principles to strengthen transparency and reproducibility. Contributors also examined how enterprise-level digital-transformation programmes can embed responsibility from the outset and how trustworthy, human-centred approaches to artificial intelligence can be realized in practice.

We invited authors to submit full manuscripts of up to 18 pages. For this inaugural edition, we received eight submissions, each assessed in a double-blind review by three independent experts from our interdisciplinary Program Committee. After this rigorous evaluation, four papers were accepted, yielding an acceptance rate of 50%. Guided by the reviewers' detailed feedback, the organising chairs selected these top-rated papers for oral presentation at the workshop and inclusion in the proceedings.

We extend our sincere thanks to every author for sharing their work, to the reviewers for their generous and timely evaluations, for their insights. We are also grateful to the ARES 2025 organizers for their unwavering support in hosting this inaugural edition of our workshop. Together we have taken an important step toward a future in which data-driven innovation proceeds hand-in-hand with privacy, fairness, and public trust.

August 2025

Mansoor Ahmed
Muhammad Irfan Khalid
Markus Helfert

RDGPT 2025 Organization

Workshop Chairs

Mansoor Ahmed   Maynooth University, Ireland
Muhammad Irfan Khalid   University of Agder, Norway
Markus Helfert   Maynooth University, Ireland

Program Committee

Farhan Safdar   Warsaw University of Technology, Poland
Aamir Anwar   University of Portsmouth, UK
Imtiaz Hussain   University of Management and
                                  Technology, Pakistan
Naveed Khan   Maynooth University, Ireland
Saif Ur Rehman Malik   Trinity College Dublin, Ireland
Tehreem Ashfaq   City St George's, University of London,
                                  UK
Syed Muhammad Usman   Bahria University Islamabad, Pakistan
Umair Yousuf   University of Calabria, Italy
Nadeem Yaqub   Beijing University of Technology, China
Azra Aryania   Maynooth University, Ireland

Behavior-Based Detection of Instagram Addiction Using Machine Learning: Accuracy and Privacy Implications

Monireh Hosseini[1], Shiva Parsarad[2(✉)], and Fatemeh Amirjani[3]

[1] K.N. Toosi University of Technology, Tehran, Iran
hosseini@kntu.ac.ir
[2] University of Basel, Basel, Switzerland
shiva.parsarad@unibas.ch
[3] University of Tehran, Tehran, Iran
fatemeh.amirjani@ut.ac.ir

Abstract. With the growing number of users on online social networks (OSNs), concerns about excessive usage and social media addiction are becoming increasingly serious. Addiction to social networks can negatively impact both physical and mental health over time. Instagram, as one of the most popular platforms, occupies a significant amount of users' time. As a result, developing methods for the automatic detection of social network addiction is essential. However, such methods also raise important privacy concerns. This paper demonstrates that it is possible to predict a user's likelihood of social media addiction solely based on their online behavior. A questionnaire based on the Bergen Social Media Addiction Scale (BSMAS) was designed and distributed to Iranian Instagram users. Profile and activity data were then collected from the respondents' pages and analyzed using machine learning algorithms, including Genetic Algorithm, Multi-Layer Perceptron (MLP),which is a type of neural network, and Support Vector Machine (SVM). Additionally, an autoencoder was used to extract key behavioral features, and its performance was compared with models trained on the original features. The results showed that the SVM with original features and the MLP with autoencoder-extracted features achieved the highest accuracy in classifying users as addicted or non-addicted. The findings indicate that social network addiction can be inferred from behavioral data alone, highlighting potential privacy risks. While behavioral analysis techniques are effective for addiction detection, they could also be misused to monitor users without their knowledge or consent.

Keywords: Online Social Network Addiction · BSMAS · Machine Learning

1 Introduction

Social networking sites (SNSs) such as Facebook and Instagram provide platforms that allow individuals to create public or private profiles within a defined

B. Coppens et al. (Eds.): ARES 2025 Workshops, LNCS 15995, pp. 161–173, 2025.
https://doi.org/10.1007/978-3-032-00633-2_10

system. These platforms have become increasingly popular, enabling users to connect with friends, build social networks, and rapidly share information. By facilitating instant communication and content sharing, SNSs have transformed the way people interact, socialize, and access information in both personal and professional contexts. Based on a survey [1],the trend toward using SNSs has increased annually across all age groups. SNSs offer a convenient way not only to manage existing social relationships but also to build new connections with others [2].

With the growing number of SNS users, problems associated with excessive use and addiction have become increasingly common. Studies have shown that active social network usage is positively linked to depression [3]. The American Journal of Psychiatry [4] has reported that the Social Network Media mmay lead to excessive use, depression, social withdrawal, and a range of negative consequences. Higher levels of social media dependency are associated with increased social media usage and online support activity [5]. There is growing evidence that social media addiction is an emerging problem [6], and internet companies often design mechanisms that increase user engagement, potentially leading to addiction and harm [7]. Unlike cigarettes, which do not adapt to become more addictive for each individual, social media platforms become increasingly addictive the more a person engages with them, tailoring their features to each user [7].

It is indicated [8,9] that adolescents suffering from a social network addiction are at a higher risk of suicidal ideation compared to non-addicted users. In 2020, a cross-sectional study [10] was conducted on 1000 students to examine social network addiction through an online survey. The results indicated that 42% of the participants were addicted to social networks. Additionally, a study investigated the relationship between social networking addiction and academic performance of students in Iran. Based on their findings, the findings revealed a significant negative correlation between social networking addiction and students' academic performance [11].

Both classic and modern approaches measure Internet and social media addiction. Classical methods typically rely on questionnaire-based assessments, while modern approaches incorporate AI-based techniques. AI-based approaches have gained significant attention in recent years for tracking and detecting the mental state of social network users. For example, in [12], deep learning algorithms are used to detect depression among Twitter users. Deep-learning techniques have been applied to automatically classify individuals' risk for alcohol, tobacco, and drug use based on the content from their Instagram profiles [13].

These studies demonstrate the potential of AI-based approaches to monitor user behavior on social media and predict mental health conditions such as depression and substance addiction. While such methods can serve as valuable tools for raising awareness and encouraging individuals to seek professional help, such as alerting users to their potential social media addiction or mental health risks, they also raise critical privacy concerns. The ability to infer sensitive psychological states from online activity presents ethical challenges, as such data could be misused or accessed without users' consent.

In this study, we examine the feasibility of predicting social network addiction based solely on users' behavioral data collected from Instagram, which is currently the second most popular social networking platform in the United States [14]. To this end, we apply and compare several machine learning models to analyze user interaction patterns and activity metrics. The results demonstrate that behavioral signals can serve as effective predictors of addiction, underscoring the potential of AI-driven techniques in identifying at-risk individuals. However, these findings also raise critical ethical concerns, particularly regarding user privacy and the potential misuse of behavioral data. Our work highlights the need for stringent privacy safeguards and the responsible use of predictive models in sensitive psychological contexts.

The remainder of the paper is organized as follows: Sect. 2 provides background on existing addiction assessment methods and prior mental state detection approaches. Section 3 outlines our methodology, including the data collection process, labeling criteria, and machine learning models used. Section 4 presents the experimental setup and results, followed by an analysis of privacy implications. Section 5 concludes the paper and highlights potential areas for future research, and an additional section outlines key limitations of our study.

2   Background

2.1   Social Network Addict Detection Methods

The Internet Addiction Test (IAT) [15], based on the Internet Addiction Diagnostic Questionnaire (IADQ) [16], consists of 20 items and was originally scored on a 5-point Likert scale ranging from "not applied" to "always". It was later modified to a 6-point scale by adding a response option: "does not apply." [15].

In [17], social networking site (SNS) addiction is measured in a sample of 402 participants using a modified version of Young's Internet Addiction Test (IAT). Eight questions are included to assess potential Internet addiction. A five-point Likert scale is used to rate an 18-item scale, where "1" indicates "rarely" and "5" indicates "always." Responses are categorized as "no" for ratings of 1 and 2 and "yes" for ratings of 3, 4, and 5. Participants who provided five or more "yes" responses are classified as addicted.

The Bergen Facebook Addiction Scale (BFAS) [18] consists of 18 items, with three items representing each of the six core features of addiction: salience, mood modification, tolerance, withdrawal, conflict, and relapse. Each item is rated on a five-point scale, ranging from 1 ("very rarely") to 5 ("very often"), with higher scores indicating greater Facebook addiction. BFAS is finalized with six core criteria, each representing one of the key elements of addiction: salience, mood modification, tolerance, withdrawal, conflict, and relapse. Within each category, the item with the highest corrected item-total correlation is retained in the final scale. Participants are asked to respond to each item using a five-point Likert scale: (1) very rarely, (2) rarely, (3) sometimes, (4) often, and (5) very often. A response of 4 or above on at least four items may indicate Facebook addiction.

A modified version of the BFAS is proposed in [19]. The primary change involves replacing "Facebook" with "social media," which is defined as platforms like Facebook, Twitter, and Instagram. The BSMAS follows the same five-point Likert scale, ranging from "very rarely" (1) to "very often" (5). Scoring "often" or "very often' on at least four items may suggest addictive social media behavior. In this paper, we use BSMAS to label our collected dataset.

2.2   Automatic Detection of User's Mental State

Various approaches have been proposed for the automatic detection of OSN users' mental states. Researchers in [20] have employed models such as BERT, RoBERTa, and XLNet to classify posts related to mental illnesses, including depression, anxiety, and bipolar disorder. These models are trained on large datasets to recognize subtle linguistic cues indicative of different mental health conditions. Similarly, in [21], pre-trained language models are fine-tuned on domain-specific datasets to improve the accuracy of mental health disorder prediction. This study demonstrated high classification performance, highlighting the effectiveness of transfer learning in detecting mental health conditions from social media posts.

While these approaches yield promising results, they require extensive amounts of labeled data for effective training and generalization. Additionally, deep learning models have a large number of parameters, making them more complex and susceptible to adversarial examples [22]–carefully crafted small perturbations that can fool the model. In contrast, traditional machine learning models such as SVM operate on simpler decision boundaries, making them generally less sensitive to such perturbations.

3   Methodology

This paper aims to investigate whether social media addiction can be detected using a limited number of data samples and simple methods for tracking user behavior on social media. In the following sections, we describe our data collection strategy and the methodologies employed in this study.

3.1   Data Collection

To collect data, a BSMAS-based questionnaire was distributed to a large number of active Iranian Instagram users. The questionnaire was initially sent to approximately 200 users via direct Instagram messages, and 80 individuals responded and completed the form. All participants were Iranian, both female and male, and over 18 years old. We invited participants to answer the BSMAS questions, defining an active user as someone who had recently posted or commented on Instagram.

Before participation, the purpose of the study was explained, and a URL link was provided directing users to a Google Form containing the questionnaire. Participants were assured that only statistical data retrieved from their publicly visible profiles would be used in the analysis and that their personal information would remain confidential and anonymized.

The BSMAS questions adapted for Instagram were as follows:

- Do you spend much time thinking about Instagram or planning how to use it?
- Do you feel an urge to use Instagram more and more?
- Do you use Instagram to forget about personal problems?
- Have you ever tried to cut down on your Instagram usage without success?
- Do you become restless or troubled if prohibited from using Instagram?
- Have you used Instagram so much that it has negatively impacted your job or studies?

Each question was answered on a five-point Likert scale, ranging from 1 ("Very rarely") to 5 ("Very often"). According to established BSMAS criteria, scoring "Often" or "Very often" on four or more items indicates addictive behavior. Based on BSMAS scores, users were classified as "normal" (non-addicted or 0) or "abnormal" (addicted or 1). A participant was labeled "addicted" if their response met the threshold of four or more items rated as "Often" or "Very often".

Next, we collected various profile and behavioral features from the respondents' Instagram pages. These features, referred to as secondary features, are detailed in Table 1. As a result, a total of 80 users participated, with 20% labeled as addicts and 80% as non-addicts. A view of the collected data is shown in Table 2.

Table 1. Feature Explanation Table

Feature	Explanation
Comment Average (CA20)	The average number of comments among the last 20 posts
Post/follower rate (Po/fwor)	Number of total posts to the number of total followers
Follower/following (fwor/folwing)	Number of followers to the number of total followings
Followers (#fwor)	Total number of followers (Po/folwing)
Post/following (Avg like 20)	Number of posts to the number of followings
Like Average (Avg like 20)	The average number of likes in the last 20 posts

3.2 Models

In this section, we discuss different models used for automating Instagram addiction detection. The general proposed idea of our approach is shown in Fig. 1.

Table 2. Overview of extracted Instagram behavioral features collected for each user. These features serve as input for model training and classification.

CA20	Po/fwor	fwor/folwing	#fwor	Po/folwing	Avg like 20
2	0.2	0.416	100	0.095	60
20	1.33	1.33	150	1.33	140
13	0.285	0.608	140	0.173	83
4	0.133	0.5	75	0.066	30
2	0.3	0.372	112	0.1	83
12	0.85	0.9	122	0.865	128
45	1.654	0.9	3672	1.2	154
3	0.1	0.2	10	0.02	14
15	0.987	0.768	110	0.97	22
12	0.234	0.564	170	0.545	87
57	1.8	0.765	1290	1.654	97
45	0.876	1.97	908	0.876	76

Neural Network (NN) based Approach We used a MLP model with a single hidden layer as our neural network-based approach. This simple architecture was chosen to evaluate whether user addiction states could be effectively predicted with a basic MLP. Additionally, given the limited size of our dataset, employing multiple layers could increase the risk of overfitting.

SVM Support-vector machines (SVMs) are supervised learning models with associated learning algorithms that analyze the data used for classification and regression analysis. In this study, we employed SVM with both linear and RBF kernels.

Genetic Algorithm A genetic algorithm is also applied to generate a set of detectors for addiction detection on Instagram users. The detectors are represented as chromosomes with numeric features. Our fitness function is defined as:

$$\text{fitness function} = a \cdot A - b \cdot B$$

, which:

- a: Correctly classified normal samples out of "A" total normal samples.
- b: Correctly classified abnormal samples out of "B" total abnormal samples.

Those fit detectors, selected based on their fitness function, undergo crossover and mutation to form a new population of detectors. In the end, we have a set of best-found detectors that can be used to detect the class of samples.

3.3   Feature Extraction

An autoencoder is a type of neural network designed to learn efficient representations of input data by reconstructing the input at the output layer. It consists of two main components: an encoder, which compresses the input into a lower-dimensional representation, and a decoder, which reconstructs the original input from this encoded representation.

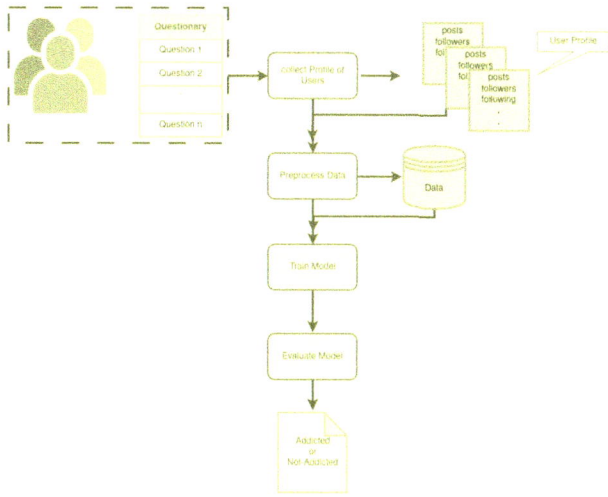

Fig. 1. Workflow of the proposed Instagram addiction detection model. It illustrates the flow from data preprocessing to classification using machine learning algorithms.

In this study, we first train an autoencoder using the training dataset. However, instead of utilizing the entire network for classification, we extract features from the encoder layers, effectively using the encoder as a feature selection mechanism. These extracted features are then fed into machine learning classifiers such as Multi-Layer Perceptron (MLP), as our neural network-based approach, and Support Vector Machine (SVM) to predict social media addiction. By leveraging the autoencoder for feature extraction, we aim to improve classification performance by capturing essential behavioral patterns in the data.

4 Experiments and Results

In this section, we present the experimental setup, implementation details, and results obtained from different machine learning models used for online social network addiction detection among Iranian Instagram users. The performance of each model is evaluated using standard classification metrics, including accuracy and F1-score.

4.1 Experimental Setup

The experiments are conducted using a dataset collected from 80 Iranian Instagram users, with addiction levels assessed using the Bergen Social Media Addiction Scale (BSMAS). Users are categorized as either addicts (abnormal) or non-addicts (normal) based on their responses. Additionally, Instagram activity features (e.g., comment frequency, likes, follower/following ratio) are extracted to supplement self-reported data. All models are implemented in Python, utilizing the following libraries:

– Scikit-learn: Support Vector Machine (SVM) implementation
– TensorFlow/Keras: Multilayer Perceptron (MLP) and Autoencoder
– NumPy and Pandas: Data preprocessing and management

Prior to training, all feature values are normalized using Min-Max scaling to ensure consistency in model input. No missing data imputation is needed. The dataset is shuffled before being split into training, validation, and test sets. We use 80% of the dataset for training and the remaining 20% for validation and testing. We report the performance by accuracy and the area under the receiver operating characteristic curve (ROC-AUC). We use ROC-AUC to focus on minority class performance. To address data imbalance, we use SMOTE or class weights. For each method, we evaluate a set of parameters to identify those that yielded the best performance.

4.2   Results Analysis

Table 3 presents the performance comparison of various machine learning models applied to the task of Instagram addiction detection. Performance is reported in terms of classification accuracy and ROC-AUC, which reflects the model's ability to distinguish between addicted and non-addicted users across thresholds.

Among the tested models, the MLP without autoencoder features achieved the highest accuracy (0.81), indicating strong classification capability based on the raw feature set. The MLP with autoencoder features yielded a balanced performance with both accuracy (0.68) and ROC-AUC (0.68), highlighting that dimensionality-reduced features extracted by the autoencoder contributed to improved generalization and threshold-independent performance.

SVM classifiers showed lower accuracy and ROC-AUC, particularly the SVM with a linear kernel (accuracy: 0.56, ROC-AUC: 0.38). The RBF kernel slightly improved accuracy (0.68) but not ROC-AUC. Interestingly, combining SVM with autoencoder features led to modest improvements in ROC-AUC (0.62) but did not significantly enhance accuracy.

Overall, the results suggest that neural network-based models, especially those leveraging autoencoder-derived features, outperform traditional SVM classifiers. While the raw feature MLP offers the highest accuracy, models incorporating autoencoder features provide more balanced and reliable performance, particularly in scenarios where ROC-AUC is critical.

The genetic algorithm was tested with three different parent selection methods: Roulette Wheel Selection, Tournament Selection, and Random Selection. The classification performance varied based on the mutation threshold. It was observed that Tournament selection achieved the best accuracy, and increasing the mutation threshold reduced false detections but also lowered detection sensitivity.

Autoencoder-based feature extraction did not lead to improved classification accuracy for either the MLP or SVM models. This may be attributed to the nature of autoencoders, which are generally more effective in high-dimensional

Table 3. Performance Comparison of Machine Learning Models

Classification Method	Accuracy	ROC-AUC
SVM (Linear Kernel)	0.56	0.38
SVM (RBF Kernel)	0.68	0.38
MLP with Autoencoder Features	0.68	0.68
MLP (without Autoencoder)	0.81	0.50
SVM with Autoencoder Features	0.57	0.62
Genetic Algorithm	0.48	0.52

feature spaces. In our case, the relatively low number of input features limits the autoencoder's ability to extract more informative representations.

Specifically, the SVM with autoencoder features performed worse than the standard SVM, both in terms of accuracy and ROC-AUC. Although the MLP with autoencoder features achieved a balanced performance and outperformed the SVM models, it still underperformed compared to the MLP trained directly on the original features.

To assess the statistical significance of our findings, we analyze the correlation between behavioral features and the binary addiction label. Pearson correlation coefficients are recalculated, and two-sample t-tests are conducted to evaluate the differences in feature distributions between addicted and non-addicted users.

Table 4. Correlation of behavioral features with Instagram addiction and statistical significance of group differences.

Feature	Correlation	Strength	p-value
CA20	0.50	Strong	< 0.001
Avg Like 20	0.47	Strong	< 0.001
#Followers	0.40	Moderate	< 0.001
Posts/Following	0.43	Moderate	< 0.001
Posts/Followers	0.38	Moderate	0.013
Followers/Following	0.12	Weak	0.15

The results are summarized in Table 4. Based on these results, most features correlate significantly with Instagram addiction, indicating meaningful behavioral differences between groups.

4.3   Privacy and Ethical Concerns

The ability to detect social media addiction using machine learning models presents both potential benefits and ethical risks. While such models can help raise awareness about problematic social media usage and facilitate timely intervention, they also introduce serious privacy concerns that must be carefully addressed.

Inference Without User Consent The proposed addiction detection system relies on behavioral data extracted from social media activity, such as comment frequency, likes, and follower-following ratios. This raises a fundamental concern: users may not be aware that their online behavior is being analyzed to infer sensitive psychological traits, such as addiction.

Unlike traditional self-reported questionnaires (e.g., BSMAS), where users voluntarily provide information about their social media habits, the machine learning approach can infer addiction without explicit consent. This lack of transparency violates informed consent principles and could lead to ethical concerns if used by third parties, such as employers, advertisers, or government agencies.

Misuse of Behavioral Data Behavioral data on social networks is often publicly accessible or obtainable through third-party applications. While the proposed model is intended for academic research and health awareness, similar techniques could be exploited for user profiling, surveillance, or targeted advertising.

- Corporations could use addiction detection algorithms to increase user engagement rather than to promote well-being. By identifying addicted users, social media platforms might optimize algorithms to further exploit addictive behaviors rather than mitigate them.
- Employers and financial institutions could potentially use inferred addiction scores in hiring decisions, loan approvals, or insurance policies, leading to discriminatory practices.
- Government agencies could apply these models for social monitoring and censorship, further compromising individual freedoms

Risk of Data Leakage and Security Breaches Machine learning models require large amounts of behavioral data to function effectively. If such datasets are not securely stored and handled, they become vulnerable to data breaches, hacking, and unauthorized access. The leakage of sensitive addiction-related data could expose users to public embarrassment, discrimination, or even mental distress. Therefore, strong data protection mechanisms must be implemented, including encryption, anonymization, and strict access controls to prevent misuse.

Algorithmic Bias and False Positives The model's classification accuracy, while high, is not perfect. Incorrect classification of non-addicted users as addicted (false positives) could have unintended consequences, such as unjustified interventions or wrongful profiling. Additionally, algorithmic bias–stemming from limited training data–could disproportionately affect certain demographic groups, leading to unfair outcomes. Ensuring fairness in addiction detection requires:

- Diverse and representative training data to minimize biases
- Transparency in algorithmic decision-making to allow users to understand and contest classifications.

5   Conclusion

The experimental results demonstrate that the Multi-Layer Perceptron (MLP) model trained on raw behavioral features outperformed all other models, achieving the highest classification accuracy (81

Although the MLP model utilizing autoencoder-extracted features demonstrated balanced performance across accuracy and ROC-AUC (both 0.68), it still underperformed compared to the raw-feature MLP in terms of accuracy. Traditional SVM models, whether using autoencoder features or not, showed lower performance overall, indicating that non-linear transformations or neural network architectures may be more suitable for this task.

These findings suggest that even with a limited dataset and relatively simple models, it is feasible to predict social media addiction based on observable user behavior. This supports the potential of behavioral data as an alternative to self-reported assessments for detecting excessive social media use.

However, while such AI-driven detection systems offer promise for early intervention, they also raise significant ethical and privacy concerns. Without careful regulation, these models may be misused for surveillance or infringe on user autonomy.

6   Limitation

The primary limitation of this study lies in the small sample size and the exclusive focus on Iranian users. This was largely due to the inherent challenges in participant recruitment for behavioral studies. To improve generalizability and robustness, future research should explore more diverse and larger datasets, apply advanced deep learning techniques, and incorporate interdisciplinary perspectives, particularly from psychology and ethics, to ensure responsible and effective deployment of addiction detection systems.

References

1. Madden, M.: "Older adults and social media," Pew Research Center, Tech. Rep., 2010.https://www.pewresearch.org/internet/2010/08/27/older-adults-and-social-media/
2. Kim, Y.., Sohn, D.., Choi, S.M.: "Cultural difference in motivations for using social network sites: A comparative study of american and korean college students," Computers in Human Behavior, vol. 27, no. 1, pp. 365–372, 2011, current Research Topics in Cognitive Load Theory.https://www.sciencedirect.com/science/article/pii/S0747563210002736

3. Nguyen, N.D., Truong, N.A., Quang Dao, P., Nguyen, H.H.: "Can online behaviors be linked to mental health? active versus passive social network usage on depression via envy and self-esteem," Computers in Human Behavior, vol. 162, p. 108455, 2025. https://www.sciencedirect.com/science/article/pii/S0747563224003236

4. Phys.org, "How social media impacts mental well-being," 2015. https://phys.org/news/2015-09-social-media-impacts-mental-well-being.html.Accessed 25 Feb 2025

5. Han, X., Han, W.., Qu, J., Li, B., Zhu, Q.: "What happens online stays online? social media dependency, online support behavior and offline effects for lgbt," Computers in Human Behavior, vol.93, pp. 91–98, 2019.https://www.sciencedirect.com/science/article/pii/S0747563218305971

6. van den Eijnden, R.J., Lemmens, J.S., Valkenburg, P.M.: "The social media disorder scale," Computers in Human Behavior, vol. 61, pp. 478–487, 2016. https://www.sciencedirect.com/science/article/pii/S0747563216302059

7. Bhargava, V.R., Velasquez, M.: Ethics of the attention economy: The problem of social media addiction. Bus. Ethics Q. **31**(3), 321–359 (2021)

8. Lin, I.H., et al.: "The association between suicidality and internet addiction and activities in taiwanese adolescents," Comprehensive Psychiatry, vol. 55, no. 3, pp. 504–510, 2014. https://www.sciencedirect.com/science/article/pii/S0010440X13003441

9. Teng, Z.: "Internet addiction and suicidal behavior among vocational high school students in hunan province, china: A moderated mediation model," Frontiers in Public Health, vol. 10, 2023. https://www.frontiersin.org/journals/public-health/articles/10.3389/fpubh.2022.1063605

10. Rahiminia, H., Soori, H., Jafari, M., Khodakarim, S.: The prevalence of addiction to social network among students in iran and its factors related: A study conducted in 2020. Clin. Pract. Epidemiol. Ment. Health **17**, 170–176 (2021)

11. Azizi, S.M., Soroush, A., Khatony, A.: "The relationship between social networking addiction and academic performance in iranian students of medical sciences: a cross-sectional study," BMC Psychology, vol. 7, no. 28, 2019. https://doi.org/10.1186/s40359-019-0305-0

12. Akhil, K., Sireesha, J., Sai, G.V., Reddy, K.S.S., Haripriya, J., "Harnessing artificial intelligence for preventing and detecting addiction in digital healthcare and social media among students of age group 12 to 18," In: 2023 5th International Conference on Advances in Computing, Communication Control and Networking (ICAC3N), 2023, pp. 936–942

13. Hassanpour, S., Tomita, N., DeLise, T., Gill, H., Rahimi, A.: "Identifying substance use risk based on deep neural networks and instagram social media data," Neuropsychopharmacology, vol. 44, pp. 487–494, 2019. https://doi.org/10.1038/s41386-018-0247-x

14. Etherington, D.: "Instagram now has 800 million monthly and 500 million daily active users," TechCrunch, 2017 . https://techcrunch.com/2017/09/25/instagram-now-has-800-million-monthly-and-500-million-daily-active-users/.Accessed   17 Sept 2018

15. Young, K.S., De Abreu, C.N.: Internet Addiction: A Handbook and Guide to Evaluation and Treatment. John Wiley & Sons, New York (2010)

16. Young, K.S.: Caught in the Net: How to Recognize the Signs of Internet Addiction-And a Winning Strategy for Recovery. John Wiley & Sons, New York (1998)

17. Wan, C.: "Gratifications and loneliness as predictors of campus-sns websites addiction and usage pattern among chinese college students," Master's thesis. The Chinese University of Hong Kong, School of Journalism and Communication (2009)

18. Andreassen, C.S., Torsheim, T., Brunborg, G.S., Pallesen, S.: Development of a facebook addiction scale. Psychol. Rep. **110**, 501–517 (2012)

19. Andreassen, C.S., Pallesen, S., Griffiths, M.D.: "The relationship between addictive use of social media, narcissism, and self-esteem: Findings from a large national survey," Addictive Behaviors, 2016. http://dx.doi.org/10.1016/j.addbeh.2016.03.006

20. Dinu, A., Moldovan, A.C.: "Automatic detection and classification of mental illnesses from general social media texts," In: Proceedings of the International Conference on Recent Advances in Natural Language Processing (RANLP 2021), R. Mitkov and G. Angelova, Eds. Held Online: INCOMA Ltd., Sep. 2021, pp. 358–366. https://aclanthology.org/2021.ranlp-1.41/

21. Ameer, I., Arif, M., Sidorov, G., Gòmez-Adorno, H., Gelbukh, A.: "Mental illness classification on social media texts using deep learning and transfer learning," 2022. https://arxiv.org/abs/2207.01012

22. Zhou, S., Liu, C., Ye,D., Zhu, T., Zhou, W., Yu, P.S.: "Adversarial attacks and defenses in deep learning: From a perspective of cybersecurity,"ACM Comput. Surv., vol. 55, no. 8, Dec. 2022. https://doi.org/10.1145/3547330

Mitigating Bias in Recruitment: A Practical Approach to CV De-identification Considering Privacy Sensitive Information

Sascha Löbner[1]([✉]) [ID], Jetzabel Serna[2] [ID], Frédéric Tronnier[1] [ID], Welderufael Tesfay[1] [ID], and Kai Rannenberg[1] [ID]

[1] Goethe University, Frankfurt am Main, Germany
{sascha.loebner,frederic.tronnier,welderufael.tesfay,
kai.rannenberg}@m-chair.de
[2] Cyber4People GmbH, Eschborn, Germany
jetzabel.serna@cyber4people.com

Abstract. Curriculum Vitae (CVs) often contain sensitive personal information, which poses risks of discriminatory use by employers during the hiring process. To address this, there have been various research approaches to de-bias the various phases of the hiring process. However, these initiatives often fall short of resolving the core issues effectively. In this paper, we propose a process and proof of concept aimed at de-identifying Privacy Sensitive Information (PSIs) in CVs. We run rigorous evaluations to de-identify relevant PSI outlined in the EU GDPR (e.g., art. 9) and synthesize findings from state-of-the-art research on text and CV de-identification. Our designed prototype is able to firstly identify PSI specific to CVs and then de-identifies these PSI within the Europass CV structure. This novel approach demonstrates a promising path towards promoting fairness and preserving privacy in the recruitment process.

Keywords: De-identification · PSI · resume · CV · privacy · fairness

1 Introduction

In recent years, technological advances and digitization efforts have significantly transformed traditional recruitment processes. The integration of data-driven tools such as Automated Hiring Systems (AHS) promise to streamline operations, enhance efficiency and mitigate biases which are inherent in conventional hiring methods [19]. However, despite the widespread adoption of such technologies and claims of neutrality and objectivity, recent studies [32] reiterate that recruitment processes remain vulnerable to human biases and prejudices, influencing the decision-making at various stages - from job posting and initial screening to interview evaluations. This susceptibility can lead to disparities in candidate selection

B. Coppens et al. (Eds.): ARES 2025 Workshops, LNCS 15995, pp. 174–192, 2025.
https://doi.org/10.1007/978-3-032-00633-2_11

and perpetuate inequalities in employment opportunities [22]. Since CVs contain many personally identifiable and Privacy Sensitive Information (PSI) [38], such as name, sex, age, ethnicity, AHS, and decision makers often fail to focus solely on candidates' qualifications and experiences. Furthermore, recruiting practices often involve outsourcing and multiple stakeholder (e.g., headhunting or job platforms). Thus, handling vast amounts of job applications loaded with PSI raises privacy concerns, and increases the risk of bias and non-compliance with, e.g., the General Data Protection Regulation (GDPR) and AI Act. In this context, de-identification of CV data could enhance the objectivity and impartiality of the employment procedures, by anonymizing or pseudonymizing relevant PSI in CVs. Data-driven tools and decision makers could then focus solely on the candidates' core qualifications, skills, and experiences, thereby fostering a fair and merit-based selection process. More precisely, CV de-identification helps mitigate bias and discrimination in the initial screening phase [22] by providing unbiased training datasets for the training of the AHS system model and reducing unconscious bias in cases where human intervention is involved. De-identification also minimizes privacy risks associated with handling (i.e., storing, sharing, and transferring) large volumes of CVs containing PSI. In the context of outsourcing, it significantly reduces the risk of inadvertently sharing personal data with third parties and potential data breach exposures. Additionally, de-identification enhances transparency by demonstrating the organization's commitment to fair and unbiased recruitment. Actively promotes diversity, inclusion, and equal opportunities, particularly for underrepresented groups, ensuring that initial screening is solely based on merits and qualifications. Ultimately, these measures support compliance with anti-discrimination laws and help mitigate liability related to discriminatory hiring practices.

This work contributes a practical road map for effective CV de-identification to systematically address the critical issue of PSI exposure in CVs, which in turn may impact fairness and reduce bias in the candidate screening phase during recruitment. Our contributions can be summarized as follows:

1. We identify key categories of PSI often present in CVs and relevant for de-identification with the aim to mitigate potential bias during job screening.
2. We propose various methods to locate and de-identify these PSI types usually present in CVs.
3. We discuss the implications and challenges of de-identifying CVs and provide implementation considerations based on a prototype.

2   Related Literature

In this section, we explore research on fairness and bias in hiring practices, the use of AI in recruitment, techniques for detecting and de-identifying PSI in CVs, and the role of synthetic data in privacy preservation.

Studies on fairness in hiring investigate data bias issues in AI-supported recruitment and related ethical implications. Raghavan et al. [32] show the interplay between algorithmic de-biasing and anti-discrimination law, while Gu et al.

[13] analyze how race, gender, and qualifications impact fair judgment in hiring. Rigotti and Fosch-Villaronga [34] define and operationalize fairness in AI recruitment, to prevent data protection violations and social discrimination. Tronnier et al. [40] categorize biases and ethical issues in digital services, discussing necessary stakeholder trade-offs. Techniques to mitigate bias include algorithm fine-tuning and anonymity in resumes. Deshpande et al. [7] present a fair matching algorithm that analyzes demographic factors using cosine similarity. Kang et al. [22] show that "resume whitening" helps minority groups, however, organizational diversity statements did not reduce discrimination. Parasurama and Sedoc [30] analyze a gender debiasing method in NLP that was found ineffective, highlighting challenges in fully anonymizing gender in resumes and limitations of lexical approaches. Using regular expressions, LSTM and BERT, Jensen et al. [19] explore the de-identification of job vacancies in stack-overflow focusing on the PSI location, organization, contact, name and profession. The detection and de-identification of privacy sensitive information (PSI) are critical in maintaining privacy. Ribeiro et al. [33] analyze automated de-identification methods in clinical textual data. They find that achieving a high privacy with recall of 100 % causes information loss and reduced readability. Tesfay et al. [37] introduce a privacy bot for detecting GDPR-related sensitive data, also included in this work. With the rise of Generative AI (GenAI) applications and services, concerns about data quality, misinformation and protection have been raised and studied [42, 46]. Recent academic research is tackling this topic from different dimensions, i.e., by studying how synthetic, GenAI-generated, data can be used as a surrogate for real data, to not contain private information. To this end, [12] provide a framework to quantify the three privacy risks of singling out, linkability, and inference risks in synthetic data. Zhao et al. [45] also study synthetic text data generation for privacy protection. The authors propose a solution that "combines the iteratively optimized mindset from genetic algorithms to align the distribution of synthetic text with that of private text." [45]. Upon evaluation, the solution maintains a high degree of utility while providing robust privacy levels. Similarly, [21] combine a generative autoencoder, federated learning, and differential privacy to generate synthetic data without revealing the original data. Utility and data protection outperform existing solutions for attribute classification tasks, and thus, show the worth of synthetic data in future use cases. Other authors focus on synthetic speech data in their analysis [20]. The authors develop a network to verify the authentication of data and identify forged segments in the data, demonstrating robust capabilities. Bias in Generative AI (GenAI) applications are also a point of study in academic research, i.e. with a systematic literature review on gender bias in AI provided in [41].

Concerning synthetic data, [3] provide a framework for the creation of synthetic datasets with different types of biases to study the interconnectedness of biases and possible mitigation mechanisms. An SoK on privacy-preserving data synthesis is provided by [16]. Skondras et al. [36] generated synthetic resumes with GPT. They use their generated data for NLP-based resume classification, achieving an accuracy for synthetic data of 85 %. This motivates the need of de-identification of synthetic CV data for resume classification scenarios. First work on resume de-identification using in-prompt anonymization is conducted in [26], whereby the authors find only limited loss in performance in their model. Schneider et al. [35] study how generative AI applications can be trained to avoid the identification of created synthetic data. Regulatory concerns from the European AI Act and GDPR compliance have been discussed by several researchers [14,39]. Memmert et al. [27] test the usability to aid of generative AI in design science research. Technological advancements also play a significant role in automated hiring processes. Zaroor et al. [44] study resume classification with real-world data, utilizing matching algorithms to maintain low error rates. Javed et al. [18] test a job role classification system using SVM-kNN, covering various taxonomies. Pal et al. [28] explore the use of Naive Bayes, Random Forest, and SVM in automated hiring, highlighting the shift towards electronic resources in recruitment.

To the best of our knowledge, there is currently no comprehensive guideline that covers all important PSI types and provides practical implications for the implementation of CV de-identification tools.

3   Methodology

In this study, we adopt a problem-centered approach to design science research [9,15,31]. We also take into consideration the work of [24] that provide a method and approach on how to employ synthetic data for use cases in academic research. Following these steps, we aim to produce a robust CV de-identification prototype that can be adapted as a starting point for organizational implementation.

Problem Identification and Motivation: Why CV de-identification is important might not be intuitive at a glance, since employers aim to collect as much information as possible about an applicant. But with the outsourcing of job application processes to job platforms and automated CV analysis, de-identification becomes essential to ensure compliance with data protection regulations (e.g. GDPR). Also for fairness and equality, PSI such as gender [30] or age [43] should be removed in CV analysis. This confronts companies with the burden to judge which PSI types should be de-identified. Thus, our approach promotes fairness in automated decision-making and contributes to fair and trustworthy use of AI.

Defining Objectives of a Solution: We set the following objectives for CV de-identification tools and demonstrate the main actions with our prototype:

Ensuring that no discriminatory PSI types are used within automated recruitment processes to effectively mitigate biases and comply with GDPR.

Maintaining the utility of CVs for job suitability assessment. This objective is in line with the privacy by design principle of full functionality [5].

Ensuring relevance of PSI de-identification. To guarantee that CV de-identifica-tion remains relevant for the standardized format across the EU.

Design and Development: To identify PSI types in CVs that may result in bias, we build on the comprehensive mapping of Chua et al. [6] who compared and combined different categorizations of PSI types from literature. We apply this framework similar to Löbner et al. [25] for the CV de-identification. The Europass [10] CV template represents the EU's efforts to standardize the presentation of individuals' skills and qualifications. To meet our objective of relevance, we analyse its free text fields. We evaluate GDPR-compliance of identified PSI types, focusing on Articles 4 and 9, that deal with the protection of personal and sensitive data processing. To identify suitable PSI detection techniques, we compare different approaches to identify PSI in texts in general, following Tesfay et al. [38]. An overview of relevant NER techniques for PSI detection is provided by Löbner et al. [25]. Identifying a suitable PSI de-identification techniques includes balancing the privacy and data utility trade-off. ISO/IEC 20889:2018-11 [17] provide different de-identification techniques such as generalization, pseudonymization or anonymization that we evaluate for each relevant PSI type.

Demonstration: To run our prototype in a controlled environment without risking exposing real world private data we decided to use synthetically generated data from ChatGPT4 2023 similar to Skondras et al. [36]. We manually validated all generated CVs to ensure the synthetic data contained realistic, diverse and correct CVs types aligned with typical resume content. For the prototype, we implement a simple model based on BERT [8] and the regex module. We have chosen BERT due to its superior performance in similar NLP tasks [23].

Evaluation: The PSI detection prototype is evaluated with the quantitative approaches of F1-score, precision and recall. We assess qualitatively the readability and utility of all de-identified text by comparing them one by one with the original.

4   Results

4.1   Design and Development

Identifying biased PSI types in CVs: In this paragraph, we present potentially biased PSI types in CVs, describe why they are might be biased and evaluate whether they are covered in the GDPR. Chua et al. [6] define six PSI categories that are Lifestyle behavior, Social Economic, Tracking, Financial, Authenticating, Medical-health. Although rare cases might exist, we exclude financial information, medical information and authenticating information because these categories were not found in our CV samples. Thus, we focus on the remaining criteria that are social-economic, tracking data and lifestyle (including behavioral) data. In Table 1 we analyse the characteristics mentioned in [6]. Moreover, we provide examples and evaluate the probability of occurrence based on how common the category is to appear in CVs. In the following, we present each characteristic and provide an assessment of whether a characteristic should be

Table 1. Classification of PSI detected, based on [6] including Occurence (Occ).

Category	Characteristics	CV Criteria	Occ.	Tag
Lifestyle-behaviour	Beliefs	Religious views, philosophical beliefs	Low	
	Preferences or interests	Hobbies	High	HOB
	Family/Relationship	Fam. structure, relationships, marriage	High	FAM
	Politics	Membership in parties, organizations	Low	ORG
Social-economic	Ethnicity	Ethnic origin, race, language	High	NATION
	Physical characteristics	Photos	High	
	Demographics	Name, date, age, date of birth, gender, sex, nationality	High	NATION, DATE, PER, PNOUN, GNOUN, TOA
	Professional career	Prev. employer, job roles/details, salary, education	High	ORG, EIN
Tracking	Contact information	email address, phone number, address	High	EMAIL, PHONE
	Location	Location	High	LOC
	Computer device details	URL	High	LINK

de-identified. To provide a more comprehensive overview, we categorize characteristics in more detailed PSI types. If we conclude that a PSI type has a high occurrence, we add a PSI tag to it and explore its de-identification. However, PSI types with low occurrence can also identify a person or cause biases what will be part of our future work. Finally, we compare the elicited tags with the GDPR (see Sect. 4.1).

Lifestyle behaviour includes all information on an individual's lifestyle and behaviors that shape their relationships, community connections, habits, preferences, beliefs, or opinions [6]. **Beliefs**, e.g., *Religious or philosophical beliefs* (cf. art. 9 of the EU GDPR) can cause bias in CV classification. Nevertheless, expressing religious or philosophical beliefs in a CV is quite uncommon, which is the reason why we do not consider it a high occurrence. **References or interests**, e.g. *Hobbies*, generally do not reveal PSI relevant to hiring decisions. However, certain hobbies, e.g. competitive sports' achievements like, Olympic participation, can increase identifiability. Additionally, some hobbies are statistically associated with gender, potentially enabling indirect gender inference [30]. Given their limited relevance to assessing job qualifications and the risk of introducing bias or indirect discrimination, we excluded hobbies from the PSI detection scope to align with fair hiring practices and promote equal opportunity. **Politics**, e.g., *membership in organizations or parties* could reveal personal affiliations, thus de-identifying could prevent bias related to perceived ideologies. Although we have not assigned a specific tag, organization-membership is covered by ORG.

Social-economic includes all PSI types that describe a person's ethnicity, physical characteristic, demographics or professional career are clustered here. **Ethnicity**, e.g., prejudices due to *ethnic origin* are a major issue for fairness in job role assignment. While removing ethnicity is often effective in mitigating ethical bias, there are reasons, such as maintaining team diversity, why it is not the sole approach. We consider ethnic related issues as highly present and classify the occurrence as high. Even indirect identifiers can reveal ethnic origin [22]. **Language** is relevant information for the application assessment but can also reveal the ethnic origin [22]. Thus, de-identification approaches should be considered carefully. **Physical characteristics** such as *photos* in traditional applications are suspected of causing bias. However, Frauendorfer et al. [11] found that including a photo on the CV does not significantly change the personality assessment. Still, the qualification of a person does in general not depend on how beautiful they look. De-identification should not cause a loss in utility. Regarding **demographics**, several important PSI types exist that should be carefully considered. *Name* is a direct identifier and should be de-identified. *Date* is an indirect identifier which can result in identification of a person when coupled with other data [29], as such it should in general be de-identified. A variety of dates exist among a CV that might require different de-identification approaches to keep utility optimal. These can contain time spans, e.g. work experience, graduation dates or age. *Date of birth/age* is an indirect identifier and should as a date be considered for de-identification. Historically, age had a huge role in salary negotiation, especially for companies that implemented a seniority based salary system. Age discrimination is a common hiring issue Zaniboni et al. [43], that we thus aim to avoid. Especially in Europe, it is common sense that fair evaluation of candidates should be based solely on qualifications and not on *gender* roles. Thus, favouring female candidates just because of quotas, or favouring male candidates just because of their gender is in the following referred to as gender biases. With our approach we aim to avoid these biases despite the challenges that exist in finding a practical implementation [30]. Regarding *national background*, national prejudice exist that are likely to bias decisions. Since national background caused biases are also ethical bias, we decided to combine them in the tag NATION. Regarding **professional career**, *previous employer* might cause a bias due to the good or bad reputation of the employer. Thus, de-identification should be considered. *Job details* are a valuable source of the actual task and experience of an applicant, and should thus not be removed. *Job roles* also provide valuable insights about an employee and might answer the question about experience in leadership or qualification for certain responsibility levels. Although they should not be removed, job roles can reveal the applicant's gender, which should be considered within the PSI type gender. *Salary* often has to be provided as expectation and thus, should be preserved. *Education* can reveal university, year of graduation, age, gender, ethnicity and even socio-economic background. Thus, de-identification can help to focus only on qualifications.

Tracking includes all information that can be utilized to locate a person, which ultimately aids in identifying an individual. **Contact information** is not required when outsourcing the initial candidate screening. When removing personal contact information, it is easier to share CVs and be privacy compliant, as many stakeholders access such information. *Email addresses* often contain fragments of the name or age and should therefore be de-identified. *Phone numbers* can be used to call a person to reveal their name but also to validate recommendation letters. Thus, de-identification should be considered carefully. An *address*

Table 2. Coverage of PSI types in the GDPR.

	EMAIL	LINK	PHONE	DATE	NATION	LOC	ORG	EIN	FAM	PNOUN	GNOUN	TOA	PER	HOB
Art. 4	✔	✔	✔	✔	✔	✔	✔	✔					✔	✔
Art. 9					✔				✔	✔	✔	✔	✔	

can be easily used to identify a person and should thus be de-identified. **Location** can be used to identify a person, especially in combination with other data and should thus be de-identified. **Computer device details**, e.g., *URLs* can point to the applicant's homepage or contain other PSI types and should be considered for de-identification.

GDPR comparison: The GDPR is designed to protect the privacy of online users by promoting privacy-by-design [5] and by default, and by prohibiting the collection and processing of certain PSI types [37]. If no specific GDPR exception applies, processing PSI without the user's consent is prohibited (see article 9).

Article 9 is of significant importance for CV analysis as it prohibits processing personal data revealing sensitive information such as racial or ethnic origin, political opinions, religious or philosophical beliefs, trade union membership, genetic and biometric data used for unique identification, health information, or data concerning a person's sex life or sexual orientation. These sensitive PSI types contribute little to assessing applicant expertise, making them a key target for de-identification. Article 4 of the EU GDPR defines personal data as any information that can be used to directly or indirectly identify a natural person, e.g., ID numbers, location data, online identifiers, or characteristics specific to their physical, mental, genetic, economic, cultural, or social identity. Table 2 maps our PSI types to GDPR art. 4 and 9 to show the relevance for GDPR-compliance.

Identifying suitable PSI detection techniques: We first discuss which different approaches are suitable to achieve the desired de-identification. Second, we assess the complexity of each PSI type and evaluate the suitability of various approaches, including regular expressions, AI-based methods, or dictionary-based techniques. The results are presented in Table 3. Against our initial considerations, we have opted not to use anonymization, and instead we recommend the application of pseudonymization based on hash values where appropriate. Since CVs are typically not very long, the risk of identifying an individual from a pseudonym is minimized, while on the other hand, the information that the same entity is meant can be highly valuable in terms of data usability.

Email addresses (EMAIL) should be removed since they are direct identifier. Due to their static structure they are easy to detect with a regular expression.

Links (LINK) should be removed because it is a direct identifier, often linking to a networking platform, e.g. LinkedIn. We indicate a pseudonym option because this could improve readability if de-identification is guaranteed. URLs exhibit a static structure and are in general easy to detect with a regular expression.

Table 3. Evaluation of PSI types and suggested de-identification techniques from ISO/IEC 20889:2018-11 [17], ● marks our implementation recommendation.

TAG	Remove	Generalize	Pseudonymize	AI	Regex	Dictionary
EMAIL	●		●		●	
LINK	●		●		●	
PHONE	●		●		●	
DATE	●	●	●		●	
NATION	●			●		●
LOC		●	●	●		
ORG		●	●	●		
EIN		●	●	●		
FAM	●			●		
PNOUN		●				●
GNOUN		●				●
TOA	●					●
PER	●		●	●		
HOB	●			●		

Phone numbers (PHONE) of the CV owner should be removed because they are direct identifiers. Since we have decided that the previous employers should not be the reason for hiring, also phone numbers of previous employers should be removed. Rare cases might exist where recommendations by previous employers or inconsistencies in letters of recommendation need clarification. In this rare cases, a conflict management should be used to subsequently reveal numbers of interest. Using pseudonyms improves readability if de-identification is guaranteed.

Date (DATE) we generally promote to remove, to prevent discrimination by age Rigotti and Fosch-Villaronga [34]. European institutions like the European Central Bank often use field experience, but it should be reasonably specified. For example, using date ranges such as 1âĂŞ3 years, 3âĂŞ10 years, or minimum experience such as more than 5 years of experience in software development offers less granular and more equitable criteria. Excessive demands, such as requiring 30 years of experience, are unreasonable and discriminatory. Because dates exhibit a static structure, they can be identified via regular expressions. Nevertheless, many date formats exists, thus it is important to include all of them. Pseudonomization can help to keep track of the same time period.

Nationalities (NATION) and all attributes towards race should be removed. According to [7,22] the so-called "resume whitening" has demonstrated a considerable reduction on discrimination of minority groups. In general, nationalities and race can often be identified directly using dictionaries. However, this straightforward approach may overlook other indirect identifiers that could reveal nationalities or race, such as former employers listed in the CV and the CV owner.

Therefore, more sophisticated methods, such as AI-based approaches, should be considered. Due methods' complexity, we have set nationalities out of scope.

Location details (LOC) can disclose significant information about the CV owner or their former employers. To still keep utility of data, we advocate generalization or pseudonomyzation. Especially generalization should be considered carefully as nationality could still be inferred, causing ethic bias. Given the diversity of location names, AI-based methods are most effective for this task.

Organizations (ORG) and *education institutes* (EIN) should be generalized or pseudonymized to prevent reputation-based hiring and unlink them from PSI types like nationality. As both represent institutional affiliations, merging them into a single "ORG" category allows for uniform pseudonymization, simplifying detection and processing while preserving linkability (e.g., repeated affiliations). Although conceptually distinct, their shared role as institutional entities justifies this approach. Hash-based pseudonymization prevents identification and reputation bias, but AI detection remains necessary due to contextual dependencies.

Detecting *relationship status* (FAM) in free text fields is challenging. Although specific lexical cues exist, automatic removal must consider the full context to be effective. In our further analysis, family status and relationships are not considered. However, it might be obfuscated, by removing family member names.

Following the approach of Cao and Daumé III [4] *pronouns* (PNOUN) should be generalized, e.g., "she" is replaced by "they" and *gendered nouns* (GNOUN) are generalized, e.g., stewardess is replaced by flight attendant. This can be implemented by using a dictionary. Due to the poor performance in generating gender related nouns, we excluded them from further investigation as explained below. Moreover, *terms of address* (TOA) should be removed [4]. This can be implemented using a dictionary pointing to an empty string. In general, it would also be possible to generalize Mr/Ms to Mx.

To remove *names* (PER), an AI-based approach is necessary due to the variety of names. A common issue are names in organization names, e.g., Mercedes. In such cases, an AI-based approach is required for context-based classification. The use of pseudonyms can be helpful to keep track of persons mentioned repetitively.

Hobbies (HOB) have no influence on job experience and expertise and should therefore be removed. We assume hobbies to appear in a respective section that is already labelled as hobbies. Thus, we will not further consider hobbies.

4.2   Demonstration

After several rounds of improvements, we derived a suitable prompt using GPT-4. For simplicity, we selected the following free-text fields, which are based on the Europass template but not identical: *Personal Statement, Work Experience, Education and Training, Personal Skills, Additional Information*. We manually checked each annotated CV for incorrectly assigned PSI. Unfortunately, we had to remove the gendered nouns because GPT-4 did not understand the task,

Table 4. Results of the PSI detection prototype tested on GPT-4 generated data.

	EMAIL	LINK	PHONE	DATE	PER	ORG	LOC	PNOUN	TOA
#	2	6	2	120	28	92	30	56	17
F1-score	1	1	1	0.89	1	0.73	1	0.56	1
Precision	1	1	1	1	1	0.57	1	0.39	1
Recall	1	1	1	0.8	1	1	1	1	1

and it generated for GNOUN, words such as "spacecraft design" or "aerodynamics" which are clearly not gender related. We also encountered that due to performance limitations, we can generate CVs only one by one. Thus, except for GNOUN, the synthetic generation was successful. The generated data was used to test the model performance in de-identifying PSI. We used the following prompt:

Objective: *Generate two synthetic CVs in JSON format, each belonging to individuals with backgrounds in technical and consulting fields, to be used as high-quality training data for a Named Entity Recognition (NER) task.*
Specifications:
1. **Template Use:** *Draw from the EUROPASS CV template, specifically utilizing sections where free text entry is permitted. These sections include: Personal Statement, Work Experience (with Descriptions), Education and Training (with Descriptions), Personal Skills, Additional Information*
2. **Content Requirements:** *Each CV must contain multiple descriptions within the free text fields, ensuring no section is left unfilled. Incorporate the following Personal Sensitive Information (PSI) across the text fields, using the stated abbreviations for annotation purposes: PER (Names), DATE (Dates), PNOUN (Pronouns), GNOUN (Gendered Nouns), TOA (Terms of Address), EMAIL (Email Addresses), LINK (Web Links), PHONE (Phone Numbers), LOC (Locations), ORG (Organizations). Ensure that the abbreviations are used within the entity fields of the annotations, not within the actual text.*
3. **Realism:** *The synthetic data should closely mimic real-world CV data, avoiding generic placeholders (e.g., "John Doe").*
4. **Output Files:** *Annotated JSON (annotated_ CV_ data.json): Contains the text with entities annotated according to the specified structure. Plain JSON (CV_ data.json): Includes only the text of the CVs without annotations.*
5. **Annotation Structure:** *For the annotated JSON, use the following format for each CV's sections, ensuring entities are correctly identified with start and end positions, types, and text: json Copy code { "CV1": { "PersonalStatement": [{ "text": "<text>", "entities": [{"start": <start>, "end": <end>, "type": "<entity type>", "text": "<entity text>"}] }] } } Plain Data Structure: For the plain JSON, structure it as follows, excluding entity annotations: json Copy code { "CV1": { "PersonalStatement": [{"text": "<text>"}] } }*
6. **Delivery:** *Generate JSON files in a human-readable manner and provide them in json format in the chat. There should be no need for displaying additional information or instructions in the chat beyond this.*

Prototype: We provide insights into the results of our algorithm. Following ISO/IEC 20889 [17] we use hashing as our standard pseudonymization technique. This allows us to assign the same hash to e.g., organizations mentioned several times in the document. Following Table 3 we also implemented regular expressions and dictionaries. Model architecture and testing process are provided in Fig. 1.

As evaluation metrics, we use precision, recall and f1-score. Especially recall is of high importance when de-identifying PSI due to the mandatory requirement of ensuring that all PSI is effectively removed or anonymized. Thus, in the CV de-identification scenario, recall is defined as the ratio of actual PSI that has been successfully identified and de-identified by our algorithm. The evaluation results of our detection approach are provided in Table 4. In the following, we will present some examples of our de-identification approach (see Table 5), structured by PSI types from Table 1. We have chosen DATE, PNOUN, TOA, PER and ORG since they represent each PSI detection technique. Each example shows the original input alongside its anonymized version, illustrating how PSI is replaced or generalized to ensure privacy while preserving the contextual structure.

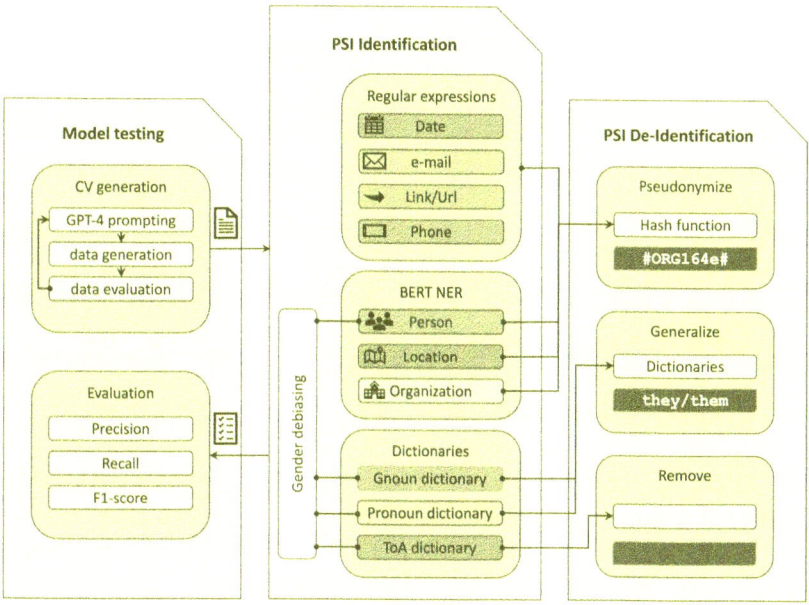

Fig. 1. Model testing, PSI identification and PSI De-identification approach.

Following our de-identification strategy from Fig. 1, we have defined several regex definitions to cover multiple *date* (DATE) types. Table 5 shows a date span that is separated with a "to" instead of a "–". Especially if further words are added between the date span e.g. "to the beginning of" a simple regex function might fail to combine the dates into one tag. While for de-identification this might not be a big deal, it might influence the accuracy metrics if the NER results differ from the actual data.

As part of our gender de-identification approach we generalize *pronouns* (PNOUN) into a neutral form as highlighted (pink) in Table 5. We implemented a conservative approach utilizing a dictionary of pronouns. This approach only covers common pronouns and fails if neopronouns are used, especially if they are fantasy based words, e.g. vix/vixelf. Training an AI on such neopronouns is a promising solution to be further researched. We remove *terms of address* (TOA)

Table 5. Selected de-identification examples of ORG, DATE, TOA, PNOUN, PER.

PSI	Original	Modified
ORG DATE	Consulting Analyst at `BizMax Solutions` from `April 2014` to `February 2019` .	Consulting Analyst at `#ORG164e#` from `#DATE8ce9#` to `#DATE7d15#` .
TOA PNOUN	Accomplished financial consultant `(Mr.)` with extensive experience in financial restructuring, risk management, and strategic investment planning. Known for `his (he/him)` ability to deliver financial solutions.	Accomplished financial consultant ▪ with extensive experience in financial restructuring, risk management, and strategic investment planning. Known for `their (they/them)` ability to deliver financial solutions.
PER TOA	Data Scientist `Alice Johnson` `(Ms.)` specializing in statistical analysis and predictive modeling.	Data Scientist `#PER4fa8#` ▪ specializing in statistical analysis and predictive modeling.

Table 6. Retained Utility and Readability of Tags, High (H), Medium (M), Low (L).

Category	Retained Utility			Readability		
	H	M	L	H	M	L
Personal Statement	1	0	0	0.55	0.45	0
Work Experience	0.85	0.1	0.05	0.05	0.85	0.1
Education and Training	0.45	0.25	0.3	0.1	0.8	0.1
Personal Skills	1	0	0	0.95	0.05	0
Additional Information	0.9	0.1	0	1	0	0

as highlighted (cyan) (see Table 5). We again use a dictionary that contains all relevant TOA. Unexpected characters around the term of address should be removed to improve readability and PSI detection accuracy.

To de-identify *names* (PER), we utilize the bert-large-NER model and its PER tag (see Table 5). As mentioned in the organization section, issues in detection can arise if a natural person's name is used as an organization name.

To de-identify *organizations* (ORG), we use the pre-trained BERT model bert-large-NER from Huggingface (2023). A common issue is the correct separation of organizations that consist of several nouns. Especially if names are part of the organization, this often resolved as a name tag. Uncommon organization names, e.g. "DevCon", are missclassified as MISC where BERT collects all entities, not labeled as ORG, PER or LOC. Thus, when training a BERT model, PSI types event and education should be considered.

Regarding retained usability we achieved a cohens kappa of 0.64 (substential agreement) and for readability a cohens kappa of 0.46 (moderate agreement). A reason for the reduced kappa in readability might be a different perception of how the reader is interrupted. Overall, we find a reduced readability and utility for *Work Experience*, and *Education and Traing*. This can be explained by excessive annonymization, de-identifying important parts, e.g. job roles (see Table 6).

5   Discussion

In this work, we aim to motivate companies and job posting platforms to implement CV de-identification by reducing implementation hurdles. Additionally, our approach supports companies and job platforms in achieving GDPR and AI Act compliance. We provide a starting point to answer which and how data should be de-identified. This groundwork is vital for future AI applications, as AI trained on de-biased, high-utility data is promising to operate with reduced bias.

5.1   Implications for Industry

Both, bias in human decisions caused by prejudice and bias trained from human behavior are both unacceptable and shold both be mitigated. Especially for model training, removing bias in advance while keeping data utility is one of our key objectives, to achieve a more effective alignment between applicants and job roles [7]. In the following, we communicate strategies and considerations:

Bias and unfairness are especially caused by PSI that are mentioned in article 9. GDPR and should not be considered for CV classification tasks. Models can profit from a better matchmaking if those PSI are de-identified.

Linkability issues are often caused by PSI from article 4, GDPR. Here, de-identification can reduce the risk of non-compliance and for a fair CV assessment.

Utility describes the usefullness of data. Pseudonymization and generalization, if applied properly, can help to maintain utility while at the same time de-identifying PSI. If applied, risks and benefits must always be carefully assessed. It should always be aimed to achieve full functionality [5] while simultaneously de-identifying data effectively.

Removal should be considered in case of uncertainties or extensive occurrence of the same PSI to break linkability or bias. This can cause reduced utility.

Pseudonymization enables linking of associated records within a CV [17]. If applied, the trade-off between de-identification and utility must be considered. Hash values for de-identification can be crucial to correctly de-identify a persons first and last name and link them to exactly one hash value. Correct start and stop values of the PSI are mandatory.

Generalization reduces granularity and allows preserving data truthfulness at the record level [17]. If used, it is important to consider the trade-off between de-identification and utility. Thus, choosing the right granularity is important.

Neopronouns are difficult to detect and can cause applicant identification, especially if rarely used.

Readability of de-identified CVs is important for human processing. Removing data completely may break the structure of a sentence. However, too many tokens in the data can decrease readability. Thus, it might be useful to summarize consecutive tokens for human readability.

5.2   Regulatory Implications of the EU AI ACT

The EU Artificial Intelligence Act [2], one of the first regulations of its kind, classifies AI systems into four risk levels: *unacceptable* (prohibited, e.g., social scoring), *high-risk* (heavily regulated, e.g., healthcare AI), *limited risk* (subject to transparency obligations, e.g., chatbots), and *minimal risk* (unregulated, e.g., AI-enabled video games). AHS, including AI-driven CV classification tools, are likely to be classified as high-risk due to their significant influence on employment decisions and their potential impact on individuals' rights. Consequently, these systems must meet strict regulatory requirements before deployment in the EU market, ensuring transparency, fairness, and bias mitigation. Ensuring compliance with the AI Act requires addressing two key aspects. First, AHS tools must be trained on high-quality, unbiased datasets to prevent unfair hiring practices. In this regard, CV de-identification plays a crucial role by ensuring that AI models assess candidates solely on skills and experience rather than demographic attributes, effectively reducing bias and enhancing fairness. Second, automated hiring decisions cannot be entirely autonomous, human oversight is mandated to review and override AI recommendations when necessary. However, human intervention does not eliminate bias either. Particularly during the initial screening phase, CV de-identification helps mitigate unconscious bias, ensuring that hiring decisions remain fair, objective, and merit-based. By prioritizing fairness and transparency, CV de-identification aligns automated hiring systems with the EU AI Act's regulatory framework, mitigating compliance risks while fostering equitable recruitment practices.

5.3   Socio-technical Framing

The adoption of CV de-identification tools depends on organizational culture, recruiter practices, and existing hiring processes. Recruiters may resist using de-identified CVs if they perceive personal information as necessary for assessing cultural fit or networking potential. Thus, integrating such tools requires raising recruiters' awareness of fairness and bias issues while balancing their information needs, making organizational training and change management essential for successful adoption. However, although de-identification enhances fairness and compliance, it may reduce recruiters' confidence or perceived completeness of a candidate's profile. Providing clear guidelines that explain the rationale of de-identified CVs, and embedding de-identification into existing hiring workflows is essential to promote acceptance and effective use.

5.4   Limitations and Future Work

While our research contributes valuable insights into de-identifying CVs to enhance fairness during the job screening phase of recruitment, subsequent recruitment phases, including interviews and final selection processes, fall outside the scope of this paper. Thus, potential biases that may arise during in-person interactions or decision-making stages not covered here, serve as opportunities for future work.

Given the current limitations of GPTs in swiftly generating synthetic testing data, our approach necessitates training our own AI model that can recognize fine-tuned CV specific PSI types such as education institutes or nationalities. We still evaluate traditional annotation approaches as more time-consuming since tremendous amounts of time and several annotators following well-structured annotation guidelines are required [1] Although we have elicited the most common PSI types from the GDPR and existing literature, some rare PSI types with high risk data might exist that are not considered yet, e.g. medical diagnosis. Whether an evaluation of all existing PSI types can be implemented depends on costs of implementation, maintenance or accuracy. Similar to Jensen et al. [19] who used real world data, some PSI types are not well represented to provide comprehensive testing results. This limitation could be solved by using larger data sets or oversampling techniques. As a next step, we aim to addres the above-mentioned limitations by implementing an advanced AI based de-identification prototype, based on fine-tuned NER trained, on synthetic training data.

6   Conclusion

In this paper, we present valuable insights on how to de-identify PSI in CVs. We elicited relevant PSI types that need to be considered in the de-identification of CVs. We provide valuable insights into the appropriate de-identification approach for different PSI types. A first PSI de-identification prototype is implemented using synthetic data, generated using GPT-4. With this research, we aim to motivate companies and job platforms by reducing the implementation hurdles of CV de-identification. In doing so, this work contributes to more fairness and de-biasing in the job market.

References

1. Al Aziz, M.M., Ahmed, T., et al.: Differentially private medical texts generation using generative neural networks. ACM Trans. Comput. Healthc. **3**(1), 1–27 (2021)
2. Artificial Intelligence Act: Proposal for a regulation of the European parliament and the council laying down harmonised rules on artificial intelligence and amending certain union legislative acts. EUR-Lex (2024)
3. Baumann, J., Castelnovo, A., Cosentini, A., Crupi, R., Inverardi, N., Regoli, D.: Bias on demand: Investigating bias with a synthetic data generator. In: Elkind, E. (ed.) Proceedings of the Thirty-Second International Joint Conference on Artificial Intelligence, IJCAI-23, pp. 7110–7114 (8 2023)
4. Cao, Y.T., Daumé III, H.: Toward gender-inclusive coreference resolution. arXiv preprint arXiv:1910.13913 (2019)
5. Cavoukian, A.: Privacy by design (2009)
6. Chua, H.N., Ooi, J.S., Herbland, A.: The effects of different personal data categories on information privacy concern and disclosure. Comput. Secur. **110**, 102453 (2021)
7. Deshpande, K.V., Pan, S., Foulds, J.R.: Mitigating demographic bias in AI-based resume filtering. In: 28th ACM Conference on User Modeling, Adaptation and Personalization, pp. 268–275 (2020)
8. Devlin, J., Chang, M.W., Lee, K., Toutanova, K.: BERT: Pre-training of deep bidirectional transformers for language understanding. arXiv preprint arXiv:1810.04805 (2018)

9. Dresch, A., Lacerda, D.P., Antunes, J.A.V.: Design Science Research, pp. 67–102. Springer International Publishing, Cham (2015)
10. Europass: Europass cv editor, European union (2024). https://europa.eu/europass/. Accessed 24 Mar 2024
11. Frauendorfer, D., Schmid Mast, M., Sutter, C.: To include, or not to include? Accuracy of personality judgments from resumes with and without photographs. Swiss J. Psychol. **74**(4), 207 (2015)
12. Giomi, M., Boenisch, F., Wehmeyer, C., Tasnádi, B.: A unified framework for quantifying privacy risk in synthetic data. Proc. Privacy Enhancing Technol. **2**, 312–328 (2023)
13. Gu, J., McFerran, B., Aquino, K., Kim, T.G.: What makes affirmative action-based hiring decisions seem (un) fair? A test of an ideological explanation for fairness judgments. J. Organ. Behav. **35**(5) (2014)
14. Gualdi, F., Cordella, A.: Theorizing the regulation of generative AI: lessons learned from Italy's ban on ChatGPT. In: 57th HICSS 2024 (2024)
15. Hevner, A.R., March, S.T., Park, J., Ram, S.: Design science in information systems research. MIS quarterly, pp. 75–105 (2004)
16. Hu, Y., et al.: Sok: privacy-preserving data synthesis. In: 2024 IEEE Symposium on Security and Privacy (SP), pp. 4696–4713 (2024)
17. ISO/IEC 20889:2018-11: Privacy enhancing data de-identification terminology and classification of techniques. Standard, International Organization for Standardization, Geneva, CH (Nov 2018)
18. Javed, F., Luo, Q., McNair, M., et al.: Carotene: a job title classification system for the online recruitment domain. In: International Conference on Big Data Computing Service and Applications (2015)
19. Jensen, K.N., Zhang, M., Plank, B.: De-identification of privacy-related entities in job postings. arXiv preprint arXiv:2105.11223 (2021)
20. Ji, Z., Lin, C., Wang, H., Shen, C.: Speech-forensics: towards comprehensive synthetic speech dataset establishment and analysis. In: Larson, K. (ed.) Proceedings of the Thirty-Third International Joint Conference on Artificial Intelligence, IJCAI-24, pp. 413–421 (2024). main Track
21. Jiang, X., Zhou, X., Grossklags, J.: Privacy-preserving high-dimensional data collection with federated generative autoencoder. Proc. Privacy Enhancing Technol. **2022**(1), 481–500 (2022)
22. Kang, S.K., DeCelles, K.A., Tilcsik, A., Jun, S.: Whitened résumés: Race and self-presentation in the labor market. Administrative science quarterly (2016)
23. Karl, F., Scherp, A.: Transformers are short-text classifiers. In: International Cross-Domain Conference for Machine Learning and Knowledge Extraction, pp. 103–122. Springer (2023)
24. Kowalczyk, P., Röder, M., Rottmann, J., Thiesse, F.: Designing a method to nudge analytics with artificially generated data. In: Proceedings of the International Conference on Information Systems (ICIS) (2023)
25. Löbner, S., Tesfay, W.B., Bracamonte, V., Nakamura, T.: Systematizing the state of knowledge in detecting privacy sensitive information in unstructured texts using machine learning. In: International Conference on Privacy, Security and Trust (PST) (2023)
26. Löbner, S., Tronnier, F., Linke, D.: De-identification of privacy sensitive information in resumes with GPT-4: An utility analysis for automated job role classification. In: Proceedings of the Hawaii International Conference on System Sciences (2025)

27. Memmert, L., Cvetkovic, I., Bittner, E.: Human-AI collaboration in conceptualizing design science research studies: Perceived helpfulness of generative language model's suggestions. In: ECIS (2023)
28. Pal, R., Shaikh, S., Satpute, S., Bhagwat, S.: Resume classification using various machine learning algorithms. In: ITM Web of Conferences (2022)
29. Pape, S., Serna-Olvera, J., Tesfay, W.B.: Why open data may threaten your privacy. In: Workshop on Privacy and Inference, pp. 1–5 (2015)
30. Parasurama, P., Sedoc, J.: Degendering resumes for fair algorithmic resume screening. arXiv preprint arXiv:2112.08910 (2021)
31. Peffers, K., Tuunanen, T., Rothenberger, M.A., Chatterjee, S.: A design science research methodology for information systems research. Journal of Management Information Systems (2007)
32. Raghavan, M., Barocas, S., Kleinberg, J., Levy, K.: Mitigating bias in algorithmic hiring: evaluating claims and practices. In: 2020 Conference on Fairness, Accountability, and Transparency (2020)
33. Ribeiro, B., Rolla, V., Santos, R.: INCOGNITUS: a toolbox for automated clinical notes anonymization. In: Conference of the European Chapter of the Association for Computational Linguistics (2023)
34. Rigotti, C., Fosch-Villaronga, E.: Fairness, AI & recruitment. Computer Law & Security Review (2024)
35. Schneider, S., Steuber, F., Schneider, J.A.G., Rodosek, G.D.: How good can machine generated texts be identified and can language models be trained to avoid identification? In: HICSS (2024)
36. Skondras, P., Psaroudakis, G., Zervas, P., Tzimas, G.: Efficient resume classification through rapid dataset creation using ChatGPT. In: 2023 14th International Conference on Information, Intelligence, Systems & Applications (IISA), pp. 1–5. IEEE (2023)
37. Tesfay, W.B., Serna, J., Rannenberg, K.: PrivacyBot: detecting privacy sensitive information in unstructured texts. In: SNAMS. IEEE (2019)
38. Tesfay, W.B., Serna, J.M., Pape, S.: Challenges in detecting privacy revealing information in unstructured text. In: PrivOn@ ISWC (2016)
39. Tronnier, F., Löbner, S., Lacombe, M.H., Rannenberg, K.: Regulatory challenges in cybersecurity – a critical analysis of the EU AI act. In: Information Security Education. Empowering People through Information Security Education. Springer Nature Switzerland (2025)
40. Tronnier, F., Pape, S., Löbner, S., Rannenberg, K.: A discussion on ethical cybersecurity issues in digital service chains. In: Cybersecurity of Digital Service Chains: Challenges, Methodologies, and Tools. Springer International Publishing Cham (2022)
41. Tronnier, F., Löbner, S., Azanbayev, A., Walter, M.L.: A systematic literature review on gender bias in AI – towards inclusiveness in machine learning. In: Proceedings of the Pacific-Asia Conference on Information Systems (2024)
42. Umbach, R., Henry, N., Beard, G.F., Berryessa, C.M.: Non-consensual synthetic intimate imagery: prevalence, attitudes, and knowledge in 10 countries. In: Proceedings of CHI 2024. CHI '24, New York, NY, USA (2024)
43. Zaniboni, S., Kmicinska, M., Truxillo, D.M., et al.: Will you still hire me when i am over 50? The effects of implicit and explicit age stereotyping on resume evaluations. Eur. J. Work Organ. Psy. **28**(4), 453–467 (2019)
44. Zaroor, A., Maree, M., Sabha, M.: JRC: a job post and resume classification system for online recruitment. In: 29th International Conference on Tools with Artificial Intelligence (ICTAI). IEEE (2017)

45. Zhao, W., Song, S., Zhou, C.: Generate synthetic text approximating the private distribution with differential privacy. In: Larson, K. (ed.) Proceedings of the Thirty-Third International Joint Conference on Artificial Intelligence, IJCAI-24, pp. 6651–6659 (2024)
46. Zhou, J., Zhang, Y., Luo, Q., Parker, A.G., De Choudhury, M.: Synthetic lies: understanding AI-generated misinformation and evaluating algorithmic and human solutions. In: Proceedings of the 2023 CHI Conference on Human Factors in Computing Systems. CHI '23, New York, NY, USA (2023)

SynthGuard: Redefining Synthetic Data Generation with a Scalable and Privacy-Preserving Workflow Framework

Eduardo Brito[1,2]✉ ⓘ, Mahmoud Shoush[1] ⓘ, Kristian Tamm[1,2] ⓘ,
Paula Etti[1] ⓘ, and Liina Kamm[1] ⓘ

[1] Cybernetica AS, Tallinn, Estonia
{eduardo.brito,mahmoud.shoush,kristian.tamm,paula.etti,
liina.kamm}@cyber.ee
[2] University of Tartu, Tartu, Estonia

Abstract. The growing reliance on data-driven applications in sectors such as healthcare, finance, and law enforcement underscores the need for secure, privacy-preserving, and scalable mechanisms for data generation and sharing. Synthetic data generation (SDG) has emerged as a promising approach but often relies on centralized or external processing, raising concerns about data sovereignty, domain ownership, and compliance with evolving regulatory standards. To overcome these issues, we introduce SynthGuard, a framework designed to ensure computational governance by enabling data owners to maintain control over SDG workflows. SynthGuard supports modular and privacy-preserving workflows, ensuring secure, auditable, and reproducible execution across diverse environments. In this paper, we demonstrate how SynthGuard addresses the complexities at the intersection of domain-specific needs and scalable SDG by aligning with requirements for data sovereignty and regulatory compliance. Developed iteratively with domain expert input, SynthGuard has been validated through real-world use cases, demonstrating its ability to balance security, privacy, and scalability while ensuring compliance. The evaluation confirms its effectiveness in implementing and executing SDG workflows and integrating privacy and utility assessments across various computational environments.

Keywords: synthetic data generation · privacy-preserving workflows · data sovereignty and governance

Funded by the European Union (TEADAL 101070186 and LAGO 101073951). Views and opinions expressed are, however, those of the author(s) only and do not necessarily reflect those of the European Union. Neither the European Union nor the granting authority can be held responsible for them. Also supported by the Estonian Centre of Excellence in AI (EXAI), funded by the Estonian Ministry of Education and Research.

B. Coppens et al. (Eds.): ARES 2025 Workshops, LNCS 15995, pp. 193–211, 2025.
https://doi.org/10.1007/978-3-032-00633-2_12

1   Introduction

In today's data-driven landscape, sectors such as healthcare [32,54], finance [13], and law enforcement [10] face stringent legal and ethical challenges in managing and exchanging data. While artificial intelligence (AI), particularly machine learning (ML) and deep learning (DL), depends heavily on access to high-quality data to enhance operations and decision-making [23,30,51], privacy concerns and regulatory frameworks such as the EU General Data Protection Regulation (GDPR) or the Directive (EU) 2016/860 [18,19] impose significant barriers to data availability. These restrictions result in lengthy compliance processes, stalling progress in data-driven innovation [27,60].

Privacy-enhancing technologies (PETs) are helping overcome these barriers, allowing data processing, analysis, and insight extraction while safeguarding personal or commercially sensitive information [31,38,61]. Among these, synthetic data generation (SDG) has emerged as a promising solution that allows organizations to use representative synthetic data for research and development without risking individual privacy [16,42,46,59]. However, existing SDG methods often involve external access to sensitive data, introducing privacy and security risks [17]. Furthermore, most research has focused on improving data generation methods or evaluating the utility and privacy of synthetic data [45], neglecting the needs and challenges of implementing secure, scalable, and adaptable SDG workflows, while maintaining data sovereignty and adhering to evolving legal and ethical standards [17,29].

Addressing these limitations may require new approaches that go beyond data generation mechanisms to tackle the operational and architectural challenges of large scale SDG workflows. Hence, we address the problem of how to enable data owners to maintain control over sensitive data and workflows while ensuring compliance with privacy regulations, supporting modularity and composability to meet diverse operational needs across heterogeneous environments. Transparency, auditability, and reliability are also essential to foster trust, ensure compliance, and enable practical deployment.

To address this problem, we propose an approach that integrates governance, scalability, and compliance into SDG workflows. Particularly, in this paper, we:

1. Present an architectural model for SDG workflows that prioritizes domain ownership, computational governance, and data sovereignty, ensuring that sensitive data and computations remain securely under the data owner's control.
2. Realize this architectural model into SynthGuard[1], a framework for modular and composable SDG workflow design that enables scalable and adaptable deployment across diverse operational environments.
3. Validate SynthGuard through practical implementation in two European Union (EU) research projects, addressing legal and technical requirements of synthetic data sharing across six distinct use cases.

---

[1] https://github.com/SynthGuard.

SynthGuard was iteratively developed with domain expert input within the two EU research projects, covering diverse use cases that highlighted the challenges and needs of SDG across domains. Structured requirement elicitation ensured alignment with legal, technical, and operational constraints and validation confirmed its effectiveness in implementing and executing SDG workflows, while integrating privacy and utility assessments across different computational environments. Our results demonstrate that the framework maintains data sovereignty, while enabling flexible and efficient SDG execution, and preserving privacy and utility requirements.

The rest of this paper is organized as follows. First, in Sect. 2, we present the background. Then, in Sect. 3, we start by outlining the requirements gathered from real-world use cases in two large-scale EU research projects, and follow with a discussion on the architectural principles needed to fulfil them, guiding SynthGuard development. In Sect. 4, we detail the technical implementation of SynthGuard and, in Sect. 5, we summarize the validation. Finally, we conclude the paper in Sect. 6, suggesting future directions.

2   Background

The increasing adoption of data-driven services, particularly in the EU, underscores the need for secure data-sharing practices [31]. However, ensuring privacy and regulatory compliance remains a significant challenge [19-21]. SDG offers a promising approach to balancing privacy, data utility, and secure data sharing by creating data with realistic statistical properties while mitigating re-identification risks [45,46,59]. Unlike traditional techniques such as anonymization, which modify real data points and often carry high re-identification risks [7,11], SDG creates new data points that closely approximate real data, offering greater privacy guarantees [49].

Research on SDG primarily focuses on developing methods to create synthetic datasets while assessing their utility and privacy [9,16]. Synthetic data can be categorized into *realistic synthetic data* (RSD), *causal synthetic data* (CSD), *artificial synthetic data* (ASD), and *hybrid synthetic data* (HSD) [8,28]. RSD replicates the statistical properties of original data using ML or DL, while CSD preserves causal relationships between data points [52,57]. ASD relies on predefined rules or aggregated statistics, making it suitable when access to raw data is restricted [36,56]. HSD combines these approaches, offering flexibility across domains [16]. Utility evaluations measure the effectiveness of synthetic data in substituting real data, often using domain-specific or statistical assessments [26]. Generic metrics, such as univariate, bivariate, and population assessments, ensure synthetic data reflects the statistical characteristics of the original data [7]. Privacy evaluations ensure compliance with legal frameworks by addressing risks of attribute disclosure, where individual characteristics might be inferred, or risks of identity disclosure, where individuals might be uniquely identified [16,35,45]. Unlike data masking, which modifies real records while preserving their structure, these SDG methods generate new, independent data and are recognized as valid forms of synthetic data generation [16,28].

Despite advancements in new methods and evaluations, typical SDG processes often require data transfer or external access, introducing further privacy risks. Data availability and exchange are often constrained by legal, technical, and ethical concerns [17]. Sectors like healthcare, finance, and law enforcement need to manage vast amounts of sensitive data but face significant restrictions on reuse due to legal uncertainties [55]. Key challenges range from obtaining necessary permissions for processing original data to addressing the legal status of synthetic data, whether pseudonymized or anonymized [17]. Furthermore, synthetic data processes must ensure compliance with evolving regulatory frameworks, balancing privacy and utility, which varies by use case [22]. Two issues emerge from these challenges: limitations on data reuse, and lack of sufficient data for certain processing tasks. To our knowledge, no previous work has addressed all these needs, spanning legal, ethical, and technical dimensions, which necessitates rethinking how data is managed, shared, and processed.

To address these multifaceted constraints, emerging paradigms such as Data Mesh offer a promising foundation for rearchitecting synthetic data workflows. Originally proposed to manage decentralized data ownership and governance [37], it advocates for a shift from centralized, monolithic data platforms to domain-oriented architectures and distributed data management. In data-intensive sectors, heterogeneous data pipelines are increasingly critical for handling diverse computational tasks and scaling to meet the growing demand for new data [58]. The Data Mesh approach introduces key principles that may help balance scalability and security in (synthetic) data generation workflows [29,37]: domain ownership, which establishes clear definitions and boundaries for what data is, where it resides, where it is processed, and by whom; computational governance, ensuring data is securely handled within environments governed by regulatory and operational constraints; and data sovereignty, emphasizing that sensitive data and computations should remain under the control of the data owner. In this paper, the terms (data) workflows and pipelines are used interchangeably. Conceptually, workflows represent the sequence of tasks involved in defining and building data processes, while pipelines refer to their specific implementation or execution [12,58].

3   Requirements and Architectural Approach

This section presents the requirements and architectural approach that guided the design of SynthGuard. It begins by detailing the structured elicitation process used to identify key needs across use cases. Based on these requirements, we outline the architectural model developed to ensure privacy, scalability, and governance in SDG workflows. The following sections describe the technical implementation of this model in the SynthGuard framework and its validation against the identified requirements.

3.1   Context and Requirements Gathering

Our work was carried out within two Horizon Europe research projects: **LAGO**[2] and **TEADAL**[3], each encompassing diverse SDG-related use cases:

- **LAGO**: Aimed to enable **law enforcement agencies** to securely share data for research, training, and testing, in line with regulatory requirements.
- **TEADAL**: Included several domains:
  - **Evidence-Based Medicine**: Secure patient data sharing for medical research.
  - **Financial Governance**: Data aggregation across banking jurisdictions.
  - **Smart Viticulture**: Business-critical data exchange via a digital platform.
  - **Mobility**: Synthetic data generation for public use.
  - **Regional Planning**: Cross-sector data sharing among public and private stakeholders.

To guide the framework design, we applied a structured requirements elicitation process. This included workshops and semi-structured interviews with domain experts, capturing operational contexts, regulatory constraints, and synthetic data needs. A use case analysis mapped data-sharing workflows, types of required data, and associated constraints, highlighting bottlenecks and opportunities for SDG to enhance compliance and security.

We also conducted surveys targeting researchers and practitioners, combining qualitative and quantitative questions on adoption barriers, preferred SDG techniques, and privacy/utility safeguards. Responses were analyzed to identify trends and gaps. In parallel, we performed a regulatory and standards review, analyzing legal frameworks such as the GDPR and the Data Governance Act, and sector-specific policies. Legal experts contributed to interpreting these regulations and embedding them into the framework. Full details of these activities are documented in the official public deliverables of LAGO and TEADAL.

This methodology yielded the requirements summarized in Table 1. Common to all use cases are **ALL_R01**, **ALL_R02**, and **ALL_R03**, which establish baseline expectations for anonymization, data sovereignty, and compliance validation. The remaining requirements map to specific use cases as follows: The **law enforcement** use case maps to **LAGO_R01**, **evidence-based medicine** and **regional planning** use cases map to **TEADAL_R01** and **TEADAL_R03**, **financial governance** and **smart viticulture** use cases are linked to **TEADAL_R02** and **TEADAL_R04**, and the **mobility** use case is associated with **TEADAL_R04**.

With the requirements defined, the following subsections present a data-sharing architectural approach designed to meet them. Drawing from Data Mesh principles, it emphasizes domain ownership, computational governance, and data sovereignty [29,37] (see Fig. 1). This model shifts SDG toward a more autonomous and programmable framework, aligning with data privacy regulations and the growing need for secure yet scalable synthetic data sharing [20,21].

---

[2] https://lago-europe.eu/.

[3] https://teadal.eu/.

Table 1. Requirements identified for LAGO and TEADAL projects.

Requirement ID	Requirement Description
ALL_R01	Ensure anonymization and secure generation of data to protect sensitive information
ALL_R02	Allow data owners to retain control over original data to uphold data sovereignty, avoiding off-premises exposure during SDG
ALL_R03	Implement compliance checks to verify the validity of synthetic data for utility and privacy before sharing it with external entities
LAGO_R01	Ensure conformance of synthetic data to legal and regulatory frameworks for non-identifiable data, supporting compliance
TEADAL_R01	Utilize standard data models and pipeline formats for interoperability across multiple organizations and environments
TEADAL_R02	Provide structured, standard workflows for managing cross-organizational data sharing, particularly in multi-cloud setups
TEADAL_R03	Ensure confidentiality and control over data prior to sharing, allowing data owners to review and validate SDG outputs
TEADAL_R04	Design scalable and modular synthetic data workflows that support large-scale data generation and flexible deployment

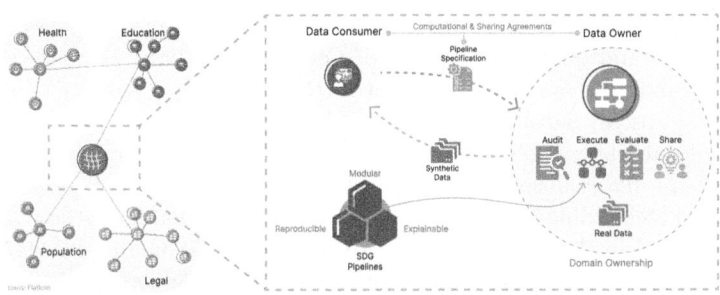

Fig. 1. SDG architectural approach, targeting Data Mesh principles of domain ownership, data sovereignty, and computational governance.

3.2 Computational Governance for Data Availability

In sensitive domains like healthcare, law enforcement, and finance, computational placement is crucial to ensure data availability without compromising sovereignty [29]. SDG processes must remain localized within clearly defined computational domains to keep data under the jurisdiction of its rightful owner. As shown in Fig. 1, real data stays within the data owner's domain, supporting **ALL_R01** and **ALL_R02**, which call for secure, owner-controlled SDG without off-premises exposure. This localized model also supports **LAGO_R01** by promoting compliance and trustworthiness, embedding privacy and transparency mechanisms throughout the SDG pipeline. Computational placement further introduces enhanced privacy guarantees—such as controlled data flows, tailored trust models, and reduced network exposure [14], reinforcing **TEADAL_R03**, which prioritizes confidentiality and pre-sharing validation.

Beyond control and privacy, this SDG model promotes a flexible, programmable approach that allows data owners to adapt workflows to evolving needs while retaining oversight [24,37]. As hybrid and heterogeneous SDG methods grow in demand, especially in AI-driven domains, pipelines must support complex operations, massive datasets, and diverse resources [5,58,62]. This requires standardized tools and processes [25,63], encompassing both the SDG method stack and the infrastructure stack (pipeline specifications, workflow, and orchestration engines). Such standardization is essential for enabling audits during the development, engineering, and deployment of SDG tools and infrastructure, as well as for meeting industry demands for reliability and trustworthiness [6]—core to **TEADAL_R02**'s emphasis on structured, cross-organizational sharing, particularly in multi-cloud setups.

Flexible deployment models are also needed to meet sovereignty and compliance goals. As with data mesh principles, deployments should reflect domain ownership and computational governance [37], ideally operating near the original data source under the data owner's oversight [38]. This includes all SDG stages, from specification to evaluation. By balancing on-premises and cloud resources, owners can scale workflows while maintaining strict data flow controls, minimizing exposure and maximizing data control and privacy [4,14,38]. Such setups further strengthen **ALL_R01**'s aim to secure and localize data generation.

Reproducibility and explainability are also essential to ensure that SDG processes remain modular, reliable, and auditable across development and deployment. Localized control paired with modular design supports transparent workflows and simplifies audits, helping meet both ethical and legal standards [24,29]. This modularity allows individual workflow components to be examined for compliance and performance, important for satisfying **ALL_R03**, which requires pre-sharing validation. It also streamlines implementation by enabling separate execution, testing, and validation phases [12]. These steps of auditing, executing, evaluating, and sharing synthetic data, under the data owner domain, are depicted in Fig. 1.

Furthermore, standardized, reusable SDG components further support cross-domain adoption, reduce redundancy, and simplify integration of new data sources and techniques. This focus on reproducibility and explainability allows pipelines to evolve with changing regulatory and ethical requirements. As privacy demands increase, the ability to validate and explain synthetic data processes becomes critical for maintaining compliance and building trust [6]. Together, these practices support the emergence of a sustainable and accountable synthetic data ecosystem that prioritizes sovereignty and responsible sharing [24,29].

3.3   Programmability and Composability in Scaling SDG Pipelines

As SDG matures, organizing modular mechanisms into structured, programmable settings becomes essential. These should be categorized by function and implemented in cross-platform languages that ensure portability. This enables SDG modules to be delivered declaratively, reliably, and reproducibly, while integrating smoothly across environments, fulfilling **TEADAL_R02** and **TEADAL_R04** requirements for structured, modular, and scalable workflows.

Python and R dominate as core tools for implementing SDG libraries [41, 48]. To support broader integration, individual modules must be transformed into portable components with consistent behaviour across environments. This allows local development and validation, followed by reliable deployment. It also facilitates auditing, as code and execution paths can be reviewed for compliance with security and reliability standards [53], potentially in automated fashion. Figure 1 illustrates these ideal properties when pipelines are executed in the data owner's domain.

In practice, Docker (for containerization) and Nix (for reproducible configuration) are widely adopted to package and manage components at scale [12, 39]. These tools offer modularity, isolation, and reproducibility, aligning with scalable workflow practices. Kubernetes adds declarative orchestration, enabling modular, composable services. When paired with workflow engines [5, 12], SDG pipelines are executed as directed acyclic graph (DAG) workflows with clear task dependencies and conditional execution. This structure allows for automated transformation of data, with each step carefully organized and controlled. Again, these choices help target **TEADAL_R02** and **TEADAL_R04**, in terms of the modularity, interoperability, and scalability of SDG workflows.

Advanced orchestration is also achievable using integrated technologies. Tasks can be labelled and scheduled to run on specific nodes [44], or securely offloaded to trusted execution environments (TEEs) in untrusted domains, realizing the concept of privacy preserving data pipelines [6]. These TEEs provide secure enclaves for privacy-preserving computation under resource-richer conditions [31]. Through these workflow engines, SDG pipelines can adopt a declarative meta-computation approach that converts pipeline specifications into shareable, auditable artifacts, thus enabling secure, transparent synthetic data sharing across domains.

3.4   Sharing SDG Pipeline Specifications

At the core of this synthetic data sharing model is the interaction between data owners (or domain experts, possibly involving data processors) and synthetic data consumers [15, 24], now facilitated through a standardized SDG pipeline specification. As shown at the top of Fig. 1, this specification is the output of computational and sharing agreements between both parties. It serves as a declarative, shareable artifact and aligns with **TEADAL_R01** by enabling interoperability through a standardized pipeline format. The specification includes a DAG outlining task orchestration, along with resource allocations, execution settings, and code for each SDG stage. Therefore, it becomes the central, controlled artifact around which data-sharing is organized [15, 24].

Nonetheless, before implementation, data owners and consumers should clarify data requirements, sensitivity levels, and regulatory constraints [15]. Designated experts can then implement, test, and validate the pipeline to ensure it meets privacy, reliability, and trustworthiness requirements [50], before handing it off to the data owner. This process allows the owner to review and approve all components before introducing sensitive data. These steps reinforce **ALL_R02**, **ALL_R03**, **LAGO_R01**, and **TEADAL_R03**, which emphasize confidentiality, compliance, and control over data prior to sharing.

For data owners, an automated deployment setup enhances sovereignty and simplifies operations. The SDG pipeline is executed within the owner's jurisdiction to comply with data locality and sovereignty mandates [21,29]. Automating the full process, from specification to result validation, reduces overhead and promotes accessible, auditable SDG practices.

This standardized, portable approach also enables future synthetic data markets, supporting secure cross-sector and cross-organization sharing [15,20,21]. Such a marketplace would allow collaboration while maintaining control over pipeline execution and output validation. As synthetic pipelines become standardized [63], organizations can use these artifacts to build interoperable and secure ecosystems. This aligns with **TEADAL_R01** and **TEADAL_R02**, which promote structured workflows for trusted data sharing. Ultimately, pipeline specifications can serve as repeatable, trustable artifacts that foster responsible, scalable synthetic data collaboration across domains and borders [20,21,27].

4   The SynthGuard Framework

Building on the architectural principles discussed, SynthGuard offers a structured SDG workflow that supports data sovereignty, scalability, and privacy. It translates the theoretical foundations into a functional system applicable across diverse use cases. This section details the framework's core components: actor interactions, requirements elicitation, pipeline specification, deployment models, and evaluation mechanisms. The final subsection presents SynthGuard's validation and Table 2 finally summarizes how its features map to the requirements in Table 1. Figure 2 supports the explanations.

4.1   Process Overview and Actor Interactions

SynthGuard structures SDG around a standardized, shareable pipeline specification, keeping computation and orchestration fully under the data owner's control. As shown in the centre of Fig. 2, this specification acts as a blueprint containing attributes, generation logic, and evaluation components, guiding collaboration between data owners and consumers.

Data owners, custodians of the original sensitive data, define requirements for synthetic data types, privacy, utility, and deployment models. These inform the construction of an SDG pipeline that aligns with organizational goals and regulatory standards. SynthGuard translates these inputs into a standard specification, jointly agreed upon by both parties and compatible with its workflow

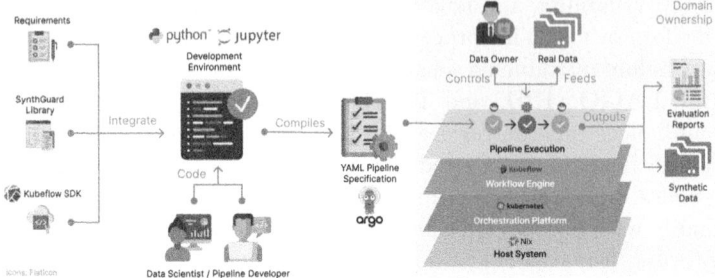

Fig. 2. SynthGuard framework overview. The pipeline specification is constructed from modular SDG components (left), compiled and orchestrated through Kubeflow/Kubernetes (centre), and executed under the data owner's control (right). Outputs include synthetic datasets and their corresponding evaluation reports.

engine. This allows the data owner to execute the pipeline independently, ensuring full control over data handling and computation.

Data consumers, such as researchers or analysts, collaborate by specifying desired statistical or causal properties of the synthetic data. SynthGuard supports this through a modular library of SDG components, enabling tailored pipeline assembly. The resulting specification is portable and reproducible, allowing data owners to audit and execute it in a secure environment. Positioned as the central artifact in the data-sharing interaction, the specification governs synthetic data generation while preserving oversight for data owners and meeting consumers' analytical needs in a transparent, compliant manner.

4.2　SDG Requirements Elicitation

Requirements elicitation is a foundational step in SynthGuard, defining parameters to ensure synthetic data aligns with intended use cases, privacy needs, and compliance constraints. It involves specifying the synthetic data type, evaluation preferences, and deployment environment—providing a structured approach for both data owners and consumers. The type of synthetic data is selected based on its intended application, with options including RSD, CSD, ASD, and HSD:

- **RSD:** Realistic synthetic data replicates the statistical structure of real data, preserving distributions, correlations, and other key patterns. It requires access to original datasets.
- **CSD:** Causal synthetic data maintains causal relationships and depends on both real data and known causal structures.
- **ASD:** Artificial synthetic data is generated from aggregate statistics or predefined rules, without needing raw data. These inputs may also carry privacy constraints.
- **HSD:** Hybrid synthetic data combines aspects of RSD, ASD, and/or CSD, offering flexibility to address diverse analytical or policy goals.

Evaluation preferences focus on utility and privacy assessments and guide SDG pipeline configuration to ensure outputs meet required standards:

- **Utility evaluation:** Measures how effectively synthetic data substitutes real data in analysis tasks, using univariate, bivariate, or multivariate assessments. This ensures that the synthetic data is useful for intended applications.
- **Privacy evaluation:** Evaluates the extent to which re-identification or disclosure risks are mitigated, supporting compliance with privacy regulations.

The deployment model defines security levels and resource configurations. Data owners choose between on-premises or cloud-based systems, and container- or VM-based isolation, depending on infrastructure and privacy requirements. On-premises deployment maximizes data control, while cloud environments offer resource scalability. VM-based isolation provides strong separation between tasks, reducing breach risk, while containers offer lightweight, efficient deployment for scalable workloads. SynthGuard's flexible model—including future support for VM-based TEEs—allows data owners to tailor pipeline isolation and infrastructure, enabling privacy, security, and scalability according to context. We clarify that SynthGuard does not define new SDG models, but rather integrates user-specified methods, such as ML-based CTGAN or rule-based generator, into modular pipelines tailored to the data context.

4.3   Pipeline Specification, Deployment and Execution

The first SynthGuard prototype is built on Nix [43], Kubernetes (via Minikube) [34,40], and Kubeflow Pipelines [33], with Argo Workflows as the pipeline specification standard [2]. As shown on the right side of Fig. 2, these components form the SynthGuard execution environment, which data owners configure and deploy locally. Nix enables reproducible, cross-platform deployment with isolated dependencies, ensuring a consistent stack across environments.

The pipeline specification begins with the SynthGuard Python library—a set of modular SDG components. Users (data owners, scientists, or developers) compose workflows by selecting and configuring modules tailored to their needs. Using the Kubeflow SDK, these are assembled into executable pipelines, often within a Python Notebook. Once tested, pipelines are exported as Argo Workflows YAML specifications. The left side of Fig. 2 depicts these concepts. This specification serves as a portable artifact which data owners can audit and review before running it against sensitive data.

Data owners then deploy these specifications within their SynthGuard stack. Kubeflow orchestrates execution, monitoring, and adjustment of components, while Kubernetes handles resource allocation and scaling, supporting both single- and multi-node clusters as needed. After execution, synthetic data and its corresponding privacy and utility reports—depicted on the right of Fig. 2—are produced directly by the pipeline. These reports help verify compliance with privacy standards and assess data utility. If validated, the synthetic dataset can be safely shared with data consumers, completing the SDG process under controlled conditions.

4.4   Privacy and Utility Evaluation Mechanisms

SynthGuard integrates evaluation mechanisms directly into SDG pipelines to balance diagnostic accuracy, utility, and privacy. Diagnostic evaluation includes essential checks to ensure synthetic data meets quality standards in format, validity, and structure [47]. For example, validity checks confirm continuous values fall within the observed real-data range, and categorical columns retain valid entries. Structural checks ensure consistency in column names and data types.

Utility evaluation measures how well synthetic data replicates the statistical properties of the original. *Univariate* comparisons assess marginal distributions, while *bivariate* evaluations capture correlations between columns. At the population level, propensity score–based metrics provide deeper insight [9,47]. Key metrics include observed propensity score mean-squared error (observed pMSE), which measures how closely synthetic data conforms to the propensity scores of real data; null-standardized pMSE (standard pMSE), which compares the observed pMSE to a distribution derived from a null model; observed-null pMSE ratio, which indicates how closely the observed pMSE matches the null model; and Kolmogorov-Smirnov distance (SPECKS), which quantifies the difference between the cumulative distribution functions of the propensity scores of real and synthetic data.

Privacy evaluation is essential in sensitive or regulated environments. Metrics assess risks of synthetic data revealing sensitive information [16,47]. CategoricalCAP estimates risks from inference attacks using public and synthetic data. NewRowSynthesis flags exact or near matches between real and synthetic rows. Inference attack scores measure the likelihood of attribute inference via statistical or ML models. Target correct attribution probability (TCAP) evaluates the probability of matching sensitive values based on key attributes. Additional metrics like minimum nearest-neighbour and sample overlap scores assess privacy risk based on proximity between real and synthetic data[4].

5   Validation

To validate SynthGuard, we followed an iterative process combining expert feedback, multi-environment deployments, and SDG quality and privacy assessment. Co-developed with domain experts from both projects, SynthGuard was refined through ongoing feedback from workshops and collaborative sessions, aligning with legal, technical, and operational requirements (Table 1). It was tested in three deployment settings: a **local** environment for testing and debugging, an **on-premises** setup to verify data sovereignty compliance, and a **cloud-based** configuration to assess scalability and distributed workflow integration.

Validation consisted of implementing SDG pipelines within the framework, executing them with varied inputs (e.g., real data, schemas, distributions) across

---

[4] CategoricalCAP and NewRowSynthesis are from SDV: https://docs.sdv.dev/sdv; other metrics are from SynthGauge: https://datasciencecampus.github.io/synthgauge/index.html.

environments, and verifying compliance through the generation of utility and privacy evaluation reports. Following the workflows described in Sect. 3, we confirmed SynthGuard's modularity, flexibility, and reproducibility, and validated pipeline execution using its modular libraries and orchestration tools.

For both projects, we generated diverse datasets (RSD, ASD, HSD) using ML-based methods like CTGAN [47], depending on data availability. For ASD, rule-based synthesis was used due to the lack of real data. Privacy and utility evaluations were integrated into pipeline execution, comparing distributions and structures to ensure representativeness and minimize disclosure risk. For ASD, direct evaluations were not conducted due to the absence of real data, though rule-based leakage checks may be explored in future work to assess privacy risks.

To assess scalability, we benchmarked SynthGuard on **law enforcement** use case datasets of 1K, 10K, and 100K rows using a cloud VM (8 vCPUs, 12 GB RAM). While the other use cases informed the architectural requirements, the validation scope focused on pipeline execution and scalability, which were sufficiently demonstrated using one use case. The pipeline included data loading, preprocessing, generation, and parallel evaluation (quality, diagnostic, privacy). As shown in Fig. 3, loading and preprocessing remained constant (~0.1 min), while generation rose from 0.14 to 5.35 min, privacy from 0.14 to 9.46 min, and quality from 0.10 to 5.59 min. Total runtime scaled sublinearly: 1.6 min (1K), 5.1 min (10K), and 16 min (100K). At 100K rows, privacy and quality evaluations accounted for over 90% of runtime, but with parallel execution via Kubeflow, their durations didn't accumulate. These results confirm SynthGuard's scalability and show how modular, concurrent design mitigates bottlenecks at scale.

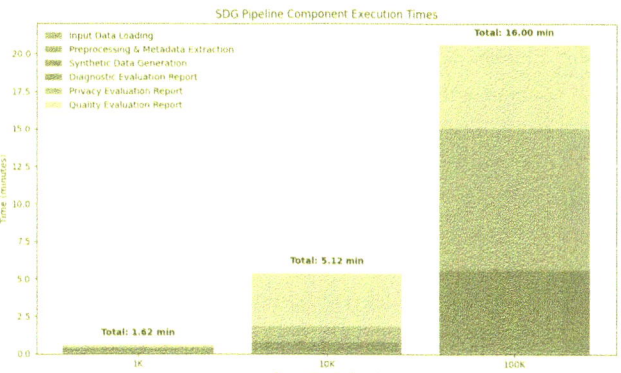

Fig. 3. Execution time per SDG pipeline component across dataset sizes.

Figure 4 illustrates a pipeline execution in the **law enforcement** use case. The pipeline specification is first loaded into the system, and the data owner provides input parameters, such as the target dataset size. The pipeline then loads the real data, generates the synthetic data, and compiles reports based on

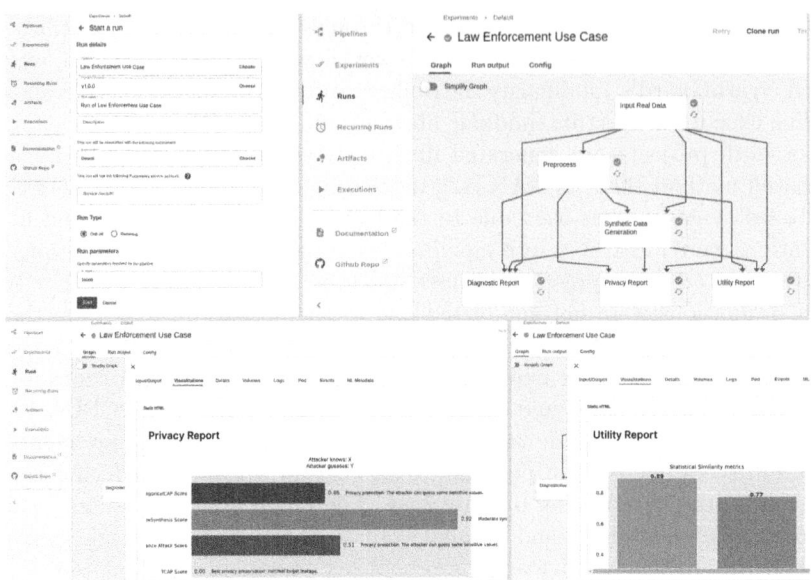

Fig. 4. Top: Example of a law enforcement SDG pipeline visualized via Kubeflow. Bottom: Privacy and utility reports accessible per pipeline component.

Table 2. LAGO and TEADAL requirements fulfilled by SynthGuard

Requirement ID	SynthGuard Features
ALL_R01	Provides on-site SDG with adaptable privacy-preserving mechanisms
ALL_R02	Enables local SDG without external transfer
ALL_R03	Includes utility and privacy validation in workflows
LAGO_R01	Enables the programmability of legally compliant SDG mechanisms
TEADAL_R01	Supports standard pipeline specifications
TEADAL_R02	Enables modular, reproducible pipelines, with flexible deployment models
TEADAL_R03	Enables local and secure output validation by data owners before sharing
TEADAL_R04	Provides modular components for SDG and flexible scaling

the chosen SDG method. Arrows represent the sequential flow and output transfers between components. Users can view execution code, logs, and download datasets and reports through the same interface.

Table 2 summarizes how SynthGuard meets project-specific requirements. The validation process confirmed SynthGuard's feasibility, adaptability, and robustness across varied environments. Future validation work includes additional performance benchmarking, large-scale deployment validation, and further automation of compliance checks.

6   Conclusion and Future Work

Privacy-enhancing technologies (PETs) are increasingly adopted to balance data utility and privacy in data-driven applications. Among them, synthetic data generation (SDG) enables representative datasets without compromising individual privacy. However, the need for secure, privacy-preserving, and scalable SDG frameworks that uphold data sovereignty and regulatory compliance, without relying on centralized processing, remains critical.

To address this, we propose SynthGuard, a modular, computational governance–oriented framework for privacy-preserving and scalable SDG. Developed iteratively with domain expert input and validated in real-world scenarios, we demonstrate through SynthGuard a balanced approach to privacy, security, and compliance, with support for SDG pipelines and utility and privacy assessments in diverse environments.

While effective in orchestrating modular pipelines, SynthGuard currently targets single-table scenarios and selected use cases. Future work includes support for multi-table relational data, integration of compliance validation, and deployment with secure multi-party computation and trusted execution environments [31]. We also plan to adopt dataspace protocols [1,3], expand compatibility with mainstream infrastructure, and explore automated workflow generation and performance optimization via GPU/TPU acceleration. As data-sharing ecosystems grow in complexity, SynthGuard will evolve with reusable pipelines, real-time generation, and regulatory alignment.

References

1. Alsamhi, S.H., et al.: Empowering dataspace 4.0: unveiling promise of decentralized data-sharing. IEEE Access **12**, 112637–112658 (2024)
2. Argo Workflows: Overview (2024). https://argo-workflows.readthedocs.io/en/. Accessed 23 Sep 2024
3. Atzori, M., et al.: Dataspaces: concepts, architectures and initiatives. In: CEUR Workshop Proceedings, vol. 3606. CEUR-WS (2024)
4. Beckman, P., et al.: Harnessing the computing continuum for programming our world. In: Fog Computing: Theory and Practice, pp. 215–230 (2020)
5. Bisong, E., Bisong, E.: Kubeflow and kubeflow pipelines. Building Machine Learning and Deep Learning Models on Google Cloud Platform: A Comprehensive Guide for Beginners, pp. 671–685 (2019)
6. Brito, E., Castillo, F., Pullonen-Raudvere, P., Werner, S.: TrustOps: continuously building trustworthy software. In: Proceeding of the 28th International Conference on Enterprise Design, Operations and Computing (2024)
7. Chandra, G., Siirtola, P., Tamminen, S., Knip, M., Veijola, R., Röning, J.: Impacts of data synthesis: a metric for quantifiable data standards and performances. Data **7**(12), 178 (2022)

8. Chang, H., et al.: A survey of data synthesis approaches. CoRR abs/2407.03672 (2024)

9. Dankar, F.K., Ibrahim, M.: Fake it till you make it: guidelines for effective synthetic data generation. Appl. Sci. **11**(5), 2158 (2021)

10. Daskal, J.: Law enforcement access to data across borders: the evolving security and rights issues. J. Nat'l Sec. L. Pol'y **8**, 473 (2015)

11. Davila, M.F., Groen, S., Panse, F., Wingerath, W.: Navigating tabular data synthesis research: understanding user needs and tool capabilities. CoRR abs/2405.20959 (2024)

12. Dessalk, Y.D., Nikolov, N., Matskin, M., Soylu, A., Roman, D.: Scalable execution of big data workflows using software containers. In: Proceedings of the 12th International Conference on Management of Digital EcoSystems, pp. 76–83 (2020)

13. Dixon, M.F., Halperin, I., Bilokon, P.: Machine Learning in Finance. Springer, Cham (2020). https://doi.org/10.1007/978-3-030-41068-1

14. Donta, P.K., Murturi, I., Casamayor Pujol, V., Sedlak, B., Dustdar, S.: Exploring the potential of distributed computing continuum systems. Computers **12**(10), 198 (2023)

15. Eichler, R., Gröger, C., Hoos, E., Schwarz, H., Mitschang, B.: From data asset to data product–the role of the data provider in the enterprise data marketplace. In: Barzen, J., Leymann, F., Dustdar, S. (eds.) Symposium and Summer School on Service-Oriented Computing, pp. 119–138. Springer (2022). https://doi.org/10. 1007/978-3-031-18304-1_7

16. El Emam, K., Mosquera, L., Hoptroff, R.: Practical Synthetic Data Generation: Balancing Privacy and the Broad Availability of Data. O'Reilly Media (2020)

17. Etti, P.: Exploring the use of synthetic data in the public sector: a framework and case study based on the example of the Estonian Police and Border Guard Board. Master's thesis, Tallinn University of Technology, Tallinn, Estonia (2024)

18. Commission, E.: Directive (EU) 2016/680 of the European parliament and of the council of 27 April 2016. Off. J. L **119**(59), 89–131 (2016)

19. European Commission: Art. 22 GDPR. Automated individual decision-making, including profiling. Intersoft Consulting (2020). https://gdpr-info.eu/art-22-gdpr

20. European Commission: Data governance act (2022). https://digital-strategy.ec. europa.eu/en/policies/data-governance-act

21. European Commission: Data act (2023). https://digital-strategy.ec.europa.eu/en/ policies/data-act

22. General Court (Eighth Chamber, Extended Composition): Judgment of the General Court (Eighth Chamber, Extended Composition) of 26 April 2023. Single Resolution Board v European Data Protection Supervisor (2023). https://eur-lex. europa.eu/legal-content/EN/TXT/?uri=CELEX%3A62020TJ0557

23. Gill, S.S., et al.: AI for next generation computing: emerging trends and future directions. Internet Things **19**, 100514 (2022)

24. Goedegebuure, A., et al.: Data mesh: a systematic gray literature review. ACM Comput. Surv. **57**(1), 1–36 (2024)

25. Hechler, E., Oberhofer, M., Schaeck, T., Hechler, E., Oberhofer, M., Schaeck, T.: The operationalization of AI. Deploying AI in the enterprise: IT Approaches for Design, DevOps, Governance, Change Management, Blockchain, and Quantum Computing, pp. 115–140 (2020)

26. Hittmeir, M., Ekelhart, A., Mayer, R.: On the utility of synthetic data: an empirical evaluation on machine learning tasks. In: ARES, pp. 29:1–29:6. ACM (2019)

27. Howe, B., Stoyanovich, J., Ping, H., Herman, B., Gee, M.: Synthetic data for social good. CoRR abs/1710.08874 (2017)

28. Hu, Y., et al.: SoK: privacy-preserving data synthesis. In: SP, pp. 4696–4713. IEEE (2024)
29. Hummel, P., Braun, M., Tretter, M., Dabrock, P.: Data sovereignty: a review. Big Data Soc. 8(1), 2053951720982012 (2021)
30. Jordan, M.I., Mitchell, T.M.: Machine learning: trends, perspectives, and prospects. Science 349(6245), 255–260 (2015)
31. Kamm, L., Bogdanov, D., Brito, E., Ostrak, A.: Blueprints for deploying privacy enhancing technologies in E-government. In: Bieker, F., de Conca, S., Gruschka, N., Jensen, M., Schiering, I. (eds.) Privacy and Identity Management. IFIP Advances in Information and Communication Technology, vol. 695, pp. 3–19. Springer (2023). https://doi.org/10.1007/978-3-031-57978-3_1
32. Kononenko, I.: Machine learning for medical diagnosis: history, state of the art and perspective. Artif. Intell. Med. 23(1), 89–109 (2001)
33. Kubeflow: Pipelines Overview (2024). https://www.kubeflow.org/docs/components/pipelines/. Accessed 23 Sept 2024
34. Kubernetes: Docs (2024). https://kubernetes.io/. Accessed 15 Oct 2024
35. Kwatra, S., Torra, V.: Empirical evaluation of synthetic data created by generative models via attribute inference attack. In: Bieker, F., de Conca, S., Gruschka, N., Jensen, M., Schiering, I. (eds.) Privacy and Identity Management. IFIP Advances in Information and Communication Technology, vol. 695, pp. 282–291. Springer, Cham (2023). https://doi.org/10.1007/978-3-031-57978-3_18
36. Lenatti, M., Paglialonga, A., Orani, V., Ferretti, M., Mongelli, M.: Characterization of synthetic health data using rule-based artificial intelligence models. IEEE J. Biomed. Health Inform. 27(8), 3760–3769 (2023)
37. Machado, I.A., Costa, C., Santos, M.Y.: Data mesh: concepts and principles of a paradigm shift in data architectures. Procedia Comput. Sci. 196, 263–271 (2022)
38. Majeed, A.: Attribute-centric and synthetic data based privacy preserving methods: a systematic review. J. Cybersecur. Priv. 3(3), 638–661 (2023)
39. Malka, J., Zacchiroli, S., Zimmermann, T.: Reproducibility of build environments through space and time. In: Proceedings of the 2024 ACM/IEEE 44th International Conference on Software Engineering: New Ideas and Emerging Results, pp. 97–101 (2024)
40. Minikube: Overview (2024). https://minikube.sigs.k8s.io/docs/. Accessed 12 Nov 2024
41. Nagpal, A., Gabrani, G.: Python for data analytics, scientific and technical applications. In: 2019 Amity International Conference on Artificial Intelligence (AICAI), pp. 140–145. IEEE (2019)
42. Nikolenko, S.I.: Synthetic Data for Deep Learning. SOIA, vol. 174. Springer, Cham (2021). https://doi.org/10.1007/978-3-030-75178-4
43. Nix: declarative builds and deployments (2024). https://nixos.org/. Accessed 5 Sept 2024
44. Oleghe, O.: Container placement and migration in edge computing: concept and scheduling models. IEEE Access 9, 68028–68043 (2021)
45. Osorio-Marulanda, P.A., Epelde, G., Hernandez, M., Isasa, I., Reyes, N.M., Iraola, A.B.: Privacy mechanisms and evaluation metrics for synthetic data generation: a systematic review. IEEE Access 12, 88048–88074 (2024)
46. Park, N., Mohammadi, M., Gorde, K., Jajodia, S., Park, H., Kim, Y.: Data synthesis based on generative adversarial networks. Proc. VLDB Endow. 11(10), 1071–1083 (2018)
47. Patki, N., Wedge, R., Veeramachaneni, K.: The synthetic data vault. In: DSAA, pp. 399–410. IEEE (2016)

48. Pezoulas, V.C., et al.: Synthetic data generation methods in healthcare: a review on open-source tools and methods. Comput. Struct. Biotechnol. J. **23**, 2892–2910 (2024)

49. Ping, H., Stoyanovich, J., Howe, B.: DataSynthesizer: privacy-preserving synthetic datasets. In: SSDBM, pp. 42:1–42:5. ACM (2017)

50. Rambert, P., Rychkova, I.: Implications of trust in cyber-physical systems design: the ASSA case study. In: International Conference on Enterprise Design, Operations, and Computing. pp. 201–218. Springer, Cham (2024). https://doi.org/10.1007/978-3-031-78338-8_11

51. Sengupta, S., et al.: A review of deep learning with special emphasis on architectures, applications and recent trends. Knowl. Based Syst. **194**, 105596 (2020)

52. Shi, J., Wang, D., Tesei, G., Norgeot, B.: Generating high-fidelity privacy-conscious synthetic patient data for causal effect estimation with multiple treatments. Frontiers Artif. Intell. **5**, 918813 (2022)

53. Shi, Y., Wen, M., Cogo, F.R., Chen, B., Jiang, Z.M.: An experience report on producing verifiable builds for large-scale commercial systems. IEEE Trans. Software Eng. **48**(9), 3361–3377 (2021)

54. Sidey-Gibbons, J.A., Sidey-Gibbons, C.J.: Machine learning in medicine: a practical introduction. BMC Med. Res. Methodol. **19**, 1–18 (2019)

55. Singh, J.: The rise of synthetic data: enhancing AI and machine learning model training to address data scarcity and mitigate privacy risks. J. Artif. Intell. Res. Appl. **1**(2), 292–332 (2021)

56. Soltana, G., Sabetzadeh, M., Briand, L.C.: Synthetic data generation for statistical testing. In: ASE, pp. 872–882. IEEE Computer Society (2017)

57. Stoian, M.C., Dyrmishi, S., Cordy, M., Lukasiewicz, T., Giunchiglia, E.: How realistic is your synthetic data? Constraining deep generative models for tabular data. In: ICLR. OpenReview.net (2024)

58. Tatineni, S., Boppana, V.R.: AI-powered DevOps and MLOps frameworks: enhancing collaboration, automation, and scalability in machine learning pipelines. J. Artif. Intell. Res. Appl. **1**(2), 58–88 (2021)

59. Taub, J., Elliot, M., Pampaka, M., Smith, D.: Differential correct attribution probability for synthetic data: an exploration. In: Domingo-Ferrer, J., Montes, F. (eds.) PSD 2018. LNCS, vol. 11126, pp. 122–137. Springer, Cham (2018). https://doi.org/10.1007/978-3-319-99771-1_9

60. Tolas, R., Portase, R., Potolea, R.: GeMSyD: generic framework for synthetic data generation. Data **9**(1), 14 (2024)

61. Wagner, P.: Privacy enhancing technologies and synthetic data. Available at SSRN 3762686 (2020)

62. Zhou, Y., Yu, Y., Ding, B.: Towards MLops: a case study of ML pipeline platform. In: 2020 International conference on artificial intelligence and computer engineering (ICAICE), pp. 494–500. IEEE (2020)

63. Zielke, T.: Is artificial intelligence ready for standardization? In: Yilmaz, M., Niemann, J., Clarke, P., Messnarz, R. (eds.) EuroSPI 2020. CCIS, vol. 1251, pp. 259–274. Springer, Cham (2020). https://doi.org/10.1007/978-3-030-56441-4_19

Designing a Framework to Tackle the Multifaceted Intricacies of Insider Threats

Rim Ben Salem[1][(⊠)], Frédéric Cuppens[1][(⊠)], Nora Boulahia-Cuppens[1][(⊠)], and Hager Khechine[2][(⊠)]

[1] Polytechnique Montréal, Montréal, Canada
{rim.ben-salem,frederic.cuppens,nora.boulahia-cuppens}@polymtl.ca
[2] Université Laval, Québec, Canada
Hager.Khechine@fsa.ulaval.ca

Abstract. Insider threats present a significant challenge to companies and organizations, resulting in severe repercussions such as asset loss, damaged reputation, and diminished shareholder trust. As long as there are human-operated tasks in a company, there is potential for abusing one's privileges or jeopardizing processes due to carelessness. A multitude of approaches have been proposed to mitigate insider threats from access management to anomaly detection, but the rate of false negatives and positives hinders these efforts. One of the challenges in this regard is the complexity of the human factor.

Existing frameworks primarily focus on recognising imminent threats. Our goal is to offer a deeper understanding of individuals long before they pose any danger. We aim to identify the states they can be in, the indicators that can be used to recognise their present state, and the factors that have led them to this point. This approach provides the opportunity to deescalate situations where an employee might transition into an insider threat and offers cybersecurity analysts early insights into problematic behaviour.

Keywords: Insider threat · Indicators · Cybersecurity · Framework

1 Introduction

There is no doubt that insider threats present a major peril to organisations across all sectors; the more sensitive the data and operations, the greater the potential impact of such threats. The Computer Emergency Response Team (CERT) at Carnegie Mellon University identifies five categories of insider threats: sabotage, theft of intellectual property, fraud, espionage, and unintentional insider threats [1]. This can include intentionally or unintentionally accessing information without legitimate reasons and/or privileges, altering data, undermining operations, submitting fraudulent reports, and mishandling assets. Managing these threats hinges on a dual approach: reactive and proactive measures.

B. Coppens et al. (Eds.): ARES 2025 Workshops, LNCS 15995, pp. 212–229, 2025.
https://doi.org/10.1007/978-3-032-00633-2_13

Reactive measures include: incident response following a security breach to mitigate damage, forensic analysis to determine the cause, impact, and methods used
by attackers, and patch management to fix vulnerabilities. Proactive measures
involve regularly scanning systems for weaknesses to address them before they
can be exploited and anticipating threats before they occur.

The first issue with these approaches is that they are often conducted in a
vacuum, whereas real-life incidents of insider threats are highly dependent on
circumstances such as triggers, emotional states, and even the device used at the
time. Second, according to CERT's taxonomy of insider threats, four out of five
categories are classified as malicious attacks. These threats are not rooted in a
lack of knowledge and, therefore, cannot be effectively mitigated through training
programs alone, despite the success of such programs in other cases. Third,
even in cases of unintentional insider threats, training is not a comprehensive
solution. Accidents tend to happen when people are stressed out, overwhelmed,
or indifferent. Fourth, organisations do not fully understand the transition that
an employee undergoes to become an insider threat. While the main focus is to
detect and report suspicious actions, understanding what individuals are feeling
and experiencing prior to the incident is not accorded the same importance. All
of this has motivated us to pursue the following objectives: defining the states
that employees can be in, detailing the indicators leading to the detection of
these states, and identifying the factors behind this transition.

We propose to retrace the root of the issue, which brings us back to the human
factor. In most cases, employees, contractors, and others do not spontaneously
become insider threats. Postmortem reports following major breaches attributed
to insiders reveal a multitude of red flags that went unnoticed, underestimated, or
filed away and forgotten. For this reason, the framework we are proposing shines
a light on the process of becoming an insider threat to serve as a cornerstone for
future mitigative measures. Deepening the understanding of the factors leading
to malicious or negligent incidents is paramount to pre-emptive approaches. We
summarise the steps taken to design the proposed framework as follows:

- We propose the notion of "state", which offers insight into an employee's
  transition to becoming an insider threat. This is different from the current
  research that focuses on generic motivations, causes, and signs of imminent
  threats.
- We identify the indicators that can be used to recognise an employee's current
  state. This highlights the feasibility of the implementation of our framework.
- We design a framework, which details the factors impacting an employee's
  state, including predispositions, personal life events, work profile, and organisational aspects.
- We demonstrate the potential of the framework using corroborating studies
  from the literature and well-known real-life examples of insider threats.

The remainder of the paper is outlined as follows: A review of related work is
provided in Sect. 2. The design of the proposed framework is detailed in Sect. 3.
Section 4 is dedicated to the discussion of the propositions and future considerations, following which we conclude this work in Sect. 5.

2   Related Work

This section is divided into two parts: the first describes and discusses the predominant approaches to insider threat mitigation and the second dives into the less explored landscape of understanding the instigators of such incidents.

2.1   Insider Threat Mitigation

Insider threat incidents often result from some form of privilege abuse. As such, a pillar of mitigative measures is Identity and Access Management (IAM), which serves as a proactive defence against such attacks by controling who has access to critical corporate information [2]. The goal of IAM is to ensure that the right individuals have the appropriate access to the right resources, at the right time, and for the right reasons [3]. Role-Based Access Control (RBAC) is a fundamental method for managing access rights within organizations [4]. It assigns access to resources based on the roles of individual users, with each role having specific permissions tailored to its needs. Advanced IAM systems extend beyond basic role assignments to include continuous verification, adaptability, and intelligent access control decisions [5]. This can be achieved thanks to the introduction of real-time, adaptive access controls that adjust permissions based on contextual information like user behaviour, location, and time of access [6,7]. These developments offer more granular, risk-based access decisions, improving security against insider threats. However, a critical friction point of these approaches is identifying and recognizing which indicators to look out for in order to assign dynamic privileges. Our framework has the potential to ease this process.

Other methods implement various behavioural biometrics [8], such as typing patterns and head and eye movements [9]. Keystroke dynamics can be continuously used to authenticate insiders based on their typing patterns [10]. In the specific context of insider threats, Babu et al. [11] rely on this information alongside access control models to detect and prevent masquerader attacks. However, using biometrics to monitor employees is highly controversial from both ethical and practical perspectives. Therefore, one of the considerations in designing our framework is the feasibility of collecting information based on the knowledge the organization already has about the employees, without further infringing on their privacy by adding more invasive monitoring.

Most mitigative solutions are intended for use when an insider threat is imminent or already underway. However, there are frameworks designed to understand the root causes of insider threats. Their value lies in the potential for early detection and prevention of such incidents.

2.2   Frameworks Offering an Understanding Of the Human Factor

Identifying and recognizing the early signs of a possible threat can be more challenging than mitigating an ongoing one because the latter involves concrete evidence, while the former relies on subtle indicators and patterns that may not be immediately obvious. Stressful events, whether work-related or personal, often precede insider attacks [12]. These events include employee dismissal, disputes with employers, perceived injustices, transfers or demotions, salary reductions, and family problems. Dissatisfaction resulting from these stressful events can trigger concerning behaviours in individuals predisposed to malicious acts. Georgiadou et al. [13] propose a cybersecurity culture framework that emphasizes human and organizational factors for detecting insider threats. By merging technical measures with human-centered insights, the framework anticipates potential risks and incorporates cultural aspects into detection strategies. Consistent with this perspective, the human-focused component detailed by Khan et al. [14] underscores the importance of lived experience and acquired knowledge as determinants of the decision-making process in the workplace. Greitzer et al. [15] propose SOFIT, an ontology encompassing sociotechnical and organizational factors for insider threats. The sociotechnical category includes the history of violations, job performance, and psychological factors, while the organizational category extends to management systems and security practices. Other researchers have tackled the subject of understanding insider threats from specific perspectives such as the work of Kandias et al. [16], which focuses on the opportunistic aspect of these incidents.

Finally, we need to seek a better understanding of employees because even the most cutting-edge anomaly detection solutions can be easily misled on their own. For example, consider Bob, who recently experienced a family emergency that disrupted his routine. A log-based system would identify his change in behaviour as anomalous and a potential indicator of a threat. However, if this approach is combined with our proposed framework, it can help eliminate false positives, allowing cybersecurity analysts to focus on more urgent cases. Clearly, our framework is not standalone; it is designed to be used in tandem with human-focused solutions to reduce both false negatives and false positives.

3   State-Centric Framework Towards Insider Threat Mitigation

There is a considerable body of research focusing on the factors leading someone to become an insider threat. However, a lot of the proposed frameworks fall short on reflecting the reality of making cybersecurity decisions. For example, most consider disgruntlement to be the leading reason to maliciously act against's the organization's best interest without studying the nuances of "disgruntlement". In the existing research, it ranges from someone who does not agree with company policies to stress in the workplace to personal life strains, etc. Due to this reductive perception of the issue, numerous threats might go unnoticed. If we cannot know the specifics of what is wrong because we group all "symptoms" as disgruntlement, how can we attempt to solve such a generic issue?

Furthermore, both reports of real-life incidents and the existing frameworks tend to present a simple timeline of events that could be summarised as: The employee experienced this, so, they decided to act upon a specific motivation.

That is far from the truth as, with the exception of negligent actions, the "degradation" of the employees' state happens over time and due to various factors.
Then, they act upon their motivation when an opportunity arises. Considering
both of these reasons, we decided to introduce the concept of "state".

3.1 A Graph Representation of the States Leading to Insider Threats

An employee can become an insider threat under specific circumstances that
align with their current state. For instance, an individual experiencing cognitive
dissonance due to a perceived misalignment between the organization's ethics
and their own would not be motivated to sell data for financial gain. Conversely,
someone undergoing personal life stress due to financial difficulties might be
driven to do so. Therefore, we no longer label both scenarios as disgruntlement.
Figure 1 illustrates the various states of an employee.

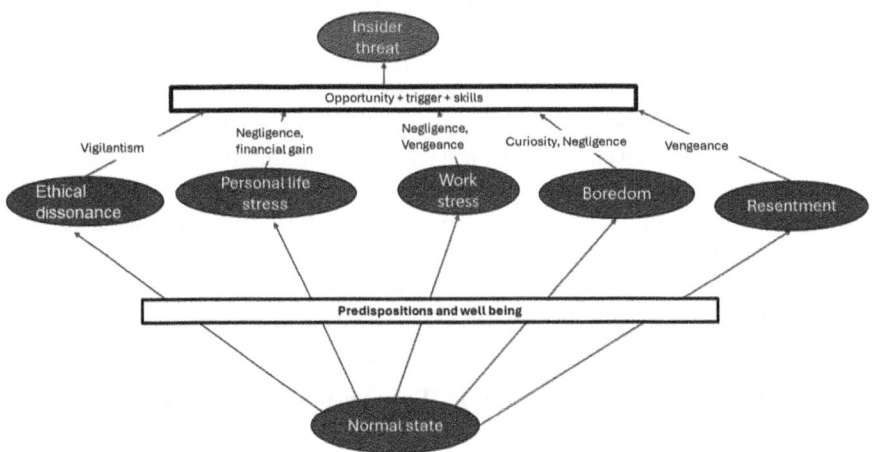

Fig. 1. Our state-based graph.

From a cybersecurity perspective, the ideal state for all employees is the
"normal state," where individuals are unlikely to transition to insider threats. In
this state, employees do not harbor ill will against their employers and are not
prone to negligent, incident-instigating actions. However, achieving this ideal can
be challenging, as each employee has unique complexities that may be beyond
the organization's control. This brings us to states that can be perceived as "one
transition away" from becoming a threat: ethical dissonance, personal life stress,
work stress, boredom, and resentment.

First, ethical dissonance refers to the feeling of a widening gap between one's
own morals and the company's. This can lead to an employee quitting their
job or changing careers. In extreme cases, it may result in actions driven by

vigilante justice, such as exposing company secrets for self-declared altruistic reasons. This leads to whistleblower ex-employees, some of whom are still seen as pariahs, such as Edward Snowden, while others have slowly gained the image of heroes, like Bradley Birkenfeld. Edward Snowden, a former NSA contractor, leaked classified information in 2013, revealing extensive global surveillance programs conducted by the NSA and other intelligence agencies. His disclosures brought to light the ubiquity of monitoring individuals without their knowledge or consent. Conversely, Bradley Birkenfeld, a former banker at UBS, exposed his employers for helping wealthy Americans hide assets in secret Swiss accounts to avoid paying U.S. taxes. His disclosures led to a $780 million fine for UBS and the release of the names of over 4,450 U.S. taxpayers. In both cases, regardless of the ethical debate around their actions, one truth remains: these individuals were indeed insider threats who revealed private information, bypassing the organization's policies and security measures. Moreover, whether it is to further their cause or for selfish reasons, individuals in this state tend to seek public recognition and acknowledgment of their actions.

Second, being in a prolonged state of personal life stress can start to affect one's professional conduct, both intentionally and unintentionally. There are records of individuals whose financial struggles led them to pursue profitable opportunities. This state is also linked to the accidental disclosure of company secrets due to sheer carelessness. An employee whose personal life is in disarray is unlikely to be fully efficient at their job and follow every cybersecurity practice.

Third, work stress is one of the most commonly cited reasons for insider incidents in the literature. While we view it as a "state" rather than a "cause" for the reasons explained earlier, we align with the existing research on the topic. Feeling burdened and overworked contributes to this stress, which, if left unattended and unaddressed by management, can lead to feelings of being overwhelmed and unfocused. Engaging in multitasking increases the likelihood of human errors and disrupts decision-making processes related to security requirements [17]. This is also evident when employees have high email loads, resulting in negative outcomes.

Fourth, while boredom is perceived as a passive, seemingly innocuous state, it can lead to dire consequences. Examples of minor incidents where individuals act out of self-interest and curiosity include using one's privileges to see the salaries of colleagues. In the literature, boredom is sometimes used interchangeably with apathy. We opt for the former because the latter is technically a personality trait, and we classify it as such in our framework. More details about this will be provided in Sect. 3.3.

Fifth, resentment is a well-documented state leading to insider threats. The difference between the third state, "work stress," and "resentment" is that while the former can lead to both negligent and intentional threats, the latter tends to be premeditated and calculated. They were not grouped into a single state because the design of this framework aims to lay the foundation for mitigating corrective measures. Hence, the solutions for overworked, stressed-out individuals (work stress) can be different from those meant to address deep-seated malice (resentment). Similar to 'rationalization' in the fraud triangle, resentment can be expressed in statements like, "I don't get paid what I'm worth."

One question arises: How can we distinguish these states from one another to determine which corrective or administrative measures to take to mitigate the potentially imminent threat?

3.2   State Indicators

In this paper, two terms are used to mean different concepts: factors and indicators. Factors refer to the contributors and catalysts that lead a person to be in a specific state. More of this will be explained in Sect. 3.3. The term "indicators," however, refers to the observed or inferred clues that can be used to determine a person's state. For example, if someone writes to their manager to express that they are feeling very overwhelmed by the workload, the message is an indicator of the employee's state. Attributes, on the other hand, are higher-level indicators or a cluster of them. For instance, an attribute could be "underperforming," with indicators such as "drop in efficiency," "increased idle time," and "missing deadlines." Given that people's behaviour and emotions are not straightforward, some indicators are more difficult to capture and interpret than others. Some industry reports have attempted to tackle the identification of the indicators and attributes associated with malicious actors [18]. However, they were solely focused on disgruntlement as a potential cause for insider threats, which is restrictive. We expand upon this to include all the states detailed in Sect. 3.1.

In our work, we divide indicators into three categories: reported, self-reported, and digital. The term "reported indicator" means that an individual other than the employee in question took note of an event and created a record of it, either by talking or writing to a manager or human resources. This can be done anonymously or not. "Self-reported" refers to the employee coming forward and disclosing information about themselves, such as being sick or asking for a pay advance due to financial hardship. "Digital indicators" are captured using activity logs and public social media posts. Figures 2 and 3 highlight our proposed model to recognize the states of "personal life stress" and "resentment." The figures for the remaining states are included in the appendix.

For example, the attributes of personal life stress are "changes in the familial structure" and "financial struggle." The first attribute includes events such as marriage, giving birth, divorce, sickness, and the death of a loved one. It can be detected based on the following indicators: requesting time off to take care of a family member (self-reported), adding or editing a family health insurance plan (self-reported), and publicly posting about grief and loss on social media (digital). The second attribute, financial struggle, has its own telltale signs, such as asking for pay advances (reported or digital through an online request), changes in lifestyle like having one's house remortgaged (can be self-reported), and asking to borrow money from coworkers (reported).

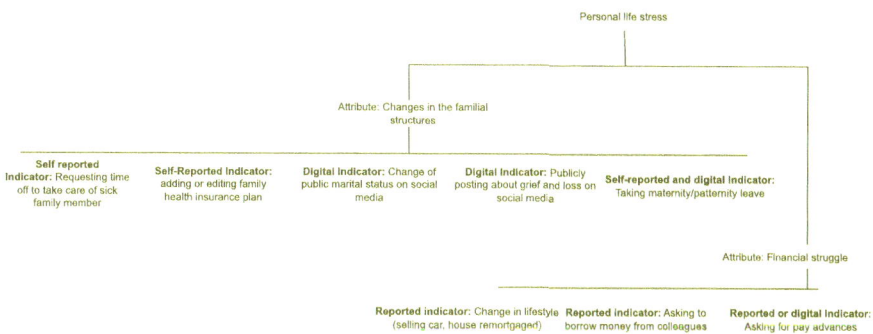

Fig. 2. The attributes and indicators of personal life stress.

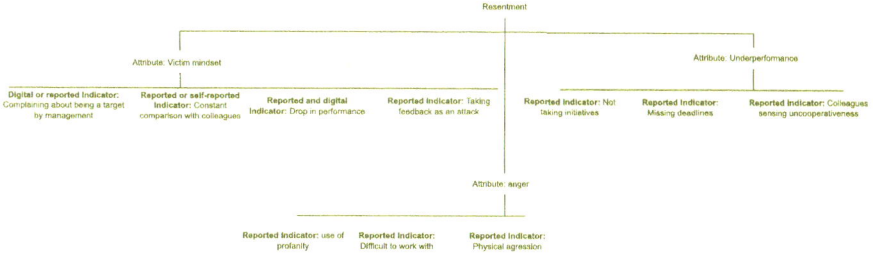

Fig. 3. The attributes and indicators of resentment.

3.3 Factors Leading to the State

The combination of states, indicators, and factors offers the following perspective: Using the collected indicators, we identified the state of employee Bob as "work life stress". So, what can be done about it? This is where the factors become relevant because knowing what led to this can allow for de-escalation in most cases. Consider a hypothetical employee, Bob, who is well-performing but whose loyalty towards the organization has been decreasing lately, and he is feeling underappreciated based on the collected indicators. If we consider recent organizational restructuring as a major contributor to this case, the company can demonstrate that its core values have not changed and that it has programs in place to keep things running smoothly. If a few employees are experiencing such hardships and difficulty adapting to the new environment, the issue might be tackled by their managers. If multiple employees are experiencing the same "symptoms", then addressing the problem can happen during the next all-hands meeting, where the entire workforce assembles. Figure 4 highlights our proposed framework. According to the person-environment fit theory, individuals experience stress in two scenarios: when the environment fails to meet their expectations and when their abilities (such as skills, time, and knowledge) are insufficient to meet the demands imposed by the environment [19]. This is why considering the organizational factor is crucial, as it is synonymous with the

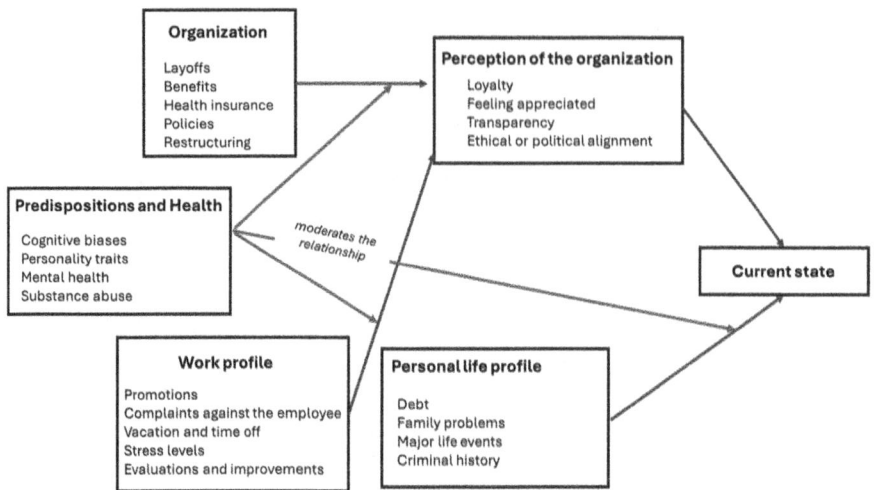

Fig. 4. The factors impacting an employee's current state (part A of the framework).

environment in this context. The direction in which the organization is headed and recent changes significantly impact employees' perception of their employers. The findings of Liu et al. [20] emphasize the negative effect of organizational change on employee performance through work pressure, which in turn reflects on the cybersecurity culture [21,22]. Furthermore, clinical psychologist and former intelligence officer Eric D. Shaw explains that changes in the organization, such as controversy, mergers, and redundancies, are major factors that drive employees to pose a risk to their companies [23]. The impact of the work profile on the perception of the organization is well-established. Higher workload stress is associated with higher psychological strain, increased negative emotions, and lower organizational commitment (loyalty) [24].

Both the organization and work life impact the way individuals perceive their organization. This connection is moderated by predispositions and health. These moderators can be catalysts or inhibitors depending on the situation. For example, the dark triad—encompassing narcissism, psychopathy, and Machiavellianism—is linked to misbehaviour and misconduct in general. As intentional insider threats fall into this category, there has been growing interest in studying the link between psychometric data and workplace behaviour [25].

Furthermore, personal life profile is a factor that determines one's current state. For example, being in debt leads to financial distress, which in turn is linked to becoming an actor against the company's best interest. Other major life events tend to have a similar link, including welcoming a newborn, divorce, becoming the caretaker of a sick loved one, etc. Figure 5 complements Fig. 4 and shows the moderator factors that impact the transition from the current state to insider threat. For example, cybersecurity skills can allow an individual to go undetected or facilitate the process of circumventing existing security measures.

Someone lacking in this department might not be confident enough to pursue this dangerous endeavor for fear of being discovered before achieving their objective. Opportunity refers to a perceived limited window of time during which circumstances are opportune, such as the manager being absent or someone forgetting to log out of their privileged account. Perceiving this as a rare fleeting chance can lead the employee to act quickly. Opportunity can be more tangible than motive [26], which is why it needs to be considered. Finally, the trigger is similar in concept to opportunity, but the difference is that a trigger tends to be an external event that heightens emotions, such as getting fired, being denied a promotion, or receiving bad news about a loved one. Such events or realizations essentially light the match and initiate the sequence of events leading to the transition to an insider threat.

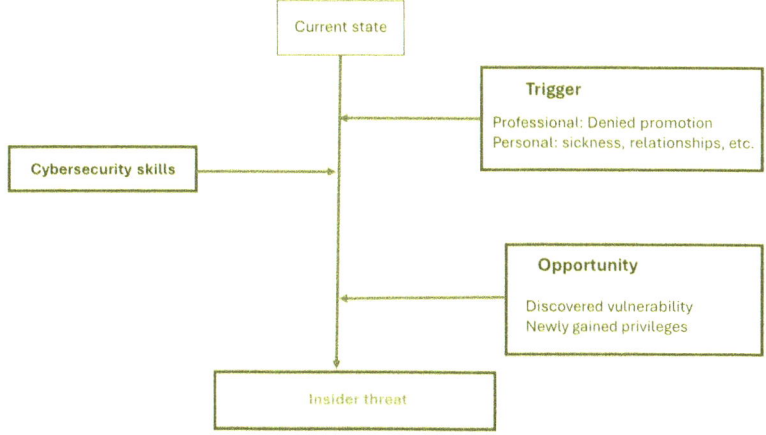

Fig. 5. Transitioning from a state to an insider threat (part B of the framework).

Figs. 6, 8, and 7 show the application of our framework to the cases of Terry Childs, Reality Winner, and Edward Snowden, all of whom are high-profile insider threat cases. The case of Terry Childs involves a former network administrator for the City of San Francisco who, in 2008, refused to provide passwords to the city's FiberWAN network, effectively locking out his superiors from accessing and managing the network. Childs, a highly skilled Cisco Certified Internetworking Engineer, had designed and built the network and was the sole administrator with access to its critical components. His colleagues reported him as being uncooperative and growing possessive over the network. As for Reality Winner, she is a former NSA contractor and U.S. Air Force veteran who became widely known for leaking a classified intelligence report about Russian interference in the 2016 U.S. elections. The factors contributing to her final decision included her mental health conditions and conflicts with her supervisor due to workplace issues.

Another point to highlight is that, while the proposed framework divides the states into five distinct ones, there are intersections between them due to

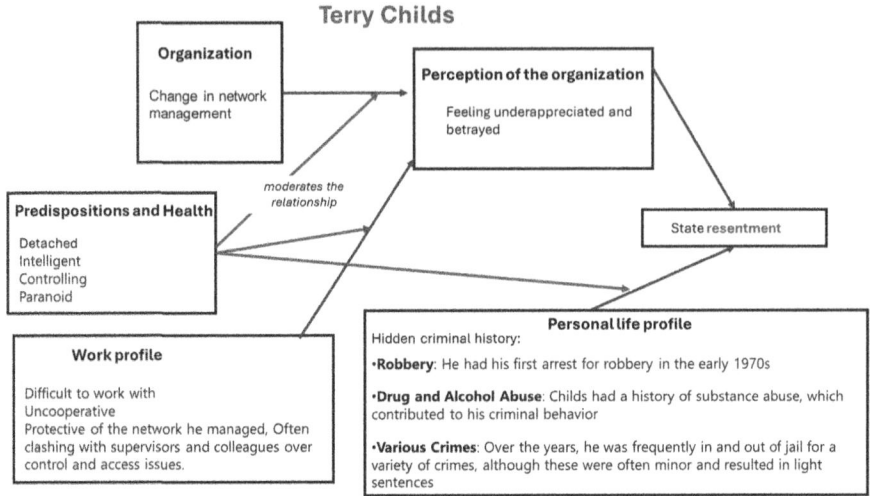

Fig. 6. Applying the framework to the case of Terry Childs.

the nuances in human psychology. In the case of Snowden, as shown in Fig. 7, he had conflicts with his supervisors and was dissatisfied with workplace conditions. This supposedly happened after he began pushing for a promotion but got into what he termed a "petty e-mail spat" in which he questioned a senior manager's judgment [27]. This type of precursor usually aligns with the state of "resentment". However, he also famously declared his motivation "to inform the public as to that which is done in their name and that which is done against them," which expresses his state of "ethical dissonance", where his own morals opposed those of his organization. Perhaps one state led to another, or he might have simultaneously existed in both states, motivated equally by vigilante justice and revenge. Our framework considers both states according to all the signs and clues prior to his actions taking place.

The relevance of applying the framework to these cases is to highlight the red flags and precursors that were present before the incident occurred. Had these pieces of the puzzle been grouped together, the outcome might have been different. Sometimes, it is not a lack of information that hinders the early detection of threats, but rather understanding the significance of seemingly isolated incidents. For example, in the case of Snowden, being injured was not his reason for becoming a whistleblower, but it sowed the seed of dissatisfaction, disappointment, and doubt in the organization he belonged to. These feelings only grew with time and further realizations. Similarly, in Terry Childs' case, his colleagues reported his misbehaviour and suspicious possessiveness over his work, but it did not result in further investigations at the time.

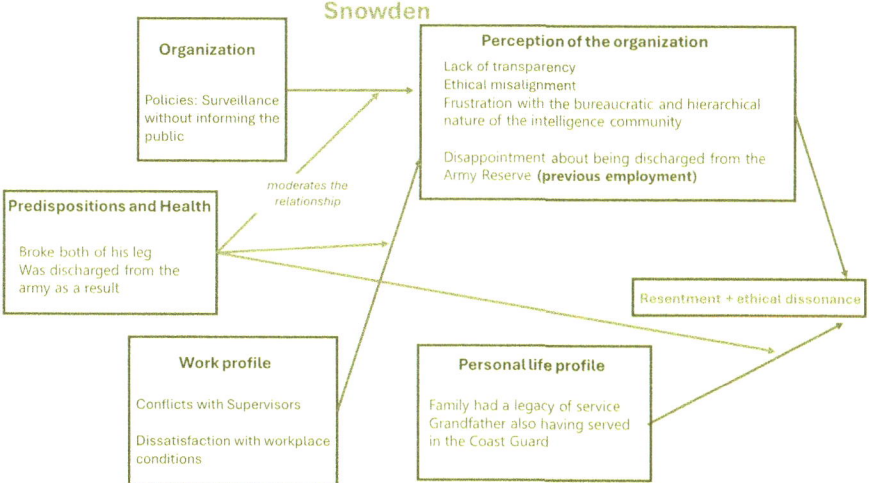

Fig. 7. Applying the framework to the case of Edward Snowden.

4 Discussion

First, we would like to acknowledge that human behaviour and predispositions are nuanced, so much so that even the eerily named "dark triad" can be linked to numerous success stories. Indeed, narcissism in CEOs has been found to have a positive influence on firm performance [28]. Furthermore, successful psychopathy is characterized by higher levels of autonomic responsivity and executive functioning [29]. The term "successful psychopathy" is used to describe people who have psychopathic traits but have achieved success despite them. The concept is controversial and has been called an oxymoron, but personality traits are not black and white. So, one might pose the question: why consider them in the framework if they are not determinants of maliciousness or a tendency to perceive the organization as a hostile entity?

It is worth pointing out that most of the existing research on the topic focuses on correlation. Correlation is not causation. However, we are essentially operating on a similar reasoning to multiple regression, where the value of a variable is predicted based on the value of two or more other variables. Personality traits, on their own, are hardly capable of pointing investigators and cybersecurity analysts in the right direction [30], but when combined with all the other factors in Fig. 4, the corroborating evidence becomes more reliable. However, this approach is not without its limitations, as experienced masqueraders and spies are adept at pretending and leaving little to no evidence behind. An insider threat at Boeing went undetected from 1979 until 2006, as he continuously fed another country military manufacturing information related to space programs [31]. This sort of data is usually kept under lock and key, yet spies persist. Zero risk does not exist in the real world, but to minimize it as much as possible, change needs

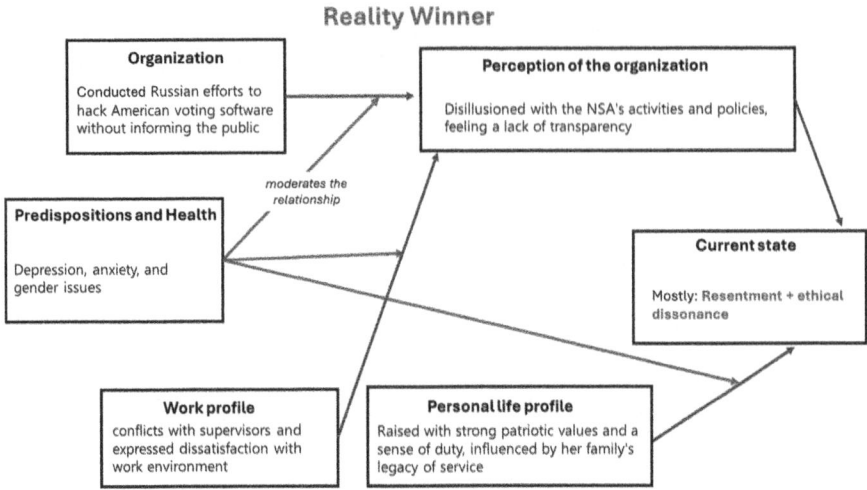

Fig. 8. Applying the framework to the case of Reality Winner.

to be brought forth at the organizational level. Additionally, we plan to research the impact of utilizing flexible fuzzy "states" to potentially overcome the lack of evidence or proof in certain scenarios. In other words, a person might not express an alarming degree of resentment towards the organization, but if coupled with personal life stress, the outcome can be different.

Another note to be made is that in the case of the aforementioned Boeing engineer, his scheme lasted for at least 27 years. It is highly unlikely that during this entire period, the employee did not raise any suspicion through his digital footprint or in real life, as observed by his colleagues and managers. Since the internal processes at his company are not public knowledge, we can only hypothesize what might have gone awry for this to last as long as it did without any intervention. One possible reason could be the sheer abundance of reports for the cybersecurity team to go through. Giving all of them the same degree of importance or criticality might have led to the worst-case scenario. As such, one aspect we aim to explore next through our work is assigning attributes to "states" that encompass the urgency and criticality of the situation. For example, if Alice and Bob are both very resentful towards their organization, but Bob has been feeling this way for months while Alice just recently transitioned to this state, with limited resources, the best choice would be to address Bob's case first. Of course, this is not a straightforward matter of assigning higher criticality or urgency based on time alone, as other factors also play a role. Continuing with the same example, Alice might be someone deemed impulsive according to her psychometric profile, a character that is further aggravated by her recent physical injury. So, what can be done in this scenario? The intricacy of human behaviour is something we are eager to explore further to answer this question.

Furthermore, in the case of Snowden or Reality Winner, the opportunity, as detailed in Fig. 5, was the discovered lax internal security measures at their organization. If we use the same terms introduced in the framework (Fig. 4), the lack of reinforcement of organizational policies and procedures, as pointed out in a redacted version of an internal report from the CIA [32], falls under the factor "organization" and impacts the "perception of the organization" as being permissive, lenient, and remiss. While it is crucial for an employee to feel valued and ethically aligned with their organization, it is equally important for them to recognize and believe that the organization is vigilant and capable of enforcing accountability. This ensures that any misconduct will be promptly identified and appropriately addressed. Figuring out where the line lies between positive and negative reinforcements, as well as between offering a welcoming yet firm and policy-abiding environment, is key to successful and secure organizations.

Considering all the aforementioned points, beyond the immediate contributions, the framework was designed with these outlined long-term goals in mind:

– Using an array of indicators and factors can reduce the number of false positives and false negatives. The former refers to instances in which someone is falsely identified as a potential insider threat. The latter pertains to cases where an insider threat falls through the cracks and is not recognized as the potential danger they present.
– Identifying the factors and indicators lays the foundation for descriptive insider threat scenarios. In the literature, one of the most cited challenges facing mitigative approaches is the lack of scenarios [33], which are needed to both train and test specific models.
– The states, as identified and described in this paper, can offer foresight into potential threats, thus contributing to the early detection of incidents before worse comes to worst. This allows the organization to take the most appropriate measures, such as offering managerial and administrative support.

5   Conclusion

The significance of insider threat mitigation is increasing annually as emerging technologies create new avenues for threats posed by both negligent employees and malicious actors seeking to harm their organization or achieve personal gain. These efforts cannot rely solely on digital indicators and anomaly detection due to the issue of false positives and negatives. Real-life incidents have proven that cybersecurity analysts are overwhelmed by a long backlog of reports requiring inspection, some of which transition to insider threats before the investigation even takes place. To alleviate their burden and lay the foundation for the prevention of such threats from the early signs, we sought out the following objectives: defining the states that employees can be in, detailing the indicators leading to the detection of these states, and identifying the factors behind this transition.

The next step is to further define the attributes of the states, such as criticality and urgency. Following this, we aim to validate our proposed design, anticipating a few challenges. We could potentially use the ubiquitous approach of recruiting participants to answer a questionnaire, based on which we can corroborate or eliminate some of the connections or correlations. However, such a method is laden with biases that we aim to minimize to be as close to reality as possible. Exploring different possibilities of achieving this without relying on self-reporting is one of our priorities.

Acknowledgments. We extend our gratitude to MITACS, National Bank of Canada, Desjardins, Mondata, and Qohash for their invaluable support and contributions to this research.

Disclosure of Interests. The authors have no competing interests to declare that are relevant to the content of this article.

A   Appendix

see Figs. 9, 10 and 11

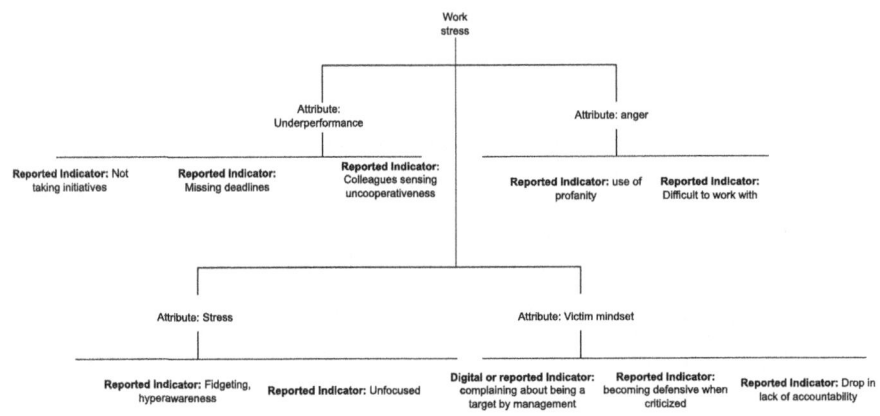

Fig. 9. The attributes and indicators of work stress.

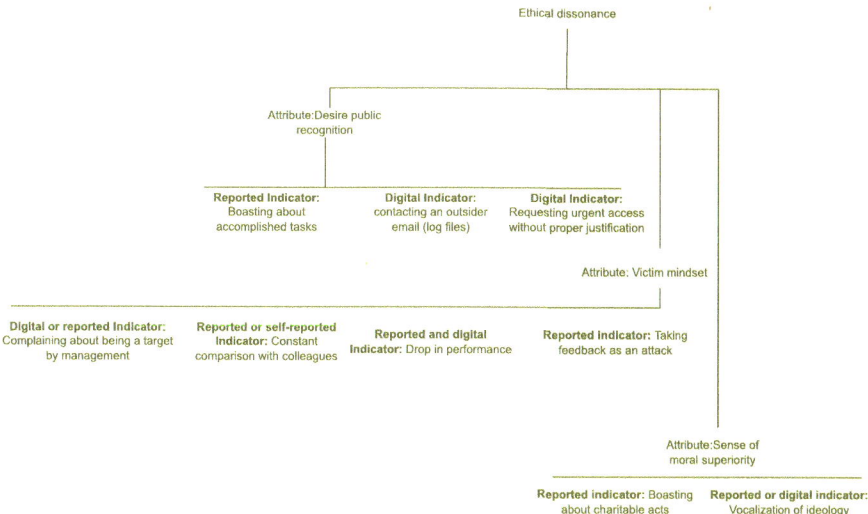

Fig. 10. The attributes and indicators of ethical dissonance.

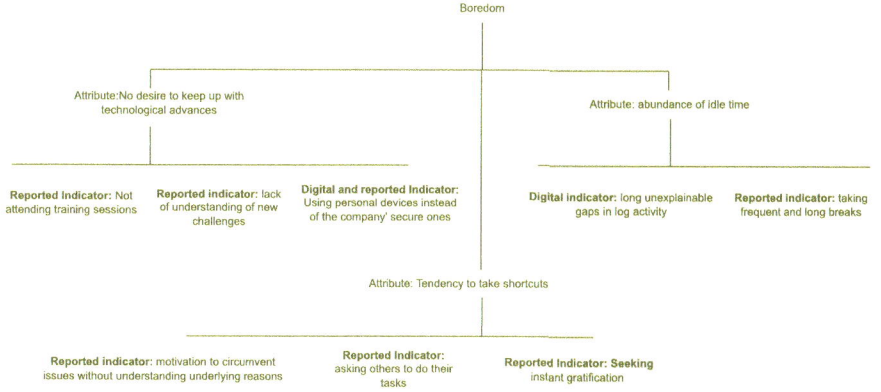

Fig. 11. The attributes and indicators of boredom.

References

1. Software Engineering Institute: Common sense guide to mitigating insider threats, seventh edition (2022). https://insights.sei.cmu.edu/library/common-sense-guide-to-mitigating-insider-threats-seventh-edition/
2. Singh, C., Thakkar, R., Warraich, J.: IAM identity access management— Importance in maintaining security systems within organizations. Eur. J. Eng. Technol. Res. **8**(4), 30–38 (2023). ISSN 2736-576X. https://doi.org/10.24018/ejeng.2023.8.4.3074
3. Vitla, S.: Pioneering IAM innovations: securing data, mitigating cyber threats, and driving compliance in the cybersecurity landscape. Int. J. Sci. Res. Arch. **10**(1), 1130–1150 (2023). ISSN 2582-8185. https://doi.org/10.30574/ijsra.2023.10.1.0714

4. Marquis, Y.A.: From theory to practice: Implementing effective role-based access control strategies to mitigate insider risks in diverse organizational contexts. J. Eng. Res. Rep. **26**(5), 138–154 (2024). ISSN 2582-2926. https://doi.org/10.9734/jerr/2024/v26i51141

5. Mandru, S.: How AI can improve identity verification and access control processes. J. Artif. Intell. Cloud Comput., 1–5 (2022). ISSN 2754-6659. https://doi.org/10.47363/jaicc/2022(1)e101

6. Jansen, W.A., Grance, T.: Guidelines on security and privacy in public cloud computing. Special Publication 800-144, National Institute of Standards and Technology (2011)

7. Bertino, E., Sandhu, R.: Database security–Concepts, approaches, and challenges. IEEE Trans. Dependable Secure Comput. **2**(1), 2–19 (2005)

8. Yampolskiy, R.V., Govindaraju, V.: Behavioural biometrics: a survey and classification. Int. J. Biometr. **1**(1), 81 (2008). ISSN 1755-831X. https://doi.org/10.1504/ijbm.2008.018665

9. Eberz, S., Rasmussen, K., Lenders, V., Martinovic, I.: Preventing lunchtime attacks: fighting insider threats with eye movement biometrics. In: Proceedings 2015 Network and Distributed System Security Symposium, NDSS 2015. Internet Society (2015). https://doi.org/10.14722/ndss.2015.23203

10. Uslu, U., İncel, Ö.D., Alptekin, G.I.: Evaluation of deep learning models for continuous authentication using behavioral biometrics. Procedia Comput. Sci. **225**, 1272–1281 (2023). ISSN 1877-0509. https://doi.org/10.1016/j.procs.2023.10.115

11. Babu, B.M., Bhanu, M.S.: Prevention of insider attacks by integrating behavior analysis with risk based access control model to protect cloud. Procedia Comput. Sci. **54**, 157–166 (2015). ISSN 1877-0509. https://doi.org/10.1016/j.procs.2015.06.018

12. Shaw, E., Fischer, L.: Ten tales of betrayal: the threat to corporate infrastructure by information technology insiders analysis and observations. p. 63 (2005)

13. Georgiadou, A., Mouzakitis, S., Askounis, D.: Detecting insider threat via a cybersecurity culture framework. J. Comput. Inf. Syst. **62**(4), 706–716 (2022)

14. Khan, N., J. Houghton, R., Sharples, S.: Understanding factors that influence unintentional insider threat: a framework to counteract unintentional risks. Cognit. Technol. Work 1–29 (2021). https://doi.org/10.1007/s10111-021-00690-z

15. Greitzer, F., Purl, J., Leong, Y.M., Becker, D.S.: Sofit: sociotechnical and organizational factors for insider threat. In: 2018 IEEE Security and Privacy Workshops (SPW), pp. 197–206. IEEE (2018). https://doi.org/10.1109/spw.2018.00035

16. Kandias, M., Mylonas, A., Virvilis, N., Theoharidou, M., Gritzalis, D.: An insider threat prediction model. In: Katsikas, S., Lopez, J., Soriano, M. (eds.) TrustBus 2010. LNCS, vol. 6264, pp. 26–37. Springer, Heidelberg (2010). https://doi.org/10.1007/978-3-642-15152-1_3

17. Brinton Anderson, B., Vance, A., Kirwan, C.B., Eargle, D., Jenkins, J.L.: How users perceive and respond to security messages: a neuroIS research agenda and empirical study. Eur. J. Inf. Syst. **25**(4), 364–390 (2016). ISSN 1476-9344. https://doi.org/10.1057/ejis.2015.21

18. Insider threat: The human element of cyberrisk — mckinsey.com. https://www.mckinsey.com/capabilities/risk-and-resilience/our-insights/insider-threat-the-human-element-of-cyberrisk. Accessed 09 Mar 2025

19. Edwards, J.R.: An examination of competing versions of the person-environment fit approach to stress. Acad. Manage. J. **39**(2), 292–339 (1996). ISSN 1948-0989. https://doi.org/10.2307/256782

20. Liu, T., et al.: Effect of organizational change on employee innovation performance: a dual mediation model. PLOS ONE **20**(2), e0313056 (2025). ISSN 1932-6203. https://doi.org/10.1371/journal.pone.0313056

21. Chowdhury, N.H., Adam, M.T., Skinner, G.: The impact of time pressure on cybersecurity behaviour: a systematic literature review. Behav. Inf. Technol. **38**(12), 1290–13081 (2019). ISSN 1362-3001. https://doi.org/10.1080/0144929x.2019.1583769

22. Chowdhury, N.H., Adam, M.T., Teubner, T.: Time pressure in human cybersecurity behavior: Theoretical framework and countermeasures. Comput. Secur. **97**, 101963 (2020). ISSN 0167-4048. https://doi.org/10.1016/j.cose.2020.101963

23. Deterrence: Crest Security Review 19 (2024). ISSN 2398-0559

24. Stich, J.F., Tarafdar, M., Stacey, P., Cooper, C.L.: E-mail load, workload stress and desired e-mail load: a cybernetic approach. Inf. Technol. People **32**(2), 430–452 (2019). ISSN 0959-3845. https://doi.org/10.1108/itp-10-2017-0321

25. Banyasz, P., Laska, P.K., Szadeczky, T., Vaczi, K.B.: The relationship between the dark triad personality and cybersecurity. In: Proceedings of the Central and Eastern European eDem and eGov Days 2024, CEEeGov 2024, pp. 195–202. ACM 2024). https://doi.org/10.1145/3670243.3670262

26. Padayachee, K.: A conceptual opportunity-based framework to mitigate the insider threat. In: 2013 Information Security for South Africa, pp. 1–8. IEEE (2013). https://doi.org/10.1109/issa.2013.6641060

27. Snowden Says He Took No Secret Files to Russia (Published 2013) — nytimes.com. https://www.nytimes.com/2013/10/18/world/snowden-says-he-took-no-secret-files-to-russia.html. Accessed 18 Feb 2025

28. Bachrach, D.G., Guedes, M.J., Harms, P.D., Patel, P.C.: CEO narcissism, top management team transactive memory systems, and firm performance: an upper echelons perspective on CEO admiration and rivalry narcissism. Eur. J. Work Organ. Psychol. **31**(1), 61–76 (2021). ISSN 1464-0643. https://doi.org/10.1080/1359432x.2021.1926989

29. Lilienfeld, S.O., Watts, A.L., Smith, S.F.: Successful psychopathy: a scientific status report. Curr. Directions Psychol. Sci. **24**(4), 298–303 (2015). ISSN 1467-8721. https://doi.org/10.1177/0963721415580297

30. Nanamou, N.K., Neal, C., Boulahia-Cuppens, N., Cuppens, F., Bkakria, A.: From traits to threats: learning risk indicators of malicious insider using psychometric data, pp. 180–200. Springer Nature Switzerland (2024). ISBN 9783031800207. https://doi.org/10.1007/978-3-031-80020-7_10

31. The Guardian: Boeing engineer sentenced for spying. The Guardian (2009). https://www.theguardian.com/business/2009/jul/17/boeing-space-technology-industrial-espionage. Accessed 4 Mar 2025

32. The Washington Post: Elite CIA unit that developed hacking tools failed to secure its own systems, allowing massive leak, an internal report found. The Washington Post (2020). https://www.washingtonpost.com/national-security/elite-cia-unit-that-developed-hacking-tools-failed-to-secure-its-own-systems-allowing-massive-leak-an-internal-report-found/2020/06/15/502e3456-ae9d-11ea-8f56-63f38c990077_story.html

33. Nasir, R., Afzal, M., Latif, R., Iqbal, W.: Behavioral based insider threat detection using deep learning. IEEE Access **9**, 143266–143274 (2021). ISSN 2169-3536. https://doi.org/10.1109/access.2021.3118297

Proceedings of the Twenty-Second International Workshop on Trust, Privacy and Security in the Digital Society (TrustBus 2025)

TrustBus 2025 Preface

Various of today's technologies (including generative AI, cloud and edge computing, and the Internet of Things) open new horizons to citizens, businesses and our whole society worldwide. All these developments ultimately aim to improve our quality of life, make it easier to generate wealth, and ensure that businesses remain competitive in the global marketplace. These developments have been made possible in a remarkably short time span because information and communication technologies move fast. Sometimes, they move too fast for society and governments. This explains why such rapid technological evolutions cannot be problem-free. In the domain of a digital society, concerns are raised regarding the lack of trust in electronic procedures and the extent to which information security and user privacy can be ensured.

The TrustBus series of events has a long tradition, dating back to 2004. In answer to the concerns mentioned above, the 22nd edition of the International Conference on Trust, Privacy and Security in Digital Society (TrustBus 2025) was held as an ARES 2025 workshop. It had the objective to provide an international and interdisciplinary forum for researchers and practitioners to exchange information regarding advancements in the state of the art and practice of trust and privacy in the digital society. Topics covered by TrustBus events include privacy enhancing technologies, privacy and identity management, secure authentication, access control and zero-trust technologies, security and privacy for data management, security management, security and trust for digital services, trust and legal compliance.

TrustBus 2025 received 17 submissions in total. All papers were peer-reviewed with a double-blind review process with at least three reviews per paper. PC members were requested to discuss and resolve any contradictory reviews. Any remaining contradictions were finally discussed by the PC chairs, who finally suggested the selected papers that were accepted. In total eight papers were accepted for TrustBus 2025.

We want to thank the members of the international Program Committee who all delivered their assigned reviews and contributed to the PC discussions. Moreover, we also thank the ARES program chairs and organisers for their support and guidance.

August 2025
Simone Fischer-Hübner
Steven Furnell

TrustBus 2025 Organization

Workshop Chairs

Simone Fischer-Hübner	Karlstad University, Chalmers University of Technology & Gothenburg University, Sweden
Steven Furnell	University of Nottingham, UK
Sokratis Katsikas	Norwegian University of Science and Technology, Norway
Costas Lambrinoudakis	University of Piraeus, Greece
Javier Lopez	University of Malaga, Spain
Günther Pernul	University of Regensburg, Germany

Program Committee

Reinhardt Botha	Noroff University College, Norway
Marijke Coetzee	North-West University, South Africa
Dionysios Demetis	University of Hull, UK
Vasiliki Diamantopoulou	University of the Aegean, Greece
Lynette Drevin	North-West University, South Africa
Davide Ferraris	University of Malaga, Spain
Stephen Flowerday	University of Tulsa, USA
Vasileios Gkioulos	Norwegian University of Science and Technology, Norway
Stefanos Gritzalis	University of Piraeus, Greece
Paul Haskell-Dowland	Edith Cowan University, Australia
Yuxiang Hong	Hangzhou Dianzi University, China
Christos Kalloniatis	University of the Aegean, Greece
Georgios Kambourakis	University of the Aegean, Greece
Maria Karyda	University of the Aegean, Greece
Vasilios Katos	Bournemouth University, UK
Sokratis Katsikas	Norwegian University of Science and Technology, Norway
Georgios Kavallieratos	Norwegian University of Science and Technology, Norway
Joakim Kävrestad	Jönköping University, Sweden
Spyros Kokolakis	University of the Aegean, Greece
Costas Lambrinoudakis	University of Piraeus, Greece
Andrew M'manga	Bournemouth University, UK
Umi Asma Mokhtar	Universiti Kebangsaan Malaysia, Malaysia

Evaluating Turnstile as a Privacy-Conscious Alternative to reCAPTCHA

Maxime Sateur, Javier Martínez Llamas(✉) ⓘ, Davy Preuveneers ⓘ, and Wouter Joosen

DistriNet, KU Leuven, Leuven, Belgium
`javier.martinezllamas@kuleuven.be`

Abstract. With the continuous increase in automated Internet traffic, bot detection systems become vital to safeguard users and website integrity, necessitating methods to differentiate between human and bot-generated traffic. CAPTCHA systems, such as Google's reCAPTCHA, serve as a primary defence by presenting tasks that only humans can solve. Nonetheless, these systems have generated privacy concerns due to their extensive data collection practices, especially considering Google's business model, heavily oriented towards advertising. This paper evaluates Cloudflare's Turnstile, a privacy-focused CAPTCHA alternative, and their claims of compliance with the European GDPR and ePrivacy Directive. A comparative analysis of reCAPTCHA and Turnstile was conducted by deploying both systems on test websites, analysing network traffic, HTTP requests, and script behaviour to assess data transfer and privacy implications. The study also reviewed relevant privacy regulations and de-obfuscated Turnstile's client-side code to examine its security mechanisms and data collection practices. Findings reveal that both systems operate similarly by issuing tokens post-verification for back-end validation, with Turnstile aligning with GDPR through its avoidance of tracking cookies. However, a vulnerability previously identified in reCAPTCHA was replicated in Turnstile, demonstrating its susceptibility to token exploitation. While reCAPTCHA, in its current form, faces challenges in conforming to GDPR requirements, Turnstile demonstrates potential as a privacy-conscious alternative offering comparable security features. Nonetheless, future regulations may challenge its compliance, highlighting the need for continuous adaptation to evolving privacy standards.

Keywords: bot · bot detection · CAPTCHA · privacy · security · GDPR

1 Introduction

The majority of Internet traffic is not attributed to human interaction, but rather to automated processes conducted by web bots [16]. These web bots are software applications designed to autonomously execute tasks on the Internet, from

B. Coppens et al. (Eds.): ARES 2025 Workshops, LNCS 15995, pp. 235–252, 2025.
https://doi.org/10.1007/978-3-032-00633-2_14

benign functions like indexing or web application testing, to malicious activities such as account takeover, Distributed Denial of Service (DDoS) attacks, or web scraping. Their growth and sophistication have been parallel to the development and expansion of the Internet and digital societies. Originally, these agents were scripts that executed rudimentary operations without evasion mechanisms, referred to as simple bots. However, the landscape rapidly evolved to include advanced bots with evasion capabilities that closely mimic human behaviour [18].

In response to this sophistication by malicious bots, and to ensure the integrity of users and websites, countermeasures are deployed for their detection. One of the most established techniques are the "Completely Automated Public Turing tests to tell Computers and Humans Apart", commonly known as CAPTCHAs [12]. These systems are designed to differentiate between humans and bots by presenting a challenge to the user, typically involving image recognition tasks (e.g., identifying patterns, letters or shapes); and rely on the assumption that humans possess superior cognitive and sensory skills compared to automated systems.

The recent surge in Artificial Intelligence (AI), particularly in image recognition, has disrupted this paradigm [1,14,15,22]. As bots have become increasingly adept at solving visual challenges on par with human capabilities, web bot detection has entered an arms race. To maintain relevance, CAPTCHAs have continuously evolved, resulting in a paradox where they became more difficult for humans to solve than for automated systems. This undermined their original purpose and led to the development of frictionless CAPTCHAs, aimed at providing a more user-friendly experience [12]. Instead of requiring users to solve a challenge, they collect and analyse data derived from user interactions with a website. This information may encompass mouse movements, keystrokes, IP addresses, or browser fingerprints.

This new paradigm introduces a trade-off for users between usability and privacy. CAPTCHAs are not without controversy, as users and regulatory agencies have raised concerns about their potential invasiveness and the use of collected data for tracking purposes [5]. The growing awareness of privacy issues in digital societies has prompted the draft of privacy laws, such as the European General Data Protection Regulation (GDPR) [7] and the ePrivacy Directive (ePD) [6], with the aim of safeguarding users' rights. Nonetheless, leading solutions such as Google's reCAPTCHA continue to raise concerns regarding their practices and handling of data, prompting competitors like Cloudflare to develop privacy-focused alternatives such as Turnstile.

Our work aims to investigate Turnstile's privacy claims and assess whether it can provide a secure, privacy-compliant alternative to reCAPTCHA. Specifically, this paper (1) evaluates Turnstile's security mechanisms and the data it collects, and (2) contextualises these aspects in relation to privacy regulations.

The main contributions are as follows:

- We conduct a comprehensive comparison of Turnstile and reCAPTCHA, with a specific focus on privacy and regulatory compliance.

- We perform an in-depth analysis of Turnstile's client-side code, assessing its security measures in comparison to those of reCAPTCHA and providing an overview of the data collected.
- We demonstrate that vulnerabilities present in reCAPTCHA can also be exploited in Turnstile, emphasising the inherent similarities among frictionless CAPTCHAs.

2   Related Work

The necessity of distinguishing between human users and automated systems (web bots) on the Internet to prevent abuses such as spamming and fraudulent account creation has been a recurring issue in the literature [19]. The term CAPTCHA was first introduced by von Ahn et al. [23] in 2003. The original CAPTCHA design utilised distorted text that users were required to decipher. This method capitalised on the superior human ability to recognise and interpret distorted characters, a task that posed significant challenges for automated systems. Since its inception, the design of CAPTCHAs has evolved considerably. Modern implementations now encompass a broader range of challenges, including not only text-based CAPTCHAs but also those involving images and audio.

Several notable commercial solutions have emerged to address new challenges and enhance security. One prominent solution is reCAPTCHA[1], which was acquired by Google in 2009. Over time, reCAPTCHA has evolved from text-based challenges to more sophisticated image recognition tasks. The latest iteration, reCAPTCHA v3, utilises risk analysis to evaluate user interactions without requiring explicit tests—an approach Google branded as NoCAPTCHA. This version aims to be less intrusive while maintaining its effectiveness. Another significant player is hCaptcha[2], which was developed as an alternative to reCAPTCHA with a particular emphasis on privacy and data protection. hCaptcha offers image-based challenges similar to those provided by reCAPTCHA but allows users to opt out of extensive tracking and includes a monetisation option for website operators.

As CAPTCHAs become increasingly integrated into online security frameworks, privacy regulations have begun to play a crucial role in shaping their design and implementation. General Data Protection Regulation (GDPR) [7], enacted by the European Union (EU) in 2018, is one of the most significant privacy regulations affecting CAPTCHAs. It imposes strict guidelines on data collection, processing, and storage, emphasising the need for transparency and user consent. CAPTCHAs that collect personal data, such as interaction patterns or behavioural metrics, must comply with GDPR requirements by ensuring that users are informed about data collection practices and that their consent is

---

[1] https://www.google.com/recaptcha/about/.
[2] https://www.hcaptcha.com/.

obtained. Additionally, GDPR mandates that users have the right to access, rectify, and delete their data, which poses challenges for CAPTCHA systems that aggregate extensive user interaction data. Complementarily, the ePrivacy Directive [6], also known as the Privacy and Electronic Communications Directive, focuses specifically on the confidentiality of electronic communications, including provisions related to cookies, unsolicited marketing, and traffic data. A significant challenge under the GDPR is the restriction on transferring personal data to non-EU countries, particularly the United States (US). The 2020 invalidation of the EU-US Privacy Shield [8] highlighted persistent concerns regarding USA government surveillance practices [11]. To ensure legal data transfers, companies now rely on mechanisms such as Standard Contractual Clauses (SCCs) [9] and the new EU-US Data Privacy Framework (DPF) [10]. However, they must still ensure that these transfers comply with the strict protections mandated by the GDPR.

As Google does not fully comply with the GDPR, it shifts the responsibility for data protection onto website owners who choose to utilise its services [13]. This delegation of responsibility has led to issues, exemplified by a recent case involving a French company that used reCAPTCHA for user registration and password recovery on its website. The CNIL (Commission Nationale de l'Informatique et des Libertés), France's independent data protection authority, determined that Cityscoot was in breach of Article 82 of the French Data Protection Act [5]. This provision, which aligns with GDPR principles, mandates that storing information on a user's device or accessing previously stored information is permissible only if the user has granted explicit consent, unless such actions are essential for transmitting a communication or providing a service explicitly requested by the user. This provision mirrors the GDPR's consent requirements, ensuring that users are adequately informed and consent to the use of cookies, with exceptions for essential cookies used solely for technical purposes.

Previous research has largely concentrated on the security of CAPTCHAs, focusing on bot detection and risk analysis while neglecting user privacy concerns. This study aims to address this gap by being the first, to our knowledge, to examine Cloudflare Turnstile with an emphasis on privacy. We assess the privacy risks associated with frictionless Google reCAPTCHA and evaluate how Turnstile mitigates these risks to strengthen user privacy protections.

3   Turnstile and reCAPTCHA Requests Analysis

3.1   Experimental Setup

To assess the performance of Turnstile and reCAPTCHA, we established a local Nginx web server to host individual test pages for each service. These pages were constructed using the default implementation code provided by the respective services, with Google's reCAPTCHA code being modified to initiate verification upon page load, as opposed to the default button-pressed process. To ensure proper isolation of the test environments, the server was configured with two distinct server blocks.

For traffic analysis, Burp Suite[3] was employed to intercept and examine the network communication between the browser, test pages, and CAPTCHA services, with a browser proxy extension implemented to route traffic through it. Additionally, Chrome DevTools[4] was employed to monitor real-time network activity, with XHR (XMLHttpRequest) breakpoints and custom functions configured to halt execution at specific network requests.

3.2 Challenge Website Integration

reCAPTCHA. As illustrated in Fig. 1a, when a user visits a website with reCAPTCHA implemented, the browser initiates a GET request to obtain the widget's code, including the website's sitekey and additional information such as the base64-encoded URL, host language, widget type (invisible), and two encoded parameters, v and cb, likely corresponding to the reCAPTCHA version and a callback parameter. In response, Google returns the widget's code. Once the user interacts with the widget and successfully completes the challenge, a response token (`g-recaptcha-response`) is generated and sent to the user's browser. The web server subsequently forwards this token, along with the website's secret key, to Google's reCAPTCHA verification servers to validate its authenticity. The reCAPTCHA server processes the token and responds to the web server with a JSON object containing the verification result. In the case of reCAPTCHA v3, web administrators can configure custom actions based on the returned score.

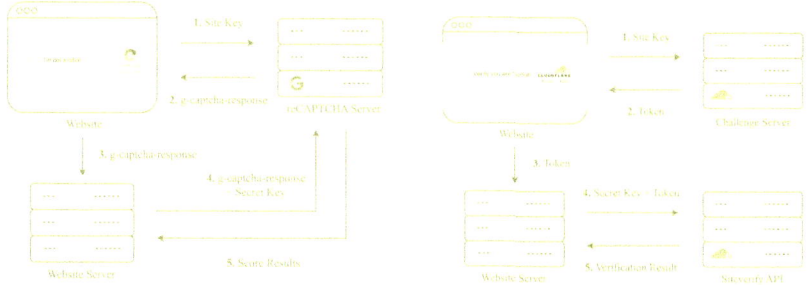

(a) reCAPTCHA's Verification Workflow   (b) Turnstile's Verification Workflow

Fig. 1. Verification workflow for the different CAPTCHA services.

Turnstile. First, it is necessary to distinguish between Cloudflare's Turnstile and its challenge page [3]. The challenge page serves as a web bot detection system with a preliminary fingerprinting mechanism that must be completed before access to the website is granted. In contrast, Turnstile is a CAPTCHA

---

[3] https://portswigger.net/burp.

[4] https://developer.chrome.com/docs/devtools.

alternative intended to replace solutions such as reCAPTCHA or hCaptcha. Despite similarities in underlying technology, their implementations differ, with Turnstile sometimes integrated into the challenge page for enhanced screening. As depicted in Fig. 1buser visits a web page with Turnstile implemented, an embedded JavaScript script executes automatically. This script sends a request to a Cloudflare challenge server, including the sitekey and basic information such as the requested domain and the visitor's IP address. In response, the server returns a script that performs various browser checks. If successfully completed, the user receives a token valid for 300 s. For subsequent interactions with the website, the server-side script sends the token, along with the secret key and the visitor's IP address, to the siteverify API. The siteverify API then confirms that the token is valid and has not been used previously, thereby preventing token forgery and reuse.

3.3   Analysis of reCAPTCHA's Requests

We recorded the network logs following the reCAPTCHA load, which revealed a total of 15 requests. However, our analysis will focus on the primary requests relevant to its core functionality or privacy. The initial request to the API, in the format `api.js?render=sitekey`, initialises the widget and triggers subsequent requests. Notably, this request also adds a meta-tag to the document's head, enrolling the user in an origin trial, which is used to test experimental features. In this instance, it disables third-party storage partitioning, a privacy measure that prevents third-party cookies and storage from tracking users across different websites. By disabling this feature, Google seems to be moving towards eliminating third-party cookies in its browser by default, while concurrently exempting its own products from adhering to privacy measures. However, this approach no longer appears to align with Google's current strategy, as the company has recently ceased its efforts to discontinue third-party cookies [20].

The following request, directed to `recaptcha_en_gb.js`, contains an obfuscated JavaScript payload. As noted in previous analyses [17], it primarily contains common code essential for reCAPTCHA's operation. Attaching a debugger revealed additional code related to the widget's functionality. This request includes several key elements, such as the `sitekey`, a base64-encoded version of the website URL, the host language, the widget type, and the encoded parameters `v` and `cb`. The response payload of this request primarily consists of a callback to the function `recaptcha.anchor.Main.init`, which includes two base64-encoded strings. One of these strings is utilised to initiate a subsequent request that includes a bytecode interpreter, while the other encodes the bytecode for a virtual machine (VM). This VM serves as an intermediary environment for executing obfuscated code, enabling developers to hide program logic and hinder bots from reverse-engineering or manipulating CAPTCHA mechanisms. The response payload also includes part of the reCAPTCHA `iframe`, specifically containing a `recaptcha-token`. Under typical circumstances, this parameter remains empty until it is populated with the token following the completion of the challenge. However, in this instance the token is already present and appears to serve a different purpose, as it remains constant for each request but varies across different websites. This observation suggests that the token may function as a unique identifier. Removing the `recaptcha-token` prior to executing the challenge leads to an error, revealing that it serves as a key API parameter.

Next, `anchor?ar=1&k=sitekey` request triggers the retrieval of fonts from Google Fonts servers. This process is mandatory and cannot be disabled, which may pose privacy challenges for certain web administrators [13]. Finally, the `reload?k=sitekey` request encompasses the resulting payload from all the challenges executed within the virtual machine. The response to this request provides the essential `g-recaptcha-response` token. Although the payload is encrypted, references [17] offer insight into the types of data being collected. This includes details like the user agent, screen resolution, execution time, time zone, number of mouse and keyboard interactions within the CAPTCHA `iframe`, canvas fingerprints, and various browser checks.

Notably, the structure of these HTTP requests remains similar to how reCAPTCHA functioned when NoCAPTCHA was first introduced [17]. Although it is highly probable that enhancements have been made to the VM obfuscation techniques and that the signals utilised for risk assessment have evolved. However, such research extends beyond the scope of this paper.

3.4   Analysis of Turnstile's Requests

Upon loading a web page that incorporates the Turnstile widget, a request is initiated to retrieve the required JavaScript file. This file contains the essential logic responsible for rendering the widget, managing user interactions, configuring the initial challenge, and facilitating communication with Cloudflare's servers.

The initial request, `auto/`, to the Cloudflare challenge platform is responsible for loading the necessary CSS for the widget. More significantly, it triggers two additional requests. The first request consistently returns a 2×2 pixel image, followed by a posterior GET request that similarly returns a small image. This behaviour suggests that Cloudflare may be verifying the dimensions and rendering of these images. The second request, `v1?ray`, delivers the primary challenge script within its payload, although the script is obfuscated. *Ray IDs* are used by Cloudflare as unique identifiers for each request [4]. This request also initiates two subsequent POST requests, each carrying URI-encoded payloads in the format `v<rayID>=<payload>`. The responses to these POST requests contain a base64-encoded payload.

We introduced XMLHttpRequest (XHR) breakpoints while reloading the request and observed numerous calls being made to the `v1?ray` script. Additionally, we detected scripts labeled *VM5* and *VM1201* being initiated by the same script. However, our ability to further investigate these scripts was hindered as the call stack disappeared upon the completion of the Turnstile challenge. Despite attempts to prevent this from occurring, we were unsuccessful, potentially due to Cloudflare's implementation of anti-debugging techniques.

Given the numerous function calls made to the initial script, along with its role in initiating the two additional requests with obfuscated payloads, it is likely that v1?ray serves as the primary challenge script. As further insights could not be obtained through dynamic debugging, we instead shift our focus to conducting a static analysis of this initialisation script.

3.5   De-obfuscation of Turnstile's Payload

To produce readable code, tools such as Babel[5] or Esprima[6] can be utilised. JavaScript relies on engines like Chrome's V8 or Firefox's SpiderMonkey to convert it into machine code for execution. This process begins with parsing the JavaScript code into an Abstract Syntax Tree (AST), which is subsequently used to generate an intermediate representation. This representation is then either interpreted as bytecode or compiled into machine code through Just-In-Time (JIT) compilation.

Listing 1.1. Snippet of Turnstile's obfuscated payload.

```
1   if (f[j9(636)](i[j9(1182)], 200) && i[j9(1182)] != 304) {
2   if (f[j9(508)](j9(726), j9(726)))
3       return void f[j9(773)](h);
```

The first notable observation when inspecting the obfuscated payload is the absence of string literals, as illustrated in Listing 1.1, employing what is known as String Array Obfuscation or String Array Mapping. We start by converting the long string variable into a string table and decoding all the strings, which are URI-encoded in their original form. This string table will be employed to retrieve the necessary strings later in the process. Using Esprima, we write a function responsible for generating the string table while traversing the AST. Once the string table is populated, the next task is to manage the ordering of the strings in the array, as they have been scrambled, with two functions already present in the payload.

Next, we examine the concept of indirection, which involves accessing data through multiple layers of references rather than directly. To address this, we implemented an Esprima function designed to iterate through the nodes of the AST in search of AssignmentExpression nodes. When identified, the function replaces all instances of these assignments. Following this procedure, we employed constant inlining, a technique wherein constant expressions or values are directly substituted for variable references or function calls that yield these values. After applying these two techniques, all strings from the string table were effectively reintroduced into the code. For illustration purposes, the line of code if(e[14(3)](14(0),1)) would be converted to if(e.Wzjdr(n,1)) for a string table of ["n", "Wzjdr"].

The final technique under consideration is the application of trivial inline functions. In this context, basic binary operations, such as $a - b$ and $a \leq b$, have been encapsulated within functions, introducing an additional layer of

---

[5] https://babeljs.io/.

[6] https://esprima.org/.

abstraction. To address this, we perform a final traversal of the AST, systematically replacing these trivial inline functions with their corresponding operations. In the last example, `e.Wzjdr()` would correspond to a function `e.Wzjdr = function(a,b){return a<=b;}`, so that the de-obfuscated statement would be `if(n <= 1))`.

3.6   De-obfuscated Request Payload

As previously seen in Sect. 3.4, the initial script is responsible for triggering two additional POST requests, each containing obfuscated payloads. Despite substantial improvements in code readability through de-obfuscation efforts, the process did not completely restore the code to its original form. To address this, we utilised a Large Language Model (LLM), specifically Copilot[7], which identified one of the functions in the script as an LZW compression algorithm [24]. Based on this recognition, we employed the *lz-string* library[8] to create a simple de-obfuscation function. Typically, we would use *lz-string*'s built-in de-obfuscation functions; however, these rely on default dictionaries, whereas Cloudflare utilises a custom dictionary that varies with each request. To identify the appropriate dictionary, we applied the following regular expression, `\\${split}([a-zA-Z0-9\\+\\-\\$]65)\\${split}`, designed to locate strings of equivalent length and character composition to those in *lz-string*'s dictionaries, though the characters may appear in any order. By employing our custom function in conjunction with the dictionary associated with the initial challenge script, we successfully de-obfuscated the payloads transmitted from the browser to Cloudflare's servers.

The first request transmits challenge parameters alongside basic attributes related to the request, such as the request URL, user agent, HTTP method, and timestamp. The second POST request payload, however, contains browser and system information. These attributes vary with each request, likely because Cloudflare verifies different elements on each occasion to prevent users from easily manipulating their browser fingerprint. Including user agent, screen size, colour depth, and other system-related metrics. Notably, screen-related data is consistently requested, with only a subset of attributes rotating per request. Additionally, the payload appears to encompass all available Web API properties, methods, and event handlers supported by the browser. This likely serves as a consistency check, verifying whether the user's browser returns all expected functionality for a particular browser type. We also identified a full list of all installed browser plug-ins. Following these attributes, we encountered several more opaque segments, which may correspond to the results of various proof-of-work challenges. Aside from the rotating nature of these challenges, the order in which their results are returned also appears to fluctuate. We identified more than 25 distinct potential challenges, with each request containing results from approximately 18 of them.

---

[7] https://copilot.microsoft.com/.

[8] https://github.com/pieroxy/lz-string.

3.7 De-obfuscated Response Payload

Upon examining the function responsible for handling the requests, we identified the logic governing the `responseText`, which is passed to another function
resembling a de-obfuscated process. Since the de-obfuscation mechanism was not
immediately clear, we resorted to the LLM for further clarification. The LLM not
only provided a partial explanation of the function but also isolated it, enabling
us to use the function to de-obfuscate the response payloads. After de-obfuscating
one of the payloads, we did not retrieve any readable code. However, upon re-
examining the request-handling function, we noticed an `if-else` statement that
checks the de-obfuscated output. Specifically, it verifies whether the payload
begins with `.window`; if it does not, the payload is passed to another function.
Tracing this secondary function revealed that it initiates the creation of a virtual
machine, where an array is constructed to serve as the internal memory. Each
function in the script is assigned a dynamically calculated index within this
array. Additionally, we observed the presence of a `for` loop that assigns random
data to dynamically calculated indices in the array using a bit-wise `XOR` operation, likely serving as an anti-debugging mechanism to hinder dynamic analysis
of the script.

The obfuscation of the virtual machine VM limits our ability to make further discoveries. Circumventing this obfuscation would require considerable time
and expertise in VM-based obfuscation techniques, which falls outside the scope
of this work. However, the specific `if-else` statement that consistently directs
the payload to the VM function is particularly noteworthy. While it could be
another form of obfuscation designed to create confusion, it does not follow the
same pattern as the other seemingly extraneous `if-else` statements. The critical
line being `if (v1.startsWith("window.")) new fw.Function(v1)(d)`. Interestingly, if the condition holds true, it appears to generate a completely new function within `fw`, the main function responsible for the challenge script. Our suspi-
cions were later confirmed through a blog post published in 2024 that explored
Cloudflare's Under Attack Mode (UAM) waiting room [25]. The authors encountered a similar line of code, `window.Function(ax(aE.responseText))()`, where
`ax` corresponds to the de-obfuscation function. It appears that this function
de-obfuscates the response payload and assigns it as a new function within
the `window` object. They further elaborate on several challenges implemented
by Cloudflare, highlighting similar obfuscation strategies and corroborating our
findings. Given that these techniques are fundamental to browser fingerprinting and bot detection, it is reasonable to assume that they continue to be used
alongside other, as-yet-unidentified methods, and new approaches.

4 Transferability of reCAPTCHA Vulnerabilities to Turnstile

In this section, we aim to evaluate the applicability of known reCAPTCHA
vulnerabilities to Cloudflare Turnstile. We consider two attacks proposed by
Sivakorn et al. [21]

4.1 Cookie Replay Attacks

Previous discussions have underscored privacy concerns surrounding the use of tracking cookies by reCAPTCHA. The attack [21] explored the potential vulnerabilities of these cookies, revealing that Google's advanced risk analysis could be circumvented by appending a 9-day-old cookie. In contrast, Cloudflare's CAPTCHA does not rely on cookies, seemingly making such exploits inapplicable. However, Cloudflare's challenge mechanism does issue a cookie that prevents users from encountering further challenges after being classified as low-risk. Tools such as Flaresolverr[9] and Playwright[10] plug-ins have exploited this mechanism by allowing users to obtain and reuse the `cf_clearance` cookie, provided the same user-agent and IP address are maintained. During the setup of Turnstile, it is observed that Cloudflare introduces a pre-clearance cookie option, similar to the `cf_clearance` cookie, which permits users who successfully complete a CAPTCHA to avoid future challenges. The degree of potential exploitation depends on how website administrators configure this feature, for instance, by limiting the cookie's validity period or restricting its application to secure API calls.

4.2 Clickjacking

Based on the local setup detailed in Sect. 3.1, we adapted the code to incorporate the `sitekey` associated with the target website, replacing the original key previously used. This adjustment led to Turnstile identifying a discrepancy between the domain specified and the `sitekey`, resulting in an error. We subsequently modified the `servername` parameter in the configuration to align with the domain name of the target website. Furthermore, we redirected traffic to the target website through our local site by altering the Windows hosts file. Following these adjustments, Turnstile permitted the use of locally generated tokens on the target website. This method, which produces one token every three seconds, significantly reduces network load and avoids potential rate-limiting by the target website. Furthermore, it is notably faster than using third-party services like Capmonster[11], which requires approximately 10 s per token.

Given the importance of speed in large-scale attacks, we aimed to optimise the volume of tokens generated within a specified time frame. Recognising that headed browsers are more resource-intensive than headless browsers, we investigated the feasibility of generating multiple tokens using a single browser window. We modified the Turnstile Dummy Log-in page used in previous experiments to render multiple Turnstile widgets simultaneously. Our tests revealed that each widget generated a unique token, and there were no restrictions on rendering multiple widgets on the same page. To investigate the limits of this approach, we gradually increased the number of widgets on the page to evaluate potential rate-limiting effects, as demonstrated in Fig. 2. We successfully configured up to

---

[9] https://github.com/FlareSolverr/FlareSolverr.
[10] https://playwright.dev/.
[11] https://capmonster.cloud/es/.

Fig. 2. Partial screenshot of the local dummy log-in page with several Turnstile widgets.

20 widgets, achieving an average token generation time of 1.5 s per token. However, further increasing the widget count resulted in diminishing returns, as the time required to solve each widget increased, leading to timeouts. Additionally, during the operation with 20 widgets, we noted a persistent issue where one widget consistently failed to resolve and necessitated manual intervention. This observation suggests that Cloudflare may intentionally allow for false negatives within its challenge mechanism, potentially requiring manual intervention even when a user is not flagged as a bot.

Subsequently, we developed a system to test daily token generation limits and identify potential patterns. Our objective was to simulate the behaviour of an attacker and determine if rate-limiting measures would be triggered. To achieve this, we implemented a Userscript function that operates directly within the browser, eliminating the need for a custom browser extension. This function executes by loading the webpage, waiting for network activity to conclude, counting the tokens present in the HTML, and transmitting this data, along with a timestamp, to a JSON database via a local API. After sending the data, the script refreshes the page and restarts the cycle.

This experiment was conducted over a three-day period, with varying token request quantities for each day: 3 tokens on Day 1, 6 tokens on Day 2, and 9 tokens on Day 3. Figure 3 illustrates the hourly distribution of token generation across these days. The results indicate that token generation was most consistent between midnight and 11 AM, while there was a significant decline in token counts during the late evening, particularly between 7 PM and 11 PM. This fluctuation may be attributed to variations in Internet bandwidth usage, which tends to be lower during early morning hours when fewer users are active online, and higher in the late evening as individuals return home and increase their Internet activity. In terms of total token generation, increasing the request from 3 to 6 tokens per session led to a 51.16% increase, while increasing to 9 tokens per session resulted in an additional 19.11% increase. These findings suggest that although generating more tokens per session reduces the time required per token, there are diminishing returns as the number of tokens per session increases. Despite these observations, we did not encounter any hard limits on

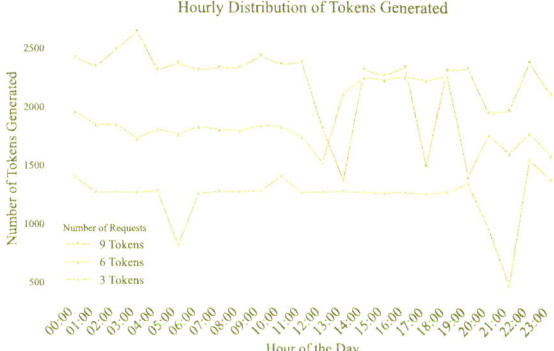

Fig. 3. Number of tokens generated per hour for a 1-day time window.

token generation, suggesting that either such a limit does not exist or that our experiment did not reach the threshold necessary to trigger it.

5 Status with Respect to Privacy Regulations

Cloudflare positions Turnstile as a privacy-focused alternative to Google's reCAPTCHA, prompting the question of how Turnstile differs in a way that justifies these privacy-related claims. A key distinction lies in reCAPTCHA's reliance on session data and user tracking. Google uses cookies to monitor users across its services, including reCAPTCHA, and the presence of a Google account can influence a user's reputation score. These cookies also store preferences across various Google services, making it difficult to opt out. However, privacy-conscious users who disable these cookies may experience lower reputation scores and more frequent CAPTCHA challenges. As discussed in Sect. 2, the French data protection authority CNIL interprets the GDPR to suggest that reCAPTCHA's use of tracking cookies and data collection for purposes beyond its core functionality violates GDPR compliance [5]. GDPR mandates explicit user consent for such tracking, which could hinder reCAPTCHA's functionality if users decline consent, rendering it less effective.

By contrast, Cloudflare Turnstile avoids the use of tracking cookies, sidestepping these GDPR-related issues. Cloudflare's privacy policy states that it processes information only for the specific purposes for which it was collected, ensuring compliance with privacy standards. Despite these advantages, Turnstile faces its own challenges. It primarily analyses browser characteristics, which can potentially create a unique identifier, or "browser fingerprint." Depending on whether this data can be used to identify a user, either directly or indirectly, it could be classified as personal information. Under GDPR, the processing of such personal data requires a lawful basis for collection and use.

According to the General Data Protection Regulation [7], the processing of personal data is lawful only if, and to the extent that, at least one of the following conditions is met:

- The data subject has given explicit consent for the processing of their personal data for one or more specific purposes.
- Processing is necessary for the performance of a contract to which the data subject is a party, or for taking steps at the request of the data subject prior to entering into a contract.
- Processing is necessary for compliance with a legal obligation to which the data controller is subject.
- Processing is necessary to protect the vital interests of the data subject or another natural person.
- Processing is necessary for the performance of a task carried out in the public interest or in the exercise of official authority vested in the data controller.
- Processing is necessary for the purposes of the legitimate interests pursued by the data controller or a third party, except where such interests are overridden by the fundamental rights and freedoms of the data subject, particularly when the data subject is a child.

Since requesting consent could undermine the functionality of Turnstile, it must meet one of the legal bases for data processing under the GDPR. Turnstile could potentially justify its data processing under the "legitimate interests" basis. Similar to the argument used by CityScoot [5], Turnstile might claim that its data processing is necessary to ensure the security of user authentication. This rationale could be valid, provided that Turnstile refrains from using tracking cookies, uses the collected data exclusively for its intended purpose, and demonstrates that the benefits of enhancing security outweigh the privacy risks associated with the data collection.

Given the complexity of the GDPR and privacy regulations, as well as their evolving nature, it is challenging to draw a definitive conclusion regarding whether Turnstile fully complies with the GDPR and the ePrivacy Directive. However, while we cannot be certain that it complies, the available evidence suggests that it does not appear to violate these regulations.

6   Discussion

6.1   Limitations

The implementation of VM obfuscation significantly restricted the information accessible for our analysis and presented considerable challenges in understanding the full extent of data collection and the specific challenges employed by Turnstile. Conducting a comprehensive de-obfuscation and complete analysis of Turnstile's operations would require substantially more resources and is beyond the scope of this paper. Consequently, our analysis is necessarily limited, requiring us to rely on assumptions and secondary sources to address the gaps in our understanding.

As external researchers, we faced another significant limitation in our inability to independently verify Cloudflare's privacy claims, particularly their assertion that the information collected is used exclusively for its stated purposes.

Although Cloudflare undergoes third-party audits to validate its privacy and security practices, our lack of direct access to their internal operations prevented us from confirming these claims ourselves. Furthermore, the dynamic and evolving nature of software development, along with ongoing updates to Cloudflare's technologies and practices, renders our assessment inherently time-sensitive. Consequently, future updates or modifications to Turnstile or Cloudflare's data practices may not be reflected in our analysis, potentially affecting the relevance and accuracy of our findings over time.

6.2   Adhering to Privacy Regulations

Similar to software development, regulations evolve to meet new societal demands or governmental ideals. Although the legislative process generally progresses more slowly than software development, regulatory agencies frequently provide advance notice of potential new regulations, enabling companies to prepare accordingly. Once a new privacy regulation is enacted, however, compliance with its requirements becomes mandatory. Regulations are inherently region-specific; for example, the GDPR applies solely to the European Union, its citizens and their data, even when it is processed or stored outside its borders. This geographic specificity often results in companies releasing products with varying features across different markets, complicating the certification of privacy compliance and requiring constant auditing of privacy claims. For instance, the forthcoming ePrivacy Regulation, intended to replace the Directive, which aims to align more closely with the GDPR's principles and address emerging privacy challenges in digital communications, could potentially impact CAPTCHA services in the EU market.

6.3   Turnstile's Security

Our successful bypass of Turnstile's polymorphic obfuscation provided a partial insight into the data being collected and the challenges presented. We found that the data requests varied with each interaction, with each response returning a subset of challenges. Some challenges reappeared, but their order varied, supporting Turnstile's claim that it periodically changes the challenges it employs. However, we observed that certain data in the payloads seemed similar to the data collected by NoCAPTCHA when it was first introduced, likely due to their fundamental nature, such as the user agent. Although Turnstile's virtual machine obfuscation prevented us from obtaining a complete picture of the data being collected, our findings suggest that Turnstile's security is comparable to reCAPTCHA's, at least from an external perspective. This does not necessarily imply that their VM implementation or challenge mechanisms are identical. Additionally, the legacy code we uncovered indicates that Turnstile did not always use virtual machine obfuscation, suggesting that its security mechanisms have evolved over time.

6.4   Transferability of Vulnerabilities

We demonstrated that a previously identified vulnerability in reCAPTCHA could be exploited in Turnstile, raising concerns about the potential for inherited vulnerabilities in newer systems. However, the attack requires approximately 1.5 s per generated token, rendering it too slow and resource-intensive for large-scale exploitation. A potential mitigation strategy for this vulnerability could involve modifying Turnstile's workflow by privatising the `sitekey`. In this approach, the website's back end would generate a unique token based on the `sitekey` upon page load and send it to the user's browser. The visitor's browser would then use this token, rather than the `sitekey`, to request a challenge, ensuring that it remains inaccessible to the user. This would effectively prevent `sitekey` reuse and mitigate the risk of such attacks. This solution highlights that addressing the vulnerability is technically feasible. The fact that it has not yet been resolved may suggest that Cloudflare is either unaware of the issue or does not view it as a significant threat [2].

7   Conclusion

This paper presents a comparative analysis of Cloudflare Turnstile and Google reCAPTCHA, focusing on their functionalities and privacy aspects. The study specifically addressed privacy concerns associated with reCAPTCHA and explored how Turnstile addresses these issues. The process involved configuring both CAPTCHA systems on test websites, capturing and analysing network logs, and examining script behaviour. Legal documents related to privacy law were reviewed to underscore the issues with reCAPTCHA, while Turnstile's client-side code was scrutinised to assess its security measures and data collection practices.

Employing de-obfuscation techniques, we overcame Turnstile's polymorphic obfuscation and decrypted the HTTP payloads. Our analysis revealed that both reCAPTCHA and Turnstile operate similarly by generating tokens based on site-specific challenges. By exploiting this similarity, we were able to replicate a vulnerability present in Turnstile, demonstrating that some of the weaknesses observed in reCAPTCHA are also evident in Turnstile. Notably, while the use of tracking cookies by reCAPTCHA raises concerns under GDPR, Turnstile avoids such tracking mechanisms, thereby aligning with the ePrivacy Directive. However, forthcoming privacy regulations on browser fingerprinting may pose challenges for Turnstile.

Although Turnstile incorporates advanced security measures comparable to reCAPTCHA, including polymorphic and virtual machine obfuscation, the latter constrained the scope of our analysis. Despite this, third-party audits of Cloudflare provide validation of its privacy and security claims. Overall, our research indicates that Turnstile represents a more privacy-conscious alternative to reCAPTCHA, yet the evolving privacy landscape necessitates continuous monitoring. This study highlights the growing importance of balancing data privacy with effective CAPTCHA solutions.

Acknowledgments. This research is partially funded by the Research Fund KU Leuven, and by the Cybersecurity Research Program Flanders.

References

1. Antal, M., Buza, K., Fejer, N.: SapiAgent: a bot based on deep learning to generate human-like mouse trajectories. IEEE Access **9**, 124396–124408 (2021)
2. Cloudflare: The end of the captcha (2023). https://blog.cloudflare.com/end-cloudflare-captcha/. Accessed 20 Sep 2024
3. Cloudflare: Cloudflare challenges: managed challenge (2024). https://developers.cloudflare.com/waf/reference/cloudflare-challenges/. Accessed 20 Sep 2024
4. Cloudflare: Cloudflare ray id (2024). https://developers.cloudflare.com/fundamentals/reference/cloudflare-ray-id/. Accessed 20 Sep 2024
5. Commission Nationale de l'Informatique et des Libertés: Délibération de la formation restreinte n° san-2023-003 du 16 mars 2023 concernant la société cityscoot (2023). https://www.legifrance.gouv.fr/cnil/id/CNILTEXT000047346903. Accessed 12 Sep 2024
6. European Parliament, Council of the European Union: Directive 2002/58/EC of the European parliament and of the council of 12 july 2002 concerning the processing of personal data and the protection of privacy in the electronic communications sector (directive on privacy and electronic communications). OJ **L 201**, 37–47 (2002)
7. European Parliament, Council of the European Union: Regulation (EU) 2016/679 of the European parliament and of the council of 27 april 2016 on the protection of natural persons with regard to the processing of personal data and on the free movement of such data, and repealing directive 95/46/EC (general data protection regulation). OJ **L 119**, 1–88 (2016)
8. European Parliament, Council of the European Union: Commission implementing decision (EU) 2016/1250 of 12 july 2016 pursuant to directive 95/46/EC of the European parliament and of the council on the adequacy of the protection provided by the EU-U.S. privacy shield (notified under document c(2016) 4176). OJ **L 207**, 1–112 (2016)
9. European Parliament, Council of the European Union: Commission implementing decision (EU) 2021/914 of 4 june 2021 on standard contractual clauses for the transfer of personal data to third countries pursuant to regulation (EU) 2016/679 of the European parliament and of the council. OJ **L 199**, 31–61 (2021)
10. European Parliament, Council of the European Union: Commission implementing decision EU 2023/1795 of 10 july 2023 pursuant to regulation (EU) 2016/679 of the European parliament and of the council on the adequate level of protection of personal data under the EU-us data privacy framework (notified under document c(2023)4745). OJ **L 231**, 118–229 (2023)
11. Court of Justice of the European Union (CJEU): Judgment of the court (grand chamber) of 16 july 2020. data protection commissioner v facebook ireland limited and maximillian schrems. C-311/18 (Schrems II) (2020). https://eur-lex.europa.eu/legal-content/EN/TXT/?uri=CELEX:62018CJ0311
12. Guerar, M., Verderame, L., Migliardi, M., Palmieri, F., Merlo, A.: Gotta captcha'em all: a survey of 20 years of the human-or-computer dilemma. ACM Comput. Surv. (CSUR) **54**(9), 1–33 (2021)

13. LG München I: Endurteil vom 20.01.2022 - 3 o 17493/20 (2022). https://openjur. de/u/2384915.html
14. Iliou, C., Kostoulas, T., Tsikrika, T., Katos, V., Vrochidis, S., Kompatsiaris, I.: Web bot detection evasion using deep reinforcement learning. In: Proceedings of the 17th International Conference on Availability, Reliability and Security, pp. 1–10 (2022)
15. Iliou, C., Kostoulas, T., Tsikrika, T., Katos, V., Vrochidis, S., Kompatsiaris, I.: Web bot detection evasion using generative adversarial networks. In: 2021 IEEE International Conference on Cyber Security and Resilience (CSR), pp. 115–120. IEEE (2021)
16. Imperva: 2024 bad bot report (2024). https://www.imperva.com/resources/ resource-library/reports/2024-bad-bot-report/
17. InsideRecaptcha (2014). https://github.com/toogle/InsideReCaptcha. Accessed 12 Sep 2024
18. Li, X., Azad, B.A., Rahmati, A., Nikiforakis, N.: Good bot, bad bot: characterizing automated browsing activity. In: 2021 IEEE Symposium on Security and Privacy (SP), pp. 1589–1605. IEEE (2021)
19. Naor, M.: Verification of a human in the loop or identification via the turing test (1996). http://www.wisdom.weizmann.ac.il/~naor/PAPERS/humanabs
20. Privacy Sandbox: A new path for privacy sandbox on the web (2024). https:// privacysandbox.com/intl/en_us/news/privacy-sandbox-update/. Accessed 20 Sep 2024
21. Sivakorn, S., Polakis, I., Keromytis, A.D.: I am robot:(deep) learning to break semantic image captchas. In: 2016 IEEE European Symposium on Security and Privacy (EuroS&P), pp. 388–403. IEEE (2016)
22. Tsingenopoulos, I., Preuveneers, D., Desmet, L., Joosen, W.: Captcha me if you can: imitation games with reinforcement learning. In: 2022 IEEE 7th European Symposium on Security and Privacy (EuroS&P), pp. 719–735. IEEE (2022)
23. von Ahn, L., Blum, M., Hopper, N.J., Langford, J.: CAPTCHA: using hard AI problems for security. In: Biham, E. (ed.) EUROCRYPT 2003. LNCS, vol. 2656, pp. 294–311. Springer, Heidelberg (2003). https://doi.org/10.1007/3-540-39200- 9_18
24. Welch, T.A.: A technique for high-performance data compression. Computer 17(06), 8–19 (1984)
25. Reverse engineering the Cloudflare JavaScript challenge (2024). https://www. zenrows.com/blog/bypass-cloudflare#bypass-cloudflare-waiting-room.   Accessed 14 Sep 2024

Hiding in Plain Sight: Query Obfuscation via Random Multilingual Searches

Anton Firc[✉], Jan Klusáček, and Kamil Malinka

Brno University of Technology, Božetěchova 2, Brno, Czech Republic
{ifirc,malinka}@fit.vut.cz

Abstract. Modern search engines extensively personalize results by building detailed user profiles based on query history and behaviour. While personalization can enhance relevance, it introduces privacy risks and can lead to filter bubbles. This paper proposes and evaluates a lightweight, client-side query obfuscation strategy using randomly generated multilingual search queries to disrupt user profiling. Through controlled experiments on the Seznam.cz search engine, we assess the impact of interleaving real queries with obfuscating noise in various language configurations and ratios. Our findings show that while displayed search results remain largely stable, the search engine's identified user interests shift significantly under obfuscation. We further demonstrate that such random queries can prevent accurate profiling and overwrite established user profiles. This study provides practical evidence for query obfuscation as a viable privacy-preserving mechanism and introduces a tool that enables users to autonomously protect their search behaviour without modifying existing infrastructure.

Keywords: user profiling · personalization · search engines · random search · anonymization

1 Introduction

Online search engines are integral to how users interact with digital information. However, these systems often rely on extensive user profiling, leveraging demographic data, search histories, and behavioural signals to personalize search results and optimize advertisement delivery. While personalization can improve user experience, it raises well-documented concerns regarding privacy, surveillance, and information bias [2,10].

Personalized search can trap users in "filter bubbles," where only algorithmically curated content is visible. Worse, search engines often collect sensitive behavioural data without explicit user consent [9,22]. These concerns have led to growing research on privacy-preserving search techniques, including anonymizing networks, private information retrieval (PIR), and query obfuscation [18,22,27].

Among these, query obfuscation presents a compelling trade-off: it requires only client-side changes, scales well, and can be deployed by privacy-conscious individuals. Tools like TrackMeNot have explored this concept by injecting decoy search traffic to obscure real interests [12]. However, prior work rarely evaluates the effectiveness of such methods under multilingual conditions or with respect to actual profile disruption over time.

This paper presents a practical approach to query obfuscation using multilingual random queries. We introduce a tool that interleaves real user queries with noise generated from language-specific dictionaries, simulating diverse user interests. Through controlled experiments using the Seznam.cz platform, which provides transparent user interest feedback, we evaluate the impact of obfuscation on search results and inferred user profiles.

The main contributions of this paper may be summarised as:

- We introduce a lightweight tool for privacy-preserving query obfuscation using multilingual random queries designed for real-world usability.
- We empirically demonstrate that query obfuscation significantly alters user interest profiles, even when search result pages remain largely unaffected.
- We evaluate how language diversity and query ratios influence obfuscation effectiveness and show that profiles can be reshaped even after initial formation.
- We provide insights into the feasibility of user-controlled privacy enhancement without requiring changes to search engine infrastructure.

The work described in this paper results from a previously completed master's thesis [15], forming the core of this research. The implementation with additional materials is available at: https://github.com/Sacek073/Protection-Against-Profiling-with-Random-Multilingual-Search.

2   Related Work

Search personalization systems rely on detailed user profiling to deliver customized results. Profiling typically involves collecting and analyzing behavioural data such as search queries, click-through history, and location [1,4,14]. Profiles are built using explicit profiling (e.g., users providing information through forms such as age or interests), implicit profiling (e.g., inferring preferences from click behaviour), or a hybrid of both approaches [2]. While this personalization enhances user experience, it simultaneously creates severe privacy risks.

Search engines do not reveal their internal profiling algorithms, which hinders third-party analysis [10]. Although patents such as [17] give some insight into legacy approaches, the current profiling mechanisms remain proprietary and continuously evolve.

2.1   Privacy-Preserving Search Techniques

To address privacy risks in web search, researchers have proposed various defence strategies categorized as *Private Information Retrieval (PIR)*, *anonymizing networks*, and *query obfuscation* [16,22].

Private Information Retrieval (PIR) allows users to retrieve data without revealing their queries. Traditional PIR schemes are computationally expensive and assume server cooperation, which is incompatible with real-world search engines [13,18]. Attempts to bypass these limitations include *h(k)-PIR* schemes, which inject fake keywords into queries to achieve plausible deniability [3].

Anonymizing networks like Tor mask users' identities by routing traffic through multiple nodes. However, such networks still expose the query content to search engines and are susceptible to de-anonymization through query content analysis [21,22]. Studies demonstrate that attackers can re-identify users from anonymized pools using only short-term search histories and standard classifiers [22].

Query obfuscation is a client-side approach where fake queries are submitted alongside genuine ones to hide user interests [12,16,22]. Tools like Track-MeNot exemplify this method by generating queries that mimic user interests based on prior search patterns. While this increases realism, it may inadvertently reinforce certain topics rather than obscure them. Moreover, TrackMeNot depends on browser extensions, lacks ongoing support, and provides limited control over the obfuscation strategy. In contrast, our approach operates independently using a headless browser, supports multilingual noise generation, and allows fine-tuning of query frequency and language diversity. These features enhance stealth, user autonomy, and the adaptability of the obfuscator in varied threat settings.

Recent work further reveals that many obfuscators, including TrackMeNot, are susceptible to filtering via semantic similarity and entropy-based models [11]. Such findings highlight the need for more configurable and dynamic obfuscation tools, which our system addresses by incorporating randomized queries, multilingual context-switching, and evaluation grounded in profile inference feedback.

2.2 Evaluation Frameworks and Limitations

Recent studies propose frameworks to assess the effectiveness of obfuscation strategies systematically. OB-WSPES [26] allows comparative analysis of obfuscation methods against modern attacks. Gervais et al. [8] introduced a general methodology to evaluate privacy using query and semantic linkage metrics.

Newer approaches explore novel obfuscation mechanisms, such as differential privacy (DP), for query rewriting. For instance, Faggioli and Ferro demonstrate that DP-based obfuscation can achieve a tunable balance between privacy and relevance, outperforming traditional dummy-based methods under specific conditions [6].

Other proposals allow users to control the semantic distance and volume of fake queries, tailoring obfuscation strength to their privacy needs [23]. These user-centric methods promote flexible trade-offs between utility and privacy but lack broad adoption or integration with real-world platforms.

2.3 Positioning of This Work

This study extends query obfuscation research by deploying a practical, multilingual obfuscator tested against real-time user profiling feedback from Seznam.cz. Unlike prior work, it directly evaluates how injected noise alters inferred user interests rather than only focusing on query-level traceability. This contributes empirical insights to an underexplored dimension of user-centric privacy tools. By enabling fine-grained control over language selection, timing, and query volume, our tool also provides a more adaptable and modular platform than existing solutions like TrackMeNot.

3 Threat Model and Assumptions

We consider a **passive profiling adversary**, modelled as the search engine itself. It collects and processes user queries to infer interests for personalization and advertising. The adversary has full access to submitted queries and session metadata but does not control the user's device or actively interfere with the content.

We aim to degrade the accuracy of inferred user profiles by injecting randomized, multilingual decoy queries. The adversary is not assumed to detect or classify obfuscated queries in real-time, though it may apply generic profiling algorithms over aggregated data.

The evaluation is conducted on Seznam.cz, which openly displays user interest profiles. This enables empirical observation of how obfuscation impacts profiling outcomes. We do not defend against semantic or behavioural de-anonymization attacks, focusing instead on practical, client-side resistance to standard profiling mechanisms.

Adversarial Capabilities. Although we model the search engine primarily as a passive profiler, real-world systems may deploy active or semi-active mechanisms to detect obfuscation attempts. These include [11, 22]:

- **Temporal anomalies**—Detection of unnatural regularity in query timing or volume.
- **Semantic incoherence**—Recognition of disjointed or unrelated topics inconsistent with typical user interests.
- **Language switching patterns**—Multilingual behaviour without corresponding context changes (e.g., UI language).
- **Lack of engagement**—Missing interaction signals such as clicks or dwell time after queries.

Our tool addresses some of these issues via randomized inter-query delays, plausible query lengths, and headless browser automation that mimics human interaction patterns. However, a powerful adversary could still filter out low-quality or suspicious queries post hoc, especially in commercial settings optimized for personalization.

We restrict our evaluation to scenarios where such detection is not yet deployed or is not sensitive enough to filter our approach reliably. Future work may extend this model to account for stronger adversaries with access to richer behavioural telemetry or multi-session fingerprinting techniques.

4   Obfuscation Tool Architecture and Workflow

We developed a custom automation tool to evaluate the effectiveness of multilingual query obfuscation, as existing solutions such as TrackMeNot[1] lacked required features and long-term maintainability [12,22]. The tool simulates user-like search behaviour by issuing genuine and randomized multilingual queries to Seznam.cz. It enables controlled experimentation on profiling disruption in a real-world environment where inferred interests are visible to the user.

The tool is implemented using Puppeteer, a Node.js library for browser automation, and extended with the `puppeteer-extra-plugin-stealth`[2] to mimic natural user interaction. It operates headless, managing login, query issuance, and result collection while minimizing detectability. All actions, including delays and query typing, emulate genuine usage patterns.

4.1   Search Generation

Obfuscating queries are generated from precompiled language-specific dictionaries comprising general vocabulary chosen to represent broad, demographically diverse topics. To ensure randomness and topic dilution, query length and language rotation follow user-defined configurations. Although ideally, the tool would simulate diverse demographic profiles, this was deemed infeasible; hence, randomness from broad lexical sources was prioritized.

4.2   Modes of Operation

The tool operates in two distinct modes:

– `the_tool`: Issues randomized queries using selected language dictionaries. Users configure the query length range and language pool. Queries are interleaved in a round-robin fashion to simulate multilingual behaviour.
– `queries`: Executes predefined queries from a provided list intended for targeted profiling or evaluation scenarios. This mode captures search results to measure post-query personalization.

---

[1] https://www.trackmenot.io/.
[2] https://www.npmjs.com/package/puppeteer-extra-plugin-stealth.

4.3   Workflow Summary

The tool's workflow includes:

1. Launching a stealth-configured headless browser.
2. Logging into a user account on Seznam.cz.
3. Loading either language wordlists or predefined queries.
4. Executing queries in a loop: entering text, triggering search, collecting result metadata, and sleeping between iterations.
5. Saving structured outputs in JSON format containing query, language, user, timestamp, and result objects with links and categorization.

   To handle unstable elements such as malformed result pages or missing CSS selectors, all browser operations are wrapped in recovery blocks that log errors and resume operation. This ensures robustness against transient failures during long-term operation.

4.4   Output Format

Search outputs are stored in JSON format for downstream evaluation. Each entry includes the query issued, the language used, the user ID, the timestamp, and a list of result objects. Results are further annotated with a boolean flag indicating whether the result is a genuine external link or a platform-specific element (e.g., videos, image results, local services), enabling finer-grained analysis of content types returned during obfuscated and targeted searches.

5   Experimental Setup

The goal of this study is to evaluate the effectiveness of multilingual query obfuscation in disrupting search engines' user profiling. We investigate this through four controlled experiments designed to answer the following research questions:

RQ1: Does multilingual query obfuscation alter displayed results or inferred user interests?
RQ2: How does the number of languages used in random queries affect profiling?
RQ3: How does varying the ratio of genuine to random queries influence outcomes?
RQ4: Can obfuscation reshape an already formed user profile?

5.1   System Configuration

All experiments were conducted using Virtual Machines (VMs) hosted on a single physical machine within a university subnet to minimize geolocation bias and temporal noise due to network routing or infrastructure differences [10]. The VMs were isolated using distinct user accounts and browser instances, ensuring independent sessions with no cookie sharing, cross-account leakage, or fingerprint carryover. Browser cache and history were cleared at the beginning of each experiment.

   Three base VMs were created:

- **Normal VM**: submits only profiling queries.
- **Control VM**: identical to Normal, used for baseline comparison.
- **Tool VM**: submits profiling queries and runs background random multilingual queries.

Each VM had a manually registered Seznam.cz account with identical demographic information (male, born 01/01/2000). No other personalization was applied. A dedicated prepaid SIM card was used to activate all accounts, avoiding any linkability to prior identity or external services.

5.2 Query Design and Execution

To simulate realistic user behaviour, profiling queries were constructed to reflect an interest in three categories: *sports*, *technology*, and *travel*. A total of 300 Czech-language queries were crafted (100 per category), spread evenly across 10 daily batches. Sample queries include: *"zimní olympiáda"*, *"stackoverflow"*, *"letenky online"*. Each VM submitted 30 queries per day (one every 960 s), mimicking natural inter-search intervals observed in human users.

The Tool VM additionally submitted 90 background queries daily, generated from dictionaries in Czech, English, French, and Spanish. These dictionaries were curated to ensure topic diversity and realism. Queries were constructed by selecting 1âĂŞ3 random words inspired by research on natural query lengths in real-world search behavior [7]. Random searches were spaced at 320-second intervals, resulting in a 3:1 ratio of random to genuine queries. These delay values were chosen to maintain operational stealth and to minimize the carryover effect [10], where rapid consecutive queries could influence search results.

All experiments were run for 8-hour periods across 10 days. Queries were issued sequentially via a headless browser controlled using Puppeteer, configured with randomized delays, human-like typing simulation, and stealth plugins to avoid detection by bot-detection heuristics.

5.3 Experiments

Experiment 1: Baseline Effectiveness. The Tool VM submitted profiling and obfuscation queries in parallel to test whether the additional traffic disrupted interest profiling or affected search results.

Experiment 2: Language Diversity. This experiment introduced:

- **Language Low VM**: uses only Czech for random queries.
- **Language High VM**: uses eight languages, including Czech, English, French, Italian, Slovak, Spanish, Turkish, and Ukrainian.

The goal was to assess whether broader linguistic diversity improves obfuscation. Both used a 1:3 profiling-to-random ratio.

Experiment 3: Query Ratio. This experiment varied the volume of random queries:

- **Ratio Low VM**: 1:1 ratio (equal number of genuine and random queries).
- **Ratio High VM**: 1:7 ratio (one genuine query to seven obfuscated ones).

This aimed to evaluate how dilution strength affects personalization.

Experiment 4: Delayed Obfuscation. The **Delay VM** performed only profiling queries for the first 5 days, then submitted random queries to evaluate if pre-established profiles could be altered retrospectively.

5.4   Search Engine Selection

Seznam.cz was selected due to its transparent profiling model and lack of restrictions on automated access. Unlike Google or Bing, Seznam.cz displays daily-updated "Areas of Interest" derived from user search history, which users can view or delete at https://ucet.seznam.cz/activity/targeting. This feature allows direct monitoring of profile evolution over time, making it uniquely suited for controlled obfuscation studies.

5.5   Evaluation Metrics and Analysis

To assess changes in personalization and content, two metrics were used:

- **Jaccard Index** [25]: measures set similarity between result or interest sets; ranges from 0 (no overlap) to 1 (identical).
- **Edit Distance** [24]: quantifies reordering and substitution cost between ranked lists.

All profiling queries captured the top-10 search results. Interest profiles were extracted daily from the Seznam interface. Comparisons were made between VM pairs (e.g., Normal vs. Tool) across days. Statistical significance was tested using the Shapiro-Wilk test for normality [19]. As no datasets followed a normal distribution, non-parametric Mann-Whitney U tests [20] were used with $\alpha = 0.05$ to determine significant differences.

6   Results

The experiments were conducted sequentially over more than 40 days. Search results and identified interests were collected daily and evaluated using the Jaccard Index and Edit Distance. Statistical significance was assessed using the Mann-Whitney U test ($\alpha = 0.05$). Table 1 summarizes the p-values for all experiments.

RQ1: Effectiveness of Multilingual Obfuscation

Experiment One showed statistically significant differences between the Tool and Normal VMs in both search results and identified interests. Although changes in search results were modest (Fig. 1), the differences in identified interests were pronounced (Fig. 2). The Tool VM's interests had consistently lower Jaccard values and higher Edit Distances, suggesting successful disruption of profiling.

Table 1. P-values from the Mann-Whitney U test for search results and identified interests.

Experiment	Search Results		Identified Interests	
	Jaccard	Edit Dist.	Jaccard	Edit Dist.
One	0.0018	0.0222	0.0001	0.0001
Two (Low)	0.0803	0.1544	< 0.0001	< 0.0001
Two (High)	0.0733	0.1324	< 0.0001	< 0.0001
Three (Low)	0.5173	0.4955	< 0.0001	< 0.0001
Three (High)	0.1108	0.1617	< 0.0001	< 0.0001
Four	0.4061	0.1568	0.0402	0.0402

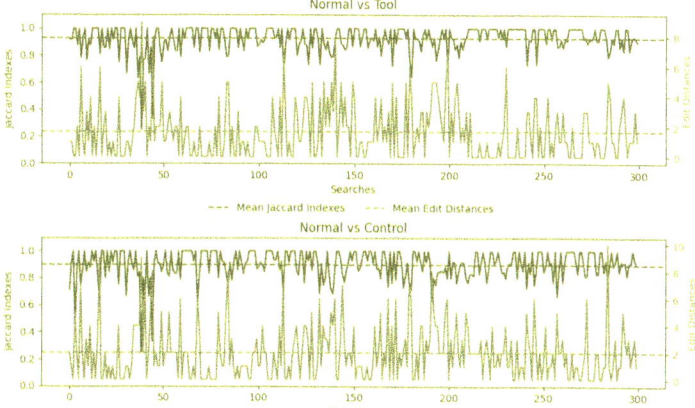

Fig. 1. Search Result Similarity (Jaccard Index and Edit Distance).

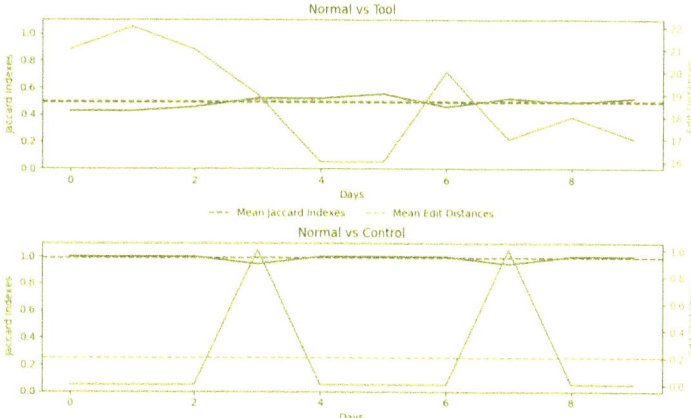

Fig. 2. Identified Interests Similarity. Note the Edit Distance scale.

RQ2: Language Diversity Impact

In Experiment Two, the number of languages used in random queries had minimal effect on search results but a significant influence on identified interests (Fig. 3). Using only Czech yielded more divergence from the Normal VM than using eight languages, suggesting that less linguistic diversity may better obscure interest profiles.

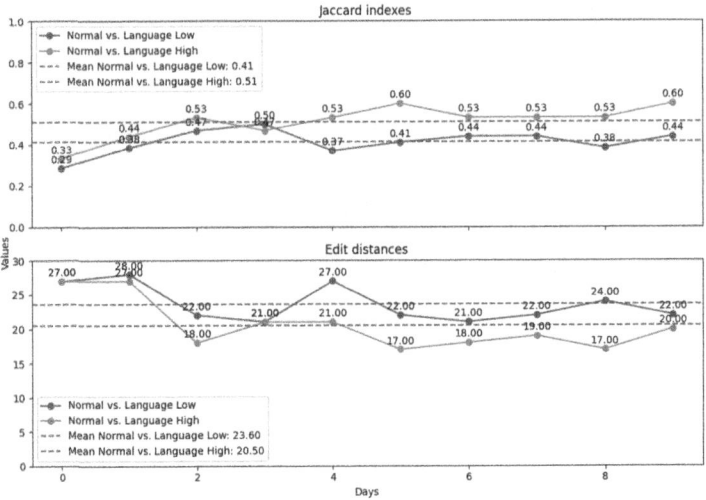

Fig. 3. Language Experiment: Identified Interests (Jaccard Index - Top, Edit Distance - Bottom).

RQ3: Obfuscation Ratio Effects

Experiment Three revealed no statistically significant changes in search results, but strong effects on identified interests. A higher random-to-genuine query ratio (1:7) led to greater divergence from the Normal VM compared to a lower ratio (1:1), as illustrated in Fig. 4. This confirms that stronger obfuscation correlates with better profile disruption.

RQ4: Overwriting Existing Profiles

In Experiment Four, the Delay VM began random queries after five days of profiling. Although search results remained largely unchanged, a shift in identified interests occurred after random queries started (Fig. 5). Edit Distance increased and Jaccard Index decreased, indicating successful profile mutation.

7   Discussion

This study provides empirical evidence that query obfuscation, particularly through multilingual random queries, can disrupt user profiling mechanisms

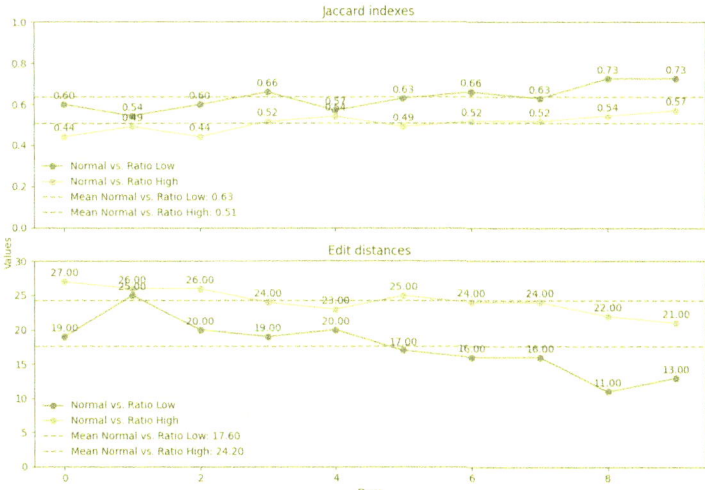

Fig. 4. Ratio Experiment: Identified Interests (Jaccard Index - Top, Edit Distance - Bottom).

used by search engines. Across multiple experiments, we observed consistent alterations in inferred user interests, even when search results remained largely stable. These findings validate the premise that obfuscation-based methods can be practical tools for enhancing search privacy, especially in user-centred, client-side deployments.

7.1   Impact on Profiling vs. Search Results

A key insight from our experiments is the decoupling between personalized search results and user profiling. While obfuscation had a limited impact on the top search results returned for specific queries, it significantly affected the interest profiles assigned to users. This suggests that search personalization pipelines operate on a longer-term behavioural model, where interest inference is more sensitive to volume and diversity of query history than short-term result ranking.

The implications are twofold. First, users concerned with behavioural profiling, e.g., for advertising or content filtering, can benefit from lightweight obfuscation without compromising search result usability. Second, this dissociation between visible results and backend profiling highlights the opacity of personalization systems and the need for tools that let users intervene in shaping or obscuring their inferred identities.

7.2   Strategic Obfuscation: Language and Volume

The experiments examining language diversity and obfuscation ratios reveal a nuanced view of obfuscation strategy. Surprisingly, obfuscation using only Czech

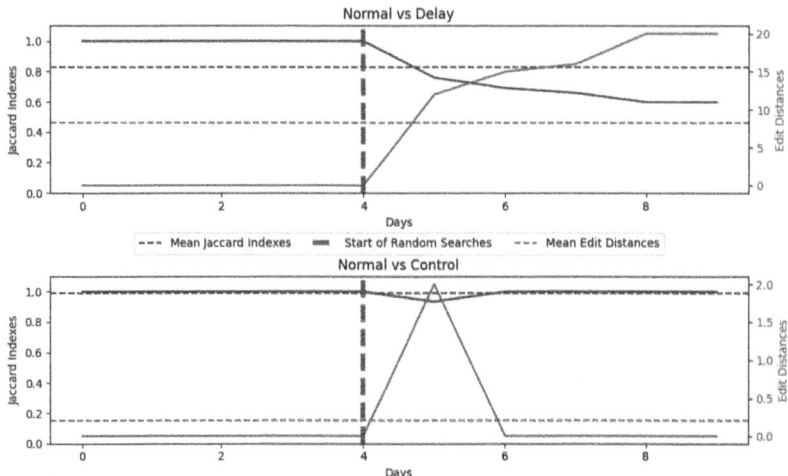

Fig. 5. Delayed Obfuscation: Changes in Identified Interests.

yielded greater disruption than multilingual approaches, likely due to the profiling engine's focus on Czech-language content. This suggests that effective obfuscation must account for the language model and cultural domain of the search engine in use and warrants further investigation across other platforms. Simply increasing linguistic variety may introduce noise without undermining the assumptions of the underlying profiling algorithms.

Additionally, increasing the volume of random queries consistently improved concealment. A 1:7 ratio of genuine to random queries yielded the most privacy-preserving profiles. This supports the conceptual intuition that in profiling systems where relevance is inferred from frequency and recency, flooding the model with decoy data can obscure meaningful signals. This finding aligns with adversarial obfuscation literature and confirms that even simple random query strategies can introduce sufficient entropy to distort user modelling.

7.3   Dynamic Reprofiling: Reversibility of Interests

A particularly promising outcome was the ability to reshape an already established interest profile. In Experiment Four, delayed obfuscation reversed the trajectory of interest inference, leading to measurable divergence from the pre-existing profile. This finding has practical significance: users who are already heavily profiled are not locked into their inferred identities. Even without deleting accounts or histories, profile trajectories can be perturbed through non-invasive means.

This also raises an important ethical and design question: Should users have the ability to audit and intervene in their profiles more actively? Search engines currently do not offer this capability, but our findings suggest it is both feasible and technically low-cost.

7.4 Positioning Within the Privacy Landscape

This work contributes to the growing class of user-controllable, zero-trust privacy mechanisms. Unlike Private Information Retrieval (PIR), which requires cooperation from service providers, and anonymizing networks like Tor, which protect identity but not content, our tool defends against profiling by polluting the data corpus used for inference. It is a pragmatic middle-ground solution: usable, scalable, and compatible with current web infrastructure.

Moreover, the use of Seznam.cz provides a unique empirical window into profiling processes that are often opaque on platforms like Google. While this limits generalizability, it provides rare observable feedback on how query history shapes user models in practice.

From a legal standpoint, our approach aligns with the GDPR principle of data minimization [5] by allowing users to interfere with excessive profiling. Since the tool operates entirely on the client side and does not alter search engine infrastructure, it respects current terms of service while offering meaningful privacy benefits.

7.5 Risks and Evasion Potential

That said, these techniques are not foolproof. Our tool assumes a non-adversarial search engine that does not actively filter or flag suspicious query patterns. In real-world deployments, engines may develop classifiers to identify and suppress obfuscation traffic. Semantic and behavioural fingerprinting (e.g., dwell time, query structure, device identifiers) could also be used to infer query authenticity.

Additionally, overuse of obfuscation may degrade the quality of personalization for users who value it. While some users may accept this trade-off for privacy, others may seek selective control over which queries are masked. This presents opportunities for future work in adaptive obfuscation—balancing utility and privacy dynamically based on context or sensitivity.

7.6 Limitations

Several limitations should be acknowledged. The use of Seznam.cz, while justifiable from a legal and operational standpoint, constrains broader applicability. Its user base, infrastructure, and profiling logic differ from global engines. The Czech language and localized query structures may have biased the obfuscation results.

Furthermore, automation limits were discovered empirically due to a lack of documentation. These constraints affected query throughput and forced serialized experiment execution, possibly introducing day-to-day search index drift.

Finally, while VMs were synchronized within minutes, they could not issue queries simultaneously. This introduces potential temporal noise, although prior work suggests such variation is minimal when comparing interest profiles rather than instantaneous result rankings.

7.7   Toward Controllable Search Privacy

Despite these limitations, this work shows that personalization and profiling can be manipulated without breaking terms of service, compromising search engines, or deploying heavyweight cryptographic tools. The results suggest a future where users actively manage their digital shadows—not by opting out entirely, but by introducing ambiguity into the systems that seek to define them.

7.8   Usability and Deployment Considerations

From a deployment perspective, our tool is lightweight and can run passively in the background during user browsing sessions. However, large-scale use may face challenges such as detection by advanced bot-filtering systems or throttling based on abnormal traffic patterns. Furthermore, while the tool simulates natural search behavior, it does not currently simulate user engagement (e.g., clicks or scrolling), which may limit realism in adversarial settings. Integrating feedback-based adaptation or browser-based query diversification may improve stealth without significantly increasing user-side complexity.

7.9   Use Case: Lightweight Daily Obfuscation

Consider a privacy-aware user performing 10 genuine searches daily. Using our tool in the background during browsing hours (e.g., 9:00âĂŞ17:00), the system automatically injects random multilingual queries at a 1:3 ratio. This lightweight activity runs in a headless browser, mimicking typical user behaviour without disrupting the user's experience.

Over time, the search engine's profile is diluted with noise, reducing personalization accuracy. This approach requires no server-side changes and minimal resources, and it aligns with terms of service, making it practical for everyday privacy protection.

8   Conclusion

This study demonstrates that random query obfuscation can effectively disrupt user profiling in search engines, particularly by altering inferred interests without noticeably impacting search results. Through experiments conducted on Seznam.cz, we showed that using a single language (Czech) and a high ratio of random to genuine queries offers strong obfuscation performance. Furthermore, obfuscation remains effective even when applied to previously established profiles, enabling retrospective privacy protection.

Our approach is lightweight, user-friendly, and compliant with search engine terms of service. It can be deployed in the background during regular browsing sessions, offering practical privacy enhancements with minimal user intervention.

Future research should investigate optimal obfuscation strategies, explore applicability to broader personalization contexts, and assess long-term effects and integration into real-world privacy tools.

Although the experiments were conducted on Seznam.cz due to its transparency and terms of service, the fundamental mechanism of query-based profiling is shared by most major search engines. Consequently, the observed effects of obfuscation are expected to transfer to platforms like Google or Bing, albeit with variations due to their more complex personalization models. Testing across these platforms remains an important direction for future research, ideally leveraging ethical frameworks or approved APIs.

Acknowledgments. This work was supported by the Brno University of Technology internal project FIT-S-23-8151. The manuscript text was refined using generative AI language models to improve clarity and grammar.

References

1. Bhopale, S.D., Sahu, A., Pandyaji, K.: Web services recommendation system using machine learning algorithms. In: 2023 4th International Conference for Emerging Technology (INCET), pp. 1–7 (2023). https://doi.org/10.1109/INCET57972.2023. 10170205

2. Bozdag, E.: Bias in algorithmic filtering and personalization. Ethics Inf. Technol. **15**(3), 209–227 (2013). https://doi.org/10.1007/s10676-013-9321-6

3. Domingo-Ferrer, J., Solanas, A., Castellà-Roca, J.: h(k)-private information retrieval from privacy-uncooperative queryable databases. Online Inf. Rev. **33**(4), 720–744 (2009). https://doi.org/10.1108/14684520910985693

4. Eke, C.I., Norman, A., Shuib, L., Nweke, H.F.: A survey of user profiling: state-of-the-art, challenges, and solutions. IEEE Access **7**, 144907–144924 (2019). https://doi.org/10.1109/ACCESS.2019.2944243

5. European Parliament and Council of the European Union: General Data Protection Regulation (GDPR) - Article 5: Principles relating to processing of personal data (2016). https://gdpr-info.eu/art-5-gdpr/. Accessed 10 June 2025

6. Faggioli, G., Ferro, N.: Query obfuscation for information retrieval through differential privacy. In: European Conference on Information Retrieval (ECIR). Lecture Notes in Computer Science, vol. 14608, pp. 278–294 (2024). https://doi.org/10. 1007/978-3-031-56027-9_17

7. Freund, L., Toms, E.: Understanding the brevity of web queries, pp. 517–518 (2005).https://doi.org/10.1002/meet.14504001103

8. Gervais, A., Shokri, R., Singla, A., Capkun, S., Lenders, V.: Quantifying web-search privacy. In: Proceedings of the 2014 ACM SIGSAC Conference on Computer and Communications Security (CCS), pp. 966–977 (2014). https://doi.org/ 10.1145/2660267.2660367

9. Guha, S., Cheng, B., Francis, P.: Challenges in measuring online advertising systems. In: IMC 2010,Proceedings of the 10th ACM SIGCOMM Conference on Internet Measurement, pp. 81–87. Association for Computing Machinery, New York, NY, USA (2010). https://doi.org/10.1145/1879141.1879152

10. Hannak, A., et al.: Measuring personalization of web search. In: Proceedings of the 22nd international conference on World Wide Web (2013). https://doi.org/10. 1145/2488388.2488435

11. Houssiau, F., Liénart, T., Hendrickx, J., de Montjoye, Y.A.: Web privacy: a formal adversarial model for query obfuscation. IEEE Trans. Inf. Forensics Secur. **18**, 2132–2147 (2023). https://doi.org/10.1109/TIFS.2023.3262123

12. Howe, D., Nissenbaum, H.: Trackmenot: resisting surveillance in web search. In: Lessons from the Identity Trail: Anonymity, Privacy, and Identity in a Networked Society, vol. 23 (2009)

13. Juárez, M., Torra, V.: Toward a privacy agent for information retrieval. Int. J. Intell. Syst. **28**(6), 606–622 (2013). https://doi.org/10.1002/int.21595, https://onlinelibrary.wiley.com/doi/abs/10.1002/int.21595

14. Kanoje, S., Girase, S., Mukhopadhyay, D.: User profiling trends, techniques and applications. Int. J. Adv. Found. Res. Comput. **1**, 2348–4853 (2014)

15. Klusáček, J.: Protection against profiling with random multilingual search. Master's thesis, Brno University of Technology, Brno, Czech republic (2024). https://www.vut.cz/en/students/final-thesis/detail/153822

16. Kumar, K.: Privacy protection in personalized web search using obfuscation. Int. J. Emerg. Trends Eng. Res. **8**(4), 1410–1416 (2020). https://doi.org/10.30534/ijeter/2020/76842020

17. Lawrence, S.R.: Personalization of web search results using term, category, and link-based user profiles (2012)

18. Maylybaeva, G.A.: The order of communication complexity of pir-protocols **18**, 505–515 (2008). https://doi.org/10.1515/DMA.2008.036

19. Mishra, P., Pandey, C., Singh, U., Gupta, A., Sahu, C., Keshri, A.: Descriptive statistics and normality tests for statistical data. Ann. Card. Anaesth. **22**, 67–72 (2019). https://doi.org/10.4103/aca.ACA_157_18

20. Nahm, F.: Nonparametric statistical tests for the continuous data: the basic concept and the practical use. Korean J. Anesthesiol. **69**, 8–14 (2016). https://doi.org/10.4097/kjae.2016.69.1.8

21. Peddinti, S.T., Saxena, N.: On the effectiveness of anonymizing networks for web search privacy. In: ASIACCS 2011, Proceedings of the 6th ACM Symposium on Information, Computer and Communications Security, pp. 483–489. Association for Computing Machinery, New York, NY, USA (2011). https://doi.org/10.1145/1966913.1966984

22. Peddinti, S.T., Saxena, N.: Web search query privacy: evaluating query obfuscation and anonymizing networks. J. Comput. Secur. **22**(1), 155–199 (2014)

23. Punagin, S., Arya, A.: A novel query obfuscation scheme with user controlled privacy and personalization. Int. J. Comput. Appl. **158**(1), 50–54 (2017)

24. Schulz, K., Mihov, S.: Fast string correction with levenshtein automata. Int. J. Doc. Anal. Recogn. **5**, 67–85 (2002). https://doi.org/10.1007/s10032-002-0082-8

25. Verma, V., Aggarwal, R.K.: A comparative analysis of similarity measures akin to the Jaccard index in collaborative recommendations: empirical and theoretical perspective. Soc. Netw. Anal. Min. **10**(1), 1–16 (2020). https://doi.org/10.1007/s13278-020-00660-9

26. Wei, C., Gu, Q., Ji, S., Chen, W., Wang, Z., Beyah, R.: OB-WSPES: a uniform evaluation system for obfuscation-based web search privacy. IEEE Trans. Dependable Secure Comput. **18**(6), 2719–2732 (2021). https://doi.org/10.1109/TDSC.2019.2962440

27. Xu, Y., Wang, K., Zhang, B., Chen, Z.: Privacy-enhancing personalized web search. In: WWW 2007, Proceedings of the 16th International Conference on World Wide Web, pp. 591–600. Association for Computing Machinery, New York, NY, USA (2007). https://doi.org/10.1145/1242572.1242652

A Time Series Analysis of Malware Uploads to Programming Language Ecosystems

Jukka Ruohonen[(✉)] [ID] and Mubashrah Saddiqa [ID]

University of Southern Denmark, Sønderborg, Denmark
{juk,msad}@mmmi.sdu.dk

Abstract. Software ecosystems built around programming languages have greatly facilitated software development. At the same time, their security has increasingly been acknowledged as a problem. To this end, the paper examines the previously overlooked longitudinal aspects of software ecosystem security, focusing on malware uploaded to six popular programming language ecosystems. The dataset examined is based on the new Open Source Vulnerabilities (OSV) database. According to the results, records about detected malware uploads in the database have recently surpassed those addressing vulnerabilities in packages distributed in the ecosystems. In the early 2025 even up to 80% of all entries in the OSV have been about malware. Regarding time series analysis of malware frequencies and their shares to all database entries, good predictions are available already by relatively simple autoregressive models using the numbers of ecosystems, security advisories, and media and other articles as predictors. With these results and the accompanying discussion, the paper improves and advances the understanding of the thus far overlooked longitudinal aspects of ecosystems and malware.

Keywords: software ecosystems · malware · vulnerabilities · dependencies · security risks · typo-squatting · security scanning · sweeps · autoregression · lags · CRA

1 Introduction

Software ecosystems—understood in the present context as programming language specific repositories from which software packages can be downloaded and updated—have greatly facilitated software development and the general software design principles, among them particularly reusability [7]. This facilitation has correlated with an enormous growth of the ecosystems, many of which contain hundreds of thousands of software packages. However, over again, software ecosystems have also been shown to be risky in terms of software security. Indeed, the security aspects of practically all major software ecosystems have been examined in recent years. The examples include, but are not limited to, PyPI for Python [13,19,26,34], CRAN for R [9], npm for JavaScript [34,36],

B. Coppens et al. (Eds.): ARES 2025 Workshops, LNCS 15995, pp. 269–285, 2025.
https://doi.org/10.1007/978-3-032-00633-2_16

Maven for Java [22], RubyGems for Ruby [9], and Packagist for PHP [27]. The overall conclusion from this already vast but still growing literature base is the general insecurity of the software ecosystems for individual developers and software development organizations, whether companies or open source software projects.

Among the primary reasons for the security risks is that many of the packages distributed in the ecosystems are of poor quality, containing various unverified security issues or already identified vulnerabilities. The security risks also increase due to a heavy use of dependencies in the ecosystems [9,22,36]. Both direct and transitive dependencies contribute to the risks, which are also related to the presence of many outdated, unmaintained, and abandoned packages distributed in the ecosystems. Also the operational security of software developers using the ecosystems has been seen as a risk factor [34,36]. Furthermore, the problems are made worse by the increasing presence of malware in some programming language ecosystems [13,19,34]. The paper aligns with and contributes to the last mentioned genre of software ecosystem research, the empirically motivated malware-specific research branch.

A traditional attack vector with the malware uploads has been so-called typosquatting; an attacker uploads a malware package with a name resembling an existing, legitimate package, trying to fool people into downloading and installing the malware-ridden package [3]. Such typo-squatting belongs to a broader class of name confusion attacks [31]. For instance, it has recently been argued that hallucinated package names by large language models might make the problem worse in the nearby future [6]. Regardless, the problem is already intensified by dependencies because it essentially may only take one misstep by one developer somewhere in a dependency network to compromise the whole network [19]. For this reason alone, it is important to gain better knowledge on the longitudinal aspects of malware uploads to popular programming language ecosystems. With this point in mind, the following three research questions (RQs) are examined:

RQ.1: How much detected malware uploads have popular programming language ecosystems seen compared to traditional vulnerability reports?

RQ.2: Which ecosystems have been particularly prone to malware uploads?

RQ.3: Can time series analysis provide insights into malware uploading trends?

To the best of the authors' knowledge, the RQs, or something analogous, have not been asked and examined in previous research. The paper thus fills a small but notable knowledge gap. The first RQ.1 also reflects a recently proposed distinction between supply chain attacks and vulnerabilities; the former can be seen to involve also an insertion of malware into an ecosystem, whereas the latter is about vulnerabilities in third-party components propagating into a software using the components [7]. Though, as was noted, also malware may propagate through dependencies. If such a propagation reaches commercial software vendors or important open source software projects, including distributors such as Linux distributions, the consequences can be catastrophic in many ways.

2   Motivation

The security risks involved are easy to demonstrate. Most—if not all—malware recently discovered from the npm ecosystem come with the following warning:

> *"Any computer that has this package installed or running should be considered fully compromised. All secrets and keys stored on that computer should be rotated immediately from a different computer. The package should be removed, but as full control of the computer may have been given to an outside entity, there is no guarantee that removing the package will remove all malicious software resulting from installing it."*[1]

This serious warning is not intensified only by the noted risk with dependencies. Among other things, many malware-ridden packages in both the npm and PyPI ecosystems have relied on installation-time infections made possible by the execution of scripts during installation or even downloading [34]. Many of the malware uploads recorded in the OSV are further referenced with CWE-506, which refers to embedding of malicious code in the Common Weakness Enumeration (CWE) framework. A similar warning is available from this framework.

The many security risks have been recognized also by policy-makers in recent years. In terms of new regulations, particularly important to acknowledge is the Cyber Resilience Act (CRA) recently enacted in the European Union (EU) [32]. This regulation is noteworthy for motivating also the present work. Among other things, the CRA's new essential cyber security requirements for most information technology products with a network functionality contain an obligation to only ship products without known vulnerabilities. This requirement applies also to vulnerabilities in dependencies distributed in software ecosystems. Although the CRA does not mention malware explicitly, its further essential requirements to ensure confidentiality, integrity, and availability [25] can be seen to cover also malware—as the above quotation also testifies. Accidentally embedding malware to a product is thus likely to face also regulatory sanctions at least in severe cases.

The CRA is important to mention also from a perspective of not software products and producers but also from a perspective of regulators. In particular, the regulation's Article 60 obliges European market surveillance authorities to conduct coordinated sweeps of particular products for checking compliance and detecting potential infringements. Regarding the paper's time series analysis, the note in the CRA's recital 114 about justifying sweeping particularly when "market *trends*, consumer complaints or *other indications* suggest that certain categories of products with digital elements are often found to present cybersecurity *risks*" (italics added). While the CRA is not meant to regulate all the world's software, sweeping software ecosystems, possibly together with other stakeholders, might improve the cyber security for everyone. To this end, it could be also argued that the new obligations placed upon regulators themselves might enhance and improve the existing tracking and monitoring

---

[1] https://osv.dev/vulnerability/MAL-2024-226.

infrastructures, among them the OSV database. After all, in the context of cyber security, the concept of a sweep, which originates from the EU's product safety laws [5], is rather close to security scanning, security audits, security monitoring, and related concepts and techniques already used to improve also the security of software ecosystems.

3   Related Work

As already noted in the introduction, the paper's closest reference point is the already large but still growing research domain on the security of programming language ecosystems, including particularly its malware-motivated branch.

Given the time series analysis pursued, a few related works are worth remarking also about longitudinal malware research—not least because such research seems to be rather limited when compared to malware research in general. For instance, a search from Scopus on 4 June 2025 with a keyword "*malware*" yields 28, 890 results when the search is restricted to papers' titles, abstracts, and author-provided keywords. When a keyword "*time series*" is added, only 233 results are returned. Although a definite conclusion is impossible to draw from these numbers, it can be still concluded that time series analysis is a nascent branch within the broader malware research domain. Adding a third keyword "*autoregressive*" yields only three papers. The first of these is a paper for forecasting malware infection rates in higher education institutions [8]. The second uses malware detection as a motivation for an idea to design a new deep learning architecture for network traffic analysis [18]. The third paper's topic is also about malware detection but its methodology is based on an autoregressive moving average model [15]. These three studies signify what time series analysis supposedly has often been about in the existing research: forecasts and detection of malware, whether through outlier detection or by other means. Although none of the three research questions explicitly fit into this simple twofold categorization, particularly RQ_3 is close to the first category because there would be only a small step from time series model-building and trend analysis to forecasts.

4   Materials and Methods

4.1   Data

The dataset examined was assembled from a bulk snapshot obtained in April 2025 from the OSV database.[2] The OSV database has recently been used also in previous research [28]. Although the database curates data from various publicly available sources, the dataset assembling was restricted to CRAN, Go, Maven, npm, PyPI, and RubyGems. Then, the following time series were constructed:

---

[2] https://osv.dev/.

1. *MalFreq$_t$* counts the number of malware entries reported for all of the six ecosystems sampled at t. The identification of malware entries was done by including those files whose names started with a MAL- character string. Even though this simple identification technique is not perfect, searching for a string `malware` from the other files indicates no major concerns.
2. *MalShare$_t$* is a percentage share of malware entries to all entries in the six ecosystems at a given t. If *VulnFreq$_t$* would be a total count of software vulnerabilities in the six ecosystems at the given t, an approximation *MalShare$_t$* $\simeq$ *MalFreq$_t$* / (*MalFreq$_t$* + *VulnFreq$_t$*) × 100 would hold.
3. *Eco$_t$* is a count of the given ecosystems that contributed to *MalFreq$_t$* at t. It follows that $\max(Eco_t) = 6$ and $\min(Eco_t) = 0$ hold for all t.
4. *Adv$_t$* is a count of security advisories curated in the OSV at t for malware entries in the six ecosystems. Given the OSV's JavaScript Object Notation (JSON) schema, the parsing was done by searching and counting the ADVISORY entries in the schema's `references` field.
5. *Art$_t$* is a count of media articles, blog posts, and related information sources recorded in the OSV database at t for malware entries in the six ecosystems. The parsing was analogous to *Adv$_t$* but by using the ARTICLE entries.

These five time series were operationalized into daily, weekly, and monthly aggregates for which the lengths are $T = 1195$, $T = 168$, and $T = 39$, respectively. The starting periods were restricted to the first day, first week, and first month (January) of 2022. The reason for this restriction is that only a few malware entries have been recorded in the OSV database prior to 2022. Regarding the daily aggregates, *MalShare$_t$* was manually set to zero in case an amount of all entries at a day t was zero. Given the date of the data collection, the end periods are March 2025 and its last day and week.

4.2   Methods

The following autoregressive distributed lag (ARDL) model is used:

$$f(y_t) = \alpha + \sum_{j=1}^{p_1} \beta_j f(y_{t-j}) + \sum_{j=0}^{p_2} \gamma_j f(Eco_{t-j})$$
$$+ \sum_{j=0}^{p_3} \phi_j f(Adv_{t-j}) + \sum_{j=0}^{p_4} \rho_j f(Art_{t-j}) + \varepsilon_t, \tag{1}$$

where y_t refers to either *MalFreq$_t$* or *MalShare$_t$*, $t = 1, \ldots, T$, α is a constant, β_j, γ_j, ϕ_j, and ρ_j are regression coefficients, and ε_t is a normally distributed residual term with a zero mean and a variance σ_ε^2. If y_t is *MalFreq$_t$*, $f(x) = \ln(x + 1)$; for *MalShare$_t$* it is an identity function, $f(x) = x$. The immediate effects of a unit change in *Eco$_t$*, *Adv$_t$*, and *Art$_t$* upon y_t are given by γ_0, ϕ_0, and ρ_0, respectively. If the unit changes are sustained, the effects are given by so-called long-run multipliers (LRMs). To use *Eco$_t$* as an example, such a multiplier is given by

$$\mathrm{LRM}_{Eco_t} = \frac{\sum_{j=0}^{p_2} \gamma_j}{1 - \sum_{j=1}^{p_1} \beta_j}. \tag{2}$$

The interpretation of these LRMs is similar to standard regression coefficients. If $MalShare_t$ and Eco_t are considered as an example, a sustained increase by one ecosystem in the Eco_t series will increase $MalShare_t$ by LRM_{Eco_t} percentage points, all other things being constant. In addition, dynamic multipliers (DMs) are useful for evaluating the dynamics of a given effect [4,20]. To again use Eco_t as an example, for some integer $k > 1$ the DMs for it are given by

$$(\mathrm{DM}_{Eco_t,1}, \ldots, \mathrm{DM}_{Eco_t,k}) = \left(\frac{\partial f(y_t)}{\partial Eco_t}, \ldots, \frac{\partial f(y_{t+k})}{\partial Eco_t} \right), \quad t + k \leq T. \tag{3}$$

For a sufficiently large k, it follows that

$$\sum_{i=1}^{k} \mathrm{DM}_{Eco_t,i} \simeq \mathrm{LRM}_{Eco_t}. \tag{4}$$

Finally, there is the tricky problem of selecting the orders p_1, p_2, p_3, and p_4. On one hand, selecting too short orders may lead to the omitted variable bias because relevant information is excluded. Too short orders often lead to also other problems, including remaining autocorrelation in the residual term ε_t. On the other hand, selecting too long orders encounters the overfitting problem.

By inspecting automatic order selection algorithms in two different implementations [23,30], it can be concluded that both implementations yield extremely long orders both with the Akaike information criterion (AIC) and the Bayesian information criterion (BIC). Therefore, a manual but still systematic three-step procedure was used. In the first step the orders were uniformly increased, $p_1 = p_2 = p_3 = p_4$, until no notable autocorrelation was present in the residual terms. In the second step p_1, as obtained from the first step, was held constant but the remaining orders, $p_2 = p_3 = p_4$, were uniformly decreased until either autocorrelation was present or any of the coefficients γ_{p_2}, ϕ_{p_3}, ρ_{p_4} were statistically significant at the conventional 95% confidence level. In the third and final step p_4, p_3, and p_2, in the order of listing, were consecutively and individually decreased by using the same stop criterion as in the second step.

5   Results

5.1   Descriptive Statistics

Th presentation of the results can be started by taking a look at the OSV's malware entries across the six ecosystems; a basic breakdown is shown in Table 1. As can be seen, npm and PyPI have garnered the most entries—as well as the most malware entries. In fact, as much as about 84% and 57% of all entries for these two ecosystems have recently (from 2022 onward) been about malware.

Although it is impossible to say how many have fallen victim to these malware uploads, the observation is still quite alarming in a sense that vetting of new uploads seems to be either working poorly or absent altogether. Interestingly, furthermore, RubyGems takes only the fifth place in terms of total entries but the third place in terms of malware uploads. At the moment, CRAN, Go, and Maven seem to have not been particular targets of malware uploads, or they have countermeasures in place, but the situation may change in the future.

Table 1. Entries Across the Six Ecosystems

Ecosystem	Frequency		Malware share
	All entries	Malware entries	
CRAN	10	0	0.00
Go	4,145	8	0.19
Maven	5,461	1	0.02
npm	24,837	20,481	82.46
PyPI	15,929	8,966	56.29
RubyGems	1,727	813	47.07

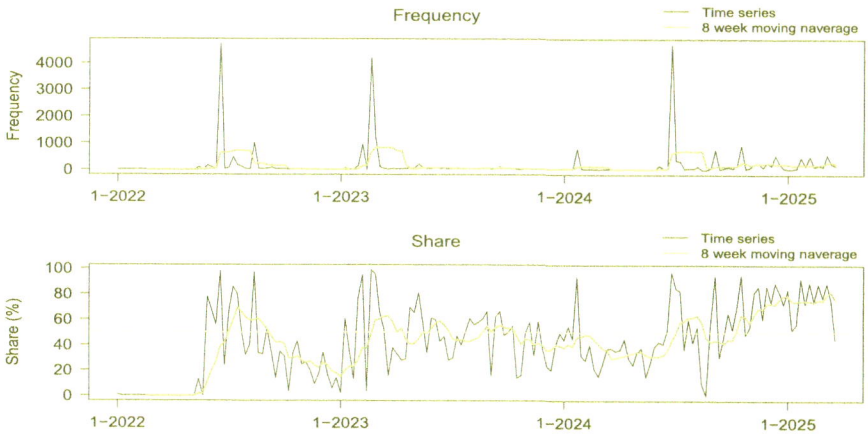

Fig. 1. The Two Malware Time Series (weekly aggregates).

The weekly $MalFreq_t$ and $MalShare_t$ time series shown in Fig. 1 further indicate the persistence of malware uploads to the three ecosystems. The former series contain three large spikes, which are likely due to specific sweeps or more general clean-up operations. Even when keeping these spikes in mind, the median is as high as 37 malware entries per week, which is again a rather striking number on its own. Then, the $MalShare_t$ time series fluctuates a lot, partially due

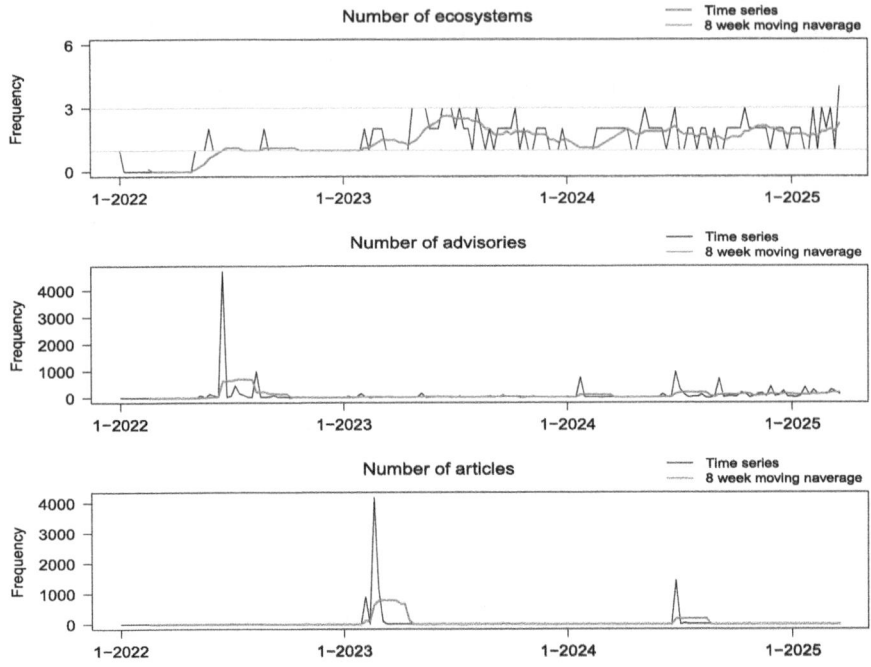

Fig. 2. The Three Explanatory Time Series (weekly aggregates).

to the spikes in *MalFreq*$_t$ but also otherwise. This observation reflects the operationalization of the time series (see Subsect. 4.1). The moving average shown was around 50% during 2023 and most of 2024, but in the early 2025 it had increased even up to 80%. This amount is almost twice the median of 41%.

Regarding the three explanatory time series shown in Fig. 2, *Eco*$_t$ fluctuates mainly between the values one and three, meaning that malware uploads into npm, PyPI, and RubyGems have sometimes been reported individually in a given week but some other times weekly malware reports have been made for all three ecosystems. However, a human eye cannot see whether the fluctuations in *Eco*$_t$ correspond with the fluctuations in *MalFreq*$_t$ and *MalShare*$_t$. This point justifies the formal ARDL modeling soon disseminated in Subsect. 5.2.

With respect to the two other explanatory time series, the three notable spikes in *MalFreq*$_t$ seem to correspond with one large spike in *Adv*$_t$ and two visible spikes in *Art*$_t$. Also this observation motivates the formal time series modeling because it seems that to some extent publicity correlates with reported malware uploads. When taking a peek at the sources behind the articles counted by *Art*$_t$, many of these have been either media articles and blogs about open source software supply-chain security or malware discovery announcements from cyber security companies and others scanning the programming language ecosystems. Given the ARDL context, it can be hypothesized that publicity may not only correlate simultaneously with the spikes but past publicity may influence a current or a future discovery rate. If there is a lot of publicity, as has been the case in the past three years, it may be that more and more companies, open source software developers, cyber security professionals, and others pay attention to the malware uploading problem. That is, it may be that $Adv_{t-1}, \ldots, Adv_{t-p_3}$ and $Art_{t-1}, \ldots, Art_{t-p_4}$, not necessarily Adv_t and Art_t alone, influence $MalFreq_t$ and $MalShare_t$. A similar reasoning applies to Eco_t. The rising trends in $MalFreq_t$ and $MalShare_t$ from late 2024 onward, and the persistence of the $[1, 3]$ range fluctuations in Eco_t, may—or should—motivate further security scans and sweeps—or, alternatively, these should not at least motivate stopping existing efforts.

5.2   Regression Analysis

The ARDL model in (1) is estimated for both $MalFreq_t$ and $MalShare_t$ by using the daily, weekly, and monthly aggregates. Thus, in total six models are estimated. Before continuing, it can be noted that both series are stationary, as also confirmed by formal Dickey-Fuller tests [10]. Another preliminary point is about the manual order selection procedure described in Subsect. 4.2. As can be seen from Table 2, the procedure resulted relatively, but not substantially, large orders for the daily aggregates, as could be expected. Somewhat unexpectedly, however, rather short orders were suitable for the weekly aggregates. A minimal model with $p_1 = 1$ and $p_2 = p_3 = p_4 = 0$ was suitable for the monthly $MalShare_t$ series. Despite these points, the procedure worked well in ensuring that no remaining autocorrelation is present. As can be seen from Fig. 3, all autocorrelation functions (ACFs) remain below the 95% confidence intervals.

Table 2. ARDL(p_1, p_2, p_3, p_4) Orders Selected

	Daily	Weekly	Monthly
Frequency	(27, 26, 22, 18)	(3, 2, 2, 2)	(3, 2, 3, 2)
Share	(23, 21, 21, 20)	(3, 0, 1, 0)	(1, 0, 0, 0)

As is typical in applied problems, the normality assumptions about ε_t is a small problem. For instance, the Jarque-Bera test [14], which is based on skewness and kurtosis, rejects the null hypothesis of normality for all residual series except those coming from the weekly and monthly estimates for $MalShare_t$. When taking a visual look at Fig. 4, however, the situation is hardly as bad as the formal test results would indicate. In other words, all residual series resemble the normal distribution; some more, some less, but all still sufficiently for proceeding.

Heteroskedasticity is also a slight problem. As can be seen from Fig. 5, particularly the residuals from the two models for the daily aggregates indicate non-random patterns. There is also a related problem: the plain ARDL model is not optimal for $MalShare_t$ because $\max(MaxShare_t) = 100$, which is exceeded by some of the estimated values. However, such exceedances are rather small: the percentage shares of estimated values exceeding one hundred are only 1.7, 1.8,

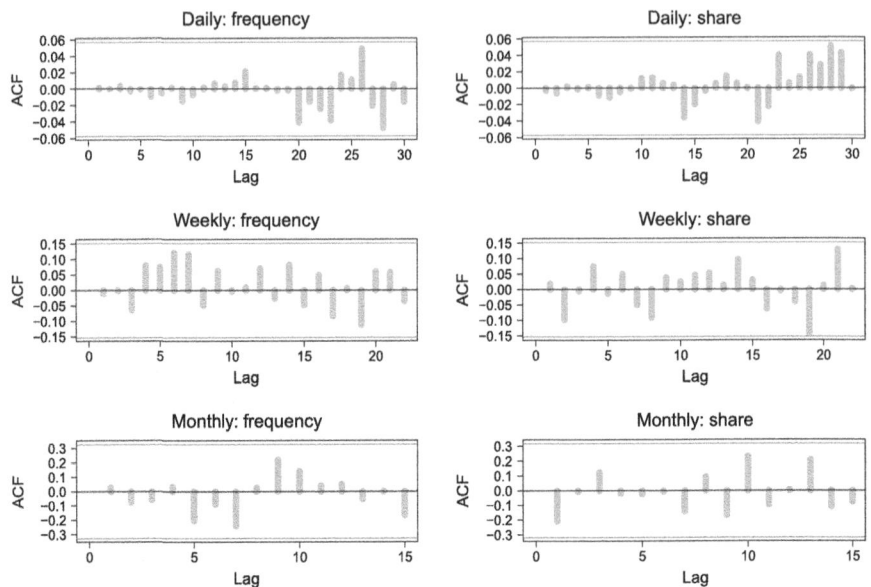

Fig. 3. Autocorrelation Functions of the Residual Terms from the Six ARDL Models (95% confidence intervals; maximum lag lengths determined by $\lfloor 10 \times \log_{10}(T) \rfloor$)

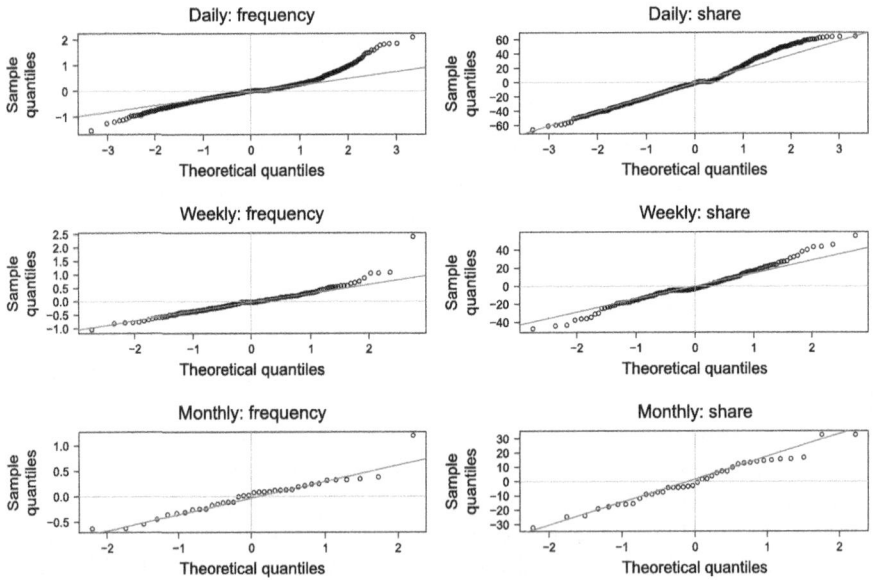

Fig. 4. Normal Quantile-Quantile Plots

and 2.6 for the three models using the daily, weekly, and monthly aggregates of $MalShare_t$, respectively. All in all, it must be acknowledged that some diagnostic problems are present, as is often the case in applied time series regression analysis, but none of the problems are severe enough to prevent proceeding into the actual results. Against this backdrop, the LRMs are shown in Table 3.

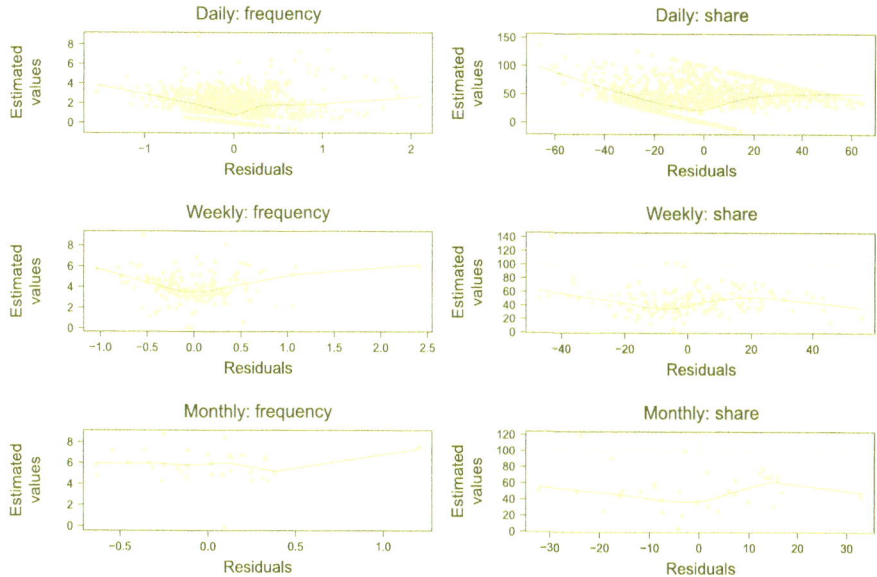

Fig. 5. Estimated Values and Residuals.

Table 3. Long-Run Multipliers[1]

	Daily		Weekly		Monthly	
	Frequency	Share	Frequency	Share	Frequency	Share
Eco_t	0.812	46.504	0.437	19.413	0.160	13.060
Adv_t	0.840	0.113	0.886	0.027	0.963	0.033
Art_t	0.519	0.061	0.311	0.041	0.169	0.015

[1] Colored entries denote statistical significance at the conventional 95% level.

All three explanatory time series indicate long-run effects, irrespective whether daily, weekly, or monthly aggregates are used. Furthermore, only three of the LRMs are not statistically significant at the conventional 95% confidence level. Having said that, the effects from Adv_t and Art_t are much lower than

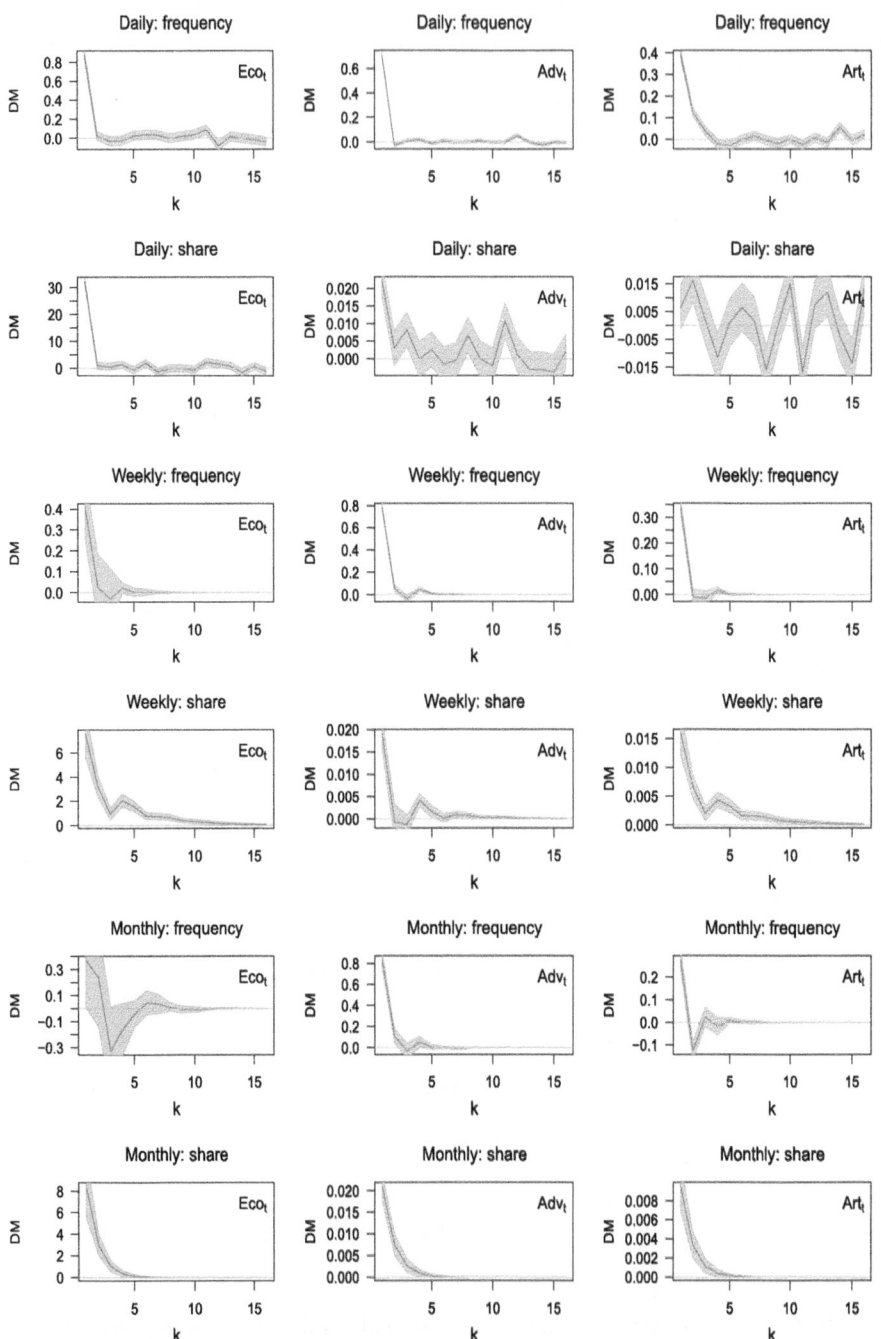

Fig. 6. Dynamic Multipliers.

those from the ecosystem count time series, which indicate substantial long-run impacts. All other things being constant, a unit increase in Eco_t increases $MalShare_t$ by 46.5% points daily, 19.4% points weekly, and 13.1% points monthly. When keeping the maximum in mind, these long-run effects are substantial but hardly surprising as such due to the concentration of malware uploads to npm, PyPI, and RubyGems. The DMs shown in Fig. 6 further indicate that the effects are not merely immediate shocks but persist relatively long before eventually dampening. Though, a similar observation applies to the other series as well. The Adv_t and Art_t time series indicate particularly disturbing dynamic shocks upon $MalShare_t$ in the model using the daily aggregates. Although the corresponding effects, as seen from the y-axes in Fig. 6 and the LRMs in Table 3, are still small in magnitude, these persistent but fluctuating shocks could be interpreted to support a conclusion that the publicity theorization is not entirely without a basis. As for the earlier speculation in the previous Subsect. 5.1 about the potential impact of the past values of the ecosystem time series, it can be concluded that—and despite for the selection of $p_2 = 0$ for two series (see Table 2)—the effects are not entirely simultaneous. Finally, the empirical exposition can be ended by noting that the ARDL models yield generally good statistical performance; the lowest and highest coefficients of determination are 0.59 and 0.95. While forecasts can be left for further work, such values indicate that even simple models could be used also in practical foresight.

6   Discussion

6.1   Conclusion

The paper examined recent (from 2022 to early 2025) malware uploads to six popular programming language ecosystems: CRAN, Go, Maven, npm, PyPI, and RubyGems. Regarding the three research questions specified, the answer to RQ.1 is simple but alarming: malware uploads have surpassed the reporting of traditional software vulnerabilities in packages distributed in the ecosystems. With respect to RQ.2, npm (over twenty thousand malware uploads), PyPI (nearly nine thousand malware uploads), and RubyGems (about eight hundred malware uploads) have been particularly prone to malware uploads, whereas CRAN, Go, and Maven have seen less than ten malware uploads in total. The answer to the third and final RQ.3 is that time series analysis can reveal insights about malware uploads and their trends. The decent statistical performance obtained—the average coefficient of determination is 0.79—indicates that forecasting could be used also in practical foresight; a hypothesis is that the increasing trend of malware uploads continues also in the nearby future. As could be expected, the number of ecosystems provides particularly good predictive power; the more there are ecosystems, the more malware uploads are also reported. Smaller but still visible effects are present for security advisories and media and other articles; publicity seems to also affect the malware upload trends. Rather analogously to recent arguments about reported vulnerabilities in open source software projects [27], the explanation might be that increasing publicity about malware uploads prompts more companies and security professionals to scan and monitor the ecosystems.

6.2   Limitations

A couple of noteworthy limitations can be acknowledged. The first is that the OSV database has not been yet validated in research. Given the well-known problems with other vulnerability databases [1,11,24], it may be that also the OSV database suffers from different reliability and validity problems. These problems cover also external validity; it is not clear how good is the database's coverage in terms of the individual tracking databases used by open source software projects.

The second limitation is more theoretical: only known and reported malware cases were observed. Rather analogously to observing only known and reported vulnerabilities [27], nothing can be deduced about what a theoretical malware count, say $TheoMalFreq_t$, might be. If $TheoMalFreq_t$ would include both $MalFreq_t$ and cases that are unknown but still true positives, $TheoMalFreq_t \geq MalFreq_t$ should hold yet $\sigma = TheoMalFreq_t - MalFreq_t$ remains unknown. This point is important because a risk analysis should assess also σ. Given the sizes of the ecosystems observed, nevertheless, it can tentatively concluded that an unconditional probability of picking a malware package is supposedly still tiny—even when dependencies are accounted for. However, further research is needed about the effectiveness of typo-squatting. Analogously to phishing and scamming [17,29], the effectiveness of typo-squatting cannot be fully understood by quantitative security metrics alone; psychology and other factors must be accounted too.

6.3   Implications

The research on ecosystems and malware has often recommended improving monitoring and detection capabilities [3,13]. In addition to publicity and awareness, it may be that this recommendation also implicitly and partially explains the answer to RQ.2. In other words, it may—or may not [12]—be that detection and monitoring capabilities might have already improved, such that more malware uploads have been detected, removed, and reported—possibly irrespective whether malware uploads have actually increased *per se*. While improving the capabilities further may improve the situation somewhat, a probability of bad apples slipping through is also dependent on the sizes of the ecosystems. When there are hundreds of thousands of packages, it is probable that some malware will slip through even with highly accurate detection engines. Against this backdrop, it is interesting to see whether the future will see curated lists for safe and secure packages. A recommendation to improve code signing [7] aligns with such curated lists. Curating has also been what Linux distributions have always done, but somewhere in recent history this quality gating function was forgotten or overridden by the emergence of programming language software ecosystems.

The results have also implications for research. For instance, reflecting a lack of data and code sharing [21,35], as well as a lack of good benchmark datasets [2,33], some studies have attempted to verify a true positiveness of a malware sample by checking that the malware packages are absent in PyPI [19]. Clearly, such a check is misleading or at least a poor choice due to the prevalence of malware in PyPI too. Instead, a starting point for further research might be to evaluate the performance of existing commercial malware detection engines in the programming ecosystem context.[3] It may be that detection accuracy is not as good as with other, more conventional malware variants usually distributed as binaries. There is also room for more practice-oriented work regarding take-down efficiency, which seems to be suboptimal according to existing research [3]. Though, takedowns and clean-ups reiterate also the point about curated lists and signing—it is debatable to which areas future efforts should be allocated. Finally, the earlier point about the effectiveness of typo-squatting should be evaluated also against the new issues brought by large language models [6,16]. By hypothesis, susceptibility to typo-squatting increases when using these models.

References

1. Anwar, A., Abusnaina, A., Chen, S., Li, F., Mohaisen, D.: Cleaning the NVD: comprehensive quality assessment, improvements, and analyses. IEEE Trans. Dependable Secure Comput. **19**(6), 4255–4269 (2022)
2. Botacin, M., Ceschin, F., Sun, R., Oliveir, D., Grégio, A.: Challenges and pitfalls in malware research. Comput. Secur. **106**, 102287 (2021)
3. Cao, A., Dolan-Gavitt, B.: What the fork? finding and analyzing malware in github forks. In: Proceedings of the Workshop on Measurements, Attacks, and Defenses for the Web (MADWeb 2022). The Internet Society, San Diego (2022)
4. Cheng, M., Liu, B.: Analysis on the influence of China's energy consumption on economic growth. Sustainability **11**, 3982 (2019)
5. Chiara, P.G.: The cyber resilience act: the EU commission's proposal for a horizontal regulation on cybersecurity for products with digital elements: an introduction. Int. Cybersecurity Law Rev. **3**, 255–272 (2022)
6. Claburn, T.: LLMs can't stop making up software dependencies and sabotaging everything: hallucinated package names fuel 'slopsquatting' (2025), the register, available online in April 2025: https://www.theregister.com/2025/04/12/ai_code_suggestions_sabotage_supply_chain/
7. Cox, R.: Fifty years of open source software supply chain security. ACM Queue **23**(1), 84–107 (2025)
8. de Souza, R.A., Silva, V.D., Junior, S.B., Zarpelão, B.B.: Forecasting malware incident rates in higher education institutions. In: Proceedings of the 38th International Conference on Advanced Information Networking and Applications (AINA 2024), pp. 226–237. Springer, Kitakyushu (2024)
9. Decan, A., Mens, T., Claes, M.: An empirical comparison of dependency issues in OSS packaging ecosystems. In: Proceedings of the IEEE 24th International Conference on Software Analysis, Evolution and Reengineering (SANER 2017), pp. 2–12. IEEE, Klagenfurt (2017)

---

[3] https://www.virustotal.com/.

10. Dickey, D.A., Fuller, W.A.: Distribution of the estimators for autoregressive time series with a unit root. J. Am. Stat. Assoc. **74**(366), 427–431 (1979)

11. Esposito, M., Moreschini, S., Lenarduzzi, V., Hästbacka, D., Falessi, D.: Can we trust the default vulnerabilities severity? In: Proceedings of the IEEE 23rd International Working Conference on Source Code Analysis and Manipulation (SCAM 2023), pp. 265–270. IEEE, Bogotá (2023)

12. Goodin, D.: Destructive malware available in NPM repo went unnoticed for 2 years (2025), ArsTechnica, available online in June 2025. https://arstechnica. com/information-technology/2025/05/destructive-malware-available-in-npm- repo-went-unnoticed-for-2-years/

13. Guo, W., Xu, Z., Liu, C., Huang, C., Fang, Y., Liu, Y.: An empirical study of malicious code in PyPI ecosystem. In: Proceedings of the 38th IEEE/ACM International Conference on Automated Software Engineering (ASE 2023), pp. 166–177. IEEE, Luxembourg (2023)

14. Jarque, C.M., Bera, A.K.: Efficient tests for normality, homoscedasticity and serial independence of regression residuals. Econ. Lett. **6**(3), 255–259 (1980)

15. Kim, K.H., Choi, M.J.: Android malware detection using multivariate time-series technique. In: Proceedings of the 17th Asia-Pacific Network Operations and Management Symposium (APNOMS 2015), pp. 198–202. IEEE, Busan (2015)

16. Luo, Z., et al.: Unsafe LLM-based search: quantitative analysis and mitigation of safety risks in AI web search. arXiv:2502.04951 (2025)

17. Ma, S., et al.: PsyScam: a benchmark for psychological techniques in real-world scams. arXiv:2505.15017 (2025)

18. Marwah, M., Arlitt, M.: Deep learning for network traffic data. In: Proceedings of the 28th ACM SIGKDD Conference on Knowledge Discovery and Data Mining (KDD 2022), pp. 4804–4805. ACM, Washington (2022)

19. Mehedi, S.T., Islam, C., Ramachandran, G., Jurdak, R.: DySec: a machine learning-based dynamic analysis for detecting malicious packages in PyPI ecosystem. arXiv:2503.00324 (2025)

20. Menegaki, A.N.: The ARDL method in the energy-growth nexus field; best implementation strategies. Economies **7**, 105 (2019)

21. Metcalf, L.B., Schwartz, E.J.: Malware Research: if you cannot replicate it, you will not use it (2025), Software Engineering Institute (SEI) Blog, Carnegie Mellon University, available online in June 2025: https://insights.sei.cmu.edu/library/ malware-research-if-you-cannot-replicate-it-you-will-not-use-it/

22. Nachuma, C., Hossan, M.M., Turzo, A.K., Zibran, M.F.: Decoding dependency risks: a quantitative study of vulnerabilities in the maven ecosystem. arXiv:2503.22134 (2025)

23. Natsiopoulos, K., Tzeremes, N.: ARDL: ARDL, ECM and bounds-test for cointegration (2023), R package version 0.2.4, available online in April 2025: https:// cran.r-project.org/web/packages/ARDL/index.html

24. Nguyen, V.H., Massacci, F.: The (Un)Reliability of NVD vulnerability versions data: an empirical experiment on google chrome vulnerabilities. In: Proceedings of the 8th ACM SIGSAC Symposium on Information, Computer and Communications Security (ASIACCS 2013), pp. 493–498. ACM (2013)

25. Ruohonen, J., Hjerppe, K., Kang, E.Y.: A mapping analysis of requirements between the CRA and the GDPR. arXiv:2503.01816 (2025)

26. Ruohonen, J., Hjerppe, K., Rindell, K.: A large-scale security-oriented static analysis of python packages in PyPI. In: Proceedings of the 18th Annual International Conference on Privacy, Security and Trust (PST 2021), pp. 1–10. IEEE, Auckland (2021)

27. Ruohonen, J., Ramadan, Q.: The popularity hypothesis in software security: a large-scale replication with PHP packages. arXiv:2502.16670 (2025)
28. Ruohonen, J., Ramadan, Q.: Tracing vulnerability propagation across open source software ecosystems. arXiv:2505.04307 (2025)
29. Ruohonen, J., Saddiqa, M.: What do we know about the psychology of insider threats? In: Proceedings of the 15th EAI International Conference on Digital Forensics and Cyber Crime (EAI ICDF2C 2024), pp. 186–211. Springer, Dubrovnik (2025)
30. Seabold, S., Perktold, J.: statsmodels: econometric and statistical modeling with python. In: Proceedings of the 9th Python in Science Conference (SciPy 2010). Austin (2010), Autoregressive Distributed Lag (ARDL) Models, statsmodels 0.15.0, available online in April 2025: https://www.statsmodels.org/devel/examples/notebooks/generated/autoregressive_distributed_lag.html
31. Snyk Limited: Name Confusion Attacks (2025). https://learn.snyk.io/lesson/name-confusion-attacks/
32. The European Union: Regulation (EU) 2024/2847 of the European Parliament and of the Council of 23 October 2024 on Horizontal Cybersecurity Requirements for Products With Digital Elements and Amending Regulations (EU) No 168/2013 and (EU) 2019/1020 and Directive (EU) 2020/1828 (Cyber Resilience Act) (Text With EEA Relevance) (2024). https://eur-lex.europa.eu/eli/reg/2024/2847/oj/eng
33. Zahan, N., Burckhardt, P., Lysenko, M., Aboukhadijeh, F., Williams, L.: MalwareBench: malware samples are not enough. In: Proceedings of the 21st International Conference on Mining Software Repositories (MSR 2024), pp. 728–732. ACM, Lisbon (2024)
34. Zhang, J., et al.: Killing two birds with one stone: malicious package detection in NPM and PyPI using a single model of malicious behavior sequence. ACM Trans. Software Eng. Methodol. **34**(4), 1–28 (2024)
35. Zheng, M., Robbins, H., Chai, Z., Thapa, P., Moore, T.: Cybersecurity research datasets: taxonomy and empirical analysis. In: Proceedings of the 11th USENIX Workshop on Cyber Security Experimentation and Test (CSET 2018), pp. 1–8. USENIX, Baltimore (2018)
36. Zimmermann, M., Staicu, C., Tenny, C., Pradel, M.: Small world with high risks: a study of security threats in the NPM ecosystem. In: Proceedings of the 28th USENIX Security Symposium, pp. 995–1010. USENIX, Santa Clara (2019)

A Role Taxonomy in Security-Safety Incident Response

Vahiny Gnanasekaran[2]([⊠]) [iD], Raphael Neudert[1]([⊠]) [iD], Poul Einar Heegaard[2] [iD],
and Günther Pernul[3] [iD]

[1] Nexis GmbH, Regensburg, Germany
raphael.neudert@nexis-secure.com
[2] Norwegian University of Science and Technology, Trondheim, Norway
{vahiny.gnanasekaran,pouleinar.heegaard}@ntnu.no
[3] University of Regensburg, Regensburg, Germany
guenther.pernul@ur.de

Abstract. Ensuring a coordinated response to safety emergencies and security incidents has become critical for maintaining operational continuity and trust, particularly within complex supply chains. As guidelines and standards attempt to tackle the problem and outline areas of responsibility, their different approaches leave them vulnerable to generalization, hindering easy comparison and understanding of how to implement the standards and regulations. Therefore, we present a comprehensive two-level taxonomy of roles in security incident and safety emergency response. It is based on relevant security and safety standards, frameworks, and regulations to identify common responsibilities and highlight differences, while also analyzing them in terms of Separation of Duty friendliness. We employed a qualitative approach to validate the taxonomy through questionnaires and in-depth interviews with industry experts. The findings indicate that such a role taxonomy needs further academic attention and is additionally needed by practitioners.

Keywords: Regulations · Compliance · Security incident response · Safety emergency response · Access control

1 Introduction

A rise in industrial cyberattacks reinforces the need for effective countermeasures and mitigation strategies. Cyber incidents escalating from IT or Operational Technology (OT) can affect functional safety in facilities and have consequences for production and human life. An incident denotes a security event that potentially causes physical consequences for equipment or human lives. As the ongoing growth of IoT systems continues to demand proper security to ensure the safety of the people involved, these two areas become ever closer and connected. Therefore, interdisciplinary incident response teams are necessary and serve as the front line in detecting, mitigating, and learning from security and safety events. Yet, despite standards such as NIST SP 800-82 [20], ISO 27035 [17], ISO 22320 [15], and ISO 15544 [14], there remains no unified view of the roles, responsibilities, and task boundaries that these teams must assume, since current standards and guidelines in incident management are primarily focused on IT systems [3,17,24]. A joint understanding of both security and safety is not only relevant for better and unified responses but also for increasing trust, knowledge, and comparability between incident responses across cooperating organizations.

To this end, we collected and analyzed standards, guidelines, and frameworks related to security and safety (hereinafter referred to as "joint") incident response and compiled the described tasks into a role taxonomy. Using these standards, guidelines, and frameworks, which we will collectively refer to as "regulations", we identify overlaps and gaps in security and safety incident management by mapping, evaluating, and comparing them to one another. To easier include these joint incident management roles into existing organizational structures, we included an evaluation on common Separation of Duty (SoD) applications. To the best of our knowledge, this represents a research gap in academia. We want to address these issues with the following contributions:

1. **We identify and analyze standards, guidelines, and frameworks related and relevant to security and safety incident response.**
2. **We create a joint incident response role taxonomy to be applied by organizations in the critical infrastructure sectors.**
3. **We provide an overview of the selected regulations and their differences regarding the identified roles.**

We seek to provide industry practitioners with a tool that helps them understand and trust others' incident procedures, enabling unified and stronger incident responses. The taxonomy is developed using regulations, literature, and standards, and validated using a qualitative approach with academia and industry experts. The rest of the paper is structured as follows: We discuss related work in Sect. 2, and Sect. 3 describes the research design. In Sect. 4, questionnaire findings are presented, and in Sect. 5 we list and discuss the selected regulations. The role taxonomy is introduced in Sect. 6, as Sect. 7 contains the interview results on the taxonomy's validity and completeness. Section 8 discusses the obtained results and future work. Finally, Sect. 9 concludes the paper.

2   Background and Related Work

Multiple theories describing roles are present in the literature [1,23]. In the context of access control, however, the concept of roles stems mainly from the RBAC approach described by Sandhu et al. [22]. Roles bundle authorizations and assign them to an identity as an intermediate step to reducing manual workload and organizational overhead. Authorizations may originate from different individual systems, such as a Microsoft AD or a SAP instance, which we will refer to as target systems. The necessity for different roles stems from the principle of least privilege (PoLP), as over-authorization represents a security vulnerability. It is enforced in many companies due to compliance with laws and regulations passed by governments worldwide, such as the US SarbanesâĂŞOxley Act or the German BSI IT certification. Groll et al. [11] show how the concepts of different types of SoD emerged from the PoLP implementation. As SoD mandates that security-critical access rights are spread across the executing factions of a process step or service, incident response teams with high profile access to organizational infrastructure are affected by it. This creates a conflict of interest, arising from the incident response team's need to grant as much access as quickly as possible to any available responder to deal with an incident. Since SoDs are in place to prevent precisely such an accumulation of access rights in small groups or single individuals, this creates a non-trivial problem to solve for organizations.

One possible solution could be the Break-Glass case [21,26], which can be implemented in access control systems. This effectively enhances a system with special policies that allow interacting users to override *deny* decisions and grant themselves temporary access. It is based on the idea that users can be aware of a current emergency that the system cannot. However, during their subsequent actions, users may be closely monitored and held responsible for misusing the granted access rights, to prevent them from using the Break-Glass case for malicious intentions. This post-process, in which the actions used must be analyzed by experts to determine if the use was justified and if any misuse occurred, can be time-consuming and resource-intensive for a company. Depending on the frequency of emergencies, this seems to be an ill-suited solution for an incident response team. As the previously presented Break-Glass case only provides an emergency solution to the problem of SoD conform incident response team roles, a correct implementation in the organizations SoD infrastructure becomes necessary. By analyzing cyber and safety incident regulations with knowledge on common SoD practices, this paper helps by providing roles that already adhere to standard SoD principles and are easier to categorize and sort into existing organizational SoD frameworks than the pure descriptions found in most regulations. The literature encompasses works that compare standards and frameworks for different purposes. Wang et al. [25] presents a comparative analysis of cybersecurity compliance frameworks, evaluating SOC 2, GDPR, PCI DSS, HIPAA, CIS Controls V8, NIST CSF, and CMMC 2.0 to unify cybersecurity compliance across these frameworks. They apply novel evaluation criteria to assess these frameworks from a risk management perspective. Djebbar and Nordström [6] conducted a comparative analysis of three established cybersecurity standards: ETSI EN 303 645 v2.1.1, ISA/IEC 62443-3-3:2019, and ISO/IEC 27001:2022, to highlight the similarities between the standards across different application areas. The authors broadly classify the standards into regulatory, region-based, and industrial. Industrial standards are further categorized into vertical and horizontal standards, where the former represents applying to a specific sector, while the latter encompasses multiple industries. Although the analysis is thorough, the review only includes three standards and does not address organizational roles or responsibilities. Baumer et al. [2] introduced a system that captures and expresses trust based on fulfilling Identity and Access Management regulations. As part of their approach, they surveyed relevant regulations and classified them.

Despite the existing compliance research, none addresses incident response roles and responsibilities in either field. Investigating the regulations to elicit the joint incident response role is needed to understand how human cooperation might occur in a potential cyber incident with significant physical consequences.

3   Research Design

This section presents the research design used in this work. The objective is to compare the distinct regulations to investigate how organizational roles in a joint incident response can be considered. Figure 1 illustrates the five key steps involved in developing the role taxonomy.

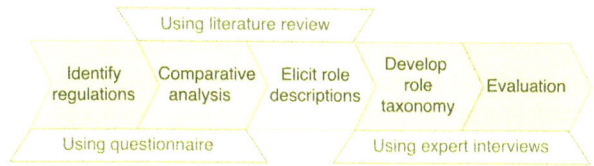

Fig. 1. Proposed research methodology.

Identify Regulations. Multiple strategies were implemented to include relevant cybersecurity and safety regulations comprehensively. First, an overview of regulations was gathered by conducting online searches with unstructured search queries, consulting peers, and prompting ChatGPT-4. Second, we manually queried and verified each regulation and included missing ones. Lastly, a questionnaire was distributed to relevant personnel at industrial companies (a detailed description is found in Sect. 3.1). The regulations included in the comparative study were selected based on their application in the oil and gas, nuclear, and power industries. Considering the wide variety of existing regulations, an emphasis was placed on horizontal and some vertical regulations in these industries. 14 safety and 21 security regulations were initially discovered.

After retrieving the regulations, each needed to satisfy specific exclusion and inclusion criteria. Regulations not publicly available, only referring to another regulation not included in the selection, and laws encouraging cybersecurity practices without offering tangible guidance were excluded from the corpus. For instance, EU directives were deemed too broad to include. The final collection consisted of five safety and seven security regulations.

Comparative Analysis. Similar to Djebbar and Nordström [6], we adopted a terminology to describe the overlap of roles and responsibilities. More specifically, the consensus among the security and safety regulations determines which definition is based on the role descriptions. If the majority of the wording of two roles is the same, they are matched with the relationship "Equivalent". Suppose the roles do not have identical wording but share the same subset of responsibilities as the equivalent relations. In that case, the type of the relationship is further analyzed, and the relationship is considered as "Related". For instance, NIST SP 800-61 [19], IEC 27035-1 [17], and the ENISA GPGIM define *incident handlers* as an organizational role, establishing the roles as "Equivalent". The role description would provide a consensus task description from the three standards. Other standards might have a subset of the tasks and minor, non-overlapping tasks in the description, which become "Related" to the broader consensus definition.

Elicit Role Descriptions. Based on the previous analysis, the role descriptions were drawn to provide the tasks and responsibilities for each role in the individual regulations. Certain regulations (e.g., ISO 22320 [15]) were task-oriented rather than role-based. The tasks were further analyzed and grouped for the next step. The primary objective is to identify distinct tasks, specific responsibilities, and their similarities and differences. As a result, a set of specific role descriptions and responsibilities emerged. Some responsibilities could not be mapped to a specific role, and such new roles were created (e.g., logistics responsible).

Develop Role Taxonomy. The role elicitation provided the foundation for constructing the role taxonomy. During this phase, the primary objective is to group similar features identified during the evaluation process. This phase involved classifying similar roles and establishing a hierarchical structure of responsibilities and clusters within the joint incident response. To ensure that the security incident response roles did not affect the identification of safety emergency roles, they were elicited separately. Each role was assigned responsibilities and tasks during a joint incident response. This systematic approach ensures an organized representation used to construct the overall taxonomy. 16 roles, organized into two layers, were included in the role taxonomy.

Evaluation. The roles of the taxonomy were presented to other researchers and practitioners through semi-structured interviews to ensure that the taxonomy was usable to a wider audience. The objective was to ensure that all aspects of security incident response and safety emergency response roles were adequately addressed. Subsection 3.2 addresses the interviews in detail.

3.1   Questionnaire

The questionnaire aimed to understand how industry practitioners apply cybersecurity and safety regulations during incident or emergency responses. The target audience was companies operating under strict safety regulations (e.g., the petroleum industry) and organizations subject to security laws and compliance demands (e.g., finance and insurance). The respondents were recruited through an industry forum, a research center in Norway, and the customer base of a consultancy firm in Germany. 19 responded to the questionnaire anonymously.

The first question was intended to separate the respondents by identifying whether they were involved in a safety emergency response at the company, skipping safety-related questions if they were irrelevant. The remaining questionnaire contained four parts. First, the common safety emergency response standards were presented as a checklist, followed by a question about their implementation of these standards within the emergency response. A similar part on security incident response was introduced. The third part contained a brief description of the taxonomy concept, along with an open-ended question for feedback and a list of requirements. Finally, the participants' years of experience, job position, and industry sector were collected.

As the questionnaire was issued to retrieve sources and measure knowledge, not all regulations presented in the final taxonomy were checkable options in the corresponding questions. The complete questionnaire is available in our repository at *GitHub*[1].

3.2   Interviews

The interviewees were recruited through the authors' network. The objective was a balanced sample of interviewees with knowledge of safety and/or security. The interviews started by asking the experts to identify critical security or safety procedures to gain an unimpeded impression of their viewpoint without bias towards our results. In the second part, we introduced the role taxonomy. The experts discussed central roles (e.g., incident handler, managerial roles), addressed future developments, and provided feedback and comments.

All interviews were recorded and lasted between 30 and 45 min each. One interview was conducted in English, two in Norwegian, and three in German. All interviews were confidential, and the interviewees preferred to stay anonymous. The recordings were transcribed using the Teams transcription tool or an institutionally approved transcription service based on OpenAI's Whisper. One researcher verified the transcription by listening to it and making corrections. Data analysis was deemed irrelevant since the interviews were only conducted to gather feedback. The feedback and suggestions were marked and summarized, and the taxonomy was improved based on the comments and feedback from the interviewees. The interview guide can be found in the repository[1].

Interviews were conducted with six relevant experts: a professor in functional safety, a PhD candidate in cybersecurity and safety, a senior scientist in functional safety, a security manager and privacy specialist from a consulting company, a security analyst from a large production company, and another from an insurance company.

4   Questionnaire Findings

The 19 respondents represented various sectors, including banking, insurance, defense, and the oil and gas industry. Eleven were security managers, three were

---

[1] https://github.com/RoleTaxonomy/RoleTaxonomy.

security analysts, and the rest held other cybersecurity positions (e.g., senior cybersecurity engineer). The years of experience ranged from 4 to 25 (Average = 12.3 and standard deviation = 6.34). Four were aware of the safety emergency procedures in their company, with three having heard about ISO 21110:2019 and two having heard about ISO 22320:2018. 17 respondents were familiar with ISO/IEC 27001 [16], 15 with NIST SP 800-61 [19], 13 with EU Cybersecurity Act [7], and 11 with the Cyber Resilience Act [8].

Standards Identifying in Emergency/Incident Response Roles. One participant revealed that *"the standards are used to guide the workflow and steps required in incident response. Although they may influence roles and responsibilities, these are ultimately determined by the existing company structure."* The respondents would rather ask for support from professional experts or listen to experiences from other companies. Another respondent said they would use *"internal stakeholders and the larger security community."*

Role Taxonomy Need and Requirements. The respondents rated the need for such a role taxonomy at an average of 6.7 (scale 1–10). They prefer such a taxonomy to possess *"short and understandable presentation of blind spots, the best requirements"*, and be a *"single source of information on what is required to be compliant with most common standards. Also, an overview of which elements are present in all standards, in some, or only in one would be useful, allowing us to prioritize the elements we require in our own processes."*

5   Selected Safety and Security Regulations

This section presents each regulation in the final corpus, as shown in Table 1, along with its justification for selection. Two global regulations (e.g., IEC, ISO, ISA) were among the selected security regulations, while the rest were regional (e.g., Canadian, EU, USA). Before we go into the details of the extracted roles, we briefly describe each regulation, focusing on key aspects and differences from other regulations.

5.1   Security Regulations

NIST SP 800-61 R3 [19]: This regulation focuses most on team composition and the different tasks for each team member. It outlines a life cycle for incident handling, including preparation, detection, analysis, containment, eradication, and recovery. It further highlights the technical details and provides practical step-by-step guidance for incident response and planning.

NIST SP 800-82 R3 [20]: A comprehensive guide tailored to the OT including supervisory control and data acquisition (SCADA). In contrast to other regulations, this guide highlights the physical and operational consequences of cybersecurity incidents in an industrial setting.

Table 1. Overview of the final regulation corpus.

Security regulations	Keywords
NIST SP 800-61 R2	IT incident response
NIST SP 800-82r3	OT incident response
ISO/IEC 27035-1:2023 & ISO/IEC 27035-2:2023	Information security incident management
ISA/IEC 62443:2020	OT security
ENISA Good Practice Guide for Incident Management (GPGIM)	IT incident response guidelines
FIRST CSIRT Services Framework v2.1	Computer Security Incident Response Team Services
FIRST PSIRT Services Framework v1.1	Product Security Incident Response Team Services
Safety regulations	**Keywords**
ISO 11320:2011	Nuclear emergency response
ISO 15544:2024	Oil and gas emergency response
ISO 22320:2018	General emergency response
CWA 18024:2023	Emergency response reporting
CWA 18018:2023	Crisis management

IEC 27035-1 and IEC 27035-2 [17]: Focus on incorporating incident handling into an organization's overall risk management strategy. Since they are process-oriented, they emphasize the need to improve security practices by incorporating lessons learned from previous incidents. While less focused on technical details, they underline the communication and coordination during and after an incident.

ENISA Good Practice Guide for Incident Management [18]: The guide emphasizes monitoring, proactive communication, coordination with external stakeholders, internal communication, and effective escalation procedures during incidents, 24/7 readiness for processing incoming incident information, and peak time resource distribution.

FIRST CSIRT Services Framework v2.1 [9]: The idea of incident handling through different services is central to the framework. It aims to standardize the capabilities and expectations directed at CSIRTs, detailing the provided services, tasks, and recommendations for achieving a certain level of quality. It fosters the ability to cooperate with other organizations to form more unified responses to threats that affect larger constructs, such as entire supply chains.

FIRST PSIRT Services Framework v1.1 [10]: The framework outlines services for vulnerability discovery, analysis, coordinated disclosure, and remediation, and emphasizes managing vulnerabilities and security incidents related to the organization's products, including software and hardware. In contrast to the CSIRT framework, it highlights product-specific risks and requires close collaboration with development and quality assurance teams.

IEC 62443 [12]: This standard belongs to the ecosystem view of the role taxonomy. Instead of providing detailed team descriptions, it emphasizes an in-depth defense approach for industrial environments where system availability and safety are paramount. In contrast to most of the included regulations, it emphasizes security by design, rather than rapid incident response.

5.2 Safety Regulations

In contrast to the response to security incidents, the safety emergency response considers unintentional faults and accidents. If a prompt response is needed, it is primarily due to the risk of losing production or the danger to lives or equipment. The safety regulations mainly focus on emergency response to manage such incidents. The safety corpus contains two vertical (i.e., nuclear and oil and gas) and three horizontal standards.

ISO 15544:2024 [14]: As a guideline for offshore structures and production installation, it focuses on immediate safety emergency response by on-site personnel while establishing communication to mainland facilities and authorities. The on-site response mostly follows a break-glass approach to maximize the available responders, while communication is divided into different responsibility areas.

ISO 22320:2018 [15]: The most comprehensive safety standard in the corpus, applicable for most organizations, and primarily focused on establishing a framework for effective command and control during emergencies. The standard is primarily task-oriented, fitting the role descriptions in the taxonomy.

ISO 11320:2011 [13]: The standard is intended for handling the emergency preparedness and response in nuclear facilities. It considers training for emergencies and the occurrence of a critical safety incident involving fissile materials, but does not address other aspects, such as legal and communication aspects of the incident. Management, technical personnel, and emergency coordinators are identified as the key roles.

CWA 18024:2023 [4]: Provides requirements and recommendations for standardized incident reporting, optimized for critical infrastructure organizations. This workshop agreement outlines tasks that the incident report should consider and identifies three key roles: infrastructure operator, security liaison officer, and first responder(s).

CWA 18018:2023 [5]: Focuses on structuring an emergency response plan for crisis management stakeholders. These actors are considered more peripheral in this context due to the likelihood that a cyber incident with physical consequences could evolve into a societal crisis (i.e., a black swan). They introduce a chain of command ranging from gold to bronze. Gold suggests the highest strategic level (e.g., top management), and silver indicates the strategic planning of the bronze command, which executes the pre-scheduled response.

6   Role Taxonomy

The roles of the taxonomy were created by searching for similar tasks described in the analyzed regulations mentioned above. Tasks that required a single executing entity would be put in a role, while tasks with multiple entities would be split into sub tasks that could be assigned to roles. The role taxonomy consists of two layers, the upper ecosystem layer and the lower joint incident response team layer, as depicted in Fig. 2. The second level describes roles designed to be part of only one organization, consisting of small groups or individual members, and focuses on tasks that require immediate attention. In contrast, the upper layer contains roles that describe the relationship between organizations during an incident, taking into account external actors. The identified roles are those that require authorizations in cyber-physical systems during emergency conditions and therefore need to be installed beforehand. External actors, such as those not affecting these systems or roles that only involve tasks that can be done without authorization, are not focused on in the taxonomy (e.g., regulators, first responders, governmental bodies).

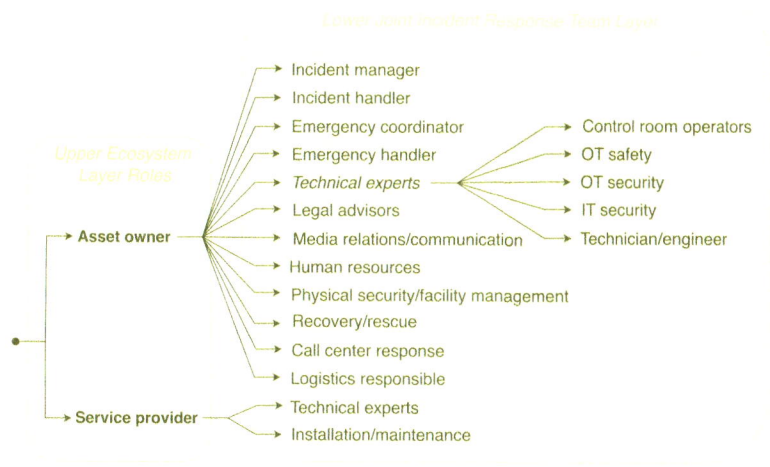

Fig. 2. Overview of the role taxonomy in joint incident response.

The exact amount of personnel assigned to each role depends on the team's size and the priorities set by the surrounding organization. Based on the used SoD framework, assignments to multiple roles might be permitted. Table 2 displays how well each selected regulation covers the developed role taxonomy.

6.1   Lower Joint Incident Response Team Layer

Incident Handler: As a foundation to all other roles in the team, this role contains the basic authorizations to conduct simple or level 1 incident handling.

Table 2. Coverage of the joint incident response roles in the regulation corpus. ◔ suggests the broader consensus ("equivalent"), ◑ indicates a subset of tasks from the consensus, and other minor tasks ("related"). In contrast, ● does not mention the role.

NIST SP 800-61 · NIST SP 800-82 · ISO/IEC 27035 · ISA/IEC 62443 · ENISA GPGIM · FIRST CSIRT · FIRST PSIRT	Role(s)		ISO 11320:2011 · ISO 15544:2024 · ISO 22320:2018 · CWA 18024:2023 · CWA 18018:2023
Security reg.	Role(s)		Safety reg.
◔◔◔ ◔ ◔◔◔	Incident manager	Emergency coordinator	◔◔◔◔◔
◔◔◔ ◔ ◔◔◔	Incident handler	Emergency handler	●◔◔◔◔
◔◔◔ ● ●◔◔	Technical experts/administration		●◔◔◔◔
◔◔◔ ● ◔◔◔	Legal advisors		●●◔●●
◔◔● ● ◔◔◔	Media relations/communication		●◔◔◔●
◔◔● ● ◔◔◔	Human resources		●●◔◔●
◔◔● ● ●●●	Physical security/facility management		●●●●●
●●◔ ● ◔◔◔	Recovery/rescue		◔◔◔●●
●●● ● ◔◔◔	Call center response		●●◔●●
●◔● ◔ ●●●	Logistics responsible		●●◔●●

This commonly includes detection, analysis, containment, eradication, and communication with other team members. While other roles may contribute more to resolving the incident, e.g., the *Technical experts/administration*, this role is usually the one to make the first contact. Depending on the SoD-rules of the organization, splitting off containment and eradication into separate roles might be enforced, as well as individual roles for each target system. The approach to this role is equivalent in some security regulations [17–19]. Other regulations derive slightly from this approach, as the service-oriented structure promotes the creation of separate incident handler roles for each aspect, with only the common authorizations shared in a more minor role of this type [9,10]. In contrast to the *Emergency handler*, the need for an absolute imminent incident response is only given in cases of threatened confidentiality.

Emergency Handler: This role has a unique function in safety regulations; it deals with injuries and provides immediate aid. Authorizations in most target systems are reduced to a minimum, yet location access might still be SoD relevant. Most safety regulations address the emergency response as either a group [15], or a facilitating individual [4,13]. Operational planning is also considered part of the emergency response [15], but this might require a distinct role depending on the systems used due to SoD. Their objective is to ensure compliance with the tactics the leader establishes.

Incident Manager: In this position, the main task consists of overseeing the incident response and conducting the level 2 incident handling, which mostly means making high-level decisions. Depending on the team size, the manager's role can contain some high-criticality authorizations; these might also be present or entirely delegated to the *Technical experts/technical administration* role. As high-level decisions are made by the entities assigned to this role, these access rights remain in place as a backup. Since this role is more managerial than others, it also includes certain access rights to human resource data. This role acts more as a second pair of eyes that coordinates rather than an active decision maker in the IEC 27035 [17]. However, two additional variations are presented in the ENISA guide [18] that use the same authorizations: The **triage officer** can be appointed to determine which actions to execute on the incident, sometimes restrained to a certain area or task. This may be necessary in times of limited resources or a high workload. Second, a **team manager** might be appointed to free the *Incident manager* from the responsibility of managing the team, thus changing the *Incident manager* into a high-criticality decision-maker. The FIRST CSIRT, FIRST PSIRT, and NIST SP 800-61 equivalently approach this role [9,10,19].

Emergency Coordinator: This role functions similarly to the incident manager in safety-related emergencies, since their primary responsibility is supervising and coordinating the emergency response, ensuring coordination between all involved roles. Specific safety standards refer to the *first responder* [4,5]; however, they specifically direct towards firefighters, police, or medics. Incident command is also applied by the ISO 22320 [15], which is mostly the exact definition as provided by the equivalent meaning of emergency coordinator in the ISO 11320 and the ISO 15544 [13,14]. They possess the highest level of responsibility and also require high criticality authorizations.

Technical Experts/Administration: Strongly depending on the SoD-rules of the organization, this role will most likely be split into at least one role for each application specific system (e.g., MySQL database, SAP application system, Honeywell safety automated system), or domain (e.g., IT layer, OT layer, control room, etc.). The two primary objectives are to provide a detailed understanding of the affected system and to increase the effectiveness of other incident responders. While regular incident and emergency handlers are more focused on managing the current case, these field experts provide knowledge on implementing distinct measures and strategies in their respective systems. The second objective is handling joint incidents with highly critical but very effective authorizations, such as root access or powerful administrative accounts. Since personnel assigned to these roles are likely already part of the administration of the respective target system, there may be an overlap with their regular administrative duties. As part of an incident or emergency response team, the role must remain functional as a standalone assignment. Therefore, reducing this role to counter redundant assignments can be problematic.

The IEC 27035 focuses more on a better knowledgeable *Incident handler* [17]. In contrast, the NIST SP 800-61 assigns them more executive power, as they operate the systems and initiate incident response protocols with their authorized access [19]. The ISO 22320 considers outsourced "expert advisors" that are different for each safety incident [15]. They might need fewer authorizations to perform their tasks, since they could also be external actors. However, similar to the NIST SP 800-61, the ISO 11320 is dedicated to in-house technical staff addressing the incident likelihood [13,19].

Legal Advisors: Depending on the legal situation, the incident handler must consider that aspects of the handling process affect data privacy (e.g., GDPR) or require communication with authorities, e.g., breach notifications or evidence handling. Their main tasks are to provide legal guidance and ensure compliance. As such, the best-known variation of this role is the data protection officer. The FIRST CSIRT and FIRST PSIRT approach this role differently, since it is considered part of the service of meeting specific contractual and regulatory requirements [9,10]. The NIST SP 800-61 deems such a role irrelevant beyond the incident response team setup [19]. Some safety regulations broadly cover the legal aspects of emergency response, stating that there should be contact with legal advisors *after* the emergency is handled [15]. Few authorizations are needed for the role and most SoD-critical access rights deal with confidential evidence. Creating a distinct role in the access control system might not even be necessary in some companies.

Media Relation/Communication: A security or safety incident may harm an organization's reputation. Therefore, how the incident is presented to authorities, business partners, or the public is crucial for maintaining trust. This role includes authorizations for public communication channels, such as social media accounts or website access. Three security regulations [10,17,19] share an equivalent definition of this role. The combination with the *Incident manager* for smaller teams is based on two regulations [9,18], but is otherwise equivalent. Only the ISO 22320 acknowledges communication as a task during emergency response [15]. As this role is minor compared to other incident response roles, its tasks are frequently performed by the *Incident manager*, or top management, especially in smaller teams.

Human Resources: A dedicated incident handler is needed to deal with internal threats or human-related security or safety vulnerabilities. The role is characterized by its access rights to human resource data, which justifies creating a separate role. Nevertheless, the SoD-rules also require an individual role in this case. In addition to monitoring internal threads, such as malicious behavior by company employees in larger or distributed incident response teams, recruiting, management tasks, and organizing personnel training can be delegated to this role from *emergency coordinator/incident manager*. Only the NIST SP 800-61 [19] recognizes the thread-related parts of the role, while two other detailed regulations [17,18] do not mention this role. The FIRST CSIRT and FIRST PSIRT [9,10] recognize only a training aspect as necessary, and ISO 22320 and ISO 11320 require having someone responsible for personnel's needs and access to their register, to e.g., alert next of kin in case of harm or death [13,15].

Physical Security/Facility Management: The physical access to compromised endpoints can be of similar importance as the digital access. This role handles tasks that require physical interaction with devices inaccessible to regular personnel and is based on two security regulations [19,20]. The role further prevents unauthorized physical access, thus reducing the risk of incidents. Due to the emergence of digital key systems, SoD-rules can be created to enforce minimal access for unauthorized entities, possibly splitting the roles due to different physical locations or security precautions, regarding e.g., backup access.

Recovery/Rescue: A minor role that considers faster recovery of digital systems. Until the incident is resolved with no active threads, this role remains inactive. However, since the follow-up steps include collecting evidence and applying digital forensics, this role ensures that they are parallelized with the recovery process, e.g., by preparing and supporting the switch to backup systems. For most SoD-rules, this does not necessarily merit its role. This role is mainly based on the IEC 27035 [17]. The FIRST CSIRT and FIRST PSIRT list the associated tasks in their services but regard them as part of the *Incident handler* role [9,10]. Safety is mainly concerned with physically recovering lives and equipment or preventing leakage. In nuclear [13], the emergency coordinator is responsible for rescue and facility re-entry, but could choose to delegate this role. The same applies for oil and gas [14], where the overall charge of the installation is co-responsible for the rescue, along with the onshore coordination center. The ISO 22320 mostly appends the recovery and life support to the roles concerning intelligence and investigations [15].

Call Center Response: This role stems from the ENISA guide and is an extension of *Incident handler*, essentially a standby operator to ensure that all incoming incident reports are delegated to available handlers [18]. Three security regulations [9,10,18] address such a role equivalently, while the ISO 22320 assigns a *liaison officer* to handle external agencies (e.g., medical services, law enforcement) [15]. As this role requires no special authorizations beyond those of the base role, it is optional and does not need to be implemented in the access control system.

Logistics Responsible: During a safety incident, additional physical resources, transportation, or supplies might need to be ordered internally. Only the NIST SP 800-82 [20] considers it a sub-role in the organizational response plan, while the ISO 22320 assigns a dedicated logistics role in their emergency preparedness plan [15]. Hence, depending on the severity of the incident and the need, a role should be responsible for contacting the relevant internal actors.

6.2   Upper Ecosystem Layer Roles

The ecosystem-level roles address a broader aspect of joint incident response, including those from the rest of the supply chain [1], and are primarily derived from IEC 62443. However, the other roles may also be considered asset owners in their own right, i.e., service providers. For simplicity, we assume the asset owner is an industrial company.

Asset Owner: This role includes the *Incident handler* role and most of its inheriting roles, as the asset owner represents the organization that contains the incident response team. As all members of the organization are already equipped with their necessary authorizations, this role is neither SoD relevant nor essential to implement in the access control system.

Service Provider: This role captures the companies providing services to the asset owner. Service in this context can mean physical components, subsystems, stand-alone systems, or assistance in response to specific faults, failures, or cyber-attacks. Its authorizations consist of access to the on-site instance of the security product, primarily through read-only access to log files, as well as access to communication channels with the incident response team. They might also possess deeper access rights than the asset owners' technical experts. SoD-rules may also merit the creation of one such role per security product or even product instance.

Installation/Maintenance: If a third party is commissioned to install or maintain a security product, its members can be assigned to this role similarly to the *Service provider* role. IEC 62443 [12] also operates with the *system integrator* role, which describes a supplier that connects various subsystems and components. These authorizations also focus on communication and on-site access to product instances. Depending on the degree of involvement, this role might differ from the *Service provider*, as one maintenance team may handle multiple products.

7   Interview Findings

Safety interviewees indicated that the role taxonomy was biased towards security incident management, rather than the safety emergency response. They highlighted the need for more specialized technical experts in emergency response. Two mentioned that the roles should be more concrete, due to the number of technical experts needed to understand the distinct underlying systems. Another layer of technical experts was added to accommodate this feedback, showing both security and safety aspects. Three recalled tasks similar to those of the *Incident handler* and *Incident manager* roles, while others alluded to different tasks associated with the *Technical expert* role.

One safety interviewee indicated that facility personnel, including control room operators, technicians, and even catering staff, were organized into emergency teams that do not necessarily reflect the ordinary organizational structure. For instance, someone from catering could be assigned as a first aid supporter. To achieve this role structure, the roles should be compatible and apply to the fewest available personnel so that the rest can be evacuated. Hence, their access rights may need to be modified to accommodate their roles during normal and emergency conditions.

A recurring feedback was the classification of roles in the lower ecosystem layer as active or passive, or consulting roles, but there was no clear consensus on where to draw the line. For a more practical application, two interviewees expressed an interest in seeing the taxonomy included in an RACI matrix, so the roles most active during specific process steps could be easily identified. Among those, there was a consensus that such inclusion would help technicians determine how well their current processes align with particular parts of the taxonomy and which parts are missing.

Multiple security and safety regulations were identified as relevant, including IEC 61511, IEC 63069, and guidelines from Norwegian regulatory bodies and a consultancy firm. These regulations did not meet our inclusion criteria for identifying concrete tasks and responsibilities related to personnel and were therefore not added to the final corpus.

Participants concurred that the taxonomy is helpful and usable. Industrial companies can use it to verify that joint incident response roles are included in their procedures. In contrast, standardization bodies can use it to understand the mapping between safety and security roles.

As some participants remarked, an application of the taxonomy may even extend beyond the currently examined sectors. According to them, it can be used as an example or overview when reviewing any organization's current incident response process. However, as the sector moves further away from the presented standards, the concrete content-related commitment of the roles for such a company is reduced. The expert from the consulting company added that it can be used to pitch incident response ideas and concepts to startups or companies that have recently developed a need for proper incident response, as they may have fallen under specific laws or compliance requirements.

8   Validating the Role Taxonomy

As seen in Table 2, no regulation covers all roles and responsibilities. Although certain regulations [17,19] provide a more in-depth scope, they seem to overlap. By close examination, we discovered that regulations consider distinct definitions of direct incident response roles, even within the security and safety field. This confirms the need for the taxonomy to unite the joint incident response roles, responsibilities, and tasks.

Despite the sparsely detailed descriptions of duties and tasks in the EU Cybersecurity Act and the Cyber Resilience Act, the questionnaire respondents seem relatively familiar with them. Their placement close to the more comprehensive NIST SP 800-61 R2 and ISO/IEC 27001 may stem from media coverage. Additionally, most respondents were unfamiliar with the safety standards because they only possess a cybersecurity background. Hence, recruiting interview participants with safety knowledge was critical. The role descriptions were generally more consistent in the security regulations than in the safety regulations. This might be due to three reasons: First, the different sectors were represented in the safety corpus. Second, cybersecurity is a relatively new field compared to functional safety, which encompasses multiple sectors that handle emergencies. Lastly, security manages broader and more general IT systems, while safety typically provides regulations specific to a particular industry. They covered more roles outside incident/emergency response than the safety regulations. The safety regulations were more concerned with the organizational roles of the incident itself.

Through our interviews with the experts, we got the confirmation that the developed role taxonomy can be applied to organizations in the critical infrastructure sector. As some experts remarked, it can also be used as a blueprint and source of inspiration for companies in other sectors, and those that need to create their own proper incident response procedure. The taxonomy does not take into account organizational size. Small and Medium-Sized Enterprises might need to assign multiple roles to fewer personnel, if their SoD framework allows for that. Future work should examine how organizational size affects allocating joint incident response roles among key personnel available. The role taxonomy only presents a snapshot of the current regulatory landscape, and the names of roles are subject to interpretation. However, it is not a fully exhaustive list, particularly from a safety perspective, since additional industries may add or modify more specific safety roles to the taxonomy. The regulation selection was based on the questionnaire, relevance, and scope. Nevertheless, its objective is to provide a brief overview of which regulations to consider when designing joint incident response roles. As we have seen with the current selection of regulations, the difference in focus affects how roles or role candidates present themselves. Future industry practitioners may use the taxonomy to map future regulations to existing roles and append upcoming roles and responsibilities to a continuously updating knowledge graph.

9   Concluding Remarks

Since incident response in both security and safety remains a topic of interest to both academia and industry, the role provides a generic overview of the relevant joint incident response roles. Real-world applicability requires sector-specific adaptation. Each sector will need to tailor and expand this framework to reflect its unique technologies, regulations, and operational practices. Hence, future work should consider the adaptation required for the industrial sectors to accommodate more specific roles, procedures, and tasks during joint incident response. Nevertheless, the methodology provides a versatile blueprint with applicable role definitions that support, for example, a potential validation app-roach for industrial companies. As new regulations emerge, they may become part of the taxonomy and possibly even influence the scope of specific roles.

Acknowledgments. This research is funded by the Research Council of Norway through *Cybersecurity Barrier Management* (project no. 326717). The authors are grateful to the interview participants for providing feedback on the taxonomy.

References

1. Aarland, M.: Digital supply chain roles in the power industry. In: IFIP Advances in Information and Communication Technology, pp. 185–199. Springer, Switzerland (2024). https://doi.org/10.1007/978-3-031-64037-7_12
2. Baumer, T., Grill, J., Adan, J., Pernul, G.: A trust and reputation system for exam-ining compliance with access control. In: Proceedings of the 19th International Con-ference on Availability, Reliability and Security. ARES 2024. Association for Com-puting Machinery, New York (2024). https://doi.org/10.1145/3664476.3670883
3. Cook, M., Marnerides, A., Johnson, C., Pezaros, D.: A survey on industrial con-trol system digital forensics: challenges, advances and future directions. IEEE Commun. Surv. Tutor. **25**(3), 1705–1747 (2023). https://doi.org/10.1109/COMST.2023.3264680
4. CWA 18024:2023: Emergency management - Incident situational reporting for crit-ical infrastructures. Workshop agreement, CEN/WS IPCI (2023)
5. CWA 18024:2023: Structuring an emergency response plan for crisis management stakeholders. Workshop agreement, CEN/WS ERP (2023)
6. Djebbar, F., Nordström, K.: A comparative analysis of industrial cybersecu-rity standards. IEEE Access **11**, 85315–85332 (2023). https://doi.org/10.1109/ACCESS.2023.3303205
7. EU: Regulation 2019/881 (2019)
8. EU: Directive 2024/2847 (2024)
9. Forum of Incident Response and Security Teams: Computer Security Incident Response Team (CSIRT) Services Framework Version 2.1 (2019)
10. Forum of Incident Response and Security Teams: Product Security Incident Response Team (PSIRT) Services Framework Version 1.1 (2020)
11. Groll, S., Fuchs, L., Pernul, G.: Separation of duty in information security. ACM Comput. Surv. **57**(7) (2025). https://doi.org/10.1145/3715959
12. ISA/IEC 62443: Industrial communication networks - Network and system security. Tech. rep., International Electrotechnical Commission (2023)
13. ISO 11320:2011: Nuclear criticality safety—Emergency preparedness and response. Standard, International Organization for Standardization (Sep 2011)
14. ISO 15544:2024: Oil and gas industries—Offshore production installations — Requirements and guidelines for emergency response. Standard, International Organization for Standardization (2024)
15. ISO 22320:2018: Security and resilience—Emergency management—Guidelines for incident management. Standard, International Organization for Standardization (2018)
16. ISO/IEC 27001:2022: Information security, cybersecurity and privacy protection — Information security management systems—Requirements. Tech. rep., Interna-tional Electrotechnical Commission (2023)

17. ISO/IEC 27035:2023: Information technology - Information security incident management - Part 1: Principles and process. Standard, International Electrotechnical Commission (2023)

18. Maj, M., Reijers, R., Stikvoort, D.: Good practice guide for incident management. Tech. rep, European network and information security agency (ENISA) (2010)

19. National Institute of Standards and Technology: Computer Security Incident Handling Guide. Tech. rep., U.S. Department of Commerce (2012). https://doi.org/10.6028/NIST.SP.800-61r2

20. National Institute of Standards and Technology: Guide to Operational Technology (OT) Security. Tech. rep., U.S. Department of Commerce (2023). https://doi.org/10.6028/NIST.SP.800-82r3.ipd

21. Break-Glass. Springer, Wiesbaden (2014). https://doi.org/10.1007/978-3-658-07365-7

22. Sandhu, R.S.: Role-based access control. In: Advances in Computers, pp. 237–286. Elsevier (1998). https://doi.org/10.1016/s0065-2458(08)60206-5

23. Sreeramagiri, P., Andrews, G., Greene, A.K., Balasubramanian, G.: Analyzing security risks in cyber-physical manufacturing systems with actor–network theory. Smart Sustain. Manuf. Syst. 6(1), 110–121 (2022). https://doi.org/10.1520/ssms20210042

24. Staves, A., Anderson, T., Balderstone, H., Green, B., Gouglidis, A., Hutchison, D.: A cyber incident response and recovery framework to support operators of industrial control systems. Int. J. Crit. Infrastruct. Protect. 37(2021), 100505 (2022). https://doi.org/10.1016/j.ijcip.2021.100505

25. Wang, W., Sadjadi, S.M., Rishe, N.: A survey of major cybersecurity compliance frameworks. In: 2024 IEEE 10th Conference on Big Data Security on Cloud (BigDataSecurity), pp. 23–34 (2024). https://doi.org/10.1109/BigDataSecurity62737.2024.00013

26. Zhang, R., Liu, G., Kang, H., Wang, Q., Tian, Y., Wang, C.: Improved bell–LaPadula model with break the glass mechanism. IEEE Trans. Reliab. 70(3), 1232–1241 (2021). https://doi.org/10.1109/TR.2020.3046768

Promoting Privacy Compliant Data Management for South African Digital Marketplaces: A Privacy-Aware Data Classification and Taxonomy Reference Model

Mmaphefo Octavia Kumalo[1](✉) ⬨ and Reinhardt A. Botha[1,2] ⬨

[1] CRICS, School of IT, Nelson Mandela University, Gqeberha, South Africa
{s220013292,ReinhardtA.Botha}@mandela.ac.za
[2] Noroff University College, Kristiansand, Norway

Abstract. Appropriate data classification is a key anchor in ensuring that data handling practices in organisations are compliant with data privacy regulations. Data classification is one of many organisational and technical measures (TOMs) obligated by regulations to reduce the risks of privacy violations and data breaches. To this end, this paper aims to provide a data classification and taxonomy reference model that digital marketplaces can utilise to understand and categorise their data to ensure that their data handling practices are compliant with data privacy regulations. A qualitative study was undertaken on three digital marketplaces in South Africa to develop a privacy-aware data classification and taxonomy reference model built on the foundations of the ISO 27002 standard. The reference model is then overlaid with privacy requirements and how to ensure its effective handling, producing a privacy-aware compliance framework. Clearly defining data classifications and their implications allows the digital marketplaces to be more transparent with users about what data is collected and how it is used and the levels of protection applied.

Keywords: Digital Marketplaces · Data Management · Data Privacy · Data Classification

1 Introduction

Digital marketplaces are defined as two- or multi-sided platforms that provide a product or service offering to potential users [25]. The digital marketplace sector in South Africa has seen exponential growth to a remarkable thirty percent in 2022, reaching more than fifty billion rands and outperforming the overall retail sector of just 1.7 % [30]. They are now poised for more significant growth, driven by innovation, improved infrastructure, and a focus on customer experience.

There are different types of digital marketplaces benefiting consumers by offering diverse products and services. The products and services offered on

B. Coppens et al. (Eds.): ARES 2025 Workshops, LNCS 15995, pp. 305–323, 2025.
https://doi.org/10.1007/978-3-032-00633-2_18

these platforms are often personalised to individual preferences [28] at competitive prices, thus increasing accessibility for consumers [27]. Data, now commonly referred to as the 'new oil' of the twenty-first century [35] allows for digital marketplaces to innovate and provide tailored customer experiences. The progressive collection of vast amounts of consumer data, including demographics, financial information, preferences, locations, consumer browsing, and photographs, to name a few, enables the prolific growth of digital marketplaces [11,26]. The consumer data collected is then processed, analysed, and often shared with third parties to generate insights for innovation, personalisation, and targeted advertising [4,24]. Many innovations, including improved fraud detection, more relevant advertising, suitable and personalised products, and pricing, rely on the consumer data provided [22].

From a consumer perspective, the benefits realised by participating in digital marketplaces may come at a value trade-off and risk [7,10]. Consumers often inadvertently and unaware give up certain freedoms and rights [36] with regard to their privacy [7,10]. Sometimes knowingly, consumers, paradoxically, disclose personal data freely, especially in exchange for convenience, personalisation, or social benefits [2]. Notwithstanding the paradox, consumers are now increasingly concerned about data privacy, particularly regarding the practices [29] related to the collection, use, and potential misuse thereof [12]. Consumers are demanding greater control over their personal data [17]. The increasing privacy concerns have necessitated regulators worldwide stepping in to provide the legal tenets and frameworks for responsible processing of personal data [29]. Regulations such as the General Data Protection Regulation (GDPR) of the European Union and the Protection of Personal Information Act (POPIA) of South Africa are examples of the many data privacy regulations. Regulators try to ensure that consumer information and data are protected from exploitation by businesses and that there is fairness and justification for certain practices [6].

Data management practices in the digital marketplace play an important role in managing the organisation's data throughout its lifecycle (from acquisition to destruction) to ensure that the data can be analysed for product and service improvements and other innovations, as expressed in previous texts. The data management practices also allow the marketplaces to have effective business operations and decision-making. There is, however, a perceived lack of transparency on the data management practices of consumer data, which leads to privacy and trust issues [6,33]. GDPR and POPIA provide the conditions of lawful processing of personal information as principles and guidelines which organisations need to comply with to allow for data processing transparency. However, compliance with these data privacy regulations is a difficult feat for digital marketplaces due to their intricate and complex structures often serving many different use cases and buyer markets.

Furthermore, from a privacy theory perspective, three data privacy concepts emerge as particularly relevant and should be considered by digital marketplaces in understanding and deconstructing privacy. First, *decicional privacy*, emphasises freedom from interference in personal choices and decisions based on data analysis [29]. This concept is violated when algorithms mine personal data to influence product recommendations or purchasing behaviours without individual consent. This can lead to concerns about manipulation and a lack of agency [22]. Thus, it is important for the digital marketplaces to be aware of the data types used for automated (algorithmic) decision-making to ensure that the necessary controls and regulatory provisions are made when dealing with these types of data.

The second concept, *informational privacy*, focuses on individual control over the flow of personal information, the ability to exert influence and autonomy over decisions, and freedom from unsolicited marketing communications [1,34]. This encompasses control over the collection, use, disclosure, and retention of data. In digital marketplaces, these manifest when individuals lack control over how their data is shared with third-party vendors or used for marketing purposes beyond the initial transaction. This can lead to feelings of unease and a loss of personal autonomy. Thus, having the necessary controls for compliant data sharing is important.

Moving beyond individual-centric perspectives, privacy as *social context, norms, and values*, recognises that privacy expectations and violations are shaped by social norms and situational contexts, also referred to as contextual integrity [23]. This concept highlights how the appropriateness of information sharing and the potential for privacy violations vary depending on factors such as the type of information, the actors involved, and the purpose of the interaction.

Establishing and maintaining trust with users in digital marketplaces means their data must be handled effectively and in compliance with privacy requirements articulated in regulations. To develop and maintain appropriate data handling practices, organisations need to firstly understand and know their data landscape; thus, a privacy-sensitive data classification and taxonomy reference model is proposed as an entry point. The model establishes a consistent method for categorising the sensitivity of data, allowing digital marketplaces to effectively navigate the complexities of privacy compliance. Furthermore, it provides clarity on what types of data exist within the digital marketplace ecosystem, how sensitive that data is, and what legal obligations apply.

This paper develops a privacy-aware data classification and taxonomy reference model within the South African context, by firstly producing a structural taxonomy of digital marketplaces to provide context, understanding, and scope for the research. Then, a conceptual data model is developed from gaining an understanding of the different use cases, business interactions, and data flows. The conceptual data model is utilised to establish the data taxonomy framework. Finally, the data taxonomy is then related to sensitivity classifications. The sensitivity classification allows the digital marketplace to relate privacy requirements to its data landscape and ensure the necessary controls are considered.

2   Research Approach

A literature review on privacy in digital marketplaces reveals a gap in detailing the personal data exchanged during user interactions (business processes); how that personal data is handled across its lifecycle; and how the data is classified based on its sensitivity. Moreover, there is limited research that aligns these aspects with regulatory data privacy requirements. This highlights the need for a more structured approach to understanding and managing data within digital marketplaces [17] in alignment with regulations. This is echoed by [26] in stating that despite the large body of research addressing Online Social Networks (OSNs) privacy issues, little differentiation of data types on social network sites is made, and a generally accepted classification and terminology for such data is missing. Furthermore, this lack of terminology has a negative impact on understanding the regulatory implications of different data types [26].

Several studies have explored privacy ontologies, taxonomies, and classifications from different perspectives and dimensions [12,26]. The contribution by [26] develops a well-founded terminology based on a thorough literature analysis and a conceptualisation of typical OSN user activities. The terminology is then organised hierarchically, resulting in a taxonomy of data types. The main contribution by [12] is an ontology for privacy requirements developed for software engineers to use when dealing with privacy requirements. These two perspectives are of particular relevance to this paper as they offer foundational insights and frameworks that inform the research approach taken. Additionally, their work confirms that having an accepted terminology for describing and differentiating data types and privacy-related concepts improves the understanding of data attribute characteristics and interrelations with privacy requirements.

This study uses qualitative research methods to mimic [26] by developing a terminology for describing and differentiating data types within the context of digital marketplaces. The study further expands on the work of [12] by relating privacy regulatory requirements to data lifecycle management practices. The regulations essentially introduce data-related rights and data transparency requirements that force organisations to substantially rework their data management practices. To comply with data protection regulations, organisations must gain a precise overview of and change the way they manage personal data from beginning to end [17].

Qualitative research methods are fitting for this study as they enable researchers to study social and cultural phenomena in their natural contexts [20]. Furthermore, to understand the social world from the experiences and subjective meanings that people attach to it, qualitative methods favour the interactions and dialogues with the studied participants, with the resulting qualitative data providing rich descriptions of social constructs [32]. For this study, post the desktop analysis undertaken to understand the customer-facing business processes and data flows, semi-structured interviews were conducted with digital marketplace stakeholders. The semi-structured interviews provided two-fold benefits: to gain a richer understanding of their experiences with interacting with the marketplaces and to ratify the assumptions made from the desktop analysis.

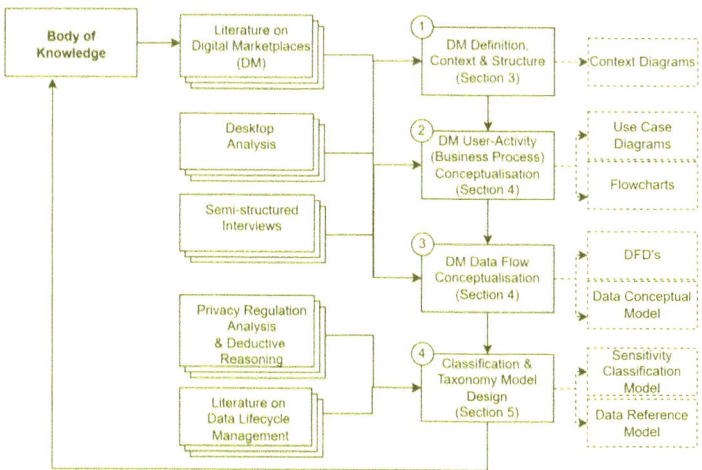

Fig. 1. Research Approach

Additionally, qualitative analysis proceeds by extracting themes or generalisations from evidence and organising data to present a coherent picture [16]. This paper focuses on three different digital marketplaces actively involved in South Africa, with one having international ownership. A comprehensive literature review on digital marketplaces indicates that while marketplaces may operate across various industries or verticals, they exhibit shared characteristics, which can be organised to provide generalisations.

The paper further introduces an aspect of data sensitivity classification to ensure that the appropriate technical controls are implemented. The ISO 27002 standard, which guides the creation and maintenance of an Information Security Management System (ISMS), emphasises the critical role of information classification in assessing data and determining the appropriate level of protection [15]. According to the standard, information should be classified based on legal requirements, value, criticality, and sensitivity to unauthorised disclosure or modification. Furthermore, the classification helps clarify the privacy risks associated with different data types and enables the identification of suitable solutions [26]. Apart from understanding how users' personal data is used throughout its lifecycle in digital marketplaces, defining and classifying personal data is of significance as it determines whether the marketplace is subject to the various obligations imposed by regulations [9]. Thus, this paper aims to respond to these research questions:

1. What are the different data types used within digital marketplaces?
2. How can we classify these data types?
3. What types of sensitivity can be attributed to these data types?
4. What do the data privacy regulations say about the handling and treatment of these data types?

The paper answers these questions by following the research approach depicted in Fig. 1.

Where the body of knowledge is created by understanding the contexts and structures of digital marketplaces in Sect. 3. Followed by understanding the business processes and data flows in Sect. 4. The classification and taxonomy data reference model is designed in Sect. 5. Section 6 discusses the research conclusions.

3   Digital Marketplace Definition, Contexts and Structures

Digital marketplaces are a type of digital platform, functioning as two- or multi-sided marketplaces. The digital platform company (platform operator) offers products or services to potential users (participants) [6] [25]. The users, including merchants, customers, and third parties, can engage with the platform through transactions and interactions such as registration or buying/selling, etc. Architecturally, digital platforms consist of products, services, technologies, or software applications that facilitate transactions and interactions between different groups of actors, each with specific roles that allow for certain actions [6,25].

Table 1 shows an example of the structure analysis for the digital marketplaces. The marketplaces are similar in their 'property values' (applicable properties are shown as grey-shaded cells in the table); however, their differences lie mainly in their industry scope and offering orientation. The digital marketplaces used as case studies for this study operate in the product, travel, and services industries.

The digital marketplaces are multi-sided, involving numerous participants who affiliate through registration and transactions. There are third-party service providers as well, providing services such as logistics, payments, insurance, etc. These platforms lean towards decentralisation, where users actively search for products or services rather than relying on centralised automated user matching. Additionally, components related to governance and control [18] further refine the definition of the marketplace. Lastly, aspects such as participant behavior, ownership, industry scope, and power asymmetries [33], highlight the types of interactions users have with the marketplace, who has authority in the marketplace, and how value is created. Table 1 illustrates the properties of the 'product' digital marketplace (which shares similar traits with the other two digital marketplaces), leading to the conclusion that the selected digital marketplaces possess comparable features, allowing for generalisation.

The next section discusses steps two and three of the research model, with a focus on understanding the business processes and data flows within the digital marketplaces.

Table 1. Example marketplace classification (Product marketplace) derived from [6, 18, 25, 33]

Property	Values			
Market Sides	One-sided	Multi-sided		
Products	Static	Dynamic		
Affiliation	Registration	Subscription	Transaction	Investment
Participation	B2C	B2B	C2C	
Offering	Product	Result	User-Specified	
Immediate Access	True	False		
Network Effects	Cross-side	Same-side		
Ownership	Independent	Consortia	Private	
Industry Scope	Horizontal	Vertical		
Market Mechanism	Exchange	Auction	Aggregator	Collaborative
Participant Behaviour	Spot Buy	Repeat Buy	System (Program) Buy	
Power Assymetries	Neutral	Biased (buyer- or seller-oriented)		
User Roles & Permissions	Buyer	Seller	Administrator	Moderator
Governance	Governance Rules	Information (streams)	Legal Aspects	
Control	Formal Control	Give up control over technology	Informal Control	
Policies	Terms of Service	User Agreement	Privacy Policy	Community Guidelines

4   Business Process and Data Flow Conceptualisation

Step two and three of the Research Model (Fig. 1) included a desktop analysis of all three marketplaces and, additionally, semi-structured interviews with merchants from the product and travel digital marketplaces. The resultant outputs from these steps were use case diagrams, business process flow maps, data flow diagrams, and a conceptual data model. These diagrams and models assisted in identifying, visualising, and analysing the user actions and activity flows as well as the information/data flowing through the business processes.

The conceptual data model depicted in Fig. 2 provides the definition framework for classifying privacy-related data within the digital marketplaces. The conceptual model is in alignment with GDPR and POPIA terminology [19], with a distinction on the use of the words information and data. POPIA refers

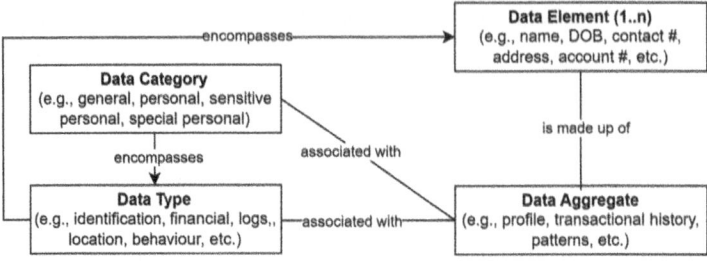

Fig. 2. Conceptual Data Model.

to personally identifiable information (PII) whereas GDPR refers to personal data. This paper refers to personal data and information interchangeably.

In the conceptual data model, the regulatory terminology and definitions of personal information represent the 'data categories.' The 'data types,' for example, financial or demographic, etc., represent the functional role or purpose of the data. The âĂŸdata element' refers to the smallest unit of information, for example, a name or date of birth. The 'data aggregate' represents the composite dataset that combines multiple data types, data elements, and sometimes categories, which are typically structured to represent a higher-level concept, for example, profile or behaviour, etc. Further to providing the basis for defining privacy-related data, the conceptual model is used to provide the logical instantiation for the privacy-aware classification and taxonomy reference models (Figs. 3 and 4).

The conceptual model highlights where privacy controls should be implemented and where the efforts for protection should be prioritised. For instance, if a physical model of the conceptual model were to be realised, a structured database implementation would materialise. The data elements, e.g., name, email, and credit card, would be stored as columns in tables. Data aggregates, e.g., customer profiles or order history, would be represented through relational table associations. Data categories could be represented as high-level metadata classification columns or classification tables and finally, the data types would be represented as specific tables with constraints. Not all privacy controls are equal nor appropriate for each data level; thus, having a structured framework helps to identify which data requires controls like encryption, tokenisation, masking, or access restrictions, etc., to ensure compliance with POPIA and GDPR [21].

4.1   Business Process and Data Flow Analysis

From a privacy perspective, three stakeholders are distinguishable in the digital marketplaces [26]: platform operators, service providers (merchants/partners), and users. The platform operators provide the related services where personal data commonly provides the basis of their business model [6, 25, 26]. The service providers provide the goods (products and services) consumed by the users, often requiring personal data to fulfill the transactions. Lastly, the users' and merchants' personal data is required to enable the interactions/actions. This illustrates the point that, from whichever stakeholder perspective, personal data is required for any interaction with the marketplace.

An excerpt of the user actions captured in Table 2 shows the common user interactions of the digital marketplace. The applicable user activities for the different marketplaces are marked with an 'x', and those that are not relevant to the marketplace are greyed out. The differences are the core business process interactions based on their business models. As an example, the core business processes for the product marketplace relate to the checkout, returns/exchanges, and delivery/logistics interactions. The travel core business processes relate to bookings, and finally, the services marketplaces' core business processes relate to the jobs that are required by a customer and performed by a merchant or service provider.

From a merchant/partner/service provider perspective, the same pattern is discovered. Interactions such as account management, profile management, login, data and analytics, financial management, reviews, and registration are all common across the marketplaces; however, they are named differently in the different marketplaces. Similarly, for the platform-operated actions provided by the digital marketplace to the various role players, e.g., manage users, manage account, etc. The overall activities from all three stakeholder perspectives can be categorised into seven buckets of business processes based on their outcomes. The generalised categorisation of the different marketplace activities allows for a structured and analytical foundation to be developed. This foundation enables simpler and less complex data mapping and alignment.

Applying the Conceptual Data Model (Fig. 2), the 'data types' and 'data elements' data constructs are then mapped to the digital marketplace's user activities. The mapping illustrates the different data elements used within the different marketplaces for the same user activity. Table 3 provides an example of a user action, *Registration* mapped to the data types that enable it: *Personal Details, Contact Details*, etc. These data types are further broken down to the data elements such as *First Name, Last name, Date of Birth (DOB)*, etc. The data elements emphasise the complexity of the data landscape in digital marketplaces, thus highlighting the importance of classifying data correctly for regulatory compliance, cost efficiencies, and operational simplicity. Additionally, the data elements from the different marketplaces can be grouped to allow for the classification and taxonomy reference model to be generalised.

Using the generalised data elements from the user activities, the next section develops the data classification and taxonomy reference model. Together with sensitivity classifications and tied together with compliance controls per data lifecycle phase, the privacy-aware classification and taxonomy reference model is completed.

Table 2. Business Process and User Activity Matrix

Business Process	User Activity	Product Marketplace	Vertical Marketplace	Service Marketplace
Onboarding	Registration	x	x	x
	Validation	x	x	x
	Profile Setup	x	x	x
Identity & Access Management	Login	x	x	x
	Authentication	x	x	x
	Forgot Password	x	x	x
Account Management	User Management	x	x	x
	Preferences	x	x	x
	Payment Details	x	x	x
	Settings	x	x	x
Transaction	Listing & Discovery	x	x	x
	Sales	x	x	
	Payment	x	x	
	Delivery/Logistics	x		
	Returns & Exchanges	x		
	Refund	x	x	
	Bookings		x	
	Cancellation		x	
	Job Requests			x
	Bidding			x
	Job Fulfilment			x
	Escrow			x
Dispute Resolution	User Reviews	x	x	x
	Mediation			x
Ratings	Review Comments	x	x	x
	Ratings	x	x	x
Analysis & Insights	Data Collection	x	x	x
	Data Organisation & Storage	x	x	x
	Data Analysis & Techniques	x	x	x
	Financial Performance	x	x	x
	Automated Decision-making	x		

Table 3. Example data mapping of user actions

User Activity	Data Types	Digital Marketplace		
		Product Elements	Vertical Elements	Service Elements
Registration	PersonalDetails	First Name Last Name Identity Number	First Name Last Name DOB Identity Number Nationality Gender	Registration is done via LinkedIn
	ContactDetails	Phone Number Mobile Number Email	Phone Number Mobile Number Email	
	SecurityDetails	Password	Password Phone Number for 2FA	
	MerchantDetails (Person)	Seller ID Date of Registration Account Status Personal Details Product Details	First Name Last Name Email Mobile Number Password Proof of Bank Account	See User Account Details
	MerchantDetails (Entity)	Business Name VAT Registration Monthly Revenue Company Registration Business Owner Name Business Owner Last Name Business Owner Email Number of Products Terms and Conditions	Company Name Business Registration Email Mobile Number Password VAT Number Proof of Bank Account	See User Account Details

5   Data Classification and Taxonomy Reference Model

A data taxonomy is a formal and organised structure based on shared characteristics for grouping data into categories and subcategories [8], thus providing a clear picture of the types of data processed by an organisation. A taxonomy further introduces common terminology and definitions to data constructs.

Figures 3 and 4 are extracts of the Data Classification and Taxonomy Reference model referencing the platform and customer-related data. The classification and taxonomy reference models are the logical instantiations of the Conceptual Data Model in Fig. 2.

As shown by the reference model in Fig. 3, the classification and taxonomy reference model from a platform perspective provides the logical understanding of the composition and interrelationships of data in a privacy-sensitive environment. The digital marketplace platform operator would typically collect data such as the user's IP address, device information, GPS location, browser, operating system, etc., to log activities on the platform [26]. The data is then aggregated to ascertain, for example, the user's behaviour when interacting with the marketplace or to keep an audit trail. The data elements are deemed sensitive personal information as they contain elements such as online identifiers [19] and thus require special conditions for processing such information, as directed by regulations. Thus, having a logical view such as this allows the organisation

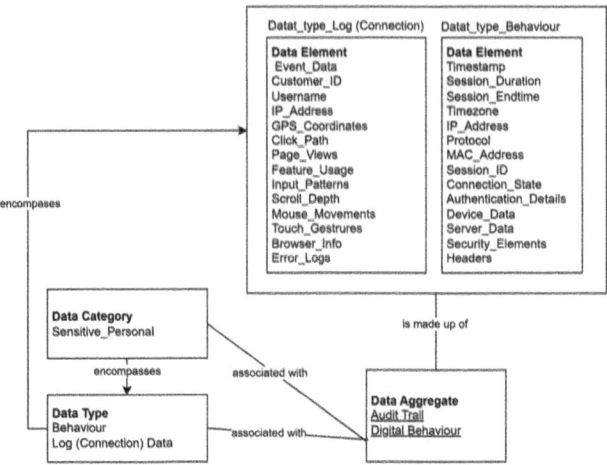

Fig. 3. Excerpt Digital Marketplace Classification and Taxonomy Reference Model (Platform).

to effect the necessary downstream controls like privacy metadata tags, access control rules, privacy data schemas, etc.

Similarly, in Fig. 4, each data element within a data type from a customer perspective is associated with and contributes to the formation of data aggregates such as Customer Profile, Spending Patterns, Risk Profile, and Customer Lifetime Value. These aggregates are pivotal in customer analytics, customer profiling, and risk assessments in the marketplaces. This taxonomy illustrates how diverse data types interrelate to enable rich, multi-dimensional digital representations of individuals within the digital marketplaces. The data types fall within the varying categories of personal, sensitive personal (payment, security, and transaction), and special personal (gender and nationality) information [19]. Thus, require special conditions for processing.

The classification and taxonomy reference model provides a holistic structure and definitions of the personal data used within digital marketplaces. Furthermore, the reference model highlights the complexity with which the digital marketplaces need to contend with for their data privacy compliance efforts. This layered taxonomy aids in the identification of where privacy risks may lie and supports the development of control mechanisms that reflect the contextual integrity of data [23]. Consequently, the model highlights where the risk of re-identification [19] of data and privacy infringements might occur when disparate data elements are aggregated. The conceptual model also demonstrates a high degree of scalability and flexibility due to its multi-layered abstraction. By decoupling the classification of data into categories, types, and granular elements, it offers a semantic architecture that accommodates both existing and emerging data forms, as well as legal and geographic contexts. Contextual changes can be

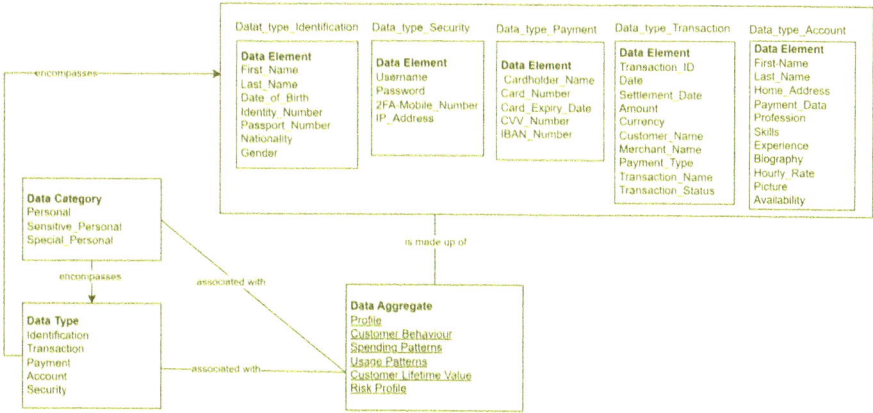

Fig. 4. Excerpt Digital Marketplace Classification and Taxonomy Reference Model (Customer)

reflected at the level of abstraction without compromising consistency across the rest of the taxonomy.

Finally, the model shows how the data conceptual model is practically realised logically. In the next section, we show how the classification and taxonomy reference model is aligned to sensitivity classifications to enable a complete privacy-aware compliance framework.

5.1   Data Protection Regulatory Requirements

The digital marketplace data classification and taxonomy reference model provides the foundation to enable data sensitivity classification. Sensitivity classification categories support the marketplaces in knowing how to treat the data constructs in compliance with regulations. Furthermore, it assists organisations in knowing the organisational impact in the event of data disclosure, alteration, or destruction without authorisation. The ISO27002 framework provides a sensitivity classification scheme [15] that can be used. Additionally, relating privacy requirements to the sensitivity classification and the marketplace data management practices, a comprehensive data privacy compliance solution is formulated. This alignment completes the research process and serves as the final step of the Research Model represented in Fig. 1.

The legal framework defined in the GDPR and POPIA lays down fundamental rules for the protection of personal data [5]. In particular, the marketplace operators should consider essential requirements such as security safeguards, transparency and openness, purpose limitation, accuracy of personal data, etc., in the processing of personal data within their procedures [3,19,31]. Moreover, both GDPR and POPIA recognise several rights that users should be granted through technical and organisational measures such as the right to access, the right to rectification, the right to erasure, etc., [31].

Furthermore, the data lifecycles and their management must be considered to ensure a holistic approach to privacy compliance. Data lifecycle management refers to the process of overseeing data from its creation or collection, through its usage and storage, to its sharing, retention, and eventual deletion. Embedding privacy protections into every phase of data handling ensures lawful collection, secure storage, responsible usage, and timely deletion, while also addressing risks such as unauthorised access, data breaches, and misuse [21].

5.2   Sensitivity Classification of Digital Marketplace Data Types

According to the Information Classification Policy of ISO/IEC 27002, a company must ensure appropriate levels of protection for information assets [15]. Information assets can be classified according to the defined information classification system, i.e. unclassified public, proprietary, client confidential data, company confidential data. The main objective of information classification is to ensure that business assets are properly handled. Different variations of this classification system have been developed depending on the context of the organisation. As defined in the Conceptual Data Model, we are concerned with a sensitivity classification that is data privacy regulation aligned, therefore, the sensitivity classification scheme is defined as such: unclassified public; internal not sensitive; internal sensitive; restricted special. It should be noted that this classification scheme is solely for the data types used within the identified user activities of the marketplaces and does not extend to other organisational information assets such as brochures, intellectual property documents, press releases, etc. [13,14].

A privacy-aware compliance framework summarised in Table 4 shows the digital marketplace data sensitivity classification in alignment with privacy requirements mapped to the data types, the data lifecycle phases, and the minimal controls required for compliance. This mapping gives the definition of the classification, the types of data that are applicable within that classification, the regulatory requirement for managing the data type within its lifecycle phase as well as the controls that should be considered to comply with the regulatory requirements. For example, financial information is considered internal sensitive information, however when aggregated with security details (e.g., passwords), nationality, and ID numbers, its classification becomes special restricted. This means that the information becomes highly confidential and sensitive and is subject to stricter restrictions and requires more privacy controls, such as explicit and informed consent, minimisation, encryption, pseudonymisation, and stricter access controls, to name a few. Another example is combining purchase history with location data could reveal sensitive spending habits and so forth. Thus, the sensitivity classification of data should be assessed not only by individual data types but also by how they are combined (aggregated) and used within the platform.

Table 4. Privacy-Aware Digital Marketplace Compliance Framework

Category	Unclassified Public	Internal Not Sensitive	Internal Sensitive	Special Restricted
Context	Information that can be disclosed or disseminated without any restrictions and poses minimal privacy risk	Information defined as personal, that is considered low-risk and not highly sensitive, but public disclosure is not intended	Information defined as personal data which if lost, stolen, or misused, could result in harm or significant consequences for the individual	Highly sensitive information if disclosed could have very significant consequences for the individual. This category includes personal data subject to the strictest regulations and controls due to its higher risk of harm (e.g., fraud, identity theft), if exposed or misused
Digital Marketplace Data Types	Public user profiles (excluding contact details or sensitive information), Product or Services listings, General platform information, Rating and Reviews	*Unclassified public data +*, First Name, Last Name, Date of Birth, Contact Details	*Internal sensitive data +*, Identity Number, Banking Details, Income Details, Online Identifiers, Dispute Resolution Details, Pricing information, Transaction Details	*Internal sensitive data +*, Gender, Nationality
Aggregation Principle	None	Combining multiple data points within this category remains classified as "Internal - Not Sensitive" unless it reveals additional sensitive information	Combining data points from this category, even with "Internal - Not Sensitive" data, elevates the classification to "Internal - Sensitive" due to the increased risk of revealing sensitive details.	Any data point classified as "Special Restricted" automatically elevates the classification of the entire dataset to "Special Restricted" due to the high level of sensitivity involved
Data Lifecycle Privacy Requirements: Acquisition	No user consent required, Inform users on what info is collected	Obtain user consent for data collection based on the specific data type, Inform users on what the data types are and why.	Obtain clear and specific user consent for data collection of the data types, Inform users what the data types collected are and why.	Limit collection of the data types to the absolute minimum necessary and only with explicit user consent, Be extremely transparent about the collection, purpose, and potential risks of sharing
Data Lifecycle Privacy Requirements: Organisation	Standard security measures are sufficient, considering the low sensitivity level	Standard security measures are sufficient, considering the moderate sensitivity level	Implement robust security measures to protect the data types due to its higher risk level	Implement the strongest possible security measures to safeguard the data types due to its extremely high-risk level
Data Lifecycle Privacy Requirements: Maintenance	Data accuracy and completeness are less critical for unclassified public data but should still be monitored	Ensure data accuracy and completeness for the data types to avoid impacting functionalities	Ensure high data accuracy and completeness for the data types, as inaccuracies can have significant consequences	Ensure the highest level of data accuracy and completeness for the data types to minimise the risk of errors or misuse
Data Lifecycle Privacy Requirements: Use	Data can be used freely for various purposes within the marketplace.	Use the data types for the purposes outlined in the privacy notice and obtained consent	Use the data types only for the purposes outlined in the privacy notice and obtain consent, Allow users to control their data usage preferences with granular options	Use the data types only for strictly authorised purposes outlined in the privacy notice and with explicit user consent, Allow users to revoke their consent for using the data types at any time

(continued)

Table 4. (*continued*)

Category	Unclassified Public	Internal Not Sensitive	Internal Sensitive	Special Restricted
Data Lifecycle Privacy Requirements: Transfer	User consent is not required for transfers of unclassified public data, but informing users about potential transfers is good practice.	Obtain user consent for transfers of the data types to third parties, especially if combined with other data that elevates the sensitivity level	Obtain explicit user consent for transfers of the data types to third parties, Partner with reputable third parties with strong data security practices	Generally, avoid transferring the data types to third parties. If necessary, obtain explicit user consent and implement the strictest security measures
Data Lifecycle Privacy Requirements: Archive	Long-term archiving of unclassified public data may be relevant depending on business needs, but retention periods can be flexible	Establish clear data archiving policies with defined retention periods based on business needs	Establish clear data archiving policies with defined retention periods based on legal or regulatory requirements	Archive the data types only if legally mandated and with the shortest possible retention period. Prioritize anonymisation before archiving
Data Lifecycle Privacy Requirements: Destruct	Secure data destruction is less critical for unclassified public data but can be implemented if required by internal policies	Ensure complete and irreversible erasure of the data types that is no longer required.	Ensure complete and irreversible erasure of the data types that is no longer required	Ensure complete and irreversible erasure of the data types that are no longer required
Minimum Controls	Minimisation, Privacy policy and notice, Firewalls, Access controls, Regular data refreshes, Secure data transfers, Standard archiving practices, Standard data deletion procedures	*Unclassified public minimum controls* plus, User consent, Opt-in & Opt-out mechanisms, Encryption, Data quality control procedures, Data governance policies, Anonymise or aggregate data before sharing with third parties and archiving.	*Internal Not Sensitive controls* plus, Privileged Access Management - need to know basis, Stricter data quality control procedures, Stricter data transfer restrictions and additional security measures in agreements, Prioritise anonymisation or strong pseudonymisation before sharing and archiving, Overwriting or demagnetisation to destroy data	*Internal Sensitive controls* plus, Emphasize the user's right to refuse consent, Strong encryption algorithms, Privileged Access Management - need to know basis, Implement multi-factor authentication, Regularly monitor and audit access, Stricter data transfer restrictions and additional security measures in agreements and sharing practices, Consider data wiping and physical destruction methods

6   Conclusion

The paper developed a privacy-aware classification and taxonomy reference model of personal information in digital marketplaces. It followed a design science-oriented methodology with diverse research methods to develop the reference model. A literature study resulted in understanding the different structures and makeup of digital marketplaces. This provided a foundation to group the marketplaces. The desktop analysis, together with process and data flow mapping ratified by semi-structured interviews, created the base for the personal data taxonomy. The taxonomy as a foundation was then related to sensitivity classifications and overlaid with privacy requirements to provide detailed guidance on implementing privacy-enforcing controls.

The privacy-aware data classification and taxonomy reference model provides a generalised data classification scheme which can be extended to other marketplaces and organisations. This general framework enables marketplaces to adhere to pertinent data privacy regulations, such as GDPR and POPIA, when classifying and managing personal data, as it ensures compliant risk-based data handling practices. Furthermore, by defining clear data types (e.g., PII, financial, etc.) and sensitivity levels, the digital marketplaces can apply privacy controls at the right level—data element, type, or aggregate, and optimise security while maintaining usability and operational efficiency.

The reference model was not validated as a stand-alone artifact, however, as it is used as a foundational input into a privacy compliance pattern language for digital marketplaces, the validation of the pattern language was conducted. Thus, the efficacy test of the model in a real-world setting was encompassed in the expert review panel of the resulting privacy compliance pattern language. The scalability, flexibility, and robustness of the privacy-aware data classification and taxonomy reference model lie in the conceptual data model and its ability to act as a blueprint for ensuring structured, secure, and compliant data management. Through the classification of the data constructs and the alignment to sensitivity levels, the digital marketplaces can implement risk-based security measures. It provides clear guidance on how to classify data, which data is considered high value, where to apply privacy controls, and generally provides a common language within the organisation.

Finally, the pattern language developed using the artifacts of this paper provides a structured way of implementing solutions to recurring common privacy compliance challenges such as governance roles and responsibilities; operationalisation of privacy-compliant data lifecycle management; and monitoring and continuous improvement of compliance practices, to name a few. Thus, the privacy-aware reference model serves as the anchor to finding appropriate management, governance, and technical compliance controls (Table 4).

Disclosure of Interests. The authors have no competing interests to declare that are relevant to the content of this article.

References

1. Gabisch, A.J., Milne, R.G.: The impact of compensation on information ownership and privacy control. J. Consum. Mark. **31**(1), 13–26 (2014)
2. Acquisti, A., Grossklags, J.: Privacy and rationality in individual decision making. IEEE Secur. Priv. Mag. **3**(1), 26–33 (2005)
3. Bhagattjee, P.: South Africa - data protection overview (2021). https://www.dataguidance.com/notes/south-africa-data-protection-overview
4. Chen, C.: Storey: business intelligence and analytics: from big data to big impact. MIS Q. **36**(4), 1165 (2012)
5. De Villiers, Z.K.: A framework for ethical data use to improve personalised customer experience in the financial industry in South Africa, Master's thesis, University of the Western Cape, Western Cape, South Africa (2022)
6. Derave, T., Gailly, F., Sales, T.P., Poels, G.: A taxonomy and ontology for digital platforms. Inf. Syst. (2024)
7. Dinev, T., Hart, P.: An extended privacy calculus model for e-commerce transactions. Inf. Syst. Res. **17**(1), 61–80 (2006)

8. Fettke, P., Loos, P.: Classification of reference models: a methodology and its application. IseB **1**(1), 35–53 (2003)
9. Finck, M., Pallas, F.: They who must not be identified—distinguishing personal from non-personal data under the GDPR. Int. Data Priv. Law **10**(1) (2020)
10. Friedman, B., Khan, P.H.J., Borning, A.: Value sensitive design and information systems. In: Human-Computer Interaction in Management Information Systems: Foundations. M.E. Sharpe, Inc, New York, NY, USA (2014)
11. Fuller, C.S.: The perils of privacy regulation. Rev. Austrian Econ. **30**(2), 193–214 (2017)
12. Gharib, M., Giorgini, P., Mylopoulos, J.: An ontology for privacy requirements via a systematic literature review. J. Data Seman. **9**(4), 123–149 (2020)
13. Information Regulator South Africa (2021). https://inforegulator.org.za/wp-content/uploads/2020/07/Guidance-Note-Processing-Special-PersonalInformation-20210628-004.pdf
14. Intersoft Consulting: GDPR - info (2021). https://gdpr-info.eu/
15. ISO/IEC: ISO/IEC 27002:2013 Information Technology - Security Techniques: Code of practice for information security controls (2013)
16. Kilani, M.A., Kobziev, V.: An overview of research methodology in information system (IS). OALib **03**(11), 1–9 (2016)
17. Labadie, C., Legner, C.: Personal data protection inside and out. In: Enterprise Modelling and Information Systems Architectures (EMISAJ), pp. 1–20 (2020)
18. Mallon, D.: A systematic literature review of digital platform business models. In: Ahlemann, F., Schütte, R., Stieglitz, S. (eds.) WI 2021. LNISO, vol. 48, pp. 389–403. Springer, Cham (2021). https://doi.org/10.1007/978-3-030-86800-0_27
19. Michalsons: Protection of Personal Information Act 4 of 2013 (2022). https://popia.co.za/
20. Myers, M.D., Avison, D.: Qualitative Research in Information Systems. SAGE Publications Ltd, London (2002)
21. National Institute of Standards and Technology: NIST Privacy Framework: A tool for improving privacy through Enterprise Risk Management, V1.0, Technical report, NIST CSWP 01162020, National Institute of Standards and Technology, Gaithersburg, MD (2020)
22. Nguyen, P., Solomon, L.: Consumer data and the digital economy: Emerging issues in data collection, use and sharing, Technical report, Consumer Policy Research Centre, Victoria, Melbourne (2018)
23. Nissenbaum, H.: Privacy as contextual integrity. Washington Law Rev. **79** (2004)
24. Ohm, P.: The rise and fall of invasive ISP surveillance. Univ. Illinois Law Rev. **2009**(5) (2009)
25. Pauli, T., Marx, E., Dunzer, S., Matzner, M.: Modeling platform ecosystems. CEUR Workshop Proc. **2716**, 17–30 (2020)
26. Richthammer, C., Netter, M., Riesner, M., Sänger, J., Pernul, G.: Taxonomy of social network data types. EURASIP J. Inf. Secur. **2014**(1), 1–17 (2014). https://doi.org/10.1186/s13635-014-0011-7
27. Saberian, F., Amirshahi, M., Ebrahimi, M., Nazemi, A.: Linking digital platforms' service dimensions to customers' purchase. Bottom Line **33**(4), 315–335 (2020)
28. Salazar, J.: Whose data? Information economics, digital privacy, and the right to be forgotten. In: Austrian Student Scholars Conference (2021)
29. Solove, D.J.: Conceptualizing privacy. Calif. Law Rev. Inc. **90**(4), 1087 – 1155 (2002)

30. Swanepoel, G.: The rise of South Africa's resilient ecommerce land-scape (2024). https://newsroom.mastercard.com/news/eemea/en/perspectives/en/2024/the-rise-of-south-africa-s-resilient-ecommerce-landscape/
31. Sánchez, D., Viejo, A., Batet, M.: Automatic assessment of privacy policies under the GDPR. Appl. Sci. **11**(4), 1762 (2021)
32. Wahyuni, D.: The research design maze: understanding paradigms, cases, methods and methodologies **10**(1) (2012)
33. Wang, S., Archer, N.P.: Electronic marketplace definition and classification: literature review and clarifications. Enterp. Inf. Syst. **1**(1), 89–112 (2007)
34. Westin, A.F.: Privacy and freedom. Wash. Lee Law Rev. **25**(1) (1968)
35. Zahid, R., et al.: Secure data management life cycle for government big-data ecosystem: design and development perspective. Systems **11**(8), 380 (2023)
36. Zuboff, S.: The Age of Surveillance Capitalism: The Fight for a Human Future at the New Frontier of Power, 1st edn. PublicAffairs, New York, NY (2019)

Dynamic Transmission Scheduling Method for High-Concurrent Zero Trust Access Control

Taisho Sasada[1]([✉]), Christophe Kiennert[2], Gregory Blanc[2], Yuzo Taenaka[1], and Youki Kadobayashi[1]

[1] Graduate School of Science and Technology, Nara Institute of Science and Technology, Nara, Japan
`taisho.sasada@naist.ac.jp`, `{yuzo,youki-k}@is.naist.jp`
[2] SAMOVAR, Télécom SudParis, Institut Polytechnique de Paris, Paris, France
`{christophe.kiennert,gregory.blanc}@telecom-sudparis.eu`

Abstract. In remote work environments, once account authentication is completed, users can continue accessing confidential data without their authenticity verification (proof of being the legitimate user with proper access rights). This poses a risk when the device or authentication credentials are hijacked by attackers after authentication, the authenticity becomes compromised. To address this, Zero Trust Access Control (ZTAC) monitors and utilizes behavior information unique to each user without trusting any access requests, enabling access control while continuously ensuring user authenticity after authentication. However, collecting behavioral information necessary for user authenticity verification creates a critical trade-off: more detailed monitoring increases traffic load, necessitating longer intervals between behavior information updates. These extended intervals create security vulnerabilities, as modern ransomware can complete lateral movement within minutes, potentially exploiting these update gaps when the system cannot respond quickly enough. In this paper, we propose a highly concurrent ZTAC architecture to address this challenge. Our system dynamically schedules monitoring intervals based on real-time network status and concurrent connection load, shortening transmission intervals when suspicious behavior is detected to intensify behavioral monitoring. However, this approach can lead to false positives, thus our verification process introduces temporary blocking as an intermediate state between permission and denial. By allowing access after a short waiting period, we minimize false detections while effectively delaying lateral movement by adversaries. Through implementation and evaluation experiments, we demonstrated that our proposed system reduced processing time in high-concurrency environments with over 10,000 concurrent connections and effectively detected and prevented unauthorized access attempts while maintaining operational efficiency.

Keywords: Zero Trust · Access Control · Transmission Scheduling · Single Packet Authorization

1   Introduction

In recent years, malware attacks targeting data, such as OrBit, WannaCry and NotPetya, have become serious threats. Data-driven services and applications continue to increase daily, making it essential to secure proper security for safe data management [1,2]. Traditionally, security measures focused on perimeter defense using firewalls and Intrusion Detection Systems to block unauthorized access by separating internal and external networks [3]. However, with the widespread adoption of cloud services and remote work becoming commonplace, the boundary between internal and external networks has become increasingly blurred. In such ambiguous network situations, it has become difficult to completely prevent attacker's penetration, leading to a growing need to control access by not trusting data access from either internal or external networks.

As a result, organizations are transitioning from perimeter defense to Zero Trust Access Control (ZTAC) [3–10]. In ZTAC, all access requests, whether internal or external, are not trusted, and authentication and authorization are performed dynamically based on monitored behavioral information for each access attempt. Specifically, ZTAC uses verification algorithms to determine allow/-deny decisions based on information such as IP address, access location, time, device ID, OS and browser versions, security patch status, antivirus software status, and security alerts, enabling dynamic access control. This enables security to be maintained without unconditionally trusting even internal networks. However, monitoring this information alone cannot guarantee user authenticity (whether the user operating an account is the legitimate account holder). Therefore, additional monitoring of user-specific behavioral information (such as keyboard typing and mouse movement patterns) [5,9,10] and device-specific information (such as device fingerprints and hardware configurations) [4,6,7] is used for access control.

Attempting to constantly monitor and collect more information to guarantee user authenticity increases the traffic load per access, resulting in the constraint of having to lengthen the monitoring information update interval (MIUI) [11]. While longer MIUIs enable more accurate collection of user behavioral data (e.g. keystroke patterns, mouse hovering behavior) leading to more appropriate access control decisions in ZTAC, they also create vulnerabilities. If anomaly conditions arise due to malware or attacker intrusion into endpoints during MIUI, access control cannot respond to and track these changes in situation. Some malware, such as OrBit, WannaCry and NotPetya, completes lateral movement in about 10 min of infection [12], spreading horizontally across the same network to expand its compromise to other endpoints. Therefore, existing technologies that require a certain amount of time to update monitoring information are clearly insufficient to respond in time. On the other hand, reducing the collected behavioral information leads to decreased accuracy in continuous authentication/authorization, which is a core function of ZTAC. Resolving this trade-off is a crucial challenge in implementing ZTAC.

To ensure authenticity and appropriate access control in multi-user access scenarios, this paper proposes a ZTAC architecture that can adaptively schedule each user's MIUI according to concurrent connection conditions and network load. We use Single Packet Authorization (SPA), which enables authentication prior to establishing communication and efficiently transmits authentication/authorization information in a single packet, to include device and user behavior information in one packet. When blocking access through packet verification, our system chooses between complete blocking or pending depending on the situation, allowing communication to resume after a certain period if it is not an attack. However, when the system detects abnormal behavior, it shortens the MIUI, and subsequently gradually adjusts the interval in accordance with increasing network load. This achieves a high-concurrent ZTAC that appropriately controls access based on behavioral information while minimizing traffic load for authentication and authorization for each user.

Outline. In Sect. 2, we review related work on ZTAC. Section 3 presents the threat model in this study. In Sect. 4, we describe the proposed system architecture. In Sect. 5, we detail the implementation and experimental evaluation. Finally, we conclude the paper with future work in Sect. 6.

2   Related Work

Security architecture in information systems has evolved from perimeter-based defense to Zero Trust Architecture (ZTA), which implements more granular control. Perimeter-based defense is a security model that prevents unauthorized access from external sources by placing firewalls and Intrusion Detection Systems at the boundary between an organization's internal and external networks. In perimeter-based defense, the internal network is treated as a trusted zone, meaning that once inside, resources can be accessed relatively freely. However, with the sophistication of targeted attacks and malware, it has become increasingly difficult to completely prevent intrusion into internal networks, and unconditionally trusting the internal network puts resources at risk.

In contrast, ZTA as defined by NIST SP800-207 [13], maintains security by following the principle of "never trust, always verify" and requires authentication and authorization based on various monitoring behaviors without placing implicit trust in access requests. Figure 1 shows the configuration of ZTA. The main components are Subject, Resource, Policy Enforcement Point (PEP), and Policy Decision Point (PDP). In this paper, Subject refers to users and endpoints. Resource is the target that Subjects access, including various network services and databases. PDP is the function that determines whether to allow or deny Subject access to Resources. PEP is installed on the communication path between Subject and Resource and allows or blocks communication according to PDP decisions.

Many ZTAC systems based on ZTA have been proposed and summarized by Azad et al. [14]. Simply collecting IP addresses and timestamps is insufficient for the PDP to verify authenticity (whether the user is the legitimate device owner or account holder) and for the PEP to implement appropriate access control. Consequently, ZTAC systems that utilize user-specific behaviors and device-specific

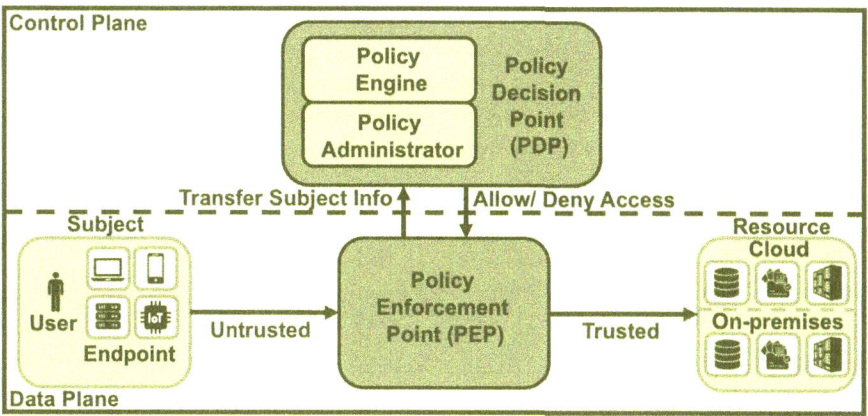

Fig. 1. Zero Trust Architecture

information for verification have been proposed. In research utilizing device-specific information, Huang et al. [7] added monitoring items such as network connection patterns and resource usage statistics including CPU/memory utilization. To block access from devices with high security risks, García-Teodoro et al. [6] monitored device patch status, security configuration values, running process lists, and installed software information. To deny access from unauthorized or tampered devices, Yao et al. [4] added monitoring items such as device hardware characteristics and firmware versions. In research utilizing user-specific behaviors, Lei et al. [15] enhanced verification capabilities by adding user location information as a monitoring item and verifying its consistency with IP addresses and timestamps. Sasada et al. [5, 10] added browser input operations such as clicks, keystrokes, and page transition speeds as monitoring items to accurately capture user behavior and cognition. However, increasing monitoring items for PDP verification results in massive data volume per packet, causing verification overload on the PDP in ZTAC systems that perform access control for each request. Additionally, since it takes time for monitoring items to be fully updated, if access occurs before changes in monitoring items are properly reflected, sequential control becomes insufficient, preventing proper access authorization or denial.

We use SPA to solve these problem, but despite having different motivations from this research, several other studies have adopted SPA in ZTA. Kataoka et al.'s NI-SPA [16] positions network devices as information providers during SPA packet forwarding, leveraging behavioral information from within the network that would be difficult for individual clients to collect. While this approach successfully achieves spatial expansion of information sources, it maintains fixed patterns for temporal control of information transmission, without implementing dynamic transmission interval adjustments based on network load or threat levels. Xu et al. [17] propose a method to address the vulnerability of the entire system when a single policy engine comes under attack by deploying multiple authentication engines in parallel, each configured with different software compositions. After each engine independently processes SPA authentication, a final decision is made through majority voting. This structural redundancy improves resistance against coordinated attacks exploiting the same vulnerability, but insufficient consideration has been given to processing time variations among multiple engines and dynamic load balancing control in response to increasing concurrent connections.

3   Threat Model

This section defines the system settings and threat model assumed in this research. As a system prerequisite, we assume deployment within an enterprise network environment similar to other works [18–20] related to this research. Specifically, the system requires a common communication path through which all TCP/UDP packets from any Subject to any Resource must pass, and where a PEP can be installed. This requirement is essential to ensure authorization decisions can be made reliably for all communications. Additionally, we assume a network environment where communication delay variations between Subjects and confidential data destinations are less than 100 milliseconds, with minimal fluctuations. This condition is necessary to properly control the timing of authorization request packets and TCP SYN packets, enabling efficient communication establishment. Particularly in countermeasures against malware, stable communication conditions are crucial as authorization processing delays directly impact defense effectiveness. These conditions are typically met in standard LANs and corporate networks.

Regarding threats, this research primarily assumes two types of adversaries: (1) Malware operators, (2) Insider threats. (1) represents operators of malware, who aim to propagate infection throughout organizational networks using malware such as OrBit, WannaCry and NotPetya. These types of malware initiate infection activities targeting other endpoints, causing damage to expand and completing infection across the entire target network in approximately 10 min [12]. (2) represents insider threats who obtain legitimate users' authentication credentials (IDs, passwords, etc.) through unauthorized means, aiming to exfiltrate organizational confidential information and intellectual property. Unlike the first type, these adversaries, being familiar with the system environment, avoid unnecessary lateral movement and attempt to access confidential resources through the shortest path. Such efficient unauthorized access cannot be prevented by standard authentication methods. Even in ZTAC, distinguishing these actors from legitimate account holders becomes difficult when relying solely on information like access time and IP addresses, necessitating access control based on access patterns and behavior.

From an attack perspective, this research excludes physical attacks, power interruptions, DDoS attacks, and direct attacks against the system's constituent software. These attacks fall outside our scope because their defense mechanisms belong to domains different than access control, which is the primary focus of this research. These threats should be addressed through existing physical security measures and availability assurance mechanisms. The User-Agent, which monitors user behavior, is assumed to have sufficient security measures in place and is not included as an attack target. The execution privileges of the User-Agent processes are constrained to the minimum necessary level, and it is designed not to collect user behavior information beyond its intended scope.

4   Proposed System

In conventional ZTAC, there exists a trade-off in continuous behavior monitoring after user authentication: attempting to collect more behavioral information increases communication overhead, forcing longer MIUI. The proposed method addresses this challenge by combining three key technologies. First, it extends SPA to design an architecture that authenticates and authorizes both endpoint and user behavioral information in a single packet. Second, it designs a multi-stage trust algorithm that selects between complete blocking or pending based on verification, depending on the circumstances. Finally, it adaptively schedules the transmission timing of authorization request packets and communication initiation packets to prevent timing attacks and control errors in MIUI.

4.1   System Design

Architecture. We show the architecture of the proposed method in Fig. 2. Similar to SPA, the proposed method consists of Subject, Resource, PDP, and PEP. The Subject incorporates a User-Agent that makes access authorization requests to the PEP based on device and user behaviors. The User-Agent is responsible for monitoring behavior, compressing information, sending authorization requests, and storing behavioral information. The PDP not only manages relatively static information such as access policies and job positions but also evaluates access requests and makes authorization decisions based on these policies. The PEP enforces these decisions by querying the PDP and acting on its responses. For information that changes infrequently and has low real-time requirements (access policy scripts, resource confidentiality levels, user positions, etc.), authorization decisions queried from PDP to PEP are cached for a certain period to reduce PDP-PEP communication volume. The PEP is located either on the same computer as the Resource or on the communication path connecting the Subject and Resource, and intercepts access request packets directed from Subject to Resource. The PEP is responsible for managing and applying access policies, validating authorization request packets, expanding compressed information, making access authorization decisions, and controlling access requests. By combining policies and static information obtained from the PDP with dynamic behavioral information sent from the Subject, it achieves fine-grained access control.

Authorization Flow. The detailed flow of access requests from Subject to Resource is explained in three phases: Request Phase, Authorization Phase, and

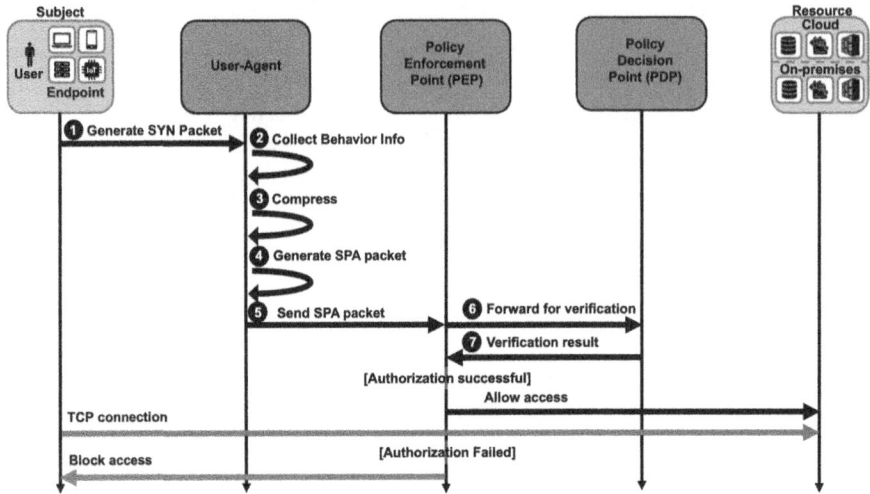

Fig. 2. Sequence Diagram of the Proposed System

Access Control Phase. At the start of the communication, the Subject generates a TCP SYN packet as a connection request to the Resource. This packet
contains essential information needed for communication, including the source
IP address, destination IP address, and destination port number (Process ❶ in
Fig. 2). Next, the User-Agent, which runs continuously on the Subject, intercepts the TCP SYN packet at the network stack. The intercepted packet is not
immediately transmitted but is temporarily buffered and remains in a pending
state until the authorization request packet is completely sent. The User-Agent
generates an SPA packet (authorization request packet) containing information
necessary for authorization decisions. First, it collects behavioral information
such as process lists, service status, and communication history (Process ❷).
Next, it applies irreversible compression to list-type information, reducing it to
a size that can fit into a single UDP packet (Process ❸). Then, it encrypts the
entire packet with an AES key and adds an HMAC for tampering detection.
Finally, it generates a digital signature using the User-Agent's private key and
appends it to the packet (Process ❹). The User-Agent sends the generated SPA
packet to the PEP using UDP protocol (Process ❺). After transmission, it waits
for an interval time dynamically determined based on past transmission history and processing status, then sends the buffered TCP SYN packet. The PEP
forwards the received SPA packet to the PDP, which performs multi-stage verification using trust algorithms (Process ❻). First, it verifies the digital signature
to confirm the packet's authenticity, then decrypts the AES-encrypted content.
Afterwards, it expands the compressed information while matching it against
keywords specified in the access policy. The PDP returns verification results
to the PEP (Process ❼). The PEP performs authorization decisions by matching the expanded behavioral information against access policy scripts. It veri-

fies Subject/Resource attributes and evaluates whether the collected behavioral information meets the specified conditions. When multiple policies exist, evaluation is conducted according to their respective priorities. Based on the policy evaluation results, the PEP implements access control. If authorized, TCP communication is allowed for the τ_{allow} period (default 3 s). In case of authorization failure, access is blocked for the τ_{deny} period, while for pending, communication is allowed for the τ_{allow} period after the τ_{deny} period expires. When authorized, the Subject's TCP SYN packet reaches the Resource, and communication is established through normal TCP 3-way handshake.

4.2   Trust Algorithm

Traditional access control with simple binary decisions (permit or deny) can lead to significant problems when misclassifications occur. Especially when classified as "deny", legitimate users are completely prevented from accessing services, severely compromising availability. On the other hand, relaxing the "permit" criteria increases the risk of data leakage through malware or insider threats. Our trust algorithm addresses this issue by introducing a multi-stage authorization with "pending". In "pending", after a denial period of τ_{deny}, access from the same device to the Resource is unconditionally permitted for a period of τ_{allow}. This provides a recovery mechanism for devices incorrectly identified as high-risk, even if they are not actually associated with insider threats or malware, by allowing a period for communication to resume later. By implementing pending rather than complete blocking, we can delay the lateral movement of malware. Simultaneously, legitimate users who were misclassified can access services after a short waiting period, thus minimizing the impact of misclassifications.

The main loop process in Algorithm 1 controls the continuous operation of the entire system, implementing the flow from packet reception to execution in an infinite loop, representing the basic operation of a continuously running system. Within this loop, verification and authorization processes are executed sequentially. The algorithm begins with packet reception function $\mathcal{R} : \emptyset \rightarrow \mathcal{P}$, where $\mathcal{P}$ denotes the packet space, followed by policy matching function $\mathcal{M} : \mathcal{P} \rightarrow \Pi$ that maps each packet p to an appropriate policy π from the policy space Π. The core verification and authorization is performed by function $\mathcal{V} : \mathcal{P} \times \Pi \rightarrow \mathcal{D}$, which returns a decision r from the decision space $\mathcal{D} = \{\text{allow}, \text{deny}, \text{pending}, \text{false}, \text{null}\}$. Based on the verification result r, the system executes appropriate actions through function $\mathcal{A} : \text{ActionType} \rightarrow \text{Effect}$. For denial cases, the system employs a pending check function $\mathcal{I} : \emptyset \rightarrow \{0, 1\}$ to determine whether to apply complete blocking or pending. When pending is selected, the scheduling function $\mathcal{S} : \text{IP} \times \mathbb{R}_{>0} \rightarrow \text{Schedule}$ manages the timing for access resumption. The cache update function $\mathcal{U} : \emptyset \rightarrow \text{CacheState}$ maintains system state consistency.

The packet verification process in Algorithm 2 performs authenticity verification and content analysis of authorization request packets. It implements digital signature verification function $\mathcal{V}_\sigma : \mathcal{P} \rightarrow \{0, 1\}$ and decryption using AES keys managed by cache function $\mathcal{C} : \mathcal{S} \rightarrow \mathcal{K}$, where $\mathcal{S}$ represents the signature space

Algorithm 1. Multi-Stage Trust Algorithm

1:	**loop**	
2:	$p \leftarrow \mathcal{R}()$	$\triangleright \mathcal{R} : \emptyset \rightarrow \mathcal{P}$ (packet reception)
3:	$\pi \leftarrow \mathcal{M}(p)$	$\triangleright \mathcal{M} : \mathcal{P} \rightarrow \Pi$ (policy matching)
4:	$r \leftarrow \mathcal{V}(p, \pi)$	$\triangleright \mathcal{V} : \mathcal{P} \times \Pi \rightarrow \mathcal{D}$ (verification)
5:	**if** $r \in \{\text{false, null}\}$ **then**	
6:	$\mathcal{A}(\text{"drop"})$	$\triangleright \mathcal{A} : \text{ActionType} \rightarrow \text{Effect}$
7:	**else if** $r = \text{"allow"}$ **then**	
8:	$\mathcal{A}(\text{"accept"})$	
9:	**else**	
10:	**if** $\mathcal{I}() = \text{true}$ **then**	$\triangleright \mathcal{I} : \emptyset \rightarrow \{0, 1\}$ (pending check)
11:	$\mathcal{S}(p.\text{source}, \tau_{\text{deny}})$	$\triangleright \mathcal{S} : \text{IP} \times \mathbb{R}_{>0} \rightarrow \text{Schedule}$
12:	$\mathcal{A}(\text{"pending"})$	
13:	**else**	
14:	$\mathcal{A}(\text{"deny"})$	
15:	**end if**	
16:	**end if**	
17:	$\mathcal{U}()$	$\triangleright \mathcal{U} : \emptyset \rightarrow \text{CacheState}$ (cache update)
18:	**end loop**	

and $\mathcal{K}$ the key space. When a signature is confirmed, the AES key is cached to improve processing efficiency by omitting public key cryptography operations in subsequent packet verifications through the AES key decryption function $\mathcal{D}_{\text{AES}} : \mathcal{P} \rightarrow \mathcal{K}$. The system converts behavior information bit arrays compressed within the packet back to original keywords using the bitmap conversion function $\mathcal{B} : \{0, 1\}^m \rightarrow 2^{\text{Keywords}}$, and matches the information obtained from the packet with access policies. It evaluates three conditions: Subject attributes, Resource attributes, and Context conditions based on behavior information through evaluation functions $\phi_s, \phi_r, \phi_c : \text{Request} \times \text{Policy} \rightarrow \{0, 1\}$. When all conditions are met, it returns an allow or deny decision according to the policy's effect. In this case, for allow decisions, a permission period of τ_{allow} is set, while for deny decisions, a blocking period of τ_{deny} is established. Conversely, when a deny decision is made, the system implements either complete blocking or pending according to system settings. In the case of pending, the system includes a mechanism to resume communication after τ_{deny} has elapsed, mitigating the impact of false detections. If packet verification fails or no appropriate policy is found, the packet is discarded according to the default-deny principle.

4.3 Dynamic Transmission Scheduling

We show the detail of dynamic transmission scheduling in Algorithm 3 and Algorithm 4. The authorization request packet scheduling algorithm proposed in this research implements a dynamic control mechanism composed of a primary control function $\mathcal{P}_{\text{req}} : \emptyset \rightarrow \perp$ and an auxiliary function $\mathcal{I} : \mathbb{R}_{\geq 0} \times \mathbb{R}_{>0} \times \mathbb{R}_{>0} \rightarrow$

Algorithm 2. Verification and Authorization Process

1: **function** $\mathcal{V}(p, \pi)$ $\triangleright \mathcal{V} : \mathcal{P} \times \Pi \to \mathcal{D}$

2:      **if** $p.\sigma \notin \mathcal{C}$ **then** $\triangleright \mathcal{C} : \mathcal{S} \to \mathcal{K}$ (AES key cache)

3:          $k \leftarrow \mathcal{D}_{\mathrm{AES}}(p)$ $\triangleright \mathcal{D}_{\mathrm{AES}} : \mathcal{P} \to \mathcal{K}$ (key decryption)

4:          **if** $\mathcal{V}_{\sigma}(p) = \mathrm{true}$ **then** $\triangleright \mathcal{V}_{\sigma} : \mathcal{P} \to \{0, 1\}$ (signature verification)

5:             $\mathcal{C}[p.\sigma] \leftarrow k$

6:          **else**

7:             **return** false

8:          **end if**

9:      **end if**

10:      $d \leftarrow \mathcal{D}_{\mathrm{AES}}(p.\mathrm{data}, \mathcal{C}[p.\sigma])$ $\triangleright \mathcal{D}_{\mathrm{AES}} : \{0, 1\}^* \times \mathcal{K} \to \mathcal{B}$

11:      $req \leftarrow \{data : d, behavior : \mathcal{B}(p.\mathrm{bitmap})\}$ $\triangleright \mathcal{B} : \{0, 1\}^m \to 2^{\mathrm{Keywords}}$

12:      **if** $\phi_s(req, \pi.\mathrm{subject}) \wedge \phi_r(req, \pi.\mathrm{resource}) \wedge \phi_c(req, \pi.\mathrm{context})$ **then** $\triangleright$ $\phi_s, \phi_r, \phi_c : \mathrm{Request} \times \mathrm{Policy} \to \{0, 1\}$

13:          **return** $\pi.\mathrm{effect}$

14:      **end if**

15:      **return** null

16: **end function**

$\mathbb{R}_{>0}$ to optimize both monitoring information volume and network load. The main processing function $\mathcal{P}_{\mathrm{req}}()$ runs continuously in an infinite loop, enabling dynamic transmission scheduling based on system state.

During normal operation, the system conducts periodic monitoring based on a standard interval τ_0. In this process, the packet capture function $\mathcal{C}_{\mathrm{pkt}} : \emptyset \to \mathcal{P}$ first captures access request packets, and the PEP address resolution function $\mathcal{G}_{\mathrm{PEP}} : \mathrm{IP} \to \mathrm{PEPAddr}$ identifies the corresponding PEP address. Then, the transmission counting function $\mathcal{N} : \mathrm{PEPAddr} \times \mathcal{P} \times \mathbb{R}_{>0} \to \mathbb{N}$ calculates the number of authorization request packet transmissions n to the PEP within the recent τ_{req} time period. The authorization packet transmission function $\mathcal{T}_{\mathrm{auth}} : \mathrm{PEPAddr} \to \mathrm{Effect}$ executes the transmission of authorization request packets when either the transmission count n is 0 or when a random number generated by $\mathcal{R} : \emptyset \to [0, 1]$ falls below the packet loss probability $\epsilon_{\mathrm{loss}}(n)$.

If the PDP detects abnormal behavior patterns, it shifts from fixed intervals to dynamic transmission scheduling. Specifically, when events such as suspicious process execution, abnormal access patterns, or matches with known attack signatures are observed, the interval calculation function $\mathcal{I} : \mathbb{R}_{\geq 0} \times \mathbb{R}_{>0} \times \mathbb{R}_{>0} \to \mathbb{R}_{>0}$ implements dynamic scheduling of transmission intervals. This function calculates the elapsed time τ_{diff} from the difference between the last transmission time τ_{last} (obtained via the last transmission time function $\mathcal{L} : \mathrm{PEPAddr} \times \mathcal{P} \to \mathbb{R}_{\geq 0}$) and the current time provided by $\mathcal{T}_{\mathrm{curr}} : \emptyset \to \mathbb{R}_{\geq 0}$. When τ_{diff} is less than τ_{req}, it applies exponential decay to significantly reduce the transmission interval. Conversely, the system autonomously reschedules transmission intervals in response to increased network load. This scheduling is executed based on recent packet transmission status and network performance metrics. Specifically, when

---

Algorithm 3. Authorization Request Packet Transmission Control

---

1: **function** $\mathcal{P}_{\mathrm{REQ}}$ $\triangleright$ $\mathcal{P}_{\mathrm{req}} : \emptyset \to \bot$ (main control loop)

2:     **while** true **do**

3:          $p \leftarrow \mathcal{C}_{\mathrm{pkt}}()$ $\triangleright$ $\mathcal{C}_{\mathrm{pkt}} : \emptyset \to \mathcal{P}$ (packet capture)

4:          $a \leftarrow \mathcal{G}_{\mathrm{PEP}}(p.dst)$ $\triangleright$ $\mathcal{G}_{\mathrm{PEP}} : \mathrm{IP} \to \mathrm{PEPAddr}$ (PEP address resolution)

5:          $n \leftarrow \mathcal{N}(a, p, \tau_{\mathrm{req}})$ $\triangleright$ $\mathcal{N} : \mathrm{PEPAddr} \times \mathcal{P} \times \mathbb{R}_{>0} \to \mathbb{N}$ (count function)

6:          **if** $n = 0 \vee \mathcal{R}() < \epsilon_{\mathrm{loss}}(n)$ **then** $\triangleright$ $\mathcal{R} : \emptyset \to [0,1]$ (random generator)

7:             $\mathcal{T}_{\mathrm{auth}}(a)$ $\triangleright$ $\mathcal{T}_{\mathrm{auth}} : \mathrm{PEPAddr} \to \mathrm{Effect}$ (auth packet send)

8:          **end if**

9:          $\tau_l \leftarrow \mathcal{L}(a, p)$ $\triangleright$ $\mathcal{L} : \mathrm{PEPAddr} \times \mathcal{P} \to \mathbb{R}_{\geq 0}$ (last transmission time)

10:         $\delta \leftarrow \mathcal{I}(\tau_l, \tau_{\mathrm{req}}, \tau_0)$ $\triangleright$ $\mathcal{I} : \mathbb{R}_{\geq 0} \times \mathbb{R}_{>0} \times \mathbb{R}_{>0} \to \mathbb{R}_{>0}$ (interval calc)

11:         $\mathcal{W}(\delta)$ $\triangleright$ $\mathcal{W} : \mathbb{R}_{>0} \to \mathrm{Effect}$ (wait/sleep)

12:         $\mathcal{T}_{\mathrm{access}}(p)$ $\triangleright$ $\mathcal{T}_{\mathrm{access}} : \mathcal{P} \to \mathrm{Effect}$ (access packet send)

13:     **end while**

14: **end function**

Algorithm 4. Auxiliary Function to Calculate Transmission Interval

---

1: **function** $\mathcal{I}(\tau_l, \tau_r, \tau_0)$ $\triangleright$ $\mathcal{I} : \mathbb{R}_{\geq 0} \times \mathbb{R}_{>0} \times \mathbb{R}_{>0} \to \mathbb{R}_{>0}$

2:      $\tau_d \leftarrow \mathcal{T}_{\mathrm{curr}}() - \tau_l$ $\triangleright$ $\mathcal{T}_{\mathrm{curr}} : \emptyset \to \mathbb{R}_{\geq 0}$ (current time)

3:      **if** $\tau_r \leq \tau_d$ **then**

4:          **return** τ_0

5:      **else**

6:          **return** $\exp\left(\ln(\tau_0) - \frac{\tau_d}{\tau_0}\right)$

7:      **end if**

8: **end function**

τ_{diff} is greater than or equal to τ_{req}, it maintains standard transmission intervals based on τ_0 while dispersing transmission timing according to network load.

The proposed algorithm executes packet transmission through the access packet transmission function $\mathcal{T}_{\mathrm{access}} : \mathcal{P} \to \mathrm{Effect}$ after waiting via the sleep function $\mathcal{W} : \mathbb{R}_{>0} \to \mathrm{Effect}$, following transmission intervals calculated by comprehensively evaluating these elements. This dynamic transmission scheduling simultaneously satisfies the conflicting requirements of efficient monitoring during normal operations, responsiveness during anomaly detection, and adaptation to network load.

5 Evaluation

5.1 Implementation

We implemented our system by using Go v1.16. The experiments were conducted on a Supermicro SYS-620U-TNR server equipped with dual Intel Xeon Silver 4316 processors (20 cores each, 2.30 GHz) and 1TB RAM, running Red Hat Enterprise Linux 8.7. The core PDP in ZTAC consolidates access control policy

Table 1. List of Major Packages Used in Implementation

Category	Go Package Name	Main Purpose
Serialization/Deserialization	binary	Network byte order conversion
Buffer Processing	bytes	Variable-length data handling
Network	net	UDP communication
Synchronization	sync	Concurrency/pool management
Encryption	crypto	Hash generation
Error Handling	fmt	Error message handling
Logging	log	Application logging
Time Processing	time	Timestamp handling
Configuration Management	flag	Command-line parsing
Performance Measurement	runtime	Profiling implementation

evaluation logic in a structure called PolicyEngine, while the PEP handles packet reception and verification through a UDPReceiver structure, and applies policy decisions received from the PDP. The communication between PDP-PEP was implemented as in-process communication using Go's goroutines and channels. The Go packages used in the implementation and their purposes are shown in Table 1.

5.2   Performance

Response Time. To evaluate the impact of concurrent connections and access requests on authorization processing time, we conducted measurements at the PEP by varying the number of Subject concurrent connections [1, 10, 100, 1000, 10000] and access requests [1, 10, 100, 1000, 10000]. In this experiment, to evaluate the impact of scheduling methods on authorization processing, we conducted a performance comparison between static scheduling (transmission at fixed-length intervals) and our proposed dynamic scheduling method. Figure 3 shows the findings from the experimental results in: Under low load conditions (1–10 requests), both methods showed relatively similar performance, with processing times ranging from 0.1 to 0.5 milliseconds. However, when the number of requests exceeded 100, the static scheduling method began to show a linear increase in processing time relative to the number of concurrent connections. Particularly under conditions with 1000 requests, the static method's processing time increased up to approximately 350 milliseconds depending on the number of concurrent connections, while the dynamic method maintained processing times around 260 milliseconds. Under high load conditions with 10000 requests, the static method's processing time increased to a maximum of approximately 2700 milliseconds as concurrent connections increased, while the dynamic method maintained processing times around 2300 milliseconds. However, the difference

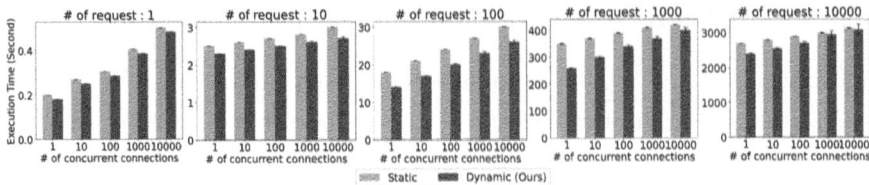

Fig. 3. Execution Time

between both decreases as the number of concurrent users increases Due to the nature of dynamic scheduling interval control in the proposed method, it exhibited larger standard deviations proportional to the number of concurrent connections compared to the static method. This characteristic inevitably arises from the dynamic adjustment of transmission intervals.

Data/Packet Size. Some of the behavioral information monitored by the User-Agent can become relatively large in data size, making it difficult to store in a single packet in its original form. Therefore, the information compression module compresses the behavioral information to reduce data size. Traditional reversible compression methods like ZIP are highly ineffective for compressing list-type hash values with high randomness. As a solution, we compressed data via Probabilistic Data Structure (PDS). When storing data in PDS packets, hash functions are applied to each element, setting corresponding bit positions to 1. During verification, high-speed compression is achieved as it only requires checking the relevant bits using the same hash functions. The total packet size remains within OpenSPA's recommended value of 1,232 bytes [21]. We conducted experiments to evaluate the compression efficiency of authorization request packets using xxHash (Bloom Filters), one of PDS. As shown in Table 2, the most notable compression effect was observed in process hash information. We achieved approximately 83% compression, reducing the size from 2,400 bytes to 412 bytes. Similarly, substantial compression was achieved for both the list of applications and patch hash information, reducing from 1,488 bytes to 284 bytes and from 1,036 bytes to 244 bytes, respectively. On the other hand, numerical data such as suspicious access, keystroke/mouse input, traffic volume, address/port scans, generated file counts, executable file counts, and idle process counts showed no change in size between pre- and post-compression. This indicates that these items are already expressed using the minimum number of bytes, leaving limited room for optimization through additional compression. When totaling all monitoring items, the pre-compression size of 5,190 bytes significantly exceeds Ethernet's maximum frame size of 1,500 bytes. However, after compression, we achieved a reduction of approximately 77% to 1,206 bytes. This result satisfies the 1,232-bytes limit recommended by OpenSPA [21], allowing for transmission within a single Ethernet packet. However, there is a constraint where the PDS's bit array length increases proportionally with the number of elements to be registered. This is particularly relevant for process hash value lists, as environments

Table 2. The Average of Data Size in Monitored Items

Item Name	Description	Original (Bytes)	Compressed (Bytes)
Process Hash	List of hash values for running process	2,400	412
Application	List of hash values for applications	1,488	284
Patch Hash	List of hash values for software patch	1,036	244
Suspicious Access	List of hash values for destination hosts connected without access history	128	128
Keystroke/Mouse	Time since last user's input (seconds)	84	84
Header Fields	Version, ID, timestamps, etc.	32	32
Traffic Volume	Maximum outbound traffic volume	8	8
Address/Port Scan	# of suspicious IP addresses connected	4	4
Generated File	# of specific file types generated	4	4
Executable File	# of executable files generated internally	4	4
Idle Process	# of processes without execution history	2	2
Total		5,190	1,206

running numerous applications require registration of more elements, leading to increased bit array lengths.

PDP Verification. In verification using PDS in the PDP, false positive assessment is crucial for determining control reliability. Due to the inherent characteristics of PDS, there can be false positives where malicious processes that are not actually running on the terminal are incorrectly identified as running. Such misidentifications can potentially cause legitimate users to be unnecessarily blocked from access. We thus evaluated verification speed, False Positive Rate (FPR), and hash collision rate using three configurations: Config A (1KB/3 hash functions), Config B (2KB/5 hash functions), and Config C (4KB/7 hash functions). The results in Fig. 4 show that verification times remained similar across configurations for fewer than 100 keywords, but Config C's processing time increased by approximately 25% at 1000 keywords due to additional hash function computation. Contrary to the original analysis, Fig. 4 demonstrates that Config C consistently delivered the lowest FPR across all keyword volumes, with Config B showing moderate values and Config A exhibiting the highest FPR. This pattern occurs because the larger bit array sizes in Config B and C (2KB and 4KB respectively) provide sufficient space to distribute bits despite using more hash functions, thereby reducing collision probability. For hash collision rates, all configurations showed increases as keywords increased, with Config C reaching approximately 0.8 at 1000 keywords while Config A remained around 0.4. This inverse relationship between FPR and collision rate highlights the inherent trade-offs. In practical implementation, Config B offers a balanced approach between verification time, memory usage, and acceptable FPR, while Config C would be preferred for systems where minimizing false positives is paramount.

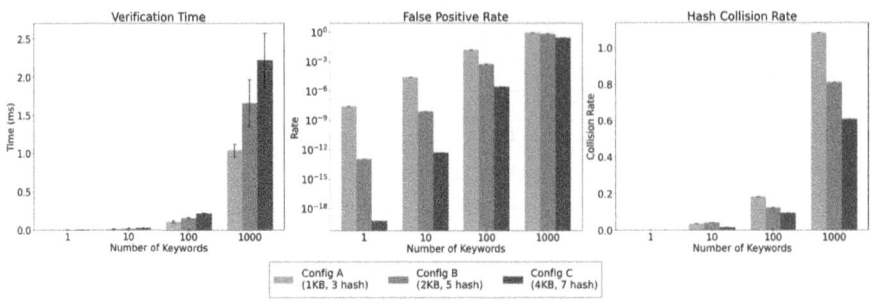

Fig. 4. PDP Verification Performance

5.3 Security Analysis

The detection performance depends on specific monitoring items. As shown in Table 2, comprehensive monitoring items such as process hash lists, running processes, HotFix lists, and suspicious access lists contribute to malware detection. Additionally, monitoring items such as the number of idle processes, creation of executable files, and PowerShell script execution are effective in detecting malware activities that exhibit unusual behavior. For internal threats, monitoring items such as keystroke/mouse hover time effectively. These serve as indicators to identify differences in behavioral patterns between legitimate users and internal threat actors (who use authentication credentials without permission). The performance of access blocking using these monitoring items directly depends on the system's response time. Experimental results in Fig. 3 show that the proposed method completes processing within approximately 300 milliseconds even under 1000 simultaneous connections and 1000 requests, and keeps processing time to about 2200 milliseconds with 10000 requests. This demonstrates the ability to respond before propagation is complete against malware, which complete lateral movement within 10 min. Furthermore, even if the number of keywords in the xxHash is increased, the PDP verification results in Fig. 4 show that verification using these monitoring items as keywords completes in about 0.5 s even with 1000 keywords. Combined with the processing time in Fig. 4, the system can make access control decisions within 3 s. This is fast enough to detect and block the activities of malware or internal threat actors that spread within 10 min, before substantial damage occurs.

In addition to addressing the threat model of this paper, this proposed architecture brought about several unexpected benefits. First, we initially use xxHash intended primarily for data size reduction, but ultimately proved valuable from a privacy protection perspective as well. The irreversible compression of user behavior information makes it difficult to reconstruct the original detailed behavioral data in the event of packet interception, reducing the risk of information leakage. Additionally, the proposed dynamic transmission scheduling, designed to dynamically adjust according to network load, has also contributed to improved resistance against DDoS attacks. The function that detects high-load conditions and automatically adjusts transmission intervals has inadvertently taken on the aspect of a mitigation measure against DDoS attacks.

Lastly, we describe limitations of proposed architecture. Temporary blocking through a multi-stage trust algorithm mitigates immediate business interruptions due to false detections, but we should consider that this mechanism itself may pose security risks. Advanced targeted attacks could potentially develop methods to exploit the timing of these blocking releases. The system proposed in the paper includes a mechanism where an allowance period τ_{allow} is automatically set after a denial period (τ_{deny}). This provides a potentially exploitable time window for attackers. Attackers can initially exhibit intentionally abnormal behavior to trigger temporary blocking and observe the system's response patterns. Once they understand this blocking/unblocking cycle, they can devise a strategy to launch concentrated attacks immediately after the τ_{deny} period ends. For example, malware lateral movement could be executed immediately following the blocking release to conduct reconnaissance activities or prepare payloads before the next blocking is activated, executing instantly at the moment of unblocking to maximize attack effectiveness. To address such vulnerabilities, countermeasures could include introducing randomness to the length of τ_{deny} and τ_{allow}, extending τ_{deny} incrementally according to patterns of abnormal behavior, or transitioning from temporary blocking to complete blocking for repeatedly detected anomalies.

6   Conclusion

In this research, we proposed a new architecture for ZTAC that combines dynamic transmission interval scheduling with a multi-stage trust algorithm capable of allow/deny/temporary deny decisions to address the balancing continuous authenticity verification with network efficiency. Through implementation and evaluation experiments, we confirmed that the proposed method reduced processing time in environments with over 1,000 simultaneous connections and achieved detection and blocking of unauthorized accesses (including malware). Additionally, the introduction of temporary blocking functionality minimized the impact of false positives. As a future work, we have to consider two additional experiments: measuring detection time of infection activities and lateral movement tolerance using actual malware samples, as well as comparatively evaluating of PDP load reduction effects between the proposed method and reverse proxy-based ZTAC.

Acknowledgements. This research has been supported by the Kayamori Foundation of Informational Science Advancement.

References

1. Alharbi, F., Kashyap, G.S.: Empowering network security through advanced analysis of malware samples: leveraging system metrics and network log data for informed decision-making. Int. J. Netw. Distrib. Comput. **12**(2), 1–15 (2024)

2. Beaman, C., Barkworth, A., Akande, T.D., Hakak, S., Khan, M.K.: Ransomware: recent advances, analysis, challenges and future research directions. Comput. Secur. **111**, 102490 (2021)
3. Teerakanok, S., Uehara, T., Inomata, A.: Migrating to zero trust architecture: reviews and challenges. Secur. Commun. Netw. **2021**(1), 9947347 (2021)
4. Yao, Q., Wang, Q., Zhang, X., Fei, J.: Dynamic access control and authorization system based on zero-trust architecture. In: Proceedings of the 2020 1st International Conference on Control, Robotics and Intelligent System, pp. 123–127 (2020)
5. Sasada, T., Masuda, Y., Taenaka, Y., Kadobayashi, Y., Fall, D.: Zero-trust access control focusing on imbalanced distribution in browser clickstreams. In: 2021 Eighth International Conference on Software Defined Systems, pp. 1–8. IEEE (2021)
6. García-Teodoro, P., Camacho, J., Maciá-Fernández, G., Gómez-Hernández, J.A., López-Marín, V.J.: A novel zero-trust network access control scheme based on the security profile of devices and users. Comput. Netw. **212**, 109068 (2022)
7. Huang, W., Xie, X., Wang, Z., Feng, J.Y., Han, G., Zhang, W.: ZT-access: a combining zero trust access control with attribute-based encryption scheme against compromised devices in power IoT environments. Ad Hoc Netw. **145**, 103161 (2023)
8. Sasada, T., Kawai, M., Masuda, Y., Taenaka, Y., Kadobayashi, Y.: Factor analysis of learning motivation difference on cybersecurity training with zero trust architecture. IEEE Access **11**, 141358–141374 (2023)
9. Matiushin, I., Korkhov, V.: Continuous authentication methods for zero-trust cybersecurity architecture. In: International Conference on Computational Science and Its Applications, pp. 334–351. Springer (2023)
10. Sasada, T., Taenaka, Y., Kadobayashi, Y., Fall, D.: Web-biometrics for user authenticity verification in zero trust access control. IEEE Access, 129611–129622 (2024)
11. He, Y., Huang, D., Chen, L., Ni, Y., Ma, X.: A survey on zero trust architecture: challenges and future trends. Wirel. Commun. Mob. Comput. **2022**(1), 6476274 (2022)
12. Akibis, M., Pereira, J., Clark, D., Mitchell, V., Alvarez, H.: An automated approach, measuring ransomware propagation patterns via network traffic analysis (2024)
13. Scott, R., Oliver, B., Stu, M., Sean, C.: NIST SP800-207: Zero Trust Architecture, Technical report, National Institute of Standards and Technology (2020)
14. Azad, M.A., Abdullah, S., Arshad, J., Lallie, H., Ahmed, Y.H.: Verify and trust: a multidimensional survey of zero-trust security in the age of IoT. Internet Things **27**, 101227 (2024)
15. Meng, L., Huang, D., An, J., Zhou, X., Lin, F.: A continuous authentication protocol without trust authority for zero trust architecture. Chin. Commun. **19**(8), 198–213 (2022)
16. Kataoka, S., Kotani, D., Okabe, Y.: NI-SPA: SPA-based dynamic access control utilizing in-network behavior. In: Proceedings of the SIGCOMM Workshop on Zero Trust Architecture for Next Generation Communications, pp. 19–24 (2024)
17. Mingyang, X., Guo, J., Yuan, H., Yang, X.: Zero-trust security authentication based on SPA and endogenous security architecture. Electronics **12**(4), 782 (2023)
18. Bashir, T.: Zero trust architecture: enhancing cybersecurity in enterprise networks. J. Comput. Sci. Technol. Stud. **6**(4), 54–59 (2024)
19. Bush, M., Mashatan, A.: From zero to one hundred: demystifying zero trust and its implications on enterprise people, process, and technology. Queue **20**(4), 80–106 (2022)

20. Ge, Y., Zhu, Q.: Trust threshold policy for explainable and adaptive zero-trust defense in enterprise networks. In: 2022 IEEE Conference on Communications and Network Security (CNS), pp. 359–364. IEEE (2022)
21. Krmelj, G.R., Pančur, M., Grohar, M., Ciglarič, M.: OpenSPA - an open and extensible protocol for single packet authorization. In: Proceedings of the Central European Cybersecurity Conference 2018, pp. 1–6 (2018)

An Empirical Measurement of Cookie Banners Potential Legal Violations in EU vs US Websites

Federica Paci[(✉)][iD], Matteo Cristani[iD], and Armando de Berti[iD]

University of Verona, Verona, Italy
{federica.paci,matteo.cristani,armando.berti}@univr.it

Abstract. Third-party tracking raises privacy concerns due to the covert collection, aggregation, and potential misuse of users' personal data, undermining individuals' sense of control and privacy online. In Europe, tracking is regulated by the GDPR and ePrivacy Directive (ePD), which require explicit user consent. In contrast, US websites, governed by a patchwork of state and federal laws, often rely on opt-out mechanisms. However, when dealing with EU residents' data, US companies must comply with the GDPR. We present an empirical study assessing compliance with GDPR and ePD consent requirements in EU and US websites through their cookie banner implementations. We identified 19 potential violations of these regulations and developed a systematic method to detect them. Our key findings are: a) none of the examined EU or US websites fully comply with GDPR and ePD consent standards; b) both EU and US websites engage in user tracking before a choice is made and even after consent is denied; c) websites that use Consent Management Platforms (CMPs) are generally more compliant than those that do not.

These findings highlight widespread non-compliance and the need for stronger enforcement and clearer guidance on valid consent mechanisms.

Keywords: Privacy · valid consent · GDPR · ePD · websites · third-party tracking

1 Introduction

Web-tracking technologies, such as cookies and fingerprinting, are widely used to analyze user behavior, personalize content, and improve marketing strategies. While beneficial for businesses, these technologies raise significant privacy concerns due to the extensive, often covert, data collection they enable.

In the EU, data collection for tracking is regulated by the ePrivacy Directive (ePD) and the General Data Protection Regulation (GDPR), which mandate user consent before processing personal data. As a result, when users visit a EU website for the first time, they are presented with a cookie banner that allows them to set their cookie preferences. In contrast, the US lacks a unified privacy

B. Coppens et al. (Eds.): ARES 2025 Workshops, LNCS 15995, pp. 342–359, 2025.
https://doi.org/10.1007/978-3-032-00633-2_20

law, relying instead on fragmented state and federal regulations such as HIPAA, COPPA, and the California Privacy Rights Act. Consequently, US websites frequently implement simplified cookie banners that offer minimal transparency about data usage. However, when handling data of EU residents, US sites must still comply with the GDPR. Indeed, several U.S. companies, including major corporations like Google and Meta, have been fined by EU Data Protection Authorities for failing to obtain valid consent.

Prior research has investigated cookie banner compliance with GDPR [6,8, 22–27,32,38,39] and the presence of *dark patterns* in cookie banners [12,15,34, 36], . However, the above studies analyzed a restricted set of violations mainly related to prior, freely-given, and unambiguous consent. Moreover, most of these studies focused on websites that use Consent Management Platforms (CMPs) to manage consent. Other studies [5,10,28,31,38] have explored geographical differences in user tracking but not in cookie banner compliance.

To address these gaps, we conducted an empirical study to investigate the extent to which websites based in the European Union and the United States adhere to GDPR and ePrivacy Directive requirements for valid user consent. We also wanted to examine whether the level of compliance with consent requirements is higher in EU and US websites that use CMPs. We assessed whether EU and US websites engage in user tracking despite a lack of user consent or after explicit denial of consent.

Our main contributions are as follows:

– **Legal Analysis**: We conduct a comprehensive review of the GDPR, the ePrivacy Directive, relevant legal guidelines, and existing literature on valid consent, identifying 19 potential legal violations in cookie banner implementations (see Sect. 3).
– **Compliance Methodology**: We develop a methodology that combines semi-automatic and manual detection techniques to evaluate website compliance with the 19 potential violations (see Sect. 4).
– **Empirical Evaluation**: Applying our methodology to 200 EU and US websites, we found that none fully comply with ePD and GDPR requirements for valid consent. Specifically, all examined websites violate rules on *prior* and *unambiguous* consent. EU websites are less compliant with the requirement for *freely-given consent*, while US websites exhibit lower compliance with requirements for *informed, specific,* and *revocable* consent (see Sect. 5.1). We found that EU and US websites not using CMPs are less compliant with ePD and GDPR consent requirements than those that do. Moreover, EU and US websites track users regardless of the consent choices they make.

The paper is organized as follows. Section 2 discusses previous works on user tracking and cookie banner compliance. Section 3 introduces the identified possible violations of GDPR and ePD consent requirements. Section 4 presents the methodology adopted in our study, while Sect. 5 reports the results and discuss the threats to validity. Section 6 discusses the main findings and provides directions for future research.

2   Related Work

In this section, we discuss prior research on user tracking and cookie banner compliance.

User Tracking and Compliance. Previous works [5,10,28,31,38] have shown that websites store cookies, especially third-party and tracking cookies without user prior consent. For instance, Dabroski et al. [5] reported that 87% of websites set persistent cookies without consent when accessed from the US, compared to 46% from the EU. Similarly, large-scale studies by Trevisan et al. [38] and Singh et al. [35] found widespread storage of cookies before consent, even in GDPR-compliant countries.

Government websites and mobile apps also track users without valid consent: Gotze et al. [10] and Samarasinghe et al. [31] documented extensive use of trackers and third-party cookies without user consent. More advanced tracking methods—such as fingerprinting and ID syncing—are often employed even when users explicitly deny consent, as noted by Papadogiannakis et al. [28]. In line with these findings, the current study confirms that both EU and US websites engage in user tracking not only when no consent choice has been made but also when consent has been denied.

Cookie Banners' Compliance. Santos et al. [33] laid the ground to assess cookie banner compliance by proposing 22 requirements that cookie banners should satisfy. They argued that verifying compliance with these requirements cannot be fully automated as most low-level requirements either necessitate manual inspection, can only be partially assessed using technical tools, or require user studies. Other studies have investigated the presence of potential violations in cookie banner interfaces implemented by websites [6,8,13,22,23,26,32,39] and mobile apps [24,25,27]. These studies [6,8,13,22,23,26,32,39] have identified widespread violations such as implicit consent, lack of a "Reject All" option, pre-selected choices, and positive consent stored before users make a decision or even after they have explicitly denied it. Similarly, research on Android and iOS apps [24,25,27] reveals extensive non-compliance, with many apps either lacking cookie banners or violating GDPR consent requirements, particularly in terms of tracking without freely-given or revocable consent.

Although our study shares similar goals with these works, there are significant differences. Unlike earlier works that focused only on a limited set of consent violations, this study offers a comprehensive assessment covering all requirements for valid consent. It also examines compliance differences between EU and US websites, and between those that use CMPs and those that do not. Third, we followed a different methodology to detect violations: we combined manual analysis to detect the potential violations related to informed, freely-given, specific, unambiguous, readable and accessible, and revocable consent, and a semi-automatic approach to detect violations of prior consent based on the actual tracking mechanisms adopted by websites. While other studies relied on the consent registered by the websites, manual analysis, or the analysis of the network traffic.

Another line of research has focused on the identification of dark patterns in cookie banner design [11,12,15,34,36,37], while other works [1,2,16] have explored how dark patterns influence users' behavior on consent decisions. Although our study does not directly investigate dark patterns, some of the violations it identifies may stem from their use, pointing to the influence of interface design on the effectiveness and legality of user consent.

3   Potential GDPR and ePD Consent Violations

The GDPR requires that web publishers and third-party trackers have a *lawful basis* for collecting and processing personal data for tracking purposes. The legal bases that are commonly used by website publishers and third-party tracking companies are *consent* and *legitimate interest*. However, according to Article 5(3) of the ePD, they must obtain users' consent before any data collected for monitoring their online activities is stored or accessed on their devices. Therefore, consent is the only valid legal basis for collecting and processing users' personal data for tracking purposes. The GDPR sets specific requirements on the validity of consent in Article 4 (11), Article 7, which are specified further in recital 32 of the GDPR. Article 4(11) establishes that consent is valid when is *freely given, informed, unambiguous*, and *specific* to each different purpose of the processing. Additionally, Article 7 states that request for consent presented by the data controllers must be *readable* and *accessible* for the users, and that they must be able to demonstrate that the user has consented to the processing of personal data. Consent must also be *revocable* at any given time, and *withdrawing* consent must be as *easy* as giving it. For each of the above requirements on valid consent, we have identified 19 potential violations based on the analysis of the ePD's Article 5(3), Articles 4(11), 7(2), 7(3), 7(4) of the GDPR, EDPB guidelines 05/2020 on valid consent [3], DPA guidelines [29], and other research papers [23,33,36] that have analyzed cookie banners' legal compliance.

Prior Consent Violations. The *prior consent* requirement imposes that website publishers must obtain consent before storing or accessing information on users' devices. There are two main violations: V_1 - *No Consent Before Storing* [36], when a website implements a cookie banner, but third-party cookies are stored in the user's browser before the user has given explicit consent; V_2 - *No Consent Before Sending* [36], when a website implements a cookie banner, but the information saved in third-party cookies is transmitted to the trackers' servers before any user consent.

Informed Consent Violations. Informed consent is infringed when a cookie banner does not provide users with information about the processed data, including details about the purposes, and who has access to it. We identified three primary violations: V_3 - *No Cookies Listed* [29]: the short notice of the cookie banner fails to clearly state that cookies or other tracking technologies are used by the website; V_4 - *No Purposes Listed* [29]: the short notice of the cookie banner fails to clearly state the processing purposes; V_5 - *No Link to Privacy and or*

Cookie Policy [29]: the cookie banner lacks a link to the comprehensive privacy policy and cookie policy.

Freely-Given Consent's Violations. Consent is not freely-given when users experience any form of coercion or undue influence in persuading them to give their consent. The main violation is V_6 - *Blocking Access* ([33], that is when a website implements a cookie wall or a tracking wall that blocks access to the website until a user expresses her choice regarding consent or has granted a positive consent.

Specific Consent's Violations. The specific consent requirement imposes that users must be able to grant consent for distinct and individual purposes of the processing. Therefore, the main violation is V_7 - *No Separate Consent per Specific Purpose* [33]: the processing has multiple purposes, but the cookie banner only allows a user to deny or grant all at once.

Unambiguous Consent Violations. Consent is unambiguous when the cookie banner allows the user to give consent through a clear affirmative action, leaving no room for ambiguity in interpreting the user's choice. Therefore, the following practices constitute a potential infringement of unambiguous consent: V_8 - *Pre-selected boxes or sliders* [36]: the cookie banner allows the user a granular choice, but some of the choices are pre-selected to grant consent; V_9 - *No labelled boxes or sliders*: when the banner presents boxes or sliders, but the options are not accompanied by labels that clarify the intended consent action; V_{10} - *No Way to Opt Out* [36]: the cookie banner does not provide the user with an option to deny consent; V_{11} - *No Easy Way to Deny Consent* [36]: the cookie banner provides an option to deny consent, but the option is not on the first layer of the banner; V_{12} - *Deceptive Button Colour and Contrast - Deny All* and V_{13} - *Deceptive Button Colour and Contrast - Configure* [4]: the cookie banner emphasizes the "Accept All" button over the "Deny All" and "Configure" buttons using contrast and colors; V_{14} - *Legitimate Interest Claimed* [4]: the cookie banner incorporates the concept of legitimate interest for subsequent processing in the "deepest layers of the banner"; V_{15} - *Non-respect of choice* [23]: the website saves third-party cookies in a user's browser, and the information saved in the cookies is transmitted to trackers' servers even though the user explicitly denied consent.

Readable and Accessible Consent Violations. For consent to be readable and accessible, the cookie banner must be presented in a manner that is easily distinguishable from other information, use clear and straightforward language, and be made readily accessible. Therefore, the following practices fail to comply with these requirements: V_{16} - *No clear and plain language* [4]: the cookie banner text uses complex language e.g. legal jargon; V_{17} - *Not Easily Accessible* [4]: the consent request and the settings page to configure consent are located far from the primary interaction with the banner.

Revocable Consent Violations. The following practices are violations of the *revocable consent* requirement: V_{18} - *No Way to Withdraw Consent* [4]: the website does not allow users to return to the "cookie settings" page where they can withdraw their consent by a means of a small hovering and permanently visible icon or a link placed in a visible and standard place; V_{19} - *No Easy Way to Withdraw Consent* [33]: the website provides an option to withdraw consent, but the user has to use a different interface than the one used to grant consent. Therefore, the number of clicks to withdraw consent will be higher than the one to give consent.

4   Methodology

In this section, we present the methodology that we followed to perform our study, which was conducted from November 2022 to August 2023. The study aimed to answer the following research questions that were derived from the analysis of the literature:

– RQ_1: *To what extent do EU and US websites comply with GDPR and ePD requirements on valid consent?*
– RQ_2: *Does the use of CMPs improve legal compliance of EU and US websites with consent requirements?*
– RQ_3: *Do EU and US websites engage in user tracking even when no consent is given or when consent is explicitly denied?*

4.1   Websites Selection

We selected the top 200 websites from the Tranco list [18], comprising 100 websites based in the European Union (EU) and 100 based in the United States (US). To determine the country associated with a website we adopted the *ip-api.com* API, which given a domain returns a set of information useful to determine a website's geographical location: continent, country, region, city, zip code, and the owner organization of the domain. 42% of the analyzed websites use CMPs to manage consent, with adoption rates of 49% among US websites and 35% among EU websites. OneTrust is the most widely used CMP both by EU and US websites. We used the McAfee SmartFilter Internet Database service [20] to associate a list of content categories with the analyzed websites. Our dataset included websites from the following categories: Internet Services, Business, Entertainment, Education, Finance and Social Networking.

4.2   Data Collection

In this section, we explain the data that we collected to answer our research questions. We visited from within the EU each website in a clean Google Chrome session and took screenshots of the cookie banners. We also stored cookies and HTTP requests and responses under three consent conditions: when the user does not make any choice (No Action), when the user denies consent (Deny All), and when the user grants consent(Accept All). To capture the cookies stored in the browser, we used *Get Cookies.txt* browser extension. We also recorded the network traffic with Wireshark [30] for about 5 min under the No Action, Deny All, and Accept All conditions.

Table 1. Cookie banner Analysis Questionnaire

Requirements	Violations	Questions
Informed	No Cookies Listed	Q_1: Does the short information notice on the first layer of the banner mention the app uses cookies or other tracking tools?
	No Purposes Listed	Q_2: Does the short information notice on the first layer of the banner specify the purposes of the processing?
	No Link to Privacy Policy	Q_3: Does the short information notice on the first layer of the banner contain a link to the privacy policy and/or to the cookie policy?
Freely given	Blocking Access	Q_4: Does the banner force the user to give consent to access the website?
Specific	No Separate Consent for Specific Purposes	Q_5: Does the banner allow to give consent for a specific purpose?
Unambiguous	Pre-selected boxes or sliders	Q_6: Does the second layer of the banner use pre-selected sliders or pre-ticked boxes?
	No labeled boxes or sliders	Q_7: Are the boxes or sliders labeled with accept/deny?
	No Way to Opt Out	Q_8: Is the design of the cookie banner interface of type Inform* or AutoAccept**?
	No Easy Way to Deny Consent	Q_9: Is the design of the cookie banner interface of type OnlyAccept***?
	Deceptive Button Colours and Contrasts - Deny All	Q_{10}: Is the "Accept all" option emphasized with respect to the "Deny all" option?
	Deceptive Button Colours and Contrasts - Configure	Q_{11}: Is the "Accept all" option emphasised with respect to the "Configure" option?
	Legitimate Interest Claimed	Q_{12}: Does the second layer of the banner use legitimate interest as the legal basis for tracking?
Readable and accessible	No Clear and Plain language	Q_{13}: Does the banner text use clear and plain language?
	No Easily Accessible	Q_{14}: Is the customization setting page easily accessible?
Revocable	No Way to Withdraw Consent	Q_{15}: Does the first layer of the banner contain a link or a button to revoke the consent?
	No Easy Way to Withdraw Consent	Q_{16}: Is revoking consent as easy as giving it in terms of number of users' clicks?

* **Inform cookie banner**: the cookie banner only informs users of the use of cookies and other tracking technologies without an option to give consent.

** **AutoAccept cookie banner**: the cookie banner informs users that by continuing navigation, they consent to the use of all types of cookies and trackers.

*** **OnlyAccept cookie banner**: the cookie banner interface makes harder for the user to deny consent.

4.3   Data Analysis

We used different analysis techniques to evaluate EU and US website compliance (RQ1) depending on the type of potential violation. To determine if a website had the potential violation *No Consent Before Storing*, we first identified the third-party cookies stored in the browser under the No Action condition. Then, we further refined them in Strictly Necessary, Performance, Targeting, and Functionality using Open Cookie Database [17], and CookieScript [21]. We label a website as having the *No Consent Before Storing* violation if third-party non-strictly necessary cookies were saved in the browser under the No Action condition. We implemented a script in Python that automatically labels a website with this violation by analyzing the file with the cookies saved in the browser when visiting the website, and then calculates the percentage of non-compliant EU and US websites.

To flag the violation *No Consent Before Sending*, we analyzed the website network traffic registered under the No Action condition. We implemented a Python script that filters the Client Hello packets associated with the start of the handshake phase of the TLS protocol. Then, from these Client Hello packets, the script extracts the Server Name Indication field, which specifies the hostname the website intends to communicate with. As in [19], the script labels each packet as related to tracking if the contacted domain is classified as a tracking domain in three dataset of third-party tracking domains: DisconnectMe [7], X-Ray Blacklist [14], and DuckDuckGO Tracker Radar [9]. The script flags a violation if third-party domains were contacted by the website under the No Action condition.

For the violations related to *informed consent, specific consent, freely-given consent, unambiguous consent, readable and accessible consent,* and *revocable consent,* we performed a systematic manual analysis of the cookie banner's screenshots. To this end, we build an analysis template based on the one we used in a previous study [27], which includes, for each possible violation discussed in Sect. 3, a set of questions that guide the analysts in identifying the violation. The full list of questions is reported in Table 1. All questions are binary, which means the only possible answers are "yes" or "no". A violation is flagged when the answer to at least one of the questions $Q_4, Q_6, Q_8, Q_9, Q_{10}, Q_{11}, Q_{12}$ is positive ("yes"), or when the answer to one of the remaining questions is negative ("no"). To facilitate the recording of the answers, we implemented the analysis template in Google Forms. Each website's cookie banner was evaluated independently by two of the authors. In the event of any discrepancies in the analysis, the authors engaged in discussions to collectively resolve disagreements and determine the appropriate revisions to the responses. Once we completed the analysis, for each possible violation in Table 1, we implemented a script that, for each question, computes the percentage of EU and US websites that have the violation and the percentage of non-compliant websites on the whole dataset. Then, to investigate whether the difference in the percentage of non-compliant EU and US websites was statistically significant, we applied the χ^2 statistical test with a significance level α of 0.05.

To detect the *Non-respect of choice* violation, we employed a different approach from previous studies [23]. Instead of verifying whether a website stored a consent preference before the user made a choice or registered the same response as the user's selection, we identified this violation when non-essential third-party cookies were stored in the browser and/or the website communicated with third-party domains despite consent being denied. The detection process was automated using a Python script.

To assess the impact of CMPs on compliance with GDPR and ePD consent requirements (RQ_2), we conducted the same comparative analysis used for evaluating potential violations across EU and US websites, distinguishing between those that use CMPs and those that do not.

To evaluate RQ_3, we analyzed the number of third-party cookies set and third-party domains contacted by EU and US websites in the three consent conditions. A t-test was used to compare the number of third-party cookies between US and EU websites under the three consent conditions. For comparisons across all three consent conditions, we used the non-parametric Kruskal-Wallis test to assess overall differences, followed by Dunn's post hoc tests to identify specific group differences.

5   Results

This section outlines the study's findings based on the main research questions.

5.1 RQ_1 - Consent Compliance Across EU and US Websites

Table 2 provides an overview of the violations we found grouped by requirements on valid consent. In particular, the third column (*EU sites*) reports the percentage of non-compliant EU websites, and the fourth column (*US sites*) reports the percentage of non-compliant US websites. The last column (*Total*) reports the percentage of the analyzed websites that are not compliant. The last row reports the percentage of websites that violate at least one of the requirements for valid consent. We can observe that neither of EU nor the US websites fully comply with privacy regulations on valid consent. Specifically, all EU and US websites fail to meet the requirements for *prior* and *unambiguous* consent. EU websites tend to be less compliant with *freely-given* (with statistical significance) consent than US websites. On the other hand, US websites are slightly less compliant with *informed*, *specific*, and *revocable* consent than their EU counterparts.

Prior Consent's Violations. We found that all the analyzed websites violate the prior consent requirement. Specifically, our findings indicate that all websites exhibit *No Consent Before Sending* violation. As shown in Fig. 1, the most popular domains contacted by US websites are www.googletagmanager.com `fonts.gstatic.com`, and `geolocation.onetrust.com`. The first two domains are owned by Alphabet, the parent company of Google, while the latter domain is owned by OneTrust. Similarly, the most popular domains contacted by EU websites are owned by Alphabet: www.googletagmanager.com `fonts.gstatic.com`,

Table 2. Observed Potential Violations

Requirements	Violations	EU sites	US sites	Total
Prior	No Consent Before Storing	40%	48%	44%
	No Consent Before Sending	100%	100%	100%
Total		100%	100%	100%
Informed	No Cookies Listed	2%	5%	3.5%
	No Purposes Listed	49%	40%	44.5%
	No Link to Privacy Policy	22%	40% •	31%
Total		62%	67%	64.5%
Freely given	Blocking Access	54% •	35%	44.5%
Specific	No Separate Consent for Specific Purposes	59%	65%	62%
Unambiguous	Pre-selected boxes or sliders	12%	17%	15%
	No labelled boxes or sliders	39%	49%	44%
	No Way to Opt Out	1%	1%	1%
	No Easy Way to Deny Consent	34%	29%	31.5%
	Deceptive Button Colours and Contrasts - Deny All	27% •	14%	20.5%
	Deceptive Button Colours and Contrasts - Configure	66%	71%	68.5%
	Legitimate Interest Claimed	23%	18%	20.5%
	Non-respect of choice	100%	100%	100%
Total		100%	100%	100%
Readable and accessible	No Clear and Plain language	5%	5%	5%
	No Easily Accessible	2%	3%	2.5%
Total		7%	7%	7%
Revocable	No Way to Withdraw Consent	82%	80%	81%
	No Easy Way to Withdraw Consent	64%	56%	60%
Total		89%	92%	90.5%
Total		100%	100%	100%

• - p-value < 0.05

and `fonts.googleapis.com`. We found that almost half of US websites (48%) exhibit the *No Consent Before Storing* violation, compared to the 40% of EU websites. The primary third-party cookies stored when visiting US websites belong to the Targeting category: `UserMatchHistory`, `bcookie` and `lidc` are set by Linkedin for advertising purposes, including tracking visitors so that more relevant ads can be presented, and collecting information about how visitors use the site. In contrast, the main third-party cookies stored when visiting EU websites are Targeting cookies related to Google. `VISITOR_INFO1_LIVE`, `YSC` are set by Youtube to provide ad delivery or retargeting, and `test_cookie` is set by doubleclick.net to check if the website supports cookies.

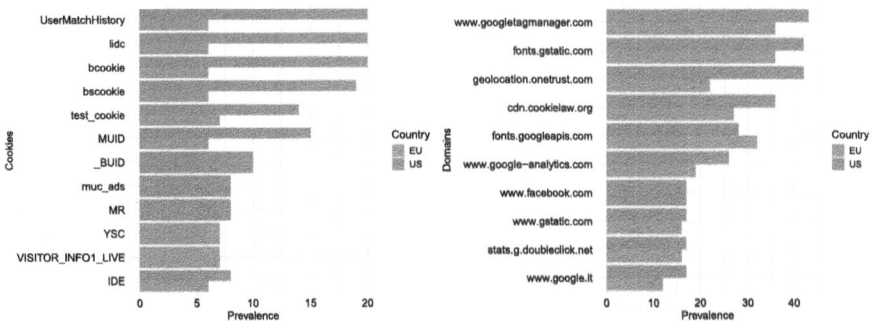

(a) Third-party cookies - No Action   (b) Third-party domains - No Action

Fig. 1. Prior Consent Violations

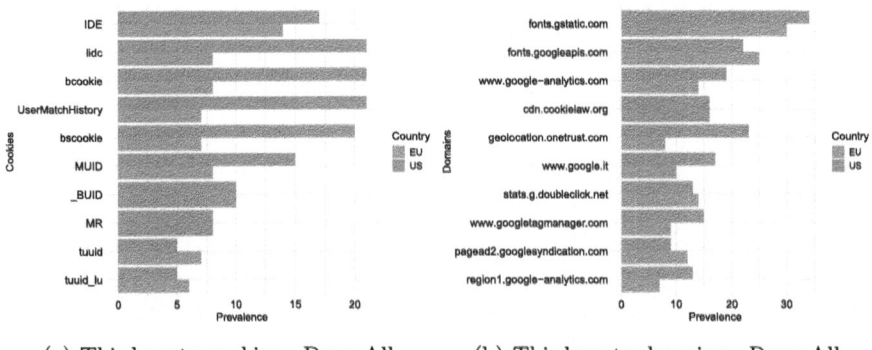

(a) Third-party cookies - Deny All   (b) Third-party domains - Deny All

Fig. 2. Non-Respect of Choice Violation

Informed Consent Violations. The percentage of US websites (67%) that fail to comply with informed consent is slightly higher than that of EU websites (62%), though the difference is not statistically significant. Specifically, the *No Purpose Listed* violation is more prevalent among EU websites (49%) compared to US websites (40%), but this difference also lacks statistical significance. However, the *No Link to Privacy* violation is significantly more common on US websites (40%) than on EU websites (22%), with a statistically significant difference (χ^2 p-value = 0.009346).

Freely-Given Consent Violations. The Blocking Access violation is more common on EU websites (54%) than on US websites (35%) with statistical significance (χ^2 p-value = 0.01043).

Specific Consent Violations. We found that 65% of US websites violate this requirement compared to 59% of EU websites, without statistical significance.

Unambiguous Consent Violations. All EU and US websites fail to comply with this requirement due to the *Non-respect of choice* violation. Figure 2 illustrates the primary third-party cookies saved in the browser and the third-party domains the websites communicate with. On US websites, the most frequently stored cookies—bcookie, UserMatchHistory, and lidc—are the same as those found when users do not interact with the cookie banner. In contrast, EU websites store different cookies compared to those detected in the *No Consent Before Storing* violation. The most common cookies—IDE, MUID, and lidc—are all targeting cookies owned by Alphabet, Microsoft, and LinkedIn, respectively. Regarding third-party domains, both EU and US websites predominantly communicate with the same ones: fonts.gstatic.com, fonts.googleapis.com, and www.google-analytics.com all owned by Alphabet.

Another observed violation is *Deceptive Button Colors and Contrast - Configure*, where the "Accept All" button is visually emphasized over the "Configure" button. This violation is slightly more prevalent on US websites (71%) than on EU websites (66%). Additionally, 49% of US websites have the *No Labeled boxes or sliders* violation compared to 39% of EU websites.

Furthermore, 34% of EU websites exhibit the *No Easy Way to Deny Consent* violation, compared to 29% of US websites. On average, users must click twice to deny consent on both EU and US websites—once to access the customization settings page and again to select the "Deny All" option. However, none of these findings are statistically significant, except for the *Deceptive Button Colors and Contrast - Deny All* violation (χ^2 p-value = 0.009346).

Readable and Accessible Consent Violations. Only a limited number of US (7%) and EU websites (7%) violate this requirement due to *No Clear and Plain Language* violation flagged on 5% of EU and US websites, but without statistical significance.

Revocable Consent Violations. We observed that US websites (92%) fail to comply more with revocable consent than EU websites (85%). The primary violation for both US and EU websites is *No Way to Withdraw Consent*, flagged on 82% of EU websites compared to 80% of US websites. The second violation *No Easy Way to Withdraw Consent* is slightly more present in EU websites (64%), than in EU websites (56%). However, none of these results is statistically significant.

5.2 RQ_2 - Impact of CMPs on Consent Compliance

The analysis (see Table 3) shows that using CMPs does not ensure full compliance with GDPR and ePD, although EU websites using CMPs display slightly better compliance for *specific* consent with statistical significance. Certain violations, such as the *No Consent Before Sending* (χ^2 p-value = 0.0027), *No Separate Consent for Specific Purposes* (χ^2 p-value= 0.03869), *Deceptive Button Colours and Contrast - Deny All* (χ^2 p-value = 0.02107), and *Non-Respect of Choice* violations (χ^2 p-value = 0.0027) were significantly more frequent on non-compliant sites. Similar patterns emerged for US websites, where websites not using CMPs had higher rates of non-compliance in areas like *prior, unambiguous, readable and accessible,* and *revocable* consent, though not all differences were statistically significant. Interestingly, some violations, including *No Labeled boxes or sliders* (χ^2 p-value = 0.005005) and *Deceptive Button Colours and Contrast - Deny All* (χ^2 p-value =0.02696), were significantly more common on US sites that used CMPs.

5.3 RQ_3 Tracking Behavior in EU and US Websites

The analysis (see Table 4) reveals that both EU and US websites continue to engage in user tracking by setting third-party cookies and contacting third-party domains under No Action and Deny All conditions. In particular, US websites store more third-party cookies and contact more third-party domains compared to EU websites. However, a statistically significant difference in the number of third-party cookies between US and EU websites is only observed in the No Action condition (t-test p-value = 0.03284).

Further statistical testing was conducted to compare tracking behaviors across three consent scenarios—No Action, Deny All, and Accept All. Results from Dunn's test indicate that for both EU and US websites, significantly more third-party cookies are stored under the Accept All condition than under No Action or Deny All, while no significant difference was found between No Action and Deny All within each jurisdiction. A Kruskal-Wallis test confirmed that the number of third-party domains contacted also varied significantly across the three consent conditions for both EU (p-value = 0.01259) and US websites (p-value = 8.693e-05). The analysis also examined the top stored cookies and contacted domains (see Fig. 3). For US websites, the same third-party cookies appeared in both No Action and Deny All conditions. In EU websites, the most common cookies included `tuuid`, `uid`, `IDE`, and `tuuid_lu`, which are known for tracking users across sites. Regarding third-party domains, similarly to what happens in the No Action and Deny All EU websites and US websites, interact with domains associated with Google services that collect user data to deliver personalized ads based on browsing behavior.

5.4 Threats to Validity

Conclusion Validity. The main limitation to conclusion validity in this study stems from the relatively small sample size of 200 websites, which was necessary due to the labor-intensive nature of manually assessing cookie banner compliance with GDPR and ePD. Since automated tools for such analysis are not yet

Table 3. Observed Potential Violations

Requirements	Violations	EU sites		US sites	
		CMP	No CMP	CMP	No CMP
Prior	No Consent Before Storing	17%	23%	22%	26%
	No Consent Before Sending	35%	*65%	49%	51%
Total		35%	65%	49%	51%
Informed	No Cookies Listed	1%	1%	3%	2%
	No Purposes Listed	18%	31%	19%	21%
	No Link to Privacy Policy	11%	11%	24%	16%
Total		24%	38%	33%	34%
Freely given	Blocking Access	21%	33%	19%	16%
Specific	No Separate Consent for Specific Purposes	26%	* 33%	33%	32%
Unambiguous	Pre-selected boxes or sliders	5%	7%	8%	9%
	No labelled boxes or sliders	17%	22%	⋆ 35%	14%
	No Way to Opt Out	0%	1%	0%	1%
	No Easy Way to Deny Consent	14%	20%	13%	16%
	Deceptive Button Colours and Contrasts - Deny All	4%	* 23%	3%	⋆ 11%
	Deceptive Button Colours and Contrasts - Configure	25%	41%	39%	32%
	Legitimate Interest Claimed	6%	17%	5%	13%
	Non-respect of choice	35%	* 65%	49%	51%
Total		35%	65%	49%	51%
Readable and accessible	No Clear and Plain language	1%	4%	1%	4%
	No Easily Accessible	0%	2%	1%	2%
Total		1%	6%	2%	5%
Revocable	No Way to Withdraw Consent	28%	54%	38%	42%
	No Easy Way to Withdraw Consent	25%	39%	23%	33%
Total		31%	58%	44%	48%

* - p-value < 0.05 - significant difference between EU websites using CMPs and
EU websites not using CMPs.
⋆ - p-value < 0.05 - significant difference between US websites using CMPs and
US websites not using CMPs.

Table 4. Tracking behaviour per consent actions

	EU sites		US sites	
	Cookies	Domains	Cookies	Domains
No Action	1.57	13.53	3.73	16.24
Deny All	3.31	8.98	4.13	9.94
Accept All	25.88	22.78	24.22	24.87

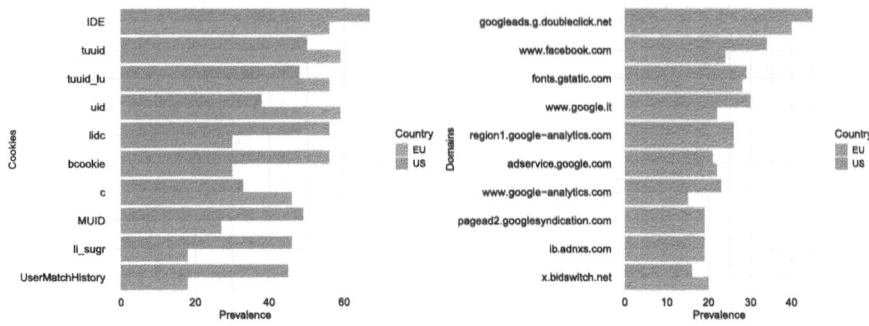

(a) Third-party cookies - Accept All   (b) Third-party domains - Accept All

Fig. 3. Accept All condition

reliable due to inconsistent banner designs, two independent researchers manually evaluated each site, enabling more accurate identification of violations that automated methods might miss. Another limitation is the study's focus on stateful tracking, primarily involving cookies with user identifiers. This may have led to underestimating certain violations, as alternative tracking techniques—such as HTML5 storage or fingerprinting—were not considered. Consequently, some instances of tracking without consent might not have been detected.

External validity. Regarding external validity, there is a potential concern about how representative the selected EU and US websites are of the broader web. To address this, we chose a diverse set of popular websites from various categories, aiming to provide a balanced and generalizable sample.

6   Discussion and Future Work

Consistent with previous research, our study shows a widespread occurrence of legal violations in cookie banners.

Consent Compliance Across EU and US Websites. The results reveal that all EU and US websites fail to comply with *prior* and *unambiguous* consent. EU websites are statistically less compliant with the *freely-given* consent requirement. In contrast, US websites exhibit lower compliance with *informed, specific,* and *revocable* consent. Our findings complement the one of previous studies on legal compliance of cookie banners [6,8,22,23,26,32,38,39], which focused only on prior, freely-given, and unambiguous consent.

Effectiveness of CMPs. We found that the use of CMPs does not guarantee adherence to GDPR and ePD but websites using CMPs showed slightly better compliance levels than those without CMPs. These findings suggest that while CMPs offer a structured approach to consent management, the flexibility they provide to their customers in configuring cookie banner interfaces may result in violations of GDPR and ePD. Future work should investigate why CMPs fail to enforce compliance with data protection regulations.

User Tracking Despite Consent Choices. We found that both EU and US websites engage in user tracking under No Action and Deny All conditions. This contradicts the GDPR and ePD requirements, which require that tracking should only occur with prior consent. Notably, US websites store more third-party cookies and contact more external domains than EU websites in these conditions. Interestingly, both EU and US websites contact more third-party domains under the No Action condition compared to the Deny All one. This suggests that tracking mechanisms operate independently of user consent actions, raising the need to find alternative methods to enforce consent.

Implications and Future Works. This lack of compliant consent notices on many websites is often driven by incentives rooted in *surveillance capitalism* [40] where companies profit from collecting, analyzing, and monetizing personal data, typically through targeted advertising. By making it difficult for users to refuse or customize their consent, these companies can maximize data collection and revenue. This business model prioritizes data acquisition over user privacy, leading to non-compliance with regulations like GDPR.

To address this issue, data protection authorities need to be equipped with suitable tools to detect and report violations. These tools could continuously scan websites for compliance issues, flagging violations and helping authorities prioritize enforcement actions. We will develop an auditing tool that will combine natural language processing to analyze the text of the cookie banner, machine learning to analyze the design of the cookie banner interface, and cookie and network inspection tools to detect the proposed potential violations.

Acknowledgments. This work was partially supported by project SHIELD (CUP: B53C22003990006) within the research program PE Security and Rights in the CyberSpace – SERICS (PE00000014) under the MUR National Recovery and Resilience Plan funded by the European Union – NextGenerationEU.

References

1. Berens, B.M., Bohlender, M., Dietmann, H., Krisam, C., Kulyk, O., Volkamer, M.: Cookie disclaimers: dark patterns and lack of transparency. Comput. Secur. **136**(C) (2024)
2. Bielova, N., Litvine, L., Nguyen, A., Chammat, M., Toubiana, V., Hary, E.: The effect of design patterns on (present and future) cookie consent decisions. In: Proceedings of the of USENIX Security 24, pp. 2813–2830 (2024)
3. European Data Protection Board: Guidelines 05/2020 on consent under regulation 2016/679 (2020). https://edpb.europa.eu/sites/default/files/files/file1/edpb_guidelines_202005_consent_en.pdf
4. European Data Protection Board: Report of the work undertaken by the cookie banner taskforce (2023). https://edpb.europa.eu/our-work-tools/our-documents/other/report-work-undertaken-cookie-banner-taskforce_en

5. Dabrowski, A., Merzdovnik, G., Ullrich, J., Sendera, G., Weippl, E.: Measuring cookies and web privacy in a post-GDPR world. In: Choffnes, D., Barcellos, M. (eds.) Passive and Active Measurement. Springer (2019)

6. Degeling, M., Utz, C., Lentzsch, C., Hosseini, H., Schaub, F., Holz, T.: We value your privacy ... now take some cookies: measuring the GDPR's impact on web privacy. In: Proceedings of the of NDSS 2019 (2019)

7. Disconnect: Disconnect list (2021). https://github.com/disconnectme/disconnect-tracking-protection

8. Fassl, M., Gröber, L.T., Krombholz, K.: Stop the consent theater. In: Proceedings of CHI 2021 (2021)

9. Duck Duck Go, Inc.: Duckduckgo tracker radar (2023). https://github.com/duckduckgo/tracker-radar

10. Gotze, M., Matic, S., Iordanou, C., Smaragdakis, G., Laoutaris, N.: Measuring web cookies in governmental websites. In: Proceedings of ACM Web Science Conference 2022 (2022)

11. Gray, C.M., Santos, C.T., Bielova, N., Mildner, T.: An ontology of dark patterns knowledge: Foundations, definitions, and a pathway for shared knowledge-building. In: Proceedings of CHI 2024 (2024)

12. Gunawan, J., Pradeep, A., Choffnes, D., Hartzog, W., Wilson, C.: A comparative study of dark patterns across web and mobile modalities. Proc. ACM Hum.-Comput. Interact. 5(CSCW2), 1–29 (2021)

13. Kampanos, G., Shahandashti, S.F.: Accept all: the landscape of cookie banners in Greece and the UK. In: Jøsang, A., Futcher, L., Hagen, J. (eds.) ICT Systems Security and Privacy Protection (2021)

14. Kollnig, K.: X-ray blacklist (2022). https://github.com/TrackerControl/tracker-controlandroid/blob/master/app/src/main/assets/xray-blacklist.json

15. Krisam, C., Dietmann, H., Volkamer, M., Kulyk, O.: Dark patterns in the wild: review of cookie disclaimer designs on top 500 German websites. In: Proceedings of the SOUPS 2021, pp. 1–8 (2021)

16. Kulyk, O., Hilt, A., Gerber, N., Volkamer, M.: This website uses cookies: users' perceptions and reactions to the cookie disclaimer. In: Proceedings of EuroUSEC (2018)

17. Kwakman, J.: Open cookie database (2021). https://github.com/jkwakman/Open-Cookie-Database

18. Le Pochat, V., Van Goethem, T., Tajalizadehkhoob, S., Korczyński, M., Joosen, W.: Tranco: a research-oriented top sites ranking hardened against manipulation. In: Proceedings of NDSS 2019 (2019)

19. Lee, D., Joo, M., Lee, W.: Net-track: generic web tracking detection using packet metadata. In: Proceedings of WWW 2023, pp. 2230–2240 (2023)

20. Musarubra US LLC: Customer URL ticketing system (2024). https://trustedsource.org/

21. Objectis Ltd.: Cookie script. https://cookie-script.com/

22. Machuletz, D., Böhme, R.: Multiple purposes, multiple problems: a user study of consent dialogs after GDPR. Proc. Priv. Enhancing Technol. 2020, 481–498 (2019)

23. Matte, C., Bielova, N., Santos, C.: Do cookie banners respect my choice? Measuring legal compliance of banners from IAB Europe's transparency and consent framework. In: IEEE Symposium on Security and Privacy (SP) (2020)

24. Nguyen, T.T., Backes, M., Marnau, N., Stock, B.: Share first, ask later (or never?) studying violations of GDPR's explicit consent in android apps. In: USENIX Security 21, pp. 3667–3684 (2021)

25. Nguyen, T.T., Backes, M., Stock, B.: Freely given consent? Studying consent notice of third-party tracking and its violations of GDPR in android apps. In: Proceedings of CCS 2022, pp. 2369–2383 (2022)
26. Nouwens, M., Liccardi, I., Veale, M., Karger, D.R., Kagal, L.: Dark patterns after the GDPR: scraping consent pop-ups and demonstrating their influence (2020)
27. Paci, F., Pizzoli, J., Zannone, N.: A comprehensive study on third-party user tracking in mobile applications. In: Proceedings of ARES 2023 (2023)
28. Papadogiannakis, E., Papadopoulos, P., Kourtellis, N., Markatos, E.P.: User tracking in the post-cookie era: How websites bypass GDPR consent to track users. In: Proceedings of WWW 2021 (2021)
29. Garante Privacy: Guidelines on the use of cookies and other tracking tools (2021). https://www.garanteprivacy.it/home/docweb/-/docweb-display/docweb/9677876#english
30. Sharpe, R., Warnicke, E., Lamping, U.: Wireshark user's guide (2024). https://www.wireshark.org/
31. Samarasinghe, N., Adhikari, A., Mannan, M., Youssef, A.: Et tu, Brute? Privacy analysis of government websites and mobile apps. In: WWW '22 (2022)
32. Sanchez-Rola, I., et al.: Can I opt out yet? GDPR and the global illusion of cookie control. In: Proceedings of CCS 2019, pp. 340–351 (2019)
33. Santos, C., Bielova, N., Matte, C.: Are cookie banners indeed compliant with the law? Deciphering EU legal requirements on consent and technical means to verify compliance of cookie banners. Technol. Regul., 91–135 (2020)
34. Santos, C., Rossi, A., Sanchez Chamorro, L., Bongard-Blanchy, K., Abu-Salma, R.: Cookie banners, what's the purpose? Analyzing cookie banner text through a legal lens. In: Proceedings of WPES, pp. 187–194 (2021)
35. Singh, N., Do, Y., Yu, Y., Fouad, I., Kim, J., Kim, H.: Crumbled cookies: exploring e-commerce websites' cookie policies with data protection regulations (2025)
36. Soe, T.H., Nordberg, O.E., Guribye, F., Slavkovik, M.: Circumvention by design - dark patterns in cookie consent for online news outlets. In: NordCHI '20 (2020)
37. Soe, T.H., Santos, C.T., Slavkovik, M.: Automated detection of dark patterns in cookie banners: how to do it poorly and why it is hard to do it any other way (2022)
38. Trevisan, M., Traverso, S., Metwalley, H., Mellia, M.: 4 years of EU cookie law: results and lessons learned. Proc. Priv. Enhancing Technol. **2019**, 126–145 (2019)
39. Utz, C., Degeling, M., Fahl, S., Schaub, F., Holz, T.: (Un)informed consent: studying GDPR consent notices in the field. In: Proceedings of CCS 2019, pp. 973–990 (2019)
40. Zuboff, S.: The Age of Surveillance Capitalism: The Fight for a Human Future at the New Frontier of Power. PublicAffairs (2019)

Large-Scale Security Analysis of Hardware Wallets

Milan Šorf$^{(\boxtimes)}$ ⓘ, Petr Švenda ⓘ, and Łukasz Chmielewski ⓘ

Masaryk University, Brno, Czechia
{xsorf,svenda,chmiel}@fi.muni.cz

Abstract. Cryptocurrency hardware wallets (HWWs) are dedicated offline devices that securely store cryptographic keys and perform internal message signing to prevent key exposure. Signing typically requires physical user interaction – such as pressing a button or using a fingerprint sensor – which provides strong protection against compromised hosts. However, this physical requirement significantly hinders independent, automated testing on real devices, often forcing reliance on software emulators or vendor claims.

We introduce a low-cost, fully automated, and reproducible testing platform to address this limitation. The platform replicates essential human interactions, including physical button presses and touchscreen inputs, incorporates Optical Character Recognition (OCR) for extracting screen content, and records precise timing metadata. These capabilities enable us to perform a comprehensive evaluation of HWWs.

Using this automated platform, we collected a dataset containing 3.4 million wallet recovery phrases, 3.4 million Elliptic Curve Digital Signature Algorithm (ECDSA) signatures, and the corresponding timing measurements. Data acquisition was performed on 17 hardware wallet models from 11 different vendors, using firmware versions available in 2023 and in 2025 to enable a comparative analysis. The data examination revealed several details about internal implementation characteristics, yet no significant cryptographic weaknesses were identified. This outcome is particularly interesting given the recent emergence of elliptic-curve cryptography (ECC) vulnerabilities, such as TPM-Fail, Minerva, or TPM-Scan, for example. Several factors are proposed to explain the comparatively stronger security posture observed in HWWs, including domain-specific design choices and operational constraints that may provide inherent resilience, even in the absence of formal certification processes.

Keywords: Hardware wallets · TRNG · ECDSA · Robotic testing

1 Introduction

The domain of cryptocurrencies requires strong protection of the cryptographic keys used to authorize digital asset transfer due to the finality of its settlement. As demonstrated by a large number of security incidents over the years [44],

B. Coppens et al. (Eds.): ARES 2025 Workshops, LNCS 15995, pp. 360–377, 2025.
https://doi.org/10.1007/978-3-032-00633-2_21

storing private keys on common devices like desktop computers or mobile phones with a large trusted computing base is prone to malware compromise. In response, purpose-built hardware wallets, such as Trezor [46], Ledger [22], and ColdCard [8], have emerged. Such a signing device typically generates, stores, and uses cryptographic keys while requiring explicit user confirmation of the operation shown on the built-in screen. Due to the value of digital assets controlled by such a device, its implementation correctness is crucial and shall undergo increased scrutiny. Additionally, the intentional backdoors, whether inserted by vendors or introduced by third parties during the device supply chain, happened in the past [35] and pose a significant risk.

Many vendors adopt open-source practices for transparency, but source code availability alone does not guarantee security. Bugs may persist, published code may not match installed binaries, and proprietary components or third-party restrictions often limit openness. Hardware design is similarly fragmented, lacking standardization and open components, leading to diverse implementations in form, interface, and security features—all requiring user interaction. Formal certifications like Common Criteria [6] or FIPS 140 [40] remain rare due to cost.

Given the situation, independent security testing, ideally carried out by end-users after receiving their own physical device, is highly desirable. Yet the manual physical authorization of every signing operation on the device not only increases the security against a compromised host computer but also hinders easy automated testing. To overcome these challenges, we developed a low-cost robotic system that emulates user interaction, enabling automated, repeatable testing of wallets. This system captures both visual outputs (e.g., recovery phrases) and timing metadata during cryptographic operations. By evaluating multiple devices and firmware versions, we can track security-relevant changes over time, forming the basis for a comprehensive, reproducible analysis of hardware wallets and guiding the following **research questions**:

RQ1: How is large-scale automated black box testing feasible for hardware wallets with a variety of physical and procedural designs in a cost-effective, replicable, and adaptable manner?

RQ2: Can we detect statistically significant biases in the initial wallet seed in the ECDSA signature nonces and recover corresponding design choices for some black box implementations?

Contributions. To answer our research questions, we contribute the following:

- Low-cost robotic system automating interactions with hardware wallets with information shown only on the built-in screen, press, touch, or fingerprint buttons to confirm any operation and with timing metadata collection capability (Sect. 3);
- Data-based analysis of cryptographic operations executed during initial wallet seed generation and ECDSA signature computation of 17 different wallets from 11 vendors, each with 200 thousand repetitions (Sect. 4 and 5);

– Discussion of reasons behind the lack of ECDSA observed cryptographic
weakness in comparison to domains of certified smartcards, TPMs, and cryptographic libraries (Sect. 6).

The data collection and processing tooling and all collected results are available under a permissive license at https://github.com/crocs-muni/wallet-scan
and https://github.com/crocs-muni/wallet-scan_results.

1.1 Related Work

The following studies have addressed large-scale security testing of cryptographic and IoT devices, particularly focusing on vulnerabilities emerging from
improper implementation and side-channel attacks. A large-scale testbed framework specifically aimed at IoT devices was presented in [37]. The framework
combines conventional techniques such as port scanning, fingerprinting, process
enumeration, and fuzz testing with advanced methods based on machine learning to identify vulnerabilities and compromised devices. It employs traffic-based
IoT device type identification and anomaly detection to uncover compromised
devices based on deviations in network behavior. Through extensive testing of
devices like smart cameras, smart speakers, and printers, the testbed effectively
identified open ports, weak authentication mechanisms, outdated software components, and behavioral anomalies. We attempt to develop a similar approach
for hardware wallets.

Similar work on large-scale security testing was also done in the context
of Trusted Platform Modules (TPMs). TPMScan [41] analysis focuses on 78
TPM 2.0 implementations from 6 different vendors. They identify numerous
previously unreported vulnerabilities, such as nonce leakage in ECC algorithms
(ECDSA, ECSCHNORR, ECDAA), including severe issues that allow private
key extraction from certain Intel fTPMs using as few as nine signatures without
requiring additional side-channel information. The study highlights the opaque
nature of TPM ecosystems, emphasizing frequent inconsistencies in vulnerability
handling and patching by manufacturers, despite extensive certification efforts.

In [11], the authors asses hardware wallet architectures, revealing fundamental security flaws due to their reliance on single points of trust. They illustrate that standard initialization and attestation methods fail to effectively safeguard against supply-chain attacks and suggest architectural modifications. The
proposed approach emphasizes collaborative cryptographic protocols, such as
mutual verification during key generation and transaction signing, to eliminate
single points of trust and significantly enhance wallet security against various
tampering scenarios.

Individual devices have been compromised through different approaches, such
as the side-channel analysis of the Trezor One [29], where physical phenomena
like power consumption and electromagnetic emanation were exploited to extract
sensitive data. These experiments enabled the successful recovery of PIN authentication data and ECDSA private keys with minimal physical interaction. Kraken
Security Labs conducted a voltage glitching attack that bypassed the Trezor's

microcontroller protections, enabling full seed phrase extraction in under 15 min using inexpensive tools [21]. Similarly, Ledger's Donjon team published several critical findings, including an unpatchable flaw in Trezor's memory access that allowed for deterministic key recovery [12]. Independent researchers, such as Colin O'Flynn, also demonstrated the feasibility of extracting secrets via electromagnetic fault injection (EMFI) through the enclosure without disassembly [26]. Collectively, these attacks underline the persistent security gaps in hardware wallet implementations and the urgent need for more robust, tamper-resistant countermeasures [13]. While the examples listed here are among the most well-documented, they represent only a subset of known and potential attack vectors as they all required manual inspection and testing of individual devices. In this work, we propose a universal, automated system for interacting with hardware wallets, enabling large-scale analysis of potential vulnerabilities.

The Minerva attack [19] exploited noisy leakage of the bit-length of ECDSA nonces to extract the ECC private key. Similarly, TPM-Fail [24] is an attack leveraging timing leakage in TPM 2.0 chips during elliptic curve cryptography (ECC) signature generation. Their black-box timing analysis demonstrates vulnerabilities in firmware-based TPMs (Intel fTPMs) and discrete TPMs (STMicroelectronics dTPMs), allowing recovery of ECDSA private keys through lattice attacks from devices with CC EAL4+ security level. This work also includes practical demonstrations, such as remotely compromising a VPN server's authentication mechanism by exploiting the vulnerabilities.

2 Hardware Wallets Background

Cryptocurrency hardware wallets are specialized devices designed to address two challenges: (1) securely storing the cryptographic keys that control digital assets, and (2) using these keys to sign transactions without exposing them to potentially compromised environments. To meet these challenges, wallet developers have adopted a range of technologies and design principles. There is no unified method of communication with the wallet; the approaches we encountered are listed in Table 1.

2.1 Core Design Features

Separated Key Storage: The keys are stored in a secure, isolated environment within the device, ensuring that they never leave the hardware.
Possibility of Recovery: Despite the need for isolated key storage, providing a secure recovery mechanism is essential for users, as it enables the restoration of funds in the event of device failure or loss.
Limited Connectivity: Reducing the communication channels available to the device minimizes potential attack vectors, thereby increasing overall security.
Transaction Details Display: A dedicated display enables users to verify the details of a transaction directly on the device, ensuring that they are aware of what is being signed.

Advanced Features: Many wallets now support sophisticated functionalities, such as handling Partially Signed Bitcoin Transactions (PSBTs).

2.2   Other Security Aspects

In addition to these core features, other aspects are important in understanding the overall context and security requirements of hardware wallets:

Threat Model and Security Objectives: Hardware wallets are designed to resist physical tampering, side-channel attacks, and supply chain threats. Their main goal is to keep cryptographic keys secure, even in hostile environments, by isolating key storage and minimizing external communication.

Hardware and Software Architecture: Most hardware wallets use secure elements or microcontrollers for cryptographic tasks, with firmware operating independently from the host system.

Usability and Human Factors: User interaction is a critical component of hardware wallet security. Most devices require direct physical input, such as pressing buttons, using fingerprint sensors, or interacting with a touchscreen to confirm transactions. This human element adds a layer of protection by ensuring that only authorized transactions are executed.

Regulatory and Standardization Considerations: Unlike many other security-critical systems, hardware wallets currently lack widely adopted industry standards or regulatory certifications. This absence of a unified framework makes it difficult for users to directly compare the security guarantees of different devices. The development of replicable and automated testing methods is therefore essential for establishing benchmarks and improving transparency across the market.

Backup Mechanism: Backups are critical to the recoverability of hardware wallets. The most common method is the BIP39 recovery phrase [27]. Some wallets implement proprietary or alternative backup methods. For instance, encrypted backups on a micro SD card or QR code-based backups. These methods can offer enhanced usability and reduce attack surfaces associated with USB or Bluetooth communication, but potentially introduce vendor lock-in or hardware dependencies.

2.3   Recovery Phrase

A *recovery phrase*, also known as a *recovery seed*, or a *mnemonic phrase*, is a sequence of words from a standardized list of 2048 terms [27] that serves as a backup for a cryptocurrency wallet. It is crucial for restoring access to funds if the wallet is lost, damaged, reset or for moving to another device. When a new wallet is created, it generates a recovery phrase by randomly selecting words from the given list. This system is codified by BIP-39 [27], which strongly recommends using the English wordlist, which is the only one supported by most wallets at the time of writing. Users are advised to store this phrase securely, as it used to derive the wallet seed, allowing direct access to the wallet contents.

The recovery phrase encodes entropy ENT in multiples of 32 bits, ranging from 128 to 256 bits. Greater entropy results in a more secure (but longer) phrase. The key derivation process described here is reversible, allowing us access to the random generator output.

After selecting the desired length (12, 18, or 24 words), the wallet's random number generator creates the initial entropy of ENT bits. Next, a checksum is calculated by taking the first $\frac{ENT}{32}$ bits of the SHA256 hash of the entropy and appending it to the initial entropy. The result is divided into groups of 11 bits, each representing an index in the wordlist. A space-separated list of these words forms the *mnemonic sentence*.

The recovery phrase is used for the remainder of the seed derivation process, rather than the binary representation. Users can provide an optional passphrase for the mnemonic sentence. Both the mnemonic sentence and passphrase can be non-English strings, so text normalization is necessary to account for different Unicode representations.

To derive a binary seed from the mnemonic, both the mnemonic sentence and the passphrase (if used) are converted to UTF-8 NFKD form. The PBKDF2 function [20] then processes the mnemonic sentence as the password, using the string "mnemonic" concatenated with the passphrase (which is an empty string if no passphrase is specified) as the salt, with an 2048 iterations of HMAC-SHA512 function. The derived seed is 512 bits long.

Since generating the mnemonic sentence and deriving the seed are separate processes, implementing new wordlists is straightforward. However, it is strongly discouraged, and as a result, the majority of BIP-39 wallets support only the English wordlist.

2.4   Signing Messages

ECDSA with the secp256k1 curve is the dominant approach across cryptocurrencies [7]. Since all tested wallets supported Bitcoin (which also uses this curve), we focus on this algorithm.

To sign a message, three values are needed: a nonce k (introduces randomness), a message hash z (typically SHA-256), and a private key d (stored in the wallet). First, compute the point $R = kG$, and extract its x-coordinate $r = R_x \bmod n$. Then compute $s = k^{-1}(z + dr) \bmod n$, where k^{-1} denotes the modular inverse. The resulting signature is the pair $S = (r, s)$ and verification succeeds if $(s^{-1}z)G + (s^{-1}r)Q = R$, where Q is the public key.

The nonce value is critical for the security of the signature. Several attacks have shown that a reused or weak nonce can allow an adversary to recover the private key [3,10,23]. Because the nonce is random, even if the same message is signed, the signatures are different.

Another approach is to use deterministic nonce generation as specified in RFC6979 [30], where the nonce is derived directly from the message and the private key. This method removes the dependency on a random number generator but introduces a different set of challenges. Deterministic schemes carry a higher risk of nonce reuse and offer reduced robustness, as malicious participants may attempt to manipulate the nonce-generation process.

3   Low-Cost Automated Physical Wallet Testing

Hardware wallets require human interaction for operations like seed generation and transaction confirmation, which complicates automated security analysis. Key steps such as initiating wallet setup, backing up the mnemonic, and verifying the seed typically depend on manual input. Likewise, confirming transactions via button presses or biometric input emphasizes the reliance on physical interaction.

To scale our evaluation across thousands of seeds and signatures, we developed 17 automation robots that simulate user actions. These systems physically interact with wallets by pressing buttons, operating touchscreens, and bypassing fingerprint checks. Integrated cameras and OCR [38] enable screen reading and behavioral monitoring, allowing tasks like recovery phrase capture or code repetition to be automated. This setup supports efficient, long-term data collection without human intervention and can be adapted for future devices.

3.1   System Overview

Our system includes coordination software running on a PC, which automates message signing, collects signatures, and records operation timing. Most wallets are controlled via Python scripts and Electrum [14], but for unsupported wallets, we rely on vendor-provided software, automated using similar scripting methods. This approach ensures compatibility with any hardware wallet regardless of native software support.

To replicate typical user interactions such as reading on-screen messages, pressing buttons, or restarting devices, we use custom-built robots tailored to each wallet's physical design. These robots automate navigation, confirm transactions, and capture on-device data (e.g., recovery phrases), with variations based on display and control differences across devices.

HWW Automation. Hardware wallets use a range of displays, from monochrome screens to full-color touchscreens. We capture on-device information like recovery phrases using a camera, with OCR software processing the output to navigate menus, read messages, and extract text. To improve timing precision, we also use a microphone (assuming an attacker could access it via a compromised host) to detect button press sounds, supplementing USB-based timing.

Each wallet is paired with a custom testing profile specifying the input sequences (buttons or touch gestures) needed for operation. These profiles allow our system to mimic user behavior and automate interaction.

For wallets with physical buttons, SG90 servo motors simulate presses, and a fingerprint module bypasses biometric authentication. For touchscreen wallets, conductive contacts emulate user input at predefined screen locations.

None of the tested wallets implemented liveness detection: all accepted silicone fingerprint forgeries, which could be enrolled and reused for automation.

Processing Software. The OCR is performed using Google's Tesseract-OCR Engine [38]. After gathering the data, we perform statistical analysis using the Dieharder test suite [4], Booltest [43], rngtest [34] (implementation of FIPS-140 [39] tests), and the NIST test suite [33]. These state-of-the-art test batteries aim to detect bias and distinguish between pseudo-random and random data.

Robot System. We present two configurations of our prototype modular setup and a universal 3D-printable version in Fig. 1.

Our setup includes four integrated modules. The **Visual Information Extraction Module** uses a camera to capture wallet display output, with a Raspberry Pi optionally processing images to extract text and detect state changes. The **Physical Interaction Module** performs input through servo-actuated button presses, a wire grid for touchscreen interaction, and a fingerprint emulator for biometric wallets. The **Control and Coordination Module** is managed by a Raspberry Pi, which orchestrates workflows, processes visual input, and runs automation scripts; an Arduino Uno ensures real-time actuator precision, and a USB sniffer monitors communication with the host computer. Finally, the **Side-channel Analysis Module** captures timing data using a camera (visual), servo feedback (mechanical), a microphone (auditory), and USB traffic (digital). The modularity of this design allows easy adaptation to wallets with varying physical and interface requirements. With the 3D-printable version, only standardized parts like screws, cameras, and the microcontrollers are required to replicate the setup.

3.2   Timing Metadata Precision

Accurate timing measurements are critical for our side-channel investigations. Depending on the measurement method used, the achievable precision and reliability can vary. To address this, we employ three distinct strategies: software-based communication timing, visual response timing, and actuator-based physical timing. Each of these methods offers different trade-offs in terms of resolution, complexity, and applicability, which we evaluate in the following paragraphs.

Full Software Communication Timing. This method measures the time from sending a command on the host to receiving the wallet's response, covering USB latency, processing, and internal delays. It is easy to implement, but limited to USB-enabled wallets. The results are imprecise, as they include operations often unrelated to security analysis.

Visual Response Timing. For this approach, we use a camera. Depending on the model, cameras running at 60 fps provide a maximal timing resolution of approximately 16.67 milliseconds between frames. Cameras capable of recording at 240 fps improve this resolution to 4.17 milliseconds, making it possible to identify when screen changes occur with finer granularity. By focusing on screen changes, we can get more granular timings if the operation includes multiple steps performed on the wallet before sending data back to the computer. This method measures the time elapsed between two screen changes. Our setup uses Raspberry Pi Camera Modules [1, 16, 17]. The system can also use a USB camera.

Actuator Timing and Consistency. We explored using actuator-triggered button presses as a timing reference. Our system employs SG90 servo motors [45]. To assess their timing consistency, we modified actuator tips to be electrically conductive and measured the delay between the actuation signal and contact with the button surface.

Across 1,000 cycles on 12 servos (three angles each), timing variability ranged from 17âĂŞ32 microseconds, with an average deviation of approximately 25 microseconds, indicating highly consistent accuracy despite the servos' low cost; these results align with prior findings [28]. This reliability enables accurate timing measurements from actuation onset. When combined with visual response timing, it yields high precision across both mechanical and touchscreen devices, where actuators are replaced by conductive touchpoints.

4   Large-Scale Data Collection Experiments

This section describes the data-gathering process and the experiments performed, including encountered difficulties and details about some unexpected behaviors of the examined wallets.

4.1   Gathering Data

Our data collection scenarios focus on the security of Random Number Generators (RNG), a foundational element for generating both wallet seeds and nonces for the ECDSA signatures. Additionally, we evaluate how these wallets handle input normalization.

Collected Data. We collected 3.4 million recovery phrases, message signatures, and timing records, split evenly across two firmware versions to assess potential changes. Simulated user interactions subjected wallets to sustained stress well beyond typical usage. Collection times varied depending on security features like fingerprint sensors or shake-based RNG initialization. On average, generating a wallet took 70 s, and signing a message took 15 s. Data collection spanned 160 days.

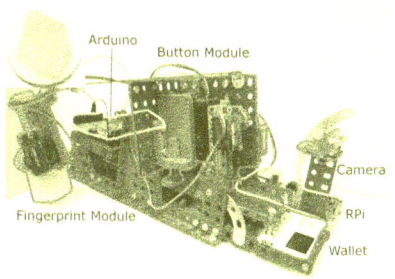
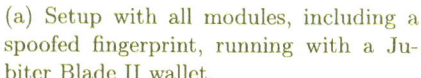

(a) Setup with all modules, including a spoofed fingerprint, running with a Jubiter Blade II wallet.

(b) A smaller combination, only with a camera, button module, and a USB sniffer, with Trezor 3.

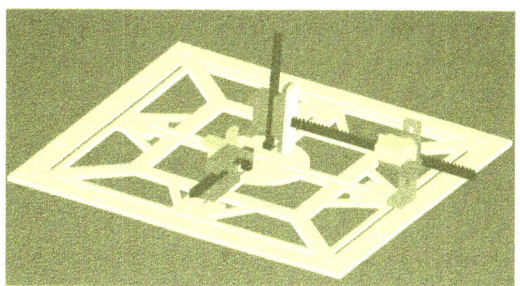

(c) A 3D-printable version for replication.

(d) A 3D-printed actuator arm.

Fig. 1. Fully assembled testing robot prototypes for different types of wallet interfaces. We have also designed a universal 3D-printable version for easy replication.

Recovery Phrases. We used 24-word recovery phrases to maximize data collection, as each of the first 23 words encodes 11 bits of RNG output, with the last serving as a checksum. Some wallets, like Trezor T and Trezor 3, only supported 12-word phrases during testing, so we collected 200,000 samples instead of 100,000; these models now support 24-word phrases. BC Vault does not support recovery phrases.

4.2   Unicode Text Normalization

When collecting text data a text normalization is important. NFKD (Normalization Form KD) is a Unicode normalization process that transforms text into a standardized form using *compatibility decomposition*. This ensures that characters with the same meaning but different binary representations (e.g., ligatures or accented letters) are converted into a consistent form [9].

In cryptographic applications like wallet seed generation, where exact byte-level consistency is critical, NFKD normalization prevents inconsistencies caused by alternative Unicode representations. Without normalization, two inputs that appear identical to a user could produce entirely different outputs. NFKD ensures that inputs are both semantically and structurally uniform before encoding them (typically in UTF-8) and processing them further.

We generate wallets with passphrases containing characters requiring normalization and verify that the wallet is created and can be accessed correctly. The expected behavior is that all character combinations leading to displaying the same string should be interchangeable. With the exception of BC Vault, all tested wallets were capable of correctly normalizing Unicode passwords. After contacting the BC Vault team, their response was that this issue is not critical.

4.3   Practical Experiences in Building Automation Systems

Below, we highlight key challenges encountered during development of multiple automation systems.

Creating Templates. Each new wallet required manual analysis of its controls and menus to create an interaction template. These templates define button layouts, expected screen flows, and helper functions to standardize wallet-specific interactions. Setup typically takes tens of minutes, after which automation can handle navigation and recognition tasks.

Servo Failures. Mechanical failures of servos disrupted data collection and required replacements, causing delays.

Space and Power Constraints. Scaling the system to 17 Raspberry Pis, matching Arduinos, and numerous servos increased demands on space and power, limiting portability outside dedicated lab environments.

Firmware Upgrades. Firmware updates were handled manually, as update processes were not included in automation.

4.4   Non-Standard/Unexpected Behavior of Wallets

BC Vault. BC Vault uses an accelerometer to seed its RNG, avoiding proprietary chips [49]. While it lacks multisig support, it enables shared control via four distinct passwords—two entered on a computer and two on the device [48].

Unlike wallets with alphanumeric passwords, BC Vault uses only directional inputs (up, down, left, right), significantly reducing password entropy. Achieving the equivalent strength of a 6-character lowercase password requires at least 14 directional inputs.

Trezor. The Trezor One wallet requires PIN entry via a computer, while displaying a randomized keypad layout on the wallet screen. Trezor Model T uses a similar layout randomization, but input is provided directly on its touchscreen. These are the only tested wallets that attempt to mitigate eavesdropping and keylogging on the computer side, providing additional security against these attack vectors.

D'CENT + Keevo Model 1. Both wallets feature fingerprint sensors. They require users to authenticate with both a fingerprint and a password, increasing the security by using another authentication factor.

Bitbox02. This was the only tested wallet that did not use deterministic nonces. In one early measurement, we observed a higher-than-expected number of high-value bytes. However, after ten additional rounds of testing (100,000 nonces each), we were unable to replicate the result. The Bitbox02 wallet has since replaced its secure element (Microchip ATECC608A) with a newer version, the ATECC608B, citing "additional security" [2] (Fig. 2).

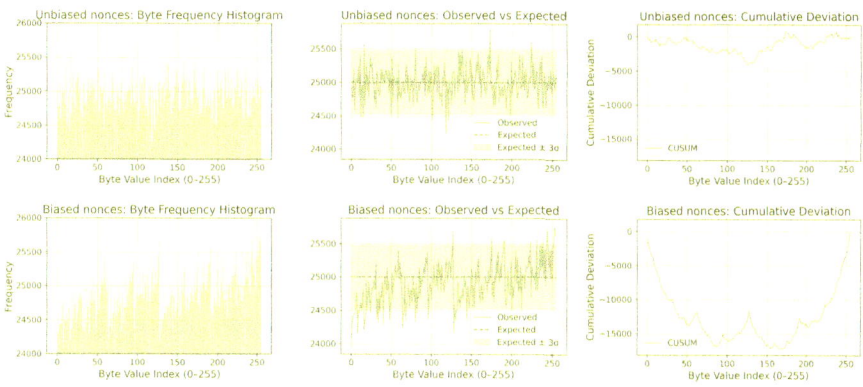

Fig. 2. Byte-wise analysis of BitBox02 nonces. The top row shows consistent, unbiased measurements; the bottom row shows a one-time, unreproducible biased sample with an elevated number of high-value bytes.

5   Analysis of Extracted Wallet Data

After preprocessing, the binary values were tested using the Dieharder test suite [4], Booltest [43], rngtest [34], and the NIST test suite.

Mnemonic Phrases. We extracted RNG outputs from mnemonic phrases and tested them using the above-mentioned suites, finding no significant entropy issues. Most wallets showed constant-time behavior, with the exception of Trezor devices, which exhibited timing variation. However, these variations were not linked to detectable entropy weaknesses. Results are summarized in Table 1.

Signatures and Nonces. ECDSA security relies on unpredictable nonces. We analyzed nonce generation in various wallets and found that sixteen used RFC 6979, ensuring deterministic, bias-free nonces. With both the message and signing key known, we verified nonce correctness by recalculating expected values. BitBox02 used a nondeterministic approach and showed one non-reproducible anomaly. Overall, statistical analysis revealed no significant deviations, confirming the reliability of deterministic nonce generation in most wallets.

Side-Channel Evaluation. Timing measurements are essential for identifying side-channel vulnerabilities. We evaluated operation latency across multiple dimensions: screen update delays (via high-speed cameras), actuator response, and USB communication. Our setup offers ~4 ms resolution by combining the actuator response and a 240 fps camera. This is less precise than specialized nanosecond-scale systems [15], but sufficient for detecting major timing flaws.

No statistically significant vulnerabilities were found under typical conditions. However, timing differences across devices and firmware versions suggest subtle implementation variances, highlighting the need for consistent, secure engineering practices.

Summary of Findings. Our analysis found that tested wallets generally uphold strong security, driven by widespread use of deterministic nonces and robust entropy handling for mnemonic creation. While current implementations appear resilient, regular automated testing remains vital to sustain security as threats evolve. Our findings are summarized in Table 1.

6   Comparison with Other Security Domains

Our extensive analysis of TRNG and ECC implementations in hardware wallets enables comparison with similar domains—such as cryptographic smartcards [19, 25, 31, 32, 36, 42], TPMs [24, 41], and embedded cryptographic libraries [5, 18, 19], where numerous vulnerabilities have been found. Despite applying similar probing and statistical methods to a broad set of devices, we observed only a minor, likely non-exploitable entropy issue in one wallet. This is especially surprising given that hardware wallets typically lack formal certification (e.g., Common Criteria or FIPS 140). We suggest five key reasons for this discrepancy:

1. **Restricted set of exposed cryptographic functions:** Smartcards and TPMs expose a wide range of cryptographic operations to support general use cases, increasing the attack surface. In contrast, hardware wallets are purpose-built for limited tasks and restrict available functions, typically to a few fixed operations like ECDSA over secp256k1. This reduces the likelihood of exploitable misconfigurations or low-level attacks.
2. **Post-processing TRNG output with hashing:** The BIP-32 [50] protocol recommends hashing initial entropy from the TRNG to whiten potential

Table 1. Summary of wallet characteristics and data gathered

Wallet Name	Firmware 2023	Firmware 2025	Interface[a]	Det.[b]	Time[c]	Sig.[d]	Notes
CoolWallet	332	341	BT	✓	const	200k	single button, menu in app
ELLIPAL	3.7.0	4.5.0	QR	✓	const	200k	
BC Vault	1.8.3	2.3.5	USB	✓	const	N/A	4 passwords replace multisig, 4-character passwords
BitBox02	9.13.0	9.22.0	USB	✗	const	1.2M[e]	male USB connector
JuBiter Blade II[f]	2.5.0	2.5.0	USB	✓	const	200k	unavailable
Keevo Model 1	1.16.0	3.3.2	USB	✓	const	200k	fingerprint sensor, removable encrypted memory
Ledger Nano S[g]	2.1.0	2.1.0	USB	✓	const	200k	retired
Ledger Nano S Plus	1.1.0	1.3.2	USB	✓	const	200k	
Trezor Safe 3	2.6.3	2.8.7	USB	✓	real	200k	eavesdropping protection
Trezor Model One	1.12.1	1.13.0	USB	✓	real	200k	eavesdropping protection
Trezor Model T	2.6.0	2.8.7	USB	✓	real	200k	
SecuX W10	2.13	2.34	USB	✓	const	200k	same firmware for all SecuX wallets
D'CENT	2.24.0	2.34.2	USB / BT	✓	const	200k	fingerprint sensor
Ledger Nano X	2.1.0	2.4.2	USB / BT	✓	const	200k	
SafePal S1	1.0.47	1.0.68	USB / BT	✓	const	200k	
SecuX V10	1.83	2.34	USB / BT	✓	const	200k	same firmware for all SecuX wallets
SecuX W20	2.12	2.34	USB / BT	✓	const	200k	same firmware for all SecuX wallets

[a] BT stands for Bluetooth.
[b] The wallet generates deterministic nonces.
[c] "const" means that the time remains constant across trials, and "real" means that we observed differences in time.
[d] Number of signatures gathered.
[e] Another million signatures were collected to try and replicate the observed bias.
[f] The application was removed from the Google Play Store, and the website is no longer functional.
[g] The device was retired, with the latest firmware released in November 2021.

Remarks: For all timing measurements, we used the actuator + video measurement method with a resolution of approximately 4 ms. We also always gathered 200k recovery seeds.

biases. Although some wallets may skip this step for a minor performance gain (typically <3ms), there's little incentive to do so. Regardless, private and public keys are deterministically derived using HMAC-SHA512, which is required for compatibility with other wallets.

3. **Use of RFC 6979 deterministic nonces:** Vulnerabilities in ECC signing often stem from biased or predictable nonces, enabling private key recovery via lattice-based attacks. As shown in Sect. 5, nearly all hardware wallets adopt RFC 6979 [30] deterministic nonces, fully mitigating this risk. In contrast, no smartcard or TPM tested in prior work [19,24,41] implemented this

defense. Adoption of RFC 6979 effectively eliminates this common attack vector in hardware wallets.

4. **High-quality open-source implementations with permissive licenses:** Unlike proprietary cryptographic modules in smartcards and TPMs, most hardware wallets today are open-source. Trezor [47], the first widely adopted hardware wallet, is fully open-sourced under the permissive MIT license, enabling reuse even in closed-source products. New vendors can adopt mature, side-channel-hardened code instead of developing their own. Shared codebases also allow faster patching of vulnerabilities across vendors—an option unavailable with proprietary implementations.

5. **Disincentives in certified implementations:** Certification schemes like Common Criteria or FIPS 140 can discourage updates to hardware wallet code, as changes often require costly re-certification. While critical vulnerabilities are typically addressed[1], non-critical, defensive improvements are often delayed until a major product revision. This increases the risk of future exploits, as evolving attack techniques target outdated, insufficiently hardened code.

We believe the above reasons not only explain the limited negative findings in our analysis despite using similar methods and a large sample as past studies, but also offer guidance for building more secure cryptographic implementations and identifying risk factors, such as fragmented proprietary ecosystems.

7   Conclusions

This paper addresses the problem of low-cost blackbox testing of functionality and cryptographic implementations on devices that intentionally prevent controlling the computer running the testing suite to see their internal state – with a focus on cryptocurrency hardware wallets. We built an accessible setup able to test a range of devices with different physical controlling mechanisms, with easy parallelization and deployability due to the low cost of a single setup unit.

Using duplicated setups, we tested 17 HWWs from 11 vendors loaded with firmware revisions from 2023 and again from 2025. Tested wallets were subjected to automatic 200 000 iterations of new wallet creation and ECDSA signature generation, practically unachievable by a human operator. Surprisingly, given the significant number of past vulnerabilities from related domains, we found no serious cryptographic weakness. The differences in the cryptocurrency wallets identified in this paper may help to improve security for related domains as well.

Acknowledgments. The Ai-SecTools (VJ02010010) project supported this work.

Disclosure of Interests. The authors have no competing interests to declare that are relevant to the content of this article.

---

[1] Vendors may alternatively revise usage conditions or move affected components outside certification scope, as seen with the EUCLeak vulnerability [31].

References

1. ArduCam: Arducam raspberry pi camera solution (2025). https://www.arducam.com/raspberry-pi-camera-solution/
2. BitBox: Bitbox 05.2021 Masnee update (2021). https://bitbox.swiss/blog/bitbox-05-2021-masnee-update/#check-your-secure-chip-variant
3. Breitner, J., Heninger, N.: Biased nonce sense: lattice attacks against weak ECDSA signatures in cryptocurrencies. In: Goldberg, I., Moore, T. (eds.) FC 2019. LNCS, vol. 11598, pp. 3–20. Springer, Cham (2019). https://doi.org/10.1007/978-3-030-32101-7_1
4. Brown, R.G., et al.: Dieharder: a random number test suite (nd), computer software, version 3.31.1. https://webhome.phy.duke.edu/~rgb/General/dieharder.php
5. Brumley, B.B., Barbosa, M., Page, D., Vercauteren, F.: Practical realisation and elimination of an ECC-related software bug attack. In: Dunkelman, O. (ed.) Topics in Cryptology – CT-RSA 2012. LNCS, vol. 7178, pp. 171–186. Springer (2012). https://doi.org/10.1007/978-3-642-27954-6_11
6. CCRA: Common criteria for information technology security evaluation, parts 1–3, version 3.1, Release 5 (2017). https://www.commoncriteriaportal.org
7. Ciulei, A.T., Crețu, M.C., Simion, E.: Preparation for post-quantum era: a survey about blockchain schemes from a post-quantum perspective. Cryptology ePrint Archive, Report 2022/026 (2022). https://eprint.iacr.org/2022/026
8. COLDCARD: Coldcard signing device (2025). https://coldcard.com/
9. Consortium, U.: Unicode standard annex #15: unicode normalization forms, version 15.1.0. https://www.unicode.org/reports/tr15/ (2023)
10. Courtois, N.T., Emirdag, P., Valsorda, F.: Private key recovery combination attacks: on extreme fragility of popular bitcoin key management, wallet and cold storage solutions in presence of poor RNG events. Cryptology ePrint Archive, Report 2014/848 (2014). https://eprint.iacr.org/2014/848
11. Dabrowski, A., Pfeffer, K., Reichel, M., Mai, A., Weippl, E.R., Franz, M.: Better keep cash in your boots: hardware wallets are the new single point of failure. In: Proceedings of the 2021 ACM CCS Workshop on Decentralized Finance and Security (DeFi '21), pp. 1–8. Association for Computing Machinery (2021). https://doi.org/10.1145/3464967.3488588
12. Donjon, L.: Unfixable seed extraction on Trezor: a practical and reliable attack (2019). https://www.ledger.com/blog/unfixable-key-extraction-attack-on-trezor
13. Donjon, L.: The ledger donjon: meet Ledger's white hat hackers (2024). https://www.ledger.com/academy/security/the-ledger-donjon
14. Electrum: Electrum bitcoin wallet (2025). https://electrum.org/
15. Eynard, J., Renault, G., Rondepierre, F., Thillard, A.: Practical timing and SEMA on embedded OpenSSL's ECDSA. In: Proceedings of SSTIC 2022 – Symposium sur la sécurité des technologies de l'information et des communications. Rennes, France (2022). https://www.sstic.org/media/SSTIC2022/SSTIC-actes/practical_timing_and_sema_on_embedded_openssls_ecd/SSTIC2022-Article-practical_timing_and_sema_on_embedded_openssls_ecdsa-thillard_rondepierre_renault_eynard.pdf
16. Raspberry Pi Foundation: Raspberry pi camera module 2 (2025). https://www.raspberrypi.com/products/camera-module-v2/
17. Raspberry Pi Foundation: Raspberry pi camera module 3 (2025). https://www.raspberrypi.com/products/camera-module-3/

18. Jager, T., Schwenk, J., Somorovsky, J.: Practical invalid curve attacks on TLS-ECDH. In: Pernul, G., Ryan, P.Y.A., Weippl, E.R. (eds.) Computer Security – ESORICS 2015, Part I. LNCS, vol. 9326, pp. 407–425. Springer (2015). https://doi.org/10.1007/978-3-319-24174-6_21

19. Jancar, J., Sedlacek, V., Svenda, P., Sys, M.: Minerva: The curse of ECDSA nonces (systematic analysis of lattice attacks on noisy leakage of bit-length of ECDSA nonces). IACR Trans. Cryptograph. Hardw. Embedded Syst. 2020(4), 281–308 (2020). https://doi.org/10.13154/tches.v2020.i4.281-308

20. RSA Laboratories: PKCS #5: Password-based cryptography specification version 2.0, rFC 2898 (2000). https://datatracker.ietf.org/doc/html/rfc2898

21. Kraken Security Labs: Kraken identifies critical flaw in Trezor hardware wallets (2020). https://blog.kraken.com/product/security/kraken-identifies-critical-flaw-in-trezor-hardware-wallets

22. Ledger: Ledger crypto wallet (2025). https://www.ledger.com/

23. de Miranda, P.A.G.C.: Attacks on ECDSA when the nonces are generated with a weak pseudo-random number generator (2019)

24. Moghimi, D., Sunar, B., Eisenbarth, T., Heninger, N.: TPM-FAIL: TPM meets timing and lattice attacks. In: 29th USENIX Security Symposium (USENIX Security 2020), pp. 2057–2073. USENIX Association (2020). https://www.usenix.org/conference/usenixsecurity20/presentation/moghimi-tpm

25. Nemec, M., Sys, M., Svenda, P., Klinec, D., Matyas, V.: The return of Coppersmith's attack: practical factorization of widely used RSA moduli. In: Proceedings of the 24th ACM Conference on Computer and Communications Security (CCS 2017), pp. 1631–1648. ACM (2017)

26. O'Flynn, C.: Glitching Trezor using EMFi through the enclosure (2019). https://colinoflynn.com/2019/03/glitching-trezor-using-emfi-through-the-enclosure/

27. Palatinus, M., Rusnak, P., Voisine, A., Bowe, S.: Bitcoin improvement proposal 39: mnemonic code for generating deterministic keys (2025). https://github.com/bitcoin/bips/blob/master/bip-0039.mediawiki

28. di Pasquo, G.: SG90 servo characterization (2021). https://doi.org/10.13140/RG.2.2.15715.89127

29. Pedro, M.S., Servant, V., Guillemet, C.: Side-channel assessment of open source hardware wallets. Cryptology ePrint Archive, Report 2019/401 (2019). https://eprint.iacr.org/2019/401

30. Pornin, T.: RFC 6979: deterministic usage of the digital signature algorithm (DSA) and elliptic curve digital signature algorithm (ECDSA) (2025). https://datatracker.ietf.org/doc/html/rfc6979

31. Roche, T.: EUCLEAK. Cryptology ePrint Archive, Report 2024/1380 (2024). https://eprint.iacr.org/2024/1380

32. Roche, T., Lomné, V., Mutschler, C., Imbert, L.: A side journey to titan. In: 30th USENIX Security Symposium (USENIX Security 2021), pp. 231–248. USENIX Association (2021). https://www.usenix.org/conference/usenixsecurity21/presentation/roche

33. Rukhin, A., et al.: A statistical test suite for random and pseudorandom number generators for cryptographic applications. Special Publication 800-22 Rev. 1A, National Institute of Standards and Technology (NIST) (2010). https://doi.org/10.6028/NIST.SP.800-22r1a

34. Rumpf, P., et al.: RNGtest: FIPS 140-2 random number generator test utility, part of the RNG-tools package (2024). https://linux.die.net/man/1/rngtest

35. Scott, A., Andersen, S.: Engineering a backdoored bitcoin wallet. In: Proceedings of the 18th USENIX Workshop on Offensive Technologies (WOOT 2024). USENIX Association (2024). https://www.usenix.org/conference/woot24/presentation/scott

36. Sedlacek, V., Jancar, J., Svenda, P.: Fooling primality tests on smartcards. In: Computer Security – ESORICS 2020. LNCS, vol. 12309, pp. 253–272. Springer (2020). https://doi.org/10.1007/978-3-030-58951-6_13

37. Siboni, S., et al.: Security testbed for internet-of-things devices. IEEE Trans. Reliab. **68**(1), 23–44 (2019). https://doi.org/10.1109/TR.2018.2864536

38. Smith, R.: An overview of the tesseract OCR engine. In: Proceedings of the 9th International Conference on Document Analysis and Recognition (ICDAR 2007), vol. 2, pp. 629–633 (2007). https://doi.org/10.1109/ICDAR.2007.4376991

39. National Institute of Standards and Technology: FIPS pub 140-2: security requirements for cryptographic modules (2001). https://doi.org/10.6028/NIST.FIPS.140-2

40. National Institute of Standards and Technology: FIPS pub 140-3: security requirements for cryptographic modules (2019). https://doi.org/10.6028/NIST.FIPS.140-3

41. Svenda, P., et al.: TPMScan: a wide-scale study of security-relevant properties of TPM 2.0 chips. IACR Trans. Cryptograph. Hardw. Embedded Syst. **2024**(2), 714–734 (2024). https://doi.org/10.46586/tches.v2024.i2.714-734

42. Svenda, P., et al.: The million-key question: investigating the origins of RSA public keys, Technical report, FIMU-RS-2016-03, Masaryk University, Faculty of Informatics (2016)

43. Sýs, M., Klinec, D., Kubíček, K., Švenda, P.: BoolTest: the fast randomness testing strategy based on Boolean functions with application to DES, 3-DES, MD5, MD6 and SHA-256. In: Obaidat, M.S., Cabello, E. (eds.) E-Business and Telecommunications, pp. 123–149. Springer, Cham (2019)

44. TheCharlatan: List of hardware wallet hacks (2025). https://thecharlatan.ch/List-Of-Hardware-Wallet-Hacks/

45. TowerPro: SG90 digital servo (2025). https://towerpro.com.tw/product/sg90-7/

46. Trezor: Trezor hardware wallet (2025). https://trezor.io/

47. Trezor: Trezor model one hardware wallet (2025). https://trezor.io/trezor-model-one

48. BC Vault: Does BC vault support multi-signature access to wallets? (2025). https://support.bc-vault.com/support/solutions/articles/43000374160-does-bc-vault-support-multi-signature-access-to-wallets-

49. BC Vault: Why choose BC vault (2025). https://bc-vault.com/why-choose-bc-vault/

50. Wuille, P.: Bitcoin improvement proposal 32: hierarchical deterministic wallets (2025). https://github.com/bitcoin/bips/blob/master/bip-0032.mediawiki

Author Index

B. Coppens et al. (Eds.): ARES 2025 Workshops, LNCS 15995, pp. 379–380, 2025.
https://doi.org/10.1007/978-3-032-00633-2

The manufacturer's authorised representative in the EU is Springer
Nature Customer Service Centre GmbH, Europaplatz 3, 69115 Heidelberg,
Germany. If you have any concerns regarding our products, please
contact ProductSafety@springernature.com

Printed and bound by CPI Group (UK) Ltd, Croydon, CR0 4YY

28/04/2026

02098527-0006